MILLER'S
ANTIQUES
PRICE GUIDE
1993

(Volume XIV)

4

MILLER'S
ANTIQUES
PRICE GUIDE
1993

(Volume XIV)

Compiled and Edited by:

Judith and Martin Miller

General Editor:
Josephine Davis

MILLERS PUBLICATIONS

MILLER'S ANTIQUES PRICE GUIDE 1993

Created and designed by
Millers Publications
The Cellars, High Street,
Tenterden, Kent, TN30 6BN
Tel: (05806) 6411

Compiled and edited by
Judith & Martin Miller

General Editor: Josephine Davis
Editorial and Production Co-ordinator: Sue Boyd
Editorial Assistants: Marion Rickman, Jo Wood
Production Assistants: Gillian Charles, Lorna Day
Advertising Executive: Elizabeth Smith
Advertising Assistants: Trudi Hinkley, Liz Warwick
Index compiled by: DD Editorial Services, Beccles
Design: Stephen Parry, Jody Taylor, Darren Manser
Additional photography: Ian Booth, Robin Saker

Bromide output by Final Word, Tonbridge, Kent
Illustrations by G. H. Graphics, St. Leonards-on-Sea
Colour origination by Scantrans, Singapore
Printed and bound in England by William Clowes Ltd.,
Beccles and London

CONTENTS

A bronze and ivory figure of a dancer, clad in a tightly fitting body suit, her arms outstretched, on a stepped onyx base, inscribed D. H. Chiparus, base replaced, depatinated, left hand reglued, c1925, 24in (62cm) high.
£14,000-18,000 *S(NY)*

Acknowledgements

The publishers would like to acknowledge the great assistance given by our consultant editors:-

POTTERY & PORCELAIN: **Peter Wain,** *7 Nantwich Road, Woore, Shropshire.*

GOSS & CRESTED WARE: **Nicholas Pine,** *Goss & Crested China Ltd., 62 Murray Road, Horndean, Hants.*

FURNITURE: **John Bly,** *50 High Street, Tring, Herts,* and *27 Bury Street, St. James's, London SW1.*

ARCHITECTURAL ANTIQUES: **Donald Cameron,** *Crowther of Syon Lodge, Buch Corner, London Road, Isleworth, Middx..*

CLOCKS: **Brian Loomes,** *Calf Haugh, Pateley Bridge, N. Yorks.*

GLASS: **Wing Cdr. R. G. Thomas,** *Somervale Antiques, 6 Radstock Road, Midsomer Norton, Bath, Avon.*

DOLLS & TEDDY BEARS: **Olivia Bristol,** *Christie's South Kensington, 85 Old Brompton Road, London SW7.*

ART DECO & ART NOUVEAU: **Audrey Sternshine,** *26 Broad Street, Salford, Manchester.*

TRIBAL ART: **Tim Teuten,** *Christie's Manson & Woods, Ltd., 8 King Street, St. James's, London SW1.*

EPHEMERA: **Trevor Vennett-Smith,** FRICS, FSVA, CAAV, *11 Nottingham Road, Gotham, Nottingham.*

A Bretby standing jardinière, the integral base with pierced sides and 3 pot holders to base, some damage, 27in (69cm) high. **£160-200** *GAK*

KEY TO ILLUSTRATIONS

Each illustration and descriptive caption is accompanied by a letter code. By reference to the followiwng list of Auctioneers (denoted by *) and Dealers (•) the source of any item may be immediately determined. In no way does this constitute or imnply a contract or binding offer on the part of any of our contributors to supply or sell the goods illustrated, or similar articles, at the prices stated. Advertisers in this year's directory are denoted by †.

ADC   *   Art Deco Ceramics, Sheep Street Antique Centre, Stratford-upon-Avon, Warwicks.

AG   †*   Anderson & Garland, Marlborough House, Marlborough Crescent, Newcastle-upon-Tyne. Tel: 091 232 6278.

AH   †*   Andrew Hartley, Victoria Hall, Little Lane, Ilkley, West Yorkshire. Tel: 0943 816363.

AI   •   Antiques & Interiors, 22 Ashford Road, Tenterden, Kent. Tel: 05806 5462.

AL   †•   Ann Lingard, Ropewalk Antiques, Ropewalk, Rye, Sussex. Tel: 0797 223486.

ALL   *   Allen & Harris, Bristol Auction Rooms, St John's Place, Apsley Road, Clifton, Bristol, Avon. Tel: 0272 737201.

ALS   †•   Allan Smith Antiques, Amity Cottage, 162 Beechcroft Road, Upper Stratton, Swindon, Wilts. Tel: 0793 822977.

AMH   •   Amherst Antiques, 23 London Road, Riverhead, Kent. Tel: 0732 455047.

ANX   •   Alan Wood, Annexe Antiques, 33 The Pantiles, Tunbridge Wells, Kent. Tel: 0892 547213.

AOS   •   Antiques on the Square, Church Stretton, Shropshire. Tel: 0694 724111.

APO   †•   Apollo Antiques Ltd., The Saltisford, Birmingham Road, Warwick. Tel: 0926 494746.

ARC   •   Architectural Antiques, West Ley, Alswear Old Road, South Molton, Devon. Tel: 07695 3342.

ASA   †•   AS Antiques, 26 Broad Street, Pendleton, Salford 6, Lancashire. Tel: 061 737 5938.

ASB   •   Andrew Spencer Bottomley, The Coach House, 173A Huddersfield Road, Thongsbridge, Holmfirth, Huddersfield. Tel: 0484 685234.

B   *   Boardman, Station Road Corner, Haverhill, Suffolk. Tel: 0440 703784.

Bea   *   Bearnes, Rainbow, Avenue Road, Torquay, Devon. Tel: 0803 296277.

BEL   †•   Bell Antiques, 68 Harold Street, Grimsby, South Humberside. Tel: 0472 695110.

BEV   •   Beverley, 30 Church Street, London, NW8. Tel: 071-262 1576.

BL   †•   Brian Loomes, Calf Haugh, Pateley Bridge, North Yorks. Tel: 0423 711163.

Bon   †*   Bonhams, Montpelier Galleries, Montpelier Street, London SW7. Tel: 071 584 9161.

BR   †*   Bracketts, 27-29 High Street, Tunbridge Wells, Kent. Tel: 0892 533733.

BTA   •   Brian Taylor Antiques, 24 Molesworth Road, Plymouth. Tel: 0752 569061.

BWA   †•   Bow-Well Antiques, 103 West Bow, Edinburgh, Scotland. Tel: 031 225 3335.

BWe   *   Biddle & Webb, Ladywood Middleway, Birmingham. Tel: 021 455 8042.

C   *   Christie, Manson & Woods Ltd., 8 King Street, St James's, London SW1. Tel: 071 839 9060.

CAG   †*   Canterbury Auction Galleries, 40 Station Road West, Canterbury, Kent. Tel: 0227 763337.

CAm   *   Christie's Amsterdam BV, Cornelis Schuystraat 57, 1071 JG Amsterdam, Holland. Tel: (3120) 57 55 255.

CAR   •   Carlton Gallery, 11 Main Street, Swanland, Nr. Hull. Tel: 0482 443954.

CB   •   Christine Bridge Antiques, 78 Castelnau, London SW13. Tel: 081 741 5501.

CD   •   The China Doll, 31 Walcot Street, Bath, Avon. Tel: 0225 465849.

CHa   •   Carol Hammond, Unit 8, Kensington Church Street Antiques Centre, 58/60 Kensington Church Street, London, W8. Tel: 071 938 4405.

CHA   •   Chapel House Antiques, 32 Pentood Industrial Estate, Pendre, Cardigan, Dyfed. Tel: 0239 614868 and 613268.

CLC   †•   The Clock Clinic Ltd., 85 Lower Richmond Road, Putney, London SW15. Tel: 081 788 1407.

CNY   *   Christie, Manson & Woods International Inc., 502 Park Avenue, New York, NY 10022, USA. Tel: (212) 546 1000. (including Christie's East).

CoH   †*   Cooper Hirst, The Granary Saleroom, Victoria Road, Chelmsford, Essex. Tel: 0245 260535.

COL   •   Collectables, PO Box 130, Chatham, Kent. Tel: 0634 828767.

CPA   †•   Country Pine Antiques, The Barn, Upper Bush Farm, Upper Bush, Kent. Tel: 0634 717982.

CR   *   Criterion Salerooms, 53 Essex Road, Islington, London N1. Tel: 071 359 5707.

C(S)   *   Christie's Scotland Ltd., 164-166 Bath Street, Glasgow. Tel: 041 332 8134.

CSK   *   Christie's South Kensington Ltd., 85 Old Brompton Road, London SW7. Tel: 071 581 7611.

DA   *   Dee & Atkinson, The Exchange Saleroom, Driffield, East Yorks. Tel: 0377 43151.

DaD   *   David Dockree, 224 Moss Lane, Bramhall, Stockport, Cheshire. Tel: 061 485 1258.

DDM   *   Dickinson, Davy & Markham, Wrawby Street, Brigg, South Humberside. Tel: 0652 53666.

DHO   •   Derek Howard, The Original Chelsea Antiques Market, 245-253 King's Road, London SW3. Tel: 071 352 4113.

DN   *   Dreweatt Neate, Donnington Priory, Donnington, Newbury, Berkshire. Tel: 0635 31234.

DOL   •   Dollectable, 53 Lower Bridge Street, Chester. Tel: 0244 344888/679195.

DRU   †•   Drummonds of Bramley, Birtley Farm, Horsham Road, Bramley, Guildford, Surrey. Tel: 0483 898766.

E   *   Ewbank Fine Art, Welbeck House, High Street, Guildford, Surrey. Tel: 0483 232134.

EP   †*   Evans & Partridge, Agriculture House, High Street, Stockbridge, Hants. Tel: 0264 810702.

FB   †•   Fenwick Billiards, Tonedale Mills, Wellington, Somerset. Tel: 0643 706165.

FD   •   Frank Dux Antiques, 33 Belvedere, Bath, Avon. Tel: 0225 312367.

GAK   †*   G.A. Key, Aylsham Saleroom, off Palmers Lane, Aylsham, Norfolk. Tel: 0263 733195.

GAZ   •   Gazelles, 31 Northam Road, Southampton. Tel: 0703 255291/780798.

G&CC   †•   Goss & Crested China Ltd., 62 Murray Road, Horndean, Hants. Tel: 0705 597440.

9

GH †* Giles Haywood, The Auction House, St. John's Road, Stourbridge, West Midlands. Tel: 0384 370891.

GIL * Gilding's, Roman Way, Market Harborough, Leicester. Tel: 0858 410414.

GRF †* Grange Farm Ltd., Grange Farm, Tongham, Surrey. Tel: 0258 2993/2804.

GRG †• Gordon Reece Gallery, Finkle Street, Knaresborough, N. Yorks. Tel: 0423 866219

GSP * Graves, Son & Pilcher, 71 Church Road, Hove, East Sussex. Tel: 0273 735266.

HCC †* H. C. Chapman & Son, The Auction Mart, North Street, Scarborough. Tel: 0723 372424.

HCH * Hobbs & Chambers, 'At The Sign of the Bell', Market Place, Cirencester, Glos. Tel: 0285 4736.

HEW †• Muir Hewett, Halifax Antiques Centre, Halifax, Yorkshire. Tel: 0422 366657.

HEY • Heyford Antiques, 7 Church Street, Nether Heyford, Northampton. Tel: 0327 40749.

HOL †* Holloways, 49 Parsons Street, Banbury, Oxon. Tel: 0295 253197.

HON †• Honan's Antiques, Crowe Street, Gort, Co. Galway. Tel: 091 31407.

HOW • Howards Antiques, 10 Alexandra Road, Aberystwyth, Dyfed. Tel: 0970 624973.

HSS †* Henry Spencer & Sons, 20 The Square, Retford, Notts. Tel: 0777 708633.

IM †* Ibbett Mosely, 125 High Street, Sevenoaks, Kent. Tel: 0732 452246.

IS †• Ian Sharp Antiques, 23 Front Street, Tynemouth. Tel: 091 296 0656.

IW • Islwyn Watkins, 1 High Street, Knighton, Powys. Tel: 0547 520145/528940.

JAC • John & Anne Clegg, 12 Old Street, Ludlow, Shropshire. Tel: 0584 873176.

JD †* Julian Dawson, Lewes Auction Rooms, 56 High Street, Lewes, Sussex. Tel: 0273 478221

JH * Jacobs & Hunt, Lavant Street, Petersfield, Hants. Tel: 0730 62744.

JHo †• Jonathan Horne (Antiques) Ltd., 66B & C, Kensington Church Street, London, W8. Tel: 071 221 5658.

JL • Joy Luke, The Gallery, 300E Grove Street, Bloomington, IL 61701, USA. Tel: (309) 828 5533.

JM * John Maxwell, 74 Hawthorn Street, Wilmslow, Cheshire. Tel: 0625 536102.

JMG †• Jamie Maxtone Graham, Lyne Haugh, Lyne Station, Peebles, Scotland. Tel: 07214 304.

JO †• Jacqueline Oosthuizen, The Georgian Village and 23 Cale Street, Chelsea, London SW3. Tel: 071 352 6071.

KEY †• Key Antiques, 11 Horsefair, Chipping Norton, Oxon. Tel: 0608 643777.

L * Lawrences of Crewkerne, South Street, Crewkerne, Somerset. Tel: 0460 73041.

LAY * David Lay, ASVA, Penzance Auction House, Alverton, Penzance, Cornwall. Tel: 0736 61414

L&E * Locke & England, Black Horse Agencies, 18 Guy Street, Leamington Spa, Warwicks. Tel: 0926 889100.

LF †* Lambert & Foster, 102 High Street, Tenterden, Kent. Tel: 05806 3233. (previously County Group).

LIO †• Lions Den, 31 Henley Street, Stratford-upon-Avon, Warwicks. Tel: 0789 415802.

LR • Leonard Russell, 21 King's Avenue, Newhaven, Sussex. Tel: 0273 515153.

LRG †* Lots Road Chelsea Auction Galleries, 71 Lots Road, London SW10. Tel: 071 351 7771.

M * Morphets of Harrogate, 4-6 Albert Street, Harrogate, North Yorks. Tel: 0423 502282.

MAT * Christopher Matthews, 23 Mount Street, Harrogate, Yorks. Tel: 0423 871756.

MCA * Mervyn Carey, Twysden Cottage, Benenden, Cranbrook, Kent. Tel: 0580 240283.

McC †* McCartney's Portcullis Salerooms, Ludlow, Shropshire. Tel: 0584 2636.

MERT • Merton Antiques, Merton, Okehampton, Devon. Tel: 08053 443.

Mit * Mitchells, Fairfield House, Station Road, Cockermouth, Cumbria. Tel: 0900 822016.

MJB †* Michael J. Bowman, 6 Haccombe House, Netherton, Newton Abbot, Devon. Tel: 0626 872890.

ML • Magic Lantern, (Josie Marsden), By George Antique Centre, 23 George Street, St Albans, Herts. Tel: 0727 53032.

MST †* Martin Spencer-Thomas, Bicton Street Auction Rooms, Exmouth. Tel: 0395 267403.

N(A) †* Amersham Auction Rooms, 125 Station Road, Amersham, Bucks. Tel: 0494 729292.

NCA • New Century Antiques, 69 Kensington Church Street, W8. Tel: 071 376 2810.

NWM †* Nigel Ward & Morris, Stuart House, 18 Gloucester Road, Ross-on-Wye, Herefordshire. Tel: 0989 768320.

OD • Offas Dyke Antique Centre, 4 High Street, Knighton, Powys, Wales. Tel: 0547 528634.

OL * Outhwaite & Litherland, Kingsway Galleries, Fontenoy Street, Liverpool. Tel: 051 236 6561.

ONS * Onslows, Metrostore, Townmead Road, London SW6. Tel: 071 793 0240.

OSc †• Simon & Penny Rumble, The Old School, Chittering Cambridgeshire. Tel: 0223 861831.

P * Phillips, Blenstock House, 101 New Bond Street, London W1. Tel: 071 629 6602.

PAG • Prinny's Antiques Gallery (F. Whitney Antiques), 3 Meeting House Lane, Brighton, Sussex. Tel: 0273 204554.

PC Private Collection.

PCh †* Peter Cheney, Western Road Auction Rooms, Western Road, Littlehampton, West Sussex. Tel: 0903 722264/713418.

P(M) * Phillips, Trinity House, 114 Northenden Road, Sale, Manchester. Tel: 061 962 9237.

P(O) * Phillips, 39 Park End Street, Oxford. Tel: 0865 723524.

POW • Sylvia Powell Decorative Arts, 28 The Mall, Camden Passage, London N1. Tel: 071 354 2977/081 458 4543.

P(S) * Phillips, 49 London Road, Sevenoaks, Kent. Tel: 0732 740310.

PSA †• Pantiles Spa Antiques, 6 Union House, Eridge Road, Tunbridge Wells, Kent. Tel: 0892 541377.

PT †• Pieces of Time, Grays Mews, 1-7 Davies Street, London W1. Tel: 071 629 2422.

P(W) * Phillips of Winchester, The Red House, Hyde Street, Winchester, Hants. Tel: 0962 62515.

RAG * Rye Auction Galleries, Rock Channel, Rye, East Sussex. Tel: 0797 222124.

RBB †* Russell, Baldwin & Bright, Fine Art Salerooms, Ryelands Road, Leominster, Hereford. Tel: 0568 611166.

RdeR †• Rogers de Rin, 76 Royal Hospital Road, Paradise Walk, London SW3. Tel: 071-352 9007.

RE • Ron's Emporium, 98 Church Lane, Sholden, Deal, Kent. Tel: 0304 374784.

RGA • Richard Gibbon, Alfie's Antique Market, 13-25 Church Street, London NW8.

RHE * R. H. Ellis & Sons, 44-46 High Street, Worthing, Sussex. Tel: 0903 238999

RIC †• Rich Designs, 11 Union Street, Stratford-upon-Avon, Warwickshire. Tel: 0789 772111.

RID †* Riddetts of Bournemouth, 26 Richmond Hill, Bournemouth, Hants. Tel: 0202 555686.

RK †• Richard Kimbell, Riverside, Market Harborough, Leics. Tel: 0858 433444.

ROS * Rosebery's, The Old Railway Booking Hall, Crystal Palace Station Road, London SE19. Tel: 081 778 4024.

ROW • Rowena Blackford at Penny Lampard's Antique Centre, 31-33 High Street, Headcorn, Kent. Tel: 0622 890682/861360.

RP	•	Robert Pugh. Tel: 0225 314713.
RPI	*	Raymond P. Inman, The Auction Galleries, 35 & 40 Temple Street, Brighton, Sussex. Tel: 0273 774777.
RWB	†•	Roy W. Bunn Antiques, 34-36 Church Street, Barnoldswick, Colne, Lancashire. Tel: 0282 813703.
RYA	•	Robert Young Antiques, 68 Battersea Bridge Road, London SW11. Tel: 071 228 7847.
S	*	Sotheby's, 34-35 New Bond Street, London W1. Tel: 071 493 8080.
S(Am)	*	Sotheby's, 102 Rokin, 1012 KZ, Amsterdam, Holland. Tel: 31 (20) 6 27 5656.
S(C)	*	Sotheby's, Booth Mansion, 28 Watergate Street, Chester. Tel: 0244 315531.
S(Ch)	*	Sotheby's, 18 Imperial Square, Cheltenham, Glos. Tel: 0242 510500.
S(G)	*	Sotheby's, 13 Quai du Mont Blanc, CH-1201 Geneva. Tel: 41 (22) 732 8585.
SHO	*	Michael Shortall Auction Centres, Highgate, Hawkhurst, Kent. Tel: 0580 753463.
SIM	†*	Simmons & Sons, 32 Bell Street, Henley-on-Thames, Oxfordshire. Tel: 0491 591111.
SMA	•	Claire & Rosemary Smale, Alfie's Antique Market, 13-25 Church Street, London NW8
S(NY)	*	Sotheby's, 1334 York Avenue, New York, NY 10021, USA. Tel: 212 606 7000.
Som	†•	Somervale Antiques, 6 Radstock Road, Midsomer Norton, Bath. Tel: 0761 412686.
S(S)	*	Sotheby's, Summers Place, Billingshurst, West Sussex. Tel: 0403 783933.
SWO	†*	Sworders, G. E. Sworder & Sons, 15 Northgate End, Bishops Stortford, Herts. Tel: 0279 651388.
TM	*	Thos. Mawer & Son, The Lincoln Saleroom, 63 Monks Road, Lincoln. Tel: 0522 524984.
TRU	•	The Trumpet, West End, Minchinhampton, Glos. Tel: 0453 883027.
TVA		Teme Valley Antiques, 1 The Bull Ring, Ludlow, Shropshire. Tel: 0584 874686.
UP	†•	Utopia Pine & Country Furniture, Holme Mills, Burton-in-Kendal, Carnforth, Lancs. Tel: 0524 781739.
VH	†•	Valerie Howard, 131e Kensington Church Street, London W8. Tel: 071 792 9702.
VS	†*	T. Vennett-Smith, 11 Nottingham Road, Gotham, Nottingham. Tel: 0602 830541.
W	*	Walter's, No. 1 Mint Lane, Lincoln. Tel: 0522 525454.
Wai	•	Wain Antiques, Peter Wain, 7 Nantwich Road, Woore, Shropshire. Tel: 063081 7118.
WAL	†*	Wallis & Wallis, West Street Auction Galleries, Lewes, Sussex. Tel: 0273480208.
WAR	†*	The Warner Auction Rooms, (William H. Brown,) 16-18 Halford Street, Leicester. Tel: 0533 519777.
WEL	†•	Wells Reclamation & Co., The Old Cider Farm, Coxley, Nr Wells, Somerset. Tel: 0749 77087/77484.
WGT		W.G.T. Burne, 11 Elystan Street, London SW3. Tel: 071 589 6074.
WHB	†*	William H. Brown, Fine Art Auctioneers & Valuers, Olivers Rooms, Burkitt's Lane, Sudbury, Suffolk. Tel: 0787 880305.
WHL	*	W. H. Lane & Son, 65 Morrab Road, Penzance, Cornwall. Tel: 0736 61447.
WIL	*	Peter Wilson, Victoria Gallery, Market Street, Nantwich, Cheshire. Tel: 0270 623878.
WIN	*	P. F. Windibank, 18-20 Reigate Road, Dorking,Surrey. Tel: 0306 884556.
WW	*	Woolley & Wallis, The Castle Auction Mart, Castle Street, Salisbury. Tel: 0722 21711.
W&W	•	Walker & Walker, Halfway Manor, Halfway, Nr Newbury, Berkshire. Tel: 0488 58693 or 0831 147480.

INDEX TO ADVERTISERS

The
Old Mint House

HIGH STREET, PEVENSEY
NEAR EASTBOURNE, EAST SUSSEX BN24 5LF
The Largest Antique Business in the South of England

ALL ENQUIRIES To Head Office (0323) 762337
(0323) 641142 (After Hours)
(0323) 762337 (Fax)

LAPADA MEMBER

Couriers Welcome

All trains met by appointment

Business hours:
Monday thru to Saturday 9.00 hrs to 17.30 hrs
(or by appointment)

The Old Mint House Antiques, established since 1901, with 33 showrooms containing a large and varied stock of Georgian, Victorian, Edwardian, inlaid and marquetry furniture, also we carry a large stock of porcelain, clocks and metalware. We can cater for a client wishing to purchase one item or an entire container.

A rapidly changing stock, but always 20,000 items available, with new consignments arriving daily.

LOCATION MAP
1 hr from Gatwick, 1½hrs from London ½hr from Brighton

Also our shipping and export division situated at
45 TURKEY ROAD, BEXHILL, E. SUSSEX. Tel: (0424) 216056
which specialises in Victorian and Pre-War oak, mahogany and inlaid shipping furniture for the large trade buyer, who wishes to find most of his requirements at one location.
This 20,000 sq. ft. purpose built warehouse contains on two levels a huge selection of goods at the absolute lowest open trade prices
Video (all systems) available for the larger buyer

16

CUNNINGHAM HART
CHARTERED LOSS ADJUSTERS SURVEYORS AND VALUERS

FINE ART, ANTIQUES AND HOUSEHOLD VALUATIONS

We prepare detailed Inventories and Valuations
of Fine Art and Antiques for Insurance purposes.
We value selected Valuable and High risk items,
or complete household contents.
We prepare professional documentation in order
to arrange appropriate insurance cover to assist
in substantiating a loss in the event of burglary
or fire, and details which assist in the recovery of stolen items.

We also prepare valuations for Capital Transfer Tax,
Sale by Private Treaty or other purposes.

For further information please contact: Peter Davy
Cunningham Hart, Valuations Office, International House
59 Compton Road, Islington, London N1 2PB
Telephone: 071-354 3504. Fax 071-354 0504

Cunningham Hart (U.K.) Ltd,
Head Office: International House, World Trade Centre
1 St Katharine's Way, London E1 9UN
Group offices throughout the United Kingdom and Europe

IF YOU BUY OR COLLECT ANTIQUES.....

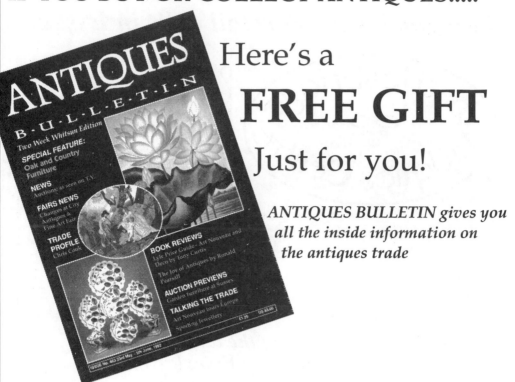

Here's a
FREE GIFT
Just for you!

ANTIQUES BULLETIN gives you all the inside information on the antiques trade

Used by dealers and collectors worldwide, **ANTIQUES BULLETIN** is *the* weekly magazine to keep you informed of news, trends and prices within the trade.

Auctions

Every week auction sales throughout the country are listed in our comprehensive **Auction Calendar** and results are printed in our **Around the Salerooms** sections.

Art

Details and prices of over 230 paintings, watercolours and drawings are listed each week in our **Art Prices Index**, which builds into an invaluable reference of national sales results.

Fairs

ANTIQUES BULLETIN produces a weekly **Fairs Calendar**, which lists national events from one-day fairs to the top quality London and regional multi-day fairs, backed up by a regular weekly **Fairs News** column.
Other regular weekly features include **Trade News, What's On,**

Letters, and a regular new series of articles by leading specialists in ceramics, furniture, silver, art etc. Monthly features include **Trade & Export News, Dealer Profiles, Book Reviews and Pine News.**

TRY A FOUR WEEK SUBSCRIPTION WITH NO OBLIGATION

Let us send you the next four issues of **ANTIQUES BULLETIN** with no obligation. If you decide to cancel, we will refund your money with no questions asked and you can keep the issues that you have already received.

FREE GIFT

If you decide to continue we will also give you, entirely free of charge, annual subscriptions to **Buying Antiques**, a regular buyers' guide to dealers throughout the UK and **The Antiques Fairs Guide**, a six-monthly calendar of events covering the fairs circuit.

WHAT TO DO

Simply post your cheque for £39.50 or credit card details with your name and address to **ANTIQUES BULLETIN, 2 Hampton Court Road, Harborne, Birmingham B17 9AE** stating that you saw your advertisement in Millers Guide and we'll do the rest!

SPEEDPHONE ORDERING SERVICE
Access/Visa/Amex
☎ **0562~700820**
Monday~Friday, 9am-5.30pm

POTTERY

The pottery market has shown no great improvement this year and contrives to be the most recession-hit of all the ceramic sections. Rumours of a scandal involving fake early English pottery being sold onto the market have not helped the top end of specialist sales, despite assurances that all of these pieces are now accounted for and have been taken off the market. The market trends of the past two or three years remain the same. The rare and unusual pieces continue to attract high prices whilst the more mundane items fail to sell. Good quality late British ceramics, such as Wemyss, Moorcroft, Minton etc. continue to sell well if they are unusual, new to the market and in perfect condition. Majolica pottery continues to attract high prices for the rare and unusual. A George Jones majolica strawberry set from around 1870 realised £2,000 at Sotheby's in Sussex.

Wemyss ware continues to attract extensive interest from collectors with surprisingly high prices being realised for the rare and unusual pieces. One of many salerooms offering Wemyss last year was Andrew Hartley of Ilkley, who sold a 12 inch wide oval basket with apple decoration for £660, a 6.25 inch high pottery goose for £560, and a 12.25 inch high black and white cat for £1,300.

Interest in Moorcroft pottery remains high although there has been a noticeable drop in prices for the more common pieces. Wedgwood's highly decorative and skilful 1920s Fairyland Lustre wares continue deservedly

A Toby jug, wearing a black hat, painted in blue, green and brown, restored, 10.5in (26cm).
£450-550 *Bea*

to rise in price for the perfect pieces. Sotheby's Sussex saw a pair of 10 inch high vases with the 'Imps on a bridge and Tree House' pattern realise a double mid-estimate £3,300 and a 6 inch diameter 'Woodland Bridge' bowl fetched nearly £2,000 against an expected £500-700. Taking into account the artistry and production difficulties of Wedgwood's Fairyland Lustre wares they still appear to be very good value for money compared to the dubious merits of many of the highly priced contemporary Staffordshire factory studio ceramics of the various popular lady designers.

A Prattware barrel, probably Bristol, c1820, 6.5in (16.5cm) high.
£400-450 *RP*

A not too often mentioned corner of the pottery market is that of the tile collector. Tiles still represent very good value for money; good examples being available for as little as £15-20 for a 19thC Staffordshire example. English 18thC delft tiles range from £50-150 whilst complete tile pictures can fetch many thousands of pounds. Andrew Hartley of Ilkley sold an interesting tile picture last year which was dated 1913 and inscribed 'After Edmund Dulac' by Mowbray Jeffrey. Comprising eighty tiles, the picture in the Art Nouveau style, measured 5ft by 4ft and realised £3,000.

A pottery flask, 16thC, 6in (15cm).
£350-450 *JHo*

English blue and white printed earthenware has always been popular with collectors and the rare and sought after patterns still continue to realise high prices. A 'Durham Ox' pattern meat plate was sold by Spencers, Retford, for £1,700. Blue and white printed earthenware Staffordshire figures and commemorative ware are all sectors of the pottery market that seem to be riding the recession with ease. This is probably because these markets are based around a sizeable and knowledgeable group of collectors.

Bottles

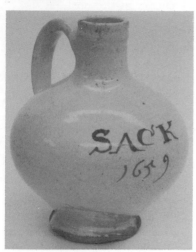

A rare delft bottle, inscribed and dated 'Sack 1659', 6in (15cm) high.
£2,500-3,000 *McC*

A Lambeth delft blue and white bowl, c1760, 12in (31cm) diam.
£3,500-4,000 *JHo*

A Wedgwood creamware bowl by Millicent Taplin, early 20thC, 8in (20cm) diam.
£500-600 *Wai*

A Bristol delftware polychrome fluted punch bowl, some chips, cracks and restoration, c1735, 12in (31cm).
£2,500-3,000 *S*

A West Country bottle, late 19thC, 6.5in (16cm) high.
£35-40 *IW*

A pair of English delft flower bowls, probably London, some chips and restoration, c1700, 7.5in (19cm).
£2,300-2,700 *S*

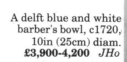

A Nevers bowl, restored, c1790, 12.5in (32cm) diam.
£400-450 *VH*

Bowls

A London delft, blue and white bowl, c1770, 9in (23cm) diam.
£220-250 *JHo*

A delft blue and white barber's bowl, c1720, 10in (25cm) diam.
£3,900-4,200 *JHo*

A Mason's posy bowl, impressed mark, c1815, 7.5in (19cm) long.
£200-240 *VH*

Boxes

A Victorian majolica sardine box, with integral stand and cover, decorated in typical palette, damaged, unmarked, 9.5in (24cm) wide.
£500-700 *HSS*

An early Quimper box and cover, c1800, 5in (13cm) diam.
£250-280 *VH*

A money box, 18thC, 4in (10cm) high.
£100-120 *IW*

A slipware money box, probably Buckley, c1890, 10in (25cm) wide.
£200-240 *IW*

Busts

A Staffordshire bust of Queen Victoria, c1820, 6in (15cm) high.
£800-1,000 *JO*

An Enoch Wood bust of Plato, decorated in coloured enamels, 13in (33cm) high.
£400-600 *LR*

A Staffordshire bust of Milton, 12in (31cm) high.
£550-650 *JO*

A bust of Alexander I of Russia, decorated in enamel and gold leaf, inscribed E. Wood on rear, c1800, 11in (28cm).
£500-600 *LR*

Commemorative

A Staffordshire pearlware plate, commemorating the death of Princess Charlotte, entitled 'Great Britain mourn her, Princes weep', all within a border moulded with fruiting vine and picked out in purple lustre, minor chips, impressed retailer's mark Clark's China Shop, Glasgow, c1817, 7in (17cm).
£350-450 *S(S)*

A commemorative plate showing Queen Caroline, the border inscribed with emblems of the British Isles, heightened in lustre, 2 chips, 7.5in (19cm) diam.
£400-450 *LR*

A commemorative plate of George III, decorated in blue, dated 29th Jan. 1820, with flower impressed border, 7in (18cm) diam.
£450-550 *LR*

A pearlware plate, transfer printed in blue with a profile portrait of Caroline Regina, with flowers of the Union cartouche and leaf moulded border, c1820, 7.5in (18cm) diam.
£300-400 *Bon*

A pottery plaque, painted in black with a portrait entitled 'William the IV, the only Royal Reformer since Alfred' with pink lustre border, restored, c1832, 6.5in (16cm) diam.
£200-250 *Bon*

A coronation plate of William IV and Adelaide, decorated in multi-coloured enamel, inscribed and dated September 1831, 7in (17cm) diam.
£475-525 *LR*

A commemorative jug of Blake with his dog Waverley, in underglaze pink, c1835.
£80-110 *HOW*

A jug, commemorating the opening of the Liverpool & Manchester Railway, damaged, early 19thC, 6in (15cm) high.
£200-250 *HSS*

A pottery plate, with puce printed portrait of the King in uniform, entitled 'His most gracious Majesty William IV' within leaf cartouche, surmounted by the crown and sceptre, with moulded border of flowers alternating with 2 children and a sheep, hand coloured, cracked, 8in (20cm) diam.
£200-250 *Bon*

A white stoneware oviform jug, with applied blue profile of Queen Caroline, the reverse with the dove of Innocence, the centre with flowers of the Union motifs, with acorn bands, garland swags, and the Bill of Pains and Penalties, c1820, 7in (17cm) high.
£250-350 *Bon*

A Doulton Lambeth stoneware jug, with white relief moulded portrait of General Gordon, within applied green cartouche, commemorating his betrayal at Khartoum in 1885, 7in (18cm) high.
£250-300 *Bon*

A creamware jug, with print commemorating Admiral Lord Rodney, damaged, c1787, 9in (23cm) high.
£300-400 *IW*

A Shelley loving cup, commemorating the Coronation of George VI, colourfully gilded and enamelled with printed double portrait medallion beneath elaborate blue acanthus swag, the reverse depicting the Royal Princesses, 4in (10cm) high.
£350-400 *Bon*

A Staffordshire jug to commemorate the Coronation of Queen Victoria, transfer printed in black with 2 bust portraits, relevant dates and a border of roses and diapering, 19thC, 6.5in (17cm) high.
£400-500 *HSS*

A Doulton Lambeth brown glazed jug, made for Bullards & Sons Ltd to commemorate the 60th year of Queen Victoria's reign, 8.5in (21cm) high.
£170-230 *GAK*

A Copeland Spode three-handled loving cup, colour enamelled with portrait of Edward VIII flanked by crusaders, Britannia surrounded by ships and elaborate Royal coat-of-arms, the inside rim with roses, restored, 5.5in (14cm) high.
£450-500 *Bon*

A Paragon china cup, saucer and plate, brown printed with portrait of Princess Elizabeth, with gilt and red lined rim, by Marcus Adams, produced with special permission of the Duchess of York.
£170-230 *Bon*

A commemorative jug depicting the marriage of Princess Louise and Marquis of Lorne.
£160-180 *RP*

British Commemorative Pottery

* the earliest wares available to collectors tend to be the blue-dash chargers of the late 17thC

* there has always been a strong royalist or political theme on chargers

* of the blue-dash chargers, the 'Royals' tend to be more valuable than, say, the Duke of Marlborough - the late delft dishes with Queen Anne or George I are very sought after

* a lot of the delftware is damaged but this does not severely affect value, rarity is more important

* the 19thC saw an absolute glut of 'royal' items particularly Victoria - these should only be bought in good condition

* American collectors always seek out Jubilee items.

An Edward VIII Coronation mug, by Ewenny potteries, c1937, 3.5in (9cm) high.
£20-30 *IW*

A pipe commemorating Admiral Nelson inscribed on the front of the bowl 'Nelson' and 'Forever' on the rear, c1802, 9in (22.5cm) long.
£900-1,100 *LR*

A Wade Heath Art Deco style jug, enamelled blue and orange, with colour printed portrait medallion of George VI and Elizabeth, the reverse with Princess Elizabeth, 5.5in (14cm) high.
£40-80 *Bon*

Cottages and Pastille Burners

A Staffordshire cottage, possibly by Walton, with a lamb lying amongst foliage, c1825, 4in (10cm) high.
£225-275 *LR*

Cow Creamers

A North Country pottery cow creamer, c1820, 6in (15cm).
£700-780 *RWB*

A South Wales pottery cow creamer, c1840, 6in (15cm).
£250-300 *RWB*

A cow creamer with flower knop on the cover, sponged in brown, ochre and yellow on green base, c1800, 7in (17.5cm) wide.
£750-900 *LR*

A Fell (Newcastle) cow creamer and cover, sponged in purple/lilac with green base.
£500-600 *LR*

A large Staffordshire Prattware cow creamer, sponged in yellow, ochre, blue and black, c1800, 8in (20cm) wide.
£750-900 *LR*

A Swansea Pottery cow creamer with red and pink lustre on a green base, c1820, 7in (17.5cm) wide.
£250-300 *HOW*

A Yorkshire type cow creamer, 19thC, 7in (17.5cm) wide.
£180-220 *IW*

A Prattware creamware cow creamer, sponged with horizontal lines in ochre and black, horns restored, 5in (13cm) high.
£400-450 *Bea*

A Prattware cow creamer and cover, sponged in ochre, brown and green, c1800, 5.5in (14cm) high.
£650-750 *LR*

Cups

A Foley faience loving cup by
Wileman & Co., depicting a
Yorkshireman's coat-of-arms,
c1892, 4.5in (11cm) high.
£30-35 *IW*

Two Quimper egg cups, c1925,
3in (7.5cm) wide.
£40-50 each *VH*

Two ironstone egg cups,
unmarked, c1818, 3in (7.5cm)
high.
l. damaged, **£70-85**
r. **£130-140** *VH*

A C. J. Mason cup and saucer,
c1830, 5.5in (14cm) diam.
£80-100 *VH*

A Quimper egg stand, c1890,
8in(20cm) high.
£250-285 *VH*

A C. J. Mason cup and saucer,
with pseudo Chinese seal mark,
c1840, 5.5in (14cm) diam.
£120-135 *VH*

A Staffordshire miniature tea
bowl and saucer, hand painted
and enamelled, salt glazed,
c1765, saucer 2.5in (6cm) diam.
£900-1,000 *JHo*

Ewers

A Prattware stirrup cup,
modelled as the Pope and the
Devil, with ochre and yellow
Papal hat and green hair, c1780,
6in (15cm) high.
£300-450 *HEY*

Two Minton majolica ewers,
impressed with the artist's
monogram and various marks,
model number 900, date code for
1862, 15in (38cm) high.
£1,500-1,800 *C*

A pair of English majolica ewers,
moulded with foxgloves on a bark
and leaf ground, with a turquoise
interior, small chip, c1860, 16in
(40.5cm) high.
£600-650 *CSK*

31

Figures - Animals

A Staffordshire bird, c1770, 3.5in (8.5cm) high.
£1,000-1,400 *JHo*

A matched pair of Staffordshire pottery birds, each with orange beak and gilt markings, perched on blue-washed rocks sprigged with moss, small crack, 11in (28cm) high, and a Staffordshire pottery group of two birds perched above a nest of three eggs.
£450-650 *S(S)*

A Prattware bird, decorated in yellow, ochre, blue and green, 8in (20cm).
£1,500-1,800 *JHo*

A Staffordshire tree group of canaries, decorated in coloured glazes, c1790, 8in (20cm).
£1,200-1,300 *LR*

A Staffordshire greyhound with a hare in his mouth, c1850, 11.5in (29cm).
£150-200 *HOW*

A Staffordshire figure of a floppy eared rabbit, with brown patched animal crouching on the oval base, 19thC, 6in (15cm).
£450-500 *S(S)*

A Yorkshire cow, calf and figure group, decorated in ochre, green, black and blue on a white ground, 6in (16cm) wide.
£1,000-1,200 *JHo*

A Staffordshire cow and milkmaid group, c1860.
£200-250 *HOW*

A pair of Staffordshire spaniels, decorated in red and white, c1860, 8in (20cm).
£200-250 *HOW*

A Staffordshire Whieldon type hollow sporting dog, in brown and green glazes, c1775, 4in (10cm).
£500-550 *LR*

A pair of Staffordshire spaniels, c1850, 5in (13cm).
£270-300 *RWB*

A pair of Staffordshire St Bernards, with dark brown decoration, c1860, 7.5in (19cm) wide.
£200-275 *HOW*

A pair of Staffordshire spaniels, brown and white with gilt collars, late 19thC, 12in (31cm).
£250-300 *S(S)*

A Staffordshire doe, c1800, 5in (13cm) wide.
£500-600 *JHo*

A pottery dog on a cushion, decorated in Prattware colours, probably Yorkshire, c1810, 2in (5cm).
£350-450 *JHo*

A pair of Staffordshire hearth dogs with children, decorated in red and white, c1860, 12.5in (32cm).
£400-450 *HOW*

An early English pointer, in brown and white enamels, standing on a flower encrusted green base, c1820, 3in (8cm).
£400-600 *HEY*

A pair of Staffordshire donkeys carrying baskets of flowers, c1870, 9in (23cm).   **£200-250** *HOW*

A Staffordshire greyhound, c1876, 11in (28cm).
£500-600 *RP*

A rare model

A Yorkshire figure of a show horse, decorated in raspberry, ochre, green and black, c1810, 7in (17.5cm) wide.
£2,700-3,000 *LR*

A North Country figure of a race horse in sponged tones of green and ochre, with blue saddle, c1810, 6in (15cm) wide.
£2,200-3,000 *LR*

A North Country horse, decorated in grey and yellow with green washed base, 5in (13cm) wide.
£2,500-3,000 *LR*

A pair of Ralph Wood stag and doe figures, decorated in translucent glazes, c1785.
£2,500-3,000 the pair *LR*

An early Staffordshire figure of a sheep, crudely splashed in manganese, on a green washed base, c1785, 4in (10cm) wide.
£500-550 *LR*

A Staffordshire cat, late 18thC, 9in (23cm).
£2,650-3,000 *JHo*

A faience cat, by George Martel, Boulogne, c1900, 10in (25cm).
£350-380 *VH*

A pair of Staffordshire zebras, c1860, 6in (15cm).
£360-400 *RWB*

A pair of Staffordshire pottery zebras, with long flaring manes and gilt bridles, slight chip to base, late 19thC, 9in (23cm).
£600-700 *S(S)*

A pair of Staffordshire pottery zebras, each beast striped black with flaring mane, c1900, 8.5in (21.5cm).
£400-500 *S(S)*

A creamware bull baiting group, decorated in enamel colours, the bull in pinkish brown, with black and white terrier, c1800, 7in (18cm).
£750-850 *HEY*

A Staffordshire model of a ram and lamb, on a mound base with bocage to rear, with green and brown enamel decoration, c1825, 5in (13cm)
£300-350 *LR*

A pair of Salt pottery bocage figures, one inscribed 'Sportsman' depicting a man with his shotgun, powder flask and hound, his lady companion entitled 'Archer' with a bow, arrow and straw target, slight damage, one inscribed Salt, 7in (17.5cm).
£550-650 *Bea*

Figures - People

A figure, probably made at Pill Pottery, Newport, run by H. Davies, c1840, 8in (20cm).
£330-380 *IW*

A Prattware figure of Bacchus, showing a domestic scene, decorated in ochre, green and brown, on a high square base, c1800, 10in (25cm).
£550-650 *LR*

A Prattware coloured figure of a girl holding oranges in her apron, c1815, 10in (25cm).
£250-300 *HOW*

35

A Pill Pottery, Newport, Gwent, figure, damaged, c1840, 7in (18cm).
£430-480 *IW*

A Leeds figure of Minerva, Goddess of Wisdom, decorated in brown, turquoise, black, blue and red, c1790, 11in (28cm).
£1,000-1,200 *LR*

A Prattware figure of a hurdy gurdy player, with acanthus leaf decoration and underglaze colours of blue, brown, ochre and green, on a square base c1800, 10in (25cm).
£550-600 *LR*

A Staffordshire Obadiah Sherratt type Dandies group, decorated in enamel colours, c1820, 7in (18cm).
£550-650 *LR*

A Prattware figure of Summer, with a cornucopia of flowers, c1810, 6.5in (16cm).
£350-400 *LR*

A hollow Prattware figure of Spring, modelled as a young lady holding a basket of flowers, decorated in yellow, brown, white, ochre, blue and green, c1800, 6in (15cm).
£350-400 *LR*

A pair of Staffordshire figures, Protestantism and Popery, c1850, 9in (23cm).
£1,250-1,400 *JO*

A Staffordshire figure group, in green, red, mauve and yellow, c1820, 5in (13cm).
£980-1,200 *JHo*

An Obadiah Sherratt figure of Faith, in green, yellow, white, red and green enamel colours, with lustre cross, c1815, 8in (20cm).
£350-450 *LR*

An Obadiah Sherratt type theatrical figure, in Turkish costume sitting on a tree stump, in yellow with blue edging and green base, c1820, 4in (10cm).
£150-200 *LR*

A pair of Staffordshire itinerant musicians with theatrical connections, Douglas and Billy Waters, c1820, 6.5 and 7in (16 and 18cm).
£1,800-1,900 *LR*

An Enoch Wood figure of Cupid disguised as a fruit seller, decorated in turquoise, black, and purple on green and brown base, c1800.
£275-350 *LR*

A hollow Staffordshire model of a lower deck sailor, standing against an anchor, with blue and white uniform, black hat and green base, c1820, 8in (20cm).
£250-300 *LR*

A rare Obadiah Sherratt figure of Flora with bocage, in multi-coloured enamels, c1820, 7.5in (19cm).
£500-600   *LR*

A hollow square based figure of Andromache, mourning the ashes of Wertha, in green, ochre and brown underglazed colours, c1800, 6in (15cm).
£350-400   *LR*

A Staffordshire figure of a lady with bird,decorated in Prattware colours, c1880, 7in (18cm).
£600-700   *JHo*

A Staffordshire Walton group, Return from Egypt, c1826, 8.5in (21cm).
£1,800-2,000   *JHo*

A pair of Staffordshire figures, Elijah and The Widow, 10in (25cm).
£700-900   *JO*

A Staffordshire figure of St George and the Dragon, decorated in coloured enamels, c1815, 10.5in (26cm).
£750-850   *LR*

A Ralph Wood figure of a bagpiper, decorated in translucent glazes of brown, yellow and green, 8in (20cm).
£1,500-1,700   *LR*

A Staffordshire religious group, c1855, 11in (28cm).
£2,500-3,000 *JHo*

A Yorkshire money box group of clock, figures and animals, 9in (23cm).
£1,200-1,500 *JHo*

A Staffordshire group of Romeo and Juliet, 12in (31cm).
£500-600 *JO*

A Wood type figure of a haymaker with bocage support, decorated in turquoise, red and yellow enamels, c1875, 8in (20cm).
£375-450 *LR*

A Yorkshire figure of the lost sheep found, decorated in sponged Prattware colours of blue, ochre and green, c1800, 9in (23cm).
£450-550 *LR*

An Enoch Wood type figure of Apollo, decorated in flesh, with white drape, on green base, c1800, 8in (20cm).
£225-350 *LR*

A Staffordshire figure of
Nicodemus, 11in (28cm).
£700-800 *JO*

A Walton figure of a shepherdess
standing against a 4-branch
bocage, decorated in blue, white
and green, impressed mark,
c1820, 5.5in (13cm).
£300-350 *LR*

An Enoch Wood type figure
of the Wise Virgin, decorated
in enamel colours, on a
hollow base, c1800,
8in (20cm).
£250-350 *LR*

Rural Pastime

A pair of Staffordshire figures,
Venus and Neptune, in pastel
shades of green, blue and ochre,
on bases, c1785, 11in (28cm).
£3,000-5,000 *JHo*

A pair of Staffordshire figures,
painted in shades of green and
brown, c1750, 7in (18cm).
£5,500-5,700 *JHo*

An R Wood type group, inscribed
Rural Pastime, depicting
musicians in a rural setting, with
underglaze and enamel
decoration in salmon pink, pale
blue and green, c1795, 8in (20cm).
£550-650 *LR*

A Staffordshire figure of the
Prince of Hesse on horseback,
c1860, 10in (25cm).
£150-180 *HOW*

Staffordshire Figures of the Victorian Era

A Staffordshire figure of Topsy and Eva, c1852, 9in (22.5cm), B.26/84.
£350-400 *JO*

A Staffordshire figure of Miss Nightingale and The Wounded Soldier, she in green skirt, pink blouse and blue veil, he in brown coat with blue sling, c1855, 10in (25cm). C/55 (143).
£850-950 *ANX*

A pair of Staffordshire figures of Havelock and Campbell, in blue coats with turquoise sashes, c1857, 9in (22.5cm), C/35 (176-177).
£750-850 *ANX*

A Staffordshire figure of William Wallace, the Scottish Champion, in plumed hat and plaid kilt, holding a round shield and a sword in his right hand, cracked, 17.5in (44cm), I/6.
£150-250 *WIL*

A Staffordshire figure entitled Soldiers Dream, the soldier wearing blue coat and white, green and red kilt, with ochre sash, c1854, 14in (35.5cm), C/73 (210).
£450-550 *ANX*

Staffordshire Figures

The letters and figures in brackets refer to the book *Staffordshire Portrait Figures,* by P.D. Gordon Pugh.

A pair of Staffordshire figures of cricketers, decorated in pale colours with blue coats, c1865, 10in (25cm), F/6 (11,12).
£800-1,000 *ANX*

A Staffordshire figure of The King of Sardinia, in blue coat and pink cape, on coloured base, c1854, 13in (33cm), C/102 (300).
£550-650 *ANX*

A Staffordshire figure of the
Begging Sailor, wearing blue coat
with pink bag, and a child
wearing a pink coat, c1854, 16in
(40.5cm), C/81 (236).
£650-750 *ANX*

A Staffordshire figure of Jenny
Lind as Alice in Meyerbeer's
opera, wearing a blue and yellow
dress, c1847, 13.5in (34.5cm),
E/80 (158).
£750-800 *ANX*

A Staffordshire figure of Romeo
and Juliet, played by the
Cushman sisters, c1852, 10.5in
(26.5cm) E/1A (1).
£700-800 *ANX*

Two Staffordshire figures of The
King of Sardinia, and Garibaldi,
c1860, 10.5in (26.5cm), C/102
(298-299).
£550-650 *ANX*

A Staffordshire figure of The
Sailors Return, c1855, 12.5in
(32cm), C/71 (197).
£600-700 *ANX*

A pair of Staffordshire figures of
Omer Pacha and The Sultan,
both in navy coats with yellow
saddle blankets,
c1854, 10in
(25cm), C/64
(166 and 167).
£700-800 *ANX*

In the Ceramics section if
there is only one
measurement it usually
refers to the height of the
piece.

Flatware

A William Adams hand decorated plate, with impressed mark, c1850, 9in (22.5cm).
£40-45 *IW*

A delft blue, white and brown plate, c1750, 8in (20cm).
£780-850 *JHo*

A London delft blue and white plate, c1760, 7in (17.5cm).
£180-220 *JHo*

A Liverpool delft plate, decorated in blue, white, green and brown, c1760, 7in (17.5cm).
£275-325 *JHo*

A delft blue and white plate, dated 1737, 9.5in (22.5cm).
£1,150-1,250 *JHo*

A Bristol delft plate depicting a peacock, in blue, white, brown and ochre, c1730, 8in (20cm).
£1,200-1,300 *JHo*

A London delft plate in blue, white and ochre, c1695, 8.5in (21cm).
£2,500-3,000 *JHo*

A London delft blue and white stand, c1725, 5.5in (13.5cm).
£1,300-1,400 *JHo*

A Buckley slipware dish, c1900, 11.5in (29cm) wide.
£240-270 *IW*

A Bristol delft blue oak leaf charger, mainly blue, yellow and green, repaired, c1700, 14in (35.5cm).
£1,200-1,900 *LR*

A Dutch Delft child's plate, c1760, 6.5in (16cm).
£60-80 *IW*

When a child left home the mother would make a hole in the plate so that it could never be used again, and it would be hung on the wall by a piece of string.

A Rothwell, Leeds, plate, decorated in sponged glazes of brown and emerald green, stippled brown to reverse, c1775, 9.5in (24cm).
£250-300 *LR*

A pair of Ashworths teapot stands, with double landscape decoration, c1865, 6in (15cm).
£100-130 *VH*

A Desvres hors d'oeuvre dish, c1890, 12in (30.5cm).
£150-190 *VH*

A Dutch Delft plate, c1760, 6.5in (16.5cm).
£60-80 *IW*

A C.J. Mason dessert plate, with painted floral bouquet, 8in (20cm).
£200-230 *VH*

A Middlesbrough Pottery child's plate, with daisy relief moulded border, the central panel with transfer printed nursery rhyme 'Hey Diddle Diddle', c1845, 7in (18cm).
£50-85 *HOW*

A child's plate, with verse by Isaac Watts, possibly Llanelly Pottery South Wales, 6.5in (16cm).
£40-50 *IW*

A Bristol delft blue charger, depicting Adam and Eve, repaired, c1700, 14in (35.5cm).
£1,750-1,950 *LR*

A Quimper comport, c1900, 9in (23cm) diam.
£150-170 *VH*

A Minton majolica 'Lazy Susan', with encaustic decoration in white, purple, ochre, brown, turquoise and green, revolving on a flared foot, cracks to rim, impressed mark and model number 799, c1873, 18in (46cm) diam.
£720-800 *C*

A Nevers plate, decorated with a peacock, 9in (23cm).
£250-300 *JH*

A Rouen plate, c1770, 9in (23cm).
£250-300 *VH*

A red painted daisy plate, 'The Sick Donkey', Anthony Scott, Sunderland, c1845, 6in (15cm).
£100-120 *IS*

A child's plate, with relief moulded border of flowers in dark red, the central panel with transfer print of 'Grandad' with related verse, probably Staffordshire, c1840, 7in (18cm).
£50-85 *HOW*

A Swansea Pottery plate, with black and white underglaze sheet pattern transfer, Lazuli pattern, Dillwyn & Co., c1850, 10.5in (26cm).
£90-120 *HOW*

Nine underglaze painted moulded miniature plates, c1810, 3in (8cm).
£240-280 *IW*

A Fremington, Devon, dish with combed slip, c1890, 12in (30.5cm) wide.
£140-160 *IW*

A Sunderland or Newcastle dish, 11in (28cm) wide.
£45-50 *IW*

A Davenport blue and white platter, impressed mark, c1830, 21in (53cm) wide.
£200-260 *HOW*

A Wedgwood majolica fish platter, moulded in relief on a pale turquoise ground, painted in shades of grey and white and with facial features and gills enriched in pink, within a shaped, reeded grey rim, cracked and repaired, impressed marks, pattern number M 2164, c1876, 25in (64cm) wide.
£420-600 *C*

A creamware ashet, Thomas Fell, Newcastle, impressed mark, c1820, 10in (25cm) wide.
£100-150 *IS*

A Staffordshire saltglazed plate, c1750.
£150-180 *RP*

A pearlware relief moulded plate, with transfer printed decoration, Dawson & Co., Sunderland, impressed mark, c1830, 9in (23cm) .
£60-80 *IS*

A Swansea Pottery plate, with a transfer print of a bird on a basket of fruit, painted in bright enamel colours, c1830.
£50-85 *HOW*

A Swiss slipware bowl, late 19thC, 10.5in (26cm) diam.
£40-50 *IW*

A slipware dish, some damage, c1800, 16in (41cm) diam.
£900-1,000 *IW*

A pair of hand decorated platters, by Clementson, c1860, 16in (41cm).
£450-500 *RP*

A hand painted dish, c1880, 9in (23cm) diam.
£35-40 *IW*

A North of England agate bodied pie dish, late 19thC, 14 by 10in (36 by 25cm).
£100-120 *IW*

A Staffordshire earthenware plate, printed in the Buffalo pattern in blue, c1820, 10in (25cm).
£40-60 *TVA*

A creamware dish, decorated with flowers in underglaze blue and dated 1778, 16in (41cm) diam.
£400-450 *HOW*

A child's plate, Joseph series, c1850, 6.5in (16cm).
£35-45 *IW*

A slipware plate decorated in brown, cream and ochre, late 18thC, 8.5in (21cm).
£2,500-3,000 *JHo*

A slipware charger, late 18thC, 13in (33cm).
£1,000-1,250 *JHo*

A rare relief moulded alphabet plate, impressed Fordy & Patterson, Sheriff Hill Pottery, Newcastle, Gateshead, c1825, 3.5in (9cm).
£350-450 *IS*

An Hispano-Moresque copper lustre charger, with central boss, painted concentric bands of stylised leaves and flowers, 16thC, 15.5in (39cm).
£1,000-1,200 *S(S)*

Inkstands

A Quimper inkstand, c1890, 10.5in (26cm) wide.
£400-480 *VH*

A Mason's Ironstone inkwell, Old School House pattern, c1815, 2.5in (6cm) diam.
£300-335 *VH*

A rare Mason's inkstand, decorated in green enamel with gilt, impressed mark, c1815, 5in (13cm).
£680-720 *VH*

A Mason's Ironstone inkstand, with black printed mark, replaced lids, c1835, 12in (31cm) wide.
£800-850 *VH*

A Georgian inkstand, decorated in blue and ochre, green shell tops, mid-19thC, 15in (38cm) wide.
£600-650 *VH*

Jardinières

A George Jones Majolica jardinière, with dark blue ground, moulded in relief with a frieze of half-length figures of sea gods and goddesses, turquoise glazed interior and yellow line rim, on a spreading foot, incised monogram, painted pattern number 2784, c1880, 23in (59cm) wide.
£3,500-4,000 *C*

A Mintons large pottery jardinière.
£850-900 *P(S)*

Jars

An English delft blue and white drug jar, 7in (18cm).
£700-900 *JHo*

A London delft, blue and white drug jar, c1730, 4in (10cm).
£680-720 *JHo*

Jugs

A Bristol pearlware puzzle jug, decorated with flower sprays, inscribed initials, dated August 11th - 1819, probably painted by William Fifield, repaired, 5in (13cm).
£500-550 *LR*

A Claypits Pottery jug, green, c1900, 7in (18cm).
£40-50 *IW*

A delft puzzle jug, probably Liverpool, c1740, 7in (17cm).
£1,200-1,300 *IW*

A pair of Davenport jugs, pink and purple lustre decorated with flowers and named, c1830, 8.5in (21cm).
£800-1,000 *LR*

A Davenport ewer, with blue and white underglaze transfer pattern, c1835, 9in (23cm).
£100-150 *HOW*

A Drabware jug, c1810, 3.5in (9cm).
£40-50 *IW*

Three Nottingham saltglazed bear baiting jugs, mid-18thC.
£10,000-12,000 *GIL*

An English delftware puzzle jug, inscribed with the usual verse, Liverpool, chipped, c1760, 7in (17cm).
£1,200-1,600 *S*

A Mason's sparrow beek jug, c1815, 2.5in (6cm).
£180-220 *VH*

Drink it up

A Quimper wall font and basin, 18in (46cm) complete.
£1,200-1,600 *VH*

A creamware beer jug, decorated with roses and flower sprigs, in the Leeds manner, inscribed Drink it up under the spout, strap handle, c1780, 7in (18cm).
£300-350 *LR*

A Staffordshire saltglazed puzzle jug, decorated in scratch blue and white, c1760, 7in (18cm).
£2,500-3,000 *JHo*

A Staffordshire bear jug and cover, decorated in tones of beige and brown, c1780, 8in (20cm).
£3,000-3,500 *LR*

A Minton 'Majolica' jug, modelled in high relief with peasant figures dancing and a man seated beneath the spout, the foot with a formal border of crosses and studding, all glazed in tones of green, blue, yellow, brown and white, registration and impressed marks, shape number and date code for 1865, 10in (25cm).
£800-1,200 *S*

A pottery jug, with black and white transfer of a ship under sail, probably Liverpool, c1810, 5in (13cm).
£100-150 *HOW*

A Mason's Ironstone jug, with green dolphin handle and animal mask supporting handle, printed and painted with oriental flowers and vessels, printed Mason's mark, c1820, 13in (33cm).
£1,100-1,300 *S(S)*

A puzzle jug, probably Pill Pottery, Newport, Gwent, c1850, 8in (20cm).
£150-180 *IW*

A Derbyshire saltglazed jug, 8.5in (21cm).
£150-180 *IW*

An underglaze harvest jug, with painted decoration, c1795, 6.5in (16cm).
£180-200 *IW*

A Staffordshire saltglaze jug, with hand painted and enamelled floral decoration, 3in (8cm).
£1,000-1,500 *JHo*

Two Mocha jugs, half gallon and quart, by Edge Malcolm & Co., c1890, 6 and 7.5in (15 and 19cm).
£250-300 *IW*

A pair of pottery jugs in the Swansea manner, each painted with a wide band of roses on a black ground above a light green base, the foliate and scroll moulding heightened in gold, early 19thC, 5in (15cm).
£400-500 *Bea*

A Swansea Pottery pouch jug and cover, Dillwyn's, in saxon blue, c1835, 8in (20cm)
£170-200 *RP*

A Swansea jug, Cymro stone china, c1835, 5in (13cm)
£90-110 *RP*

A Staffordshire lustre jug, depicting scenes from the cotton trade and inscribed Success to the Friendly Cotton Spinners and Liberty to the Sons of Britain, decorated in coloured enamel, c1835, 5in (13cm).
£250-300 *LR*

A yellow pottery jug with silver lustre decoration and a green transfer of Burdett, c1815, 5in (13cm).
£250-300 *HOW*

A Swansea, Landore marked, jug, c1830, 8in (20cm).
£120-140 *RP*

A pearlware jug, decorated in colour enamels and inscribed Gamelia Bingley 1800 surrounded by swags of flowers, strap handle, 7in (18cm).
£400-450 *LR*

A Swansea Pottery jug in Lazuli pattern, c1850, 16in (41cm).
£280-320 *RP*

A silver lustre jug with panels of leaves and vines, in yellow, orange and black, c1820, 4in (10cm).
£250-300 *LR*

A silver lustre jug, with flowers and bird decoration, c1820, 5.5in (14cm).
£300-350 *LR*

A pair of Staffordshire jugs, shaped as begging spaniels, coloured in red and white, c1860, 10.5in (26cm).
£400-450 *HOW*

A Napoleonic silver lustre jug, with enamelled panels of mounted Cossacks, c1815, 4in (11cm).
£350-400 *LR*

A Sunderland Pottery jug and basin, with underglaze black transfer of 'Feather' pattern highlighted with enamel colour decoration, c1845, Jug 9in (23cm).
£120-160 *HOW*

A pottery jug with black transfer scenes showing 'Courtship' and 'Matrimony', c1815, 6in (15cm).
£140-160 *HOW*

A moulded cream jug, decorated colours, c1800, 3in (8cm).
£100-120 *IW*

> **Miller's is a price GUIDE not a price LIST**

A creamware jug depicting Toby Fillpot, dressed in red coat, pink waistcoat and yellow breeches, on one side, the other The Farriers Arms, in the middle the date 1810, 7.5in (19cm).
£300-350 *HEY*

An earthenware jug, with transfer printed scenes from the Prodigal Son in Georgian costume, 6in (15cm).
£120-150 *IW*

An underglaze decorated jug, c1795, 7in (18cm).
£200-240 *IW*

A gravel finish jug, with gadrooned band, c1830, 3in (8cm).
£25-30 *IW*

A pink lustre jug, 'Female Archers', marked Fen, 5.5in (14cm).
£300-350 *RP*

A gaudy lustre jug, c1840, 6.5in (16cm).
£90-100 *RP*

A Walton squat type overglaze enamel Toby jug, with blue swirled coat, pink trousers and green base, c1800, 7in (18cm).
£200-300 *HEY*

Toby Jugs

A creamware A Neale & Co.,Toby jug, modelled as a jovial man holding a mug of frothing ale, wearing black hat, green waistcoat, dark brown jacket and light brown breeches, square base with canted angles, minor chip and restoration, impressed mark, incised 15, c1795, 10in (25cm).
£850-1,100 *C*

A Neale & Co., Toby jug, decorated with overglaze enamels of turquoise coat, buff breeches and blue socks, c1800, 10in (25cm).
£750-850 *HEY*

An overglaze enamel 'Gin Woman' Toby jug, with yellow hat, black hair, pink face, green and rust dress, c1840, 10in (25cm).
£200-300 *HEY*

A collection of 11 Wilkinson Ltd., WWI Toby jugs, each designed by Sir F. Carruthers Gould, the characters include King George V, President Wilson, Lord Kitchener, Earl Haig, Sir John French, Marshal Foch, General Botha, Marshal Joffre, Admiral Beatty, Admiral Jellicoe and Lloyd George, each jug decorated in bright colours, restoration to President Wilson's hat, crack to hat of Marshal Joffre, printed mark, facsimile signature and retailer's mark for Soane and Smith 10 to 12in (25 to 31cm).
£4,000-5,000 *P(S)*

A Wilkinson Ltd. Toby jug, from WWI series, designed by Sir F. Carruthers Gould, in the form of Lloyd George, a shell between his knees, inscribed 'Shell Out', 10in (25cm).
£350-400 *Bea*

A Wilkinson Ltd. Toby jug, from WWI series, designed by Sir F. Carruthers Gould, in the form of Marshall Joffre, sitting with a shell on his knee, 10.5in (26cm).
£350-400 *Bea*

An underglaze Toby jug, with blue coat, pink breeches and face, black hat and shoes, on a stippled base, c1840, 10in (25cm).
£150-250 *HEY*

A pair of Minton majolica Toby jugs, 'The Barrister', 'The Fan Lady', impressed date mark 1867, restored, 11.5in (29cm).
£1,000-1,200 *LR*

A Hearty Good Fellow Toby jug, with branch handle, in coloured enamels , marked Walton, c1820, 11in (28cm).
£900-1,100 *LR*

A pearlware Toby jug, with manganese glazed hat, hair breeches and shoes, blue splashed coat, ochre waistcoat, Staffordshire or Yorkshire, chipped and cracked, c1780, 10.5in (26cm).
£600-700 *C*

A Prattware Toby jug, decorated in yellow and blue patterned jacket and socks, blue waistcoat, yellow breeches, brown hat and shoes, c1790, 10in (25cm).
£900-1,000 *HEY*

A cross-legged Toby jug, wearing blue and white transfer printed Willow pattern jacket and hat and brown trousers, c1890, 8in (20cm).
£150-250 *HEY*

An underglaze Toby jug, decorated in Pratt colours of blue coat, yellow waistcoat and ochre breeches, c1840, 10in (25cm).
£150-250 *HEY*

Dr Johnson or 'The Drunken Parson' Toby jug, dressed in black underglaze colours, sitting on a rust Georgian style chair, c1840, 8in (20cm).
£450-550 *HEY*

The Nightwatchman or George Whitfield Toby jug, dressed in grey and black coat, the spout forming the chair back, c1890, 7in (18cm).
£200-250 *HEY*

An underglaze snuff taker Toby jug with blue jacket, red breeches, and yellow waistcoat, c1900, 9in (23cm).
£60-80 *HEY*

Mugs

An English delftware blue and white chequer pattern mug, probably Bristol, repaired, l8thC, 5in (12.5cm) high.
£1,700-2,000 *S*

An early Victorian pearlware frog mug to commemorate the signing of the Peace Treaty of the Crimean War, printed in underglaze black and naively overpainted in colours with a French and English soldier shaking hands, beneath the scrolled legend 'May They Ever Be United', within Sunderland pink lustre rims and waved line decoration, damaged, 1856, 5in (12cm) high.
£270-320 *HSS*

An English delft named and dated mug, probably Lambeth, with small deep grooved strap handle, painted in blue with a pair of birds perched upon a zig-zag fence flanked by flowering branches, inscribed 'Richard Latham, 1744', below a diapered and stylised flower border, worn, 6.5in (16.5cm) high.
£8,500-10,000 *HSS*

An English delft mug, probably Bristol, painted in blue, 18thC, damaged and restored, 5in (12.5cm) high.
£800-1,000 *S*

A pottery mug with transfer print in red, inscribed 'Loyal Volunteer', c1800, 4.5in (11cm) high.
£220-250 *JHo*

An orange lustre decorated frog mug, 'The Unfortunate London', Anthony Scott, Sunderland, c1860, 5in (12.5cm) high.
£170-190 *IS*

A Mason's Ironstone mug, decorated in Japan pattern, with wavy edging, c1830, 4in (10cm) high.
£200-250 *HOW*

An orange lustre decorated primitive Methodist love feast mug, inscribed on verso, probably A. Scott, Sunderland, c1870, 5in (12.5cm) high.
£100-150 *IS*

A creamware mug, inscribed 'Patrick', c1830, 3.5in (8.5cm) high.
£100-130 *RP*

A Ralph Wood type creamware Bacchus mask mug, decorated in green and brown translucent glazes, c1780, 4.5in (11cm) high.
£150-200 *HEY*

A creamware mug in the form of Admiral Lord Rodney, his shoulders in green translucent glaze, decorated in pale manganese, brown and ochre, with yellow headband, inscribed 'Success to Lord Rodney' in relief, c1785, 4.5in (11cm) high.
£400-500 *HEY*

A Prattware mug modelled as Admiral Lord Rodney, decorated in blue, orange, green, ochre and brown, restoration to base, c1790, 6.5in (16cm) high.
£300-400 *HEY*

A child's mug, decorated with the alphabet, c1880, 3in (7.5cm) high.
£40-60 *IW*

A child's mug, c1820, 2in (5cm) high.
£60-80 *IW*

A child's mug, with alphabet painted in underglaze colour, c1790, 2.5in (6cm) high.
£280-320 *IW*

A child's mug, Scottish, c1885, 3.5in (8.5cm) high.
£40-50 *IW*

A child's mug, c1860, 4in (10cm) high.
£60-80 *RP*

A child's mug, c1870, 3in (7.5cm) high.
£60-80 *IW*

A marblised tankard, in blue, black and cream on white, cl800, 6in (15cm).
£500-650 *JHo*

A small banded mug, c1860, 3in (7.5cm) high.
£50-60 *IW*

A Mocha half-pint mug, c1890, 4in (10cm) high.
£80-100 *IW*

Plaques

A Staffordshire pearlware plaque, depicting Peace and Plenty before a brazier, with a classical swag surround and decoration, c1790, 5in (12.5cm) high.
£700-800 *LR*

A Prattware plaque, depicting the head of a classical female, decorated in typical Prattware palate, c1800, 7.5in (18.5cm) high.
£600-700 *LR*

A Staffordshire plaque, inscribed 'Du of York', decorated in blue, white, ochre and yellow, c1800, 4.5in (11.5cm) high.
£350-450 *JHo*

A creamware plaque of Paris and Oenone in a woodland setting, decorated in enamel with leaf moulded borders, c1800, 9in (22.5cm) high.
£400-500 *LR*

A Prattware plaque of Bacchus and Venus, decorated in blue, ochre, green, and brown, impressed EC 1801 on reverse, c1801, 8in (20cm) high.
£600-700 *LR*

A pink lustre decorated plaque inscribed 'Duke of Wellington - 131 guns', Anthony Scott, Sunderland, c1840, 9in (22.5cm) wide.
£150-170 *IS*

Pots

A rare Prattware plaque of a horse grazing in a rural setting, c1800, repaired, 4.5in (11cm) high.
£450-500 *LR*

A brownware storage pot, with relief moulding of Victoria and her mother, c1840, 6in (15cm) high. £80-110 *HOW*

A Desvres (Pas de Calais) Revolutionary faience mustard pot, c1872, 7.5in (18.5cm) high.
£145-165 *VH*

A Sarreguemines majolica pot, formed as a tree stump with dogs chasing a rabbit into its burrow, complete with handles, 7in (17.5cm).
£100-130 *GAK*

An English delftware bulb pot, London or Bristol, c1760, restored, 5in (12.5cm) high.
£750-850 *S*

A pearlware baluster shaped mustard pot, decorated in underglaze blue, lid missing, c1790, 4.5in (11.5cm) high.
£130-150 *IW*

An English delftware blue and white posset pot with lid, London or Bristol, c1720, 8.5in (21cm) high.
£2,000-2,500 *JHo*

Posset pots were also made in lead glazed and manganese glazed earthenware and white and brown saltglazed ware. They always had two handles but did not necessarily have a drinking spout. Posset was a wholesome gruel sold in inns and consisted of ale, oats and honey. It was often fortified with brandy.

Services

A Mason's Ironstone dessert service, decorated with a scroll chinoiserie pattern of Orientals seated and standing taking tea in a rocky garden reserved on a tight scroll ground with a lobed panel of trophies, on an elaborately moulded surface, comprising: 13 plates, 2 sauce tureens, covers and stand, 8 various shaped dishes, and a comport, c1820, some damage, plates 9in (22.5cm)
£1,800-2,200 *S*

A Mason's Patent Ironstone part dinner service, comprising: 2 tureens with covers and stands, 16 plates and 11 dishes, early 19thC.   **£400-500** *N(A)*

A Wedgwood dessert service comprising: 6 plates, 4 dishes, 1 comport, c1810, comport 5in (12.5cm) high.
£1,000-1,250 *VH*

Tea and Coffee Pots

A teapot from the William Greatbatch factory, depicting The Hun August Keppel, hand painted, coloured transfer print, c1780, 6in (15cm).
£2,500-3,000 *JHo*

A Jackfield teapot, c1755, 3.5in (8.5cm).
£150-180 *IW*

A Mason's miniature teapot and cover, 3in (7.5cm).
£350-380 *VH*

A Wedgwood creamware teapot and cover, decorated with a Chinaman in a rocky landscape, the reverse with sprays of roses, with Crabstock spout and handle, damaged, c1765, 5.5in (13.5cm).
£750-850 *LR*

A Wedgwood teapot and cover, finely decorated with bouquets of flowers, with Crabstock handle and spout, c1765, 4in (10cm).
£800-900 *LR*

A Mason's teapot and sucrier, decorated with waterlilies, c1815, 7.5in (19cm).
£500-570 *VH*

Two Whieldon type teapots, 18thC.
l. **£2,800-3,200**
r. **£750-800** *N(A)*

A Minton majolica teapot and cover, modelled as a yellow gourd with leaves, flowers and a branch handle, the cover as a mushroom, spout restored, impressed marks c1870, 5in (12.5cm).
£950-1,200 *CSK*

An English pearlware pottery tea kettle, decorated with red lines, in the manner of Wedgwood, late 19thC, 6in (15cm).
£60-100 *GAK*

A Bargeware kettle and stand, inscribed 'A Happy New Year', c1890, 10in (25cm).
£170-200 *RP*

A Staffordshire Agateware 'pecten shell' teapot with cover, the green ground body veined in colours and modelled in relief, the spout as a dragon's head and neck, the C-scrolled handle as a tail, the cover with rampant Dog of Fo finial, connected with a metal chain to the handle, c1740, 5.5in (13.5cm).
£2,400-2,600 *CAm*

A Staffordshire stoneware teapot, decorated with Chinese pattern, with replacement antique silver spout, c1765, 6in (15cm) high.
£440-500 *JHo*

Two Mason's miniature coffee pots and covers, 2in (5cm).
l. Argyle, c1815, restored. **£200-250**.
r. c1820. **£200-275** *VH*

A saltglazed teapot and cover with blue ground, decorated with enamelled red, green and yellow roses, with Crabstock handle and spout, finial repaired, c1760, 4.5in (11.5cm).
£1,100-1,300 *LR*

A pearlware teapot and cover, decorated with 8 dancing figures, picked out in enamel colours in red, blue and green, c1810, 5.5in (13.5cm).
£425-475 *LR*

A Redware glazed engine turned teapot, c1770, 4.5in (11cm).
£150-180 *IW*

A saltglazed teapot and cover, decorated in coloured enamels with roses and blossoms, with Crabstock handle and spout, c1740, 5.5in (13.5cm).
£600-700 *LR*

A Leeds teapot and cover, Dutch decorated with sprays of roses, c1780, 5.5in (13.5cm).
£450-550 *LR*

Tiles

A London delft blue and white tile, depicting Lazarus in Heaven, and The Rich Man in Hell, c1740.
£40-50 *JHo*

A Liverpool delft blue and white tile, c1760, 5in (12.5cm) square.
£30-40 *JHo*

A Liverpool woodblock transfer print tile, c1757.
£400-450 *JHo*

A Liverpool delft blue and white tile, c1770, 5in (12.5cm) square.
£30-40 *JHo*

A Liverpool delft blue and white tile, c1760, 5in (12.5cm) square.
£30-40 *JHo*

A Liverpool tile, partly restored, 5in (12.5cm) square.
£55-70 *JHo*

A London delft blue and white tile, depicting The Miracle of the Loaves and Fishes, c1740.
£35-55 *JHo*

A London delft blue and white tile, depicting Jesus and The Woman of Samaria, c1740, 5in (12.5cm) square.
£40-70 *JHo*

A London delft blue and white tile, 5in (12.5cm) square.
£50-70 *JHo*

A London delft blue and white tile, depicting Christ carrying the Cross, c1740, 5in (12.5cm) square.
£40-80 *JHo*

A London delft blue and white tile, depicting Christ and the Woman of Canaan, c1740, 5in (12.5cm) square.
£35-70 *JHo*

A Liverpool red transfer print tile, c1765, 5in (12.5cm) square.
£200-220 *JHo*

A Liverpool red transfer print tile, c1765, 5in (12.5cm) square.
£185-250 *JHo*

A Liverpool black and white transfer print tile, c1770, 5in (12.5cm) square.
£100-120 *JHo*

A Bristol delft blue and white tile, c1750.
£60-65 *JHo*

A Liverpool black and white transfer print tile, c1765, 5in (12.5cm) square.
£150-200 *JHo*

A Liverpool polychrome tile, c1750, 5in (12.5cm) square.
£195-230 *JHo*

A London delft blue and white tile, depicting Peter and John healing a cripple at the gate of the Temple, c1740, 5in (12.5cm) square.
£40-45 *JHo*

A collection of 11 Dutch Delft tiles, each painted in blue with a different animal subject, repaired, 19thC, 6in (15cm) square. **£450-550** *S(S)*

Tureens

An Italian tin glazed maiolica tureen and cover, decorated in blue and white, c1900, 11in (28cm) high. **£100-150** *VH*

A Dillwyn & Co. Swansea Pottery lidded tureen, decorated in underglaze blue and white, c1815, 7in (17.5cm) wide. **£100-135** *HOW*

A swan cheese dish and cover, c1870, 12in (30.5cm). **£200-220** *RP*

A Staffordshire pottery bird tureen, decorated in yellow, green, red, grey, brown and blue, 5in (12.5cm) high. **£450-550** *JHo*

Vases

A faience mandolin vase, 11in (28cm). **£200-220** *VH*

A pair of Mason's Ironstone vases and covers of Chinese inspiration, printed and hand coloured with covers similarly decorated beneath an entwined dragon finial, one chipped, impressed and black printed marks, red painted pattern number Λ/9447/3, c1825, 25in (64cm). **£1,000-1,500** *S*

A London delft blue and white vase, c1750, 5.5in (14cm). **£1,400-1,800** *JHo*

An English delft blue and white vase, 7in (18cm). **£250-300** *JHo*

A garniture of 3 Mason's Ironstone two-handled vases and covers, printed and coloured with an elaborate chinoiserie pattern against a gilt ground, flanked by 2 blue dragon handles, covers similarly decorated and surmounted by a gilt seated shishi finial, matching internal flat covers, pseudo Chinese markings in underglaze blue, red painted numerals 537, c1825, tallest 15.5in (39cm).
£850-1,000 *S*

A Staffordshire saltglaze vase, with hand painted and enamelled Oriental design in pink, blue, green and yellow, c1760, 8in (20cm).
£2,500-3,000 *JHo*

A majolica vase of baluster form, decorated in colours, the body signed Walter and the foot inscribed O Milet, Sevres, 40in (101.5cm).
£780-850 *P(S)*

Spill Vases

A pair of Continental blue and white tin glazed earthenware two-handled vases, depicting 16thC Italian scenes, with acanthus leaf scrolling borders, some damage, late 19thC, 15in (39cm).
£300-500 *HSS*

A Wood type lion spill vase in enamel colours, c1800, 5in (13cm).
£1,000-1,200 *LR*

A Staffordshire zebra spill vase, with black and white zebra, orange inside vase and blue outside, c1870, 11.5in (29cm).
£300-350 *HEY*

A pair of Staffordshire spill vases, modelled as setters, c1860, 6in (15cm).
£600-650 *RWB*

A Staffordshire spill vase, modelled as a rustic man holding a bird's nest, seated by a tree with birds in the branches, with a dog at his side, c1820, 9in (23cm).
£450-500 *RWB*

A Staffordshire bull baiting spill vase, coloured brown, white and green, c1800, 8in (20cm).
£2,000-2,500 *JHo*

A Staffordshire spill vase group entitled 'The Rivals', c1855, 13in (33cm).
£175-195 *RWB*

A pair of Staffordshire creamware triple spill vases of Ralph Wood type, each modelled as entwined green dolphins supporting 3 reed moulded vases enriched in grey and yellow translucent glazes, on foliage moulded brown quatrefoil bases, chipped, c1780, 7.5in (19cm).
£700-1,000 *C*

A pair of Staffordshire figures of zebras being attacked by snakes with spill holder in the form of a tree trunk, c1860, 6in (15cm).
£200-250 *HOW*

Wemyss

A Wemyss three-handled mug, painted with geese, 5.5in (14cm).
£300-400 *RdeR*

A Wemyss 'combe' flower bowl, painted with large roses and foliage, cracked and chipped, impressed and painted Wemyss, c1900, 8in (20cm).
£400-500 *S(C)*

A Wemyss cockerel candlestick, 12in (30cm).
£200-300 *RdeR*

A Wemyss honey pot and cover, painted with bees, 7in (18cm).
£1,500-2,000 *RdeR*

A Wemyss cherry basket, c1920, 4.5in (11cm).
£700-900 *RdeR*

A Wemyss biscuit barrel and cover, painted with apples, 5in (12cm).
£200-250 *RdeR*

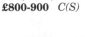

A Wemyss honey pot and cover modelled as a straw skep, the cover painted with bees on a shaded base, impressed and painted Wemyss, T. Goode & Co., 7in (18cm).
£800-900 *C(S)*

A Wemyss preserve jar and cover, painted with raspberries, chipped, impressed and painted Wemyss, and stamped T. Goode & Co., c1900, 5in (13cm).
£250-350 *S(C)*

A Wemyss Earlshall jug, painted in black and inscribed 'As the many wintered crow, that leads the clanging rookery home', and 'Earlshall Faire 1914', impressed and painted mark, 6in (15cm).
£450-650 *C(S)*

A Wemyss Earshall jug, painted in black with crows nesting in tall spindly trees, divided by a cartouche with 'Earlshall Faire, A.D. 1914' beneath the inscription 'Or whiles a clan o'roosty craws cangle the gether', handle repaired, impressed and painted Wemyss, 8in (20cm).
£270-350 *C(S)*

A Wemyss ewer, with high lip, painted with cherries on branches, impressed and painted Wemyss, stamped T. Goode & Co., c1900, 10in (25cm).
£300-350 *S(C)*

A Wemyss honey pot, painted with bees and hive, 5in (13cm).
£250-300 *RdeR*

A Wemyss preserve jar and cover, painted with brambles, 5in (13cm).
£150-200 *RdeR*

A Wemyss three-handled mug, painted with plums, 7in (18cm).
£700-900 *RdeR*

A Wemyss mug, painted with Jubilee pink ribbon, 5.5in (14cm). **£300-400** *RdeR*

A Wemyss child's mug, painted with apples, 3.5in (9cm). **£200-250** *RdeR*

A Wemyss crimson glazed pig, tail missing, impressed mark, Wemyss ware R H & S, 17in (43cm) long. **£2,500-3,000** *WAR*

Three Wemyss graduated models of ducks, each with green, yellow, blue, black, pink and red plumage on a circular tapering foot with yellow, blue and green swags, cracked and restored, impressed Wemyss marks, 6 to 8in (15 - 20cm). **£700-900** *C(S)*

A Wemyss Plichta pottery pig, its blue eyes framed by curly black lashes, and body painted with cherries, damaged, green painted marks Nekola, Pinxt, 25, Plichta, London, Made in England, 1920s, 18in (46cm). **£400-600** *S(S)*

A Wemyss burgundy pig, 6.5in (16cm) long. **£300-400** *RdeR*

A Wemyss pig, painted with clover leaves, minor glaze rubbing, impressed Wemyss Ware R.H. & S., printed T. Goode & Co., South Audley St., London, c1900, 6in (15cm) long. **£600-700** *S(S)*

A Wemyss black and white cat, with green eyes, 13in (33cm). **£1,500-2,500** *RdeR*

A Wemyss pig painted with shamrocks, repaired, impressed mark, 6in (15cm) long. **£400-450** *C*

A Wemyss green pig, 7in (18cm) long. **£200-300** *RdeR.*

A Wemyss 'combe' jardinière, painted by Edwin Sandland, with yellow and pink chrysanthemum beneath a green dentil rim, cracked, impressed and painted Wemyss mark, 9.5in (24cm) diam.
£650-750 *C(S)*

A Wemyss Earlshall jardinière, painted within green line rims, chipped, impressed Wemyss, 10.5in (26cm).
£1,000-1,200 *C(S)*

A Wemyss Gordon plate, painted with blackberries, 8in (20cm).
£150-250 *RdeR*

A Wemyss tray, painted with roses, 10 by 8in (25 by 20cm).
£150-200 *RdeR*

A Wemyss heart shaped tray, with red border and painted with cherries, c1890, 12 by 10.5in (31 by 26cm).
£300-400 *RdeR*

A Wemyss gypsy pot, painted with thistles, 4in (10cm).
£250-300 *RdeR*

A Wemyss dish, painted with buttercups, 5in (13 cm) wide.
£150-200 *RdeR*

A Wemyss vase, painted within green borders, cracked, impressed mark, c1900, 5in (13cm).
£400-500 *C*

A Wemyss Bonjour breakfast set, each piece painted with black cockerels in the grass, comprising: a teapot and lid, 2 cups, 2 saucers, 2 side plates, milk jug and sugar bowl, chipped, impressed Wemyss Ware R.H. & S., stamped T. Goode & Co., c1900.
£650-1,000 *S(C)*

A Wemyss plaque, painted with thistles, 5.5 by 4in (14 by 10cm).
£200-250 *RdeR*

A Wemyss pen tray, painted with cherries, 11in (28cm) wide.
£150-200 *RdeR*

A Wemyss ewer and basin, painted with a band of black cockerels in green grass, both cracked, both painted Wemyss, T. Goode & Co., the basin impressed Wemyss, c1900, jug 10in (25cm).
£600-800 *S(C)*

A Wemyss goblet commemorating Queen Victoria's Jubilee, 5.5in (14cm).
£300-400 *RdeR*

A Wemyss inkwell, painted with sweet peas, 10in (25cm) wide.
£200-300 *RdeR*

A Wemyss quaiche, painted with cherries, 8in (20cm) wide.
£150-200 *RdeR*

A Wemyss Lady Eva vase, painted by Karel Nekola, 11.5in (29cm).
£400-550 *RdeR*

A Wemyss Japan vase, painted with blue wisteria and foliage beneath a green swag band, impressed Wemyss Ware R.H. & S., 13in (33cm).
£1,500-1,800 *C(S)*

Two Wemyss Plichta pigs, 3in (8cm) long.
£20-25 each *RdeR*

A Bristol delftware bowl, with floral design, c1760, 9in (23cm).
£1,000-1,450 *JHo*

Three Bristol delftware fluted bowls, probably Brislington, restored, c1830, 7in (18cm) **£900-1,500** and a porringer or bleeding bowl, restored, c1725. **£2,000-2,500** *S*

A set of 5 Dutch Delft plates, De Roos factory, each painted with a biblical subject after Lucas van Leyden, rim chips, R mark in underglaze blue, 9in (23cm), c1678.
£4,000-5,000 *S*

An Adam and Eve charger, cracked and chipped, London, c1660, 16.5in (42cm).
£26,500-30,000 *S*

l. An English delftware dated christening bowl, London or Bristol, the exterior with figures and carriages near The Plough Inn, cracked and restored, 1752, 10.5in (26cm).
£22,500-25,000 *S*

A 'Midnight Modern Conversation' punch bowl, the exterior with rural landscape panels, restored, Liverpool, c1750, 10in (25cm).
£10,500-12,000 *S*

An armorial Lambeth delftware caudle cup, inscribed 1674, with paper label, 3.5in (9cm). **£19,000-22,000** *S*

l. A Castelli armorial dish, c1592.
£3,500-4,000 *S*

r. A Castel-durante tondino.
£2,700-3,700 *C*

A dated armorial marriage charger, restored, London, 1673. **£45,000-50,000** *S*

A pair of Staffordshire rustic musicians, decorated in enamel, possibly by John Dale of Burslem, 4.5in (11cm). **£1,000-1,200** *LR*

A pearlware 'Tee Total' figure group, of Obadiah Sherratt type, on a black sponged base, c1830, 7.5in (19cm). **£2,500-3,500** *S*

A pair of figures of Neptune and Venus, by Obadiah Sherratt, on table base, c1825, 9.5in (24cm). **£1,800-2,400** *LR*

A Yorkshire pottery horse, c1860, 7in (18cm) wide. **£2,000-2,500** *JHo*

A selection of Staffordshire models of watch holders and a money box, painted in Pratt enamels, 8 to 11in (20 to 28cm). **£400-1,400 each** *Bea*

An Obadiah Sherratt group of Dr. Syntax playing cards, c1825. **£3,000-3,500** *S(S)*

A Staffordshire lion, c1820, 7in (18cm) wide. **£1,200-1,500** *JHo*

A Dixon Austin & Co., watch stand, c1822, restored. **£800-1,000** *S(S)*

A Staffordshire pearlware cow group, chipped, c1800, 13in (33cm). **£4,000-4,500** *S*

A creamware
Ralph Wood jug,
c1770.
£500-700 *HEY*

A Ralph Wood
'Admiral Lord Howe'
Toby jug, c1775, 10in
(25cm).
£4,700-5,000 *S*

An Enoch Wood figure
of Fortitude.
£1,400-1,600 *LR*

A pearlware Toby jug,
c1790, 10in (25cm).
£850-1,000 *HEY*

'The Sinner' Toby
jug, c1800.
£2,000-3,000 *HEY*

A Prattware Toby jug,
c1790, 8in (20cm).
£850-950 *HEY*

A pair of pearlware figures of
Faith and Charity, c1800, 7in
(18cm).
£150-200 *HEY*

A Palissy type
figure of 'La
Nourrice,
probably Avon,
mid-17thC.
£4,000-4,500 *S*

A Prattware Rodney's
sailor Toby jug, c1790.
£2,000-3,000 *HEY*

An Obadiah Sherratt group,
c1830. **£400-500** *HEY*

A Maiolica group of The
Virgin and Child, probably
Faenza, c1540.
£15,500-16,500 *C*

A 'Lohan' of
Whieldon type,
derived from a
Meissen model,
c1750, 4.5in
(11cm).
£17,000-18,000
S

A Staffordshire group of Jenny
Jones and Ned Morgan, c1860, 9in
(23cm).
£400-500 *HOW*

l. A Queen Mary Royal portrait charger, Brislington, c1690, repaired, 13in (33.5cm).
£5,500-6,500 *S*

r. An equestrian charger, London, c1670, probably depicting Charles II, repaired crack, 13in (32.5cm).
£18,000-20,000 *S*

A delft Queen Anne charger, c1705, probably Bristol, 13.5in (34.5cm).
£10,000-11,000 *S*

A delft Queen Anne charger, c1705, probably Bristol, 10in (25cm).
£17,500-18,500 *S*

An English delftware charger, probably London, c1690, 12in (30cm).
£2,600-3,600 *S*

A Bristol delft tulip charger, c1690, 14in (35.5cm).
£1,800-1,900 *JHo*

A set of 6 octagonal 'Merryman' plates, c1690, 3 repaired, slight glaze flaking, 8in (19.5cm) diam.
£19,000-20,000 *S*

l. A Bristol charger, depicting Prince George of Denmark, glaze chip to rim, c1705, 13.5in (34cm).
£10,500-11,500 *S*

r. An armorial charger, Southwark, 1651, repaired, 15in (38cm).
£36,000-40,000 *S*

A delft tulip blue dash charger, probably Bristol, glaze damage, 13.5in (34cm). **£1,700-1,900** *Bea*

An Urbino dish, the reverse inscribed Pluto e Proferpina. **£6,100-6,500** *S*

A Dutch Delft charger, extensively repaired, 13.5in (35cm). **£280-320** *Bea*

Two Dutch Delft Royalist lobed dishes, with William of Orange and Queen Mary, 9in (22cm). **£600-800** *Bea*

A polychrome delft dish, with allover floral pattern, 13in (33.5cm). **£500-600** *Bea*

A polychrome delft plaque with 2 Chinese figures in a garden, 14in (35cm). **£1,000-1,100** *Bea*

A pair of English polychrome delft dishes, with willow and flowering plants, 12in (30.5cm). **£650-850** *Bea*

A blue and white delft plate, with a lion, 10.5in (26cm). **£600-700** *Bea*

An English delft polychrome plaque, probably Bristol, 14in (35cm). **£300-400** *Bea*

A blue and white delft dish with figures in a landscape, 14in (35cm). **£400-500** *Bea*

An English delft polychrome plaque, 14in (36cm). **£1,400-1,600** *Bea*

An English delft dish, with a Chinaman by a rock, 12.5in (32.5cm). **£575-625** *Bea*

A polychrome delft dish, probably London, 14in (35cm). **£550-650** *Bea*

An Urbino Istoriato dish, painted with the Contest between Pierides and the Muses, repaired, c1540, 15.5in (40cm).
£31,000-33,000 *C*

A slipware charger, early 18thC.
£10,000-11,000 *JHo*

An Istoriato tondino, painted with St Paul healing a woman, perhaps Pesaro, cracked and repaired, c1580, 9in (22.5cm).
£3,500-4,000 *C*

A Staffordshire dated slipware dish, with stylised bird, minor surface chips, c1790, 14in (35cm).
£5,000-6,000 *S*

An Urbino maiolica dish, painted by Francesco Xanto Avelli with a scene from Virgil's Aeneid, restored, dated 1539, 12in (30.5cm). **£34,000-35,000** *S*

A Montelupo dish, depicting figures in a bakery, some damage, late 16thC, 20in (50.5cm). **£12,000-13,000** *C*

A tondino, Deruta or Siena, some damage, c1510, 9.5in (24cm). **£2,500-3,000** *C*

A Palissy type dish, probably Le Prè d'Auge, moulded with a coiled snake, rim cracked, early 17thC, 22in (55cm).
£1,400-1,600 *S*

A Staffordshire slipware dish, with a spotted bird surrounded by smaller birds within a pie crust rim, dated 1777, 16.5in (42cm).
£8,000-10,000 *S*

A Deruta lustred dish, depicting a mythical beast, minute rim chips, c1525, 17in (43cm). **£31,000-35,000** *C*

An inscribed mug, London, some damage, dated 1696, 7in (18cm).
£11,500-12,500 *S*

Two Faenza waisted albarelli, named in Gothic script, some damage and repairs, c1545, 10. 5in (26cm).
£8,000-9,000 *C*

A Cambrian Pottery jug, painted by Thomas Pardoe, depicting a tiger in Indian landscape, chip to spout, c1800, 10.5in (26.5cm).
£4,500-5,500 *S*

A Don Pottery pearlware jug, early 19thC, 6in (15.5cm).
£1,700-1,800 *S(S)*

A Staffordshire saltglaze bear jug and cover, c1750, 8.5in (21cm).
£1,700-2,000 *C*

A Pratt type pearlware jug, painted with flowers, 1817, some damage, 7in (16.5cm).
£450-550 *S(S)*

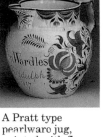

A Famiglia Gotica albarello, late 15thC, 11.5in (30cm).
£8,000-10,000 *C*

A Faenza albarello with Gothic script, c1525, damage and restoration, 12.5in (31.5cm).
£6,500-8,000 *C*

A Staffordshire glazed jug, c1820, restored, 6in (16cm).
£250-350 *S(S)*

A Montelupo albarello, cracked, 8in (20.5cm).
£900-1,200 *S(S)*

A creamware baluster jug, possibly Leeds, damaged, dated 1786, 9in (23cm).
£800-900 *S(S)*

A Faenza albarello, mid-16thC, 6.5in (16.5cm).
£3,000-4,000 *S*

A sgraffito puzzle jug, from Ewenny Pottery, dated June 19th, 1830, slight damage, 13in (33cm).
£1,300-1,800 *S*

A North Italian maiolica albarello, hair crack, with collector's label, 10in (25cm).
£1,700-1,800 *S*

A selection of Wemyss baskets, painted with roses, flowers and fruit, c1900. **£500-1,500 each** *S*

An Urbino cistern, repaired, c1580, 29in (73cm). **£9,000-12,000** *C*

A botanical creamware dessert service, early 19thC, dessert plate 9in (22cm). **£2,800-3,500** *S*

Two Wemyss ewers and basins, c1900. **£900-1,300 each** *S*

An Annaberg tankard with pewter lid, c1667. **£14,500-15,500** *S*

A George Jones majolica dessert service, c1870. **£2,000-3,000** *S*

A Nevers faience crucifix base, c1775. **£700-800** *S*

A French papier mâché model for a tea service, mid-19thC. **£5,500-6,000** *S*

A Wemyss tyg and bucket, c1900, tyg 9in (23cm). **£680-1,200 each** *S*

A mug, London or Bristol, c1730. **£2,700-3,000** *S*

A Dutch Delft tureen and cover, c1750. **£2,300-2,800** *S*

A creamware mug, c1782, 6in (16cm). **£550-700** *S*

A Minton majolica centrepiece, repaired, impressed marks, c1877, 40in (102cm). **£2,500-3,000** *S*

A Wemyss bucket and cover, restored, c1900, 11.5in (29cm). **£2,000-2,500** *S*

A Newcastle earthenware tea set, c1820, 6in (14.5cm). **£1,100-1,300** *S*

A delft posset pot and cover, mid-18thC, 8.5in (21.5cm).
£1,400-1,800 *S*

A Dutch Delft vase, in Chinese Transitional style, restored, GK monogram in underglaze blue, c1700.
£2,700-3,000 *S*

An early delft posset pot, Southwark, Pickleherring, restored, c1630, 5in (13cm) high.
£20,000-22,000 *S*

A pair of dated English delftware shoes, probably London, one tongue restored, 1695, 5in (13cm).
£18,000-19,000 *S*

A London delftware plaque, initialled AML and dated 1716.
£4,500-5,000 *S*

A hand warmer, in the form of a book, with an aperture at either end, probably London, chipped and restored, late 17thC, 6in (15cm).
£6,600-7,000 *S*

Two views of a dated English delftware triangular salt, the sides with a lion, unicorn and dragon in relief, the well inscribed and dated E C 1674, restored.
£33,000-34,000 *S*

An English delft drinking vessel, c1650.
£12,500-13,000 *C*

l. A pair of English delft child's head flower vases, some damage, c1685, 6.5in (16cm).
£11,000-12,000 *S*

r. An English delft candle niche, cracked and chipped, mid-18thC.
£3,000-4,000 *S*

A Meissen gold mounted snuff box, painted with a river god, slight rubbing, c1750, 2.5in (6cm).
£12,000-14,000 *C*

Two Meissen quatrefoil centrepieces, painted with Holzschnitt Blumen, chipped, c1740, 14.5in (37cm).
£5,500-6,000 *C*

A Meissen gold mounted circular snuff box, c1745, 2in (5.5cm). **£42,000-45,000** *C*

A St. Cloud silver mounted snuff box, minor rubbing, c1740, 3in (8cm) wide. **£4,000-4,500** *C*

A Chelsea fluted teacup and saucer, tiny chips, painted red anchor mark, c1754, saucer 5in (13cm).
£1,300-1,500 *S*

A Meissen box and cover, chipped and restored, restoration and slight chips, blue crossed swords mark, c1725, 8in (19.5cm) long.
£22,000-25,000 *C*

A Meissen Hausmaler bowl, crossed swords and J mark, impressed 6, c1745, 7in (18cm).
£3,500-4,000 *S*

A Meissen gold mounted yellow ground oval snuff box, c1740, 3in (7.5cm) wide.
£42,000-42,500 *C*

A pair of Worcester green camaieu baskets, some chips, 7in (18cm), c1775.
£2,500-3,000 *S*

A Meissen gold mounted snuff box, c1750, 5.5in (13cm) diam.
£5,500-6,000 *C*

A Meissen armorial chinoiserie teabowl and saucer, 1731.
£5,000-8,000 *C*

A Derby group of Europa and the Bull, c1765.
£1,300-1,500 *S*

A Chelsea figure of a Judge, c1760.
£2,200-2,800 *S*

A group of Juno and a Peacock, Derby, c1765.
£1,250-1,500 *S*

A Chelsea figure group of Britannia lamenting, c1751, 10in (25.5cm).
£14,500-16,500 *S*

A Böttger pagoda figure, c1715, 5in (13cm).high.
£8,000-10,000 *C*

A Meissen armorial teabowl and saucer, marked, c1730.
£7,000-8,000 *S*

A pair of Derby figures, John Wilkes and General Conway, c1765. **£1,500-1,700** *S*

A pair of Ludwigsburg figures by Franz Anton Pustelli, c1760, 5in (13cm) high.
£3,200-4,000 *C*

A Meissen teabowl and saucer, incised and gilder's mark, c1730. **£3,000-4,000** *S*

A Meissen yellow ground coffee cup, c1730, 3in (7cm) high.
£13,500-14,500 *C*

A Meissen chinoiserie tea bowl and saucer, c1735.
£30,000-35,000 *C*

A Fürstenberg figure of Frederick the Great, c1800, 19in (48.5cm).
£2,000-2,500 *S*

A Sèvres biscuit
figure of Thalie,
impressed, c1808,
12in (30cm) high.
£2,700-3,000 *C*

A pair of Chantilly wolves, chipped
and repaired, c1740.
£10,000-15,000 *C*

A Meissen figure of Count
Bruhl's tailor, restored, c1880,
marked, 17in (43cm).
£5,500-6,000 *S*

A Frankenthal model of
a stork, restored, c1760.
£2,600-3,000 *C*

A Meissen
model of a
dove, chipped
and restored,
c1740.
£3,000-3,5000
C

A Strasbourg model of a pug
dog, impressed H above F738
above A3, c1770, 4in (10cm).
£4,200-5,000 *C*

A Meissen model of a
parrot, damaged, c1740,
7in (18cm) high.
£8,500-9,000 *C*

A pair of Chelsea sporting hounds, with a hare and brace of partridges
under each dog's forepaws, minor chips, c1749, 7.5in (19cm).
£60,000-65,000 *S*

A Meissen Paduan
cockerel, incised
L3144, damaged and
restored, crossed
swords mark and
incised, c1880.
£3,500-4,000 *S*

A Meissen model
of a guinea fowl,
by J. J. Kändler,
some damage
and restored,
c1745, 6.5in
(16cm).
£2,500-3,000 *C*

Two Meissen models of playing bears, by J. J. Kändler, blue
crossed swords at back, minor chips, c1740, 3 and 3.5in (7.5
and 8cm) high. **£6,600-8,000** *C*

A Derby trompe l'oeil plate, minor wear, marked, c1805, 8.5in (22cm).
£2,000-2,500 *S*

A Chelsea two-handled dish, with Arcadian river landscape, stilt marks, c1755, 7in (18.5cm).
£2,800-3,200 *S*

A Swansea dessert plate, painted by Henry Morris, c1820, 8in (21cm).
£1,000-1,500 *S*

A Meissen Schmetterling part dinner service, marked, mid-18thC.
£9,500-10,000 *S*

A pair of Chelsea dishes, restored, marked, c1755, 8in (20cm).
£950-1,000 *S*

A Meissen dish from the Swan service, marked, c1740, 15in (38cm).
£42,000-45,000 *C*

A Meissen two-handled lobed tray, marked, c1740, 10in (25cm).
£4,500-5,000 *S*

A Meissen Kakiemon dish, blue crossed swords mark, c1735, 13in (33.5cm).
£6,000-6,500 *C*

A Worcester dish, marked, c1770, 8in (20cm). **£600-650** *S*

A pair of Chelsea bowls, red anchor marks, c1755, 9in (22.5cm). **£2,000-2,500** *S*

A Nantgarw plate, London decorated, c1820, 10in (25cm).
£3,000-3,500 *S*

A pair of Worcester dishes, one cracked, c1770, 13.5in (34.5cm).
£3,000-3,500 *S*

A Chelsea botanical plate, restored, marked, c1755, 11in (28cm).
£6,800-7,200 *S*

A Meissen cabinet tray, painted with a view of Dresden, c1870, 20.5in (52cm). **£5,500-6,000** *S*

A Sèvres tureen, cover and stand, marked, c1760, 20in (50.5cm). **£22,500-30,000** *S*

A pair of flower tubs and stands, probably Chamberlain's Worcester, c1790, 5in (12.5cm). **£4,500-5,000** *S*

A Longton Hall lobed tureen and cover, restored, c1755, 5in (12.5cm). **£9,000-12,000** *S*

A Vincennes écuelle, cover and stand, damaged, marked, 1753, stand 8in (20.5cm). **£4,500-6,000** *S*

A Coalport botanical dessert service, some damage, impressed and script marks, c1820, 9in (23.5cm). **£3,500-4,000** *S*

A pair of Sèvres bleu lapis ground orange tubs, restored, marked, 1765, 7in (18cm). **£7,000-12,000** *S*

A pair of bough pots, possibly Chamberlains, early 19thC, 8.5in (21.5cm). **£3,000-3,500** *S*

A 'Vienna' tray, painted after F. Laufberger, c1880, 24.5in (62cm). **£2,500-3,000** *S*

Ten Meissen topographical plates, crossed swords in underglaze blue, c1870, 9in (22.5cm). **£9,000-10,000** *S*

A Vienna Du Paquier, plate, enamels rubbed, c1730, 5.5in (13.5cm) diam. **£3,000-4,000** *C*

DERBY PORCELAIN
TAKES THE BISCUIT

A Derby Porcelain Group of "Three Graces Distressing Cupid" Modelled by Pierre Stephan

**EXHIBITS AT THE INTERNATIONAL CERAMICS FAIR & SEMINAR
THE PARK LANE HOTEL, LONDON W1   VISIT US ON STAND B18
JUNE 1993 STAND TELEPHONE 071-753 6779
WITH EVERY BOOKLET PURCHASED WE WILL GIVE YOU
A FREE TICKET FOR THE INTERNATIONAL FAIR VALUED AT £8.00**

The 1992 Sixth colour booklet, *Derby Porcelain Takes The Biscuit* is available in a limited edition, price £15 + £1.50 postage & packing.
Previous editions are also available, *Derby Porcelain Sweetmeats and Surprises, The Doris Wheatley Collection of Derby Porcelain, The Dynamic Brilliance of Derby Porcelain: The First 100 Years, Cabaret Stars and Illustrious Derby Porcelain, Derby Porcelain: The Fruits of Perfection.* Each available for £15 + £1.50 postage & packing.

Peter Jackson Antiques (MG)

3 Market Place, Brackley
Northants NN13 5AB
Tel: (0993) 882415, (0280) 703259
0860 772860 (Mobile) 0860 820028 (Carphone)

A Coalport botanical part dessert service, minor wear and restoration, c1810. **£5,500-6,000** *S*

A Spode botanical part dessert service, minor wear, puce painted mark and pattern number 1100, c1800. **£1,300-2,000** *S*

A Derby dessert service, crowned D and crossed batons mark in iron red, small chips and cracks, c1820. **£2,000-2,500** *S*

A Vienna coffee pot and domed cover, marked, 1796, 8in (20cm). **£5,500-6,000** *C*

A Derby dessert service, painted crown, D and crossed batons, some damage, c1790. **£2,000-2,500** *S*

A pair of Meissen flattened scent bottles, c1745. **£10,000-12,000** *C*

A Höchst part tea and coffee service, puce and gilt wheel marks, gilder's crescent marks, various incised marks, some damage, c1765. **£15,500-16,000** *C*

A Coalport feldspar porcelain botanical dessert service, c1820. **£3,000-4,000** *S*

A Meissen dessert service, painted with reserves of rural landscapes, crossed swords in underglaze blue, incised numerals, one dish with hair crack, c1870. **£10,000-11,000** *S*

A Meissen cabaret set, incised numerals and crossed swords in underglaze blue, c1870. **£8,000-9,000** *S*

A Meissen cabaret set incised numerals and crossed swords, late 19thC. **£1,350-1,500** *S*

A Barr, Flight & Barr dessert service, incised factory marks, c1802, the large oval dish 14in (36cm). **£7,500-9,000** *S*

A pair of Sèvres gilt metal mounted vases, late 19thC, 25.5in (65cm). **£6,000-8,000** *S*

A Copenhagen cornucopia vase and cover, c1923, 24in (61.5cm). **£3,500-5,000** *S*

A pair of Sèvres pattern gilt metal mounted vases, late 19thC, 43in (110cm). **£14,500-16,500** *C*

A pair of Sèvres pattern gilt metal mounted vases, late 19thC, 50.5in (128cm). **£26,500-28,500** *C*

A French vase, late 19thC, 30.5in (77.5cm). **£2,000-3,000** *S(S)*

A garniture of Sèvres-pattern vases, late 19thC, largest 62in (157.5cm). **£35,500-37,500** *C*

A pair of Grainger Lee & Co. Worcester pot pourri vases, c1825, restored, 14in (35cm). **£1,500-2,000** *S*

A pair of Sèvres two-handled vases, damage and repair, late 19thC, 17in (43cm). **£2,500-3,000** *S(S)*

A garniture of Sèvres vases on gilt stands, marked, c1780. **£1,850-2,000** *S(S)*

A Vienna faux bois ground part coffee service, blue beehive marks, various impressed marks, c1790. **£5,000-6,000** *C*

A Flight, Barr & Barr urn, c1825, marked, 12in (31cm). **£1,200-1,500** *S*

A garniture of Bow 'frill vases', c1770, marked, 12in (31cm). **£2,000-2,500** *S*

A famille rose punch bowl, 2 restored cracks, Qing Dynasty, 14.5in (37cm), late 18thC, 14.5in(37cm). **£16,500-17,500** *S*

A Chinese Lotus pattern tea bowl and saucer, late 18thC. **£120-140** *Wai*

A famille rose hunting punch bowl, rim restored, Qianlong, 15.5in (40cm) diam. **£5,000-6,000** *C*

A blanc de chine figure of a seated luohan, 17thC. **£5,000-6,000** *C*

A tileworks figure of a lion, chips restored, Ming Dynasty. **£2,500-3,000** *S*

A Compagnie-des-Indes hound, Qianlong. **£4,500-5,500** *S*

A painted pottery horse, restored, Tang Dynasty, 17in (42.5cm) high. **£2,000-3,000** *C*

A Compagnie-des-Indes dog, Qing Dynasty. **£5,500-6,000** *S*

A polychrome bowl, restored, Kangxi, 14.5in (37cm). **£4,700-5,700** *S*

A Kakiemon style shishi, restored, late 17thC. **£10,500-11,500** *S*

A famille rose figure of Budai, 18thC. **£3,000-4,000** *S*

A famille rose punch bowl, Yongzheng, on wood stand, 15in (38cm). **£5,000-6,000** *S*

A set of famille rose figures of Immortals, chipped and restored, Qianlong, 9in (23cm). **£3,500-4,500** *S*

A Sancai pottery ox and cart, minor restorations, Tang Dynasty. **£5,000-6,000** *C*

A set of three doucai dishes, chipped and cracked, 18thC, 15in (38cm) diam. **£6,600-8,000** *C*

A foliate charger, painted in Yuan style, Kangxi, 26.5in (67.5cm) .**£2,000-2,500** *C*

A Ming style dish, chipped and restored, Qianlong seal mark and of the period. **£4,000-6,000** *C*

A Ming style dish, with Qianlong seal mark and of the period. **£30,000-31,000** *C*

An Imari shaped dish, 17/18thC, 18in (46cm) diam. **£4,500-5,500** *C*

A Northern celadon saucer dish, Song Dynasty, 7in (18cm) diam. **£6,500-7,000** *C*

A kraak porselein dish in delft style, frits, late Ming Dynasty, c1600, 14in (36cm). **£2,000-2,500** *S*

A kraak porselein dish, late Ming Dynasty, c1643. **£2,500-3,000** *C*

A Ming dish, hairline crack, with encircled Hongzhi six-character mark and of the period, 10.5in (26cm). **£90,000-95,000** *C*

A pair of dragon dishes, with Qianlong seal marks and of the period, 7in (17.5cm). **£9,000-10,000** *C*

A Junyao barbed rim dish, Song Dynasty, 7in (18cm). **£22,000-23,000** *C*

A Kakiemon jar, painted with birds among rocks and peonies, restored, late 17thC, 8.5in (21.5cm). **£10,000-12,000** *S*

A jardinière, with scrolling lotus and key pattern, 19thC, 28in (71cm) diam. **£7,500-8,500** *C*

A ormolu mounted famille rose baluster vase, Yongzheng, 19thC, 18.5in (47cm). **£8,000-10,000** *C*

A pair of famille rose jardinières, with metal liners, on scroll feet, restored, Yongzheng, 13.5in (34.5cm). **£7,500-10,000** *C*

A rouleau vase, painted with phoenix, Kangxi, 18.5in (46.5cm). **£1,800-2,200** *C*

An enamelled moulded baluster vase, Qianlong, 14in (36cm). **£3,750-5,000** *C*

A hu-shaped vase, with 2 taotie fixed-ring handles, Han Dynasty, 17in (43cm). **£3,250-3,750** *C*

An Arita vase, with flowers and Buddhist objects in Wanli style, late 17thC, 21in (51cm). **£6,000-7,000** *S*

A boar's head soup tureen and cover, restored, Qing Dynasty, 18thC, 16in (40cm). **£15,500-16,000** *S*

A Chinese Imari baluster jar, Qianlong, 23.5in (60cm). **£5,500-6,000** *Bea*

A Henan vase, Song Dynasty, 10.5in (27cm). **£11,500-12,000** *C*

A famille rose ormolu mounted five-piece garniture, restored, Qianlong.
£10,500-12,000 *C*

A pair of Canton enamel vases, mid-19thC, 24in (61cm) high.
£1,800-2,200 *Wai*

A beaker vase, restored rim, Kangxi, 17.5in (44cm) high.
£800-900 *Wai*

A bottle vase, damaged, Tao Kuang mark, Ching Dynasty.
£500-600 *N(A)*

A pair of Japanese Imari flasks, marked Shin, c1710.
£10,000-11,000 *WW*

A Transitional wucai baluster vase, c1640, 11.5in (30cm) high.
£4,500-5,000 *C*

A famille verte rouleau vase, Kangxi, 18.5in (47cm) high.
£16,500-18,000 *C*

A pair of gilt decorated mirror black vases, Kangxi.
£16,500-17,500 *S*

A famille rose garniture of vases, well painted, some damage and repair, 1 cover matched., Qianlong, 10.5in (27cm). **£4,500-6,000** *S*

A famille rose mandarin pattern garniture, some restoration, baluster vases, Qianlong, 13.5in (35cm) high.
£9,000-10,000 *C*

A pair of Japanese porcelain vases, one with interior firing crack.
£1,200-1,800 *Bea*

Four wine glasses, on facet cut knopped stems, with cut conical bowls, cl849, 5.5in (14cm). **£350-450** *Som*

A pair of ogee rib moulded finger bowls, c1830, 3.5in (8.5cm) **£200-300** *Som*

A pair of amethyst carafes, c1850, 7.5in (19cm) **£480-520** *Som*

Three finger bowls, 3 to 4in (8 to 9.5cm). **£90-130 each** *Som*

A spirit flagon, with loop handle and metal mount, c1830, 7.5in (19cm). **£180-200** *Som*

A cranberry enamelled decanter, English, c1890. **£90-120** *CB*

An onion shaped carafe, engraved with fruiting vine, 8.5in (21cm). **£250-350** *Som*

A pair of spirit bottles, with flute cut bodies, c1840. **£600-700** *Som*

A Nailsea bottle, with small loop handle, 8.5in (21.5cm). **£560-600** *Som*

A cylindrical jar and cover, c1810, 3in (8cm). **£260-280** *Som*

Three spirit bottles, c1835, 11 to 12.5in (28 to 32cm). **£260-420 each** *Som*

A rare wine glass, with multiple spiral air twist stem, c1750, 6.5in (16.5cm). **£4,600-5,000** *Som*

A set of 3 Bristol decanters, c1800. **£1,400-1,600**, and sauce botles, 5in (12.5cm). **£80-150 each** *CB*

Two cream jugs with applied loop handles, *l.* c1800, *r.* North Country soda glass, c1790.
£200-300 each *Som*

A Baccarat concentric mushroom paperweight, c1850.
£2,500-3,000 *S*

Two wine glasses: *l.* with ogee fluted bowl. **£80-100** and *r.* with cup bowl, c1840. **£170-200** *Som*

A Baccarat thousand petalled rose weight, mid-19thC.
£3,500-4,000 *S*

A glass cream jug, 3.5in (9cm) high, c1860.
£150-250 *Som*

A selection of Victorian hyacinth vases, c1860-1920. **£20-50 each** *CB*

A Stourbridge Webb claret jug, c1897.
£800-1,200 *CB*

Two Nailsea type water jugs: *l.* c1800, 4.5in (11cm) high and *r.* Wrockwardine, 4in (10cm) high.
£250-450 each *Som*

A Baccarat dated close millefiori weight, marked B/1847, 3in (8cm).
£1,100-1,500 *S*

A cranberry goblet.
£50-70 *CB*

A St. Louis fruit weight, mid-19thC.
£550-1,000 *S*

A set of 5 wine glasses, with ovoid bowls and flute cut stems, c1840, 5in (12.5cm) high. **£250-350** *Som*

Two cream jugs, c1830, 2.5 and 4in (7 and 9.5cm) high and circular salt, c1840, 2.5in (7cm) high.
£100-250 each *Som*

A wine jug, c1800, 8in (20cm) high.
£750-850 *Som*

A pair of scent bottles, decorated with enamel and gilt, gold caps and fitted shagreen case, c1760, 1.5in (4cm) high. **£3,000-3,500** *Som*

A Victorian cranberry glass épergne, with baskets, 21in (53cm) high. **£350-450** *CB*

An overlay lustre, c1880, 12in (31cm) high. **£650-750** *CB*

A Bohemian cameo glass vase, c1896. **£250-300** *CB*

An English cased glass vase, c1880. **£350-400** *CB*

Three glass scent bottles with brass and silver gilt mounts, *l.* and *c.*c1880, and *r.* c1870, 4 to 5.5in (10 to 14cm) long. **£150-400 each** *Som*

A Peking glass vase, c1860, 10in (25cm) high. **£500-650** *CB*

A Webb three-coloured cameo vase, attributed to William Fritsche, c1880, 18.5in (47cm). **£5,000-6,000** *S*

A set of 4 cut salts, with moulded lemon squeezer diamond feet, c1810, 3in (8cm) high. **£800-1,000** *Som*

Two pairs of English citrine cornucopia, mounted on white marble bases, c1820. **£800-900 each** *CB*

Three glass bells, the green one c1890, the 2 cranberry c1880, 13 to 13.5in (33 to 35cm) high. **£100-200 each** *CB*

Miscellaneous

A Staffordshire cradle with a baby, decorated in yellow ochre and white, early 19thC, 5in (12.5cm) wide.
£350-450 *JHo*

A Victorian pottery flour bin, with two lug handles, decorated in underglaze blue with chinoiserie fishermen beneath flower filled baskets and scroll border, damaged, 12.5in (31.5cm) high.
£600-700 *HSS*

A Buckley pottery brewing jar, 15in (38cm).
£35-40 *IW*

A Swansea pottery pierced basket stand, in underglaze blue and white transfer, with 'Ladies of Llangollen' pattern, c1820, 11in (28cm) wide.
£400-475 *HOW*

A Staffordshire pottery watch holder, c1830, 7in (18cm).
£360-400 *RWB*

A Ewenny pottery butter churn with lid, c1870, 23in (58cm) high.
£110-130 *IW*

A Yorkshire puzzle pipe, decorated in Prattware colours, c1800, 11in (28cm) long.
£800-900 *RWB*

A pair of delft flower bricks, possibly Liverpool, decorated in blue and white, c1750, 5in (12.5cm) wide.
£850-950 *JHo*

A sauceboat in blue printed Longbridge pattern, 6in (15cm) wide.
£60-80 IW

An English delftware cornucopia wall pocket, probably Liverpool, small crack, inscribed I G I and dated 1748 on reverse, 8in (20cm).
£2,300-2,700 *S*

A Minton majolica cheese dish and cover in the form of a bee-skep, with a branch-moulded loop handle, exterior with fruiting blackberry branches, base glazed in mottled pale-blue, on branch-moulded feet, damaged, impressed mark and model number 969, date code for 1865, 14in (35.5cm).
£2,500-2,800 *C*

An English delft flower brick, chipped and restored, 1737, 6in (15cm) wide.
£3,500-4,000 *S*

A West Country pitcher, mid-19thC, 17in (43cm).
£70-90 *IW*

An English red pottery watering can, with pulled loop handle and press moulded semi-cover, the ovoid body applied with a large pierced rose, partly glazed in brown and moss-green, 13in (33cm).
£1,500-2,000 *Bea*

A rare Prattware pipe, depicting John Bull smoking, with a lion at his side, decorated in strong Prattware colours, bowl restored, c1800, 6in (15cm).
£750-850 *LR*

A Quimper bagpipe wall pocket, c1890, 9.5in (24cm).
£190-210 *VH*

An English delftware mask wall pocket, probably Liverpool, small chips, inscribed PM and dated 1769 on reverse, 9in (22cm) high.
£5,300-5,800 *S*

A Desvres wall pocket, c1885, 10in (25cm) high.
£175-195 *VH*

A Quimper pipe rack, c1890, 11in (28cm) wide.
£200-270 *VH*

A delft flower brick, possibly Liverpool, decorated in blue and white, 5in (12.5cm) wide.
£350-400 *JHo*

Three Mason's miniature chamber sticks, c1820.
l. 2.5in (6.5cm)
£250-270
c. 1.5in (4cm)
£220-250
r. 1.5in (4cm).
£135-160 *VH*

PORCELAIN

There has been little change in the porcelain market over the last twelve months. If anything, the pattern of the past two or three years has intensified, with buyers willing to pay record prices for the best items and leaving the regular pieces unsold. There has been a slight increase in interest in 18thC porcelain figures, particularly from the Bow factory, but there has been no real increase in values for some two or three years. The demand for the later British ceramics such as Minton, Crown Derby and Royal Worcester has remained firm but values have not increased. Tablewares have retained their popularity if sold in complete tea or dinner sets but individual pieces are slow selling unless decorated with a rare pattern. After the poor showing of 18thC figures in the auction rooms over the past two or three years the auctioneers have had to readjust their estimates to reflect recent price levels.

A Crown Derby tea service, of Empire inspiration, each piece painted with laurel swags between blue ground borders, gilt with scrolls and foliage above or enclosing a band of flutes picked out in royal blue and gilding, comprising: cream jug, bowl, 2 circular dishes, 12 tea cups, 6 coffee cups, 18 saucers and 12 plates, small hairline cracks, orange printed mark and year code, painted Pattern No. 1654, c1885.
£1,000-1,500 *S(S)*

These lower estimates have perhaps encouraged more private buyers into the market with the result that figures are beginning to sell again. Phillips, London, sold a Bow figure of Columbine for £1,550, more than treble the estimate. Similarly, at the same sale, a rare Chelsea red anchor figure, modelled by Joseph Willem as an old beggar wrapped in a cloak, sold for £2,500.

Tablewares are traditionally sub-divided into flatware (plates, saucers etc.) and hollow ware (tureens, teapots etc.). Flatware has always been difficult to sell as individual pieces unless they are examples of a particularly rare pattern or an individual item from a unique service. Hollow wares, with the added interest of shape, are much more decorative and are therefore of more interest to the collector. During the 19thC many factories, such as Minton and Derby, produced specialist cabinet plates, hand painted and gilded to the highest quality, for the sole purpose of display. These plates are miniature works of art and as such are still under valued at £200-500.

Complete tea or dinner services are always sought after either by the wealthy collector or the decorator with wealthy clients. Even late services can fetch large sums of money. £4,000 was paid for a 1930s Coalport part tea and dinner service, of 135 pieces, at Sotheby's, Sussex. At some £30 a piece it was probably good value. Had the service been split by the auctioneer the individual prices would probably have averaged much more than £30 and the general collector may have been fortunate enough to own a piece of that particular service. An example of this dilemma for the auctioneer or dealer was the sale of the Barr, Flight and Barr 'Gordon Service' in 1980. Made originally for Sir Willoughby Gordon and kept in the family until the sale, it caused something of a minor furore when Phillips, Edinburgh, divided it into 19 lots. This splitting of the service enabled collectors to have a unique piece of Worcester that would have been denied them had the service been sold complete. It also ensured that these pieces would circulate amongst collectors and reappear on the market from time to time. A pair of plates from the 'Gordon Service' were recently sold by Phillips, London, for £4,200 the pair, having been sold the first time round in 1980 for £850 the pair! Other examples of

A Royal Worcester pierced oviform ewer, the silver form possibly painted by Henry Chair, washed in turquoise and picked out with gilt dots, with foliate scrollwork between bands of white jewelling and joined by the single scroll handle with mask terminal and beadwork border, puce printed mark with year code, registration numbers and shape number 1944, brown printed TIFFANY NEW YORK retailers mark, 1897, 7in (18cm).
£2,000-3,000 *S*

the highly decorative Regency painted porcelains continue to sell well. A Flight and Barr 10 inch high yellow ground pot pourri vase and cover with decoration of full blown roses realised £1,700 at the same Phillips sale. Welsh ceramics from the same period, always sought after by a dedicated breed of collectors, have had a boost this year with the sale of the Sir Leslie Joseph Collection. The demand for the later British ceramics, such as Minton, Crown Derby and Royal Worcester, continues on an even keel.

Baskets

A pair of Caughley pierced baskets, decorated in underglaze blue, 8.5in (21.5cm) wide.
£600-800   *P(M)*

A Worcester quatrefoil pierced chestnut basket and cover, moulded with yellow centred puce flowerheads, damaged and repaired, c1765, stand 10.5in (26cm) wide.
£1,500-2,000   *C*

Bowls

A pair of Fürstenberg baskets, painted with green and blue flowerheads, the handles and rims enriched with gilding, gilding rubbed, blue F marks inside baskets and impressed NO3 to underside of bases, incised S to one, c1770, 7.5in (19cm) wide.
£1,700-2,000   *C*

A Worcester footed bowl, colour enamelled with chinoiserie figures, the inner rim decorated in underglaze blue with an ornate border pattern, interior rubbed, blue painted open crescent mark, c1768, 6in (15cm) diam.
£200-300   *Bon*

A Worcester footed bowl, painted in blue with the Precipice pattern, painted open crescent mark, c1765, 8in (20cm) diam.
£200-300   *Bon*

A Bow white squat baluster bowl and cover with loop handles, applied with prunus sprigs, the cover with branch finial, c1752, 5in (13cm) diam.
£2,000-3,000   *C*

A Meissen écuelle, cover and stand, painted with scenes of country figures before buildings, bordered by applied trailing vine and foliage, branch handles, gilded details, chipped, crossed swords in underglaze blue and impressed 13, c1880, stand 8.5in (21.5cm).
£2,000-2,500   *S*

A Pinxton bowl, enamelled with iron red sprigs, c1799, 2.5in (6cm).
£100-180   *TVA*

A Worcester footed bowl, transfer printed in blue with the Laterre and Mother and Child patterns, hatched crescent mark, c1775, 5.5in (13.5cm) diam.
£200-250   *Bon*

A Worcester bowl, transfer printed in underglaze blue with uncommon European landscapes, c1780, 4.5in (11.5cm) diam.
£100-180   *TVA*

A Worcester blue and white bowl and cover, with shell-moulded handles and pine cone knop, damaged, 18thC, 13in (32.5cm) wide.
£400-500   *Bea*

A Worcester footed bowl, colour enamelled upon transferred outlines with various chinoiserie figures, the interior similarly decorated, the inner rim in underglaze blue with an ornate border pattern, unmarked, c1765, 9in (22.5cm) diam.
£650-750 *Bon*

A Worcester First Period punch bowl, painted in blue and white with the Precipice pattern, with open crescent mark, c1765, 9in (22.5cm) diam.
£425-525 *TVA*

A Meissen Kakiemon sugar bowl and cover, the cover with a flower finial and a brown line rim, cracked, blue crossed swords mark, c1735, 4.5in (12cm) high.
£1,200-1,600 *C*

A Meissen Kakiemon sugar bowl and cover, painted with a tied bouquet and trailing flowering branches with turquoise stems, the cover with purple cone finial and a chocolate line rim, chipped, blue crossed swords mark and Dreher's p for Pfitzner, c1735, 4.5in (11.5cm) diam.
£1,700-2,000 *C*

A Chamberlain's Worcester shallow bowl and cover modelled as a basket with loop handle, the centre to the interior painted with a loose bouquet within a gilt scroll well, the border and cover encrusted with shells and aquatic plants, printed marks to cover, c1840, 6.5in (16cm) diam.
£1,500-2,000 *C*

A Worcester bowl, transfer printed in blue and white with Bat pattern, c1780, 6in (15cm) diam. **£100-125** *TVA*

A Worcester First Period blue and white basin, chinoiserie decorated with a house by a lake to one side, trees in a landscape to the other, 6in (15cm) diam.
£100-150 *MJB*

A Minton covered bowl encrusted with flowers, painted on one side with a titled view of Warwick Castle and on the other side with a bouquet of flowers, green glazed handles, pomegranate knop, slight damage, blue crossed swords marks, 10.5in (26.5cm) wide. **£600-700** *P(S)*

Boxes

A German casket with gilt metal mounts, painted with battle scenes alternating with panels of flowers inside an oval gilt frame against a puce scale ground, the inside cover painted with a Royal portrait, impressed eagle mark, late 19thC, 9.5in (24cm) wide.
£2,500-3,000 *S(S)*

A French snuff box and cover, with silver mounts, probably St. Cloud, 18thC, 3in (8cm) wide.   **£500-700** *Bea*

A Berlin gilt metal mounted snuff box, the green scale ground reserved with pink ground panels painted in imitation of cameos with The Three Graces and trophies, the base with Cupid blowing bubbles and the interior of the cover finely stippled in colours with a lady at her dressing table trimming her pigtail accompanied by a gallant, base repaired, c1780, 3.5in (8.5cm) wide.
£3,200-4,000 *C*

A French silver gilt mounted bonbonnière, painted with flowers, the mount with carved borders, 19thC, 3in (7cm).   **£650-750** *S(S)*

A St. Cloud silver mounted snuff box, modelled as a kneeling Chinaman, in an Oriental flowered robe with 3 scattered flying insects, the cover with Oriental flowersprays, reeded silver mounts, damaged and repaired, c1740, 2in (5cm) wide.
£700-800 *C*

Busts

A Copeland parian bust, modelled as a young maiden with a wreath of ivy tied into her long hair with a ribbon, her head turned slightly to the right, raised on a socle base, restored, impressed COPELAND L 84 and Copyright, c1865, 25in (64cm).
£2,500-3,000 *S*

A Copeland parian bust of Juno, modelled by W. Theed, after the Antique, raised on a low socle base, impressed COPELAND T 28 and copyright, c1851, 23in (59cm).
£3,500-4,000 *S*

A pair of Meissen portrait busts of Prince Louis Charles and Princesse Marie Zéphirine de Bourbon, after the original models by J. J. Kändler, she wearing turquoise, blue, pink, black and gilt, he in gilt, yellow, blue, white and lilac, the bases enriched in gilding, restored, blue crossed swords marks, Pressnummer 77, incised 2764, painted numbers 15, c1880, 6in (15cm).   **£1,000-1,400** *C*

Centrepieces

A Sèvres porcelain, silvered and gilt bronze centrepiece, the red-brown campana-shaped urn with turquoise lining, supported by rope twists and putti, reputedly stamped C. H. Ficquemet Sèvres under the gilt mounts, c1870, the gilding later, 16in (40cm).
£1,200-2,000 *S(S)*

A Continental white ground centrepiece, designed as a conch shell, with external applied rose and floral decoration, supported by 3 standing cherubs, damaged, c1880, 11in (28cm).
£120-160 *GH*

Miller's is a price **GUIDE** not a price **LIST**

A Meissen comport, applied with flowers, with a couple dancing around the high foliate scroll base, 19.5in (49.5cm).
£3,500-4,000 *Bea*

Clock Cases

A Minton majolica centrepiece, painted in typical enamel colours, impressed mark and date code for 1872, 17in (44cm) wide.
£1,500-2,000 *Bea*

A Meissen porcelain framed timepiece, surmounted by a pair of cherubs holding a flower festoon, restored, the movement inscribed Howell, James & Co., late 19thC, 9in (22.5cm).
£600-700 *S(S)*

An Italian porcelain watch stand, the shell form watch case supported by male and female figures, each wearing pale yellow and green drapery, all modelled on a base of overlapping rocks, restored, c1770, 9in (22.5cm).
£300-500 *S(S)*

Cups

A Miles Mason cup, saucer and bowl, pattern No. 128, The Seasons, bat printed and gilded, c1805, bowl 6.5in (16.5cm) diam.
£160-190
cup and saucer, cup with hairline crack. **£60-80** *VH*

An English two-handled cup, cover and stand, probably Coalport, painted with flowers in yellow and gilt edged cartouches in a deep blue ground between a pair of angel handles, butterfly finial, late 19thC, 5in (12.5cm).
£550-650 *S(S)*

A Miles Mason cup and saucer, c1810, saucer 5.5in (14cm) diam.
£75-85 *VH*

A Miles Mason cup and saucer, with relief moulded decoration, landscape painted panels and gilding, c1805, saucer 5.5in (14cm) diam.
£150-180 *VH*

A Worcester fluted cup and saucer of Lord Henry Thynne type, each piece painted with a central turquoise and gilt framed circular landscape panel surrounded by arrangements of fruit and scattered insects, within an underglaze blue and gilt rim, saucer cracked, underglaze blue crescent mark, c1772.
£300-400 *S(S)*

A Worcester coffee cup, with grooved loop handle, painted in an unusual and bright palette, c1765.
£950-1,200 *C*

A Miles Mason cup, decorated with Boy at the Door pattern, 1796, 2.5in (6.5cm).
£75-85 *VH*

A Worcester transfer printed coffee cup, with grooved loop handle, printed in sepia with a scene from the Italian Comedy showing Harlequin and Columbine seated beside a table being surprised by Pierrot, c1756.
£450-650 *C*

A Böttger Augsburg decorated Goldchinesen two-handled beaker and saucer, gilt in the workshop of Bartholomäus Seuter, the interior and borders richly gilt and edged with C-scrolls, slight damage, stencilled lustre MF monogram marks and incised line to footrim of saucer, c1725.
£7,000-8,000 *C*

A Miles Mason cup and saucer, with red bat prints heightened with gilding, c1808, saucer 5.5in (14cm) diam, cup and saucer.
£100-120
bowl 6in (15cm) diam.
£150-170 *VH*

A Miles Mason Shepherd's bat print and enamelled cup, saucer, and saucer dish, c1805, saucer 5.5in (14cm) diam. cup and saucer **£90-105**,
saucer dish 8in (20cm)
£130-160 *VH*

A Miles Mason cup and saucer, decorated with Boy at the Door pattern, c1805, saucer 5in (12.5cm) diam.
£80-100 *VH*

A Sèvres style blue ground chocolate cup, cover and saucer, painted within circular cartouches, the ground enriched with dots in gilding, slight damage, porcelain 18thC, decoration later, 4in (10cm).
£550-750 *CSK*

A Worcester bucket shaped coffee cup and saucer, painted with the rare Two Quail Kakiemon pattern in direct imitation of Meissen gilt open crescent mark, saucer 5in (12.5cm) diam.
£800-1,000 *TVA*

A Dresden chocolate cup, lid and saucer, in pale blue ground with hand painted vignettes, gilt handles and edges, early 19thC, 2.5in (6.5cm).
£250-300 *GAK*

A Meissen octagonal cup, decorated in the Kakiemon style, of a pair of quail in garden landscapes, iron red, blue, gilt and green, underglaze blue cross swords, c1735, 4.5in (11.5cm) wide.
£350-550 *WW*

A Meissen cup and cover, the bowl supported by four huntsmen in green coats, black tricorn hats and black boots, the cover with a huntsman in a red coat and breeches, damaged and repaired, gilt metal mounts to cover and footrim, c1735, 16.5in (42cm).
£6,000-7,000 *C*

A Vincennes bleu celeste coffee cup and saucer, painted with sprays of pink and yellow roses within gilt palm, flower and foliage borders and gilt dentil rims, slight damage, blue interlaced L marks enclosing date letter B for 1754, painter's marks for Taillandier, incised 'oni' to cup and 'o' to saucer.
£800-1,200 *C*

Vincent Taillandier working at Vincennes and Sèvres from 1753-90.

Ewers

A Sèvres ormolu mounted ewer, the ormolu handle moulded with leaves and bulrushes, damaged, blue interlaced L marks, flanked by Z for 1777 and y for Bouillat, the ormolu handle slightly later, 10in (25cm). **£900-1,200** *C*

A pair of Coalport 'jewelled' ewers, decorated beneath a salmon pink ground, green printed marks, gilt pattern numbers V1285, c1885, 8in (20cm). **£500-700** *S*

A Derby blue ground ewer, with gilt painted scroll handle, damaged, printed red mark, 14in (35.5cm). **£200-300** *CSK*

A Royal Worcester blush ivory handled ewer, with floral body decoration with gilding, shape number 1162, puce mark, c1880, 10in (25cm). **£300-350** *GH*

Figures - Animals

A Meissen pug dog, after a model by J.J. Kändler, with grey markings and a black muzzle, wearing a green and gilt collar with a purple bow, restored, c1740, 4.5in (11.5cm). **£2,500-3,500** *C*

An English porcelain ewer, probably Coalport, the ovoid body applied with a handle, neck and spout in the form of a swan, painted on either side with landscapes and applied with flowers, slight damage, mid-19thC, 11in (28cm). **£300-350** *Bea*

A Royal Crown Derby ewer, decorated in cisele gilt with musical trophies, hung from a ribbon tied swag on a salmon pink ground, printed mark in burnt orange, incised 877, 10in (25cm). **£200-300** *HSS*

A pair of Bow models of finches, on pierced scroll moulded bases enriched in turquoise and gilding, damaged, c1765, 6in (15cm). **£1,400-1,900** *CSK*

A pair of Meissen porcelain models of hunting birds, each supported on a tree stump tearing the prey, damaged, l8thC, 11in (28cm).
£4,000-4,500 *S(S)*

A pair of Meissen models of thrushes, their plumage naturalistically coloured in shaded brown and grey and with brown markings, on white and blue bases, slight damage, blue crossed swords marks, Pressnummern 123 and 16, incised 113X, painted number 40, c1880, 8in (20cm).
£650-850 *C*

A Royal Copenhagen model of an owl, after an original by P. Herder, the bird perched on a cluster of pine and naturalistically coloured, signed, 1911, 13ın (33cm).
£650-750 *S(S)*

A Meissen white model of a royal eagle, wearing a 'jewelled' gilt crown with white bosses, its beak open aggressively and with boldly painted features, its yellow claws with black talons clasping a 'jewelled' gilt sceptre and a silvered and gilt sword, restored, blue crossed swords mark, Pressnummer 343, incised S63, c1880, 20in (50cm).
£2,700-3,500 *C*

Two English models of spaniels, on yellow tasselled puce cushions, mid-l9thC, 3in (8cm).
£350-500 *S(S)*

A group of 3 Meissen monkey band figures, comprising: a conductor, a female harpist and a female hurdy-gurdy player, the conductor's arm damaged and wrist repaired, crossed swords in underglaze blue, incised and impressed numerals, 6.5in (16cm), and a group of 4 Volkstedt monkey band figures, comprising a violinist, a bagpipe player and 2 figures with wind instruments, chips, 19thC.
£1,500-2,000 *S(S)*

An English model of a greyhound, on a yellow tasselled puce cushion, restored, mid-l9thC, 4in (10cm). **£150-250** *S(S)*

A group of Continental monkey band figures, various factories, comprising a conductor and various instrument players, each standing on a circular base moulded with scrolls picked out in gilding, some damage and repair, printed marks, late l9thC, 6in (15cm).
£850-950 *S(S)*

A set of 13 French dog band figures, adapted from the Meissen monkey band figures, including the conductor, his stand, wind players, brass players and a percussionist, crossed arrow marks in blue enamel possibly for Bourdois & Bloch, 4.5in (11cm).
£1,200-1,700 *S(S)*

A matched pair of Bow white glazed porcelain figures of recumbent lions, each with a paw resting upon a sphere, damaged, the smaller lion marked B, 3.5 and 4.5in (9.5 and 10.5cm) long.
£1,500-2,000 *HSS*

Figures - People

A pair of Derby figures of a shepherd, in black hat, yellow ground floral trousers, playing a flute, and a shepherdess holding a bouquet of flowers, on rococo pierced scroll moulded bases enriched in turquoise and gilding, c1770, 9in (23cm).
£1,200-1,700 *CSK*

A Copeland parian figure of Sunshine, after William Brodie, minor chips to flowers, impressed factory mark, sculptor's name and title, c1860, 19in (48cm).
£500-600 *S(S)*

A Derby porcelain group of Procris and Cephalus, in a yellow robe bending over his dying wife touching the arrow in her breast, modelled on a grassy base beneath a stunted tree, chips and restoration to extremities, c1770, 8in (20cm).
£350-500 *S(S)*

A Minton parian figure of Clorinda after an original by John Bell, chips to inner rim of base, impressed marks and incised February 1848, impressed date code for 1862, 13in (33cm).
£450-650 *C*

A Robinson and Leadbeater tinted parian figure group, entitled 'How Like Grandma', the girl wearing a pink lace trimmed dress with blue sash, dressing a Jack Russell in a white lace cap and coat, seated on a bamboo framed pink plush easy chair, on a shaped base, impressed R & L, 13in (33cm).
£450-500 *HSS*

A pair of Chelsea figures of a shepherd and shepherdess, wearing puce and gilt flowered clothes, he in a green hat and his companion in a blue hat, standing before blue and pink flowering bocage, on bases enriched with gilding, damage and restoration, gold anchor marks, c1768, 11in (28cm).
£3,000-4,000 *C*

A pair of Chelsea Derby figures he in a red cloak and floral jacket and knee breeches, she in blue bodice and flowered dress, with a sheep at her feet, on a matching base, some damage, 13in (33cm).
£4,500-5,000 *WW*

A Royal Worcester figure of The Dodo, modelled by F. G. Doughty, printed mark in black, 3in (8.5cm).
£250-300 *HSS*

A pair of Royal Worcester figures of a huntsman and a fishergirl, coloured in brown and pink with gilt details, one with ends of stick restored, printed and impressed crowned circle mark, c1870, 18in (45cm).
£2,000-2,500 *S*

A pair of Royal Worcester figures of Grecian water carriers, each modelled as a Classical maiden wearing bronzed orange, yellow and green robes, carrying an amphora in one hand and with a vase balanced on the head, puce printed shape numbers 2/125 and 'shot enamel' mark, impressed numerals, c1907, 20in (51cm).
£1,700-2,200 *S*

An Ansbach group of musicians modelled as a gallant, playing a flute, in a white gilt-trimmed jacket, flowered waistcoat and puce breeches, his companion in a flowered skirt, puce bodice and blue trimmed apron, arbour lacking, restoration, c1770, 4.5in (12cm).
£1,500-2,000 *C*

A Dresden figure of a classical lady, blue crossed swords mark, mid-19thC, 10.5in (26cm).
£350-400 *GAK*

A pair of Royal Dux figures of maidens, in green and gold flowing robes, one playing a mandolin, the other a tambourine, standing on rocky bases strewn with leaves, some damage, pink patch marks, mid-19thC, 29in (74cm).
£1,500-2,000 *HSS*

A Berlin erotic group, 'The Model', slight restoration, KPM mark, c1870, 13in (33cm).
£500-585 *TVA*

A pair of Royal Dux figures of Eastern carpet sellers, coloured in tones of green, red, cream and green, detailed in gilding, her arm repaired, applied pink triangle mark, impressed 465 and 466, early 20thC, 16in (41cm).
£900-1,200 *S(S)*

A pair of Meissen figures of a fisherman and companion, after models by J.J. Kändler, both restored, c1748, 7in (18cm).
£2,000-2,500 *S(S)*

A Höchst figure of a boy as a cooper, after the model by J.P. Melchior, in a puce hat, puce waistcoat, yellow breeches and a brown apron, slight blemish to back, blue wheel mark and incised N97:M48, c1770, 4in (10.5cm).
£1,200-1,700 *C*

A pair of Royal Dux figures of water and fruit vendors, each decorated in 'shot enamels', raised on circular bases, minor chip, applied pink triangle mark, impressed 441 and 442, early 20thC, 15in (38cm).
£600-700 *S(S)*

Johann Joachim Kändler (1706-1775)

The first of the 910 monumental animal figures, as commissioned in 1730 by the Elector Augustus for his new palace, were very lifeless and quite unrealistic. Their quality only improved in 1731 when the young J.J.. Kändler began modelling at Meissen. Although Kändler was unable to overcome the firing problems, he studied the animals in the Elector's menagerie and produced lifelike, animated figures.

The project ended in 1733, shortly after the Elector's death and Kändler applied his talents to designing on a smaller scale. From around 1740 until Kändler's death in 1755 Meissen figures replaced table wares as the most sought after of the factory's produce.

The most popular series of figures was the Kändler Harlequins, modelled between 1738-1744.

A pair of Royal Dux figures of a man and woman in rustic dress, each carrying baskets on their shoulders, minor chips to base, applied marks, cl900, 15.5in (40cm).   **£500-600** *S(S)*

A French group, modelled as a classical bearded man wearing a crown and loose drapes supporting a young woman, pseudo Derby mark in red, late l9thC, l7in (44cm).
£500-600 *S(S)*

A Meissen figure of a wheelwright, from the series of Craftsmen modelled by J.J. Kändler and P. Reinicke, in a turquoise tunic, pink breeches, black buckled shoes and a brown apron, arm restored, hammer lacking, chips, blue crossed swords mark to back of base, c1748, 8in (20cm).
£1,500-2,000 *C*

A Meissen figure of a boy with a hen, the boy wearing a flowered pink edged robe, on a moulded base with scrolls picked out in gilding, restored chip to base, restoration to fingers and toes, crossed swords in underglaze blue, 19thC, 5.5in (14cm).
£450-650 *S(S)*

A Meissen group of rustic lovers, modelled as a shepherd and shepherdess, crossed swords in underglaze blue, incised A.41, late l9thC, 7.5in (19cm).
£800-1,000 *S*

A Fürstenberg figure of a miner, after the model by Anton Carl Luplau, in a black pill box hat, black jacket, apron, breeches and shoes, and red tunic, damaged, blue F mark, late l8thC, 5in (13cm).
£4,000-5,000 *C*

A Meissen figure of a chinaman, after a model by P. Reinicke, in a long jacket with indianische Blumen, iron red breeches with yellow edging, black stockings and red shoes, restored and one finger missing, faint blue crossed swords mark, c1740, 6in (15cm).
£900-1,200 *C*

A Meissen 'Poussah' figure, wearing an orange ground robe scattered with indianische Blumen over his flesh toned body, with green hat, one hand repaired, chip to wing of bird, indistinct crossed swords mark on base, c1745, 7.5in (18cm).
£6,000-7,000 *CAm*

A Lladro group, with figures in a rowing boat on a lake with willow trees, on contemporary base, 18in (46cm).
£500-550 *GAK*

A Meissen figure of a youth, clutching a cockerel under one arm, in turquoise hat with puce rosette, white jacket over pale blue trousers and yellow shoes with red bows, repaired, parts lacking and chips, blue crossed swords mark to back of base, c1750, 6in (15cm).
£850-950 *C*

A Meissen Marcolini group of a music lesson, modelled as a young girl in blue and yellow striped dress, her male companion wearing a pale turquoise jacket and purple tunic, attempting to teach her to play a wind instrument, small chips and areas of restoration, crossed swords and dot in underglaze blue, c1800, 5.5in (14cm).
£1,000-1,500 *S(S)*

Two Meissen Marcolini figures of a gardener and companion, he in a pink hat, green jacket and patterned breeches, she in a brown bodice and striped skirt, on scroll mound bases enriched with gilding, some damage, blue crossed swords and star marks, impressed H to back of his base and 2 to back of her base, c1790, 5.5in (14cm).
£800-1,200 *C*

A Royal Worcester Hadley shot silk figure, 'Kruger', shape 223/10, Hadley mark to base, signed Hadley to reverse, c1900, 8in (20cm).
£300-350 *GH*

A Meissen figure of a beggar musician playing the hurdy-gurdy, modelled by Kändler, wearing a black hat, a yellow coat, dark brown trousers with holes, a grey sack on his back, repaired, chip to hat, glaze rubbed, blue crossed swords mark, Pressnummer 33, c1750, 5.5in (14cm).
£1,200-1,500 *CAm*

A Meissen figure of an Oriental nun, wearing a flowing garment scattered with florets, a yellow dress with stripes over a lilac gown, black shoes, fingers chipped, marked with blue crossed swords, c1750, 5.5in (14cm).
£700-1,000 *CAm*

A Meissen model of a sawyer, from the Craftsmen series after a model by J.J. Kändler and P. Reinicke, in a black tricorn hat, white jacket, puce waistcoat, turquoise breeches, brown apron and black shoes, restored, blue crossed swords mark to back of base, c1750, 9in (22cm).
£4,000-5,000 *C*

A Meissen figure group, a gallant seated on a barrel holding a wine bottle, a faun on his shoulders, a young boy and girl at his feet, raised on an oval scroll moulded base picked out in gilt, damage, crossed swords mark in underglaze blue, incised D13, late 19thC, 8in (20cm).
£450-550 *S(S)*

A Meissen figure of a seamstress, from the Craftsmen series after a model by J.J. Kändler and P. Reinicke, in a turquoise and white bonnet, yellow jacket and her skirt with indianische Blumen, holding a ruler and knife, part of a jacket over her right arm, restoration, minor chips, blue crossed swords mark to back of base, c1750, 9in (22.5cm).
£1,500-2,000 *C*

A Meissen figure of a lightly draped maiden, with red and gilt border to her skirt, slight chip to rear of base, underglaze mark in blue and incised M158, c1880, 19.5in (50cm).
£1,700-2,000 *CAG*

A Meissen group of 2 men in 18thC costume, with tricorn hats, a globe and navigational instruments between them, some damage, painted mark, pattern No.376.
£1,200-1,500 *Bea*

A Meissen group, in the form of Jupiter on the back of an eagle in flight, thunderbolts in one hand, incised No.327X, 10.5in (26.5cm).
£450-550 *Bea*

A Meissen figure of a boy gardener, clad in a swirl of pink drapery, losses and restoration to stump and flower pots, spade handle restored, crossed swords in underglaze blue, incised C100, late l9thC, 5in (12.5cm).
£450-650 *S(S)*

A Vienna figure of a girl, emblematic of Spring, in a yellow and green conical hat, yellow bodice and scarf over a pink skirt and yellow shoes, flower in left hand lacking, minor chips to fingers on left hand, impressed W mark, incised X mark, c1760, 6.5in (16cm).
£1,200-1,700 *C*

A Meissen figure group, The Hairdresser, 9in (23cm).
£500-550 *GAK*

A pair of Meissen gardener figures, the gentleman in lilac knee breeches, the lady in a pink dress, 13in (33cm).
£2,500-3,000 *WW*

A Volkstedt-Rudolstadt figure of 3 young cherubs, 6in (15cm).
£120-170 *GAK*

A pair of Continental putti with goat and sheep groups, richly encrusted with flowers and fruit, on blue magenta and gilt decorated scrolled bases, repaired, 9in (23cm).
£300-400 *LF*

A Meissen figure of Touch, depicting a young woman seated wearing flowered lace trimmed costume beside a birdcage on a table, chip to edge of dress, crossed swords in underglaze blue, incised E4, late l9thC, 6in (14.5cm).
£850-1,000 *S(S)*

A Vienna group of child musicians, in coloured jackets and breeches, on a green mound base edged with gilt foliate scrolls before a tree, tree repaired, chips to hats, bugle and tree, and a group of a peasant and companion in coloured and patterned clothes, arms and hand repaired, chips to extremities, blue beehive marks to both and various incised marks, c1765, 7in (17cm).
£900-1,200 *C*

A pair of Meissen figures of a shepherd and shepherdess, small chips and areas of restoration, crossed swords in underglaze blue, 19thC, 6in (15cm). **£2,500-3,000** *S(S)*

A Vienna group of a peasant and companion, he with a moustache and black hat, buff jacket, patterned shirt, purple breeches with green braces and black boots, she in a yellow bodice, white apron, pink skirt and yellow shoes, on a green mound base edged with gilt scrolls, slight hairline crack to back of her skirt, blue beehive mark, c1770. **£2,000-2,500 C**

Flasks

A Meissen chinoiserie pilgrim flask, painted within gilt quatrefoil cartouches, with Böttger lustre panels, iron red and puce foliage scrolls and gilt shelves supporting purple vases between female mask heads and above moulded gilt gadroons, the neck moulded and gilt with ribs, damaged and repaired, c1730, later gold cover, 3in (7cm). **£3,700-4,200** *C*

A Meissen figure of a gallant, wearing a long red coat, gilt edged waistcoat and puce breeches, a green sash over one shoulder, restoration to wrist and hand, crossed swords in underglaze blue, incised 550, 19thC, 9in (23cm). **£350-450** *S(S)*

Flatware

A Caughley melon shaped dessert dish, blue transfer printed with the full Nanking pattern, c1790, 10.5in (26.5cm). **£100-140** *TVA*

A Sèvres saucer, painted by Falot and gilded by Prevost, reserved on a gold and pink dotted ground within a gold foliate rim, date mark for 1781. **£250-350** *Bea*

A Meissen pilgrim flask, painted within gilt quatrefoil panels with purple scrolls and between female mask heads with iron red plumes, the neck with gilt ribs, damaged, blue crossed swords mark, c1730, later gold cover, 3in (7cm). **£4,000-4,500 C**

A pair of Chamberlain's Worcester Royal Gadroon armorial plates, red script mark, c1820, 10in (25cm). **£600-650** *TVA*

A Caughley dessert plate, blue printed with the full Nanking pattern, c1790, 8in (20cm). **£100-165** *TVA*

A Caughley blue and white fluted bread and butter plate, transfer printed with Temple pattern, c1780, 7.5in (19cm).
£100-120 *TVA*

A Bow plate, enamelled with the Quail pattern, c1758, 9in (22.5cm)
£400-500 *TVA*

A Chelsea strawberry-leaf dish, with incised vein markings enriched in puce, painted beneath a chocolate brown rim, the underside with puce veining, iron red flowers and moulded in relief with a curled strawberry plant terminating in a loop handle, slight damage, red anchor mark, c1756, 9in (22.5cm) long.
£900-1,200 *C*

A Chelsea shallow dish, painted beneath a brown line rim, slight damage, c1753, 10.5in (26.5cm).
£1,000-1,500 *C*

A pair of Coalport shell shaped dessert dishes, painted by John Randell, c1840, 10in (25cm) wide.
£600-700 *TVA*

A Derby plate, painted in the Japanese taste, decorated in tones of green, iron red, lilac and blue with gilt detail, slight wear, pseudo seal mark in blue, c1765, 9.5in (24cm).
£150-250 *WIL*

A pair of Coalport plates, each painted with a landscape, pattern No. 4/414, c1840, 8.5in (21.5cm).
£200-280 *TVA*

A Miles Mason porcelain teapot stand, decorated in Boy at the Door pattern, c1805, 7.5in (18.5cm) wide.
£100-140 *VH*

A Worcester sweetmeat dish of scallop shell form, painted in blue with the Two Peony Rock Bird pattern, blue painted workman's marks, c1755, 4.5in (11.5cm) **£900-1,200** *Bon*

A Spode blue and white Indian Sporting pattern meat plate, impressed Spode One, 17in (42.5cm) wide.
£500-700 *HSS*

A set of 6 Hammersley & Co. dessert plates, each painted with a named bird in its natural setting, within gold decorated pink foliate moulded rims, one damaged, signed E. J. Garnett, 8.5in (21.5cm). **£350-400** *Bea*

A pair of Worcester blue scale ground dishes, painted with exotic birds and butterflies, with brown tendril handles, blue seal marks, c1770, 8in (20cm) wide.
£1,500-2,000 *C*

A pair of Worcester blue scale plates of Lady Mary Wortley Montagu type, decorated in the atelier of James Giles, within gilt line circular cartouches, the borders with exotic birds within gilt scroll and flowering foliage cartouches, reserved on blue scale grounds beneath scalloped gilt rims, slight damage, blue square seal marks, c1770, 9in (22.5cm).
£1,600-2,000 *C*

A Worcester plate, transfer printed in blue with the Pine Cones and Butterflies pattern, hatched crescent mark, c1770, 12in (30.5cm).
£250-350 *Bon*

A Worcester saucer dish, reed moulded with shaped rim, painted in blue with the Hollow Rock Lily pattern, blue painted open crescent mark, c1760, 7in (17.5cm).   **£300-400** *Bon*

A Chamberlain's Worcester meat dish with gravy well, and 3 matching deep plates, each painted with the crest of Nevile of Thornley, reserved on a wide orange band painted with scrolling foliage, the centre painted with a flowerhead and gold foliage, meat dish repaired, early 19thC.
£450-650 *Bea*

A Worcester junket or salad dish, transfer printed in blue with the Pinecone Group pattern, the interior moulded in low relief, the exterior transfer printed in blue, hatched crescent mark, c1770, 10in (25cm).
£500-600 *Bon*

A Worcester Flight Barr & Barr dessert plate with gilded rim, central ivory reserve with painted decoration attributed to Henry Stinton, with gilt scroll and white jewelled border, on deep blue ground, red printed mark, c1825, 10in (25cm).
£3,500-4,500 *AH*

This pattern was later employed for the 1830 William IV Coronation service, with the Royal Insignia replacing the floral group.

A set of 6 Mintons Cabinet plates, each enamelled with a double rose spray against gilt and silvered stem and leaves, printed and impressed marks and date code for 1885, painted pattern no. G4419/5, 9.5in (23.5cm).
£700-1,000 *S(S)*

A Worcester blue and white deep dish, printed with the Pine Cone pattern within a diaper and foliate border, slight damage, late 18thC, 15in (39cm).
£650-1,000 *Bea*

Miller's is a price
GUIDE not a price
LIST

A Worcester footed water basin, painted in blue with the Willow Bridge Fisherman pattern, slight crack, blue painted 'w' workman's mark, c1758, 10.5in (26.5cm).
£900-1,200 *Bon*

A Meissen saucer, the centre painted with a bird in flight over a flowering shrub raised on a pierced rock, the underside with birds in flight amongst twigs slight chips, engraved in Dresden, on a café-au-lait ground, underglaze blue caduceus mark and a script letter A, c1725, 4.5in (12cm).
£2,000-2,500 *S(S)*

A Meissen blue and white plate, painted within a shaped chocolate line rim, the reverse with a flowering tree and the border with trailing flowering branches, slight chip, blue crossed swords and dot mark, Pressnummer 20, c1740, 10.5in (26cm).
£3,000-3,500 *C*

A Meissen armorial plate, painted in purpurmalerei and enriched with gilding, with scattered indianische Blumen, the border with the Arms of the Münchhausen, slight chip, blue crossed swords mark and Pressnummer 16, c1740, 9in (23.5cm).
£3,000-3,500 *C*

A Royal Worcester white ground plate, with cobalt blue border, pink panels and gilding, the central panel decorated with still life fruit, pears and damsons, signed R. Sebright, 1913, 9in (22.5cm).
£350-450 *GH*

A Meissen cabinet plate, entitled 'Meleagar u Atalante', after P. Rubens, with the 2 scantily clad figures being united by Cupid, within an elaborate gilt frame and a pierced blue ground border gilt with ovolos and overlapping cash, crossed swords in underglaze blue, impressed numerals and title in black script Meleagar Atalante, nach P. Rubens, c1880, 10in (24.5cm).
£2,000-2,500 *S*

A pair of Berlin plates, each painted with figures before Roman ruins, sceptre mark in blue, printed KPM and orb, 19thC, 12.5in (31.5cm).
£950-1,200 *S(S)*

A Vienna portrait plate, the young girl wearing a white headdress, blue dress with a white lace frilled collar, signed Volk, the dark blue border richly gilt, blue beehive mark, 9.5in (23.5cm). **£1,500-1,700** *P(S)*

A Meissen lobed quatrefoil spoon tray, painted within 2 iron red lines, the border with a band of gilt interlocking scrolls and lines, blue crossed swords mark, Pressnummer 30, gilder's marks 52.L, c1740, 5.5in (14cm) wide.
£800-1,200 *C*

A Bow Middle Period powder blue plate, c1760, 8in (20cm).
£200-225 *TVA*

The old price label for £6. 10s. 0d. on the reverse.

A set of 4 Minton dessert plates, each hand painted with a different marine scene, probably by J. B. Evans, pattern no. B1486, c1860, 9in (22.5cm).
£500-600 *TVA*

Jars

A pair of Vienna Augustus Rex jars and lids, against a cerise background, gilt detail, mid-19thC, 15in (38cm).
£550-600 *GAK*

A Meissen pedestal jar and cover, with handles in the form of writhing snakes, painted in green enamel and gold with figures in gardens, insects and flowers, 18thC, 12.5in (31.5cm).
£600-800 *Bea*

A Worcester plate, with scalloped rim, painted in blue with the Rubber Tree Plant pattern, slight chip, individual pseudo-Chinese four-character mark, c1775, 7.5in (19cm).
£450-550 *Bon*

Jugs

A Worcester mask jug, moulded with stiff leaves enriched in yellow, puce and purple, the neck with flowersprays, the rim with a band of moulded leaves and dot pattern and with moulded bearded mask spout, chips to spout and restored footrim, c1770,7.5in (19cm).
£1,200-1,500 *C*

A Worcester baluster sparrow beak cream jug and cover, with loop handle, painted with gilt borders on a dark blue ground, the domed cover with flower finial, hairline crack and minute rim chip, blue crescent mark, c1770, 5.5in (14cm).
£400-600 *C(S)*

A pair of Vienna yellow ground topographical plates, with panels painted with named views of Ankunft des Holländischen/Schiffes-Amsterdam im Donaukand beim Schanzel./1846 and Der Josefplatz, within broad gilt bands, slight rubbing, blue beehive marks, 1846, 8.5in (21cm).
£1,600-2,000 *C*

A Royal Worcester blush ivory jug, with coral handle, floral decoration and gilding, puce mark, 1892, 6in (15cm).
£150-200 *GH*

A Worcester baluster mask head jug, with scroll handle, transfer printed in blue with the Plantation pattern, body crack near spout, unmarked, c1760, 6.5in (16cm).
£150-250 *Bon*

A Lowestoft baluster form sparrow beak jug, painted with Long Elizas in pink, purple, yellow, green and iron red, late 18thC, 4in (9cm) high.
£600-700 *HSS*

Mugs

A Derby mug, decorated in polychrome with glaze enamels, late 18thC, 4.5in (11cm).
£1,200-1,500 *HSS*

A Longton Hall mug, painted in colours, the rim enriched with a brown line, the handle and surrounding area restored, chip to rim, c1755, 4in (10cm).
£450-550 *CSK*

A Plymouth mug, with reeded handle, distinctly painted in coloured enamels below a gilt strapwork border, mid-18thC, 6in (15cm). **£2,000-3,000** *HSS*

An English mug, with foliate handle, with gold initials, minor damage, 4in (9cm).
£200-250 *Bea*

A buff glazed pearlware mug, bat printed and inscribed in gilt 'Success To The Roe Buck Oyster Club', within a gilt banded border, slight damage, 19thC, 5.5in (14cm).
£120-200 *HSS*

Plaques

A pair of Royal Worcester miniature plaques, each signed by Raymond Rushton, in original pierced silver mounts, Birmingham 1912, 4in (10cm).
£800-1,000 *TVA*

A Worcester plaque, painted by R. F. Perling, with a stag, hind and doe in a highland setting, signed Worcester and R. F. Perling, 8 by 9.5in (20.5 by 24cm).
£1,000-1,500 *S*

A Staffordshire plaque, painted by Woodhouse, with a pensive family group seated beside trees at the head of a river valley, signed Woodhouse 1838, 6 by 4.5in (15 by 12cm).
£600-900 *S*

A Doccia plaque, after the model by Anton Filippo Weber, with 10 profile bust portraits of various Roman emperors, c1750, 6in (15cm).
£1,500-2,000 *C*

A Berlin plaque, painted with the Madonna wearing a diaphanous veil, pink dress and blue robe, seated on a marble bench, unsigned, impressed KPM, impressed Berlin mark, 9 by 7in (22 by 17cm), in a gilt frame.
£800-1,000 *HSS*

A 'Vienna' plaque, painted by J. Schiller, within a dark brown border painted and gilt with scrolling foliage and flowers, titled on the reverse H. Makart, Gruppe aus dem Einzug Carl van Antwerpen, underglaze blue beehive mark, painted title, 19thC, 20.5in (52cm), gilt frame **£1,500-2,000** *S(S)*

A Berlin plaque, painted in pastel colours with a mother and child, impressed KPM and sceptre, c1890, 9.5 by 7in (24.5 by 18.5cm) framed. **£1,200-1,600** *S(S)*

A Berlin plaque, painted with a portrait of Princess Louise in full court dress of ermine trimmed cloak, gold coronet and gold embroidered white court gown, signed 'C.L.', impressed KPM and sceptre mark, retailer's label and Florentine carved giltwood frame, 9 by 6in (23 by 15cm). **£2,000-2,500** *C(S)*

A Berlin plaque, painted in the English style with a bouquet of crimson, pink and white blown roses on a powder green ground, unsigned, impressed KPM and sceptre, 13.5in (35cm). **£550-750** *HSS*

A Vienna plaque, the centre with hand painted panel depicting Samson and Delilah, within a puce and pale blue border overlaid with gilt rococo motif, marked on the reverse Simsons Gefangennahme, 19.5in (49cm) diam, gilt frame. **£2,000-2,500** *RID*

A Meissen plaque, in the Sèvres manner, painted with a view of Pillnitz on the river Elbe, within a gold foliate reserve and blue rim, set in a gilt plaster frame, inscribed Pillnitz, crossed swords mark, 6in (15cm) wide. **£1,500-2,000** *Bea*

A pair of Sèvres plaques, depicting Buffoon and Marionette, in velvet frames, 6in (15cm) high. **£620-670** *GAK*

A Vienna plaque, painted with a panel of Roman Charity, inscribed Cigniani, L. Zeiser, 8.56, impressed beehive mark, numerals 954, late 19thC, 13 by 16in (33 by 41cm), framed and glazed. **£1,100-1,600** *S(S)*

A pair of Sèvres type plaques, painted with portraits of Madame de Maintenon and Marie Antoinette, with gilt and blue borders, gilt brass frames, 19thC, 5in (12.5cm). **£400-500** *P(S)*

A group of 4 Continental plaques, printed marks, late 19th/early 20thC, 3.5in (9cm) high. **£750-850** *S(S)*

A German plaque, depicting Amor and Psyche, each scantily clad, flying above the clouds, 10 by 8in (25 by 17cm), in a gilt Florentine frame. **£1,200-1,500** *Bea*

Pots

A Caughley spittoon, transfer printed with Temple pattern, c1785, 4in (10cm).
£900-1,200 *TVA*

A Minton Dresden match holder, design 28, c1835, 5in (12.5cm).
£200-300 *TVA*

Sauceboats

A Sèvres Empire sauceboat and stand, modelled as a white swan, its head and neck forming the handles, the interior solid gilt, the oval stand gilt inside a white feather moulded border, some wear to stand, factory mark in red M. Imp le de Sèvres, c1810, 5.5in (14cm) long.
£500-750 *S(S)*

Services

A Coalport part dessert service comprising 7 plates, 9in (22.5cm), and 2 oblong comports, each piece painted and named with an English or Scottish view, signed J. Oldfield, A. Perry, and P. Simpson, with gilt rococo decoration to the blue borders, the views include Loch Awe, Kilchurn Castle, Ullswater, on the Thames, Bassenthwaite Lake, Loch Long, Langdail Pikes, St Michael's Mount and Rydel Water, printed marks, some hairline cracks.
£600-800 *P(S)*

A sauceboat, probably Bow, decorated in relief with a raised border, hand painted and underglazed with blue flower and foliate designs, damaged and cracked, late l8thC.
£60-100 *WIL*

A Worcester sauceboat, moulded with fluted sides, scalloped rim and scroll handle, painted in blue with the Doughnut Tree pattern, unmarked, c1775, 7in (17.5cm)
£350-450 *Bon*

A Copeland dessert service, decorated with salmon pink border and gilt, comprising: 2 oval scallop rimmed bowls with leaf grips, 10in (25cm), 4 square dishes, 8.5in (21.5cm), 3 lobed dishes, 9in (22.5cm), and 20 plates, 9.5in (24cm), with differing pattern numbers.
£2,200-2,700 *WW*

A Copeland & Garrett Feldspar dessert service, comprising: a comport, 3 shaped dishes and 6 plates, each brightly painted with sprays of flowers within gold foliate reserves on a decorative green band, printed mark, mid-19thC.
£600-800 *Bea*

A residue of a Meissen early morning tea service, painted by C. F. Herold, in red and dark blue, comprising: a teapot and cover, jug and cover, basin, 6 teabowls, and one saucer, crossed swords marks in blue, some chipping.
£24,000-26,000 *RID*

A Spode part tea service, comprising: a teapot, cover and stand, sugar basin and cover, milk jug, slop bowl, 22 cups and 9 saucers, some damage, Pattern No. 2/578, early 19thC.
£1,500-2,000 *Bea*

A Grainger's Worcester Japan pattern tea and coffee service, decorated with formal floral designs in typical Japan colours, comprising: teapot and cover, sucrier and cover, milk jug, slop bowl, bread and butter plate, 20 cups and 12 saucers, Pattern No. 2013, and a similar bread and butter plate.
£900-1,200 *P(S)*

A Coalport blue ground part tea and dessert service, brightly painted in iron red, green, blue, yellow and gilding, comprising: a sugar bowl and cover, base inscribed Lord Milford, finial repaired, a milk jug, 2 slop bowls, one inscribed Lord Milford by T. Pardoe, Bristol, 4 muffin dishes and 3 covers, 2 bread plates, one inscribed Pardoe, 28 Bath Street, Bristol, 8 coffee cans, 5 teacups, 10 saucers, one inscribed Lord Milford and another with For Lord Milford by T. Pardoe, Bristol (/) 1812, and 12 side plates, some damage, c1812.
£3,500-4,500 *C*

A Meissen tea and coffee service, each painted with small colourful flowersprays, within richly gilt leaf moulded rims, comprising: teapot and cover, a coffee pot and cover, a sugar bowl and cover, a cream jug, 12 cups, saucers and plates, and a cake plate, cancelled crossed swords in underglaze blue, black printed Made in Germany, impressed and painted numerals, 20thC.
£2,000-2,500 *S(S)*

A Royal Crown Derby dessert service, with painted central floral bouquets and gilt edges, comprising: 18 plates, 4 dishes, and 2 comports, red printed and impressed marks and pattern number 7698H in red.
£780-880 *P(S)*

A Paris Empire style teapot, sucrier and bowl.
£200-250 *P(S)*

Miller's is a price GUIDE not a price LIST

A Chamberlain's Worcester part breakfast and tea service, comprising: 5 plates, 8.5in (21.5cm), 8 plates, 7.5in (18.5cm), 2 slop bowls, 25 cups, and 13 saucers, each piece brightly painted within a white and buff flower embossed border, together with 7 matching cups and 9 saucers, some damage, printed marks, early 19thC.
£1,000-1,500 *Bea*

A New Hall tea service, painted in famille rose style, with a pink diaper border, comprising: a silver shaped teapot, cover and stand, slop bowl, milk jug, and 6 tea bowls and saucers, slight damage and repair, pattern number 173, c1790.
£550-770 *CSK*

An English part tea service, comprising: a teapot and cover, sugar basin and cover, milk jug, slop bowl, 2 plates and 12 cups and saucers, each decorated in the Chinese manner with vases, scrolls, boxed and flowers in famille verte enamels, some discolouration, early 19thC.
£300-500 *Bea*

A Meissen composite purple ground part tea and coffee service, painted with sprays of Holzschnitt and Deutsche Blumen within brown line quatrefoil shaped reserves, enriched with gilding, comprising: a teapot and cover, hot-milk jug and cover, sugar bowl and cover, 2 coffee cups, 6 teacups and saucers, some repairs and chips, blue crossed swords marks and Pressnummern to some pieces, c1740.   **£7,500-8,500** *C*

A Bloor Derby tea and coffee service, decorated with a turquoise band and gilt flowering branch outline, comprising: pot, stand, slop basin, sucrier and cover, milk jug, 2 dishes, 22 cups, and 12 saucers, red crown and baton mark, c1825.
£3,000-4,000 *WW*

A Miles Mason blue and white sucrier with cover, cream jug, and tea bowl and saucer, with gilding, c1805. **£250-300** *VH*

A Derby part tea and coffee service, decorated in blue, pink and gilt with a chantilly sprig type decoration, comprising: a teapot and cover, sucrier and cover, milk jug, quatrefoil spoon tray, 2 saucer dishes, 3 coffee cups and 6 tea bowls and saucers, sucrier cover handle restored, and other damage, crown over crossed swords over D over III.
£700-750 *HSS*

A Meissen outside decorated tête à tête, each piece enamelled with shipping in an estuary scene within gilt borders on a solid turquoise ground, comprising: a tray, 2 cups and saucers, coffee pot and cover, sucrier and cover, and milk jug, slight damage, repaired, deleted swords marks in underglaze blue, late 19thC.
£1,200-1,600 *S(S)*

An extensive New Hall tea and coffee service, comprising: 10 saucers, 10 coffee cans, 11 tea bowls, bread and butter plate, sucrier and cover, slop basin, milk jug, teapot, cover and stand, and coffee pot, some damage, pattern No. 480. late 18thC.
£700-1,000 *HSS*

Tea & Coffee Pots

A Coalport boat-shaped teapot and cover by Anstic, Horton & Rose, painted with an Imari pattern, c1805, 6.5in (16.5cm).
£250-300 *GAK*

A Meissen teapot and cover, with gilt highlighted animal spout and wishbone handle, painted in colours, with gilt decorated pineapple finial, damaged, crossed swords mark in underglaze blue, and inscribed L in puce, mid-18thC, 4in (10cm) high.
£1,000-1,200 *HSS*

A Miles Mason teapot and cover, with relief decoration and gilding, restored, c1805, 11in (28cm) wide.
£300-325 *VH*

A Lowestoft teapot and cover, painted in the famille rose palette, within cartouches reserved on an iron red foliate whorl pattern ground with lesser panels of purple foliage, the domed cover with knop finial, c1775, 6in (14.5cm).
£750-950 *C*

A Böttger Hausmalerei teapot and cover, painted in the workshop of Johann Friedrich Metzsch in purpurmalerei, with a purple monogram beneath the spout, chipped and restored, the porcelain c1720, the decoration later, 4.5in (12cm) high.
£4,000-5,000 *C*

A First Period Worcester teapot and cover, in underglaze blue, with the Three Ladies pattern, hatched crescent mark, slight chip to cover, c1770, 6in (16.5cm) high.
£800-925 *TVA*

Vases

Tureens & Butter Tubs

A Chelsea melon tureen and cover, naturally modelled and enriched in yellow and green, repaired, red anchor marks to base and cover, c1756, 6.5in (17cm) wide.
£4,200-5,500 *C*

A Meissen tureen and cover, with Dulong moulding and painted with birds within gilt scroll cartouches and scattered Deutsche Blumen, the scroll handles enclosing cauliflower and asparagus, the cover applied with mushrooms, a cauliflower sprig, 2 almonds, a stem of asparagus and a lemon finial, damaged, c1750, 11.5in (30cm) wide.
£3,000-4,000 *C*

A pair of Worcester, Flight, Barr & Barr green ground two-handled vases, with apple green grounds, the richly gilt foliage moulded scroll handles with anthemion terminals, the rims and feet moulded with a band of white and gilt flowerhead and leaf ornament, on square bases enriched with gilding, damaged and repaired, impressed and script marks, c1820, 8.5in (22cm) high.
£2,500-3,500 *C*

A Worcester butter tub and cover, transfer printed in blue with the Fence pattern, the cover with applied open flower finial, hatched crescent mark, c1770, 4in (10cm) wide.
£550-650 *Bon*

A Caughley garniture of 3 vases, painted in the Chamberlain studio at Worcester, probably by George Davis, the necks with blue S-scrolls enriched with gilt flowerhead, foliate and dot ornament, the rims gilt, gilding rubbed, large vase cracked, c1788, 6in (15cm) and 5in (13cm) high. **£1,200-1,500** *C*

A pair of Chelsea blue ground slender lobed bottle vases, painted within gilt scroll and diaper pattern cartouches reserved on dark blue grounds gilt with flowering foliage, gilt foliate rims, chipped and repaired, c1765, 11.5in (29cm). **£2,000-2,500** *C*

A Royal Worcester biscuit ground vase, with raised floral gilded body decoration, shape No.1764, puce mark, 1896, 14in (35.5cm) high. **£500-600** *GH*

A Worcester, Kerr & Binns vase, painted by James Bradley Snr., named 'On The Scheld, Holland', c1853, 6in (15cm) high. **£200-255** *TVA*

A Royal Worcester biscuit ground vase, with gilded and floral body decoration, shape No. 1149, puce mark, 1894, 17in (43cm) high. **£600-700** *GH*

A Grainger Lee & Co. two-handled pedestal vase, painted below a gold foliate band, the pedestal base enhanced in gold, early 19thC. **£250-350** *Bea*

A pair of Worcester, Flight & Barr vases, with applied gilt scroll handles, painted with The Queen Charlotte pattern, chipped and restored, c1800, 20in (51cm) high. **£6,000-9,000** *C*

A pair of Royal Worcester vases, with covers and inner liners, painted by Stinton on a white ground, signed, one repaired, printed mark in puce, shape number 1927, date cipher for 1905/6, 6.5in (16.5cm) high. **£600-700** *HSS*

A pair of Meissen Schneeballen vases and covers, applied with flowers and floral clusters on the end of green stems and foliage, amongst which small yellow birds perch, the covers similarly decorated and applied with a floral cluster and green stem surmounted by a yellow bird finial, gilt rims, minor restoration, crossed swords in underglaze blue, c1880, 13in (33cm) high. **£3,000-4,000** *S*

A Worcester, Kerr & Binns vase, painted with an Arctic snowy owl and prey by Luke Wells, slight restoration, shield mark, dated 1862, 10in (25cm) high.
£900-1,200 *TVA*

A Royal Worcester biscuit ground, two-handled footed vase with cover, having floral and gilded decoration, shape No.2336, puce mark, 1899, 14in (35.5cm) high.
£300-350 *GH*

A Royal Worcester vase and cover and two slender oviform ewers, the shaded pale green grounds painted by Roberts with continous of harebells painted in shades of lilac, green and mauve, reserved in ivory, enriched in gilding, damaged and repaired, artist's signatures, green printed marks, model Nos 2007 and 2156, date codes for 1901, vase 23in (58cm) high, ewers 14in (35cm) high.
£1,500-2,000 C

A Royal Worcester ivory and biscuit ground two-handled footed vase, having wild thistle and floral decoration with gilding, shape No. 1683, puce mark, 1905, 7in (17.5cm) high.
£250-300 *GH*

A Coalport vase, designed by Francis Brewer, with painted flowers, attributed to Thomas Dixon, c1830.
£170-240 *TVA*

A Royal Worcester vase with gilded neck and foot, decorated with landscaped scene, cottages and figures, shape 304, signed Lewis, green mark, 1910, 10in (25cm) high.
£250-300 *GH*

A pair of Royal Crown Derby two-handled vases, painted and signed by Darlington, with a gilt frame over a central deep blue ground, red printed mark with year cypher, painted and incised numerals 1658, dated 1919, 7.5in (18.5cm) high.
£900-1,200 *S*

A Royal Worcester biscuit ground bottle shaped bulbous footed vase, with raised floral gilded body decoration, shape No. 1661, puce mark, 1895, 9in (22.5cm) high.
£200-250 *GH*

A Royal Worcester vase, decorated on a peach ground, No. 2249, 9in (22.5cm) high.
£350-450 *RBB*

A Royal Worcester vase, signed by Raymond Rushton, dated 1929, 8in (20cm) high.
£1,000-1,150 *TVA*

A Royal Worcester vase, painted on a turquoise ground, with pierced neck, moulded foliage handles and gilt, signed C. Baldwyn, No. 1927, 8in (20cm) high.
£1,200-1,800 *RBB*

A Royal Worcester vase and cover, with 2 angular Persian type pierced handles, the slightly blushed ivory ground decorated in green, brown and gilt with fern fronds, shape number 1071, printed mark in purple, initialled GN in gilt, 16in (40cm) high.
£400-600 *HSS*

A pair of English blue ground rococo scroll moulded two-handled vases, painted in colours, damaged, 8in (20cm) high.
£200-300 *CSK*

A Royal Worcester biscuit ground vase, with floral body decoration and gilding, shape No. 1911, puce mark, 1913, 14in (36cm).
£400-450 *GH*

A pair of German vases and covers, each painted with gilt framed panels of Watteauesque figures at leisure against a turquoise ground, crossed swords marks in blue, c1880, 16in (40.5cm) high. **£1,500-2,000** *S(S)*

A pair of Dresden bottle vases, each heavily encrusted with flowers, fruit and vine and painted between with various colourful insects and butterflies, chips, indistinct blue printed marks, 19thC, 7in (18cm) high.
£900-1,200 *S(S)*

A Meissen pot pourri vase group, slight damage, faint cancelled crossed swords mark in underglaze blue, 18thC, later decorated, 10in (26cm) high.
£900-1,200 *S(S)*

A pair of Sèvres style blue ground two-handled vases and covers, with acorn finials, painted in colours with gilding, on socle bases, one vase cracked and gilding worn, 13in (33cm) high.
£500-700 *CSK*

A Vienna vase, painted with a scene after Wouvermanns, on blue and gilt background, gilt handles, 5in (12.5cm) high. **£120-170** *GAK*

A KPM Berlin two-handled vase and cover, printed and overpainted in colours, between gilt, pink and green borders, Berlin mark in underglaze blue, KPM printed in brown, 17in (43cm) high.
£800-1,200 *HSS*

A Meissen pot pourri vase and cover, painted with exotic birds between gilt edged puce scale borders, the domed cover with pomegranate finial, repaired, crossed swords mark in underglaze blue, c1770, 8in (21cm) high, with gilt metal base.
£3,000-3,500 *S(S)*

A Meissen vase, painted with a view of Wesenstein, other panels painted with coloured sprays of flowers within gold scrolling foliate reserves on a deep blue ground, inscribed Wesenstein, crossed sword mark, 12.5in (32cm) high. **£2,500-3,000** *Bea*

A pair of Helena Wolfsohn vases, painted in the Meissen manner, within ornate gold reserves on a turquoise ground, 19thC, 14.5in (37cm) high. **£1,400-1,800** *Bea*

A Royal Worcester shot silk bamboo double vase, with central handle, shape No. 858, puce mark, 1906, 10in (25cm) long.
£200-250 *GH*

A pair of large Paris vases, with vine handles, painted on one side with groups of Eastern figures in a garden, on the other a fountain or vases in a similar garden setting, embellished in gold, chipped, 22in (55.5cm) high.
£1,200-1,700 *Bea*

A Meissen (Augustus Rex) vase and cover, with a flower finial, damaged, blue AR mark, incised /// to rim, c1730, the decoration later, 12.5in (32cm) high.
£4,500-5,500 *C*

Goss China

The Goss factory produced a wide range of high quality porcelain between 1858 and 1939. There were three periods of manufacture, the first period (1858-87) encompasses parian busts, statuettes and ornamental ware. The second period (1881-1934) concentrated on the popular heraldic Roman and Saxon urns and ewers and coloured cottages, with the third period (1929-1939) producing coloured pottery and elegant ladies dressed in colourful crinolines.

Many people choose to collect Goss with a particular coat-of-arms while others collect such themes as lighthouses, crosses or fonts.

For further information collectors are recommended to read *The Concise Encyclopaedia and Price Guide to Goss China* and *The Price Guide to Arms and Decorations on Goss China,* both by Nicholas Pine, available from Milestone Publications, 62 Murray Road, Horndean, Hants. The definitive biography: *William Henry Goss, The Story of The Staffordshire Family of Potters who Invented Heraldic Porcelain,* by Lynda and Nicholas Pine, is also available from Milestone Publications and provides fascinating reading for those interested in the history of the family and the factory.

Tenby Gateway, brown.
£275 *G&CC*

Blue handled taper vase and Fourshire stone.
£35-40 *G&CC*

Three Goss models. **£15** *G&CC*

Cheshire cat and shetland pony.
£160-180 each *G&CC*

Oxford Jug.
£25 *G&CC*

Goss Evangeline.
£275 *G&CC*

A selection of models, all with matching coats-of-arms.
£20-35 each *G&CC*

A selection of containers.
£6-25 each *G&CC*

A selection of Goss shapes and models.
£6-350 each *G&CC*

Richmond market cross.
£50 *G&CC*

Eddystone and Portland
lighthouses.
£30-75 *G&CC*

Exeter vase with a primrose
decoration.
£50 *G&CC*

George and Mary
Coronation
commemorative
item.
£35 *G&CC*

St. Columb Major
and St. Martin's
crosses.
£70-170 *G&CC*

A selection of Goss decorations and models.
£10-245 *G&CC*

Night Lights showing Mary
Queen of Scots and Durham
Abbey Sanctuary knocker.
£95-130 each *G&CC*

Antwerp Oolen pot.
£7.50 *G&CC*

Las Palmas Earthen jar.
£12.50 *G&CC*

Crested China

While Goss concentrated on the accuracy and quality of the reproduction of models, other factories, such as Arcadian, Carlton, Shelley and Willow Art, produced a quick succession of comic novelty shapes.

In 1914, with the outbreak of WWI, the demand for crested china fell. The manufacturers soon produced a range of military souvenirs in an attempt to appeal to the patriotic fervour of the time. This range was very successful, but by the late l930s trade was virtually at a standstill and production ceased.

For further information, collectors are recommended to read *The Price Guide to Crested China* by Nicholas Pine, published by Milestone Publications, 62 Murray Road, Horndean, Hants. This contains the histories and marks for over 500 factories and lists every model, together with over 1,000 illustrations.

Animals.
£7-75 each   *G&CC*

A selection of transport.   **£20-65 each**   *G&CC*

Clocks.
£11-16 each   *G&CC*

Boots and shoes.
£4-22 each   *G&CC*

Souvenirs from the seaside.
£5-17 each   *G&CC*

127

Home/Nostalgic collection.
£3.50-20 each   *G&CC*

Upright piano by Corona.
£12   *G&CC*

Assorted figures by Grafton,
Carlton, Shelley and Arcadian.
£12-60 each   *G&CC*

Man in the sun,
by Willow Art.
£50   *G&CC*

A selection of animals.   **£9-75 each**   *G&CC*

Buildings.   **£30-40 each**   *G&CC*

Pillar boxes.
£10-16 each
G&CC

128

A wheelbarrow and garden bench.
£7-10 each *G&CC*

'Blighty is the place for Me-e', by Shelley. **£90** *G&CC*

Miscellaneous

A pair of Royal Dux book ends, formed as standing elephants, with white, blue and gilt decoration, 6in (15cm).
£120-180 *GAK*

A Royal Crown Derby '1952' pattern dressing table set, painted in Imari colours, reserved within gilt frames against a deep blue ground, comprising: tray, pair of candlesticks, one large pot and cover, two smaller pots and covers, rectangular pot and cover, shaped pin dish and ring stand, some repair, orange printed and impressed marks, painted No.1952, 1913.
£750-850 *S(S)*

A Chamberlain's Worcester pen tray, the interior painted with a frieze of red roses, script mark in iron red, c1825, 8.5in (21cm).
£170-220 *S(S)*

An English salt cellar, modelled as a scallop shell on a mythological sea creature base, gilded, early 19thC, 3.5in (9cm).
£200-250 *GAK*

A Meissen yellow ground cane handle, the pug's head terminal with brown fur markings and a purple lustre collar enriched with gilding, chips to ears, c1740, 5in (13cm) long.
£2,200-2,500 *C*

A Meissen style figural salt, modelled as a lady holding a flower decorated dish.
£400-500 *JL*

A Ludwigsburg rococo scroll moulded inkstand, after the model by Johann Gottfried Trothe, on 4 paw feet, the scrolls enriched with puce, turquoise and gilding, slight chips to claws on back feet, blue crowned interlaced C mark, c1760, 8.5in (21cm) wide.
£4,000-4,500 *C*

A Georgian porcelain milk pail, with cast brass handle
£350-500 *CHA*

A pair of Davenport ice pails, covers and liners, some cracks, repair and rubbing, printed Davenport mark in red, c1830, 11in (28cm).
£1,000-1,500 *S*

Make the Most of Miller's

Every care has been taken to ensure the accuracy of descriptions and estimated valuations. Price ranges in this book reflect what one should expect to pay for a similar example. When selling one can obviously expect a figure below. This will fluctuate according to a dealer's stock, saleability, at a particular time, etc. It is always advisable to approach a reputable specialist dealer or an auction house which has specialist sales.

Belleek

Belleek is currently enjoying a steady and deserved growth in popularity and collectability. Founded in 1857, the pottery is still in production on its original site in the little village from which it takes its name in County Fermanagh, Northern Ireland.

It owes its existence to the drive and ambition of three men - John Caldwell Bloomfield, a local entrepreneur and benefactor who donated the site in order to bring work and fame to the area; William Armstrong, a Dublin architect and potter from Worcester who designed, built, and managed the pottery; and William McBirney, a Dublin businessman who financed the venture. Apart from the ready availability of labour and water power, one of the main reasons for the choice of site was an abundance of local deposits of good quality feldspar and other raw materials, but these have since been worked out and now have to be imported.

Initially the pottery only made earthenware, turning out a large range of products including sanitary ware. However, this was not the market in which the founders wished to succeed and Armstrong ploughed back any profit from the earthenware into experiments on parian. Even so it was not until 1863, after at least ten men, together with their knowledge, had been enticed from England (notably the Goss potteries), that Belleek achieved a parian that was marketable.

Belleek won its first Gold Medal at the Dublin Exhibition in 1865. Thereafter it won orders from Queen Victoria and the Prince of Wales and soon this small pottery had become fashionable amongst the nobility. Since then its fortunes have waxed and waned a number of times but

always the high reputation of its work has been maintained.

All Belleek is marked and is relatively easy to date.

A Belleek comport, of a boy and a swan, 1st Period.
£2,500-2,500 *PC*

* **1st Period 1863-1890**. This mark shows a seated Irish Wolfhound with its head turned to face a Round Tower, on the right of which is an Irish Harp. Below this two sprigs of shamrock border each end of a banner carrying the word Belleek. This mark is usually coloured black, and although other colours are sometimes found this has no special significance.

* **2nd Period 1891-1926**. A furled banner with the words Co. Fermanagh Ireland was added under the first mark.

* **3rd Period 1926-1946**. A circular stamp bearing the Gaelic words 'Deanta in Eirinn' (made in Ireland) and a registration trade mark number 0857 was added below the banner.

All the above marks are known as the black period.

A Belleek four strand woven tray, 24in (61cm) long.
£4,000-5,000 *PC*

* **1st Green 1946-1955**. The mark remained the same but there was a colour change to green.

* **2nd Green 1955-1965**. To show that the Belleek mark was registered in the USA the letter R within a circle was added above the banner carrying the words Co. Fermanagh Ireland.

* **3rd Green 1965-1981**. The mark was reduced in size and the words Fermanagh were deleted leaving the word Ireland.

* **1st Gold 1981** (still in production). The mark design remained the same but the colour changed to gold.

l. A Belleek spill vase depicting a boy holding a fish, 1st Period, 9in (22.5cm). **£750-850**
r. A spill vase of a fish, brown and green with gilded fins, 1st Period, 7in (17.5cm).
£350-450 *PC*

Baskets are more difficult to date. As a rough guide, early baskets are seldom coloured, are usually three strand and carry the word Belleek or Belleek Co. Fermanagh impressed on pads stuck on the base of the basket. Around 1900 four strand baskets were introduced.

A letter R after the word Belleek is found in Baskets after 1955.

Unlike the parian, Belleek earthenware is not very popular or collectable. Nonetheless, some very handsome and well decorated examples exist and perhaps deserve more credit than they are given.

Irish Ceramics

A Belleek 'Rathmore' basket, minor restoration to handles, applied ribbon with impressed mark, post 1891, 11in (28cm).
£900-1,200 *S*

A Belleek bust of Clytie, First Period.
£800-900 *PC*

A Belleek 'Rathmore' basket, with a three-strand basket weave base and criss-cross latticework sides, raised on looped branches forming the feet and applied with trails of intricately modelled flowers strung from ribbons around the looped rope-twist rim, the whole with a creamy lustrous glaze, minor restoration, applied ribbon with impressed mark, c1880, 11in (28cm).
£1,500-2,000 *S*

A pair of Belleek candlesticks, First Period.
£350-400 *PC*

A Belleek basket, the three-strand basket centre within a plaited border below threaded sides rising to a looped rim applied with flowers and foliage, mounted with a pair of briar stem handles, small rim chips, applied ribbon mark impressed Belleek Co. Fermanagh, c1880, 12in (30cm).
£600-700 *S*

A Belleek ring handle cup and saucer, with Masonic decoration, First Period.
£300-350 *PC*

A Belleek appletop earthenware bathroom set, First Period.
£250-300 *PC*

A Belleek triple tulip vase, Second Period.
£700-800 *PC*

A Belleek centrepiece, First Period.
£400-450 *P*

A Belleek Cleary miniature mug, decorated for the 1902 Cork Exhibition, Second Period.
£75-100 *PC*

A Belleek Celtic part tea set, the handles, finials and outlines painted in green, Second Period.
£400-450 *PC*

A Belleek tazza on flowered pedestal, First Period.
£1,200-1,500 *PC*

A Belleek 'Greek' dessert plate, highlighted with turquoise and gilded, First Period.
£250-300 *PC*

A Belleek vase, painted on one side with a titled view of The River Erne, Ballyshannon, the handles picked out in gilding, black printed mark, title in black script, post 1891, 10in (25cm).
£1,000-1,500 *S*

A Belleek tea set with shamrock pattern, comprising: teapot, sugar bowl, creamer, and 4 cups and saucers, black mark.
£300-400 *JL*

A pair of Belleek baskets, with applied flowers and entwined briar handles.
£200-250 each *PC*

Two Belleek Nile vases, First Period.
Large **£375-400**
Small **£300-350** *PC*

A Belleek three-strand covered basket, c1890.
£3,500-4,000 *PC*

A Belleek shamrock cabaret set, Second period.
£850-900 *PC*

One of 35 different sets produced by Belleek.

A Belleek thistle vase, and a previously unrecorded shortened example, Second Period.
£300-350 each *PC*

A Belleek Blarney monogrammed cup and saucer, Second Period.
£300-350 *PC*

A Belleek shell cup and saucer, slight hairline crack, black mark, c1895, saucer 4in (10cm).
£20-50 *TVA*

FURTHER READING

BELLEEK

By Marion Langham
Published by Quiller

ORIENTAL CERAMICS

High quality, combined with an element of the rare and unusual, has been the pre-requisite for high prices and demand during the present economic climate. The top end of the Oriental porcelain market, more than perhaps any other, is prone to the fluctuations of international money markets, collecting fashions and effects of the worldwide recession. Early Chinese ceramics of the Song and Tang dynasties are still depressed, although high prices have been attained for good quality Tang tomb figures. The recent fashion for Qing mark and period pieces has continued but only will the rarer, previously unseen pieces fetch record prices. Rare and unusual Chinese export wares of the 18thC continue to be popular but routine famille rose export pieces are having a difficult time. Highly decorative Canton enamel pieces of the 19thC continue to sell for high prices, the demand coming from the decorator market, rather than from collectors.

Good pieces of export ware will fetch high prices no matter where they are sold as international trade buyers search them out. A village hall sale in Yorkshire, saw £3,800 being paid for a good and rare 18thC Chinese porcelain punch bowl painted with a European fox hunting scene encircling the bowl.

Japanese buyers are still in the market for the best of their own ceramics, but at much more subdued price levels than were being fetched two or three years ago. After seeing incredibly high prices recently, Japanese Imari from the last 17thC has now settled down to a steady price level. A pair of 24 inch high Imari vases and covers from the late 17thC sold at Sotheby's Maxwell House sale for the top estimate of £7,000.

Japanese Satsuma pottery is still much sought after, particularly if from one of the well known studios. A signed Kinkozan cabaret set of 9

pieces reached £1,500 in a Heathcote Ball, Leicester, sale. An interesting Satsuma vase, decorated with figures and warriors on a blue ground realised £1,150 at Drewett Neate, Newbury, against a pre-sale estimate of £150-200.

Condition is one of the most important factors in determining the price of Oriental ceramics. A Qianlong mark and period two-handled moon flask was sold by Phillips, Edinburgh, for £15,500. The flask, decorated in underglaze blue and red with the dragon and flaming pearl pattern, had a small, 2 inch, crack to the rim. A perfect example of this type of flask has previously sold for £50,000. To the collector who doesn't worry too much about a small amount of damage there are often bargains to be acquired, normally at about one tenth of the perfect price.

Chinese
Bowls

A Canton famille rose punch bowl, with a gilt ground at the rim, restored, 19thC, 18.5in (47cm) diam.
£4,000-5,000 *C*

A Cantonese bowl, the interior and exterior decorated in famille rose enamels, within gilt and burnt orange key borders, restored, mid-19thC, with later cast gilt brass beaded mounts with Empire style handles and fruit swags, on a quatrefoil foot, 19in (48cm) wide.
£350-550 *HSS*

A Cantonese bowl, painted and gilt with alternating panels of figures on terraces, birds and butterflies among flowers, on a green scroll ground, damaged, 14.5in (37cm) diam.
£550-650 *CSK*

A Chinese famille rose blue ground medallion bowl, small chips, Qianlong seal mark and of the period, 6in (15cm) diam.
£1,000-1,500 *C(S)*

Bearing label for John Sparks Ltd., 128 Mount Street, West London.

A doucai bowl, painted with ducks among lotus beneath bands of dragons chasing pearls and lanca characters, cracked, underglaze blue Daoguang seal mark and of the period, 6.5in (16cm) diam.
£1,000-1,500 *CSK*

A Chinese bowl, on short foot, painted in aubergine with 2 dragons chasing flaming pearls among clouds, above a band of stylised rocks and breaking waves, on a green ground, plain interior, underglaze black Daoguang seal mark and of the period, 6in (15cm) diam.
£3,200-3,700 *CSK*

Chinese dynasties and marks

Earlier Dynasties

Shang Yin, c.1532-1027 B.C.
Western Zhou (Chou) 1027-770 B.C.
Spring and Autumn Annals 770-480 B.C.
Warring States 484-221 B.C.
Qin (Ch'in) 221-206 B.C.
Western Han 206 BC-24 AD
Eastern Han 25-220
Three Kingdoms 221-265
Six Dynasties 265-589
Wei 386-557

Sui 589-617
Tang (T'ang) 618-906
Five Dynasties 907-960
Liao 907-1125
Sung 960-1280
Chin 1115-1260
Yüan 1280-1368

Ming Dynasty

Hongwu (Hung Wu)
1368-1398

Yongle (Yung Lo)
1403-1424

Xuande (Hsüan Té)
1426-1435

Chenghua (Ch'éng Hua)
1465-1487

Hongzhi
(Hung Chih)
1488-1505)

Zhengde
(Chéng Té)
1506-1521

Jiajing
(Chia Ching)
1522-1566

Longqing
(Lung Ching)
1567-1572

Wanli (Wan Li)
1573-1620

Tianqi
(Tien Chi)
1621-1627

Chongzhen
(Ch'ung Chêng)
1628-1644

Qing (Ch'ing) Dynasty

Shunzhi
(Shun Chih)
1644-1661

Kangxi (K'ang Hsi)
1662-1722

Yongzheng (Yung Chêng)
1723-1735

Qianlong (Ch'ien Lung)
1736-1795'

Jiaqing (Chia Ch'ing)
1796-1820

Daoguang (Tao Kuang)
1821-1850

Xianfeng (Hsien Féng)
1851-1861

Tongzhi (T'ung Chih)
1862-1874

Guangxu (Kuang Hsu)
1875-1908

Xuantong
(Hsuan T'ung)
1909-1911

Hongxian
(Hung Hsien)
1916

A Wucai bowl, painted with ruyi cartouches of peony and chrysanthemum on a cell pattern ground, underglaze blue six-character mark, 17thC.
£550-650 *CSK*

A pair of Doucai bowls, the exteriors painted with foliate roundels, sprigs of flowers between, the foot painted with a scroll pattern, Jiaqing mark, with ebonised stands, 6in (16cm) diam.
£450-650 *Bea*

A Canton famille rose crested punchbowl, painted around the exterior, with a crest beneath the inscription Alexander Crawford Rhodes, 19thC, 16in (41cm) diam.
£4,500-5,500 *C*

A famille rose basin, the interior enamelled with 2 pheasants and peonies amidst rocks, the well with 4 floral panels reserved on a diaper and trellis pattern ground, the border with ribboned composite flowersprays below a band of trellis pattern, Qianlong, 15.5in (39cm) diam.
£3,000-3,500 *CAm*

A pair of blue and white soft paste bowls, glaze lines, 18thC, 6.5in (16cm) diam.
£700-800 *CAm*

A late Ming Swatow enamelled bowl, the interior containing Arabic script in turquoise and black enamels, an iron red line around the rim, cracked and restored, early 17thC, 15.5in (40cm) diam.
£950-1,050 *CAm*

An export bowl for the Dutch East India Company, decorated in tones of underglaze blue, the interior with monogram V.O.C., 9in (23cm) diam.
£3,600-4,200 *HSS*

A famille rose bowl, the interior with gourds on a leafy stem, Jiaqing seal mark, 7in (18cm) diam.
£500-550 *CAm*

Cups

A Chinese beaker and saucer, Guangxu 4 character seal mark and period, c1895.
£300-400 *Wai*

A Transitional blue and white tripod surprise cup, modelled in the shape of a lotus leaf, the interior paint with leaf veining, the exterior with a poem, mid-17thC, 2.5in (7cm) diam.
£1,200-1,500 *CAm*

Five famille rose semi eggshell tea bowls, 4 enamelled with a butterfly and flowersprays, a single bloom to the interior, 3.5in (9cm) diam, and one larger, similarly enamelled, 4in (10cm) diam Qianlong.
£1,500-2,000 *CAm*

Figures

A pair of white glazed cockerels, modelled in mirror image, decorated in black, their combs and wattles red, lightly moulded and incised plumage, restored, 18thC, 14.5in (37cm).
£3,200-4,200 *CAm*

A pair of polychrome pheasants, each standing on an outcrop of aubergine with green splashes, their yellow claws naturalistically incised, their feathers brightly enamelled in flame, violet, green, blue and yellow with black details, 19thC, 13.5in (34.5cm).
£4,000-4,500 *C*

A pair of white glazed phoenix, modelled in mirror image, with short gold beaks, red crests and beards, cracked and restored, 19thC, 16.5in (42cm).
£1,600-2,000 *C*

A pair of blanc de chine cockerels, 19thC, 16in (40cm).
£1,200-1,600 *S*

A buff pottery ox and cart, with 2 large detachable wheels with spokes and large hubs, Tang Dynasty, 9.5in (23cm) long, on fitted wood stand.
£2,700-3,500 *CAm*

A stoneware eagle, modelled on a rockwork base, slight touches of ash glaze, chipped, engraved mark kitsu, Bizen Provence, 19thC, 15.5in (39cm).
£900-1,200 *S*

A Sancai glazed pottery horse, all under brown, amber and straw glazes, chipped and restored, Tang Dynasty, 13.5in (34cm).
£6,000-7,000 *C*

A pair of famille rose export figures of elegant lady candle holders, each modelled in mirror image holding a gu-shaped beaker vase wearing long robes with full sleeves, hair tied in a topknot, restored, Jiaqing, 16in (40cm).
£4,250-5,000 *CAm*

A pair of ormolu mounted famille noire figures of boys, wearing tunics, baggy trousers and boots, one with a sword the other mounted as a lamp, damaged, the porcelain 19thC, 13in (33cm).
£4,600-5,600 *CAm*

A set of 9 famille rose figures of Immortals on floral bases, wearing brightly coloured robes and holding their various attributes, some restoration, late Qianlong, 10in (25cm).
£4,200-4,700 *C*

A set of 8 famille rose figures of Immortals, on wave pattern bases, wearing brightly coloured robes and holding their various attributes, some restoration, late Qianlong, 9in (23cm).
£1,800-2,200 *C*

A Tang painted pink pottery figure of a polo player, extensive areas of pigment remaining, restored, 16in (40.5cm) long.
£8,000-9,000 *C*

A blanc de chine group modelled as Guanyin and a child, seated on a rocky base, chipped, 18thC, 11in (28cm).
£1,500-2,000 *C*

A pair of blanc-de-chine figures of Guanyin and a child, she wearing loose robes and a shawl, the child holding an ingot, restored, 18thC, 16in (40.5cm).   **£1,700-2,000** *C*

A Chinese famille verte figure of Li Tie guai, and a famille rose Immortal, holding a fan and standing on a mound base, both damaged, early 19thC, 8 and 8.5in (20 and 21cm).
£450-650 *C(S)*

Two famille rose Daoist Immortal groups, each modelled with the 8 Immortals and Shoulao standing on a rockwork and holding their attributes, chipped and repaired, 19thC, 6.5in (16cm).
£175-275 *CAm*

Two blanc de chine figures of Guanyin, chipped, 18thC, 9.5in (24cm).
£1,200-1,600 *C*

A blanc de chine figure of Guanyin, the even glaze with a green tinge, chipped, the back with an impressed mark He Chao Cong, 17thC, 15in (37.5cm) on wood stand.
£9,500-10,500 *C*

Flatware

A pair of dragon dishes, painted in underglaze blue and washed in yellow with a dragon in pursuit of the flaming pearl amidst clouds, the border with 2 further dragons, all against a blue ground, some damage, seal mark of Daoguang in blue, and period, 10in (25cm).
£1,200-1,600 S(S)

A famille verte charger, 19thC, 21in (53cm).
£350-400 MJB

A Chinese dish, minor rubbing to glaze, Qianlong, 17in (43cm).
£900-1,200 Bea

A Junyao saucer dish, with shallow sides, under a pale blue glaze, thinning at the rim, the centre with a crescent shaped purple splash and 2 small circles, Song Dynasty, 7in (17cm).
£3,600-4,200 C

A pair of famille verte deep dishes, painted with scrolling peony flowerheads and foliage, minute rim frits, Kangxi, 11in (28cm).   £400-600 CSK

A set of 7 famille rose plates, 4 octagonal and 3 circular, decorated within an underglaze blue border, some cracked, Qianlong, 9in (23cm).
£600-900 S(S)

A pair of famille rose dishes, decorated in bright enamels, the ground enriched with multi-coloured blooms, small chips, Qianlong, 15in (38cm).
£3,000-3,500 CAm

A Chinese saucer dish, Daoguang mark and period, c1845, 10in (25cm).   £600-700 Wai

A Chinese saucer dish, cracked and restored, Tongzhi mark and period, c1868, 9in (23cm).
£700-800 Wai

A late Ming Japanese market blue and white moulded saucer dish, rim frits, encircled Chenghua six-character mark, Tianqi, 8.5in (21.5cm).
£1,200-1,500 CAm

A late Ming blue and white saucer dish, Jiajing six-character mark and late in the period, 14in (36cm).   £1,800-2,000 C

A famille rose saucer dish, the interior enamelled, exterior plain, rim chip, encircled Yongzheng six-character mark and of the period, 8in (19.5cm).
£1,200-1,700 C

A famille rose dish, painted at the centre beneath a band of pink trellis pattern, the well reserved with 4 cartouches of precious emblems, the border with 8 Daoist Immortals, slight rubbing and chip, early Qianlong, 13.5in (35cm).
£3,500-4,000 *CAm*

A Longquan celadon dish, the interior carved with a peony spray below petals, beneath everted rim, the countersunk base with an unglazed ring burnt orange in the firing, rim crack, 14th/15thC, 17in (43cm).
£1,500-2,000 *C*

A Chinese blue and white deep dish, decorated with trailing floral border, the centre with figures in a landscape and pagodas, c1750, 15in (38cm).
£400-450 *WW*

A famille rose dish, Qianlong, 14in (35cm).
£1,500-2,000 *CAm*

A famille rose meat dish, painted and gilt within a gilt chain border, minute rim frits, Qianlong, 12.5in (31cm) wide.
£700-800 *CSK*

A Canton famille rose commemorative plate, painted in the centre with 3 Portuguese ships within a band inscribed QUARTO CENTENARIO DO DESCOBRIMENTO DA INDIA, surmounted by the Royal arms of Don Carlos I, within 2 rows of butterflies, ducks, fish and floral sprays, minute rim chip, 19thC, 10in (25cm).
£850-950 *CAm*

Four Cantonese warming dishes, 19thC.
£950-1,200 *P(S)*

An enamelled plate, the interior painted en grisaille and gilt, the border with a blue enamelled Y-pattern ground below a band of scrolling foliage, rim chips, Yongzheng, 8.5in (21cm).
£2,200-2,500 *CAm*

Nanking

In the 18thC the bulk of Chinese export porcelain for the West was the now well known blue and white, commonly called 'Nanking' after the port from where it was shipped. Nanking is on the lower Yangtze river, to which the porcelain was sent by boat from Ching tê Chên via the Po-yang lake in Kiangsi province.

Three Chinese Imari dishes, each with a vase of flowers within a central medallion below a qilin, birds and prunus, lotus sprays at the well, early 18thC, two 11.5in (29cm), one 13in (33cm).
£2,000-2,500 *CAm*

A blue and white deep dish, painted with 4 exotic fantailed fish swimming amongst lotus heads and water plants within a band of peony, lotus, hibiscus and dense foliage at the well, the border with 4 broad clusters of peony and stylized flowers, small rim chips and frittings, c1750, 17.5in (45cm).
£6,150-6,500 *CAm*

A pair of Chinese Imari 'Dame-au-Parasol' plates, painted after a design by Cornelis Pronk, on an iron red diaper ground, restored, c1735, 9in (23cm).
£1,600-2,000 *C*

An iron red European subject baptism plate, painted with the Baptism of Christ in a wooded riverscape below the Holy Spirit in Dove form, surrounded by 4 winged cherubs and a bird holding ribboned flowersprays above a cartouche inscribed Mat.3.16, small rim chip, Qianlong, 10.5in (27cm).
£1,700-2,200 *C*

Jars

Garden Seats

A pair of Canton famille rose garden seats, painted with figure and bird panels around pierced cash between gilt stud borders, late 19thC, 19in (48cm).
£2,500-3,000 *S(S)*

A blue and white baluster jar and cover, cracked and restored, Kangxi, 20.5in (52cm).
£1,500-2,000 *C*

A Chinese Imari silver mounted milk jug, the domed silver cover with coat-of-arms below a crest and the motto Recte Faciendo Neminem Timeas, handle chipped and cracked, the porcelain 18thC, the mounts 19thC, 10.5in (26cm).
£3,500-4,000 *CAm*

A pair of Canton famille rose baluster jars and covers, with Buddhistic lion finials, on wood stands, late 19thC, 17.5in 45cm).
£2,000-2,500 *S(S)*

A Cantonese garden seat, in famille rose et verte enamels and gilt, 19in (48cm),
£800-1,000 *HSS*

A pair of blue and white soft paste miniature jugs and covers, the covers and handles pierced, minute chips, jade character mark, Kangxi, 4in (10cm).
£1,600-2,000 *CAm*

A Transitional oviform jar, c1640, 11.5in (29cm).
£1,500-2,000 *C*

Hollow Ware & Services

A Chinese famille rose teapot, c1770, 4in (10cm). **£200-300** *Wai*

Two Chinese blue and white vegetable tureens and domed covers, with strawberry finials, painted with fishermen in mountainous river landscapes, early 19thC, 9in (23cm) diam. **£250-400** *CSK*

A Canton 'Cadogan' wine pot, the peach shaped body painted on one side with figures and on the other with birds, insects and flowers on a foliate decorated gold ground, minor damage, 6in (16cm). **£150-200** *Bea*

A Canton 'Cadogan' famille verte wine pot, painted with 6 panels of figures and birds on branches, 6.5in (16cm). **£150-200** *Bea*

A famille rose tureen, cover and stand, with iron red hare head handles and knop finial, enamelled with mixed floral sprays within flame shaped aubergine hatched borders and spear head around the foot, Qianlong, 14.5in (37cm) long. **£4,200-4,700** *C*

A famille rose monogrammed teapot and cover, each side of the body enamelled with a cypher containing the letters spelling Sir Joshua Reynolds for whom the service was made, below an underglaze blue Fitzhugh pattern border repeated around the flat cover, with a straight spout and entwined double strap handle, c1785, 9.5in (23cm) wide. **£3,700-4,000** *C*

A white glazed rococo style tureen and cover, modelled from a European faience original, supported on 4 paw feet, moulded with irregular flutes and ridges, the sides set with scrolling handles, the cover modelled as a curled leaf with spiralling stem finial, small chips, Qianlong, c1760, 12in (31cm) wide. **£5,400-6,000** *CAm*

A famille rose tureen and cover, modelled after a European silver original, supported on 4 claw feet, decorated with flowersprays, applied at either side with elaborate frond handles, the cover similarly decorated and surmounted by a rococo scroll finial, chipped, Qianlong, 12.5in (32cm) wide. **£2,500-3,000** *C*

A famille rose armorial tureen, cover and stand, decorated predominantly in blue enamel, iron red and gilt with a crest above the motto Sub Umbra Alarum Tuarum, crack to rim of stand, c1800, stand 14in (36cm) wide. **£2,500-3,500** *C*

A famille rose Mandarin pattern part tea service, enamelled with a dignitary seated in a chair being attended by his wife, a child and a female servant in the garden of a dwelling, with floral panels reserved on gilt and grisaille borders, comprising: a silver mounted teapot and domed cover, a milk jug and domed cover, baluster tea caddy and domed cover, an octagonal lobed spoon tray, a hexagonal lobed spoon tray, a large tea bowl and saucer, 6 tea bowls and saucers, Qianlong. **£2,000-3,000** *CAm*

A Chinese exportware toy tea service, each piece painted with flowersprays and a puce scale border, comprising: teapot, cover and stand, hot milk jug and cover, tea caddy, spoon tray and 6 cups and 4 saucers, some damage, Qianlong.
£550-750 *S(S)*

A Chinese export child's tea service, comprising: a teapot and cover, milk jug and cover, tea caddy, sugar bowl, spoon tray, 2 tea bowls, 2 coffee cups and 2 saucers, each piece painted with figures in conversation by a table, Qianlong. **£800-900** *Bea*

The residue of a Canton famille rose dinner service, each piece with a panel of figures meeting by a veranda framed by a border of butterflies amongst scattered flowers, comprising: an oval dish, oval vegetable dish and cover, 4 rectangular vegetable dishes and 2 covers, a pair of oval dishes, 4 liners and 2 covers, some damage, early 19thC.
£1,600-2,000 *S(S)*

A blue and white dinner service, painted with figures amidst pavilions in a river landscape, comprising: 4 tureens, 3 wine coolers with mask handles, a sauceboat, 5 oval dishes, 95 plates, 13 soup plates, 2 strainers, 1 hot water plate, 16 saucer dishes, 37 foliate rim plates, 4 foliate rim saucer dishes, a sauceboat stand and a blue and white part dinner service painted with a boy riding a buffalo beside 2 figures and a pavilion in a wooded river landscape, comprising: a floral rim dish, 12 floral rim plates, 8 floral rim soup plates, and 11 plates painted with ladies on a terrace, 9in (22.5cm), 2 shaped octagonal dishes, painted with rocks, trees and peonies on a terrace, 10in (25cm) and 2 sauceboats, 10.5in (26cm), and 8in (20cm), cracks and chips, all Qianlong.
£17,000-18,000 *CAm*

Vases

A Chinese blue and white bottle, Wanli period, 11.5in (29cm) high.
£1,500-2,000 *S(S)*

A pair of Transitional Wucai baluster vases and covers, each enamelled on an iron-red trellis pattern ground, beneath an underglaze blue bud finial, slight damage, c1640, 15in (38.5cm) high.
£2,700-3,000 *C*

A pair of Chinese famille verte vases of square tapering form, with waisted cylindrical necks, decorated with exotic birds, flowers and foliage, one rim damaged, retrospective Kangxi marks, 19thC, 16in (41cm) high.
£800-900 *GAK*

A pair of Canton famille rose baluster vases, each with swan handles, 3 handles restored, 19thC, 25in (64cm) high.
£2,500-3,000 *C*

A pair of Chinese blue and white vases, the low baluster body filled with leaf shaped landscape panels in insect medallions in a lotus scroll ground, under a broad neck with bell shaped mouth, one rim chipped, 19thC, 17in (43.5cm) high.
£1,200-1,500 *S(S)*

A Chinese famille rose vase, 18thC, 6in (15cm) high.
£250-300 *Wai*

A bottle vase, painted in underglaze blue and copper-red with kylins, with gilt metal mounts, cracked, 18in (46cm) high.
£800-1,000 *S*

A pair of Canton famille rose square baluster vases and domed covers with Guanyin finials, reserved on a ground of scrolling flowers and fruit embellished with exotic birds and butterflies, the covers similarly decorated, slight damage, 19thC, 21.5in (55cm) high. **£4,000-4,500** *C*

A famille rose vase, with tall flaring neck painted and gilt with shou medallions, surrounded by flowerheads and scrolling leaves, underglaze blue Guangxu six-character mark and of the period, 15.5in (39.5cm) high.
£800-1,000 *CSK*

A Chinese vase, delicately decorated in pastel shades and iron red, 19thC, 10.5in (26.5cm) high.
£350-450 *HSS*

A Chinese finely enamelled vase, Daoguang, 5.5in (13.5cm) high.
£400-500 *Wai*

Locate the Source

The source of each illustration in Miller's can be found by checking the code letters below each caption with the list of contributors.

A pair of famille noir vases, decorated and heavily gilt with scrolling lotus and shou symbols between bands of lappets, underglaze blue Kangxi six-character marks, l8in (45.5cm).
£950-1,000 *CSK*

A pair of Samson famille rose rouleau vases painted with birds and butterflies among peonies issuing from pierced rockwork on blue grounds, 18.5in (47cm) high.
£600-700 *CSK*

A pair of Chinese famille verte vases, the necks applied with iron red Buddhistic lions, hairline cracks, 19thC, 24in (61cm) high, on wood stands.
£1,000-1,200 *S(S)*

A lustrous black glazed garniture comprising: a pair of squat baluster vases and domed covers with knop finials, and a pear shaped vase decorated in gilt, 19thC, vases 17.5in (44.5cm).
£3,000-4,000 *C*

A Chinese famille rose vase, 24in (61.5cm) high.
£300-400 *P(S)*

A pair of Chinese clobbered flattened vases, with angular handles, painted and gilt with bands of scrolling lotus and peonies on green, red and black grounds, 11in (28cm) high.
£450-650 *CSK*

Clobbered: In the late 18thC it was the practice in Europe to enhance the value of simple blue and white porcelain from China with overglaze enamelling - now called clobbering. Most clobbering was done in Holland but a small amount was done in the London decorators' workshops.

A pair of Canton vases, each brightly painted with panels of strolling figures in conversation, reserved on a green hatched ground, damaged, 24in (61cm) high.   **£900-1,200** *Bea*

Locate the Source

The source of each illustration in Miller's can be found by checking the code letters below each caption with the list of contributors.

A pair of Cantonese vases, decorated in famille rose colours, with reserved panels of warriors and other figures in interiors and alternate panels with vases of flowers and insects, restored, 19thC, 10in (25cm) high.
£200-250 *GAK*

A famille rose oviform enamelled vase, the interior and base with a turquoise glaze, Qianlong seal mark, 9in (22.5cm) high.
£1,800-2,200 *C*

A pair of Canton famille rose flaring vases, with pierced covers, each painted with figure panels divided by relief gilt squirrels and vines, with gilt handles, the lightly domed pierced covers with matching decoration, 19thC, 9in (23cm) high. **£2,500-3,000** *CAm*

A pair of famille rose lobed baluster enamelled vases and covers, the shoulders with 2 lion mask fixed ring handles, the domed covers with flowersprays below a Buddhistic lion finial, one cracked, one restored, Qianlong/Jiaqing, 24in (61cm) high.   **£5,000-5,500** *CAm*

An Imari triple gourd vase, brightly painted in iron red, green and yellow enamels, with gilt on underglaze blue, rim chipped, Kangxi, 12.5in (32cm) high. **£3,250-3,750** *CAm*

A carved celadon meiping, decorated under a thick creamy celadon glaze stopping around the foot to expose the body burnt orange in the firing, 14thC, 10in (25.5cm) high. **£2,500-3,000** *C*

Miscellaneous

A Chinese blue and white bidet, of waisted form, Qianlong/Jiaqing, 24in (61cm) long, on a four-footed mahogany stand. **£900-1,500** *S(S)*

A blue and white jardinière, painted in smokey blue tones, l9thC, 21.5in (54in). **£2,000-2,500** *C*

A Transitional blue and white double gourd ewer, painted with lotus and peony sprays and cloud scrolls, strut crack, c1640, 9in (23cm).   **£1,500-2,000** *C*

A pair of Rhodes Kuthaya style baluster jars and domed covers, with twin lion head loop handles, painted with flowering stems on a whorl pattern ground, 15in (38cm) high. **£1,500-2,000** *CSK*

A painted Cizhou pillow, modelled as a recumbent tiger with a broad mouth, pierced nostrils and bold eyes, freely painted with black stripes on a flame coloured ground, its back with a cream ground panel containing a bird within a lozenge, Jin Dynasty, 14.5in (37cm) wide. **£2,500-3,500** *C*

A Chinese blue and white pilgrim flask, replacement silver neck and cover, 19thC, 9in (23cm). **£300-400** *WW*

Japanese
Bowls

An Imari bowl, painted against a predominantly iron red ground between further brocade borders, ho-o mon within, Meiji period, 15in (38cm).
£700-800 *S(S)*

An Imari bowl, painted and gilt to the interior, the exterior with panels of chrysanthemum sprays and stylised heads on geometric grounds, damaged, c1700, 10in (25cm). **£1,300-1,500** *CSK*

An Imari barber's bowl, painted and gilt within a border of panels of trees, rockwork and buildings, chipped, c1700, 11in (28cm).
£620-720 *CSK*

A Satsuma bowl, the exterior enamelled with a dragon, the inside filled with the 18 Rakkan, signed, Meiji period, 5in (13cm).
£400-500 *S(S)*

An earthenware bowl by Kizan, painted in enamels and gilt with 2 panels showing a formal and an informal picnic, the interior with mille fleur, the base with ho-o, Meiji period, marked Dai Nihon Kizan tsukuru, 5in (12.5cm).
£2,500-3,000 *S*

A fluted Imari bowl, decorated in typical coloured enamels and gilt on underglaze blue, early 18thC, 8.5in (21.5cm).**£2,000-2,500** *CAm*

A Kenji Imari style bowl, kiku signature, mid-18thC, 12.5in (31.5cm). **£2,200-3,000** *S(S)*

An Imari bowl, painted and gilt with a design of bijin holding parasols, 10in (25cm), and a set of 6 quatrefoil bowls painted and gilt with flowersprays and geometric patterns, 7in (17.5cm). **£250-300** *CSK*

An Imari barber's bowl, early 18thC, 11in (28cm).
£1,200-1,500 *Bea*

A porcelain bowl by Zengoro Hozen, his son Wazen, or grandson Tokizen, finely painted in underglaze blue in late Ming style with 2 immortals on a raft, the exterior with dragons and Buddhist objects, the rim with brown edge, signed Dai Nihon Eiraku tsukuru, 19thC, 7.5in (19cm) wide. **£1,000-1,200** *S*

A Kakiemon bowl, decorated in enamels and slight gilt with pine and prunus, the everted rim with scrolling peonies within a brown edged rim, footrim drilled with one hole, late 17thC, 5.5in (13.5cm).
£1,300-1,700 *S*

Imari

Most Japanese porcelain was manufactured in and around the town of Arita, in the province of Hizen. The factories of Arita were within eight miles of the port of Imari, the market town of the district, and the place to which all porcelain was carried before being shipped to Nagasati for export to Europe.

The term 'Imari' survives to describe a certain type of decoration on Arita wares, namely underglaze blue, with on-glaze iron red and gold decoration.

Ewers

An Arita blue and white moulded kendi, late 17thC, 8in (20cm).
£1,000-1,500 *CAm*

A large Arita ewer, decorated in underglaze blue with peonies between floral and geometric bands, drilled towards the foot, c1670, 11in (28cm).
£900-1,200 *S*

An Arita ewer.
£650-700 *P(S)*

A pair of Arita ewers, decorated in underglaze blue with figures in a garden, damaged, c1670, 10in (25cm). **£1,400-1,600** *S*

Figures

A Kutani group of 5 cats, comprising: a mother and 4 kittens, each asleep with their paws tucked beneath them, with gilt fur markings and orange bows, Taisho period, 11in (28cm) and 2.5in (6.5cm) wide.
£600-900 *S(S)*

A porcelain duck, the plumage ornithologically correct, the eyes touched in black, slight damage, possibly Mahuzu Kozan, Meiji period, 8in (20cm) wide.
£600-700 *S(S)*

A Satsuma earthenware figure of Fugen Bosatsu, by Kizan, the female deity seated on an elephant, decorated in enamels and gilt, foot of goddess restored, marked Dai Nihon Satsuma yaki Kizan, Meiji period, 13in (33cm) high.
£2,500-3,500 *S*

A pair of Imari figures of ladies, wearing high cowls and flowing robes, each holding a flowerspray, slight damage and repair, 16in (41cm) high.
£400-800 *CSK*

An Hirado white glazed model of a tiger, 6in (15cm) high.
£400-500 *CSK*

Flatware

An Arita dish, decorated in underglaze blue with floral designs, late 17thC, 12.5in (31.5cm).
£800-1,200 *S*

Two Imari dishes, decorated in underglaze blue, iron red, black enamel and gilding with a bijin and attendants, both with a rivetted crack, 19in (49cm) and 18in (45.5cm).
£3,500-4,000 *S*

An Imari charger, decorated in underglaze blue, iron red, enamels and gilding, 19thC, 17.5in (45cm).
£2,200-2,700 *S*

An Imari plaque painted with panels, 18in (46.5cm).
£300-400 *Bea*

A large Imari dish, the iron red ground filled with a profusion of peony painted in underglaze blue, detailed in black lacquer, slight damage, 25in (63cm).
£800-1,200 *S(S)*

An Arita dish, framed by a border of panels filled with dots between intersecting blue lines, Meiji period, 21.5in (54.5cm).
£400-600 *S(S)*

An Imari charger, painted and gilt with a central ho-o medallion within a border of three panels of cranes, sages and birds among the Three Friends, on a floral and geometric design ground, 24.5in (63cm).
£1,500-2,000 *CSK*

An Imari saucer dish, decorated in iron red and gilt on underglaze blue, c1700, 21in (54.5cm).
£4,750-5,250 *CAm*

An Arita blue and white charger, containing the letters V.O.C., surrounded by a ho-o bird perched among flowers and foliage, the rim with 6 shaped rectangular panels alternately containing the shochikubai.
£14,500-15,000 *CAm*

An Imari foliate rimmed charger, decorated in iron red and gilt on underglaze blue, late 19thC, 25in (64cm).
£2,500-3,000 *CAm*

Two Imari chargers, painted and gilt with shaped and scroll panels of maple, wisteria, bijin and landscapes, 18in (46cm).
£400-500 *CSK*

A Imari charger, painted with panels of mountain landscape and kara shi shi on gilt and blue ground with cranes amidst clouds, and gilt and red phoenix in shaped panels, 21.5in (54.5cm). **£350-450** *ALL*

A Nabeshima style dish, decorated overall in underglaze blue with finely scrolling foliage, the exterior with larger scrolls, the tall tapering foot with 'comb' design, 19thC, 19in (48cm). **£1,700-2,000** *S*

An Arita blue and white charger, painted with a roundel enclosing the letters V.O.C., surrounded by 3 ho-o birds, one perched on a rock, the other in flight amongst pomegranate and peony sprays, within a border of 6 alternate panels of peony and shochikubai sprays divided by vertical bands of stylised flowerheads and foliage, late 17thC, 14.5in (37.5cm). **£13,000-15,000** *C(S)*

An Arita blue and white charger, late 17thC, 23in (58cm). **£5,000-5,500** *CAm*

An Imari charger, decorated with 2 galloping fabulous animals with a phoenix overhead, the floral lattice border with groups of pendant hexagons painted with flowering branches and formal designs, 24in (61cm). **£800-850** *P(S)*

Hollow Ware

A large blue and white jardinière, raised upon 3 dwarf cabriole legs, 19thC, 25in (64cm) diam. **£1,200-1,400** *B*

A Kakiemon cup and an Arita saucer, the cup decorated in iron-red, green, blue and black enamels and gilding with floral sprays, the saucer of multi-lobed form with floralsprays, damaged, late 17thC, cup 2.5in (6.5cm), saucer 5in (13cm). **£800-1,200** *S*

An Arita blue and white silver mounted coffee pot and cover, on 3 shaped feet, the loop handle decorated with scrolling foliage, the porcelain late 17thC, the mounts 19thC, 13in (33cm) high. **£4,000-4,500** *CAm*

> **Miller's is a price GUIDE not a price LIST**

An Hirado jar and cover, modelled as a conch shell in blue, brown, cream and green glazes, the shell encrusted conch moulded with crabs and limpets, slight damage, 18thC, 11in (28cm). **£2,200-2,600** *CSK*

Vases

Three Arita blue and white jars and covers, damaged and covers repaired, late 17thC, 18.5in (47cm). **£7,750-8,250** *CAm*

A Imari fluted jar, painted and gilt in coloured enamels and underglaze blue, c1700, 16in (41cm).
£4,000-5,000 *CSK*

A pair of Imari vases, painted against an iron red ground, damaged and repaired, Meiji period, 36in (92cm), on wood stands. **£500-800** *S(S)*

A pair of Satsuma vases, damaged, signed in gold within the pattern, 6in (15cm).
£500-600 *MJB*

A pair of Satsuma vases, painted and gilt with continuous scenes, damaged, 11in (28cm) high.
£900-1,200 *CSK*

A pair of Satsuma vases, painted and gilt with continuous scenes, signed Renji, 7in (17.5cm).
£700-1,000 *CSK*

A pair of Satsuma vases, reserved on a brocade ground, fitted with pierced gilt brass stands, 12in (30.5cm).
£1,500-2,000 *Bea*

An Imari vase, traditionally decorated with blue, rust and gilt floral designs, early 19thC, 18in (46cm).
£450-550 *GAK*

A Samson Imari jar and domed cover, with knop finial, painted and gilt, 33in (83.5cm).
£7,200-8,000 *CSK*

A pair of Kutani vases, applied with butterfly handles, one repaired.
£900-1,200 *S(S)*

An Imari bottle vase, moulded in relief and painted in underglaze blue, iron red and gilding with sprays of kiku and peonies, c1800, 7in (17.5cm) high.
£1,000-1,200 *S*

A pair of Kutani vases, enamelled, with mask and tongue handles, 11in (28cm).
£800-1,200 *S(S)*

A pair of Imari vases, each in the form of Benkei clinging to a giant leaping carp, decorated in underglaze blue, iron red, enamels and gilding, damaged, c1800, 9in (23cm).
£3,000-4,000 *S*

Benkei, a hero of the 12thC, as a boy was nicknamed Oniwaka (young demon) and is often depicted exhibiting great feats of strength.

A Satsuma vase, of butterfly outline, one side filled with a panel of bijin, the other with samurai on a shore, signed, Meiji period, 4in (10cm)
£450-550 *S(S)*

A large Satsuma quatrefoil vase, painted and heavily gilt with panels of officials, ladies and children before buildings in mountainous landscapes, 19.5in (49.5cm).
£1,500-2,000 *CSK*

An Imari garniture, comprising: jar and cover, and a pair of beaker vases, all decorated in underglaze blue, iron red, slight black enamel and gilding, beaker vases restored, c1800, jar and cover 19in (48cm).   **£2,700-3,200** *S*

An Imari vase and cover, decorated in underglaze blue, iron red, enamels and gilding, with panels of bijin and attendants, with a wood stand, Meiji period , 25in (64cm) high.
£1,700-2,000 *S*

A pair of Satsuma double gourd vases, painted with Rakkan, signed, Meiji period, 8.5in (22cm) high.
£500-700 *S(S)*

An Imari vase, decorated in underglaze blue, iron red and gilding with ho-o among flowering trees, c1800, 13in (33cm) high.
£1,500-2,000 *S*

A Kutani millefiori vase, signed, Meiji period, 12in (30.5cm).
£1,200-1,500 *S(S)*

An Imari vase, painted beneath the shoulder with a repeated panel showing a bird descending to a blossoming branch, 3 ho-o panels on the shoulder reserved in a flower strewn blue ground, c1800, 10.5in (26.5cm).
£400-600 *S(S)*

A pair of Kutani vases, each painted in brilliant enamels and gilding with figures in a landscape, marked fuku (happiness), Meiji period, 11.5in (29.5cm) high.
£1,700-2,200 *S*

A Kutani vase, decorated in white and coloured enamels and gilding with chrysanthemum, marked Kutani Taniguchi, Meiji period, 14in (36cm).
£1,500-2,000 *S*

A blossom vase for the tea ceremony room, (Hanaike), Ko-Kiyomizu-Edo, 14in (36cm).
£2,000-2,500 *Wai*

A pair of Satsuma earthenware vases, decorated in typical palette, 17.5in (44cm).
£5,700-6,000 *HSS*

A pair of Satsuma earthenware vases, by Fuzan, each with 4 panels of bijin, birds and flowers, reserved on a blue ground, marked Fuzan, Meiji period, 6.5in (16.5cm).
£2,000-2,500 *S*

A pair of Imari moulded trumpet necked vases, decorated in iron red and gilt on underglaze blue with 2 panels of vases of flowers divided by massed flowers and foliage, late 19thC, 22.5in (58cm).
£5,000-5,500 *CAm*

A pair of Imari vases, each painted with cockerels, bats, chrysanthemum, peony and blossoming branches, within moulded hexagonal panels, late 19thC, 18in (46cm).
£3,000-3,500 *C(S)*

A pair of Satsuma earthenware vases by Gyokushu, each decorated in enamels and gilt with landscapes and still life, signed Gyokushu, one rim chip repaired, 4in (11cm) high.
£1,500-2,000 *S*

An Imari bottle vase, decorated in underglaze blue, iron red and gilding, with shaped panels of kiku and peonies reserved on birds and trees, c1800, 10.5in (26.5cm) high.
£1,700-2,000 *S*

An Hirado reticulated and double skinned vase, c1860, 6in (15cm).
£1,000-1,200 *Wai*

A Satsuma vase, the slim ovoid body painted with figures in conversation in a garden and on a verandah, reserved on a brocade ground, 15.5in (40cm).
£400-500 *Bea*

A Satsuma gilt bronze mounted vase, decorated in enamels and gilding with sages amid bamboo and geese by a stream, mounted with gilt bronze handles and base, Meiji period, 21.5in (54.5cm) high.
£1,200-1,500 *S*

An Imari trumpet-shaped vase, decorated with panels of flowers on a floral ground in rust, blue and gilt, 16.5in (42cm).
£900-1,200 *RID*

A pair of Imari vases, of baluster form with frilled rims, 18in (45.5cm).
£600-900 *S(S)*

A Sota ware blue and white vase, cover and liner, with birds perched amongst flowers and foliage, the decoration being continuous and extending over the cover, 11.5in (29cm).
£250-450 *P(M)*

An Hirado vase, decorated in underglaze blue with a group of 4 kirin beneath a dragon, slight firing fault, Meiji period, 15.5in (39cm) high. **£3,200-3,700** *S*

A Satsuma vase, reserved on a dark blue/green ground painted with wisteria and other blossom on silver and gold, 5in (13cm).
£550-600
and a Satsuma saucer dish, the cavetto finely painted with houses and figures in an extensive mountain landscape, on the reverse flowerheads in an encircling river, 5in (12.5cm).
£650-700 *Bea*

A pair of Satsuma earthenware vases, decorated in coloured enamels and gilt, one neck restored, 7.5in (19cm).
£1,600-2,000 *HSS*

A garniture of 3 Kutani vases, the central covered jar with Buddhist lion knop, each painted on one side with a woman and children in a garden and on the other with peafowl and foliage, reserved on a gold decorated multi-coloured ground, 11.5in (30cm).
£650-750 *Bea*

GLASS

Bowls

A green glass finger bowl, c1800, 4.5in (11cm) diam.
£60-70 *WGT*

Two Stourbridge bowls, c1880, 5.5in (14cm) and 6.5in (16.5cm) diam.
£40-90 each *CB*

A butter dish, with prism cutting above and below a band of relief diamonds, star cut base, notched rim with 2 fan cut handles, c1810, 7.5in (18.5cm) wide.
£450-500 *Som*

An English sugar bowl, engraved with a fruiting vine, with pedestal stem and star engraved foot, c1880, 5in (12.5cm) diam.
£50-60 *CB*

A butter dish, cover and stand with diamond, prism and blaze cutting, the domed cover with a mushroom finial, c1825, 5in (12.5cm).
£250-320 *Som*

A fruit bowl, with kettle drum body, turn-over rim and cut with diamonds and splits, on a bobbin knopped stem and square lemon squeezer foot, c1800, 9.5in (24cm) diam.
£900-1,200 *Som*

A pair of Georgian style cut glass bowls, with crenellated rims over steep diamond faceted sides, late 19thC, 9in (22.5cm) diam.
£600-900 *S(S)*

An opalescent vaseline bowl, 5.5in (14cm) diam.
£40-60 *CB*

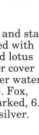

A Victorian glass bowl and stand with silver cover, etched with trailing water lilies and lotus blossoms, the flat silver cover crested and with further water lily finial, by C. T. & G. Fox, London, 1859, fully marked, 6.5in (16.5cm) diam., 9oz of silver.
£800-900 *S(S)*

Decanters

A dish, cut with small diamonds and fluting, serrated on a short cut stem and notch cut rim, conical star cut foot, c1810, 6in (14.5cm).
£200-300 *Som*

A pair of plain decanters, with three neck rings and cut mushroom stoppers, c1800, 8in (19.5cm).
£700-900 *Som*

A pair of cut glass decanters, with an engraved crest, c1780, 12.5in (32cm) high. **£1,500-2,000** *WGT*

GLASS - PRICE TRENDS

In my previous three reviews I made the point that glass had bucked the trend compared with other areas of collecting by moving up sharply in price. Over the past year, however, as the recession has deepened, prices have stabilised and are generally not very different from twelve months ago.

The demand for early English glass is still strong, with good quality pieces being very much in demand. Victorian glass on the other hand has fared poorly, this is due in part to the lack of interest being shown by overseas buyers, particularly the Americans who are normally avid collectors.

Continental glass is selling but when one looks at the sale results ordinary façon de Venise, Venetian and South German glass make up most of the unsold lots.

Returning briefly to English glass, there seem to be quite a lot of 'Beilby' enamelled glasses appearing on the market. The quality of these does vary a lot and while a glass with poor decoration or restoration can be had for as little as £500 a good glass with ordinary fruiting vine decoration and a gilt rim cannot be had for much less than £1,200. Jelly glasses are becoming quite hard to find and it is not unusual to find an early or mid-18th century example with, perhaps, a ribbed bowl, air beaded knop and domed foot making in excess of £80.

In conclusion, I sense that more glass is now coming on to the market and, if the economy does pick up as predicted, prices should not advance too rapidly. Now, therefore, is a good time to buy good quality examples when they become available.

R. G. Thomas
April 1992

An octagonal moulded decanter, with annulated string ring, c1730, 8in (19.5cm).
£450-500 *Som*

A pair of decanters, engraved 'WMW' below a hatched rose and laurel leaf garland, with target stoppers, c1770, 10in (25cm).
£1,300-1,500 *Som*

A Bristol blue decanter, engraved with gilding and 'Noyeou', French, c1760, 9in (22cm). **£400-500** *CB*

A pair of decanters with ovoid bodies, broad flute cut, 3 neck rings and target stoppers, c1820, 8.5in (21cm).
£600-800 *Som*

A set of 3 cruciform decanters, with bladed string rings, c1730, 11.5in (29cm).
£1,500-2,000 *Som*

A pair of near Rodney type plain decanters, with monogram 'BB', 3 plain neck rings and target stoppers, c1800, 8in (20cm).
£1,000-1,200 *Som*

A pair of heavy cut decanters, with cut mushroom stoppers, c1810, 8.5in (21cm).
£1,000-1,200 *Som*

A pair of tapered decanters, with a band of looped egg and tulip engraving, with lunar cut bevelled lozenge stoppers, c1780, 9in (23cm). **£1,000-1,200** *Som*

Three spirit decanters, with ovoid bodies, c1810:
l. flute cut base and angular neck rings, with mushroom stopper, 7in (18cm)
c. plain body and neck rings, with target stopper, 7in (18cm)
r. flute cut base and neck, cut neck rings, with mushroom stopper, 7.5in (19.5cm).
£100-150 each *Som*

A magnum decanter, cut with flutes, prisms, diamonds, cut neck rings, star cut base and cut mushroom stopper, c1810, 10.5in (27cm).
£850-1,000 *Som*

Three decanters with ovoid bodies, c1810:
l. fluted base and neck, with mushroom stopper, 8.5in (21.5cm)
c. plain body, target stopper, 9in (22.5cm)
r. fluted base and neck, with mushroom stopper, 8.5in (21cm).
£200-300 each *Som*

A green glass Whiskey decanter, c1850, 10in (25cm).
£100-150 *WGT*

Three cut decanters:
l. body cut with strawberry diamonds and flutes, with cut mushroom stopper, c1820, 8.5in (21cm)
£220-250
c. body cut with diamond and flute cutting, with cut mushroom stopper, c1810, 8in (20.5cm).
£200-230
r. body cut with strawberry diamonds, flutes and prisms, with mushroom stopper, c1825, 8in (20.5cm).
£220-250 *Som*

A pair of Continental enamelled glass decanters, with titled oval portrait medallions of Field Marshal, Duke of Wellington and Admiral Nelson, 19thC, 9.5in (23.5cm).
£600-700 *S(S)*

A blue glass Claret decanter, c1850, 10in (25cm).
£100-150 *WGT*

Three decanters:
l. with ovoid plain body, 3 plain neck rings, with plain mushroom stopper, c1800, 9in (23cm)
£200-250
c. with straight sided body flute, diamond and prism cut, 2 cut and one annulated neck rings, with cut mushroom stopper, c1820, 9in (23cm)
£220-270
r. with tapered body, 3 bladed neck rings, with cut lozenge stopper, c1800, 9in (23cm).
£220-270 *Som*

A liqueur decanter and 2 glasses, 9.5in (24cm) and 3.5in (9cm).
£80-120 *CB*

A green glass Rum decanter, c1850, 10in (25cm). **£100-185** *WGT*

A Betjeman's Patent tantalus, comprising a chromium plated locking frame and 3 cut glass decanters with stoppers, sitting in recesses, held when locking bar shut, stamped Betjeman's Patent London with crown and G.B. & S., 13.5in (34.5cm).
£300-350 *P*

A washstand flask and tumbler, engraved with grapes and vine leaves, flask 6.5in (16cm).
£40-60 *CB*

A set of 2 decanters and a claret jug, with diamond and printy cut ovoid bodies, facet cut necks and diamond cut ball stoppers, c1880, 9.5in (23.5cm).
£400-600 *Som*

Drinking Glasses

A Bohemian tumbler, engraved with the four Continents, Europa, Asia, Africa, and America, 4.5in (11.5cm).
£800-900 *CB*

A water glass, the bellied bowl engraved with a Jacobite rose, sunflower and daffodil, c1750.
£900-1,100 *Som*

An engraved tumbler, c1820, 4in (10cm).
£30-40 *CB*

A conical sided beaker, engraved with a 3 masted sailing ship, the reverse side with monogram 'W.E.R'., c1820, 4in (10cm).
£200-300 *Som*

A commemorative rummer, the cup shaped bowl engraved with Nelson's catafalque, plain stem, plain conical foot, c1806, 5in (13cm).
£750-850 *Som*

A green glass flask/ tumbler, 4in (10cm).
£5-8 *CB*

A Georgian cut glass tumbler, 3.5in (9cm).
£30-40 *CB*

A commemorative rummer, the ovoid bowl engraved with Admiral Lord Nelson's catafalque, the reverse side engraved 'Lord Nelson, Jan'y 9, 1806', 5.5in (14.5cm).
£1,000-1,500 *Som*

An ale glass, engraved with hops and barley, on lemon squeezer foot, c1790, 4.5in (11.5cm).
£120-140 *FD*

A rummer, the ovoid bowl on a collared stem with domed, moulded, lemon squeezer base, c1800, 5.5in (14cm).
£60-80 *Som*

A rummer, the ovoid body engraved with Nelson's funeral car, the reverse side 'Jan'y 9, 1806', 5.5in (14.5cm).
£1,200-1,400 *Som*

A set of 4 pale green wing flutes, with drawn slice cut stems, engraved with fruiting vines, c1830, 4.5in (11cm).
£240-280 *FD*

Three flutes, the conical bowls on cut baluster stems, c1850, 7in (17.5cm).
£150-200 *Som*

A bucket rummer, with hollow knop containing a silver coin for 1817, 6in (15cm).
£200-300 *Som*

A drawn trumpet bowl wine glass, with air-twist stem and domed partially folded foot, c1740, 6.5in (16.5cm).
£350-400 *WW*

A pair of bucket shaped bowl rummers, engraved with monogram WB, within a leaf cartouche, with knopped stems, and plain conical feet, c1825, 6.5in (16cm).
£150-200 *Som*

Three panel moulded rummers, the ovoid bodies with a band of floral and leaf decoration, c1810, 4.5 to 5in (11 to 12.5cm).
£70-100 each *Som*

An Anglo-Venetian ale glass, the deep round funnel bowl with wrythen and pincered decoration, a short knopped stem and folded conical foot, c1700, 5in (13cm).
£850-950 *Som*

A rummer, the cup shaped bowl engraved with the rare motif of St George slaying the dragon, the reverse side with monogram T.E.B. and date 1818, plain stem, square, domed, lemon squeezer foot, 6.5in (16cm).
£1,200-1,400 *Som*

An English wine glass, with opaque spiral twist stem, 18thC.
£1,100-1,500 *N(A)*

A set of 14 wine glasses, with deep round funnel bowls on stems with single series spiral cable air-twists, on plain conical feet, c1745, 7in (18cm).
£6,700-7,000 *Som*

A Lynn wine glass, the horizontally ribbed round funnel bowl on a stem with a double series opaque twist and plain conical foot, c1760, 5.5in (13.5cm).
£800-900 *Som*

Three wine glasses, with double series opaque twist stems, and plain conical feet, c1760, 5 to 6in (13 to 15cm).
£200-280 each *Som*

A trumpet bowl wine glass, drawn stem with multiple spiral air twist, plain conical foot, c1750, 6.5in (16.5cm).
£300-400 *Som*

l. A firing glass, with trumpet bowl, on a drawn stem with multiple spiral air-twists, on a thick flat foot, c1745, 4.5in (11cm)
£300-350
r. A wine glass with similar bowl and stem, on a plain conical foot, c1745, 6.5in (16cm).
£320-370 *Som*

A glass, with multiple series opaque twist stem on a thick foot, c1760, 4.5in (11.5cm).   **£150-170** *FD*

A large drawn trumpet bowl wine glass, with air-twist stem and folded conical foot, c1745, 8in (20cm).   **£350-400** *WW*

Three wine glasses, bowls, with double opaque twist stems and plain conical feet, c1760, 5.5 to 6in (13.5 to 15cm).
£220-360 each *Som*

Two wine glasses, the ogee bowls engraved with a Jacobite rose and bud, and thistle, double series opaque twist stems, plain conical feet, c1760, 6in (15.5cm).
£450-500 each *Som*

A pair of wine glasses, with round funnel bowls, engraved and polished with a floral band, on stems with double series opaque twists and plain conical feet, c1760, 6in (15cm).
£700-750 pair *Som*

A gilded green wine glass, 18thC, 5in (13cm).
£150-200 *CB*

Two opaque twist wine glasses with round funnel bowls, engraved with fruiting vines, double series opaque twist stems and plain conical feet, 6in (15.5cm).
£300-350 each *Som*

Three glasses with double series opaque twist stems, and plain conical feet, c1760:
l. with a bell bowl, 6.5in (16.5cm)
c. with an ale bowl, engraved with hops and barley motif, 7.5in (19cm)
r. with ogee bowl, 6in (15cm).
£250-380 each *Som*

A wine glass, the ogee bowl engraved with a sunflower and sprig, on a stem with a double series opaque twist, and plain conical foot, c1760, 5in (13cm).
£200-250 *Som*

A trumpet drawn wine glass, with spiral air-twist stem and basal knopped stem with domed foot, 7in (18cm).
£400-450 *CSK*

A mixed twist flute, with slender trumpet bowl on a stem with central opaque white gauze, and outer pair of spiralling air-twist threads, on a plain conical foot, c1760, 7.5in (19cm).
£480-550 *Som*

A Beilby funnel bowled wine glass, enamelled in white with trailing grapes and vine leaves on a double series opaque twist stem, on spreading foot, foot chipped, c1760, 6in (15cm).
£550-600 *C*

A wine glass, with round funnel bowl engraved with fruiting vine motif, on a double series opaque twist stem and plain conical foot, c1760, 6in (15cm).
£300-350 *Som*

A Beilby wine glass, the ogee bowl decorated with white enamel fruiting vine, on a stem with a double series opaque twist, with plain conical foot, c1775, 5.5in (14.5cm).
£2,400-2,800 *Som*

A wine glass with round bowl, finely engraved with Jacobite rose and moth, polished in parts, with double series opaque twist stem and plain conical foot, c1765, 6.5in (16cm).
£750-800 *Som*

A mixed twist flute, the trumpet bowl on a stem with annulated collar and slender stem, with a central opaque white gauze and a pair of outer air threads spiralling, on a plain conical foot, c1770, 7.5in (19cm).
£900-1,200 *Som*

A firing glass, with ogee bowl on a short stem with double series opaque twist stem, thick terraced firing foot, c1760, 3.5in (9.5cm).
£470-530 *Som*

An ale glass with deep round funnel bowl, engraved with hops and barley motif, with double series opaque twist stem and plain conical foot, 7.5in (19cm).
£300-350 *Som*

An unusual ale glass, with deep ogee bowl engraved with hops and barley, on a stem with multiple spiral air-twist and plain conical foot, c1750, 7.5in (18.5cm).
£750-800 *Som*

Firing Glasses

Firing glasses are always short stemmed. They are dram glasses or small wines made with a specially strong, thick foot for use at meetings. When a toast was drunk the members would strike the table simultaneously with their glasses, the noise was said to resemble the firing of a musket.

A large drawn wine glass with tear drop stem, domed and folded foot, c1720, 9in (22.5cm).
£250-350 *WW*

One goblet and two wine glasses, with trumpet bowls and plain drawn stems with air tears, c1745, 6 to 7.5in (15.5 to 18.5cm).
£150-180 each *Som*

A short cordial glass, the trumpet bowl on a drawn stem with multiple spiral air-twist, and plain conical foot, c1745, 4.5in (11cm).
£450-500 *Som*

A wine glass with trumpet bowl engraved with fruiting vine, on a plain drawn stem, and folded conical foot, c1740, 7in (18cm).
£350-375 *Som*

Locate the Source

The source of each illustration in Miller's can be found by checking the code letters below each caption with the list of contributors.

Two wine glasses, with plain stems and folded conical feet, c1748, 7 to 7.5in (18 to 19cm).
£300-350 each *Som*

l. An ale glass, with deep round funnel bowl engraved with a barley motif, on a plain drawn stem, and plain conical foot, c1750.
£200-250
r. A wine glass, the ogee bowl on a plain stem, and folded conical foot, c1750.
£150-170 *Som*

A Jacobite wine glass, the trumpet bowl engraved with Jacobite rose, two buds and a star, on a plain drawn stem with air tear, and plain conical foot, c1750, 6.5in (16cm).
£1,200-1,500 *Som*

A green wine glass, late 18thC, 5in (13cm).
£80-100 *CB*

A glass with bell bowl, engraved with a vine and grapes, on a drawn stem with tear and folded foot, c1770, 6in (15cm).
£100-200 *CB*

An ale glass, with deep round funnel bowl engraved with hops and barley motif, on a plain stem and folded conical foot, c1750.
£250-300 *Som*

A dwarf ale glass, engraved with hops and barley, plain stem and folded foot, c1770, 6in (15cm).
£50-60 *CB*

An English glass with bucket bowl, engraved with grapes and vines, on a plain stem and folded conical foot, c1770, 6in (15cm).
£100-200 *CB*

A green wine glass, c1780, 6in (15cm).
£100-200 *CB*

A Jacobite wine glass with trumpet bowl, engraved with a Jacobite rose, two buds and an oak leaf, on a plain drawn stem and plain conical foot, c1750, 6in (15.5cm).
£1,700-2,000 *Som*

A green wine glass, with baluster stem, c1880, 4in (10cm). **£30-50** *CB*

A green wine glass, on a faceted stem, with gilding, c1820, 6in (15cm).
£80-150 *CB*

A Newcastle light baluster wine glass, with Dutch engraving.
£4,000-5,000 *CB*

This glass is engraved with the Arms of the Count van der Stragen of Brabant, created Count in 1698.

A toastmaster's glass, the deceptive conical bowl straight on to an inverted baluster knop with air tear, on a folded conical foot, c1720, 4in (10.5cm).
£850-900 *Som*

A heavy baluster wine glass with conical bowl, mushroom and base knop stem, on domed folded foot, c1720, 6in (15cm).
£950-1,000 *Som*

Two heavy baluster wine glasses, with solid sections to bowls containing an air tear, knopped stems, folded conical feet, c1720, 5.5 to 6in (14to 15cm).
£900-1,200 each *Som*

Three balustroid wine glasses:
l. with waisted bucket bowl, inverted baluster knopped stem, and folded conical foot, c1720, 5.5in (14cm)
£620-650
c. with trumpet bowl, multi-knopped stem, and plain conical foot, c1740, 7in (18cm)
£750-800
r. with bell bowl, hollow inverted baluster knop stem, and folded conical foot, c1720, 6.5in (16cm).
£720-850 *Som*

A balustroid cordial glass, the bell bowl on a stem with cushion drop and true baluster knops, on a domed folded foot, c1720, 5.5in (14cm).
£650-700 *Som*

Three balustroid wine glasses:
l. with trumpet bowl, drawn with swelling knop and air tear stem, on plain conical foot, c1720, 6.5in (16.5cm)
£850-900
c. with bell bowl, stem with annulated and base knops, folded conical foot, c1720, 6in (15cm)
£770-820
r. with bell bowl, stem with central ball knop, plain conical foot, c1725, 6.5in (17cm).
£550-600 *Som*

A gin glass, the trumpet bowl on a balustroid stem with shoulder, inverted baluster and base knops, on a folded conical foot, c1720, 5in (12.5cm).
£250-300 *Som*

A baluster wine glass, with a bell bowl, on inverted baluster and base, knopped stem, on plain domed foot, c1720, 6in (15cm).
£650-700 *Som*

A heavy baluster wine glass, the conical body with solid section, on a stem with inverted baluster and base knops and air tear, on a domed folded foot, c1710, 7.5in (19cm). **£1,500-2,000** *Som*

Three balustroid wine glasses, two with bell bowls and domed, folded feet, one with trumpet bowl, 'kit-kat' stem, and plain conical foot, c1720, 5.5 to 6.5in (14 to 16cm).
£300-750 each *Som*

A balustroid wine glass, the bell bowl on a stem with base ball knop, on a plain folded foot, c1740, 6.5in (16.5cm).
£320-360 *Som*

A balustroid wine glass, the conical bowl on a stem with an unusual cylinder knop with air tear, on folded conical foot, c1720, 5.5in (14cm).
£850-950 *Som*

A heavy baluster wine glass, the bell bowl on a stem with annulated and base knops, with air tears, on a domed folded foot, c1710, 6in (15.5cm).
£1,000-1,400 *Som*

A heavy baluster wine glass, with trumpet drawn bowl, tear to stem and knop, domed foot, small chip to foot, c1720, 6.5in (16.5cm).
£450-500 *WW*

A Christening glass, engraved 'Born Febr. 19. 1750' and initialled, 5.5in (14cm). **£900-1,200** *CB*

A Newcastle type goblet, the round funnel bowl engraved with fine band of scrolling and floral decoration, with Newcastle type knopped and air beaded stem, on a plain conical foot, c1750, 7in (18cm).
£1,400-1,650 *Som*

A 'Newcastle' light baluster goblet, the round funnel bowl engraved with a border of floral swags pendant from tied tassels, on a multi-knopped inverted baluster air beaded knopped stem, on a plain conical foot, c1750, 7in (18cm).
£1,700-2,000 *Som*

A balustroid wine glass, the round funnel bowl engraved with a band of fruiting vine, on a stem with shoulder, angular inverted baluster and base knops, domed folded foot, c1730, 7in (17.5cm).
£750-800 *Som*

A balustroid wine glass, on a folded conical foot, c1750, 6in (15cm).
£300-350 *Som*

A 'Newcastle' light baluster goblet, on a multi-knopped stem, with a plain conical foot, c1750, 7in (18cm).
£1,000-1,200 *Som*

A Newcastle type goblet, engraved with the Royal coat-of- arms, Newcastle knopped air beaded stem, c1750, 7.5in (18.5cm).
£1,500-1,800 *Som*

A Newcastle type wine glass, engraved with a band of floral meander with perched parrots, on a light baluster stem, with shoulder ball and inverted baluster knops, on a plain domed foot, c1750, 7in (18cm).
£1,000-1,300 *Som*

A balustroid goblet, engraved with a band of scrolling, foliage and exotic birds, with a multi-knopped stem, on a plain domed foot, c1750, 7.5in (19cm).
£1,200-1,500 *Som*

A green mead glass with incised knop stem, c1760, 5.5in (14cm).
£800-1,000 *CB*

Two facet stem wine glasses with round funnel bowls, diamond cut stems, and plain conical feet, c1770, 4.5 to 5.5in (11.5 to13.5cm).
£150-180 each *Som*

l. A wine glass with diamond cut knopped stem, c1770, 6in (15cm).
£150-180
c. An ale glass, engraved with a band of stars and printies, on a diamond cut stem, c1770, 7in (18cm).
£200-230
r. A wine glass with pan top bowl, on a drawn hexagon cut stem, c1770, 5.5in (14cm).
£650-700 *Som*

A Bristol blue moulded goblet, c1810, 6in (15cm).
£100-200 *CB*

A Newcastle engraved goblet, the stem with angular and inverted baluster air-beaded knops, on a plain conical foot, c1750, 7.5in (18.5cm).
£1,200-1,400 *Som*

A green glass facet funnel bowl on balded knop stem, c1840, 4.5in (11.5cm).
£40-50 *CB*

A set of 10 green cut glass wine glasses, c1830, 5.5in (14cm).
£300-400 *CB*

A green cut glass wine glass, 4.5in (11cm).
£40-50 *CB*

An amethyst cut glass wine glass, c1840, 5.5in (14cm). **£60-80** *CB*

A Newcastle light baluster goblet, on a plain domed foot, c1750, 7in (18cm).
£1,000-1,500 *Som*

Three wine glasses, with multiple spiral air-twist stems, on plain conical feet, c1750, 6 to 7.5in (15.5 to 18.5cm).
£380-570 each *Som*

l. A wine glass, with bell bowl on a stem with multiple spiral air-twist and shoulder knop, on a plain conical foot, c1745, 6.5in (16.5cm).
£400-450
r. A wine glass, with trumpet bowl on a drawn stem with multiple spiral air-twist, on a folded conical foot, c1745, 7in (18cm).
£250-290 *Som*

A composite stem wine glass, with a trumpet bowl on multiple spiral air-twist section and inverted baluster air-beaded knop, on a plain domed foot, c1745, 7in (18cm).
£750-800 *Som*

A set of 6 wine glasses, the round funnel bowls on stems with multiple spiral air-twists and shoulder and centre knops, on a plain conical feet, c1750, 6in (15cm).
£2,000-2,400 *Som*

l. A flute, the flared trumpet bowl on a slender drawn stem with double series opaque twist, on a plain conical foot, c1760, 7.5in (19cm).
£300-350
r. A dwarf wrythen ale glass, with conical bowl, on a short stem with cushion knop, on a plain conical foot, c1800, 5in (13cm).
£35-42 *Som*

A wine glass, engraved with a fruiting vine, on a stem with multiple spiral air-twist and shoulder knop, on a plain conical foot, c1750, 6.5in (16cm).
£550-600 *Som*

Dessert and Jelly Glasses

A sweetmeat glass, the double ogee bowl with a dentillated rim, on a stem with centre ball knop, on a plain domed foot, c1750, 3.5in (9cm).
£350-400 *Som*

An unusual sweetmeat glass, on a moulded pedestal stem, on a plain domed foot, c1750, 5.5in (14cm).
£250-280 *Som*

A sweetmeat glass, with double ogee bowl and dentillated rim, on a Silesian moulded stem with star studded shoulders with coiled collars at each end, on a domed folded foot, c1730, 5.5in (14cm).
£650-700 *Som*

Jugs

A Bristol blue cream jug, c1800.
£100-200 *CB*

A water jug, the pillar with moulded decoration, with prism cut neck and serrated rim, on star cut base, with applied strap handle, c1830, 7in (18cm).
£150-180 *Som*

A Georgian cut glass footed jug, with applied handle, c1800, 10in (25cm).
£100-200 *CB*

A North Country clear soda glass jug, with wrythen body and translucent blue rim, with applied handle, c1800, 5in (13cm).
£250-280 *Som*

A jug, the bowl engraved with a barrel and coopers tools, with inscription 'Mr N. Player, P.O.K.H.S., and date July lst 1828', with heavy strap handle, 8.5in (22cm).
£900-950 *Som*

A cut cream jug, on scalloped cut foot, with cut strap handle, on star cut base, c1810, 4.5in (11.5cm).
£200-260 *Som*

A water jug, cut with small diamonds below a deep band of flute cutting, notched rim, and cut strap handle, c1810, 6.5in (16cm).
£550-600 *Som*

A pair of enamelled Continental glass claret jugs and stoppers, each painted with clusters of vine and holly between pincered ribs, late 19thC, 9in (23cm).
£350-450 *S(S)*

A cranberry and opaque cider set, moulded with irises, comprising a jug with applied loop handle, and six cylindrical tumblers.
£300-400 *CSK*

A Bristol blue cream jug, c1800, 4.5in (11.5cm).
£60-80 *CB*

A wrythen Bristol blue cream jug, with folded rim, c1840, 3in (8cm).
£60-80 *CB*

A late Victorian silver mounted glass claret jug, decorated with a satyr mask, vines and bunches of grapes, with wrythen decorated handle, the hinged cover with heraldic lion and shield finial, having a star cut flared base, London, 1876, maker's mark C.B., 11in (28cm).
£600-700 *GC*

A cut glass magnum claret jug, c1790, 10.5in (26.5cm).
£1,200-1,500 *WGT*

A pair of Victorian frosted glass and silver mounted claret jugs, raised on a circular foot, inscribed on foot Green & Co. Fecit London, 1867, 13.5in (34.5cm).
£6,500-7,500 *P(O)*

A late Victorian cut glass claret jug, engraved with flowers and scrolls in a rock crystal effect, the silver top embossed with foliage and a humming bird, the hinged gadrooned edge cover with a chased finial, the handle decorated with a cartouche and garrya flowers, makers William Hutton & Sons, London 1894, 11in (28cm).
£900-1,200 *WW*

A late Victorian diamond, hob nail and panel cut glass claret jug, with silver mounts to the rim, the hinged cover with baluster finial and acanthus capped inverted S scroll handle, Birmingham 1889, maker's mark H & T, 10.5in (26cm).
£500-600 *HSS*

Paperweights

Scent Bottles

Two cut glass scent bottles with silver gilt mounts:
l. c1880, 3.5in (9cm) long
£50-90
r. c1860, 3.5in (9cm) long
£170-220 *Som*

A millefiori glass paperweight, the four central white and green cut canes surrounded by 2 concentric circles of coloured canes, possibly Clichy, 2.5in (6cm) diam. **£400-700** *HSS*

A pair of blue moulded scent bottles, English, c1890, 8in (20cm).
£100-200 *CB*

An Italian micro-mosaic paperweight, the oval panel depicting St Peter with lapis lazuli border and mounted on a black slate base, c1860.
£500-700 *S(S)*

A silver topped quilted satin scent bottle, with Jules Barb decoration, 2.5in (6.5cm).
£150-250 *CB*

A purple glass double scent bottle, with scroll engraved silver gilt stoppers.
£250-300 *S(S)*

A pair of Edward VII silver mounted engraved glass scent bottles, decorated with anthemion shells and daisies, with similarly decorated hinged covers with glass stoppers, William Comyns, London 1907, 7in (18cm).
£500-600 *Bea*

A scent bottle in the form of a two handled amphora, applied with vari-coloured agates, with slide-action dispensing mechanism and chain and loop attached, late 19thC, 2.5in (6.5cm). **£250-300** *CSK*

A gold mounted gem set bloodstone scent bottle, the neck and hinged cover chased and engraved with acanthus leaves and scrolling foliage and set with red stones and a pearl, 19thC, 2in (5cm).
£1,200-1,500 *C*

A Webbs cameo glass scent bottle, the blue body etched with flowers, leaves and a bee, the cover engraved with flowers, 5in (13cm).
£200-250 *S(S)*

Vases

A cut glass and gilt-metal mounted vase, the crenellated horn rising from a ram's head terminal resting on a marble slab base, late 19thC, 8in (20.5cm).
£400-600 *S(S)*

A pair of opaque green glass vases, on veined marble bases, late 19thC, 7.5in (18.5cm) high.
£450-550 *S(S)*

An opalescent vaseline glass fan- shaped vase, 6in (15cm).
£50-80 *CB*

Two English celery vases:
l. with moulded pedestal, 1880, 10in (25cm)
£40-60
r. gadrooned and scalloped, c1770, 10in (25cm).
£40-60 *CB*

A turquoise trailed posy vase, with clear collar, English, c1890, 4in (10cm).
£40-60 *CB*

A Victorian engraved hyacinth vase, 8.5in (21cm).
£40-50 *CB*

A Continental hyacinth vase, with enamel decoration, c1870, 5.5in (14cm).
£60-80 *WGT*

A selection of hyacinth vases.
£40-50 each *CB*

A cut glass celery vase, c1880, 10.5in (26.5cm).
£50-60 *CB*

A pair of gilt-bronze, white marble and glass cornucopia vases, each in the form of a fluted vase supported by ram's mask, 1830, 11in (28cm).
£1,700-2,000 *S(S)*

Miscellaneous

Two unusual toddy lifters, c1810, 5.5 and 6.5in (14 and 16cm). **£100-160 each** *Som*

A tankard with baluster body, folded rim, and gadrooned base, on a plain conical foot ring, with reeded handle, c1790, 6in (15cm). **£450-500** *Som*

Two toddy lifters, c1810, 5.5 and 6in (13.5 and 14.5cm). **£100-130 each** *Som*

A storm shade candlestick, on an ormolu mounted blue drum base, c1790, 18.5in (47cm). **£600-700** *WGT*

A pair of cut pickle jars, on lemon squeezer feet, c1810, 6in (15cm). **£450-500** *Som*

A cut glass pickle jar and cover, c1825, 5.5in (14cm). **£150-200** *Som*

An unusual wine glass cooler, with two pouring lips, c1820, 4in (10cm). **£100-160** *Som*

A pair of ormolu and cut glass candle lustres, c1830, 16.5in (42cm). **£10,000-15,000** *WGT*

A storm shade candlestick, ormolu mounted, with a Wedgwood base, c1800, 16.5in (42cm). **£800-900** *WGT*

A Stourbridge green opalescent over white night light, c1880, 4.5in (11cm). **£150-195** *CB*

A pair of confitures, with slice cut rims, raised on stepped circular bases with slice and star cut feet, mid-19thC, 8.5in (21cm).
£150-200 *HSS*

An unusual wine urn, c1790, 13in (33cm). **£8,000-9,000** *WGT*

A pair of cranberry glass salts, 2.5in (6.5cm) diam.
£50-100 *CB*

A Victorian blue glass bird feeder, with blue stopper, 5.5in (14cm).
£40-70 *CB*

A storm shade candlestick, with blue and gilt drum base, c1800, 13.5in (34.5cm).
£400-475 *WGT*

A Victorian glass centrepiece, engraved with holly leaves and berries, 16.5in (42cm).
£100-200 *CB*

An Irish boat-shaped fruit bowl, with knop stem, on a moulded oval foot, c1700, 12in (31cm).
£1,600-1,850 *WGT*

Two Stourbridge pink opalescent night lights, c1880, 4 to 5in (10 to 13cm). **£150-195 each** *CB*

A pair of 18thC style candlesticks, the cylindrical stems terminating in bell shaped feet, all facet cut, chipped, 10in (25.5cm).
£300-350 *HSS*

Irish Glass

An Irish cut glass footed bowl, c1825, 10in (25cm) diam.
£1,000-1,250 *WGT*

An Irish cut glass bowl and cover, c1790, 11in (28cm).
£650-750 *WGT*

An Irish spirit bottle, c1800, 9in
(23cm). **£75-125** *WGT*

An Irish bowl, with typical
herringbone design, c1800, 10in
(25cm) diam.
£185-285 *WGT*

Two Irish cruet bottles,
for oil and vinegar,
c1800, 6.5in (16.5cm).
£40-50 each *WGT*

An Irish cut glass preserve dish
and cover, c1800, 7in (18cm)
diam.
£300-400 *WGT*

An Irish jug, c1790, 6in (15cm).
£400-500 *WGT*

An Irish cut glass decanter,
c1810, 8.5in (21.cm).
£100-200 *WGT*

An Irish glass library candlestick,
c1790, 5in (13cm).
£150-195 *WGT*

An Irish cut glass decanter,
c1785, 11in (28cm).
£125-225 *WGT*

An Irish butter dish, the body and
domed lid cut with small
diamonds and prisms, c1810,
6.5in (16cm) diam.
£450-480 *Som*

An Irish rummer, c1790, 6in
(15cm).
£100-200 *WGT*

l. An Irish decanter, with 3 annulated neck rings, and moulded mushroom stopper, probably Cork Glass Co.,c1810, 8in (20cm).
£320-350
r. An Irish decanter, with base moulded fluting extending underneath, a plain lozenge (disc) stopper, indistinctly marked Waterford Co. Cork, 9in (23cm).
£450-500 *Som*

An Irish decanter, with engraved anchor design, on a rib moulded base, c1790, 12in (31cm).
£400-500 *WGT*

An Irish moulded glass tantalus, with japanned wood base and metal trim, c1800, 9.5in (24cm).
£250-350 *WGT*

A pair of Irish glass salts, c1790, 3in (8cm).
£200-300 *WGT*

A set of 4 Irish glass salts, c1790, 3in (8cm).
£600-700 *WGT*

A rummer, possibly Irish, c1800, 4.5in (11.5cm).   **£70-80** *WGT*

An Irish cut glass decanter, c1820, 9.5in (24cm).
£150-250 *WGT*

An Irish ribbed glass rinser, c1790, 4.5in (11cm) diam.
£90-125 *WGT*

An Irish spirit decanter, with moulded fluting at the base, and 2 bladed neck rings, the body engraved with 3 thistle sprays, with flat circular grid moulded stopper, marked underneath Edwards Belfast, c1810, 7in (18cm).
£600-800 *Som*

OAK AND COUNTRY FURNITURE
Beds

A carved oak tester bed, with the date 1662 and the initials S.T., altered and restored including later timber, together with 2 interior sprung mattresses, 82in (208cm) high.
£4,000-5,000 *S(S)*

A 17thC style oak cradle, with arched canopy, panelled sides and ball finials, 44in (111.5cm) long.
£550-650 *Bea*

An oak tester bedstead, the headboard with 2 nulled panels above rectangular panels and channel-moulded stiles and muntins, the tester with lozenge carved panels and on 2 turned posts with square feet, 17thC and later, 54.5in (138cm) wide.
£7,000-8,000 *Bea*

An oak tester bed, dated 1517, 51in (130cm) wide.
£3,000-4,000 *CSK*

An oak cot, 18thC.
£300-400 *N(A)*

An oak bed, the headboard basically 17thC with later top, the footboard incorporating some 17thC pieces, with 2 associated side-rails, 84in (213cm) long.
£2,500-3,000 *C*

An oak headboard, some pieces deficient, incised E D K D, mostly 17thC with later braces, 65.5in (166cm).
£600-800 *C*

Bureaux

An early Georgian oak bureau, with fitted interior, on bracket feet, 29.5in (75cm).
£2,000-2,500 *AH*

An oak bureau, with fall front and 2 long drawers having moulded decoration, on 2 baluster front legs, c1940, 30in (76cm).
£150-200 *LF*

An oak bureau cabinet, with double domed cornice and 2 conforming fielded panel doors, fitted interior, on bun feet, early 18thC and later, 38in (96.5cm).
£1,500-2,000 *Bea*

MONARCH CHRONOLOGY

Date	Monarch	Period
1558-1603	Elizabeth I	Elizabethan
1603-1625	James I	Jacobean
1625-1649	Charles I	Carolean
1649-1660	Commonwealth	Cromwellian
1660-1685	Charles II	Restoration
1685-1689	James II	Restoration
1689-1694	William & Mary	William & Mary
1694-1702	William III	William III
1702-1714	Anne	Queen Anne
1714-1727	George I	Early Georgian
1727-1760	George II	Georgian
1760-1812	George III	Late Georgian
1812-1820	George III	Regency
1820-1830	George IV	Late Regency
1830-1837	William IV	William IV
1837-1860	Victoria	Early Victorian
1860-1901	Victoria	Late Victorian
1901-1910	Edward VII	Edwardian

An oak bureau bookcase, 18thC.
£900-1,200 *P(S)*

An oak bureau cabinet, early
18thC, 32in (81cm) wide.
£2,200-2,500 *AH*

An oak bureau, with brass
handles and escutcheons, on
bracket feet, 18thC, 37.5in
(95cm).
£2,000-3,000 *DDM*

An oak bureau, with sloping fall
front enclosing a fitted interior
above 4 graduated long drawers,
on later bracket feet, 39in (99cm).
£600-900 *CSK*

An 18thC style oak bureau, with
later all-over carved decoration of
religious panels, the fall flap
enclosing a fitted interior, over
one dummy, 2 short and 2 long
drawers, on bracket feet, 36in
(91.5cm).
£600-700 *DDM*

An oak bureau, with stepped
interior and well, applied skirt
moulding, c1735.
£1,800-2,200 *OSc*

An oak bureau, with brass drop
replacement handles, supported
on carved bracket base, mid-
18thC, 34in (86cm).
£700-800 *GAK*

A George III oak bureau, the fall revealing mahogany veneered stationery compartments, c1760, 39.5in (100cm).
£1,200-1,600 *S(S)*

A walnut and oak bureau, with crossbanded fall, on bracket feet, mid-18thC with later veneered on oak carcass, 37in (94cm).
£1,000-1,500 *CSK*

Chairs

A Charles I oak open armchair, incised 'RM 1640' with 3 smaller 'RM', the scroll arms and splayed seat on turned supports joined by a box stretcher, with carved apron, additional support to base of back.
£1,000-1,500 *C*

Cabinets

An oak cabinet-on-stand, veneered in walnut and ebony, 17thC, the stand of later date with plain turned supports, 40in (101.5cm).
£2,000-2,500 *CAG*

An oak cabinet, carved with initials 'M.E.', early 18thC, adapted, 62.5in (159cm).
£2,500-3,000 *CSK*

A Charles II oak panel back armchair, with a fluted and scroll cresting rail, the back with mitred mouldings flanked by stop fluting, the solid seat above square and turned legs joined by peripheral stretchers, reconstructed.
£350-400 *S(S)*

A Charles II oak open armchair, carved with scrolls and flowerheads and 'THOMAS IEPSON', with scrolling arms on baluster supports, restored.
£2,500-3,000 *C*

A Charles II oak and parquetry cabinet-on-stand, the stand with spirally-twisted legs and double gateleg action to the front, on bun feet, restorations to interior, 45in (114cm).
£2,000-2,500 *C*

A Charles II oak armchair, with old repairs, c1670.
£800-1,000 *S(S)*

A set of 4 Charles II oak side chairs, on bobbin-turned legs joined by a turned front stretcher, the back seat-rail incised 'WS'.
£4,000-5,000 *C*

An oak child's wainscot chair, 17thC, 33in (83.5cm) high.
£900-1,200 *B*

A James II oak open armchair, the toprail carved '1686', flanked by animal scrolls, with later solid seat, on baluster legs joined by square stretchers, one front foot with later section, the feet shortened, Westmoreland.
£2,200-2,500 *C*

The serpent strapwork and snail-like creatures flanking the cresting are two of the most distinctive features of Lake District furniture. Distinctive forms appear on dated furniture continuously from as early as the 1620s until as late as the 1740s.

A George III birchwood rocking chair, the webbed seat above a solid panel front and open panel sides, on rocking bases, c1780.
£1,000-1,500 *S(S)*

A North Country shepherd's wing chair, with original painted decoration, c1780.
£2,500-3,000 *RYA*

A pair of William and Mary oak chairs, South Yorkshire/Derbyshire, c1690.
£800-1,000 *S(S)*

A set of 4 ash spindle back chairs, on pad and ball feet joined by stretchers, late 18th/early 19thC.
£800-1,000 *S(S)*

An oak wainscot chair, 17thC.
£1,500-2,000 *N(A)*

A set of 6 elm Lancashire spindle back dining chairs with rush seats and club front legs, 19thC.
£1,700-2,000 *JM*

A pair of panel back chairs, with foliate carved shaped cresting rails, the panels carved with scrolling foliage and flowers and the solid seats on baluster turned legs with similar front stretchers, late 17thC.
£500-700 *Bea*

A Yorkshire ash panel back open armchair, with planked seat and on bobbin turned legs joined by box stretchers, with additional later back stretchers and front seat moulding, mid-17thC.
£2,500-3,500 *C*

A pair of William and Mary beechwood chairs, with cane splats, the cane seats above square and turned legs joined by stretchers, restored, c1690.
£500-700 *S(S)*

A set of 6 Yorkshire cottage chairs, 19thC.
£2,000-2,500 *MAT*

A Welsh primitive oak and ash comb back armchair, with semi-circular seat and triple splayed legs.
£600-800 *S(S)*

A yew wood and elm Windsor armchair, with a pierced splat back and turned splayed legs joined by crinoline stretchers, on later turned ash feet, early 19thC.
£650-850 *S(S)*

A set of 4 yew, ash and elm low back Windsor chairs, on turned legs with crinoline stretchers.
£2,500-3,000 *DDM*

A pair of James II oak side chairs, on C-scroll legs joined by turned stretchers and by a high pierced scrolled front stretcher.
£2,000-2,500 *C*

Two elm and fruitwood Mendlesham open armchairs, each with spindle back inlaid with boxwood, one with vase-shaped splat, with solid seat on turned tapering legs joined by turned H-shaped stretchers, early 19thC. **£1,200-1,700** *C*

A matched set of 8 North Country spindle back dining chairs, in fruitwood and ash, including one elbow chair, with rush seats, turned legs and stretchers, early 19thC. **£2,300-2,800** *P(S)*

A yew wood comb back elbow chair, on cabriole legs with crinoline stretcher, 18thC. **£550-650** *JD*

A pair of yew and elm Windsor low-back armchairs, the horseshoe arms with scroll terminals, the solid seats on turned legs joined by stretchers, late 18th/early 19thC.   **£2,500-3,000** *Bea*

A set of 8 oak and ash spindle back chairs, including a pair of armchairs, with rush and woven seats, on turned legs ending in pad and ball feet joined by stretchers, spindle splats partially lacking, seats differ, early 19thC. **£1,500-2,000** *S(S)*

A yew wood Windsor chair, with crinoline stretcher and pierced splat, c1850. **£750-850** *OSc*

A Windsor low back chair, with shaped seat and single bow back, c1780.   **£550-750** *OSc*

An ash, elm and fruitwood Windsor high back chair, with 'Christmas tree' decorated splat, c1860. **£350-450** *OSc*

A child's yew wood and elm Windsor armchair, with an arched stick back and turned splayed legs joined by crinoline stretchers, early 19thC. **£1,000-1,500** *S(S)*

A set of 6 Windsor back chairs, and 2 armchairs, c1840. **£2,200-2,500** *OSc*

A yew and elm Windsor chair, 19thC.
£260-350 *HCH*

A matched set of 8 ash and beechwood spindle back chairs, including 2 armchairs, with rush seats, on turned tapering legs ending in pad and ball feet, late 18th/early 19thC.
£3,000-3,500 *S(S)*

A yew and elm Windsor armchair, with spindle filled hoop back and horseshoe arms, solid seat and on baluster turned legs joined by stretchers, stamped Hubbard, early 19thC.
£550-650 *Bea*

A pair of William and Mary walnut side chairs, each with vertical railed back surmounted by a scroll cresting and flanked by turned supports, the planked seat on turned legs joined by a turned front stretcher, on bun feet, one with repair to one front and one back leg.
£3,000-4,000 *C*

An elm and yew wood child's Windsor armchair, the back legs fruitwood, 19thC.
£650-800 *C*

An oak settle, dated 1740, 44in (111.5cm).
£2,800-3,000 *JAC*

A set of 8 Windsor elbow chairs, 19thC.
£2,500-3,000 *P(S)*

An elm rocking chair, c1820, 39in (99cm) high.
£350-400 *AL*

An oak chair, with folding steps, turned spindle back and legs and solid seat, 19thC.
£350-450 *WIL*

An elm and fruitwood Windsor chair, with comb back, solid splat and cabriole front legs.
£850-1,250 *OSc*

A set of 6 spindle back chairs and 2 armchairs, in ash, with rush seats, c1840.
£2,500-3,000 *OSc*

A Gothic carved oak pew, the uprights carved with foliage and heraldic beasts, the associated solid seat with crewel-work loose cushion, on solid supports, lacks back, restored, late 15th/early 16thC, 44in (112cm).
£1,600-2,000 *CSK*

Chests

A George III oak chest-on-chest, 39in (99cm).
£800-1,200 *GIL*

An oak chest of drawers with hinged lid, c1690.
£1,300-1,700 *OSc*

An oak chest of drawers, with original yew wood handles, c1680, 36in (91.5cm).
£1,400-1,800 *OSc*

An oak chest of drawers, with oak drawer linings on side runners, with applied mouldings to drawer fronts, lozenges with painted black centres, c1665, 36in (91.5cm).
£1,300-1,700 *OSc*

A William and Mary oak chest, with later top, above 4 moulded doors with panelled sides, on later bracket feet, 40in (102cm).
£500-800 *CSK*

An oak chest of drawers, with bracket feet, c1770, 36in (91.5cm) wide.
£650-850 *OSc*

A bone-inlaid oak and fruitwood chest, in 2 sections, with star-shaped inlay flanked and divided by simulated fluting above 2 drawers with conforming decoration, on bun feet, restored, 17thC, the applied decoration probably later, 44in (112cm).
£2,000-3,000 *C*

An oak chest of drawers, with applied geometric mouldings and bun feet, c1690, 36in (91.5cm).
£1,500-1,800 *OSc*

An oak coffer, with plain top over 4 carved panels to the front, 18thC, 48in (122cm).
£450-550 *DDM*

An oak laburnum and fruitwood chest, in 2 parts, with cleated top, dentil frieze, conforming uprights and on later bracket feet, late 17thC, 45in (114cm).
£2,000-3,000 *Bea*

A Queen Anne oak and mahogany chest, with crossbanded drawers, on later bun feet, c1705, 34in (86cm).
£900-1,200 *S(S)*

A James I style carved oak coffer, the hinged top above a gadrooned frieze flanked by grotesque masks, the triple arched front with foliate carving and central heraldic shield surmounted by the date '1625' and flanked by figural pilasters, on stile feet, early 20thC, 68in (173cm).
£1,200-1,500 *S(S)*

A panelled oak coffer, outlined with chip carved mouldings, the top inlaid with various devices and the date '1588', the front with crosses within lozenges, the sides applied with later lozenges, on stile feet, 16thC, 37.5in (95cm).
£1,000-1,500 *Bea*

An oak six-plank chest, with scratch carved decoration, c1700, 24in (61.5cm).
£550-750 *OSc*

A Charles II carved oak coffer, the moulded hinged top above a strapwork scroll frieze and twin lunette panel front, on tall stile feet headed by shaped angle brackets, 47in (120cm).
£1,000-1,500 *S(S)*

An oak coffer, with plain triple panelled hinged lid over 2 plain panels to the front, on block supports, 18thC, 43in (109cm).
£300-350 *DDM*

Miller's is a price GUIDE not a price LIST

An oak chest, with 3 panelled carved front and plank top, c1670, 51.5in (130cm).
£550-750 *OSc*

An elm chest, with plank top and carved panelled front, c1670, 42in (106.5cm).
£550-700 *OSc*

An oak commode, on bronze lion paw feet, late 19thC.
£1,500-1,600 *LRG*

Reputedly once the property of Sir William Russell Flint.

A Charles II oak coffer, with hinged top enclosing an interior with till, the panelled front carved with '1671 IT', on stile fcct, with later cleats, one back foot spliced, 50in (127cm).
£1,200-1,700 *C*

A carved oak chest, with 3 panels and quatrefoil motif, c1670, 48in (122cm).   **£850-1,200** *OSc*

An oak chest, with scratch carved decoration, c1670, 36in (91.5cm).
£550-750 *OSc*

A Charles II oak coffer, with hinged moulded top, inscribed on the reverse 'P.R. 1680' within a circle, the front carved with scrolling foliage and sea monsters around 3 geometric carved and inlaid panels, above 2 drawers inlaid with scrolling foliage, restored, South Yorkshire, 58in (147cm).   **£3,000-3,500** *C*

An oak coffer, with plain hinged top and front, 18thC, 35in (89cm).
£200-250 *DDM*

An oak and fruitwood chest, lead scratch carved with compass decoration, c1690, 42in (106.5cm).
£600-900 *OSc*

A carved oak coffer, c1800, 44in (111.5cm).
£600-700 *MJB*

Cupboards

An oak cupboard, the top and sides carved with Romayne panels flanked and divided by foliate capitals, on moulded canted rectangular base and gothic bracket feet, Flemish or French, extensive restoration, later top, drawer, supports, back and base, 34in (86.5cm).
£1,700-2,200 *C*

An oak court cupboard, early 18thC.
£2,000-2,500 *GIL*

A mid-Georgian oak cupboard, back feet replaced, restorations to cornice, West Wales, 59.5in (151cm).
£2,000-2,500 *C*

A Yorkshire oak press cupboard, with turned bulbous supports, the frieze drawer with gadrooned decoration over 2 panelled doors, carved strap work surround and stile supports, 17thC, 50.5in (128cm).
£3,500-4,500 *AH*

An oak tall standing corner cupboard, in 2 sections, the panel doors enclosing shaped shelves, 18thC, 85in (216cm) high.
£850-950 *DDM*

A Queen Anne oak press cupboard, the moulded cornice above a pair of arched fielded panelled doors, the base with a triple fielded panel front and a pair of drawers below, on stile feet, c1700, 60in (152cm).
£1,300-1,700 *S(S)*

An oak spice cupboard with rosewood inlay, c1690, 12in (31cm) square.
£325-450 *OSc*

A George III oak press, with moulded cornice above 2 arched fielded doors divided by reeded pilasters, the base with 3 short and 2 long drawers, on block feet, 55in (140cm).
£1,500-2,000 *CSK*

A Continental oak and ebony inlaid cupboard, 17thC, 38in (96.5cm).
£1,700-2,200 *LAY*

A Welsh oak press deuddarn, the moulded cornice with turned pendant finials above triple recessed ogee panel doors, the base with 3 frieze drawers and a pair of panelled cupboard doors, on stile feet, 18thC, 58in (147cm).
£2,500-3,500 *S(S)*

An oak clothes press, with later moulded cornice, 2 doors with ogee moulded fielded panels, 3 false and 3 real drawers below, on stile feet, mid-18thC, 53in (134.5cm).
£1,000-1,500 *Bea*

A two-stage oak cupboard, with wave pattern cornice, centre ogee panel flanked by similar doors, over 3 fielded panels with 2 drawers below, panelled sides and ogee feet, mid-18thC, 63.5in (161cm).
£2,000-2,500 *AH*

A George III oak aumbry, the sides in pine, the base now with 2 dummy frieze drawers and a pair of panel doors, on stem feet, the interior now with hanging space and a shoe rest, altered, c1790, 39in (99cm).
£1,200-1,500 *S(S)*

An oak press cupboard, outlined with punched decoration, with projecting frieze, on turned supports, on reeded stile feet, 51in (129.5cm).
£2,500-3,000 *Bea*

A carved oak livery cupboard, in 2 sections, the upper portion with 2 ornately carved doors, the lower portion with 2 doors, with a fitted shelf, 46in (116.5cm).
£500-600 *LF*

A French Provincial oak armoire, with conforming front apron, on cabriole front supports, 18thC, 60in (152cm).
£3,500-4,500 *CAG*

An enclosed oak cupboard, with yew wood inlay and applied geometric mouldings, c1645.
£2,400-2,800 *OSc*

A French provincial elm and fruitwood armoire, with arched moulded cornice, above a pair of arched fielded panelled doors enclosing an interior with a drawer, on angled cabriole legs, late 18th/early 19thC, 48in (122cm).
£1,700-2,200 *CSK*

Dressers

A Charles II oak dresser base, with associated moulded top, the back re-supported, 79in (201cm).
£2,700-3,000 *CSK*

A William and Mary oak dresser base, the baluster turned legs joined by stretchers, drawers relined, c1690, 74in (188cm).
£2,600-3,200 *S(S)*

A William and Mary oak dresser base, with an open plate shelf, the 3 frieze drawers with mitred mouldings and walnut veneers, with 3 panelled doors and bun feet, partially reconstructed, 72in (183cm).
£2,500-3,500 *S(S)*

A William and Mary oak dresser base, the drawers with mitred mouldings and fruitwood veneers, on square and baluster turned legs, restored, 72in (183cm).
£2,500-3,500 *S(S)*

An oak dresser, on bracket feet, restored and with alterations, 18thC, 58in (148cm).
£2,500-3,000 *S(S)*

An oak dresser base, with 3 frieze drawers with mitred mouldings and walnut veneers... An oak dresser base, on stile feet, part early 18thC, 58in (147cm).
£2,000-3,000 *S(S)*

An oak dresser, the inverted breakfront base with 4 central drawers flanked by a pair of fielded panel cupboard doors, on bracket feet, part 18thC, 76in (193cm).
£1,200-1,500 *S(S)*

An oak dresser, 18thC, 70.5in (178cm).
£2,000-2,500 *P(S)*

A George II oak dresser base, with shaped apron and cabriole legs ending in pad feet, formerly with an open shelf back, 71in (180cm).
£2,000-2,500 *S(S)*

An oak dresser base, with unusual legs, c1740, 80in (203cm).
£5,000-6,000 *JAC*

A George II oak dresser, the raised open shelf back with a moulded cornice and valanced frieze, the base with 3 drawers, on turned tapering legs ending in pad feet, c1750, 68in (172cm).
£2,000-3,000 *S(S)*

An oak dresser base, with 3 fascia drawers with brass drop handles, contemporary delft rack with stepped and moulded cornice, shaped frieze, 3 moulded shelves, on shaped supports, early 18thC, 76in (193cm).
£3,000-3,500 *AH*

A mahogany banded and inlaid oak low dresser, with some original pierced handle plates, mid-18thC, 72in (182.5cm).
£2,300-2,700 *MJB*

A Welsh oak dresser, with 3
lipped drawers, 4 square front
legs with brackets and pot shelf,
brass knobs, 18thC, 56in (144cm).
£1,700-2,000 *WIL*

An oak 3 drawer dresser, with ogee shaped cornice,
cock beading to drawers with brass swan neck drop
handles, 18thC, 75in (190.5cm).　　　**£3,000-3,500** *GH*

An inlaid oak dresser,
18thC.
£3,000-3,500 *SIM*

An oak dresser, with extended
stile supports, 18thC, 59in
(150cm).
£2,000-2,500 *HSS*

A late George III oak dresser,
on slender turned supports
joined by an undertier, 72in
(182.5cm). **£2,000-2,500** *Bea*

An oak dresser, 19thC.
£3,000-3,500 *P(S)*

A mid-Georgian oak dresser,
banded overall in mahogany,
on ogee bracket feet,
79.5in (202cm).
£3,200-4,000 *C*

An oak Welsh dresser, the later delft rack with stepped and dentil pediment over 2 shelves with panel backs, over a base with mahogany crossbanding to the top, fluted pillar sides, enclosing 9 drawers with mahogany crossbanded fronts and brass swan neck handles, the whole supported on short bracket feet, 93in (236cm).
£1,200-1,700 *DDM*

A George III oak and pine dresser, with chamfered square legs joined by a platform stretcher, restored, late 18thC, 55in (139cm).
£4,000-5,000 *S(S)*

A late George III oak and pine Welsh dresser, with arched panelled doors below, flanking 3 simulated drawers, on block feet, 53in (134cm).
£2,500-3,000 *CSK*

An oak dresser and rack, with dentil moulded cornice and open shelves above 3 drawers, on square legs, part 18thC, 75in (190cm).
£1,000-1,500 *CSK*

A George III oak dresser, the moulded cornice above an open shelf back, the pair of frieze drawers above baluster turned and square legs joined by a platform stretcher, on bracket feet, possibly reduced in width, c1790, 46in (117cm).
£2,000-3,000 *S(S)*

A pair of oak dresser bases, probably adaped from a single dresser base, each with rectangular top above 2 frieze drawers and waved apron, on baluster turned uprights and block feet, part 18thC, 46in (117cm).
£3,000-3,500 *CSK*

An oak dresser, with baluster turned uprights and bun feet, joined by an undertier, 94in (239cm).
£1,400-2,000 *CSK*

An oak dresser and rack, with moulded dentil cornice and waved frieze, 18thC and later, 70in (178cm).
£2,500-3,000 *CSK*

An oak Welsh dresser, with chamfered legs joined by an undershelf, on block feet, 18thC, 61in (154.5cm).
£2,700-3,200 *CSK*

An oak dresser base on straight feet, having 3 fielded panelled doors and 3 drawers over, 18thC, 71in (180cm).
£2,500-3,000 *JD*

Stools

A child's joint stool, with baluster turned legs, c1640, 14in (35.5cm) square.
£500-700 *OSc*

A country stool, 19thC, 25in (64cm) high.
£40-50 *JAC*

A Charles II oak bench, lacking 2 spandrels, 81in (205cm) long.
£3,000-4,000 *C*

An oak joint stool, c1650, 18in (45cm).
£600-900 *S(S)*

A pair of oak benches, with plain tops and reeded friezes, on turned legs with plain stretchers, 17thC, 63in (160cm).   **£470-520** *DDM*

An oak joint stool, 17thC, 23in (59cm) high.   **£1,600-1,800** *JAC*

Tables

An oak oval gateleg dining table, with plain top, frieze drawer, turned supports and plain stretchers, 60in (152cm) extended.
£1,200-1,700 *DDM*

A small oak side table, with turned legs and box stretchers, c1700.
£450-650 *OSc*

A Charles II oak gateleg table, with bobbin turned supports and gates, feet reduced, 56in (142cm).
£3,000-4,000 *GIL*

An oak gateleg table, with twin-flap top and one panelled drawer, on later bun feet, restorations to top, some replacements to legs, top extended, part late 17thC, 60in (153cm).
£1,500-2,000 *C*

A Charles II oak and later painted double action gateleg table, made up, 49in (125cm).
£1,000-1,500 *S(S)*

A George I oak gateleg table, the top with a frieze drawer, c1720, 60in (151cm) extended.
£2,000-3,000 *S(S)*

Oak & Country Furniture
TURNED TABLE LEGS

A Tuscan 17thC style walnut refectory table, made up, on shaped trestle supports, 57.5in (146cm).
£2,000-2,500 *S(S)*

A cherrywood refectory table, with plank top and plain frieze, formerly with slide, now fixed, on square legs joined by plain stretchers, early 19thC, probably French, repaired, 90.5in (230cm).
£1,800-2,200 *C*

An oak refectory table with detachable elm top, 18thC, 75in (190.5cm).
£1,200-1,700 *GH*

A oak gateleg table, with later top, associated frieze drawer, on twist-turned legs joined by similar stretchers, mid-17thC, 62in (157cm).
£3,500-4,000 *Bea*

An Elizabeth I style carved oak refectory table, made up, including 17thC components, 69in (176cm) long.
£900-1,400 *S(S)*

A William and Mary oak side table, the overhanging moulded top above a frieze drawer, on baluster turned and square legs joined by stretchers, c1690, 27.5in (70cm).
£1,000-1,500 *S(S)*

A William III oak gateleg table, the associated top with a frieze drawer, the turned and square legs joined by stretchers, c1700, 56in (143cm).
£2,000-2,500 *S(S)*

An oak cricket table from West Wales, c1780.
£350-400 *JAC*

A Charles II oak side table, on bobbin turned legs joined by a conforming front stretcher, 34in (87cm).
£2,500-3,500 *C*

A William and Mary small oak side table, c1690, with later bun feet, 24in (61cm).
£500-800 *S(S)*

An oak gateleg table, 31.5in (80cm).
£1,000-1,500 *S(S)*

A William and Mary oak gateleg table, the top with a frieze drawer, the baluster turned and square legs joined by stretchers, top restored, c1690, 59in (150cm).
£900-1,400 *S(S)*

A lowboy, with 3 drawers, shaped frieze and pad feet, c1750, 26.5in (67.5cm).
£1,000-1,200 *OSc*

An oak side table, with moulded edge to the elm top, frieze drawer, on baluster turned legs with square stretchers, 17thC, 34in (86.5cm).
£550-600 *Bea*

An oak side table, on turned baluster legs joined by box stretchers, late 17th/early 18thC, 36in (91cm).
£800-1,000 *C*

A George II oak side table, on cabriole legs with pad feet, damaged, 31in (79cm).
£1,000-1,500 *S(S)*

An oak side table, with swan neck brass handles and escutcheons, shaped central and side aprons, supported upon shaped legs with pad feet, 19thC, 28in (71cm).
£400-500 *GH*

An oak lowboy, the 3 drawers with herringbone inlay, on rounded cabriole legs terminating in pad feet, c1725.
£1,700-2,000 *OSc*

An oak side table, with 2 early additional frieze drawers, late 17th/early 18thC, 36in (91cm).
£800-900 *MJB*

An oak lowboy, early 18thC, 36in (91cm).
£700-1,000 *MAT*

An oak lowboy, with square
cabriole legs, and shaped frieze,
c1740.
£1,200-1,500 *OSc*

An oak lowboy, c1780, 30in
(76cm).
£1,800-1,900 *JAC*

A George I oak side table, the top
with cusped corners, c1720, 32in
(81cm).
£1,200-1,700 *S(S)*

An oak side table, with
2 plank top, single drawer to
frieze, supported on 4
chamfered square legs,
18thC, 29in (74cm).
£400-500 *GAK*

An oak lowboy, with 3 plank top
and moulded edge, with a single
oak lined drawer, brass swan
neck handles and escutcheons,
late 18thC, 31.5in (80cm).
£800-1,000 *WIL*

A Flemish oak centre table, the
bulbous turned legs joined by
peripheral stretchers, on bun feet,
top split, part 17thC, 50in
(127cm).
£1,000-1,500 *S(S)*

An oak hall table, with full width
fitted drawer with brass peardrop
handles, supported upon turned
legs with stretchers, early 18thC,
32in (81cm).
£1,600-2,000 *GH*

A William and Mary oak tea
table, the double fold-over top
revealing a well, the turned and
square legs joined by stretchers,
minor restoration, c1690, 30in
(76cm).
£2,500-3,000 *S(S)*

An oak 17thC style draw-leaf
table, 75.5in (192cm).
£3,000-3,500 *CSK*

An oak livery table, with
cupboard, c1625.
£1,500-1,800 *OSc*

A pine tavern table, with
scrubbed top and cream painted
base, c1820, 30in (76cm).
£500-700 *OSc*

A George IV oak dining table, by Alexander Norton, with central section and 2 rectangular end sections, the moulded top inset with simulated green leather, the gothic panelled frieze on turned tapering arcaded legs carved with acanthus and headed by paterae, each end painted in Gothic script 'KESTEVEN', with trade label of JAMES LATHAM LTD. HIGH CLASS VENEERS BANDINGS MOULDINGS INLAYS TIMBER 124 CURTAIN RD LONDON EC, inscribed in ink 'Curtis Mawer Silver St. Lincoln', some replacements to frame, 216in (549cm).
£5,000-6,000 *C*

This table was part of the furnishing of Kesteven Sessions, at Sleaford, Lincolnshire by the firm of Alexander Norton of 14 Bulstrode Street, Manchester Square, London. The building itself was designed by Henry Edward Kendall (1776-1875) and completed in 1830. The account of the furnishings, totalling £537. 19s. 0d. was 'allowed and confirmed' by the Sessions on 23rd October 1830 and still exists in the Lincolnshire Archives Office.

A South German walnut and oak side table, with moulded top above one fielded panelled drawer, with later flat stretcher and block feet, restored, part late 17thC, 42in (107cm).
£3,000-3,500 *C*

An oak serving table, the top with foliate carved edge above a scroll carved frieze, on 6 foliate carved baluster uprights on block feet joined by stretchers, part 17thC, reconstructed, 84in (214cm).
£1,700-2,000 *CSK*

A James I style oak refectory table, early 20thC, 120in (305cm).
£1,600-2,000 *S(S)*

Miscellaneous

An oak apprentice piece kitchen cabinet, inlaid with mahogany, Welsh, early 19thC, 21in (53cm).
£800-900 *JAC*

A set of Victorian oak 3 tread library steps in Gothic Revival style, with a turned post and chamfered legs, c1870.
£1,500-2,000 *S*

An oak door surround, the top rail carved with a crest of a mask flanked by scrolls and shields and the date 1614, early 17thC, 51in (129.5cm).
£1,500-2,000 *B*

An elm dough bin, c1820, 48in (122cm).
£250-350 *OSc*

Locate the Source

The source of each illustration in Miller's can be found by checking the code letters below each caption with the list of contributors.

FURNITURE

Another year has passed and the antique furniture business appears as difficult to summarise as ever. The major auction houses have all seen a reduction in turnover during the past year, but this is due just as much to the lack of quality items offered for sale as to the prices attained.

Early English furniture has, for many years, been considered of significantly less value than comparable items of a later period; this has been particularly true of chests of drawers. However, there are signs of movement in this area. Bonhams recently sold a Charles II oyster veneered and marquetry chest for £12,500 which represents an unusually high price when compared with its Regency equivalent. At a Midland saleroom a few months ago three court cupboards sold for well over their pre-sale estimates, making between £6,000 and £8,000 each. Of early furniture, small oak and country pieces remain most popular. At Lawrence's of Crewkerne a rare Charles II food hutch recently made over £5,280, and a Queen Anne oak chest nearly £6,000.

A Chippendale period mahogany serpentine fronted commode, c1760, 45in (114cm) - sold for £23,100 at Phillips Oxford.

Georgian furniture, probably the backbone of the British antiques trade, has followed the same trend as in previous years. Genuine pieces with a fine colour, impeccable provenance and in good condition have been selling as they always will. Christie's sold the Messer Collection, some of the finest furniture to come on the market in recent times, and attained excellent prices, including the St Giles

armchairs (a pair) at £275,000, and a superb pair of dolphin armchairs at £286,000. A stunning mahogany commode, attributed to the workshop of Thomas Chippendale and one of the best examples available of the English Director period, was sold for £935,000.

A George II walnut elbow chair - sold for £53,900 at Phillips Cornwall.

Phillips have also reported excellent prices and interest in English furniture from their provincial rooms. Among their most notable sales are a Chippendale period serpentine front commode, sold for £23,100 at Oxford and a glorious George II walnut elbow chair sold for £53,900 in Cornwall.

Regency furniture continues to be sought, often, at present, by interior designers and decorators rather than dealers and collectors. Sotheby's Sussex recently sold a Regency sofa table at twice the pre-sale estimate.

Victorian furniture, again, must be of the highest standard of both crafts- manship and materials to tempt a buyer and, as before, furniture of high quality has been selling very well. Bonhams report a very healthy demand for good Victorian furniture, especially small walnut pieces.

The market for Continental furniture is enjoying a buoyancy unusual in the United Kingdom. Most French and Italian furniture,

especially fine quality examples that demonstrate the style of the country of origin, has been selling extremely well. Biedermeier furniture, long a favourite of the cognoscenti, is now enjoying a more popular appeal and consequently enjoys a very steady demand with both dealers and in the salerooms.

It is fair to say that good lots, realistically reserved, do continue to sell, while less worthwhile items remain a block on the market. Significant exceptions to this rule are the well-publicised house sales that appear very successful. Sotheby's raised £2 million at Castle Howard in Yorkshire late last year, with just about every lot doubling or trebling their estimate.

There is a popular belief that there has never been a better time to buy, this depends entirely on what you are looking for. It is certainly a good time to buy ordinary pieces whose values are depressed, but it is as difficult today to find a wonderful piece at a bargain price as it has ever been.

A Charles II oyster veneered and marquetry chest - sold by Bonhams for £12,500.

Hopefully the next year will see more and more furniture of better and better quality offered for sale. The prices will certainly be keen. However, the old warnings and advice are as relevant as ever. Buy what you like and what you can live with rather than for investment. Buy the very best you can afford and buy from reputable auction houses and dealers, who will always be willing to offer help and advice.

Beds

A mahogany framed child's cot, with caned sides and hood, on turned supports, 19thC.
£300-500 *LRG*

A Napoleon III ormolu mounted mahogany day bed, covered with white and beige striped silk, the mattress covered in conforming material, with 2 bolsters and 2 shaped cushions, 83in (210cm) long. **£2,500-3,500** *C*

A mahogany and boxwood strung four poster bed, with moulded arched canopy and polygonal uprights with stiff-leaf headings, 52in (132cm) wide.
£800-1,200 *CSK*

A Dutch marquetry double bed, with mattress, mid-19thC, 52in (132cm).
£2,200-2,600 *WW*

A French walnut bedroom suite in the Louis XV style, comprising: a double bed with rococo scroll carved surmounts, floral carved foot on dwarf cabriole supports, 66in (167.5cm) wide, an armoire, 54in (137cm) wide, and a bedside cupboard with inset marble.
£2,000-3,000 *RBB*

An Empire ormolu mounted mahogany lit-en-bateau, with velvet head and footboard, the plinth base with a Bacchic mask within a wreath of roses flanked by rose trails, lacking mattress, 49in (124.5cm) wide.
£3,000-4,000 *C*

An ormolu mounted mahogany daybed, the back and seat covered in pale yellow material, above a plain seat rail centred by a patera flanked by laurel leaves, on turned baluster legs headed by paterae and on tapering feet, 57.5in (145cm) long.
£1,500-2,000 *C*

An Empire ormolu mounted mahogany lit-en-bateau, the panelled head and footboard with turned toprail and a column headed by a swan below a star, with dished panelled frontrail, on bun feet, lacking mattress and box spring, with inscription *meuble 3 a Cigne* (sic), 78in (198cm) long. **£3,000-4,000** *C*

An Empire style cream painted and parcel gilt lit-en-bateau, the conforming footboard with fruiting finials, on turned feet carved with acanthus, 42in (106.5cm). **£3,500-4,500** *C*

A French ormolu mounted mahogany lit-en-bateau, with later panelled headboard and side boards mounted with ducks' heads, the scrolled end board centred by billing doves and a laurel wreath, on giltwood paw feet, with modern mattress, some mounts probably re-casts and some later, lacking finials, 19thC, 80.5in (205cm) long. **£4,000-5,000** *C*

A French double bedstead in the Japanese style, the beechwood framed panelled head and foot inset with 2 panels boldly carved with floral sprays and with gold lacquer shibayama panel of flowers and leaves and 2 small panels inlaid with mother-of-pearl, stamped G Siardot (?), 19thC, 62in (157cm) wide **£1,500-2,000** *CAG*

Bonheur du Jour

A Louis XVI green painted lit d'alcove, with arched padded sides within conforming moulded frame, carved with entrelac and headed by pinecone finials, on short tapering fluting legs headed by paterae, upholstered in celadon floral silk, 71in (180.5cm) long. **£3,250-3,750** *CNY*

Miller's is a price GUIDE not a price LIST

An Edwardian inlaid rosewood bonheur du jour, with inlaid urn decoration, satinwood stringing and shell motifs, with brass gallery, inset leather surface, and 2 frieze drawers, supported on square tapering legs, 36in (91.5cm). **£800-900** *DDM*

An Italianate bonheur du jour, the doors inset with pietra dura vase and floral design, brass stringing, drawer and slide below, 19thC.
£1,500-2,500 *RPI*

An inlaid rosewood bonheur du jour, with brass fretwork decoration, on cabriole supports, with bronze mounts, 19thC, 34.5in (88cm).
£2,000-2,500 *P(M)*

A George III satinwood and tulipwood veneered bonheur du jour, the superstructure with a pierced brass gallery, concave central shelf to an open compartment, flanked by a pair of oval panel doors, enclosing a drawer, banded in ebony above a leather inset writing flap and a fitted drawer, later gilt brass handles to the segmented front, on square tapering legs, c1790, 29.5in (75cm).
£12,000-14,000 *WW*

A German rosewood bonheur du jour, with leather lined writing surface, above 3 frieze drawers, on foliate carved baluster turned legs, mid-19thC, 44in (112cm).**£800-1,000** *CSK*

A Louis XV style ormolu-mounted kingwood bonheur du jour, with hand painted and gilded porcelain plaques, supported upon shaped cabriole legs, 19thC, 28in (71cm).
£3,000-4,000 *GH*

Breakfront Bookcases

A late George III mahogany architectural breakfront library bookcase, the upper section with broken apex pediment over dentil carved cornice, with 4 sets of adjustable shelves, brass shaped lock escutcheons, 94in (238cm).
£7,000-9,000 *HSS*

A mahogany breakfront library bookcase with moulded cornice, 63in (160cm) wide.
£4,500-5,500 *Bea*

A Victorian mahogany breakfront bookcase, the glazed upper section fitted with 4 doors enclosing adjustable shelves, the lower portion fitted with 4 drawers to frieze and 4 panel doors below, on plinth base, 111in (282cm). **£6,500-7,500** *RBB*

197

A carved mahogany library breakfront bookcase, the arched cavetto and dentil cornice above 4 astragal glazed doors enclosing fixed shelves, the lower fitted with cupboards and standing on a plinth form base, 133in (287cm).
£4,000-5,000 *OL*

A mahogany breakfront bookcase, the lower section with 4 arched panel doors on plinth base, parts 19thC (adapted), 122.5in (311cm).
£2,500-3,500 *CSK*

A George IV mahogany breakfront bookcase, with moulded cornice, 4 glazed doors with arched astragals and on a plinth base, 117in (297cm).
£2,000-3,000 *Bea*

A Regency mahogany breakfront bookcase.
£6,000-7,000 *P(S)*

A Victorian mahogany breakfront library bookcase, with arched and moulded cornice, glazed and leaf carved doors enclosing adjustable shelving, over 3 arched cupboard doors, on plinth base, 64in (162.5cm).
£4,000-5,000 *AH*

An Edwardian mahogany crossbanded Georgian style breakfront library bookcase, crossbanded and inlaid with satinwood, with angled broken trellis fretwork pediment with urn finial, triple opening astragal glazed doors with 3 internal shelves, base with 3 upper drawers, brass swan neck handles with pierced backplates, cupboards beneath having single panelled doors with fitted shelves, 72in (182.5cm).
£3,500-4,500 *GH*

Bureau Bookcases

An Edwardian mahogany boxwood and ebony strung bureau bookcase, with overall rosewood bands, on bracket feet, 39in (99cm).
£1,000-1,500 *CSK*

An Edwardian mahogany and boxwood strung bureau bookcase, with moulded cornice above a pair of astragal glazed doors and hinged slope enclosing a fitted interior, above 4 drawers, on bracket feet, 42in (106.5cm).
£1,500-2,000 *CSK*

Use the Index

Because certain items might fit easily into any number of categories, the quickest and surest method of locating any entry is by reference to the index at the back of the book.
This has been fully cross-referenced for absolute simplicity.

A late George III mahogany bureau bookcase, the later top with moulded dentil cornice above astragal glazed doors, the hinged fall enclosing a fitted interior, on geometric carved bracket feet, 38.5in (98cm).
£2,000-3,000 *CSK*

A George III mahogany bureau with associated bookcase top, with dentil moulded cornice above a pair of astragal glazed doors, the hinged fall enclosing fitted interior, on bracket feet, the top stamped *James Sibson, 102 London Street, Glasgow, 702,* 45.5in (115cm). **£2,500-3,500** *CSK*

A late George III mahogany bureau with associated bookcase top, with dentil moulded cornice and pair of astragal glazed doors enclosing shelves above hinged fall enclosing a fitted interior with 4 graduated drawers below, on bracket feet, 44in (112cm).
£2,000-3,000 *CSK*

A George III mahogany bureau and associated bookcase, with later moulded cornice, 2 astragal glazed doors, sloping flap and fitted interior, on bracket feet, 39.5in (100cm). **£2,000-3,000** *Bea*

A walnut and burr walnut veneered bureau cabinet, with ovolo carcase mouldings, on bracket feet, 86.5in (219cm) high.
£3,000-4,000 *Bea*

A late George III mahogany bureau bookcase, the associated top with moulded dentil cornice and pair of astragal glazed doors above hinged fall enclosing fitted interior, with 4 graduated drawers below, on bracket feet, 45in (115cm).
£2,000-2,500 *CSK*

A Georgian mahogany bureau with additional bookcase, the top with stepped pediment over 2 glazed astragal doors enclosing adjustable shelves, over an inlaid fall flap enclosing a fitted interior, over 3 small and 3 long drawers, on bracket feet, 45in (114cm).
£900-1,200 *DDM*

A lady's Sheraton Revival satinwood bureau bookcase, painted with baskets, floral garlands and ribbands, the upper section with swan neck pediment above a bookcase enclosed by glazed doors, the base with fitted bureau, on bracket feet, 32in (81cm). **£7,000-9,000** *RID*

A walnut bureau bookcase, the upper part with a cavetto moulded cornice above 2 glazed doors enclosing adjustable shelves and 4 small drawers, 2 candle slides, the fall front enclosing a fitted interior, the drawer fronts and interior feather and cross-banded, on bracket feet, 37in (94cm).
£5,500-6,500 *P(S)*

Dwarf Bookcases

A Regency brass inlaid rosewood and simulated dwarf bookcase, the frieze with panels of stylised foliage above open shelves flanked and divided by foliage, on later turned feet, adapted, 72in (182.5cm).
£4,000-5,000 *C*

A mid-Victorian walnut breakfront dwarf bookcase, with moulded cornice, above open shelves between acanthus carved mouldings on plinth base, 94in (239cm).
£1,500-2,000 *CSK*

Library Bookcases

A Regency rosewood dwarf bookcase, with scrolling foliate brass inlay, the crested ledge back above 3 open tiers between walnut banded side panels, on bracket feet, 46.5in (118cm).
£1,500-1,800 *CSK*

An early Victorian oak library bookcase with moulded cornice applied with roundels above open shelves flanked by similar roundel uprights with 2 slides below, on a plinth base, 76in (193cm).
£1,700-2,300 *CSK*

A George III mahogany bookcase, with dentil cornice, 2 astragal glazed doors, 2 panelled doors on a plinth, astragals altered, 66.5in (168cm). **£2,500-3,000** *Bea*

A mahogany bookcase with moulded cornice, damaged, above a pair of astragal glazed doors and frieze door with a pair of panelled doors below, on a plinth base, late 18thC, adapted, 48in (122cm).
£900-1,200 *CSK*

A mahogany bookcase with moulded cornice above a pair of arched astragal glazed doors with a pair of panelled doors below, on a plinth base, late 18thC, adapted, 98in (249cm).
£2,000-2,500 *CSK*

A mahogany breakfront library bookcase of mid-Georgian style, with broken triangular pediment and moulded cornice above 4 glazed doors enclosing shelves with 4 cupboard doors below, on a foliate carved plinth base, 84in (165cm).
£3,000-3,500 *CSK*

A Victorian mahogany bookcase, with glazed doors and panelled cupboard doors, 62in (157cm).
£4,000-5,000 *SWO*

A mahogany bookcase in the Georgian manner, the upper part fitted with adjustable shelves enclosed by a pair of astragal glazed doors, with reeded edge and a pair of panel doors under, on splay feet, 41in (104cm).
£1,500-2,000 *GC*

A Regency style mahogany standing bookcase, with three-quarter gallery, 2 graduated shelves, crossbanded drawer below, shaped sides with brass ring handles, and on tapering square legs, 18.5in (47cm).
£600-900 *Bea*

An Edwardian mahogany bookcase, inlaid overall with boxwood lines and chequer stringing, with moulded cornice above a pair of astragal glazed doors enclosing shelves above 2 drawers and 2 panelled doors, on a plinth base, 49in (125cm).
£1,700-2,200 *CSK*

Secrétaire Bookcases

A late Victorian walnut secrétaire bookcase.
£900-1,200 *HCH*

A George III secrétaire bookcase.
£2,000-3,000 *P(S)*

A Regency mahogany secrétaire bookcase, with moulded cornice above 2 glazed cupboard doors enclosing shelves, the base with deep secrétaire drawer with cockbeaded panel, above panelled doors enclosing 3 sliding shelves, flanked by fluted pilasters, on fluted melon feet, 43in (109cm).
£3,000-4,000 *WHB*

A George III mahogany secrétaire bookcase.
£3,000-4,000 *P(S)*

A mahogany secrétaire bookcase, with broken arch pediment above 2 glazed doors enclosing 2 fixed shelves, the base with a moulded edge above 5 long drawers, enclosing a fitted interior, on shaped ogee bracket feet, early 19thC, 48in (121cm).
£1,500-2,000 *P(M)*

A George III mahogany secrétaire bookcase.
£2,000-3,000 *P(S)*

A late Victorian walnut secrétaire bookcase, with pierced broken scroll pediment above a pair of leaded glazed doors with coloured glass flowers, above a hinged foliate carved fall enclosing fitted interior with a pair of doors below, on plinth base, 47.5in (121cm).
£900-1,200 *CSK*

Bookcases

A William IV bookrack, with central division and scroll ends, with bobbin turned uprights, on bun feet, 16in (41cm).
£800-1,200 *CSK*

A satinwood revolving bookcase, the brass bound top decorated with trellis pattern inlay, the open tiers below fitted with brass wirework panels, on dwarf cabriole legs with pad feet, 18.5in (47cm).
£2,500-3,000 *AG*

A late Victorian stained oak revolving bookcase, with gabled top and simulated tiling, carved with the inscription 'The Tabard Inn' and on the frieze 'The True University of These Days' above asymmetrically arranged shelves carved with various other inscriptions, on 4 splayed legs, attributed to Richard Norman Shaw, 76in (193cm) high.
£600-800 *CSK*

Bureaux

An early Georgian walnut bureau, inlaid overall with feather and crossbanding, the hinged fall enclosing fitted interior, on bracket feet, restored, 36in (92cm).
£3,000-4,000 *CSK*

A walnut and feather banded bureau, with ledged fall enclosing fitted interior, on bun feet, top and base associated, restored, 18thC, 32.5in (82cm).
£1,700-2,500 *CSK*

A walnut and feather banded bureau, on bracket feet, later veneer, fall front damaged, mid-18thC, 30in (76cm).
£3,500-4,500 *CSK*

A walnut bureau, with satinwood line inlay, the fall enclosing fitted stepped interior with numerous shaped drawers, 2 short and 3 long drawers beneath, on bracket feet, 18thC, 36in (92cm).
£2,000-2,500 *RBB*

A walnut and feather banded bureau, with hinged fall enclosing a fitted interior, on bracket feet, restored, possibly previously with bookcase top, 18thC, 33in (84cm).
£2,200-2,600 *CSK*

A Georgian mahogany bureau, the fall front fitted with pigeon holes and a well, 2 drawers below flanked by fluted side columns, opening to reveal 4 small drawers, 24in (61cm).
£900-1,200 *M*

An early Georgian fruitwood bureau, with hinged fall enclosing a fitted interior, on later bracket feet, the fall warped, restored, 34in (86cm).
£1,500-2,000 *CSK*

A walnut bureau, early Georgian design, with crossbanded top and sloping fall front enclosing a fitted interior, on bracket feet, 37.5in (95cm).
£1,200-1,700 *CSK*

A walnut and feather banded bureau, the sloping fall front enclosing a fitted interior and well, on bracket feet, 18thC and later, 37in (94cm).
£1,700-2,200 *CSK*

A George III mahogany bureau, with fall front enclosing a fitted interior, above 4 graduated long drawers, on bracket feet, 41in (104cm).
£1,700-2,200 *CSK*

A mahogany bureau, the drawers with brass rococo handles, on bracket feet, 18thC, 36in (92cm).
£2,300-2,500 *RBB*

A Georgian mahogany bureau, 34in (86cm).
£1,700-2,200 *N(A)*

A George III mahogany bureau, the fall front opening to reveal fitted interior including semi-secret document drawers, with later brass loop handles, pierced back plates and lock escutcheons, on bracket feet, 36in (92cm).
£1,200-1,700 *HSS*

A mid-George III mahogany bureau, with hinged fall front enclosing a fitted interior, above 4 graduated drawers, on later bracket feet, 38in (97cm).
£1,500-2,000 *CSK*

A George III mahogany bureau, the hinged fall front above 4 long graduated drawers, on bracket feet, 36in (92cm).
£900-1,200 *CSK*

A Georgian mahogany bureau, the plain fall front enclosing an interior of drawers, pigeon holes, small cupboard and secret compartments, over 4 long drawers with brass swan neck handles, on turned supports, 42in (106cm).
£1,500-2,000 *DDM*

A mid-George III mahogany bureau, with replaced top above hinged fall front enclosing fitted interior, with 4 graduated drawers below, on bracket feet, one foot loose, one missing, 42in (106cm). **£1,200-1,700** *CSK*

An early Victorian mahogany cylinder bureau, with three-quarter galleried top above hinged fall enclosing fitted interior with leather lined slide and central ratcheted writing slope, above 3 drawers to either side, on plinth base, 48in (122cm).
£1,700-2,000 *CSK*

A mid-George III mahogany bureau, with hinged fall enclosing fitted interior with central mirrored compartment, on shaped bracket feet, the fall front warped, 39.5in (101cm).
£1,500-2,000 *CSK*

A George III mahogany bureau, with inlaid interior, on ogee bracket feet.
£3,500-4,500 *LRG*

A George III mahogany bureau, with 4 long graduated drawers, on bracket feet, 33in (84cm).
£1,500-2,000 *CSK*

A George III mahogany bureau.
£1,200-1,700 *CoH*

A mahogany bureau, with hinged fall enclosing fitted interior, on outswept bracket feet, possibly Danish, late 18th/early 19thC.
£1,200-1,700 *CSK*

A Georgian mahogany bureau, the plain fall front enclosing an inlaid and fitted interior, on splayed feet, 39in (99cm).
£1,500-2,000 *DDM*

A George III mahogany bureau, with sloping fall front enclosing small drawers and a cupboard, on later bracket feet, some restoration, 34in (86cm).
£1,700-2,000 *Bea*

A mid-George III mahogany bureau, the hinged fall front enclosing fitted interior, on bracket feet, 42in (106cm).
£800-1,200 *CSK*

A French mahogany and floral marquetry bureau à pente, the hinged front enclosing fitted interior above 2 frieze drawers, on cabriole legs with gilt clasps and sabots, 26in (66cm).
£750-1,000 *CSK*

A French bureau de dame, decorated with kingwood crossbanding and inlaid flowers, surmounted by a pierced scrolling balustrade, the serpentine shaped fall front with ormolu border opening to reveal 3 small drawers and a well, on scrolling tapering legs terminating in sabots, 19thC, 28in (71cm).
£1,500-2,000 *AG*

A late George III mahogany and later inlaid bureau, with hinged fall enclosing fitted interior, above 4 graduated drawers, on bracket feet, 42.5in (108cm).
£2,000-2,500 *CSK*

A late Louis XVI ormolu mounted mahogany bureau à cylindre, with three-quarter pierced galleried inset white and grey marble top, above 2 panelled drawers and a cylinder enclosing a gilt tooled inset leather writing slide and a pair of open compartments above a pair of open drawers, the frieze fitted with a pair of panelled drawers, on circular tapering fluted legs, 32.5in (82cm).
£4,500-5,000 *CNY*

A French Vernis Martin mahogany and ormolu mounted bureau de dame, the top with 3 frieze drawers above a panelled cylinder and hinged fall decorated with pastural scenes, opened by a frieze drawer below, on square tapering legs, 35in (89cm).
£2,000-2,500 *CSK*

A French kingwood and parquetry bureau de dame, the sloping fall front opening to reveal a fitted interior, green baize writing surface, shaped apron, on square section cabriole supports, with gilt metal foliate cast mounts to the top, lock escutcheon and knees, mid-19thC, 24in (61cm).   **£2,500-3,000** *HSS*

A marquetry bureau de dame, of bombe form, on cabriole legs, 19thC.
£2,500-3,000 *RPI*

A French tulipwood and kingwood banded bureau à pente, with hinged fall front enclosing fitted interior above 2 frieze drawers and waved apron, on cabriole legs with gilt sabots, 33.5in (85cm).
£1,500-2,000 *CSK*

A French Louis XVI style mahogany and brass mounted cylinder bureau, with three-quarter galleried marble top and 3 frieze drawers, above Vernis Martin painted fall enclosing leather lined fitted interior, on fluted tapering legs, 35in (89cm).
£1,800-2,200 *CSK*

A Queen Anne miniature walnut bureau, with crossbanding and feather stringing throughout, on bracket feet, later interior fittings, some restoration, 15.5in (39cm). **£1,800-2,500** *Bea*

A rosewood bureau, with marquetry inlay and hatched detail, brass handles, on cabriole legs, early 19thC, 23in (59cm). **£800-1,000** *GAK*

A French kingwood, marquetry inlaid and ormolu mounted bombé bureau de dame of Louis XV design, the parquetry and radially inlaid banded top with concave borders above a sloping fall front enclosing a fitted leather lined interior, on cabriole legs, 29in (74cm). **£3,500-4,000** *CSK*

Bureau Cabinets

A Milanese walnut and ebony bureau cabinet, 31in (79cm).
£2,500-3,000 *APO*

A Dutch walnut and marquetry bureau cabinet, 18thC, 40in (101.5cm).
£21,000-23,000 *M*

A mahogany bureau and associated cabinet, with cavetto cornice, mid-18thC, on later bracket feet, 39.5in (100cm).
£2,000-3,000 *Bea*

A George III mahogany bureau and associated cabinet, the sloping flap enclosing a cupboard, drawers and pigeon holes, a brushing slide and 4 graduated long drawers below, on moulded bracket feet, some alteration, 45.5in (115cm).
£2,500-3,500 *Bea*

Display Cabinets

A George III mahogany corner display cabinet, with broken pediment, upper doors enclosing a white and painted arcaded interior with gilt cherub motifs, 48in (122cm).   **£1,700-2,200** *Bea*

A George III style mahogany display cabinet, with pierced swan neck pediment and double astragal doors, the stand with 3 drawers, on reeded and tapered legs, 43in (109cm).
£1,200-1,700 *Bea*

An Edwardian mahogany Art Nouveau style display cabinet, with central leaded glass door flanked by similar bowed side panels above stylised foliate marquetry panels, inlaid with pewter and copper, on tapered square legs, c1910, 35in (90cm).
£1,000-1,500 *S(S)*

A Victorian walnut breakfront display cabinet, applied with gilt brass foliate mouldings, the cavetto frieze inlaid with scrolling foliage, 60in (152cm).
£3,000-3,500 *Bea*

A Victorian walnut breakfront display cabinet, applied throughout with gilt brass foliate mounts, banded with partridgewood and with boxwood stringing, the frieze and uprights inlaid with trelliswork panels, 71.5in (181cm). **£2,200-2,600** *Bea*

A Victorian burr walnut veneered display cabinet, with moulded cornice, acanthus carved frieze, 2 pairs of glazed doors applied with acanthus roundels, similarly applied moulded uprights, glazed sides, on plinth base, 51in (130cm). **£3,000-3,500** *Bea*

Locate the Source

The source of each illustration in Miller's can be found by checking the code letters below each caption with the list of contributors.

An Edwardian mahogany inlaid bowfronted display cabinet, with 3 internal lined shelves, on square tapering legs, 42in (107cm). **£1,700-2,200** *GH*

A late Victorian rosewood and marquetry display cabinet, the crested tiered superstructure interspersed by bevelled mirror plates and turned columns, on turned feet, 54in (137cm). **£900-1,500** *CSK*

An Edwardian inlaid mahogany china cabinet, with fixed bowed centre panel, 44in (112cm). **£650-750** *MJB*

An Edwardian inlaid walnut display cabinet, 23in (59cm). **£150-200** *LF*

An Edwardian satinwood and marquetry vitrine, crossbanded overall and inlaid with geometric lines, with mirror backed interior, 3 velvet lined shelves, with convex fronted glazed sides, on square tapering legs and block feet, 50in (128cm). **£1,500-2,000** *C*

A Sheraton Revival period mahogany display cabinet, with moulded cornice and top frieze, on splayed rectangular legs, 42in (107cm). **£400-500** *GAK*

A mahogany corner display cabinet, with moulded cornice, canted corners, an astragal glazed door and 2 panelled doors above a shaped apron, 39.5in (100cm). **£2,000-2,500** *Bea*

A French gilt metal mounted, tulipwood, parquetry and marquetry display cabinet, inlaid overall with trellis and rosette on an amaranth ground, with green velvet lined interior, on cabriole legs headed by floral clasps, marble top repaired, reverse stamped 1883G, inscribed in chalk GORDON LAWERENCE 27382, 20thC, 49.5in (126cm). **£3,000-4,000** *C*

A Dutch 18thC style walnut bombé display cabinet, with brass loop handles, pierced shaped back plates and lock escutcheons, on heavy claw-and-ball front feet, 50in (127cm). **£4,500-5,000** *HSS*

A French rosewood and gilt metal mounted bombé vitrine, with C-scroll arched cresting and a pair of glazed panel doors with painted panels below of 18thC figures in pastoral settings flanked by similar panels, on angled splayed legs with gilt sabot, one pane damaged, late 19thC, 32in (81cm). **£2,000-2,500** *CSK*

A French ormolu mounted tulipwood, kingwood and mahogany display cabinet, banded overall in fruitwood, with later chamfered rectangular white marble top, pale silk lined interior with 2 shelves, on short cabriole legs with foliate sabots, probably adapted from a Louis XVI secrètaire à abattant, 38in (96cm).
£1,000-1,500 *C*

A Venetian walnut display cabinet, with moulded broken pediment cornice above 2 long glazed doors with later latticework, on short bracket feet, 3 later glass shelves, one glass plate cracked, restored, mid-18thC, 41in (104cm).
£6,000-7,000 *C*

An Edwardian inlaid and painted mahogany china cabinet, 27in (69cm).
£500-600 *MJB*

A mahogany bowfront china cabinet, early 20thC.
£300-400 *GAK*

A French walnut and marquetry display cabinet, with plain top, the frieze, sides and glazed door with marquetry decoration, inlaid stringing and ormolu type mounts, 19thC, 30in (76cm).
£550-700 *DDM*

An ebonised corner display cabinet, with shaped and carved sides, platform base, on square curving legs, early 20thC, 27in (69cm).
£200-250 *DDM*

A mahogany display cabinet, with plain gallery back, inlaid stringing decoration and painted ribbon and garland designs, 2 glazed astragal doors, enclosing shelves, over 2 drawers, on square tapering legs, 42in (107cm).
£550-750 *DDM*

A Louis XV style kingwood vitrine, with bronzed metal mounts, serpentine fronted internal green velvet lined shelves with matching back, on shaped legs and rouge marble detachable top, 19thC, 33in (84cm).
£1,700-2,000 *GH*

A Hepplewhite style mahogany breakfront display cabinet, the pediment with carved gadrooning, leaf and wheat ear designs, each door with a central oval floral medallion, Prince of Wales feathers and carved acanthus leaves, 76in (193cm).
£3,500-4,000 *DDM*

A George III style satinwood cabinet-on-stand, with kingwood crossbanding, boxwood and ebony stringing and inlaid with urns, swags and scrolling foliage, on tapering square legs with spade feet, 22in (56cm).
£800-1,200 *Bea*

A Louis XV style kingwood and marquetry secrétaire cabinet-on-stand, of serpentine outline, applied with gilt brass foliate mounts, the scagliola top with pierced brass gallery, the conforming stand with a fitted drawer, on cabriole legs joined by an undertier, 33in (84cm).
£2,500-3,500 *Bea*

A Continental red tortoiseshell display cabinet, with mirrored back, plinth base, on bracket feet, one section of back foot lacking, one detached, hinges stamped JC PATENT, 19thC, 48in (122cm).
£8,000-10,000 *C*

Cabinets-on-Stands

A Spanish tortoiseshell and ivory inlaid cabinet-on-stand, late 18thC, 33in (84cm).
£2,500-3,000 *APO*

Side Cabinets

A George IV rosewood breakfront dwarf side cabinet, 52.5in (133cm).
£2,500-3,500 *C*

A Georgian satinwood demi-lune side cabinet, with shaped apron, the 3 crossbanded doors with string inlay and original brass escutcheons, 4 hexagonal tapering legs surmounted ormolu mounts, 29in (74cm).
£650-750 *DA*

A Regency rosewood side cabinet, with later hardwood top, the doors flanked by gilt brass mounted freestanding columns, on reeded bun feet, 38in (97cm).
£700-900 *Bea*

A William IV rosewood side cabinet, with an associated coromandel tapering three-tier galleried superstructure, with a pair of glazed doors and a plinth base, c1830, 28.5in (72cm).
£1,700-2,000 *S*

A Chinese cabinet, with ivory panelled doors, 19thC, 45.5in (115cm).
£800-900 *APO*

A William IV rosewood side cabinet, with arched ledged scroll carved mirrored back, on plinth base, 76in (193cm).
£1,500-2,000 *CSK*

A William IV rosewood inverted breakfront side cabinet, with brass grilles and green cloth backing, on plinth base.
£1,800-2,200 *CSK*

A Regency rosewood dwarf side cabinet, with three-quarter pierced brass gallery, 52in (132cm).
£1,700-2,000 *CSK*

A Regency rosewood side cabinet, with brass inset frieze, tapering side pillars with ormolu capitals, the cupboard with 2 adjustable shelves, double opening doors with floral needlepoint glazed panels with black background, on crescent shaped base, 45in (114cm).
£2,200-2,600 *GH*

A Victorian walnut side cabinet, crossbanded with rosewood and with satinwood stringing, 2 fitted red velvet lined shelves, double opening ormolu mounted panelled doors with hand painted and gilded portrait plaques and ormolu ribbon finial, 45in (114cm).
£1,500-2,200 *GH*

A Victorian burr walnut veneered breakfront credenza, with moulded edge top, inlaid frieze with stringing and gilt brass mounts, the central cupboard plush lined with a shelf, enclosed by a panelled door with floral porcelain plaque, the serpentine sides with shelves enclosed by glazed doors, on a shaped plinth, 53in (135cm).
£3,500-4,500 *WW*

A Victorian figured walnut and ormolu side cabinet.
£1,200-1,700 *HCH*

A mid-Victorian inlaid walnut breakfront side cabinet, the top with brass beaded edge above a central glazed door flanked by turned uprights with gilt cappings and open compartment with doors below centred by jasperware plaques, on turned feet, 68.5in (173cm).
£3,000-4,000 *C*

A Victorian burr walnut credenza.
£3,000-3,500 *P(S)*

A Victorian ebonised and burr walnut credenza, with curved ends, painted porcelain door panel, foliate brass mounts and beaded outlines, 60in (152cm).
£1,500-2,000 *CoH*

A brass mounted mahogany side cabinet, with hinged lid enclosing a fitted interior above a panelled frieze and 2 panelled doors, on toupie feet, probably Dutch, late 18thC, 52in (132cm).
£3,000-4,000 *S*

A Victorian burr walnut inlaid breakfront credenza, with gilt brass appliques, 61in (155cm).
£2,500-3,000 *GIL*

An Edwardian inlaid rosewood side cabinet, with satinwood stringing and marquetry inlaid decoration of urns and scrolling leaves, the back with nine bevelled glass panels, numerous display shelves with turned galleries, 48in (122cm).
£800-1,200 *DDM*

A mid-Victorian walnut floral marquetry and ormolu mounted side cabinet, with foliate scroll inlaid frieze and similarly inlaid glazed panelled doors flanked by female mask mounts, on plinth base with waved apron, 31in (79cm).
£1,800-2,500 *C*

A walnut and amboyna pot cupboard, 31in (79cm).
£250-300 *APO*

A Napoleon III ebonised, ormolu mounted, tortoiseshell and brass inlaid credenza, of broken D-shaped outline, the top with egg-and-dart border above a frieze with female mask mounts, on plinth base, slight damage, 84in (213cm).
£2,000-3,000 *CSK*

A Victorian walnut breakfront credenza, with inlay and gilt metal mounts.
£1,500-2,000 *LRG*

A Dutch kingwood side cabinet, the panelled door set with a ribbon tied Japanese lacquer dish, on square tapering legs, c1790, 28in (71cm).
£3,000-4,000 *S*

Chiffoniers

A Regency rosewood and banded chiffonier, with brass three-quarter galleried mirrored ledged back top with turned supports, above a frieze drawer flanked by ormolu maidens with 2 panelled doors below, on turned feet, 36.5in (93cm).
£1,500-2,000 *C*

A William IV chiffonier, veneered in rosewood.
£1,000-1,500 *SIM*

A Regency mahogany and ebony string inlaid two-stage chiffonier, the lower stage with reel and leaf decoration enclosing shelving and 2 drawers, on reeded base with turned supports, 44in (111.5cm).
£800-1,000 *AH*

A William IV rosewood chiffonier, the mirrored back carved with lotus, acanthus and scrolls, the top with gadrooned edge, the reeded supports also carved with lotus and acanthus and on a concave plinth base, 54in (137cm).
£1,000-1,500 *Bea*

A William IV mahogany chiffonier, the raised back with moulded edged shelf with turned and gadrooned column supports and shaped smaller shelf below on similar supports, 2 glazed and brass grille cupboard doors enclosing adjustable shelving, on bun feet, 42in (106.5cm)
£1,700-2,000 *AH*

A William IV mahogany chiffonier, with half-reel turned beading, the shelved upstand above base with 2 frieze drawers and 2 cut velvet inset doors, on lobed bun feet, 56in (142.5cm).
£1,500-2,000 *ALL*

A late Regency rosewood chiffonier, the triple tiered ledge back with pleated silk panels and scroll bracket supports, above a rectangular top and 2 frieze drawers with 2 silk panel doors below, on plinth base, possibly adapted, 28in (72cm).
£1,000-1,500 *CSK*

Chiffoniers

The chiffonier became popular during the late 18thC and is basically a small shallow cabinet with a shelf and perhaps a drawer below the top of the cabinet section. Many cheap chiffoniers were produced in the Victorian era, lacking the refinement of those made in the Regency period.

Canterburies

A George III mahogany music
canterbury, the hooped divisions
above a drawer with turned legs
on brass casters, c1805.
£2,000-2,500 *WW*

A late George III mahogany
canterbury, with wavy rail
uprights, swept rectangular top
and a drawer to the base with
turned knob handles, on ring
turned tapering supports with
brass caps and casters, 16in
(41cm).
£2,000-2,500 *HSS*

A Regency mahogany folio
canterbury, with 4 divisions, on
turned feet with casters, c1810.
£3,000-3,500 *S*

A late Georgian mahogany
canterbury.
£1,500-2,000 *MAT*

A late George III mahogany
canterbury, with 4 divisioned top
above a drawer, on square
tapered legs, 18in (46cm).
£2,000-2,500 *C*

A Victorian rosewood canterbury,
20in (51cm).
£1,200-1,700 *C(S)*

A Victorian walnut canterbury,
with 4 arched divisions, on turned
tapering spindle supports, shaped
and pierced sides with carved
scroll decoration, single drawer
with turned knob handles, turned
baluster supports with brass toes
and casters.
£1,400-1,700 *AH*

A late George III mahogany
canterbury, the top with spindle
turned sides and apron drawer
below, on baluster turned legs
and casters, some slat divisions
missing, 55.5in (140cm).
£1,500-2,000 *CSK*

A mid-Victorian figured walnut
canterbury, the oval top with 2
handles, 3 division undershelf
and drawer, on casters, 24in
(61cm).
£900-1,200 *McC*

A William IV rosewood 3 division
canterbury, with pierced lyre
ends carved with flowerheads
flanked with spindle turned
uprights, with single frieze
drawer, on gadrooned and turned
tapering legs.
£1,500-2,000 *CSK*

A William IV mahogany double canterbury, the crested toprail with egg-and-dart moulding above 6 slatted divisions and baluster turned lotus leaf lappeted lower rail between reeded and finial supports, the base with 2 apron drawers, on reeded turned tapering legs and brass casters, 55in (140cm).
£7,000-8,000 *CSK*

A Regency mahogany 4 division canterbury, c1810, 20in (51cm).
£1,000-1,500 *S(S)*

A Victorian walnut canterbury, 19in (48cm).
£650-700 *APO*

Open Armchairs

A pair of George II mahogany armchairs, the upholstered seats now covered with floral tapestry, the chamfered square legs joined by H-shaped stretchers, damaged and old repairs, c1750.
£2,500-3,000 *S(S)*

A George III mahogany Gainsborough type open armchair, upholstered in olive green floral damask, on square chamfered legs.
£2,000-3,000 *P(O)*

A George III black japanned and gilt armchair, with cane seat and turned splayed legs, c1800.
£800-1,200 *S(S)*

A Regency reclining library chair.
£900-1,000 *JAC*

An ebonised and parcel gilt Regency style modern armchair, in the manner of Henry Holland, covered in black moiré fabric, on reeded turned legs with casters.
£1,500-2,000 *S(S)*

A George I walnut armchair, with a solid vase shaped splat and an upholstered seat, on cabriole legs joined by waved H-shaped stretchers, minor restorations, c1720.
£1,500-2,000 *S(S)*

A pair of William IV mahogany library armchairs, upholstered in red ochre leather, on reeded legs.
£2,000-2,500 *C*

A Restauration mahogany fauteuil, the padded back and seat covered in floral patterned cotton, the scrolled arms with reeded terminals on sabre legs headed by lotus leaves, repair to end of one arm.
£1,200-1,700 *C*

A pair of Louis XVI beechwood fauteuils by Pierre-François-Joseph Corbisier, each covered in patterned cotton, with moulded frame, on turned tapering fluted legs headed by paterae and pointed feet, stamped P F J CORBISIER, previously gilt.
£2,000-2,500 *C*

A matched pair of Flemish walnut open armchairs, each upholstered in pale blue silk with dished arms and on spirally twisted legs joined by conforming stretchers, restorations, late 17thC.
£2,000-3,000 *C*

A pair of French giltwood open armchairs, each with laurel band padded seat, arms and seat covered in grey striped floral silk, the seat rails carved with entrelac, on fluted beaded twilled tapering legs headed by lotus leaf, late 19th/early 20thC.
£4,500-5,000 *C*

A pair of carved walnut Louis XIV style high back elbow chairs, with floral tapestry backs and stuffover seats, on turned legs united by a floral and scroll arched stretcher to the front.
£1,000-1,500 *P(O)*

A pair of Louis XVI grey painted fauteuils, each covered in floral needlework in imitation of tapestry, the moulded frame on turned tapering stop fluted legs headed by paterae, on turned feet.
£3,000-3,500 *C*

A Victorian walnut and button upholstered armchair, together with a companion occasional chair, the frames with simulated figuring and stylised leaf crestings, the serpentine seats on cabriole legs with casters, slight worm damage, c1860.
£1,200-1,700 *S(S)*

A Victorian walnut open armchair, upholstered in floral woolwork and crimson velour, on fluted cabriole front supports carved at the knees with flowerheads, terminating in knurl and peg feet and ceramic casters.
£700-1,000 *HSS*

A Victorian mahogany salon armchair, on leaf carved cabriole legs, c1860.
£1,800-2,200 *S(S)*

A mid-Victorian oak master's chair, the arched back with dentil moulded cornice above a pair of carved figures on lion's mask brackets flanking geometric panels with cherub masks with carved inscription above, the drop-in loose cushion seat with acanthus carved baluster turned legs headed by lion's masks, the Greek inscription translated reads: God is not mocked; for what a man soweth that shall he also reep, the seat carved Made 1841, carved on seat rail J Sutt, 1841.   **£550-850** *CSK*

A pair of French beech fauteuils of Louis XV design, with floral needlework upholstery back and seat, foliate carved outswept arms and cabriole legs with scroll feet. **£1,500-2,000** *CSK*

A pair of Edwardian Sheraton revival painted satinwood open armchairs, each with crested shield shaped cane panel back decorated with an oval portrait of a lady above a serpentine fronted cane seat, flanked by swept arms, on square tapering legs and splayed feet, including squab cushion.   **£900-1,200** *CSK*

A George III mahogany open armchair, covered in blue cotton, on square chamfered legs carved with trellis pattern joined by H-shaped stretchers with later blocks, formerly with casters, the front legs strengthened. **£1,500-2,000** *C*

A pair of carved giltwood Adam period armchairs, the seats covered in blue dralon, moulded paterae fronts to turned fluted leaf carved legs and fluted feet, one repaired, c1770. **£3,000-4,000** *WW*

A pair of Regency carvers. **£1,600-1,800** *JAC*

A Louis XV giltwood fauteuil, with padded back and seat upholstered in pale floral brocade, with foliate cresting and scroll arms, on cabriole legs, re-gilded, and a matched giltwood fauteuil. **£1,200-1,800** *CSK*

A George III mahogany library armchair, with upholstered back and overstuffed seat with later covering, acanthus leaf and flower carved arm supports and similarly decorated cabriole front legs with claw-and-ball feet. **£3,500-4,000** *AH*

A Flemish walnut open armchair, covered in blue velvet with dished acanthus carved and beaded arms, on baluster turned legs joined by turned stretchers, restored, late 17thC. **£2,000-3,000** *C*

Upholstered Armchairs

A pair of mahogany wing armchairs of mid-Georgian design, upholstered in green floral damask, on mask headed cabriole legs with paw feet.
£2,200-2,700 *CSK*

A chair, upholstered in faded and worn rose pink velvet, with applied Berlin work panel to the back, on 4 cabriole legs with pad feet.
£250-350 *LF*

A George IV mahogany and button upholstered armchair, covered in nailed green hide, ring turned legs on brass casters, c1825.
£1,500-2,000 *S(S)*

A late George III mahogany bergère armchair, with panelled cresting rails and stiles, red leather upholstered arm pads, baluster turned arm fascias applied with split balusters, cane panelled back, arms and seat, panelled seat rail and short sabre front supports with casters, damaged.
£1,500-2,000 *HSS*

A Georgian style mahogany porter's chair, the canopy supported by 4 detachable carved pillars, with upholstered seat and back, on reeded baluster legs with casters, 76in (193cm) high.
£800-1,000 *Bea*

A Regency mahogany library armchair, with red leather upholstery, button winged back, outswept arms carved with paterae and padded seat, on reeded tapering legs.
£1,500-2,000 *CSK*

A small upholstered low seat drawing room chair.
£200-300 *LF*

A Victorian rosewood drawing room chair.
£450-500 *HCH*

A rosewood and simulated rosewood nursing chair, on foliate headed cabriole legs, possibly Continental, mid-19thC.
£450-650 *CSK*

A matched pair of mid-Victorian ebonised shell shaped bergères, each covered in floral silk brocade with turned tapering legs, some restoration.
£2,000-3,000 *C*

A late Victorian stained beechwood and nailed hide Patent reclining wing armchair, with adjustable back and hinged sides, the baluster turned legs with stretcher rails and sliding footrest with twin ratchet rising action, on brass casters, c1900.
£3,000-4,000 *S(S)*

A mahogany wing armchair, with padded back, arms and squab cushion covered in yellow silk damask, on canted square legs joined by an H-shaped stretcher.
£800-1,200 *C*

A pair of Biedemeier armchairs, with cherrywood veneer and needlework covers.
£300-350 *LRG*

A Regency simulated rosewood reclining armchair, upholstered in green dralon, with adjustable back, outscrolled and reeded arm fronts, pull-out adjustable footrest, on reeded legs with brass casters.
£700-1,000 *Bea*

A Victorian walnut framed armchair, with fluted legs and ceramic casters.
£1,000-1,500 *WHB*

Pembrook Chair Collection

A comprehensive selection of
Wing Chairs, Stools, Sofas and Settees
manufactured to a high standard

For details of stockists or
to become one please contact:

A pair of Edwardian drawing room armchairs, the show wood with bone and marquetry inlay, padded to the back, arms and stuffover seats, one chair has been re-upholstered in printed cotton, the other in green brocade.
£400-500 *LF*

A Victorian open armchair, with mahogany show frame carved with foliate scrolls, buttoned rounded back and seat in green velvet, scroll arms, and leaf carved cabriole legs.
£550-750 *DN*

A William IV mahogany bergère, with deeply curved caned back, sides and seat, the padded arms and squab cushion covered in buttoned green leather, on lotus carved turned legs and brass caps, restored.
£2,000-3,000 *C*

A Directoire grey painted and parcel gilt bergère, upholstered in yellow patterned cotton, on turned tapering feet headed by paterae, later blocks, the seat rail with later fillets to front and back.
£1,200-1,700 *C*

A set of 4 French walnut framed fauteuils, the shaped show wood frames with carved leaf cresting, C and S-scroll mouldings, scroll arm terminals, on cabriole supports with carved cartouche ornament to knees, upholstered in cream floral brocade, 19thC.
£2,000-2,500 *CAG*

An Anglo-Indian hardwood bergère armchair, the scroll back with reeded uprights and arms, on turned and reeded front supports, 19thC.
£700-900 *CAG*

A black lacquered and gilt chinoiserie decorated four-piece bergère suite, comprising a sofa, a pair of armchairs and a stool, each with caned back and solid vase splat and double caned arms, on cabriole legs with pad feet, the sofa 66in (168cm).
£2,200-2,700 *CSK*

A Victorian mahogany framed shaped back gentleman's chair, with shaped arm terminals, leaf carved to serpentine frieze and squat circular front legs.
£700-900 *GAK*

Miller's is a price
GUIDE not a price
LIST

A pair of Victorian walnut show frame armchairs, with tulip carved moulded crests and terminals to the arms, serpentine front seats to front cabriole legs, on china casters.
£2,500-3,000 *WW*

Corner Chairs

A Victorian satinwood frame corner seat, upholstered in buttoned green damask, on moulded cabriole legs with scroll toes and casters, restored.
£500-700 *Bea*

A Louis XV Provincial walnut fauteuil de bureau, the moulded frame carved with scrollwork and with arched back, rounded seat and moulded cabriole legs, mid-18thC.
£3,000-3,500 *S*

A pair of Italian carved walnut armchairs, the solid tub shaped backs with foliate scroll crestings above griffin cartouches and griffin arms, the serpentine seats on splayed legs with scrolled knees and hairy paw feet, including loose squab cushions, c1870.
£1,500-2,000 *S(S)*

Dining Chairs

A set of 6 George III mahogany shield back dining chairs, including 2 similar style carvers, each with carved wheat ear back supported upon square tapering legs with spade feet, the seats upholstered in red leather.
£2,000-2,500 *GH*

A set of 11 Queen Anne style walnut dining chairs, including 2 open armchairs, each with floral needlework drop-in seat, on C-scroll and shell headed cabriole legs with trefid pad feet, damaged.
£3,700-4,200 *CSK*

A set of 4 mid-George III mahogany ladder back dining chairs, each with waved toprail and horizontal bars above drop-in seats, on square chamfered legs joined by stretchers.
£800-1,000 *CSK*

A set of 5 Queen Anne walnut dining chairs, with vase shaped splats, drop-in seats and cabriole legs with pad feet joined by turned stretchers, with replaced seat rails, c1710.
£1,500-2,500 *S(S)*

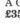

A George I walnut dining chair.
£350-500 *HSS*

A set of 6 late George III design mahogany dining chairs, including 2 open armchairs, each with shield shaped back, pierced vase splat with inlaid paterae and carved husks above bowed padded seat, on square channelled tapering legs with spade feet.
£1,500-2,000 *CSK*

A set of 8 George III style mahogany dining chairs, including 2 armchairs, with pierced vase shaped splats and drop-in seats, on chamfered square legs, c1900.
£1,500-2,000 *S(S)*

A set of 6 George III design mahogany dining chairs, each with pierced interlaced splat above a padded drop-in seat, on cabriole legs with claw-and-ball feet and foliate headings.
£800-1,200 *CSK*

A set of 4 George III mahogany chairs, the serpentine crestings above pierced splats and drop-in seats, the chamfered square legs joined by stretchers, c1770.
£1,500-2,000 *S(S)*

A set of 6 George III mahogany ladder back dining chairs, with pierced interlaced splats and dished tapestry upholstered seats, on moulded square legs joined by stretchers, c1770.
£2,500-3,000 *S(S)*

A set of 8 George III mahogany dining chairs, including 2 later armchairs, the slat backs carved with flower heads, with floral needlepoint covered padded seats, on tapered square legs and spade feet, damaged, c1790.
£1,500-2,000 *S(S)*

A set of 6 late George III mahogany dining chairs, each with arched back with pierced vase splat above drop-in seat, on square chamfered legs joined by stretchers, re-blocked.
£1,000-1,500 *CSK*

A set of 6 late George III mahogany dining chairs, each with channelled uprights and 2 pierced bars above drop-in seat, on square tapering legs joined by stretchers.
£1,500-2,000 *CSK*

A set of 6 George III mahogany dining chairs, with arched crest, wave patterned splat backs, dished upholstered seats and chamfered square supports and stretchers.
£900-1,200 *AH*

A set of 6 George III mahogany dining chairs, with green damask covers, the backrails inset with spheres, on ring turned supports.
£2,000-2,500 *LRG*

A set of 6 William IV dining chairs, each with scroll carved bar toprail and horizontal splat above drop-in seat, on sabre legs joined by stretchers, restored.
£1,500-2,000 *CSK*

A set of 14 George III style mahogany dining chairs, including a pair of armchairs, with pierced vase shaped splats above nailed hide uphostered seats, on fluted tapered square legs with spade feet, c1905.
£6,000-7,000 *S(S)*

A set of 18 George III style mahogany dining chairs, including 2 armchairs, with pierced strapwork splats and drop-in seats, on chamfered square legs, 20thC.
£3,000-5,000 *S(S)*

A set of 7 Regency mahogany dining chairs, including one carver and a matched carver, each with a bowed toprail and crossbar, above a padded drop-in seat, on sabre legs.
£3,000-4,000 *CSK*

A set of 6 mid-Victorian rosewood balloon back dining chairs, on cabriole legs with scroll feet, and 2 similar mid-Victorian rosewood dining chairs, one damaged.
£1,000-1,500 *CSK*

A set of 6 early Victorian mahogany dining chairs, each with deep bar toprail and channelled uprights above padded seats, on turned tapering legs.
£1,500-2,000 *CSK*

A set of 6 late Regency mahogany dining chairs, each with a scroll bowed bar toprail and crossbar above a padded drop-in seat, on sabre legs.
£1,700-2,200 *CSK*

A matched pair of Regency beech dining chairs, in simulated rosewood finish, with canework seats, one stamped I.C., brass inlaid roundels to backs. **£200-300** *MJB*

225

A set of 6 mid-Victorian mahogany dining chairs, with pierced scroll carved waisted splats, with stuffover serpentine seats upholstered in gold and rust weave, on formal foliate sheathed baluster turned front supports with brass caps and casters.
£1,000-1,500 *HSS*

A set of 6 George III mahogany dining chairs of Sheraton design, including 2 armchairs, the curved crest rails with reeded borders, reeded uprights and splats, upholstered drop-in seats, on square front supports.
£1,500-2,000 *CAG*

A set of 6 Victorian mahogany dining chairs, the spoon backs with a lotus carved rail, with padded seats, on reeded tapering legs, c1840.
£1,200-1,600 *S(S)*

A set of 4 Victorian rosewood dining chairs, with reeded and curved waisted backs, carved scroll splats and cabriole legs, the seats upholstered in gold dralon.
£700-800 *MAT*

A set of 8 early Victorian rosewood balloon back dining chairs, each with padded drop-in seat upholstered in green velvet, on turned tapering lotus leaf lappeted legs.
£2,000-3,000 *CSK*

A set of 6 mid-Victorian rosewood balloon back dining chairs, each with foliate scroll carved horizontal splat and serpentine padded seat, on cabriole legs with scroll feet. **£1,700-2,000** *CSK*

A set of 6 Victorian mahogany dining chairs, with curved back rails and padded seats, on lobed tapering legs, c1850.
£1,500-2,000 *S(S)*

A set of 8 mahogany dining chairs, with leaf carved crests, pierced vase shaped splats and drop-in seats, 6 in needlework, on straight legs, 19thC, including 2 elbow chairs of a later date.
£2,000-3,000 *DN*

A set of 12 Victorian walnut framed dining chairs, the backs and seat covered in red leather cloth, on front turned supports and casters.
£3,000-4,000 *LRG*

A set of 7 Victorian mahogany
dining chairs, with stuffover
seats, upholstered in apricot
velour, serpentine seat rails, on
melon fluted baluster turned
front supports with peg feet.
£1,700-2,000 *HSS*

A set of 6 Victorian mahogany balloon back dining
chairs, with carved beadwork decoration, stuffover
serpentine seats, on slender cabriole legs.
£1,500-2,000 *BWe*

A set of 6 mahogany dining
chairs, 19thC.
£1,500-2,000 *HCH*

A set of 8 Hepplewhite design
mahogany dining chairs,
including 2 carvers, c1900.
£3,000-4,000 *MAT*

A set of 4 Regency mahogany dining chairs, with scroll
carved backrails and spiral turned supports.
£500-700 *LRG*

A dining room suite, comprising 10 chairs, with hide
covered seats, a conforming D-end table, 95in
(241cm) long, including 2 centre leaves, and a
sideboard, 72in (182.5cm) wide.
£6,000-7,000 *P(S)*

A set of 8 Hepplewhite style mahogany dining chairs, with woolwork drop-in seats, on square tapering supports tied by plain stretchers, two with outward scroll arms, late 19thC.
£2,000-2,500 *HSS*

A set of 8 Victorian carved walnut balloon back chairs.
£4,000-5,000 *P(S)*

A set of 6 Victorian mahogany dining chairs. **£900-1,200** *HCH*

A set of 4 Victorian rosewood dining chairs.
£500-600 *HCH*

An Edwardian seven-piece inlaid mahogany drawing room suite, with square tapering legs, and varying upholstered seats, including 4 dining chairs, an open armchair, a two-seater settee, and a tub chair.
£700-1,000 *GH*

A set of 6 Victorian mahogany single dining chairs, with upholstered backs and seats, each with a paper label for Urquhart & Adamson, 13 & 15 Bold Street, Liverpool. **£800-1,200** *DDM*

A set of 6 dining chairs, carved in Carolean taste, with needlework seats, late 19thC.
£2,500-3,000 *LRG*

Hall Chairs

A pair of Gothic revival rosewood hall chairs, on square moulded tapering legs and block feet.
£900-1,200 *CSK*

A pair of George III mahogany hall chairs, the fan fluted shield-shaped backs centred by painted armorial crests, the serpentine solid seats with fluted rails, on moulded square legs joined by stretchers, c1780.
£750-1,000 *S(S)*

A pair of Regency mahogany hall chairs, lacking one block.
£800-1,200 *C*

A pair of Victorian mahogany hall chairs, each with shield backs, solid seats, on turned front supports. **£300-400** *DDM*

A pair of Milanese ebonised hall chairs, with ivory and bone intarsia panels, the crested C-scroll backs above panelled seats with tortoiseshell panelled aprons, on carved baluster turned legs joined by H stretchers.
£800-1,200 *C*

A set of 4 George III mahogany hall chairs, each with a moulded waisted back with oval toprail with a circular painted crest, the horseshoe solid seat upon ring turned tapering legs, c1810.
£3,500-4,000 *S(Ch)*

A pair of Victorian mahogany framed hall chairs, with pierced backs, turned bobbin columns, turned ring front, and sabre back legs.
£320-380 *GAK*

A pair of Victorian mahogany hall chairs, each with shield backs with carved scroll edges, solid seats, on turned front legs.
£300-400 *DDM*

Side Chairs

A Victorian low seat nursing chair, with deeply buttoned back and seat with original bead work panel to back and seat, with ebonised and gilded framework, on turned front legs, 37in (94cm) high.
£500-600 *ROW*

A set of 4 mid-Victorian mahogany Gothic revival side chairs, after a design by Charles Bevan, each with red leather upholstered outswept back with turned toprail above similarly upholstered padded seat on chamfered X-framed support, stamped Gillows Lancaster, *No. L2450,* 3 stamped *L. Brumfitt (?).*
£1,000-1,500 *C*

An early Victorian walnut salon chair, with upholstered backing panel flanked by wrythen carved supports, stuffover seats with gros point needlework covering depicting polychrome bird and flower decoration, opposing spiral front supports with brass toes and casters.
£700-1,000 *AH*

A pair of ebony side chairs, carved overall with foliate scrolls and flowerheads, each with pierced rectangular back filled with spirally twisted spindles beneath pierced scrolls, with padded seats covered in later blue and red silk brocade, on spirally twisted turned legs joined by conforming stretchers and later bun feet, Coromandel Coast, India, minor restorations, mid-17thC.
£1,500-2,000 *C*

Ebony chairs of this type were imported into England during the second half of the 17th century, and a pair at the Ashmolean Museum are claimed by tradition to have been brought from Portugal in 1661 as part of Catherine of Braganza's dowry.

Chests of Drawers

A George III mahogany chest, with green baize lined brushing slide, on ogee bracket feet, restored, 34in (86cm).
£2,000-3,000 *C*

A mahogany dressing chest, with brushing slide above 4 drawers, on bracket feet, mid-18thC and later, 34.5in (87cm).
£1,500-2,000 *Bea*

A mahogany bowfronted chest, with wood knob drawer handles, on splayed bracket feet, 19thC, 40in (102cm) high.
£300-400 *AG*

An Edwardian walnut carved window seat, 25in (64cm) wide.
£400-500 *APO*

A fruitwood and burr walnut veneered chest, inlaid with ebony lines, on bracket feet, early 18thC, 36in (92cm).
£1,200-1,700 *LAY*

A George III mahogany dwarf chest, with brushing slide, on bracket feet, 31.5in (80cm).
£1,200-1,700 *CSK*

A walnut bachelor's chest, with quarter veneered top with crossbanding, each drawer crossbanded with ornate handles and key escutcheons, on bracket feet, 18thC, 30in (76cm).
£1,800-2,200 *GAK*

A George I walnut bachelor's chest, made up, inlaid with feather banding, with fold-over top, on shaped bracket feet, top warped, 39in (99cm).
£4,000-5,000 *S(S)*

A mid-George III mahogany chest, with moulded top above 4 graduated drawers, on bracket feet, 36in (92cm).
£1,500-2,000 *CSK*

A Queen Anne walnut chest, inlaid with featherbanding, on bracket feet, 38.5in (98cm).
£1,600-2,000 *Bon*

A George I walnut veneered chest, the crossbanded top geometrically inlaid with boxwood lines, the drawers similarly banded and inlaid, on later bracket feet, 38in (97cm).
£2,500-3,500 *Bea*

An early George III walnut chest, with cockbeaded drawers, pierced brass handles and lock plates, the top three-quarter moulded, on bracket feet, 37in (94cm).
£1,500-2,000 *HSS*

A Victorian mahogany bowfronted chest of drawers, with inlaid banding, the drawers with cock beading.
£450-550 *LF*

A William and Mary walnut and seaweed marquetry chest, with banded and boxwood line borders, on later bun feet, 39.5in (100cm).
£6,000-7,000 *C*

A George III mahogany chest, the moulded crossbanded top inlaid with stringing, on bracket feet, c1760, 34.5in (88cm).
£1,500-2,000 *S(S)*

A William and Mary walnut veneered chest, with later rectangular top, the drawers with crossbanding and ebony stringing, ovolo carcase mouldings, on later bun feet, 39in (99cm).
£600-800 *Bea*

A mid-George III mahogany serpentine chest, with 4 graduated drawers, on ogee bracket feet, 41in (104cm).
£1,700-2,700 *C*

A mid-Georgian mahogany bachelor's chest, the moulded edge top with incurving corners, 4 graduated drawers with brass drop handles, bracket feet, 30in (76cm).
£4,000-4,500 *AH*

A mahogany chest of drawers, with oak lined drawers, brass plate handles and escutcheons, on bracket feet, 18thC, 38in (97cm).
£2,000-2,500 *WW*

A George III mahogany chest, the moulded top above 2 short and 3 long graduated drawers, on ogee bracket feet, handles replaced, c1780, 33in (84cm).
£1,200-1,800 *S(S)*

A George III mahogany serpentine chest of drawers, 47in (119cm).   **£900-1,200** *GIL*

A George III mahogany plan chest, with brass swan neck handles, on block feet, 43in (109cm).
£900-1,500 *M*

A mahogany serpentine fronted chest of drawers, the top with rosewood border band and decorative string lines, the 4 drawers similarly banded to the top, the canted corners banded and veneered in satinwood, on bracket feet, 44in (112cm).
£2,000-2,500 *P(S)*

A George III mahogany chest, on ogee bracket feet, 41.5in (105cm).
£1,200-1,700 *AG*

A mid-Georgian mahogany chest, with original pierced brass drawer handles and key plates, on bracket feet, 31in (79cm).
£1,200-1,700 *ALL*

A pair of walnut chests, with geometric mouldings, on moulded spreading bases and bun feet.
£1,700-2,500 *CSK*

A walnut dwarf chest, inlaid overall with boxwood and ebony lines, with rectangular moulded top, on bracket feet, 29.5in (75cm).
£3,200-3,700 *CSK*

A Regency apprentice chest of drawers, 11.5in (29cm).
£300-320 *JAC*

A George III mahogany veneered bowfront chest, the top banded in satinwood and inlaid stringing, oak lined drawers, with brass plate handles, on swept French feet, 37in (94cm).
£2,200-2,700 *WW*

A George II mahogany chest of drawers, the moulded top above a brushing slide and 4 long graduated drawers, on shaped bracket feet, c1770, 33in (84cm).
£2,200-2,700 *S(S)*

A Regency mahogany bowfront chest of drawers, with reeded pilasters, on reeded tapering feet, c1810, 42in (105cm).
£900-1,500 *S(S)*

A George III mahogany chest of drawers, the caddy top crossbanded and with ebony edge above a brushing slide, the drawers with original brass swan neck handles, on shaped bracket feet, 36in (92cm).
£2,000-2,500 *B*

A walnut and crossbanded bachelor's chest, the folding top with re-entrant corners, above 2 short and 3 long drawers, on bracket feet, 28in (71cm).
£3,200-3,700 *CSK*

Locate the Source

The source of each illustration in Miller's can be found by checking the code letters below each caption with the list of contributors.

A Regency mahogany chest of drawers, with stringing, bowed centre section, 4 long drawers and reeded sides, on sabre legs, 47in (119cm).
£700-900 *LRG*

A Dutch walnut and marquetry bombé chest of drawers, inlaid overall with vases, birds and flowers, on splayed front legs, late 18th/early 19thC, 33in (84cm).
£1,500-2,500 *RID*

A Dutch mahogany and marquetry bombé chest, the top centred by a bird perched on an urn of flowers within acanthus scrolls, above 3 long drawers with foliate inlay, on later bun feet, 37.5in (95cm). **£3,200-4,000** *Bon*

A Dutch mahogany and marquetry bombé chest of drawers, with ornate brass handles, the shaped top inlaid with urn and flowers, the scroll sides on front paw feet, late 18thC.
£4,000-4,500 *WW*

Chests-on-Chests

A walnut and featherbanded chest-on-chest, with moulded cornice, on bracket feet, the sides split, early 18thC and later, 40in (102cm).
£2,000-3,000 *CSK*

An early George III mahogany tallboy, with cavetto cornice, on bracket feet, 41.5in (105cm).
£1,500-2,000 *Bea*

A George III style crossbanded mahogany tallboy, 44in (112cm).
£1,200-1,700 *MJB*

A George I walnut chest-on-chest, featherbanded throughout, with brass swan neck handles, on later bracket feet, 40in (102cm).
£3,500-4,500 *GIL*

A Channel Islands walnut tallboy, with inlaid string lines, fluted and canted corners, ogee bracket feet, 18thC, 42.5in (107cm).
£3,500-4,500 *P(S)*

A George III mahogany tallboy, with cavetto cornice, on bracket feet, 43.5in (110cm).
£1,200-1,700 *Bea*

A George III mahogany tallboy, in 2 parts, the upper with dentil and blind fret cornice, the lower with 3 long drawers below a slide, on bracket feet, 43in (109cm).
£1,500-2,000 *P(O)*

A George II mahogany tallboy chest-on-chest, the base drawers with original brass open plate handles and escutcheons, on bracket feet, 39in (99cm).
£2,000-3,000 *WW*

A Queen Anne style walnut and oyster laburnum veneered small chest-on-chest, on bun feet, c1930, 23in (59cm).
£1,500-2,000 *S(S)*

A mid-George III mahogany chest-on-chest, with dentil moulded cornice and blind fret frieze above 2 short and 3 long drawers, flanked by fluted quarter angles, with brushing slide and 3 further drawers below, on bracket feet, damaged, 44in (112cm).
£1,000-1,500 *CS*

A Regency bowfronted mahogany tallboy, with a shaped pediment, reeded mouldings at the corners, shaped aprons, splay bracket feet, lion mask and ring handles, inlaid ebony string lines, 45in (114cm).
£2,000-2,500 *P(S)*

A George III mahogany chest-on-chest, with dentilled cavetto cornice, and chamfered corners, on bracket feet, cornice lacking a corner moulding, c1760, 43.5in (110cm).
£2,000-3,000 *S(S)*

A George III mahogany tallboy, with stepped pediment, on splayed bracket feet, 44in (112cm).
£1,200-1,700 *DDM*

A George III mahogany tallboy, with dentil cornice, all with original gilt brass handles and escutcheons, on shaped bracket feet, 43in (109cm).
£1,500-2,000 *Bea*

A walnut chest-on-later stand, the cavetto moulded cornice projecting at the corners, featherbanded, fluted and canted corners, the conforming stand with 3 drawers, on cabriole legs, early 18thC, 42.5in (107cm).
£950-1,100 *P(S)*

A walnut and feather banded chest-on-stand, the stand with arched apron, on bun feet, re-veneered, early 18thC, 41.5in (105cm).
£2,200-2,700 *CSK*

Chests-on-Stands

A walnut and featherbanded chest-on-stand, the stand with 3 drawers, arched apron and bun feet, early 18thC, top and base later, partly re-veneered, 38.5in (97cm).
£1,500-2,000 *CSK*

A black and gold lacquer decorated chest-on-stand, with moulded cornice, the base with a shaped frieze and 3 oak lined drawers, cabriole legs with pad feet, 18thC with later restoration, 42in (107cm).
£2,500-3,000 *WW*

A William and Mary oyster veneered chest, with fruitwood crossbanding throughout, the top geometrically inlaid with boxwood lines, on a later stand with twist turned supports, bun feet and flat stretchers, restored, 33.5in (85cm).
£2,200-2,700 *Bea*

A Dutch walnut and marquetry chest-on-stand, decorated overall with scrolling foliate and bird motifs, the banded top with oval panel, on later stand with cabriole legs and pad feet, 18thC and later, 37.5in (95cm).
£2,500-3,000 *CSK*

Miller's is a price GUIDE not a price LIST

A Dutch Colonial chest-on-stand, applied throughout with pierced and engraved brass mounts, brass studs and loop handles, the stand with a drawer, on cabriole legs with claw-and-ball feet, 32.5in (82cm).
£800-1,000 *Bea*

A Queen Anne walnut veneered chest-on-stand, outlined with featherbanding and with a cavetto cornice, the stand with shaped underframe, on cabriole legs with pad feet, restored, 43in (109cm).
£1,500-2,000 *Bea*

A Spanish iron bound and bone inlaid walnut chest-on-stand, with 8 panelled drawers inset with cube pattern, the top layer with spirally twisted columns, around a cupboard door with portico, lacking 3 bun feet, the sides with iron carrying handles, the associated, possibly Portuguese, stand with single drawer, on bobbin turned legs and block feet, 2 feet detached, 39in (99cm).   **£4,000-5,000** *C*

A walnut and burr veneered chest-on-stand, with moulded cornice, on cabriole legs, top early 18thC, base later, 38.5in (97cm).
£1,200-1,700 *CSK*

Wellington Chests

A late Victorian walnut secrétaire Wellington chest, the 2nd and 3rd of the 6 graduated drawer fronts falling to reveal the writing compartment, 24in (61cm).
£1,000-1,500 *MJB*

A Victorian walnut secrétaire Wellington chest, with 6 graduated drawers and locking style.
£1,500-2,000 *RPI*

A Victorian mahogany Wellington chest, with 7 graduated drawers, behind hinged stile locks, on a plinth base, 22in (56cm).
£1,000-1,500 *Bea*

Coffers

Wellington chests were first seen during the 1820s and are identified by their tall narrow shape. They are most commonly found in mahogany but were made in a variety of other woods, such as maple and sycamore, and, in the Victorian period, veneered walnut.

A South German walnut and inlaid coffer, with hinged domed top and tapered sides applied with gilt metal carrying handles, on moulded plinth, 18thC, 48in (122cm).
£1,000-1,500 *C*

A Scandinavian painted marriage coffer, the domed lid with initials HRH and MWM above a panelled front painted with legendary scenes, flanked by carrying handles, on block feet, late 19thC, 47.5in (121cm). **£800-1,200** *CSK*

A North Italian walnut cassone, carved with winged dragons and scrolling acanthus, the top inlaid with ebony lozenges and centred by an armorial motif, on bun feet, with carrying handles to the sides, early 18thC, later carving, 55in (140cm). **£900-1,500** *CSK*

A Tuscan walnut cassone, with panelled front and sides, paw feet, 17thC, 55in (139cm). **£600-800** *S(S)*

A George III mahogany bedside commode, the tray top pierced with carrying handles and quatrefoils, above 2 cupboard doors and a sliding commode drawer, on square legs, 22in (56cm). **£1,000-1,500** *C*

Commodes

A George III mahogany bedside commode, the tray top with waved gallery above 2 cupboard doors and a single drawer as 2 false drawers, on square legs, adapted, 19in (48cm). **£900-1,200** *CSK*

Commode Chests

A George III mahogany bedside commode, the tray top with a gallery pierced with carrying handles, above a cupboard door and a sliding commode drawer, on square moulded legs, 21in (53cm). **£650-750** *CSK*

A George III mahogany concave front tray top commode, the waved gallery above a tambour front cupboard and deep drawer, on divided square legs, back panel missing, c1780, 23in (58cm). **£1,500-2,000** *S(S)*

A South German marquetry serpentine commode with bombé sides, inlaid with satinwood and ivory, the legs and sides with scrolling foliage, 19thC, 30in (77cm). **£1,800-2,200** *GSP*

A Louis XV style kingwood and marquetry bombé commode, applied with foliate cast brass mounts, escutcheons and handles, the pink veined marble serpentine top, drawers inlaid sans travers with scrolling foliage and flowers, on slender splayed legs.
£1,000-1,200 *Bea*

An Edwardian satinwood and tulipwood banded serpentine commode, with chequer inlay, the eared top above a central door with circular panels painted in the manner of Angelica Kauffmann, on spade feet, labelled on reverse The Property of Savoy H, No 101 and maker's label Gill and Reigate, London, W, 48in (122cm).
£4,500-5,500 *C*

A French rosewood and kingwood veneered small commode, with brown marble top, drawers with canted sides and gilt bronze mounts throughout, the whole chevron veneered in rosewood with shaped tulipwood crossbanding, c1880, 25.5in (65cm). **£1,000-1,500** *S(S)*

A George III harewood and tulipwood crossbanded demi-lune commode, the top inlaid with a half fan patera, on square tapered feet, 50in (127cm).
£8,000-10,000 *Bon*

A satinwood demi-lune commode, with rosewood crossbanding, painted with oval plaque after Kauffman and other classical attributes, c1900.
£2,000-2,800 *LRG*

A gilt metal mounted tulipwood and marquetry bombé commode, with moulded serpentine liver marble top, above 2 long drawers inlaid sans travers with flowerheads and foliage, the keeled angles mounted with acanthus and flowerheads, with waved apron, on cabriole legs and scroll sabots, late 19th/early 20thC, 48in (122cm).
£1,500-2,000 *C*

A George III mahogany serpentine fronted commode, in the manner of Thomas Chippendale, the top with a floret edge, the cockbeaded drawers with later rococo brass drop handles, the top one fitted with divisions and a frieze covered internal slide, the chamfered angles carved with scrolling acanthus and flowering foliage, the shaped apron carved with C-scrolls, on foliate carved shaped bracket feet, 45in (114cm).
£22,000-25,000 *P(O)*

The carved angles also bear a resemblance to the famous 'Moccas Court' commode, from Childwick Bury, Hertfordshire.

An Italian walnut commodino, banded overall in fruitwood, on angled cabriole legs and pad feet, adapted, part 18thC, label with ink inventory number 555, 20in (50cm).
£1,000-1,500 *C*

A Regency brass mounted kingwood and walnut commode, with moulded serpentine orange breccia marble top, on bracket feet, remounted, broken marble, with later ink inscription HEDOUIN PERE.
£4,500-5,000 *C*

A French commode, with serpentine front and ends, drawer front with matched veneers, ebonised edges and white stringing, decorated with applied gilt metal mounts in the form of female figures, leaves and stalks, fitted with black veined marble top, 19thC, 45in (114cm).
£1,200-1,700 *WIL*

A Louis XV style ormolu mounted kingwood and marquetry serpentine fronted bombé commode, with grey ground multi-coloured marble top, walnut internal veneered doors, tapering legs with pad feet and ormolu mounts, 19thC, 63in (160cm).
£10,000-12,000 *GH*

A French mahogany commode, with shaped frieze drawer above 3 long drawers, early 19thC.
£800-1,200 *LRG*

A Scandinavian brass inlaid mahogany commode, the associated canted black and white variegated marble top above 3 drawers, on tapering feet, restored, formerly with wooden top, 39in (99cm).
£1,700-2,500 *C*

A Dutch marquetry bombé commode, inlaid overall, on angled scroll feet, modern, 35in (89cm).
£1,500-2,000 *CSK*

A Dutch rosewood and floral marquetry bombé commode, the undulating top centred by a floral arrangement within a strapwork border, the S-shaped front with 4 long drawers, on bracket feet, late 18th/early 19thC.
£4,000-5,000 *P(O)*

A parquetry and marquetry prie dieu commode, on lion front supports, reconstructed incorporating early 18thC German/Italian veneers and inlays, 35in (89cm).
£2,000-2,500 *Bea*

A painted Italianate commode chest, with 3 drawers and brown and red mottled marble top.
£200-250 *LF*

A French traditional style inlaid walnut commode, with marble top, 3 drawers with ormolu mounts. **£300-400** *LF*

Cupboards-Armoires

A French walnut armoire, in 2 sections, the red painted interior with 6 shelves and rounded angles, on bun feet, the back feet replaced, mid-18thC, 72in (183cm).
£3,000-4,000 *C*

A Franco-Flemish walnut armoire, with rectangular moulded cornice and a lunette carved frieze above 2 panelled doors with large raised cartouche mouldings between pilasters, on inverted plinth base, 64in (163cm).
£1,200-1,500 *CSK*

A French marquetry armoire, inspired by commode made for Louis XV by Jean-Henri Riesener, in Transitional manner, the door inlaid with a marquetry trophy, the lower panel applied with a similar trophy in gilt bronze, with convex corner cupboards, the whole inlaid in pearwood and tulipwood on a kingwood ground, with key, c1885, 73in (185cm).
£18,000-25,000 *S*

Corner Cupboards

A pair of mid-Victorian rosewood bowfront corner cupboards, each with scroll crested glazed panelled door enclosing velvet lined interior flanked by pilasters with foliate headings, on plinth bases, 33in (84cm).
£1,500-2,000 *CSK*

A Regency mahogany inlaid bowfronted corner cupboard, with dentil cornice, blind fretwork beneath, double opening doors with central oval inlaid satinwood and sycamore shell motifs, 3 internal shelves, 30in (76cm).
£600-800 *GH*

A Dutch painted bowfront hanging corner cupboard, the doors depicting St. Catherine of Siena meeting Pope Gregory XI, the interior with shelves, 18thC, 23in (59cm).
£800-1,000 *S(S)*

A George III mahogany corner cupboard, the dentilled cornice above a lancet astragal door enclosing shaped shelves, the lower part with a pair of panelled cupboard doors, on later bracket feet, alterations, c1790, 42in (107cm).
£1,500-2,000 *S(S)*

A George III mahogany bowfront hanging corner cupboard, inlaid with chequer stringing, the interior with shelves and 3 small drawers, c1760, 31in (79cm).
£900-1,200 *S(S)*

A late George II mahogany corner cupboard, on plinth base, 86.5in (220cm) overall.
£1,500-2,500 *P(M)*

A George III mahogany bowfronted hanging corner cupboard.
£550-650 *HCH*

A Dutch painted corner cupboard, with shelved cresting and bowed hinged door, enclosing 2 shelves, repaired, 18thC, 19.5in (50cm).
£800-1,000 *C*

A Georgian bowfronted corner cupboard, c1780.
£1,100-1,200 *JAC*

A walnut corner cupboard, the projecting cornice above a panelled door flanked by fluted and stop fluted pilasters with Ionic capitals, on moulded bracket feet, Italian or German, c1740, 44in (111cm).
£3,000-4,000 *S(S)*

A Dutch marquetry double corner cupboard, 18thC.
£9,000-10,000 *APO*

A George III mahogany standing corner cupboard, the cavetto cornice with a blind fret carved frieze, 2 astragal doors enclosing shaped shelves, on later ogee bracket feet, restored, c1770, 42in (107cm).
£1,500-2,000 *S(S)*

Cupboards and Linen Presses

A mid-George III mahogany linen press, on bracket feet, 49in (125cm).
£800-1,200 *CSK*

A Dutch mahogany press cupboard, the open pediment carved with egg-and-dart and bead-and-reel, flanking a flaming urn, over slight breakfront frieze and 2 double panelled doors with gilt metal Corinthian capitals, flanked by half columns, on leaf scroll bases to the corners, enclosing drawer and shelf interior, above 3 graduated drawers with crossed branch and wreath carved apron, on rectangular section fluted feet, 84in (211cm).
£5,500-6,000 *APO*

A George III mahogany clothes press, with key pattern carved broken pediment centred by a plinth, above a band of blind fretwork above a pair of panelled doors enclosing 5 slides, the base with 3 graduated long drawers, the top partially fitted, on ogee bracket feet, one back foot replaced, 52in (132cm).
£5,000-6,000 *C*

A late George III mahogany clothes press, with broken scroll pediment and pendant moulded cornice, above a pair of panelled doors, on outswept bracket feet, damaged pediment, 57in (145cm).
£1,800-2,500 *CSK*

A late George III mahogany clothes press, crossbanded and ebony strung, the dentil cornice with 2 marquetry flowerheads above sliding trays, enclosed by 2 oval panelled doors, the base drawers with brass ring handles, on square tapering legs with ebony flutes, 51.5in (130cm).
£1,200-1,500 *DN*

A late George III mahogany linen press, with dentil moulded cornice above a pair of panelled doors, on bracket feet, 49in (125cm). **£1,200-1,700** *CSK*

A George III mahogany linen press, with broken arch top and cavetto cornice, the doors with mahogany crossbanded, boxwood and ebony stringing, on bracket feet, 50in (127cm). **£1,800-2,200** *HCH*

A Regency mahogany linen press, with brass lion's head mounts, the broken swan necked pediment above 2 panel doors flanked by reeded columns, on reeded scroll bracket feet, 49.5in (126cm). **£1,700-2,000** *CSK*

A late George III mahogany linen press, on bracket feet, 51in (130cm). **£900-1,400** *CSK*

A George III mahogany linen press. **£650-750** *HCH*

A mahogany linen press. **£700-900** *W*

A George III mahogany linen press, inlaid throughout with stringing, the fluted cornice carved with a swag and paterae above a pair of doors with oval bandings enclosing sliding trays, on later bracket feet, c1780, 51in (130cm). **£1,700-2,200** *S(S)*

> **Miller's is a price GUIDE not a price LIST**

A mahogany linen press, with moulded cornice, 2 panelled doors applied with beaded brass mouldings, enclosing sliding trays, the drawers with moulded brass knob handles, on splayed bracket feet, early 19thC, 53in (135cm). **£1,800-2,200** *Bea*

Cupboards-Wardrobes

A mahogany breakfront wardrobe, the broken pediment pierced with trelliswork and centred by an urn above a dentil frieze decorated with ribbons and flowerheads, above 2 blind fret carved panelled doors applied with paterae, the side cupboard doors each with 3 false drawers, the fluted plinth on bracket feet, 19thC, 98in (249cm).
£5,000-8,000 *C*

An Edwardian mahogany breakfront wardrobe, with satinwood crossbanding and inlaid with trelliswork, husk swags and lines, on bracket feet, lacking trays to central section, 40in (101.5cm). **£900-1,200** *Bea*

A William IV mahogany miniature inverted breakfront wardrobe, of architectural form, with cedar lined drawers flanked by a tall cupboard with panelled door to each side, 21in (53cm).
£2,200-2,700 *P(O)*

A Regency mahogany wardrobe, the drawers with ebony handles, flanked by 2 long doors each simulated as 2, flanked and divided by reeded and spirally twisted columns, with waved apron, on turned feet, the cornice with 2 later hinged secret compartments, 98in (249cm).
£2,700-3,500 *C*

A Victorian curled ash breakfront triple wardrobe, with central mirror door enclosing slides and drawers, flanked by hanging cupboards, on plinth base, 83.5in (212cm). **£550-750** *ALL*

Davenports

A Victorian rosewood davenport, the sliding top with fretwork gallery and inset writing surface, the side with pull-out and hinged pen drawer, over brushing slide and 4 real and 4 dummy drawers, the sides on bun feet, one drawer stamped Johnstone Jupe & Co. New Bond, 21in (53cm).
£2,000-2,500 *DDM*

A Victorian figured walnut and marquetry davenport, with inlaid scrolling leaf and flowerhead decoration, tooled leather writing surface enclosing a typical plain interior, over 4 real and 4 dummy drawers, on platform base with carved, curving front supports, 22in (56cm). **£1,500-2,000** *DDM*

A Victorian mahogany davenport, with a leather inset top above twist columns, with 4 graduated drawers at the side, c1850, 21in (53cm). **£1,200-1,700** *S(S)*

A William IV figured satinwood veneered davenport, with leather inset flap enclosing fitted interior, oak lined drawers, turned feet, 19in (48cm). **£2,000-2,500** *WW*

A George IV davenport, with three quarter spindle turned gallery, leather lined fall and fitted interior, flanked by a hinged pencil drawer, on reeded bun feet, stamped M Wilson, 68 Great Queen Street, 24in (61cm). **£2,000-2,500** *CSK*

A mid-Victorian inlaid walnut davenport, the hinged superstructure with pierced three-quarter brass gallery above leather lined fall enclosing a fitted interior, one drawer stamped 20172, 21in (54cm). **£1,700-2,200** *CSK*

A Burmese carved rosewood davenport, late 19thC, 24in (61cm). **£550-650** *GIL*

A Victorian walnut veneered davenport, with small drawers and pigeonholes to the rising stationery compartment, the piano front enclosing a fitted interior, the cabriole front supports carved with flowers and foliage, on turned feet with brass casters, lacking brass gallery, 23in (59cm). **£3,500-4,500** *Bea*

A William IV rosewood davenport, the sliding top section with a three-quarter gallery, pen drawer and leather lined slope enclosing short drawers, 23in (59cm). **£1,500-2,000** *CSK*

A Victorian walnut veneered davenport, with raised stationery compartment, sloping flap, foliate carved C-scroll front supports, on bun feet with casters, 21in (53cm). **£1,200-1,700** *Bea*

A Victorian figured walnut harlequin davenport, the rising stationery rack with gilt brass gallery, fitted with 4 real and 2 dummy drawers, veneered in bird's-eye maple, leathercloth lined sliding slope, with carved scroll front brackets, on turned bun feet, 24in (61cm). **£2,500-3,000** *CAG*

A Victorian walnut davenport, with crossbanded slope, leather inset reveals a 4 drawer interior, on carved and decorative front supports, 19in (48cm). **£900-1,200** *GAK*

An unusual late George III mahogany davenport, the sliding top with a three-quarter gallery and a hinged slope with tooled morocco inset, enclosing 3 small drawers, 3 long drawers at the front, re-lined, a drawer to the left hand side fitted with an adjustable writing slope, and a drawer and hinged pen drawer to the right hand side, turned feet, casters, stamped Williams and Gibson, 37in (94cm).
£2,400-2,800   *P(S)*

Desks

A Georgian style walnut kneehole desk, with later leather writing surface, brass handles, carved cabriole supports, claw-and-ball feet, c1920, 43in (109cm).
£1,000-1,200   *GIL*

A Regency mahogany partners' desk.
£2,700-3,200   *N(A)*

A George I walnut kneehole desk, outlined in featherbanding, on bracket feet, the top re-veneered, 39in (99cm).
£2,000-2,500   *Bon*

An early Victorian mahogany pedestal desk, with leather inset top above 3 frieze drawers, 3 drawers to each pedestal, on plinth bases, c1840, 48in (122cm).
£1,500-2,500   *S(S)*

A mid-Victorian mahogany partners' desk, with leather lined top, each pedestal with a cupboard opposed by a cupboard enclosing pigeon holes, on shallow plinth base, 63in (160cm).
£2,500-3,000   *CSK*

An inlaid walnut kneehole desk, with brass ring handles and escutcheons, recessed centre cupboard, distressed, early 18thC. **£1,000-1,500** *Bea*

A mid-Victorian burr walnut pedestal desk, with leather lined top of broken outline above 3 frieze drawers, 3 drawers to each pedestal, on plinth bases, damaged, 57in (145cm). **£1,700-2,200** *CSK*

A mahogany kneehole desk, with moulded top above a frieze drawer and an open drawer, above a cupboard flanked by 3 drawers either side, on shaped bracket feet, adapted, late 18thC, 42.5in (108cm).
£700-1,000 *CSK*

A George III mahogany kneehole desk, on bracket feet, 31in (79cm). **£2,200-2,700** *CSK*

A Victorian mahogany partners' desk, with rounded leather cloth inset top, above an arrangement of 9 drawers with gadrooned knop handles, opposed by 3 further drawers and a pair of panelled doors, on plinth bases, stamped T. Wilson, 68 Great Queen Street, London, c1850, 72in (183cm). **£5,000-6,000** *S(S)*

A Victorian mahogany veneered partners' desk, with cloth inset top, wood knob handles, on plinths, 66in (168cm). **£2,500-3,500** *WW*

A burr walnut and featherbanded partners' desk, with leather lined top, above 6 frieze drawers, 6 drawers to each pedestal, on plinth bases, 60in (152cm). **£2,000-2,500** *CSK*

A late Victorian mahogany and ebony strung partners' desk, with leather lined top with reeded edge, on shallow plinth bases, restored, 71in (180cm). **£2,500-3,000** *CSK*

A mahogany roll top desk, with additional shelved top over a tambour slide affording access to the pull-out writing surface with fitted interior, on brass casters, early 19thC, 36in (92cm).
£1,200-1,700 *DDM*

A George III mahogany roll top desk, with a tambour shutter, brass floret knob handles, fitted interior with a pull-out baize inset ratcheted slope, the drawers with brass lion mask ring handles, brass carrying handles to the sides, square tapering legs on brass casters, 46in (117cm).
£3,000-4,000 *WW*

A mahogany roll top desk, inlaid with marquetry, with fitted interior and pull-out writing top, the drawers with chased brass swan neck handles, on bracket feet, 39in (99cm).
£4,000-5,000 *WW*

A walnut veneered pedestal desk, inlaid with panels of seaweed marquetry, the top with tooled leather insert, each pedestal with ovolo mouldings and 3 drawers, on ogee bracket feet, 51.5in (130cm).
£1,500-2,000 *Bea*

A Victorian walnut pedestal desk, the leather inset top with 3 frieze drawers, 3 graduated drawers to each pedestal, on plinth base, c1880, 42in (107cm).
£3,500-4,000 *S(S)*

A mahogany partners' desk, with leather lined top, on foliate headed cabriole legs, claw-and-ball feet, 66in (168cm).   **£4,000-5,000** *CSK*

A Victorian mahogany pedestal desk, 60in (152cm).
£1,500-2,000 *SIM*

A George III mahogany tambour top pedestal desk, the interior with small drawers, pigeonholes and adjustable writing inset, the frieze with a real and dummy drawer, fitted as a dressing compartment, c1780, 48in (122cm).
£3,500-4,500 *S(S)*

A mahogany Carlton House desk, inlaid with satinwood bands and ebony and satinwood lines, with three-quarter brass gallery, adjustable leather lined writing surface, on square tapering legs, 55in (140cm).
£5,000-6,000 *C*

A French style Edwardian lady's kneehole writing desk, with cylinder action, inlaid to drawer fronts and cylinder with coloured woods, 37in (94cm).
£3,000-4,000 *LF*

A walnut Wooton desk, with amboyna panels, the moulded top and hinged frieze compartment above 2 semi-dome fronted hinged panelled doors enclosing a fall front fitted satinwood and leather lined secrétaire, flanked by numerous stationery compartments, with letter box to the front, on reeded bracket feet, with dummy letter box marked Wooton Desk Co. Indianapolis, IND, Patent October 1874, 39in (99cm).   **£2,500-3,500** *CSK*

A French mahogany piano top desk, the elevated canted top enclosing 3 fall front drawers above a fall front lid, enclosing a pull slide leather lined fitted interior with 3 frieze drawers below, on baluster turned fluted legs, mid-19thC.
£1,000-1,500 *CSK*

A Victorian mahogany pedestal desk, one drawer with paper label inscribed 'Solomon's Office & Household Furniture, Queen Victoria Street, 49in (124cm).
£1,200-1,500 *HSS*

A walnut, ebonised and marquetry kneehole desk, with spindle turned shelved gallery, gadrooned edge and scroll and parquetry inlay, each pedestal similarly inlaid, with cupboard door flanked by fluted uprights, on bun feet, mid-19thC, 55in (140cm).
£2,700-3,500 *CSK*

A Carlton House style mahogany and satinwood banded desk, the raised bowed back with an arrangement of small drawers, compartments and an architectural cupboard, the breakfront frieze with a slide and 3 drawers, on slender tapering square legs and spade feet, c1930, 29.5in (75cm).
£1,200-1,500 *S(S)*

An inlaid writing desk.
£1,000-1,200 *WLT*

An Edwardian inlaid satinwood bowfront desk, with ledged back and finials, above a frieze drawer between 2 quarter veneered panelled doors, on reeded turned tapering legs with gadroon headings, 48in (122cm).
£900-1,500 *C*

An inlaid satinwood kidney shaped desk, with leather lined top, the frieze drawer with hidden locking mechanism, flanked by 2 further drawers to each side, on bulbous turned tapering legs, 69in (175cm).
£2,000-2,500 *CSK*

This desk is reputedly a copy, made by the same maker, of the example commissioned by the Scottish Co-operative Society as a present for Stalin in gratitude for grain sent over from Russia during WWII.

Dumb Waiters

A late Regency mahogany dumb waiter, with 2 dished tiers joined by turned supports on ring turned shaft and tripartite hipped splayed reeded legs, 23in (59cm) diam.
£2,000-2,500 *CSK*

A George IV mahogany three-tier buffet, the graduated and moulded stages connected by oblong uprights, on foliate carved bases with paw feet, c1825, 54in (137cm) high.
£2,500-3,000 *S(Ch)*

A George III mahogany two-tier dumb waiter, moulded edge trays, on vase turned stems to 3 cabriole legs, 23in (59cm).
£700-900 *WW*

A late George III mahogany dumb waiter, with 2 graduated circular drop leaf tiers on vase turned stems to the down turned tripod base with brass casters, 36.5in (93cm) high.
£900-1,200 *Bea*

An early Victorian oak three-tier telescopic dumb waiter, with dual supports and bun feet, 48in (122cm).
£1,000-1,500 *CSK*

Mirrors and Frames

A William and Mary oyster veneered walnut mirror, with bevelled plate in a moulded convex frame, formerly with candle branches, the plate re-silvered, 26in (66cm).
£2,500-3,000 *C*

A William and Mary walnut dressing glass, 22in (56cm) high.
£600-800 *HSS*

A George III carved and gilded frame, the top with eared corners, centred with flowersprays and pendant festoons of husks at the sides, raised egg-and-dart outer edge, alternating rope twist and flower head sight edge.
£500-600 *CSK*

A George III design giltwood mirror, the plate between 2 pilasters, on a pierced foliate surround with flowerhead cresting, 49 by 23in (125 by 59cm).
£800-1,200 *CSK*

A George III style giltwood architectural wall mirror, with broken pediment, scroll finial and floral decorated shaped frieze, 19thC, 45 by 24in (114 by 61cm).
£700-900 *GH*

A George I chinoiserie scarlet and gilt dressing table mirror, made up, with gilt decoration on a scarlet japanned ground, the base with a fall front revealing small drawers and pigeonholes, a serpentined drawer below, on block feet, 37 by 18in (93 by 46cm).
£1,000-1,500 *S(S)*

A George IV gold painted overmantel mirror, the plate with an ebonised reeded band, with a foliate cornice and tied reeded pilasters, c1825, 36 by 56in (92 by 122cm).
£500-800 *S(S)*

A mid-George III giltwood and gilt gesso mirror, within C-scroll and trailing foliate surround, 45 by 24in (114 by 61cm).
£900-1,200 *CSK*

A George III style satinwood cheval mirror, outlined throughout with ebonised stringing, on down turned splayed legs with brass casters, 68.5in (174cm) high.
£900-1,200 *Bea*

A George III giltwood overmantel, 62.5 by 55in (159 by 140cm). **£2,000-2,500** *CSK*

A mahogany framed upright wall mirror, with a boxwood strung frieze, tulipwood crossbanded and boxwood and ebony strung borders, flanked by turned and reeded columns, headed by ebony strung panels, 19thC, 37.5 by 27in (95 by 69cm). **£500-700** *DN*

A George III style gilt framed pier mirror, the plate with a wave and flame pierced surround, with foliate festoons, with a cabochon surmount and conforming apron, c1900, 60 by 25in (152 by 63cm). **£1,600-2,000** *S(S)*

A George I walnut veneered and giltwood frame mirror, with applied carving to the top and base, sides with trailing fruit, later bevelled glass, missing the surmount, 43 by 25in (109 by 64cm).   **£1,200-1,700** *WW*

A William IV mahogany framed cheval glass, with reeded uprights, on scroll carved bases. **£700-900** *LRG*

A Regency convex girandole, the ball studded and moulded giltwood frame with a U-shaped candle arm to each side, surmounted by an eagle with scrolling foliage, 40 by 23.5in (101 by 60cm). **£1,500-2,000** *Bea*

A Regency giltwood convex mirror, the plate in a reeded border edged with foliage and a moulded surround, below a foliate plinth, with an eagle flanked by dolphins, with foliate boss, re-gilt, traces of old gilding, 41.5 by 22in (105 by 56cm). **£1,200-1,800** *C*

A George IV mahogany cheval mirror, in the manner of Gillow, the plate with a reeded frame, the reeded turned and square supports with mushroom finials, the conforming splayed legs ending in brass capped casters, c1820, 58 by 31in (147 by 79cm). **£2,000-2,500** *S(S)*

253

A Regency giltwood triple-plate overmantel mirror, the frieze applied with ebonised flowerheads and stars above cluster column uprights, c1810, 61 by 29in (155 by 74cm).
£900-1,200 *S(S)*

A Victorian giltwood and gesso overmantel mirror, the surmount decorated in relief with mermaids above a 3 section glass interspersed with turned columns, 64.5 by 31in (163 by 79cm). **£550-650** *OL*

A pair of German gilt mirrors, the plates within 6 subsidiary plates divided by a border of foliate C-scrolls with scallop shells at each corner, surmounted by a rockwork motif flanked by 2 putti, the surround incorporating foliate scrolls, one labelled Carl Brassart, Hgl. Hof-Vergolder, Stuttgart, Specialitat In Zimmer decorationen Von Cartonpierre, re-gilt and slight differences in carving, mid-19thC, 68.5 by 38in (173 by 97cm).
£2,500-3,500 *Bon*

An Italian giltwood mirror, with divided plate centred by a patera, the frame carved with radiating rays, some losses to extremities, 69 by 62in (175 by 157cm).
£2,500-3,500 *C*

A Regency style giltwood overmantel, the moulded cornice with ball decoration, acanthus leaf finial fluted side columns, 3 bevelled mirror glass panels surmounted by classical urn, ribbon and swag decoration, 19thC, 42 by 28in (107 by 71cm).
£550-650 *GH*

A George III giltwood and gesso pier glass, the 2 plates surmounted by a husk carved pediment, frieze set with 3 classical roundels and flanked by reeded columns with leaf carved capitals, 78 by 36.5in (198 by 93cm).
£1,000-1,200 *Bea*

A Victorian mahogany and satinwood cheval mirror, the plate on pierced shaped serpentine supports, on splayed feet with casters.
£650-750 *Bea*

A Transitional grey painted and parcel gilt overmantel mirror, with later plate in a moulded foliate surround below a fluted urn with floral cresting and flanked by acanthus scrolls, the sides with leafy trails, the rectangular backboard with later egg-and-dart cornice, part of framing moulding later, 59 by 48in (150 by 122cm).
£2,500-3,500 *C*

A pair of oval carved giltwood wall mirrors, 18thC.
£8,500-9,500 *P(S)*

A Viennese ormolu mounted mahogany and parcel gilt mirror, the cresting with pediment centred by a Bacchic mask above a tablet mounted with Cupid and Psyche, c1830, 62 by 22.5in (157 by 57cm). **£800-1,000** *C*

A Louis XVI grey painted and parcel gilt pier glass, the later divided plate in a lotus leaf and beaded moulded surround with flowerhead top angles, the reverse inscribed in pencil n°1480, reduced in height, 74.5 by 31in (189 by 79cm).
£1,800-2,500 *C*

A Victorian giltwood pier glass, c1840, 73in (185cm) high.
£650-750 *GIL*

A Provincial French carved and gilded frame, 18thC, 50 by 42in (127 by 106.5cm).
£900-1,200 *CSK*

An Italian giltwood mirror, with later plate, reduced in height, regessoed and re-gilded, late 17thC, 59 by 46.5in (150 by 118cm).
£6,000-7,000 *C*

A pair of Swedish gilt lead mirrors, with shaped plate in a foliate border above an apron centred by a double flowerhead, with filled candle branch sockets, late 18thC, 20 by 8in (51 by 20cm). **£1,000-1,500** *C*

An Italian carved giltwood mirror, the plate engraved with a figure carrying a torch and a coat-of-arms, within a rococo frame with trophies, damaged, 18thC, 49 by 31in (125 by 79cm).
£1,700-2,200 *WW*

A Louis XIV carved and gilded frame, with scrolling foliage and flowers flanked by opposed C-scrolls on cross hatched ground, foliate sight edge, 20 by 19in (51.5 by 48cm). **£500-600** *CSK*

A Victorian giltwood serpentine console and mirror, the arched glass plate surmounted by intersecting scrolling acanthus, the veined white marble top above a similarly carved frieze, on conforming cabriole supports, 126 by 58.5in (319 by 148cm).
£1,250-1,750 *Bea*

A Regency inlaid mahogany toilet mirror, the plate with beaded surround and a patera to each corner, flanked by turned uprights, the D-shaped platform crossbanded in satinwood above 3 frieze drawers, flanked by turned uprights and bun feet, one drawer stamped T Wilson, 38 Great Queen Street, London, 44 by 27in (112 by 69cm).
£900-1,200 *CSK*

Screens

A Victorian mahogany pole screen, with a floral tapestry panel, on a tripod dolphin support.   **£250-300 M**

A pair of Regency pole screens, decorated in penwork, on gilt brass mounted ebonised stands with tripod bases, 63.5in (161cm) high.
£800-1,000 Bea

A mid-Victorian rosewood pole screen, with polychrome woolwork panel in scrolled surround, baluster column support and tripod base with scroll feet, 54in (137cm).
£350-400 AH

An early Victorian maple pole screen, the banner with a needlework panel of a dove and prayer book amongst flowers, the triform base with scroll feet.
£300-400 P(O)

An early Victorian mahogany pole screen, the lobed banner painted with humming birds, in a cut paper and grisaille decorated foliate border, the triform base with scrolled leaf feet.
£400-500 P(O)

Miller's is a price GUIDE not a price LIST

An early Victorian stained rosewood cheval firescreen, with profusely carved foliate scroll surround and cartouche shaped woolwork panel in many colours, 45in (114cm).
£600-900 CSK

A Victorian rosewood pole screen, with woolwork panel of a young lady, on a tripod platform base.
£120-170 M

A Victorian oak three-fold screen, with carved paterae scrolls and a balustrade above the specimen wood panels of rosewood, bird's eye maple, satinwood, mahogany, kingwood, tulipwood, amboyna, walnut, burr walnut, pollard oak, ash, boxwood, birch and others, 76in (193cm) high.
£700-900 AG

A Victorian carved mahogany three-fold graduated draught screen, with brocade fabric panels. **£200-230** *MST*

A pole firescreen, the woolwork panel on a dark green background and standing on a mound, 20 by 16.5in (51 by 42cm), on a mahogany baluster tripod stand with hoof feet, 18thC. **£400-500** *Bea*

A mahogany triple chair back sofa, on shell headed cabriole legs with pad feet, restored, mid- 18thC, 66in (168cm). **£2,000-2,500** *C*

Settees

A George I style giltwood sofa, upholstered in tapestry, the out scrolled arms carved with bell flowers, terminating in eagle masks, on hipped cabriole legs and claw and ball feet, 65in (165cm). **£3,000-3,500** *CSK*

A George III mahogany triple shield back open arm settee, with pierced wheatsheaf style back, supported on square tapering legs with stretchers, upholstered in rose coloured velvet, 57in (145cm) long. **£600-800** *GH*

A Regency chaise longue, with scroll end, on curved supports, decorated in white and gilt, green damask cover. **£1,000-1,200** *LRG*

A George III mahogany sofa, with urn shaped arm supports, on turned tapering legs joined by turned stretchers, c1795, 73in (185cm). **£2,200-2,600** *S(S)*

A George III mahogany sofa, the padded serpentine back, scroll arms and seat, on reeded square legs, c1770, 64.5in (164cm). **£3,000-3,500** *S(S)*

A mid-Georgian design mahogany
and yellow upholstered sofa, on
foliate headed cabriole legs with
claw-and-ball feet, one arm
damaged, 82in (208cm).
£700-1,000 *CSK*

A George III brown painted sofa, covered in floral
cotton, on turned tapering fluted legs with brass
caps, repaired, 71.5in (181cm). **£1,000-1,500** *C*

A George III mahogany settee,
the padded seat covered in pale
striped cut velvet, on square
tapering legs joined by a later
central pine stretcher, repaired,
59.5in (151cm).
£800-1,200 *C*

Provenance:
*Princess Helen Frederica Augusta
of Waldeck and Pyrmont was the
wife of Prince Leopold, Duke of
Albany (d.1884), youngest son of
Queen Victoria. She lived at
Claremont from 1882-1922. She
was the mother of Princess Alice,
Countess of Athlone (d.1981).*

A mid-Georgian style mahogany
sofa, with machine made floral
upholstery, the arms with
flowerhead terminals, on foliate
headed cabriole legs with claw-
and-ball feet, 82.5in (209cm).
£800-1,000 *CSK*

A Regency style
ebonised and gilt
sofa, with crimson
and blue striped
upholstery, scroll
ends, scroll arm,
reeded seat rail
and outswept legs
headed by
rosettes,
77in (196cm).
£1,200-1,700
CSK

A Regency carved rosewood
chaise longue, the back and seat
with green and cream striped
upholstery, the seat rail and
turned tapering legs with lotus
carved decoration, 79in (201cm).
£2,000-2,500 *C*

A Regency mahogany scroll end
sofa, of slightly assymetric form,
the waved gadrooned top rail,
lotus leaf and acanthus carved
arms enclosing a floral
upholstered back and seat with
bolster cushions, on scroll bracket
feet, 95in (241cm).
£1,600-2,200 *CSK*

A rosewood framed couch, with
single end, carved frame,
outswept carved legs, porcelain
casters, loose squab and bolster,
covered in red brocade, c1830.
£600-900 *WIL*

A Regency mahogany sofa, the back, downswept arms and padded seat with green moiré upholstery, on reeded tapering legs headed by paterae, restored, 78in (198cm). **£2,500-3,000** *CSK*

A cream painted and parcel gilt blue upholstered canape, with spiral twist uprights, serpentine seat, on fluted tapering legs headed by paterae, previously with caned seat, restored, late 18thC, 70in (178cm). **£700-1,000** *CSK*

A William IV mahogany sofa, upholstered in green striped moire, above a rope twist apron on splayed legs with ebony moulding and brass paw casters, 81.5in (206cm). **£2,000-2,500** *C*

A Regency mahogany sofa, the back, arms and seat with striped upholstery within reeded surround, the arms with vase turned terminals, on turned tapering legs, 76in (193cm). **£900-1,500** *CSK*

A William IV mahogany frame sofa, with scroll detail to the back and sides, in crimson damask, on short reeded supports. **£900-1,200** *LRG*

A George IV white painted and parcel gilt sofa, with dished back, cushions and acanthus carved outscrolled arms covered in yellow silk damask, one caster missing, 96in (243cm). **£7,000-8,000** *C*

A Victorian walnut settee, with 3 button back panels, each with carved scroll and garland decoration, linked by curving open arms, on an upholstered serpentine seat, on cabriole front legs.
£2,000-2,500 *DDM*

A mid-Victorian satinwood sofa, the back and seat with channelled surround and striped upholstery, vase turned arm supports, square tapering legs headed by paterae, 66in (168cm).
£1,500-2,000 *C*

A Victorian love seat, the walnut frame supported by 4 scrolled decorative legs with casters, upholstered in red moquette.
£600-700 *GAK*

A George III style satinwood and painted settee, the caned back with an ebonised oval caned seat, swag decorated seat rail, on fluted gilt turned legs with brass casters, c1900, 46in (117cm).
£2,700-3,200 *S(S)*

An Edwardian mahogany morning room suite comprising: a two-seat settee, inlaid with floral sprays in bone and stained wood, upholstered in gold floral coloured tapestry, on scrolling supports, 2 tub shaped easy chairs and 4 single chairs.
£1,500-2,000 *AG*

A Victorian carved rosewood and upholstered matching drawing room suite, covered in green moquette, comprising: a sofa and a pair of tub shaped armchairs, with similarly carved supports, c1845. **£2,000-3,000** *S(S)*

A mid-Victorian carved walnut couch, with serpentine leaf decorated and button upholstered back, upholstered seat with shaped apron, leaf carved cabriole legs with white china casters, 75in (191cm).
£1,000-1,200 *AH*

A Victorian walnut serpentine chaise longue, the button upholstered back with pierced end rail above seat, on short cabriole legs, with scroll feet.
£800-1,200 *BWe*

An Edwardian two-seater open arm settee, in mahogany show wood, re-upholstered in flame pattern material.
£350-400 *LF*

A Victorian mahogany frame settee, with carved leaf and scroll decoration, buttoned and upholstered back and seat, carved, curving front supports, on cabriole legs, 82in (208cm). **£1,500-2,000** *DDM*

An Anglo Indian hardwood sofa, the pierced back with reeded uprights and scrolling reeded horizontals carved with paterae and shells, the ends similarly carved, on reeded baluster turned legs headed by shells, mid-19thC, 104in (264cm).
£900-1,200 *CSK*

A French mahogany and gilt metal mounted sofa, of Empire design, applied with gilt paterae and foliate decoration, downswept arms with sphynx uprights, on angled griffin legs, upholstered in green patterned fabric, 65in (165cm).
£2,500-3,000 *CSK*

An Edwardian painted satinwood sofa, the bowed caned back with central panel of figures in a pastoral setting, the bowed caned seat with loose cushion, on turned tapering legs, 47in (119cm).
£3,000-3,500 *C*

A walnut framed three-piece bergère suite, comprising: 2 arm-chairs and a three-seater settee, with caned back and sides, carved arms with scroll ends, on cabriole legs with carved shoulders, upholstered loose cushions.
£1,500-2,000 *WIL*

A Regency chaise longue, in simulated rosewood frame, with scroll end and back, on turned supports with brass casters.
£1,000-1,400 *LRG*

A late Victorian painted satinwood double chairback settee, the back with cane panels centred by cherubs, the downswept arms with double cane panels, the upholstered seat with loose squab, on tapering turned legs with brass casters.
£2,200-2,600 *Bea*

Shelves

A pair of mahogany display shelves, with pierced fret sides and fret mouldings, late 19thC, 30in (76cm).
£2,000-2,500 *WW*

A George III mahogany three-tier open wall shelf, with fretwork tracery sides and galleries, above 2 apron drawers, c1770, 24in (61cm).
£2,000-2,500 *S(S)*

A Georgian inlaid and crossbanded mahogany shaped front sideboard, the top with 3 brass finials over a central drawer, flanked by a drawer and cupboard door to one side and a dummy double drawer cellaret to the other, on square tapering legs, 54in (137cm).
£2,500-3,000 *DDM*

A late George III mahogany bowfront pedestal sideboard, outlined with boxwood and fruitwood stringing, the back with double brass rail, crossbanded top, with tambour shutter, on slender bracket feet, 72.5in (183cm). **£2,200-2,600** *Bea*

A George III Sheraton style mahogany inlaid serpentine fronted sideboard, with brass side carrying handles, having satinwood stringing, original brass octagonal shaped ringed handles, on 6 square tapering legs with spade feet, 54in (137cm).
£2,200-2,600 *GH*

A late George III mahogany inlaid and satinwood crossbanded sideboard, of broken D-shaped outline, the top inlaid with a shell motif, on turned legs, 43in (109cm).
£2,000-2,500 *P(O)*

Sideboards

A late George III mahogany bowfront sideboard, with central frieze drawer and arched apron drawer, flanked by a deep drawer and cupboard, on turned reeded tapering legs, the top possibly associated, 63.5in (161cm).
£1,800-2,200 *CSK*

A Regency mahogany D-shaped sideboard, inlaid with ebony lines, on ring turned tapering legs, 48in (122cm).
£2,500-3,500 *CSK*

A George III inlaid mahogany bowed breakfront sideboard, 52in (132cm).
£1,700-2,000 *MJB*

A Regency brass inlaid mahogany sideboard.
£3,500-4,000 *P(S)*

A George III style semi-circular sideboard, inlaid throughout with boxwood and ebonised stringing, on moulded tapering square legs with spade feet, 60in (152cm).
£3,500-4,500 *Bea*

A mahogany and inlaid sideboard, three quarter scroll fretted brass gallery, ribbed panels and inlaid oval fan medallions, the whole inlaid with floral festoons, ribbons, fan medallions, and decorative bands, square section tapering legs, spade feet, late 19thC, 90in (229cm).
£5,200-6,000 *P(S)*

A mahogany and chequer strung bowfront sideboard, with satinwood banded top, on square tapering legs with spade feet, restored, late 18thC, 73in (185cm). **£2,000-2,500** *CSK*

A carved walnut sideboard, the mirror panelled back of architectural form, the drawer stamped Johnstone, Jeanes and Co, 67 New Bond St., London, 5078, 101in (257cm).
£2,000-3,000 *P(S)*

A Regency mahogany and ebony strung sideboard, with ledge back above central bowed frieze drawer and apron drawer flanked by a deep lead lined cellaret drawer and a cupboard, on reeded tapering legs, 48in (122cm).
£2,500-3,500 *CSK*

An Edwardian mahogany sideboard, on turned legs, 48in (122cm).
£800-1,000 *AG*

A George III mahogany sideboard, on turned legs.
£750-950 *RPI*

A Regency mahogany sideboard, of broken D-shaped outline with foliate scroll carved galleried back above central frieze drawer and arched apron drawer flanked by a deep drawer and a cupboard, on ring turned tapering legs, 61in (155cm). **£1,500-2,000** *CSK*

A George IV mahogany sideboard, on ring turned and reeded supports with ball feet, 83in (211cm).
£2,500-3,500 *CSK*

Make the Most of Miller's

CONDITION is absolutely vital when assessing the value of an antique. Damaged pieces on the whole appreciate much less than perfect examples. However a rare, desirable piece may command a high price even when damaged.

An early Victorian mahogany sideboard, the raised mirror back with scallop carved surmount and panelled pilasters with rosette capitals, the base fitted with 2 frieze drawers on scroll carved front supports and platform base, 69in (175cm).
£550-650 *RBB*

Stands

A late Victorian mahogany folio stand, with slatted adjustable sides of slight serpentine outline with incised scroll decoration, on dual reeded scroll uprights joined by a flattened stretcher, 29in (74cm). **£1,500-2,000** *C*

A George III mahogany stand. **£550-650** *MAT*

A wrought iron lectern, with oak plank top and fleur-de-lys detail. **£150-200** *LRG*

An ebonised and parcel gilt umbrella stand, on a moulded stepped plinth base, 32in (81cm) high. **£1,500-2,000** *C*

A William IV music stand, the painted and gilt adjustable rest, in the form of a laurel wreath and shell centred by a lyre, the telescopic brass column on a painted cast iron triform base, 55in (140cm) high. **£700-900** *Bea*

Locate the Source

The source of each illustration in Miller's can be found by checking the code letters below each caption with the list of contributors.

A hall/umbrella stand, made from WWI mahogany propeller, 32in (81cm) high. **£65-70** *RE*

A late Victorian rosewood and marquetry duet music stand, the twin ratchet adjustable panels inlaid with musical trophies, the adjustable fluted and spiral turned stem on bell flower inlaid splayed tripod supports, c1890, 16in (41cm). **£1,500-2,000** *S(S)*

A Victorian mahogany folio stand with drop side panels, 4 splayed feet and a stretcher. **£1,700-2,200** *MST*

Steps

A set of mahogany library steps, with gilt tooled leather to the treads, on an open frame, folding over to form a low table, the turned feet on brass casters, early 19thC. **£2,200-2,700** *WW*

A set of Regency mahogany and ebony strung library steps, with 3 leather lined rectangular treads, fitted with a commode, and cupboard door with brass handle, 16.5in (42cm). **£3,500-4,000** *C*

A Georgian mahogany framed and metal rung folding library ladder. **£1,500-2,000** *GAK*

Stools

A George II giltwood stool, the stuffed seat covered in grey velvet, the scroll apron with diaper and scallop shells, on moulded cabriole legs, re-gilt and restored, c1755, 26in (66cm). **£2,500-3,000** *S*

An early Victorian rosewood stool, in the Gothic style, with upholstered drop-in seat, on triple cluster legs with carved oak leaf cluster knops and moulded and fretted arched sides, 21 by 17in (53 by 43cm). **£700-800** *CAG*

A George III mahogany stool, with padded top covered in pale floral damask, on chamfered square legs carved with blind strapwork below a scallop shell, on block feet, repair to one leg, 31.5in (80cm). **£3,000-3,500** *C*

A mahogany piano stool, 19in (49cm) high. **£300-350** *APO*

A pair of Victorian oval rosewood footstools, with padded seats above flower carved aprons, on cabriole legs with scroll feet, c1860, 15in (38cm). **£600-800** *S(S)*

A mid-Georgian mahogany metamorphic library stool, with padded drop-in seat, on turned legs joined by turned stretchers and short vertical planks forming step treads, 39in (99cm). **£2,500-3,000** *CSK*

A Victorian giltwood simulated bamboo stool, with canted padded seat covered in chinoiserie pattern material, with pierced apron, on splayed turned legs joined by X-shaped stretcher with turned boss, redecorated, 24in (61cm). **£900-1,000** *C*

A pair of late Victorian stools of Regency design, with green and gilt decoration, rectangular seats upholstered in buttoned yellow velvet, on ribbon tied X-frame supports with paterae headings, 21.5in (54cm).
£1,200-1,500 *CSK*

A George III mahogany stool, with padded top covered in close nailed yellow leatherette, on 6 canted square supports joined by box stretchers, on block feet, adapted, stretcher restored.
£2,000-2,500 *C*

A Victorian grey painted X-framed stool, with a leopard skin seat, c1850, 24in (61cm).
£1,500-2,000 *S*

A piano stool with glass marble feet, 20in (51cm) high.
£250-300 *APO*

A pair of Venetian giltwood stools, with stuffed drop-in seats, pierced aprons, on 4 cabriole legs, mid-18thC, 41in (104cm).
£8,000-9,000 *S*

A mahogany duet stool, with well and 4 cabriole legs with shell carved shoulders and claw and ball feet, 20thC, 39in (100cm).
£320-400 *WIL*

A walnut stool, with serpentine drop-in padded seat covered in green damask, damaged, 26in (66cm).   **£900-1,200** *C*

A Victorian rosewood stool, the upholstered seat with a valanced apron, above cabriole legs, c1850, 29in (74cm).
£800-1,000 *S(S)*

A rococo style carved and giltwood hearth stool, 19thC.
£550-850 *LRG*

A Victorian mahogany duet stool, with carved decoration and rising seat, on cabriole legs.
£300-350 *LRG*

A pair of Victorian mahogany stools, with overstuffed close studded seats on turned fluted legs, 30in (76cm). **£1,200-1,700** *CSK*

An Italian walnut stool, with serpentine padded seat with tassels, a foliate scroll bar to each end, on bearded satyr supports, with later turned feet, late 19thC, 40in (102cm). **£1,500-2,000** *C*

An early Victorian giltwood stool, the upholstered seat covered in salmon pink fabric, the scroll carved X-frame supports joined by twin turned stretchers, with trade label of Robert Strahan, 24 Henry Street, Dublin, c1850, 22in (55cm). **£1,200-1,500** *S(S)*

An early Georgian walnut stool, on cabriole legs with square tops and shaped angles, on pad feet, the underside indistinctly inscribed in ink Mont Row, 21in (53cm). **£3,000-3,500** *C*

A pair of George IV white painted and parcel gilt stools, with padded seats covered with floral needlework, on X-shaped end supports carved with acanthus scrolls and centred by a patera, joined by a turned stretcher, on scrolled feet, one with repairs to 3 legs. **£1,200-1,700** *C*

TABLES

Architects Tables

An early George III mahogany architects' table, with fitted frieze drawer with beize lined slide, brass side handles, on square supports concealing columns with brass casters, some alteration, 26in (66cm). **£1,500-2,000** *Bea*

A George II mahogany architect's table, the double rising top self-activating a rising fiddle, with candleslides to the side and split front legs supporting a pull-out drawer, with baize topped surface and compartments beneath, 33in (84cm). **£3,000-3,500** *B*

A walnut architect's table, the hinged ratcheted top with adjustable ledge, re-entrant corners and feather-banding flanked by brass candle holders, the front legs sliding open to reveal fitted interior, 36in (92cm). **£3,000-3,500** *CSK*

Breakfast Tables

A George III mahogany snap-top pedestal breakfast table.
£1,000-1,500 *MAT*

A late George III mahogany breakfast table, with reeded edged patent supported top, ebony stringing and wide crossbanding, on tapering ring turned column with 4 splayed legs, brass caps and casters.
£3,000-4,000 *Bea*

A Regency mahogany breakfast table, with rounded corners and reeded edge, on a turned column and reeded downswept legs, with lion's paw feet, c1810, 51in (130cm).
£1,500-2,000 *S(S)*

A mahogany breakfast table, with radially veneered top and gadrooned shaft, on scroll carved splayed legs with paw feet, probably German, mid-19thC, 48in (122cm).
£1,000-1,500 *CSK*

A Regency style mahogany crossbanded with satinwood tip-up top breakfast table, with turned central pillar with 4 shaped scroll fluted legs, brass lion's paw feet and casters, 19thC, 48in (122cm) square.
£1,200-1,500 *GH*

A Regency rosewood breakfast table, the parquetry tip-up top with satinwood banding, on faceted tapering shaft, spreading to tripartite scroll feet, damaged, 42in (106cm).
£1,000-1,500 *CSK*

A Regency mahogany breakfast table, with single plank top, on turned central column and reeded quadruple splay supports with brass caps and casters.
£1,300-1,700 *RBB*

A late Regency mahogany breakfast table, with tip-up top, baluster turned shaft, on 4 splayed legs with paw feet, restored, 46in (117cm).
£1,200-1,700 *CSK*

A Regency mahogany breakfast table, the top inlaid with mahogany segments, tilting on a pedestal base with 3-way plateau and carved paw feet, 54in (137cm).
£2,000-2,500 *B*

A Regency design mahogany breakfast table, with crossbanded top in rosewood, on turned shaft and splayed legs, modern, 84in (213cm).
£1,500-2,000 *CSK*

A William IV rosewood breakfast table, with tip-up top, on polygonal baluster turned shaft and circular platform with paw feet, 49in (125cm) diam.
£1,000-1,500 *CSK*

A William IV rosewood breakfast table, with tip-up top and faceted shaft on trefoil platform with paw feet, 47in (119cm).
£1,500-2,000 *CSK*

An early Victorian rosewood breakfast table, with moulded tip-up top, a baluster turned foliate carved shaft, on tripartite hipped splayed legs with cartouche headings and scroll feet, 49.5in (125cm).
£1,500-2,000 *CSK*

A mid-Victorian walnut breakfast table, with quarter veneered shaped oval tip-up top, on baluster turned shaft and splayed scroll legs, 57in (145cm).
£2,000-2,500 *CSK*

A mid-Victorian walnut breakfast table, with quarter veneered tip-up top, foliate carved baluster shaft, on 4 acanthus and scroll carved splayed legs, 46.5in (118cm).
£1,000-1,500 *CSK*

A mid-Victorian burr walnut breakfast table, with tip-up top, baluster turned shaft and quadripartite hipped splayed legs with foliate carved headings, 54in (137cm).
£1,000-1,500 *CSK*

A mid-Victorian burr walnut breakfast table, with oval quarter veneered top, gadrooned shaft, on splayed scroll carved legs, 47in (119cm).
£1,500-2,000 *CSK*

A Victorian walnut and marquetry oval breakfast table, the top inlaid with foliage and flowers, on a carved column and 4 downswept legs with scroll feet, stamped J.L. VIII, c1860, 53.5in (136cm).
£2,000-2,500 *S(S)*

A mid-Victorian rosewood breakfast table, of serpentine outline with tip-up top, on faceted bulbous shaft and 4 splayed scroll carved legs, 55in (140cm).
£1,000-1,200 *CSK*

A Victorian burr walnut breakfast table, the quarter veneered top with satinwood crossbanding, on a fluted column and 4 leaf carved downswept legs, c1870, 51in (129cm).
£3,200-4,000 *S(S)*

A Victorian coromandel breakfast table.
£1,500-2,000 *HCH*

Card Tables

A George III inlaid mahogany folding card table.
£600-700 *HCH*

A Queen Anne style walnut and featherbanded card table, the eared hinged top with baize lined surface and playing counters, above a frieze drawer, on shell headed cabriole legs with pad feet, 33in (84cm).
£800-1,000 *CSK*

A George III mahogany concertina action card table, with hinged green baize lined top and square legs with scroll angles, on block feet, 36in (92cm).
£3,200-3,700 *C*

A George III mahogany D-end folding card table, the frieze drawer with boxwood stringing, on square tapered legs.
£1,500-2,000 *LF*

A George III mahogany D-shaped fold-over card table, crossbanded and inlaid with satinwood, 36in (92cm).
£900-1,200 *MAT*

A late George III satinwood demi-lune card table, inlaid overall with boxwood and ebony lines and rosewood bands, with hinged top, on tapering legs, 38in (97cm).
£2,500-2,800 *C*

A George III mahogany and satinwood crossbanded card table, the hinged fold-over top on square tapering legs with spade feet, 37in (94cm).   **£2,000-2,500** *RID*

A George III mahogany card table, inlaid overall with boxwood and ebonised stringing, the top crossbanded with satinwood and tulipwood, the frieze with simulated panelling, the legs with double gateleg action, the satinwood crossbanding possibly later, restored, 35.5in (90cm).
£2,000-2,500 *C*

A George III mahogany fold-over demi-lune card table, with satinwood crossbanded border, on tapering legs with line inlay and brass casters, 36in (92cm).
£600-700 *GAK*

A pair of George III satinwood demi-lune card tables, the tops with satinwood and tulipwood crossbanding, on square tapered legs inlaid with boxwood and ebony stringing, 36in (92cm).   **£8,000-9,000** *P(O)*

A Regency rosewood and brass inlaid table, the D-shaped fold-over swivel top with baize lining, turned and reeded column support with gadrooned collar, on circular base, 4 splayed feet with star decorated knees and brass lion paw toes and casters 36in (92cm).
£3,500-4,500 *AH*

A Regency period rosewood fold-over card table, the revolving top crossbanded with rosewood and shark skin and brass line inlay, on legs with brass inlays and toes, on casters, 36in (92cm).
£3,500-4,000 *GAK*

A Regency period rosewood veneered card table, with brass inlay, the D-shape swivel top baize lined, the frieze with a raised panel, concave panelled stem to a quatreform base, on feet with casters, 36in (92cm).
£1,000-1,500 *WW*

A Regency rosewood D-shaped card table, with hinged swivel top and beaded frieze, on square shaft with gadrooned base, on quadripartite platform with scroll feet, 36in (92cm).
£900-1,200 *CSK*

A made-up Regency mahogany card table, on lyre shaped supports, 36in (92cm).
£900-1,500 *S(S)*

A Victorian figured walnut serpentine card table, on swept supports and cabriole legs with floral carved knees, 32in (81cm).
£1,500-2,000 *GSP*

A George II mahogany card table, with fold-over top, single drawer with brass swan neck handle, on rounded supports with scroll ears on pad feet, 29in (74cm).
£2,500-3,000 *M*

A William IV rosewood fold-over top card/games table, one side of the interior leaf fitted with a draught board and pegging area, swivel top reveals card storage box, on octagonal tapering column, shaped base, on squat circular feet, 23in (59cm) long when folded. **£800-1,200** *GAK*

A late Regency mahogany card table, with rounded swivel top, scroll carved spandrels, on foliate scroll carved shaft and quadripartite platform with paw feet, 36.5in (93cm).
£1,200-1,500 *CSK*

A mid-Victorian walnut card table, with serpentine quarter veneered top, on 4 scroll uprights with central finial and 4 splayed legs with scroll feet, 37in (94cm).
£1,500-2,000 *CSK*

A Victorian walnut card table, with satinwood crossbanded top, on cabriole legs with gilt metal mounts at the knees and sabots, c1860, 39in (99cm).
£2,200-2,700 *S(S)*

A Regency rosewood card table, with rounded fold-over top enclosing a baize lined interior, 36in (92cm).
£1,400-2,000 *CSK*

A Regency fold-over card table, on plain column with platform base and 4 carved claw supports.
£900-1,200 *M*

A Victorian walnut card table, with hinged quatrefoil top, on leaf carved cabriole legs, c1860, 40in (102cm). **£2,200-2,500** *S(S)*

An Edwardian mahogany crossbanded and string inlaid envelope card table, the revolving top with baize lined interior, single frieze drawer with brass knob handles, circular undershelf, on 4 scrolled supports and 4 squared tapering legs with brass toes and casters, 19.5in (49cm).
£450-600 *AH*

A mahogany demi-lune folding card table, with green baize lined top, on 4 square tapering legs and brown porcelain casters, 24in (61cm) diam.
£300-400 *LF*

A satinwood demi-lune card table, in the Sheraton manner, the top with crossbanded edge, segmented panels and inlaid Prince of Wales feathers motif, the frieze with crossbanding, stringing, ribbon, swag and shell decoration, the interior with 8 green baize segments, bordered by boxwood stringing, enclosing a central inlaid chequerboard, 36in (92cm). **£1,000-1,500** *DDM*

A Victorian burr walnut serpentine fronted fold-over swivel top card table, with original green baize lining, supported on a turned central column with 4 shaped legs having scroll carved knees, on original casters, 36in (92cm).
£1,200-1,500 *GH*

A rosewood folding card table, with baize lined swivel top, brass inlay to frieze, on twin supports and spider leg base, decorative brass toes and casters.
£1,700-2,000 *LF*

Centre Tables

A William IV rosewood centre table, on polygonal ends and dual supports with turned feet, 57.5in (146cm). **£900-1,200** *CSK*

A Regency rosewood centre table, with leather-lined top and beaded frieze on turned tapering legs, 54in (137cm) wide.
£1,200-1,700 *CSK*

A Victorian ebonised and bird's-eye maple card table.
£350-450 *HCH*

A Victorian walnut centre table, English, inlaid with foliage, on carved cabriole legs, c1855, 59in (150cm) wide.
£1,400-1,800 *S(S)*

A burr-elm and parcel-gilt centre table, the top with central ebony and stained yew parquetry feather pattern medallion with yew border, on tapering shaft and inverted tripartite platform base with gilt lions' paw feet, early 19thC, re-veneered, 46in (117cm) diam. **£3,500-4,500** *C*

A late Victorian walnut and marquetry centre table, the tilt top with central scroll decoration, bordered by scrolling flower and leaf designs, over an inlaid freize supported on a pedestal with 4 turned supports and splayed legs, 34.5in (87cm) wide.
£500-600 *DDM*

A Victorian satinwood centre table with serpentine sided top, foliate cartouche and scroll carved frieze, acanthus and cabochon carved baluster end supports, on splayed legs with scroll toes and casters, 54.5in (138cm).
£900-1,200 *Bea*

A mahogany centre table,
c1830, 29in (74cm) high.
£300-400 *JAC*

A Victorian walnut centre table,
with burr walnut veneered tip-up
top, cabochon carved bulbous
stem, on 4 acanthus carved
hipped splayed legs with scroll
toes and casters, 57.5in (145cm)
wide.
£900-1,200 *Bea*

A Regency rosewood centre table
in the manner of George Bullock,
the tip-up top inlaid in cut brass
with a wide band of stylised ivy
leaves, the altered baluster stem
on a concave sided platform with
splayed legs inlaid with brass
stars and stringing, ending in
brass casters, 50in (127cm) diam.
£3,000-3,500 *Bea*

A mahogany centre table, with
gadrooned edge and faceted
baluster shaft, on platform with
paw feet, mid-19thC, 45in
(114cm) diam.
£1,000-1,500 *C*

A mahogany centre table, top
inset with various specimen
marbles, on baluster turned shaft
and 4 splayed legs with scroll
feet, mid-19thC, adapted, 26in
(66cm) diam.
£1,200-1,500 *C*

A Burmese hardwood centre
table, the tip-up top with egg-and-
dart moulded edge and pierced
foliate frieze, on lotus carved
baluster turned shaft, on
quadripartite platform with scroll
feet, mid-19thC, 60in (152cm)
diam.
£1,500-2,000 *CSK*

A mid-Victorian walnut,
marquetry and ormolu mounted
centre table, with cross-banding
and floral border, on cabriole legs
with gilt clasps trailing to sabots,
42in (107cm) wide.
£1,500-2,000 *CSK*

A late Victorian satinwood and
marquetry centre table, inlaid
overall with beaded banding, the
top centred by a sun-burst with
radiating fan pattern and green
stained demi-lunes, the frieze
with 2 drawers and 4 simulated
drawers, reconstructed and
adapted from an earlier table, 2
legs re-supported, 54in (137cm)
diam.
£5,000-6,000 *C*

A Milanese ebonised centre table,
decorated overall with ivory and
bone intarsia panels, on square
tapering supports with moulded
plinth bases, joined by a platform
stretcher, damaged, mid-19thC,
55in (140cm) wide.
£1,700-2,000 *C*

An Italian rosewood and
marquetry table, the top centred
by a floral spray within a leafy
border, the paterae inlaid frieze
including a drawer at one end, on
ebonised fluted turned legs,
restored, 23.5in (60cm) wide.
£1,700-2,200 *S(S)*

An Italian walnut centre table, with inlaid marble top and carved border, the tripartite base carved with masks and foliate scrolls, on paw feet, 19thC, 36in (91.5cm) diam. **£800-1,000** *WHB*

A Victorian burr walnut centre table, the quarter veneered tip-up top inlaid with floral swags and motifs, the baluster stem and 4 splayed legs carved with foliage, the toes inlaid with flowers and on casters, 63.5in (161cm) diam. **£1,700-2,000** *Bea*

A Napoleon III rosewood, ebonised and marquetry centre table, banded with amboyna inner border above waved floral inlaid apron, on cabriole legs with gilt sabots, one sabot missing, 41.5in (105cm) wide. **£1,500-2,000** *CSK*

A centre table, the top raised on fluted central pillar and 4 subsidiary pillars, the scroll feet with knop surmounts and recessed brass casters, 62in (157cm) diam. **£12,000-15,000** *RBB*

A Continental centre table, ebonised, with inlaid designs in bone, 19thC. **£450-550** *LRG*

Console Tables

A Regency walnut console table with brocatelle marble top, on pieds-de-biches, repaired, 38.5in. (98cm). **£2,000-3,000** *C*

A pair of Italian giltwood demi-lune console tables, with marble veneered tops, early 19thC, 29.5in (75cm). **£1,500-2,000** *P(O)*

A stained wood and gesso console table in the Neo-Classical style with black marble top, oak leaf and acorn frieze, lion monopodia supports and mirrored back, 57in (144.5cm). **£2,000-2,500** *Bea*

A Louis XVI white painted and parcel-gilt console table, with red and grey veined fossil marble top above a pierced frieze with scrolling foliage centred by a flowerhead, possibly Italian, re-gilt, 32in (81cm). **£1,500-2,000** *C*

A Sheraton style painted semi-eliptical console table, the top centred by a scene of cherubs riding on fishes, contained in a reserve hung by swags and ribbon from a pole, the frieze fluted and decorated with rosettes, on turned fluted legs, united by a concave sided undertier, 19thC, 39.5in (100cm) wide. **£1,500-2,000** *P(O)*

Dining Tables

A late Regency mahogany and ebony strung drop-leaf extending dining table, with rectangular top on tapering ring turned legs, including 4 extra leaves, 119.5in (303.5cm) long.
£3,000-4,000   *CSK*

A late Regency mahogany dining table, the tilt-top with a leaf carved edge, on a turned and leafy scroll carved cylindrical tapering pillar, the concave platform base, on 3 carved claw and scroll feet, 50.5in (128cm) diam.
£1,200-1,500   *P(W)*

An early Victorian rosewood veneered dining table, with tip-up top, octagonal stem, concave sided platform, on lion paw feet, 53.5in (136cm) diam.
£2,000-2,500   *Bea*

A Victorian mahogany extending dining table, with 2 leaves, c1850, 92in (233.5cm) long extended.
£1,700-2,000   *GIL*

A George III mahogany dining table, with 2 end sections and drop leaf centre section.
£3,500-4,000   *SWO*

An Edwardian mahogany extending dining table, on reeded tapering legs, stamped on mechanism *Edwards & Roberts*, including 3 extra leaves, 100in (254cm) extended.
£3,000-4,000   *CSK*

A George IV mahogany fold-over extending dining table, with concertina action, fitted with 2 loose centre leaves, 96in (243.5cm) long.
£2,500-3,000   *MAT*

A Regency D-end mahogany dining table.
£8,500-9,500   *P(S)*

A mahogany gateleg dining table, supported on shaped legs with carved knees and horse hoof feet, 19thC, 72in (182.5cm) long extended.
£800-1,000 *GH*

A mid-Victorian mahogany extending dining table, on cabochon carved and fluted tapering legs, including 3 extra leaves held in a leaf carrier, 132in (335cm) long extended.
£4,000-5,000 *CSK*

A mid-Victorian mahogany extending dining table, on reeded baluster turned legs on later turned tapering supports, including 5 extra leaves, 131in (333cm) extended.
£2,500-3,000 *CSK*

Display Tables

An Edwardian mahogany inlaid and crossbanded vitreen table, glass cracked, 24in (61cm).
£400-700 *GH*

A mahogany framed two-tiered display table, standing on 4 tapering legs with spade feet, carved detail to borders, late 19thC, 24in (61cm).
£700-1,000 *GAK*

A French kingwood and gilt-metal mounted vitrine table of Louis XV design, with gilt clasps and sabots, 27in (69cm) wide.
£1,700-2,200 *CSK*

A pair of gilt-metal mounted mahogany display tables of Louis XVI style, enclosing a velvet lined interior, with panelled sides on fluted turned tapering legs and toupie feet, both locked, one with one foot replaced in wood, c1900, 31.5in (80cm).
£2,000-3,000 *C*

An Edwardian mahogany vitreen table, inlaid with brass, 26in (66cm) wide. **£400-600** *GH*

Dressing Tables

A dressing table which is part of a mid-Victorian coromandel and amboyna banded ebonised bedroom suite.
£3,200-4,000 *CSK*

An English mahogany veneered bowfront dressing table, the top inlaid with stringing, ivory escutcheons and chased brass bail handles, on swept bracket feet, late 18thC, 43in (109cm).
£4,200-5,000 *WW*

Dropleaf Tables

A Victorian inlaid rosewood occasional table, the pair of dropleaves opening to form an oval top above a deep frieze and standing on square tapering supports joined by an under platform, 26.5in (67cm).
£850-1,200 *OL*

A small Georgian mahogany dropleaf Pembroke table, fitted with 2 small drawers and 2 dummy drawers with brass knob handles, on bobbin turned legs with brass casters, one missing, damaged, 30in (76cm) extended.
£450-550 *LF*

A Victorian burr walnut and scrolling marquetry inlaid combined games and work table, the top enclosing an inlaid backgammon and chess board above a fitted frieze drawer, 27in (69cm) wide.
£1,700-2,200 *CSK*

Games Tables

A Victorian figured and carved walnut work and games table, the hinged top inlaid for chess, backgammon and cribbage, with fitted drawer and well below, 23in(59cm).
£800-1,000 *RID*

An early Victorian inlaid marble chess top table, bordered with bands of coloured geometric and leaf motifs, on burr walnut triform stem with carved base and scroll feet, with plate glass protector, 36in (91.5cm) diam.
£4,500-5,000 *GSP*

An Anglo Indian games table, the marble top with chequer board inset, on a parcel gilt mahogany base, 19thC, 31in (78.5cm) diam.
£2,500-3,000 *SWO*

Miller's is a price GUIDE not a price LIST

A Victorian walnut combined games and work table, inlaid throughout with arabesques and stringing, the fold-over top revealing backgammon and chessboards, the frieze drawer above a solid well, on turned end supports with splayed bases joined by a turned stretcher, c1865, 24in (61cm).
£1,500-2,000 *S(S)*

A Syrian parquetry and mother-of-pearl inlaid games table, the swivelling hinged lid with baize lined interior flanked by counter compartments, hinged to reveal backgammon and chess boards on 4 angled faceted uprights joined by a spindle turned upright on 4 splayed legs, late 19thC, 36in (92cm).
£1,700-2,200 *CSK*

A games table, the mahogany veneered reversible top with counter wells and baize one side, the veneered frieze with slides and small drawers, centred with a scallop shell, on shell carved cabriole legs to claw and ball feet, 31.5in (80cm).
£2,200-2,700 *WW*

Library Tables

A Victorian light oak library table, each side with 3 drawers, each end with a tooled leather lined writing slide, on spiral turned and carved legs with low 'H' stretchers, 72in (182.5cm).
£2,500-3,000 *LAY*

A William IV rosewood library table, the moulded top lined in gilt tooled black leather with key pattern border with 4 frieze drawers, on solid end standards applied with scrolling volutes and joined by a turned stretcher, on bar and bun feet, 54in (137cm).
£2,200-2,700 *CSK*

A mid Victorian mahogany partners' library table, with leather lined top above 8 frieze drawers, on reeded tapering legs, 96in (244cm).
£4,500-5,000 *CSK*

An early Victorian mahogany library table, with rectangular top above 2 frieze drawers and 2 false drawers with a pendant finial at each corner, on pierced spindle turned and scroll carved standard ends joined by a lotus carved inverted U-shaped stretcher, on dual scroll feet, 66in (168cm).
£2,200-2,700 *CSK*

A Regency rosewood library table inlaid with brass stylised foliate motifs and paterae mouldings, on converging C-shaped end-standards and scroll legs joined by a turned stretcher, with paper trade label, Edwards and Roberts, Upholstery Warehouses, Wardour St, London, 48in (122cm).
£4,500-5,500 *C*

A late Victorian walnut library table, with moulded leather lined top, on carved arched supports and twin column end standards with scrolling bar bases joined by a stretcher, 88.5in (224cm) extended.
£1,500-2,000 *CSK*

A William IV mahogany partners library table, with rounded leather lined top above 2 frieze drawers to either side and beaded frieze on reeded tapering legs, stamped W. Priest, 17 & 24 Water St., Blackfriars labelled Priest's Temple Furniture Mart. 17 & 24 Water Street, Bridge Street, Blackfriars, City, Established for the sale of Superior New and Secondhand Furniture and Office Fittings. Improved Fire-Proof Safes, Doors, Chests....SH and Deed Boxes, 60in (152cm).
£2,000-2,500 *CSK*

William Priest, an Auctioneer and Appraiser, is recorded at this address between 1837-1839; it is probable that he marked secondhand items which were then sold from his warehouse premises.

A William IV rosewood library table, with 2 flush frieze drawers, the leaf scroll volute feet with inset casters, 57in (144.5cm).
£1,000-1,500 *MJB*

Nests of Tables

A set of George IV rosewood quartetto tables, the largest table with D-shaped lidded side compartments for chess pieces, the second table top inlaid with a chess board, raised on turned legs united by a turned stretcher, 27in (68cm).
£4,500-5,500 *P(O)*

A nest of 4 George III style thuyawood occasional tables, the ebonised beading within tulipwood crossbanding, on simulated bamboo legs and ebony strung splayed feet, largest table 19.5in (49cm).
£1,200-1,500 *S(S)*

A nest of 4 George III style mahogany occasional tables, the crossbanded fiddle-back tops centred by an oval flame veneered panel within a band of beading, on simulated bamboo end supports and splayed feet, damaged, c1910, largest table 20in (50cm).
£1,700-2,000 *S*

A nest of black lacquered and burr walnut tables, with inlaid satinwood and triangular patterned side stringing, 19thC, largest table 23in (58.5cm).
£1,000-1,200 *GH*

Occasional Tables

An Edwardian occasional table, on 4 legs with crossed supports, 24in (61cm) diam.
£100-120 *LF*

An Easter hardwood occasional table, with front and rear single drawer, on 8 legs richly inlaid with floral patterned bone decoration, 19thC, 24in (61cm).
£200-250 *GH*

A mid-Victorian papier mache and gilt decorated occasional table, with tip-up top, 24in (61cm).
£1,500-2,000 *C*

A hand carved Indian table, the top one piece of solid teak, 19thC, 28in (71cm) square.
£250-350 *ROW*

A walnut octagonal inlaid table, 31in (79cm) diam.
£500-600 *APO*

A pietra dura occasional table, with central spray of flowers in various coloured marbles and lapis lazuli, inscribed on reverse Fratelli Bencini, Grande Fabbica Mosdico, 2 Via Leopardi 2, Firenze, Italy, on carved giltwood tripod base with scroll feet, mid-19thC, 26.5in (67cm) diam.
£3,000-3,500 *GSP*

A mahogany snap top occasional table, on vase pedestal and tripod, with felted cover for the top, 28in (71cm) diam.
£150-180 *LF*

A Dutch satinwood occasional table, with parquetry tilt-top pierced brass gallery, on tripod base, top and base possibly associated, c1800, 25.5in (65cm) diam.
£1,000-1,500 *S(S)*

A mahogany snap top occasional table, with pie-crust top, on vase pedestal and tripod, 21in (53cm) diam.
£220-260 *LF*

A French occasional table, 2nd Empire period, 32in (81cm).
£300-350 *APO*

Pembroke Tables

A mahogany pedestal Pembroke table with plain top, real and dummy frieze drawers on a turned bulbous stem with quatrefoil base, on 4 fluted curving legs, ending in lion paw casters, 19thC, 40in (101.5cm).
£500-600 *DDM*

A late Georgian mahogany and rosewood crossbanded table, with reeded edge, fitted 4 drawers, 2 blind bone knobs, on 4 turned legs, brass casters, some knobs missing, c1820, 19in (48cm).
£650-850 *WIL*

A late George III mahogany Pembroke table, with tulipwood banded top above a frieze drawer, on square tapering legs, 39in (99cm). **£2,000-2,500** *CSK*

A Regency mahogany and satinwood banded pedestal Pembroke table, with brass casters, bearing paper label This table was bought by Thos. Gibson about 1817 for the back drawing room in their house in Great Coram Street, Bloomsbury, it stood in the library at 10 Broadwater Down, Tunbridge Wells, original label transcribed by the same hand, 46in (116.5cm).
£1,500-2,000 *CSK*

A late George III mahogany Pembroke table, with rosewood banded hinged top and frieze drawer, on square tapering legs, 39in (99cm).
£2,000-2,500 *CSK*

A George III mahogany and rosewood banded Pembroke table by George Simson, with rounded leaves, on square tapering legs headed by satinwood tablets, outlined overall in boxwood stringing, the drawer with George Simson's trade label, 31in (78cm).
£2,000-2,500 *Bon*

George Simson established his own business by 1787 at 19 St Paul's churchyard where he continued trading until 1839. He subscribed to Sheraton's drawing book in 1793 and was included in the list of master cabinet makers in the 'Cabinet Dictionary' in 1803.

A Sheraton style mahogany inlaid Pembroke table, with oval twin flap top, fitted drawer, on square tapering legs and casters, 19thC, 36in (91.5cm) extended.
£350-450 *GH*

A George III kingwood Pembroke table, with a broad border crossbanded within a narrow satinwood band, crossbanded end drawer, square section tapering legs with collared feet, gee string lines, brass terminals, casters, 32in (81cm). **£3,200-3,700** *P(S)*

A late George III 'plum pudding' mahogany Pembroke table, with kingwood crossbanding and boxwood and ebonised stringing, on tapering square legs with later brass casters, 44in (111.5cm).
£3,000-3,500 *Bea*

Serving Tables

A late George III mahogany serpentine Pembroke table, the kingwood banded top with later painted decoration, on associated channelled moulded legs, 37in (94cm).   **£800-1,000** *CSK*

A William IV mahogany serving table, the top with a shallow raised back and gadrooned mouldings, on reeded and foliate carved turned supports headed by paterae, c1835, 57.5in (146cm).
£900-1,200 *S(S)*

A Chippendale style mahogany serving table, with bressia marble top on profusely decorated base, with blind fret Chinese carving, 72in (182.5cm) long.
£2,500-3,000 *B*

An Irish George II style carved mahogany serving table, the frieze with acanthus, scallop shell and mask motifs, cabriole legs with claw and ball feet, c1900, 60in (153cm) long.
£1,700-2,500 *S(S)*

A mahogany serving table, 19thC.
£3,000-4,000 *RBB*

A George III mahogany D-shaped serving table, with veneered frieze, on turned tapering legs, c1780, 60in (153cm) long.
£1,500-2,000 *WW*

Side Tables

A Queen Anne walnut veneered and elm side table, the quarter veneered top with crossbanding and diagonal banding, on square cabriole legs with pointed pad feet, 31in (79cm).
£2,500-3,000 *Bea*

A Queen Anne oyster veneered walnut and elm side table, the top geometrically inlaid in boxwood, on square cabriole legs, restored, 31.5in (79cm).
£1,500-2,000 *Bea*

A mid-Georgian walnut side table, one drawer with compartments and a simulated short drawer to the front, one short drawer with compartments and candle stand to the side, on lappeted club legs and pad feet, 27in (69cm).
£1,500-2,000 *C*

A George III mahogany bowfront side table, c1790, 36in (91cm).
£650-750 *S(S)*

A Cuban George II side table, with a brass plate handle above a bracketed frieze, on plain turned tapering legs and pad feet, 27.5in (70cm).
£1,200-1,700 *WW*

A walnut side table, with moulded edge, long frieze drawer, on baluster turned legs joined by square stretchers, early 18thC, 33in (84cm).
£1,200-1,700 *Bea*

A burr elm side table, inlaid overall with kingwood featherbanding, on turned feet, late 17thC, 29.5in (75cm).
£2,200-2,700 *C*

A Regency D-shaped side table, the top and frieze with rosewood panels, crossbanded with satinwood and inlaid with string borders, 43in (109cm).
£5,000-5,500 *N(A)*

A Victorian mahogany side table, fitted with 2 frieze drawers, turned wood handles, on turned legs.
£250-300 *LF*

An Italian neo-classical giltwood side table, with liver and green marble top, on turned tapering fluted legs filled with chandelles and headed by paterae, on toupie feet, probably Piedmontese, restored, late 18thC, 53.5in (136cm).
£4,200-5,000 *C*

A Dutch mahogany and floral marquetry side table, with dished top above 2 end frieze drawers, on cabriole legs and pad feet, the drawers reconstructed, 31in (79cm).
£1,500-2,000 *CSK*

A grey painted and parcel gilt side table, of Empire design, the concave fronted top with foliate scroll ledge back, on winged female monopodia uprights, 50in (127cm).
£1,000-1,500 *CSK*

A Regency mahogany and ebony strung breakfront serving side table, on reeded tapering legs with paw feet, 80in (203cm).
£2,500-3,000 *CSK*

A Dutch mahogany and marquetry half-round side table, inlaid overall, on square tapering legs, late 18th/early 19thC, 32in (81cm).
£500-1,000 *CSK*

A walnut veneered side table, with panels of oyster veneers, oak lining on side liners, spiral twist legs with a shaped stretcher rail, inlaid parquetry 3 pointed stars in ivory, on bun feet, possibly North Italian, 70in (178cm).
£3,500-5,000 *WW*

Sofa Tables

A mahogany and ebony strung sofa table, on ring turned uprights and dual splayed legs joined by a stretcher, reduced in size, early 19thC, 39.5in (100cm).
£1,000-1,500 *CSK*

A Regency brass inlaid rosewood sofa table, the top with 2 frieze drawers, on shaped centre pillar support and umbrella base, with casters, 56.5in (143cm) when extended.
£2,500-3,500 *Bea*

A Sheraton period faded rosewood veneered sofa table, banded in satinwood with stringing, the frieze with 2 mahogany lined drawers with brass knob handles, the reverse with dummy drawers, on stretchered trestle ends and splay legs, the brass sabots on casters, c1800, 39in (99cm).
£6,500-7,500 *WW*

A Regency mahogany pedestal sofa table, with rectangular twin flap top and frieze drawer, on baluster turned shaft and 4 channelled splayed legs, 40in (102cm).
£1,200-1,700 *CSK*

A George IV mahogany sofa table, with crossbanded top, on moulded and hipped sabre legs, c1825, 58in (147cm) when open.
£1,500-2,500 *S(S)*

A Regency mahogany sofa table, with rosewood crossbanded top, 2 drawers and 2 false drawers outlined with ebony, on splayed and reeded legs with paterae and brass casters, 61in (155cm).
£2,500-3,500 *Bea*

A rosewood sofa table, on square end standards and spade feet joined by a turned stretcher, adapted, 19thC and later, 57in (145cm).
£1,000-1,500 *CSK*

A Regency mahogany and ebony strung pedestal sofa table, with hinged top, on baluster turned shaft and 4 splayed legs, the drawer with label Lord Addington, '7 Gabels', Addington, Nr Winslow, Bucks, 41in (104cm).
£900-1,200 *CSK*

A Regency mahogany and calamander crossbanded sofa table, fitted with 2 drawers to one side opposing side with dummies, applied with anthemion decorated brass mounts, 63in (160cm). **£4,700-5,000** *P(O)*

A late Regency rosewood and brass inlaid sofa table, with 2 frieze drawers opposing dummies, on drum feet and casters, allover profusely inlaid with cut brass in a formal floral and foliate design, original turned handles available, 59.5in (151cm) when extended. **£2,500-3,000** *P(S)*

A Regency rosewood sofa table, with satinwood and foliate scroll marquetry inlay, on an inverted tapering octagonal column with concave holly wood banding, brass claw terminals and casters, 61in (155cm) when extended. **£3,000-3,500** *GC*

A Regency rosewood sofa table, on a rectangular shaft and inverted quadripartite platform base with hipped splayed legs, extensive restorations, 60in (152cm). **£900-1,200** *CSK*

A George III mahogany sofa table, crossbanded in satinwood, above a pair of real drawers opposing a pair of dummies, with brass box casters, restored, 24in (61cm). **£850-950** *HSS*

A Regency mahogany sofa table, with twin flap top crossbanded in kingwood and edged with gadrooning, the panelled frieze with 2 mahogany lined drawers, 56in (142cm). **£2,500-3,000** *C*

Use the Index

Because certain items might fit easily into any number of categories, the quickest and surest method of locating any entry is by reference to the index at the back of the book.
This has been fully cross-referenced for absolute simplicity.

A George IV figured rosewood veneered sofa table, inlaid satinwood and burr wood stringing and banding, gilt brass stamped handles and inlaid brass stringing, the turned stem with a cast gilt brass egg-and-dart moulding, the 4 shaped top splay legs with brass paw sabots, on casters, the twin flaps with restoration, 35in (89cm). **£3,500-4,500** *WW*

A Charles II oak
box seat joint
stool, c1680.
£2,000-2,500
S(S)

A pair of Regency oak
window seats, restored,
c1815. **£7,500-8,500** *S*

An oak boarded
chest, late
l6thC, 39in
(99cm).
£1,100-1,300
S(S)

A Jacobean fruitwood inlaid and carved oak
tester bedstead, 17thC and later, 103in
(261cm) long. **£16,000-18,000** *S(NY)*

A mid-Georgian oak
bookcase.
£3,500-4,500 *C*

A Charles I carved
oak armchair, mid-
17thC.
£2,200-2,500 *S(S)*

A James I oak open
armchair, some
replacements.
£5,500-6,000 *C*

A George III oak bureau, the
fall revealing stationery
compartments, c1760.
£1,700-2,000 *S(S)*

A Charles I oak coffer, c1620,
48in (122cm).
£2,000-2,500 *S(S)*

A George II oak chair, c1670.
£800-1,200 *PHA*

A George I oak bureau
bookcase, c1720, 37.5in
(95cm).
£5,500-6,000 *S(S)*

A late Elizabethan oak X-
frame chair.
£4,500-5,000 *C*

A mahogany crossbanded and inlaid oak low dresser, mid-18thC. **£2,200-2,800** *MJB*

A cedarwood chest, painted with maritime scenes, early 17thC. **£2,000-2,500** *S(S)*

An English oak low cupboard, restorations, late 17thC, 23in (59cm). **£1,800-2,200** *C*

A Dutch oak cupboard, with ebony enrichments, mid-17thC, 72in (182cm). **£9,000-11,000** *S*

A German carved oak chest, c1600, 74in (188cm). **£3,200-3,500** *SWO*

A Queen Anne oak chest of drawers, c1710. **£2,000-3,000** *PHA*

A William III carved oak press cupboard, altered, c1700, 69in (175cm). **£2,000-2,500** *S(S)*

A Continental carved oak cupboard, early 19thC. **£180-200** *PCh*

An early Georgian oak low dresser. **£7,000-8,000** *C*

A North Wales oak dresser, in 2 sections, mid-18thC, 64in (162.5cm). **£8,000-10,000** *C*

287

A Charles II oak refectory table, with four-plank top, c1660, 100in (254cm).
£8,500-9,500 *S(S)*

A George IV oak double sided library table, with a slide at either end, c1820. **£3,500-4,500** *S*

A George III oak dresser, with matching plate rack, 65.5in (166cm).
£3,500-4,000 *SWO*

A George III oak dresser, restored, c1780.
£2,000-2,500 *S(S)*

A George III oak dresser, cl780, 73in (185cm).
£4,000-5,000 *S(S)*

A George III inlaid oak Welsh dresser, the back of the upper section of later date. **£6,000-8,000** *S(NY)*

A Charles II walnut, elm and ash hanging cupboard, restored, 33in (84cm)
£4,000-5,000 *S(S)*

A Charles I oak armchair, restored.
£1,300-1,500 *S(S)*

A pair of William IV oak card tables.
£3,500-4,500 *C*

A Charles I carved oak credence table, the fold-over top with rear gateleg, c1640, 35in (89cm).
£3,000-3,500 *S(S)*

An Anglo-Flemish oak cupboard, in 2 parts, c1680.
£2,500-3,000 *S(S)*

Paul Hopwell Antiques

Early English Oak

Top: A set of eight (four showing) Georgian ash wavyline ladderback dining chairs. Excellent colour, condition and patination. English c1800.

Centre: A rare George II oak dresser base with a superb arched moulded apron. Standing on cabriole legs with spade feet. Good colour and patination. English c1745.

Bottom: A superb 18th century dresser in oak. Excellent condition, colour and patination. N. Wales c1770.

Furniture restoration service available
30 High Street, West Haddon, Northamptonshire NN6 7AP
Tel: (0788) 510636

A George III mahogany breakfront library bookcase, the lower part cut in 2 parts, c1770, 111in (282cm). **£13,000-15,000** *S*

A George III four-poster bed, with painted cornice, 77.5in (197cm). **£9,000-10,000** *S*

A George III mahogany tester bedstead, adapted, c1760, 76in (193cm) long. **£18,500-20,000** *S(NY)*

A George III mahogany breakfront library secrétaire bookcase, 91in (231cm). **£9,000-11,000** *S*

A Queen Anne bureau bookcase, 19thC decoration. **£16,000-18,000** *S(NY)*

A George III mahogany breakfront library bookcase, the cornice with serpentine pediment, c1770, 97in (246cm). **£22,000-25,000** *S*

A George III satinwood secrétaire bookcase, the lower part with a fitted secrétaire drawer, c1790, 33.5in (85cm). **£30,000-32,000** *S*

A Queen Anne bureau bookcase. **£18,000-20,000** *S(NY)*

A Second Empire mahogany and ormolu mounted lit en bateau, feet adapted, 91.5in (232cm) long. **£5,000-6,000** *C*

A mahogany and cream painted four-poster bed, part 18thC, 78in (198cm). **£3,500-4,000** *C*

A mid-Victorian mahogany bookcase. **£4,500-5,500** *CSK*

A George I elm bureau,
c1730.
£8,500-10,000 *S*

A George I walnut bureau,
c1725, 41in (104cm).
£4,500-5,000 *S*

A Louis XVI ormolu mounted bois satine
bonheur du jour. **£5,000-6,000** *C*

A William and Mary
marquetry bureau, restored.
£7,000-8,000 *S*

An early Georgian walnut and burr
walnut bureau, inlaid with
featherbanding, extensively restored and
re-veneered. **£2,500-3,000** *C*

A William and Mary stained
burr elm bureau, banded in
walnut.
£3,000-4,000 *C*

A French tulipwood,
parquetry and ormolu
mounted bonheur du
jour.
£7,000-9000 *CSK*

A George III
bonheur du jour.
£3,500-4,000 *C*

A Louis XVI bonheur du
jour.
£34,000-36,000 *S(NY)*

A Dutch marquetry bureau,
c1770 and later.
£7,000-8,000 *S*

A Dutch mahogany and
marquetry bureau, c1780,
marquetry possibly later.
£6,000-8,000 *S(S)*

A George II burr elm
bureau, with chequer
stringing, c1750.
£3,500-5,000 *S*

A Dutch marquetry bureau,
mid-18thC and later.
£6,500-8,000 *S*

An Italian lacca povera bureau, the sloping front enclosing a fitted interior, mid-18thC, 41in (103cm). **£7,500-8,500** *S*

A Portuguese rococo jacaranda bureau, the panelled and carved lid enclosing a fitted interior, 45in (114cm). **£6,500-8,000** *CNY*

An Edwardian inlaid satinwood and crossbanded cylinder bureau, 42in (107cm). **£5,300-6,000** *CSK*

A French gilt bronze mounted kingwood free-standing bureau, by Millet of Paris, with 11 drawers and 2 cupboards, 61in (155cm). **£23,000-25,000** *S*

A walnut veneered table bureau, the flap with a book rest and fitted interior, Queen Anne, c1710, 16in (41cm). **£5,500-6,500** *S*

An Italian late Baroque inlaid walnut slant front bureau, with fitted interior, mid-18thC, 50in (127cm). **£10,000-12,000** *CNY*

An Italian walnut and marquetry bureau, with fitted interior, c1730, 45.5in (115cm). **£42,000-43,000** *S*

A German black and gilt lacquer bureau, with fitted interior, 2 oak lined drawers, on cabriole legs, late 18thC. **£8,500-10,000** *C*

A Louis XIV oyster veneered kingwood and walnut bureau mazarin, the moulded top inlaid with circles and geometric patterns, restored, 30.5in (77cm). **£12,500-14,000** *C*

l. A Louis XVI ormolu mounted mahogany bureau, with fitted interior, c1789, 39.5in (100cm). **£7,200-8,000** *C*

r. A Louis XIV ormolu mounted ebony and amaranth bureau, inlaid in brass and pewter, mid-19thC, 46.5in (118cm). **£40,000-50,000** *C*

A Regency chinoiserie vitrine, with 2 paper labels PIETRO E GAET.
£32,500-40,000 *S(NY)*

A Regency pedestal cupboard, with tambour cupboard, c1805, 15.5in (39cm).
£3,200-3,500 *S*

A Regency mahogany pedestal cabinet, each with a pair of panelled and grille filled doors, c1800, 22in (55cm).
£2,500-3,000 *S*

A George III serpentine front mahogany side cabinet, in the manner of Thomas Chippendale, the serpentine shaped fielded doors opening to marblized lined sliding shelves, c1775, 47in (119cm) long.
£8,000-9,000 *S(NY)*

A pair of Neapolitan painted and parcel gilt display cabinets, mid-18thC.
£3,500-4,000 *S*

A Sheraton revival inlaid mahogany and crossbanded display cabinet.
£1,500-2,000 *PCh*

A Venetian red and gilt japanned bureau cabinet, with 2 mirrored doors enclosing fitted interior, mid-18thC.
£33,000-35,000 *C*

A Queen Anne walnut bureau cabinet, with fully fitted interior, restored, c1700, 93in (236cm) high.
£22,500-23,500 *S*

An Italian late Baroque scarlet and silver japanned bureau cabinet, with fully fitted interior, mid-18thC, 88in (224cm) high.
£62,000-70,000 *CNY*

A Dutch amboyna display cabinet, the astragal doors enclosing shelves, above 3 long drawers.
£4,700-5,500 *S(S)*

A George III semi-circular mahogany side cabinet, with crossbanded top and 11 drawers, 35in (89cm) high.
£3,000-3,500 *S*

A Victorian inlaid walnut display cabinet, 32in (81cm).
£400-500 *PCh*

A George III mahogany breakfront side cabinet, with 4 central drawers and 1 drawer and a door each side, c1770, 60in (152cm). **£3,500-4,000** *S*

A Goanese rosewood, teak, ebony and bone inlaid cabinet-on-stand, late 17thC, 35.5in (90cm).
£18,000-20,000 *C*

A William and Mary walnut and marquetry cabinet-on-stand, reconstructed.
£4,500-5,500 *S(S)*

An Augsburg marquetry cabinet, possibly originally with a fall front, c1600, 35in (89cm).
£7,500-9,000 *S*

A marquetry cabinet, Augsburg or Ulm, the later conforming stand with spirally turned legs and waved stretchers, c1610, 39in (99cm).
£5,000-6,000 *S*

A bone, tortoiseshell and ebony cabinet, Neapolitan or Spanish, mid-17thC.
£3,400-4,500 *S*

A mahogany and satinwood banded side cabinet, in the Dutch manner, c1900, 35in (89cm).
£2,600-3,000 *S(S)*

A Queen Anne walnut cabinet-on-chest, the doors enclosing a fitted interior, c1710, 43in (109cm). **£3,500-4,500** *S*

A pair of George III style bronze mounted fruitwood inlaid satinwood cabinets, after a commode attributed to John Cobb.
£11,000-13,000 *S(NY)*

A Dutch walnut and marquetry cabinet-on-stand, adapted.
£7,000-9,000 *C*

A boulle and ebonised side cabinet, c1860, 81in (205.5cm).
£2,500-3,500 *S(S)*

An Antwerp painted cabinet, mounted with repoussé metal figures, on later ebonised stand with cabriole legs, 42in (105cm).
£14,000-16,000 *S*

A late George III mahogany canterbury, c1810, 18in (46cm). **£2,000-2,500** *S*

A George III mahogany armchair, in French Hepplewhite style, c1770. **£1,700-2,200** *S*

A pair of George II style mahogany library armchairs, with 18thC needlepoint upholstery, on acanthus carved cabriole legs with claw-and-ball feet. **£18,500-20,000** *S(NY)*

A George II mahogany library armchair, with cabochon cabriole front legs, c1750. **£3,500-4,000** *S*

A late George III mahogany plate canterbury, 25.5in (64cm) long. **£4,600-5,000** *S*

A Queen Anne walnut shepherd's crook armchair, with needlepoint upholstery, restored, and a similar chair of a later date. **£7,500-9,500** *S(NY)*

An early George III mahogany library armchair, covered in tan leather, with moulded arm supports and moulded chamfered legs. **£3,500-4,000** *S*

r. A George IV mahogany canterbury, with a drawer at one end, c1820, 18in (46cm). **£1,600-2,000** *S*

A pair of George III mahogany armchairs, with stuffed backs, arms and seat, c1770. **£4,000-5,000** *S*

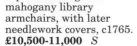

A pair of George III mahogany library armchairs, with later needlework covers, c1765. **£10,500-11,000** *S*

A pair of George III mahogany open armchairs, in the French manner, covered in associated 18thC Aubusson tapestry, restored. **£16,500-18,000** *C*

A Regency mahogany plate canterbury, c1820, 25in (63cm). **£2,500-3,000** *S*

A pair of George III mahogany armchairs, c1780.
£10,000-11,000 *S*

A set of 9 George III mahogany chairs, c1770.
£4,000-4,500 *S*

An early George III carved mahogany armchair, with flower carved arms and supports, c1760.
£3,000-4,000 *S*

A pair of giltwood fauteuils, with carved moulded channelled frames, with clasp cresting and centres to the seat rails, on cabriole legs stamped, BAUVE.
£12,500-15,000 *C*

A George II carved mahogany armchair, with later wool floral needlework, c1750.
£6,500-7,000 *S*

A pair of George III mahogany armchairs, c1770.
£4,700-6,000 *S*

A matched pair of Anglo-Dutch mahogany metamorphic wing-backed open armchairs, each with hinged back and seat, in later leather covers, opening to a daybed, restored, mid-18thC, 84in (213cm) long extended.
£21,000-23,000 *C*

A Louis XIV Franco-Flemish armchair, covered in painted leather, c1680.
£3,500-4,500 *S*

A George II carved mahogany armchair, in the style of Thomas Chippendale, with drop-in seat, on carved cabriole front legs with claw-and-ball feet, c1755.
£9,500-10,500 *S*

r. A Queen Anne walnut armchair, with pierced vase splat, the arms with shepherd's crook supports, drop-in seat, on cabriole front legs, c1710.
£3,500-4,500 *S*

A Regency mahogany metamorphic library armchair/steps, in the manner of Morgan and Sanders, c1810.
£4,600-5,000 *S*

A set of 6 satinwood and painted open armchairs, each splat painted with a mythological figure, restored.
£10,000-12,000 *C*

A Regency mahogany
library bergère, repaired.
£15,500-17,000 *C*

A George I walnut needle-
point wing armchair, repaired
c1720. **£32,000-35,000**
S(NY)

A pair of early George III mahogany
armchairs, with carved and pierced
splats. **£10,000-12,000** *S*

A walnut wing armchair,
one foot spliced, labelled.
£7,500-9,000 *C*

A George I wing
armchair, some
restoration.
£3,000-3,500 *Bea*

A George III
mahogany framed
and buttoned
leather porter's
armchair, c1780.
£2,500-3,000 *S*

A George III mahogany
wing armchair, c1770.
£3,000-4,000 *S*

A Queen Anne walnut
wing armchair, restored.
£9,000-11,000 *C*

A pair of mid-Victorian
ebonised spoonback
chairs. **£3,600-4,000** *C*

A set of 6 Regency chinoiserie
japanned armchairs, with caned seats,
c1805. **£14,000-15,000** *S*

A set of 9 George III mahogany
dining chairs, c1790.
£9,500-10,500 *S*

A George II walnut
armchair, c1750.
£1,500-2,000 *S*

A George II mahogany wing armchair, with carved front cabriole legs, c1730.
£9,000-10,000 *S*

A pair of walnut bergères, with channelled cabriole legs, restored.
£4,000-5,000 *C*

An assembled suite of Empire mahogany and parcel gilt seat furniture, early 19thC, 3 pieces.
£4,500-5,500 *S(NY)*

A Regency caned mahogany bergère, with anthemion carved toprail, scrolled arms and leaf carved front legs, c1815.
£7,000-8,000 *S*

A pair of ormolu mounted mahogany bergères, the moulded frames mounted with entrelac, very distressed cover, late 19thC. **£12,500-15,000** *C*

A Louis XV white painted and gilded bergère, stamped I.B. Boulard.
£8,000-9,000 *C*

A William IV mahogany bergère, in leather cover, c1830.
£3,500-4,000 *S*

A set of 8 walnut dining chairs, with velvet seat covers, extensively restored, part 18thC.
£12,500-15,000 *C*

A Queen Anne walnut easy chair, probably Rhode Island, c1770, 48in (122cm) high.
£23,000-25,000 *CNY*

l. A George IV caned mahogany library bergère, with panelled frame and circular reeded front legs, c1825.
£2,600-3,500 *S*

A set of 8 rosewood and gilt chairs, with curule legs set with bosses, c1810. **£14,000-16,000** *S*

A set of 14 Regency mahogany dining chairs, with curved toprail and crossbar, c1825. **£9,000-9,500** *S*

A set of 12 George III style mahogany 'Gothick' dining chairs, by Edwards & Roberts. **£16,000-16,500** *S(NY)*

A set of 14 mahogany dining chairs, with cabriole legs. **£14,500-15,000** *CSK*

A pair of Piedmontese giltwood chairs, with curved backs. **£9,000-9,500** *S*

A pair of George III mahogany hall chairs, c1805. **£1,500-2,000** *S*

A pair of George II mahogany hall armchairs, with solid shell shaped seats, on cabriole front and raked back legs, 40in (101cm) high. **£39,000-41,000** *C*

A set of 4 George II walnut side chairs, on cabriole legs with later eagle-head brackets, restored, c1745. **£20,000-25,000** *S(NY)*

A pair of George II mahogany hall chairs, c1766. **£4,000-5,000** *S*

A set of 8 grained rosewood and gilt dining chairs, c1810. **£12,000-12,500** *S*

A George III mahogany library bergère chair, c1780. **£3,500-4,000** *S*

A set of 6 mahogany dining chairs, c1815. **£2,500-3,000** *S*

A pair of George I style walnut dining chairs. **£450-500** *PCh*

A walnut and marquetry chest-on-stand, late 17thC and later, 48.5in (123cm) high.
£4,700-5,500 C

A William & Mary japanned chest-on-stand.
£4,000-6,000 C

An early Georgian walnut chest-on-chest, 69.5in (176cm) high. **£6,000-7,000** C

A George I burr walnut tallboy, with chevron and crossbanding, c1720, 70.5in (179cm) high.
£10,500-12,000 S

A Queen Anne walnut veneered chest, with pine sides, c1710.
£2,000-2,500 S

A George II walnut veneered tallboy, c1730, 69in (175cm) high. **£6,500-7,500** S

A William & Mary oyster veneered walnut and marquetry chest, on later bun feet, 37.5in (95cm).
£5,500-6,500 Bea

A George III mahogany chest-on-chest. **£9,500-10,500** S(NY)

A George III mahogany chest, on scroll bracket feet, c1760, 36in (92cm).
£4,000-5,000 S

A George I inlaid burr walnut bachelor's chest, restored.
£5,500-6,500 S(NY)

l. A William & Mary walnut and marquetry chest-on-stand, with elaborate floral inlay, 2 short and 3 long drawers, the stand with an inlaid drawer, restored, c1690, 51in (129cm) high.
£16,500-18,000 S

A George I walnut bachelor's chest, in feather banded wood, c1720, 36in (92cm).
£17,500-20,000 S

A German walnut chest of drawers, with 4 long drawers and cabriole feet, c1740, 36in (92cm). **£11,000-12,000** *S*

A parcel gilt walnut chest, North German or Danish, mid-18thC, later marble top, 34.5in (87cm). **£20,000-22,000** *S*

An Irish Georgian mahogany blanket chest-on-stand, the stand with 2 drawers and a carved apron, cabriole front legs with claw feet, mid-18thC. **£2,700-3,500** *S*

A pair of George III serpentine mahogany chests, c1770, 44in (111cm). **£5,800-6,500** *S*

A mahogany veneered chest, on turned feet, mid-19thC, 13.5in (34cm). **£150-200** *PCh*

A Victorian mahogany military chest, with recessed handles, on turned legs. **£1,000-1,200** *PCh*

A Hepplewhite period yew wood secrétaire chest. **£8,000-9,000** *SHO*

A Genoese walnut chest, the 4 panelled drawers with cherub head handles, with carved decoration, late 17thC, 60.5in (153cm). **£9,000-10,000** *S*

A walnut and crossbanded chest, on later cabriole feet, possibly Swedish, c1720, 28in (72cm). **£8,000-9,000** *S(S)*

A Regency mahogany bowfront chest, c1800, 28.5in (72cm). **£2,000-2,500** *S*

A Wellington chest, early 20thC, 42in (107cm) high. **£350-400** *N(A)*

A German parquetry chest, with serpentine front, 3 long drawers, carved projecting corners and paw feet, mid-18thC, 43in (109cm). **£7,200-8,000** *S*

An Italian walnut chest of drawers, of inverted breakfront form, with panelled top and 4 long drawers, 35in (90cm). **£5,500-6,500** *S*

A George III pair of semi-circular harewood commodes, crossbanded in satinwood, c1780, 33in (84cm) high. **£5,000-6,000** *S*

A satinwood serpentine commode, crossbanded overall in amaranth, with one mahogany lined and 3 cedar lined drawers, on splayed bracket feet, restored, 41in (104cm). **£4,700-5,500** *C*

A Louis XV ormolu mounted kingwood and tulipwood marquetry commode, mid-18thC, 31in (78.5cm). **£9,000-10,000** *S(NY)*

A Louis XV ormolu mounted tulipwood parquetry commode, with marble top, signed M. Criard, 34in (86cm). **£5,000-6,000** *S(NY)*

A George II mahogany chest of drawers, c1755, 38.5in (98cm). **£3,000-4,000** *S*

A pair of George III sycamore, rosewood and tulipwood inlaid satinwood commodes, on moulded plinths, composed in part of 18thC elements, 50in (127cm) long. **£18,500-20,000** *S(NY)*

A Louis XV ormolu mounted tulipwood commode, signed P. Roussel, JME, mid-18thC. **£5,500-6,500** *S(NY)*

A Louis XV ormolu mounted amaranth and marquetry bombé commode, restored, stamped J.C. ELLEAUME JME. **£6,500-7,500** *C*

A French Louis XV kingwood serpentine commode, with moulded breccia marble top, 2 drawers veneered with end-cut marquetry and overlaid with acanthus, alterations, c1750, 55in (139cm). **£12,500-14,000** *S*

A George III marble top inlaid satinwood and harewood demi-lune commode, with marble top. **£6,000-7,000** *S(NY)*

r. A Louis XV ormolu mounted lacquer commode, with serpentine moulded marble top above 2 veneered doors with a rural scene in tones of gold on a black ground, with scrolled ormolu sabots, distressed, mid-18thC, 42in (107cm). **£52,000-60,000** *S(NY)*

302

A painted and lacca povera commode, with a marble top, Southern French or North Italian, mid-18thC. **£22,500-25,000** *S*

A North Italian walnut inlaid commode, c1790, 49in (124cm). **£15,500-17,000** *S*

A Louis XVI tulipwood commode, with grey marble top, c1780, 44in (111cm). **£6,500-7,500** *S*

An early George III serpentine fronted mahogany chest, the top with gadrooned edge, c1760, 44in (111cm). **£8,000-10,000** *S*

A George III satinwood and marquetry demi-lune commode, c1775. **£132,000-135,000** *S*

A pair of German rococo walnut and tulipwood commodes. **£81,000-85,000** *CNY*

A German rococo brass mounted kingwood commode, with marble top, restored. **£8,000-10,000** *CNY*

A Louis XV ormolu mounted tulipwood, kingwood and fruitwood marquetry commode. **£28,000-30,000** *S(NY)*

An Italian marquetry commode, c1830, 52in (132cm). **£4,000-6,000** *S*

A Louis XV/XVI ormolu mounted tulipwood and fruitwood marquetry commode, with marble top, signed M.B.Evald, late 18thC, 37in (94cm). **£8,500-10,000** *S(NY)*

A French mahogany commode, after the model by Beneman and Stockel, locked shut, c1910. **£6,500-8,000** *S*

r. A pair of German parquetry commodes, each with a rectangular top, inlaid with panels of lozenge parquetry, c1785. **£17,000-18,000** *S*

A satinwood davenport, English, c1830, 22in (26cm). **£2,500-3,000** *S*

A George IV mahogany writing desk, c1820, 36in (91cm). **£3,000-3,500** *S*

A Victorian walnut kidney shaped desk, with moulded top and 8 drawers, c1840, 51.5in (131cm). **£10,000-15,000** *S*

A George IV mahogany Carlton House desk, with hinged bookrest above 3 drawers and turned legs, c1820, 55in (140cm). **£8,500-9,000** *S*

A George III satinwood and later gilt tambour top writing desk, crossbanded in mahogany, restored, 42.5in (108cm). **£4,000-5,000** *S(S)*

A George IV rosewood davenport, inlaid overall with boxwood lines, 18in (46cm). **£2,000-2,500** *C*

A Franco-Flemish marquetry and ebony kneehole desk, with 5 small drawers within hinged cover and fall front, 40in (102cm). **£7,000-8,000** *S(S)*

A German rococo walnut and parquetry cylinder desk, on cabriole legs and scroll feet, late 18thC, 47in (119cm). **£26,500-27,500** *CNY*

A Victorian mahogany partners' desk, with leather lined moulded top above 3 drawers, and 3 drawers in each pedestal, 67.5in (172cm). **£4,000-5,000** *S*

A burr walnut veneered kidney shaped walnut desk, with leather lined top, 7 drawers and ebonised mouldings, 60in (153cm). **£10,000-11,000** *S*

A George II walnut wall mirror, c1730, 30in (75cm) high. **£2,750-3,250** *S*

A George II parcel gilt walnut wall mirror, 31in (79cm) high. **£3,000-3,500** *S*

A walnut mirror, c1730, 41in (104cm) high. **£2,000-2,500** *S*

A William and Mary seaweed marquetry mirror, with bands of scrolling foliage, with a barber's pole moulding, 31.5in (80cm) high. **£4,000-4,500** *Bea*

A pair of George II giltwood pier mirrors, each with coat-of-arms and eagle's heads, 64in (163cm) high. **£22,000-24,000** *S(NY)*

A giltwood and gesso mirror, c1730, 43in (110cm) high. **£6,000-7,000** *S*

A giltwood wall mirror, c1725, 60in (151cm) high. **£4,000-4,500** *S*

A George I giltwood pier mirror, c1715, 49in (124cm) high. **£4,500-5,000** *S*

A pair of George II giltwood mirrors in the Kent style, repaired, 76.5in (194cm) high. **£100,000-120,000** *C*

A George I giltwood wall mirror, with leaf decorated moulded frame, 33in (84cm) high. **£8,500-9,000** *S*

A George I, James Moore style, giltwood wall mirror, 55.5in (141cm) high. **£17,000-20,000** *S*

A Queen Anne giltwood wall mirror, c1710, 36in (90cm) high. **£4,000-4,500** *S*

COLOUR REVIEW

A George II giltwood and plaster overmantel mirror, c1755.
£5,000-6,000 *S*

A pair of George III giltwood oval mirrors, each with later plate.
£9,000-11,000 *C*

A George III giltwood mirror, restored.
£5,000-6,000 *C*

A George II carved giltwood mirror, c1755, 62in (157cm) high.
£6,800-8,000 *S*

A Scottish giltwood pier mirror, late 18thC, 67in (170cm) high.
£12,000-14,000 *S*

A George II giltwood wall mirror, c1730, 34in (86cm) high.
£3,000-4,000 *S*

A George III giltwood pier mirror, c1755.
£13,000-14,000 *S(NY)*

A George III giltwood mirror.
£10,000-12,000 *S(NY)*

A pair of George III giltwood mirrors.
£12,500-13,500 *C*

A George II giltwood wall mirror, c1730.
£3,000-4,000 *S*

A pair of Queen Anne giltwood wall mirrors, with replaced plates, c1710, 51in (130cm) high.
£11,000-12,000 *S*

A George III giltwood wall mirror, the frame carved with rococo scrolls and flowers, c1765, 55.5in (141cm) high.
£6,000-7,000 *S*

A giltwood wall mirror, c1755.
£7,000-8,000 *S*

A Queen Anne
black japanned
toilet mirror,
c1705.
£2,500-3,500 *S*

An Italian gilt
framed mirror.
£1,700-2,500
S(S)

A mahogany shield shaped
box base toilet mirror, with 3
drawers, early 19thC.
£175-250 *PCh*

A Swedish Baroque polychrome
painted dressing mirror, early
18thC, 30.5in (77cm) high.
£23,000-25,000 *CNY*

A Scandinavian ebonised
and tortoiseshell mirror.
£3,500-4,500 *C*

A Spanish mirror, c1680, 67.5in
(171cm) high.
£24,500-26,000 *S*

A pair of Venetian mirrors, in a
framework of engraved glass panels,
c1700. **£66,500-68,000** *S*

An Irish oval wall
mirror, early 19thC.
£4,000-5,000 *S*

A German black and gilt
japanned mirror, early
18thC, 57.5in (146cm) high.
£4,000-6,000 *C*

A George III giltwood overmantel
mirror, 48in (122cm) high.
£5,500-6,500 *C*

A George II carved grey
painted wall mirror, c1750,
68.5in (173cm) high.
£23,500-25,000 *S*

A mahogany sideboard, c1780, 66.5in (169cm). **£4,000-4,500** *S*

A satinwood inlaid mahogany sideboard, c1780, 60in (163cm). **£10,000-10,500** *S(NY)*

A George III mahogany bowfront sideboard, c1780. **£6,000-7,000** *S*

A George III inlaid sideboard, 18thC, 62in (157cm). **£9,000-10,000** *S(NY)*

A George III mahogany sideboard, c1780, 84in (214cm). **£10,000-11,000** *S*

A mahogany serpentine sideboard, remodelled, 18thC, 71in (181cm). **£4,500-5,000** *S*

A George III mahogany bowfront sideboard, c1785, 72in (183cm). **£9,000-10,000** *S*

A George III mahogany sideboard, c1800, 66in (168cm). **£3,000-4,000** *S*

A George III bowfront mahogany sideboard, c1780, 66.5in (169cm). **£5,000-6,000** *S*

A George IV bowed breakfront mahogany sideboard, c1820, 84in (214cm). **£2,500-3,000** *S*

A George III painted sofa, with stuffed back, arms and seat, the beaded frieze on reeded circular legs, 88in (224cm) long. **£2,000-2,500** *S*

A George III mahogany camel back sofa, with stuffed back, arms and seat, Chinese fret legs and stretchers, c1760. **£6,500-7,500** *S*

A George III mahogany sofa, with stuffed back, arms and seat, on 3 square front legs with stretchers, c1770. **£5,500-7,000** *S*

A George II carved mahogany settee, with upholstered back, arms and drop-in seat, mid-18thC, 62in (157cm) long. **£8,000-9,000** *S(NY)*

A George III mahogany settee, with needlework upholstery, on stop fluted square chamfered legs, restored, c1770, 96in (246cm) long. **£6,500-7,500** *S(NY)*

A George II walnut settee, with out-turned arms terminating in lion's heads, carved cabriole legs, c1740. **£4,000-5,000** *S(NY)*

A Queen Anne giltwood sofa, the wing back and out-scrolled arms detachable from the padded seat, restored, c1700, 99in (252cm) long. **£3,000-5,000** *S*

A George II mahogany double chair back settee, restored, c1755, 55in (140cm) long. **£9,500-10,500** *S*

A George III fine carved mahogany sofa, with serpentine back and seat, moulded padded arms and 4 fluted circular front legs, c1780, 81in (205cm) long. **£9,500-11,000** *S*

A Swedish painted and parcel-gilt sofa, perhaps by Ephraim Ståhl, c1810, 92in (233cm) long. **£4,500-6,000** *S*

An Italian neo-classic beechwood settee, with loose cushion seat, on circular tapering stop-fluted legs headed by paterae, 79in (200cm) long. **£4,500-5,000** *CNY*

Two mahogany camel back sofas, one mid-18thC, one modern, 86in (218cm) long. **£9,000-10,000** *S*

A carved mahogany couch or window seat, probably Scandinavian, c1830, 94in (238cm) long. **£12,000-13,000** *S*

A suite of giltwood furniture, comprising a sofa and 8 armchairs, with piastre moulded frames, Rome or Turin, c1780, 98in (249cm) long. **£50,000-70,000** *S*

A Victorian walnut double backed settee, with serpentine seat, cabriole legs, scroll feet with ceramic casters. **£1,000-1,500** *SHO*

An Italian grey painted settle, with putti and a winged angel, late 17thC, 84in (213cm) long. **£14,500-15,500** *C*

A Venetian cream painted and parcel gilt sofa, painted overall with flowers, on cabriole legs, damaged and restored, mid-18thC, 87.5in (222cm) long. **£3,250-4,000** *C*

A Louis XV beechwood marquise, with flower carved moulded frame, cabriole legs, possibly reduced from a sofa, mid-18thC, 34in (86cm). **£3,500-4,500** *S*

A mahogany sofa, covered in yellow silk, with scrolled terminal arms and acanthus headed cabriole legs, 62.5in (159cm). **£4,500-5,500** *C*

A George III mahogany low whatnot, with 3 shelves and slatted ends, the tapering legs with brass caps and casters, c1800, 29.5in (75cm) wide.
£2,000-3,000 *S*

A George IV mahogany stick stand, c1820, 28in (71cm).
£5,000-5,500 *S*

A George II mahogany two-tier dumb waiter, with revolving tiers, c1760, 35in (89cm) high.
£4,500-5,500 *S*

A George IV mahogany whatnot, with bead and reel turned frame, c1820, 40in (101cm) high.
£2,500-3,000 *S*

A George III mahogany whatnot, c1800, 52in (130cm).
£3,500-4,500 *S*

A George III mahogany whatnot, 60in (152cm).
£2,000-2,500 *S*

A Regency mahogany two-tier dumb waiter, c1810, 27.5in (70cm) diam.
£3,000-3,500 *S*

A George III mahogany dumb waiter, c1780, 46in (117cm) high.
£2,200-3,000 *S*

A George IV mahogany four-tier whatnot, with drawer, c1820, 60.5in (154cm) high.
£1,500-2,000 *S*

A mahogany four-tier whatnot, with drawer, 19thC.
£550-650 *WW*

A Swiss or Austrian carved wood hall stand, late 19thC, 85in (216cm) high.
£1,200-1,800 *S(S)*

An Empire giltwood tabouret pliant, on
channelled carved X-shaped supports,
restored, later seat base, 25.5in (65cm).
£8,500-9,500 *C*

A pair of Italian neo-classic green painted and parcel gilt
tabourets, with panelled carved seat rails, on circular
tapering legs, both seat rails branded MR, late 18thC.
£10,500-11,500 *CNY*

A painted stool, with Louis-
Philippe's inventory mark, LP
beneath a crown, c1800.
£2,700-3,700 *S*

A pair of Dutch
walnut stools, c1720,
17in (43cm).
£11,500-12,500 *S*

A Louis XVI painted stool, with loose
cushioned seat, c1780, 30.5in (77cm).
£3,000-3,500 *S*

A pair of Regency marble
mounted parcel gilt
rosewood pedestals,
c1820, 37in (94cm) high.
£8,000-9,000 *S(NY)*

A George II style carved
and silver painted stool,
c1920, 36in (92cm).
£2,200-3,000 *S(S)*

A monumental Regency giltwood stool, with
needlework covered drop-in seat, leaf carved legs
on block bases, damaged, 29in (74cm).
£13,000-14,000 *C*

A pair of North European
white painted and parcel gilt
window seats, with cane filled
arms and seats, late 18thC.
£2,750-3,750 *C*

r. A George II walnut stool, with
contemporary embroidery drop-
in seat cover, 18in (46cm).
£8,000-8,500 *S*

A pair of Empire mahogany tabourets,
carved with laurel leaves, joined by
baluster shaped stretchers with claw feet,
early 19thC, 20in (51cm).
£6,500-7,500 *S(NY)*

A pair of George II red
walnut stools, restored,
c1740, 32in (55cm).
£11,000-12,000 *S*

r. A pair of
William IV
mahogany
stools, with
rococo
carving,
c1835, 24in
(61cm).
£4,000-5,000
S

312

A George III serpentine mahogany card table, c1770, 37in (94cm). **£3,000-3,500** *S*

An Irish Georgian walnut card table, with candlestand corners and counter wells, c1740. **£3,000-4,000** *S*

A George II concertina action card table, the cabriole legs with foliate cabochons, c1755. **£2,500-3,000** *S*

A Dutch marquetry and mahogany card table, the fold-over top revealing a baize inset and playing card motifs, the frieze and sides with drawers, on cabriole legs with claw-and-ball feet, c1750, 30in (76cm). **£3,500-4,000** *S(S)*

A pair of George III inlaid satinwood crossbanded and painted demi-lune card tables, each hinged flap opening to reveal a baize lined surface, minor restorations to veneers, decoration of a later date, late 18thC, 38.5in (97cm) wide. **£25,000-30,000** *S(NY)*

A pair of George III rosewood card tables, each with a fold-over top above a boxwood strung frieze, c1790, 38in (96.5cm). **£6,000-7,000** *S(Ch)*

An Irish Georgian card table, with baize lined interior, candlestands and counter wells mid-18thC, and a modern copy. **£3,000-3,500** *S*

A George III satinwood and marquetry card table, the top crossbanded in mahogany, c1775, 36in (92cm). **£2,000-2,500** *S*

A George II concertina action card table, with interior candlestands and wells, c1740, 33in (84cm). **£2,000-2,500** *S*

A late Louis XVI mahogany card table, with hinged semi-circular top and square tapering legs, 44in (112cm). **£3,000-4,000** *S*

A William and Mary walnut card table, with crossbanded top, restored, c1690, 30.5in (78cm). **£7,000-8,000** *S*

313

A George IV brass inlaid rosewood card table, with swivel top, c1820, 36in (92cm). **£3,500-4,500** *S*

A pair of satinwood card tables, the fold-over tops crossbanded in rosewood, c1825, 35.5in (90cm). **£3,500-5,000** *S*

An ebonised and inlaid fold-over top card table, the top with brass reeded border, on 4 turned supports, early 19thC, 35.5in (90cm). **£600-650** *PCh*

A Regency amboyna, maple, bird's-eye maple, specimen-wood and parcel gilt centre table, with tilt-top, 52.5in (133cm) diam. **£25,000-27,000** *C*

A late George II mahogany centre table, with associated crossbanded top, c1755, 25.5in (64cm). **£15,500-16,500** *S*

A George IV pollard elm and marquetry card table, with swivel top, c1820, 36in (92cm). **£2,500-3,500** *S*

A pair of William IV mahogany card tables, with swivel crossbanded tops, c1835, 36in (92cm). **£3,500-4,000** *S*

A Russian brass mounted mahogany, walnut and marquetry card table, late 18thC. **£5,000-6,000** *C*

A pair of late George III mahogany card tables, c1805, 36in (92cm). **£3,500-4,500** *S*

A Regency mahogany centre table, with 2 frieze drawers each side, 45in (114cm). **£5,000-6,000** *C*

A pair of George III giltwood consoles, with white marble tops, restored, c1770, 44.5in (114cm). **£36,000-40,000** *S(NY)*

A Regency calamander and coromandel banded centre table, 54in (137cm). **£3,500-4,500** *Bon*

314

A Restauration mahogany centre table, with granite top, c1825, 43.5in (110cm) diam. **£7,000-9,000** *S*

A William IV brass mounted parcel gilt rosewood and burr elm centre table, c1835, 51.5in (131cm). **£9,000-11,000** *S(NY)*

A Restauration mahogany centre table, with marble top, stamped Jacob, c1830, 37.5in (96cm). **£34,500-35,500** *S*

An Empire centre table, attributed to Jacob-Desmalter, after a design by Percier and Fontaine, c1805, 36in (91cm) diam. **£36,500-40,000** *S*

A William IV rosewood centre table, the top inlaid with squares of specimen marble and hardstone, c1835, 31in (79cm). **£19,000-20,000** *S*

A George IV brass inlaid rosewood centre table, with tilt-top banded with foliage, 60in (152cm) diam. **£6,500-7,500** *C*

A mahogany and gilt brass mounted centre table, 24in (61cm) diam. **£2,000-3,000** *Bea*

A brass inlaid mahogany centre table, c1820, 31.5in (80cm). **£2,500-3,000** *S*

A George IV mahogany centre or breakfast table, with rosewood crossbanding to top, c1820, 56in (142cm) diam. **£6,500-7,500** *S*

A Regency giltwood centre table, with moulded marble top and heavily carved supports, some damage, 36in (92cm). **£20,000-25,000** *S(NY)*

A George II mahogany concertina action card table, banded in pearwood, c1740. **£4,500-5,500** *S*

A Regency mahogany breakfast table, the tilt-top with reeded edge, repaired, 59in (150cm) diam. **£7,000-8,000** *C*

A George III crossbanded satinwood card table, c1785. **£4,000-5,000** *S*

A pair of Italian giltwood stools, with serpentine stuffed seats, the moulded front seat rails centred by rococo cartouches, on cabriole legs, mid-18thC, 21.5in (55cm). **£5,500-6,500** *S*

A George III mahogany architect's table, c1765, 36in (92cm). **£3,000-3,500** *S*

A George III mahogany card table, crossbanded in satinwood and veneered in segments, c1780. **£2,500-3,500** *S*

A George III mahogany breakfast table, the finely figured top with a broad mahogany crossbanding, restored, 60in (152cm) long. **£3,000-4,000** *S*

A pair of Swedish painted stools, c1800, 15in (39cm) wide. **£3,000-3,500** *S*

A George IV brass inlaid rosewood veneered card table, the top crossbanded in calamander, c1820. **£3,000-3,500** *S*

An Italian giltwood stool, the sides and legs ornately carved, possibly Sicilian, mid-18thC, 24in (61cm) wide. **£7,000-8,000** *C*

An Italian neo-classic walnut and parquetry card table, with inlaid playing surface, late 18thC, 35in (89cm). **£7,000-8,000** *CNY*

A Regency style mahogany dining table, the top inlaid with ebony lines, with downward reeded base, 54in (137cm). **£5,500-6,500** *S*

An early George III mahogany twin pedestal dining table, with one leaf, on turned spreading shafts, 77.5in (197cm). **£10,000-15,000** *C*

A George III mahogany three-pedestal dining table, c1810 and later, 126in (320cm) extended. **£8,500-12,000** *S*

An Anglo-Irish mahogany two-pedestal dining table, with reeded edge, c1825, 80.4in (204cm) extended. **£5,000-7,000** *S*

A Venetian walnut marquetry dressing table, c1770, 38.5in (98cm). **£12,000-15,000** *S*

A George II mahogany triple-top games table, with baize lined interior, c1740, 34.5in (88cm). **£2,750-3,750** *S*

A Dutch fruitwood and marquetry centre table. **£3,000-5,000** *C*

A George III mahogany games table, c1805. **£4,000-4,500** *S*

A Venetian black japanned dressing table, mid-18thC. **£6,500-7,500** *S*

A George IV mahogany twin-pedestal dining table, with later extra leaf, restored, top and bottom possibly associated. **£5,500-7,000** *C*

A French kingwood extending table, c1920. **£4,500-5,500** *S*

A George III mahogany Wilkinson's patent dining table, with 3 leaves, c1810, 88.5in (224cm) extended. **£8,000-10,000** *S*

An Irish Regency mahogany draw-leaf pedestal dining table, leaf scratched, c1820, 72in (183cm) extended. **£4,000-5,000** *S*

A pair of marble inset rosewood
tables, c1840, 36in (91cm).
£9,000-10,000 *S*

A rosewood and calamander library
table, c1805. **£8,500-10,000** *S*

An red tortoiseshell
boulle occasional table,
c1850. **£4,500-5,000** *S*

A Regency inlaid mahogany library table,
restored, c1820, 66in (168cm) long.
£7,000-10,000 *S(NY)*

A Federal mahogany library table, with inset green
leather lining, Boston, early 19thC, 85in (216cm) long.
£9,000-12,000 *CNY*

A Charles X ormolu mounted
rosewood guéridon, mid-
19thC, 33in (84cm) diam.
£9,000-11,000 *S(NY)*

A George IV mahogany
library table, with curved
ends, 2 drawers, and
spindle filled end
supports, c1820, 40in
(102cm).
£3,000-3,500 *S*

A marble topped
rosewood occasional
table, 25in (63cm)
diam. **£2,200-3,000** *S*

A George IV
occasional table,
c1820.
£1,500-2,000 *S*

l. A parquetry games
table, German or
Austrian, mid-18thC.
£8,000-10,000 *S*

r. A mahogany 3-
pillar dining table,
c1820, 123.5in
(314cm).
£18,250-20,000 *S*

l. A mahogany library
table, with moulded
leather lined top, 3
drawers and pierced fret
brackets, c1770, 59.5in
(151cm) long.
£7,000-8,000 *S*

r. A pair of mahogany
toilet tables, each with
divided top enclosing
apertures and rising
mirror, c1770.
£17,500-19,000 *S*

A pair of George III inlaid mahogany tulipwood and rosewood crossbanded Pembroke tables, c1770, one pair of stretchers later. **£19,000-23,000** *S(NY)*

A George IV marble topped pedestal table, c1825. **£2,500-3,000** *S*

A pair of George IV mahogany pier tables, c1820, 42in (106cm). **£4,250-5,000** *S*

A pair of George III harewood and satinwood oval occasional tables, c1780, 16.5in (42cm). **£3,000-4,000** *S(S)*

A pair of Italian neo-classic walnut night tables, each with a frieze drawer and hinged fall front, on square tapering legs, 16in (41cm). **£12,500-14,000** *CNY*

A George III inlaid satinwood Pembroke table, late 18thC. **£4,000-5,000** *S(NY)*

A Regency brass mounted ebony Pembroke table, early 19thC. **£18,500-20,000** *S(NY)*

A pair of Federal mahogany Pembroke tables, each with 2 drop leaves, a single long drawer with incised moulded edge, on square tapering legs, New York, c1800, 30in (76cm) long. **£5,000-6,000** *CNY*

A Russian ormolu mounted Empire centre table. **£12,000-14,000** *C*

A satinwood veneered Pembroke table, c1780. **£3,000-4,000** *S*

An English serpentine mahogany centre table, in Chippendale style, 42in (106cm) long. **£3,000-5,000** *S*

l. A George III oval satinwood Pembroke table, the moulded top crossbanded in tulipwood, c1775, 35in (89cm) extended. **£6,500-8,000** *S*

A George III yew wood Pembroke table, the twin flap top crossbanded with mahogany, 38in (97cm) open **£7,500-8,500** *C*

A pair of George IV pier tables, c1820, 26.5in (68cm).
£2,300-2,500 *S*

A George IV mahogany side or serving table, the moulded frieze with a drawer, on carved scrolling front legs, 88in (224cm) wide.
£3,500-4,000 *S*

A George III mahogany serving table, with rosewood crossbanded top, 36in (92cm) wide.
£2,000-2,500 *S*

A Dutch satinwood centre table, inlaid with sycamore, c1790, 40in (102cm) wide.
£2,200-2,500 *S(S)*

A George III harewood Pembroke table, c1780, 35in (89cm) wide open.
£2,000-2,500 *S*

A pair of giltwood pier tables, in the manner of Thomas Johnson, each with removable marble tops supported on a tree with rocky base, 19thC, 33in (84cm) wide.
£30,000-32,000 *S*

A William IV mahogany side table, c1830, 96in (243cm).
£7,000-9,000 *S*

An Anglo-Indian rosewood veneered library table, c1830, 60in (152cm).
£3,200-3,600 *S*

A satinwood Pembroke table, c1785. **£3,000-3,500** *S*

A George III painted mahogany Pembroke table, c1780, 40in (102cm).
£5,000-6,000 *S*

A pair of Italian carved giltwood pier tables, depicting Summer and Autumn, c1800, 34in (87cm) wide.
£27,000-30,000 *S*

A pair of George IV mahogany side tables, with brown English marble top, 72.5in (184cm) wide.
£4,000-5,000 *C*

A Regency ebonised and parcel gilt console table, c1810, 50in (127cm).
£3,200-3,800 *S*

A George I walnut lowboy, restored, c1715, 30in (76cm).
£6,500-7,500 *S*

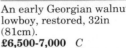

An early Georgian walnut lowboy, restored, 32in (81cm).
£6,500-7,000 *C*

A pair of Portuguese rosewood side tables, each with 2 drawers in the panelled frieze, part 18thC, 47.5in (121cm). **£7,000-8,000** *S*

An Irish George II style mahogany side table, c1900, the top possibly associated, 55in (140cm).
£4,500-6,000 *C*

A George III satinwood and marquetry side table, the top crossbanded in kingwood, c1775, 68in (173cm). **£6,000-7,000** *S*

A George II mahogany side table, c1730, 27.5in (70cm). **£4,500-5,000** *S*

A Regency plum pudding mahogany side table, the top banded in amboyna, 42in (106.5cm).
£4,500-5,500 *C*

A pair of Louis XV rococo painted console tables, each with serpentine fronted moulded white marble top, possibly reduced in size, 28.5in (72cm).
£7,000-8,000 *S(NY)*

A George III mahogany Pembroke table, by George Simson, with flame figured top, the drawer with maker's label, 40in (101.5cm).
£8,500-10,000 *S*

A George II mahogany lowboy, c1740.
£3,500-4,000 *S*

A Queen Anne gilt gesso side table, restored and re-gilt, c1710.
£2,200-2,600 *S*

A George III rosewood sofa table, the top with partridgewood banding between double lines of boxwood, 63in (160cm) long. **£13,000-15,000** *S*

A carved giltwood side table, with painted top, and carved legs, Italian or Austrian, mid-18thC, 66in (168cm). **£2,500-3,000** *S*

A Restauration mahogany centre table, c1820. **£3,500-4,500** *S*

A Regency ebonised and bird's-eye maple sofa table, restored, 58.5in (148cm). **£4,000-6,000** *C*

A Régence ormolu mounted boulle marquetry side table, with marble top, the front and sides veneered with panels of boulle marquetry and brass, c1725, 39in (99cm).
£200,000-225,000 *S(NY)*

A George III mahogany 3-pedestal dining table, with 3 additional leaves, late 18thC. **£12,000-15,000** *S(NY)*

A Restauration parcel gilt mahogany centre table, c1825, 38in (97cm) diam.
£14,000-16,000 *S*

A pair of Biedermeier Hungarian ashwood side tables. **£4,000-6,000** *S*

Two Roman carved giltwood side tables, with marble tops, c1730, 48.5in (123cm).
£21,000-23,000 *S*

A late George III rosewood sofa table, with amboyna and kingwood crossbandings, 56in (143cm). **£6,500-8,000** *S*

A George II mahogany card table, with a drawer, 32.5in (82cm). **£2,500-3,000** *S*

An Austrian walnut centre table, with parquetry top, mid-18thC. **£5,500-7,000** *S*

A Regency satinwood veneered sofa table, cross-banded with calamander, c1810, 63.5in (161cm) open. **£4,000-4,500** *S*

A mahogany sofa table, on leaf carved reeded hipped sabre legs, part c1820, 58.5in (149cm) open. **£2,200-2,800** *S*

A George II mahogany tripod table, c1730. **£2,000-2,500** *S*

A George III japanned side table, chinoiserie decorated within floral borders, c1770. **£7,000-8,000** *S*

An inlaid mahogany tripod table. **£2,500-3,000** *C*

An early George III mahogany tripod table, with birdcage support. **£11,000-12,000** *C*

A George II mahogany tripod table, top split. **£4,000-5,000** *S*

A George II carved mahogany tripod table, c1755, 33in (84cm) diam. **£16,000-20,000** *S*

A Piedmontese giltwood console table, in the manner of Bonzanigo, late l8thC. **£7,000-8,000** *S*

An early George III mahogany tripod table, 24.5in (62cm) diam. **£22,000-24,000** *C*

A George II mahogany tripod table, c1755, 30in (76cm) diam. **£5,500-7,000** *S*

A Regency mahogany wine cooler, with metal liner, on paw feet, 39in (100cm) wide. **£20,000-21,000** *C*

A George III brass bound mahogany wine cooler, with metal liner, 20in (51cm) wide. **£9,000-10,000** *C*

A set of Edwardian library steps, converting to a chair. **£550-600** *JH*

A Victorian ormolu mounted hexagonal mahogany wine cooler, with pomegranate finial, 20in (51cm) wide. **£2,000-2,500** *C*

A mahogany cellaret, c1780, 21in (54cm) wide. **£2,500-3,000** *S*

A mahogany and iron library ladder, 19thC, 59in (150cm) high. **£2,500-3,000** *S*

A George III mahogany cellaret, c1780, 19.5in (50cm) wide. **£3,000-3,500** *S*

A pair of George III mahogany buckets, with pierced sides, brass band and liner, late 18thC, 13in (32cm) high. **£6,000-6,500** *S*

A mahogany cellaret, c1770, 19in (48cm) wide. **£3,500-4,000** *S*

A Regency mahogany wine cooler, restored, 29in (74cm) wide. **£4,000-4,500** *C*

An Irish mahogany brass bound turf bucket, mid-18thC. **£3,250-3,500** *S*

A five drawer chest, c1880, 42in (107cm). **£400-450** *UP*

A Co.Clare bed, c1820, 66 by 70in (168 by 178cm). **£1,000-1,700** *UP*

A harness cupboard, c1820, 60in (152cm). **£1,250-1,450** *UP*

A linen press, with brushing slide, c1790, 48 by 80in (122 by 203cm). **£1,250-1,350** *UP*

A housemaid's cupboard, c1890, 96in (244cm) high. **£1,000-1,600** *UP*

A bureau, c1780, 42in (107cm). **£1,500-1,750** *UP*

A Scandinavian chest of drawers, c1860, 48 by 50in (122 by 127cm). **£400-500** *RK*

A French glazed cupboard, c1870. **£950-1,200** *UP*

A French cupboard, c1870, 76in (193cm) high. **£1,250-1,350** *UP*

An English corner cupboard, c1770. **£600-650** *RK*

A breakfront bookcase, c1820, 168in (427cm) wide. **£2,200-2,400** *UP*

An Irish food cupboard, c1850, 58in (147cm) wide. **£1,250-1,350** *UP*

An Irish glazed cupboard, c1850, 82in (208cm) high. **£1,250-1,450** *UP*

A Welsh dresser, c1820, 58in (147cm) wide.
£1,000-1,400 *RK*

An Irish fiddle front dresser, c1820, 50in (127cm) wide.
£1,250-1,350 *UP*

A Scottish dresser, c1860, 52in (132cm) wide.
£500-600 *RK*

An Irish dresser, c1840, 78in (198cm) high. **£700-800** *RK*

An Irish dresser, c1850, 49in (124.5cm) wide.
£700-800 *RK*

An Irish dresser, c1880, 80in (203cm) high.
£600-700 *RK*

A Scottish dresser, c1860, 55in (139.5cm) wide.
£750-850 *RK*

An Irish dresser, c1860, 80in (203cm) high.
£750-850 *RK*

An Irish dresser, c1860, 60in (152cm) wide.
£1,650-1,850 *UP*

An Irish dresser, c1880, 52in (132cm) wide.
£850-950 *UP*

An Irish settle, c1880, 75in (190.5cm). **£400-450** *UP*

A French buffet, c1850, 52in
(132cm) wide.
£650-750 *UP*

An Irish cupboard, c1820,
54in (137cm) wide.
£800-900 *RK*

An English press cupboard,
c1840, 88in (223.5cm) high.
£700-800 *RK*

A single wardrobe, c1850,
40in (101.5cm) wide.
£550-650 *UP*

A Danish single door
wardrobe, c1870, 40in
(101.5cm). **£375-425** *RK*

A French buffet base, c1880, 44in (111.5cm)
wide. **£375-425** *UP*

An Irish four-door cupboard,
c1850, 65in (165cm).
£800-900 *RK*

A double wardrobe, c1890,
48in (122cm).
£450-500 *UP*

A Southern Irish corner
cupboard, c1850, 45in (114cm).
£1,000-1,200 *RK*

A set of 4 Coade stone figures representing The Seasons, designed by John Bacon, c1779, 73in (185cm) high. **£75,000-85,000** *S(S)*

A pair of carved stone urns, early 18thC, on associated plinth. **£7,000-8,000** *S(S)*

A Flemish marble figure of Minerva, early 18thC, 72in (183cm) high. **£41,000-45,000** *S(S)*

An Italian white marble fountain bowl-on-stand. **£2,200-3,000** *S(S)*

A bronze figure, early 20thC. **£5,200-6,000** *S(S)*

A pair of French cast iron figures of putti, late 19thC, 51in (130cm) high. **£5,000-6,000** *S(S)*

A carved sandstone model of a lion passant gardant, c1880, 85in (216cm) **£11,000-14,000** *S(S)*

l. A pair of Japanese bronze cranes, late 19thC, 81in (206cm) high. **£3,000-4,000** *S(S)*

Two matching serpentine brass fenders, pierced and engraved with unicorns and cherubs, mid-19thC, 53in (135cm) wide. **£5,500-6,000** *S*

An English marble chimney surround, early 19thC, 75in (190cm) wide. **£3,500-5,000** *S*

A Victorian steel fire curb and 3 steel and brass fire irons, c1860, 54.5in (138cm). **£1,200-1,500** *S*

A Regency Coalbrookdale floral pattern seat, seat rails damaged, 46in (116.5cm) wide. **£1,700-2,000** *SWO*

A George III steel basket grate, with Royal arms, 32.5in (82cm). **£1,500-2,000** *S*

A brass and steel basket grate and surround, c1800, 38in (96cm) wide. **£1,500-2,000** *S*

A set of 3 Regency brass fire irons, shovel 27.5in (70cm). **£1,200-1,300** *C*

A William IV brass fender, c1835, 35.5in (90cm). **£2,500-3,000** *S*

A set of 3 Regency steel fire irons, shovel 30in (75.5cm). **£700-800** *C*

A Regency cast-iron, steel and brass fire grate, by Burton & Co., of Roman sarcophagus shape, c1820, 33in (84cm). **£4,700-5,000** *S*

Sutherland Tables

A mahogany Sutherland table on turned legs and stretchers, mid-19thC, 33in (84cm).
£300-500 *GAK*

A Victorian rosewood and simulated rosewood Sutherland table, on tapering turned end supports with down-turned feet joined by pole stretchers, 42in (106.5cm).
£600-800 *Bea*

A Victorian mahogany double tier Sutherland table, lower tier 30in (76cm) extended.
£220-270 *LF*

A Victorian walnut Sutherland table with quarter veneered burr walnut oval top, spiral turned baluster end supports, on splayed legs with scroll toes and casters, 42in (106.5cm).
£650-850 *Bea*

A Victorian burr walnut miniature Sutherland table with carved dual stretchers and turned supports, 21in (53cm).
£550-600 *GAK*

Tea Tables

An inlaid mahogany semi-circular folding tea table, on double fly-leg action, late 18thC, 35in (89cm).
£750-900 *MJB*

A George II mahogany fold-over top table, with well interior, fitted single swinging leg, supported on 5 cabriole legs, the front with carved shell and swag motifs and shaped brackets, all supported on pad feet, top restored, 35in (89cm).
£2,500-3,000 *WIL*

A red walnut semi-circular folding tea table, early 18thC, 30in (76cm).
£800-1,000 *MJB*

A George III mahogany crossbanded with satinwood stringing, fold-over demi-lune tea table having double opening rear gateleg, on square tapering legs, 36in (92cm).
£1,000-1,500 *GH*

A George III mahogany tea table, on chamfered beaded square legs, restored, 35in (89cm).
£1,700-2,000 *CSK*

> In the Furniture section if there is only one measurement it usually refers to the width of the piece.

A Regency rosewood tea table with plain frieze and U-shaped support on a concave sided platform with 4 sabre feet, brass foliate caps and casters, 36in (92cm).
£900-1,200 *Bea*

A William IV rosewood D-shaped tea table, with beaded edge on turned lotus-carved shaft with gadrooned base and 4 acanthus carved splayed legs with scroll feet, 36in (92cm).
£1,500-2,000 *C*

A William IV rosewood tea table with D-shaped top and baluster-turned faceted shaft with lappeted base, on quadripartite platform with scroll feet, 42in (107cm).
£800-1,000 *CSK*

An early Victorian rosewood D-shaped tea table, the hinged top inlaid with butterflies and sprays of flowers, on cabochon carved baluster turned shaft and 4 floral headed cabriole legs with scroll feet, 39in (99cm).
£1,000-1,200 *CSK*

A Dutch mahogany tea table, the double fold-over breakfront top revealing a well with compartments, the frieze containing a small drawer, on fluted and stop-fluted tapered square legs ending in block feet, 31in (79cm).
£1,500-2,000 *S(S)*

A late George III mahogany fold-over tea table, on 4 turned columns and raised on quadruple platform base, with 4 reeded swept sabre supports, all having brass cappings and casters, 40in (101.5cm).
£900-1,200 *P(M)*

This table is probably Scottish, and is similar to the work of William Trotter, the Edinburgh cabinet maker.

A Scottish Regency mahogany, rosewood crossbanded, boxwood and ebony lined tea table, on bobbin turned tapering supports, 38in (97cm).
£750-950 *C(S)*

Tripod Tables

A mid-George III mahogany tripod table, with bird cage action lobed top, on vase turned shaft and 3 splayed legs, restored, 20.5in (51cm).
£1,200-1,500 *CSK*

A George III mahogany tripod table with bird cage action, the tip-up top above a baluster turned shaft, on hipped splayed legs with pad feet, 36in (92cm).
£1,000-1,200 *CSK*

A Dutch mahogany and marquetry inlaid tripod table, the tip-up top decorated with flowers, parrots and butterflies with a chequered border, on hipped splayed legs and pad feet, damaged, c1800, 29.5in (75cm).
£900-1,200 *CSK*

A Georgian red walnut bird cage top tripod table, c1780.
£800-900 *JAC*

A George III style mahogany tripod table, the shaped tilt-top on cabriole legs ending in egg and claw feet, 37.5in (95cm).
£650-950 *S(S)*

A George III mahogany tripod occasional table, with dished top above a bird cage and gun barrel turned column, on ogee supports and pad feet, 20in (50.5cm).
£1,200-1,700 *HCH*

Work Tables

A late Regency crossbanded work table in rosewood, with original silk bag, double fronted frieze and dummy drawers, 18in (46cm).
£1,500-1,800 *MJB*

A Regency rosewood work table with sliding well on column uprights with brass cappings, on dual splayed legs joined by a turned stretcher, 21in (53cm).
£1,000-1,200 *CSK*

A Regency rosewood crossbanded mahogany drop-leaf work table, with 2 frieze and 2 dummy drawers, the wooden sewing box re-covered, the table in need of further restoration, 32in (81cm) extended.
£800-1,200 *MJB*

A Victorian walnut games and work table, the burr walnut fold-over top set with a Tunbridge ware panel depicting Eridge Castle within geometric bands and opening to reveal chess and backgammon boards, the frieze with a drawer above sliding work compartment, on turned end supports with foliate carved splayed feet joined by a pole stretcher, 23in (59cm).
£1,000-1,200 *Bea*

A George III mahogany work table of Louis XV style, the eared serpentine fronted top with a silk lined rising firescreen behind, above a velvet lined slide and false drawer, with one side drawer and waved apron, on cabriole legs joined by an undertier, screen replaced, restorations, 20in (50.5cm).
£1,800-2,200 *CSK*

A Victorian burr walnut veneered top work table, inlaid stringing, the fitted interior with fretwork above a fabric covered work box, the turned spiral twist supports, on leaf carved open scroll capped legs with casters, turned connecting stretcher, 25in (64cm).
£500-600 *WW*

A mahogany work table with line inlay, single drawer, tapestry pull out drawer, 4 tapering legs with scale and line inlay and brass casters, late 19thC, 19in (48cm).
£350-450 *GAK*

A Regency rosewood work table inlaid throughout with brass lines and foliate motifs, the sarcophagus top with brass drop-ring handles, on a lyre support with 4 hipped splayed legs, brass lion paw caps and casters, 17in (43cm).
£1,200-1,500 *Bea*

A mahogany sewing table, c1830, 27.5in (70cm) high.
£1,200-1,400 *JAC*

An Austrian Biedermeier brass mounted mahogany sewing table, with canted hinged top, the reverse with detachable mirror, the fitted interior with lidded compartments and glass bottles, one glass engraved Schloss Brunn Sauerbrunn in Karlsbad, on turned shaft with spreading octagonal base, c1840, 18.5in (47cm) wide.
£1,000-1,500 *C*

A Victorian walnut trumpet shape work table, the hinged top enclosing a mirrored and fitted interior, on a turned stem and 3 carved tripod legs, 18in (46cm).
£550-750 *DDM*

A mahogany work table, the swivel top above a single drawer, raised on arcaded end supports and corbelled bun feet with a baluster turned stretcher, possibly Continental, c1840, 34in (86cm).
£800-1,200 *S(S)*

An Edwardian painted satinwood work table, decorated with Neo Classical floral swags and oval medallions, enclosing a fitted interior with drawer below, 21in (53cm).
£1,500-2,000 *CSK*

An Edwardian portable sewing box, with 2 sloping panelled lids on a stand, with square outswept legs, velvet lined, maker J. C. Vickery, 179-183 Regent Street, W., 30in (76cm) high.
£400-600 *WIL*

A Regency mahogany work table, crossbanded in rosewood and inlaid with satinwood, divided interior, on a turned column with scrolled quadruple supports.
£600-700 *M*

Writing Tables

A Victorian marquetry and ormolu mounted writing table, decorated within a bird's eye maple border, on fluted tapering legs with saltire stretcher, 51.5in (130cm).
£3,000-4,000 *GSP*

A rosewood kidney shaped writing table.
£1,500-2,000 *P(S)*

A Regency mahogany writing table, with single frieze drawer and writing compartment, with ebony string inlay, 26in (66cm).
£1,500-2,000 *NA*

A mahogany partners' writing table, with leather lined top above 2 frieze drawers opposed by 2 false drawers, on turned lotus leaf lappeted legs, 59in (149cm).
£3,500-4,000 *C*

An Italian writing table, probably Milan, inlaid with Renaissance style ivory foliage and grotesques on an ebonised ground, set with hardstones including lapis coloured sodalite, c1880, 34.5in (88cm).
£1,000-1,200 *S(S)*

A mid-Victorian mahogany writing table, the leather lined top with hinged fitted compartment above 2 frieze drawers on fluted tapering legs, stamped Gillow, L1126, restored, 36in (92cm).
£1,800-2,200 *C*

An Edwardian mahogany and marquetry writing table, the writing surface lacks lining, on tapering legs inlaid with trailing foliage, stamped Joseph Hide, Market Place, Kingston, 42in (107cm).
£2,500-3,000 *C*

A George III zebrawood veneered writing table, outlined throughout with boxwood stringing, the crossbanded top enclosing a fitted interior with adjustable tooled leather writing slope, 19in (48cm).
£1,200-1,700 *Bea*

Teapoys

A Victorian walnut teapoy, the crossbanded top enclosing a fitted interior containing 2 oval caddies above a band of lobing, raised on a fluted column and 3 leaf carved scrolling legs, c1850, 18.5in (47cm).
£1,000-1,200 *S(S)*

A George IV golden wood veneered sarcophagus shaped teapoy, inlaid with chequer banding, the sides with brass decorative ring handles, the interior with a mahogany lift-out mixing box and 2 caddies with fielded sliding covers, the leaf carved stem on shaped top splay legs, the brass sabots on casters, 18in (46cm).
£400-600 *WW*

A mahogany teapoy, c1830.
£1,200-1,400 *JAC*

Whatnots

Washstands

A Sheraton period washstand.
£400-500 *SIM*

A mahogany washstand in the Gillows manner, the interior with lidded compartment and provision for bowl and accessories, the frieze with one false and 2 real drawers, on tapering reeded legs with brass casters, early 19thC, 33in (84cm).
£450-650 *Bea*

A George IV mahogany two-tier whatnot, the top hinged to form an adjustable reading slope, the lower tier with a drawer, on turned supports and turned lopped feet, fitted casters, c1825, 20.5in (52cm).
£1,000-1,200 *S(S)*

A Victorian walnut whatnot, with shaped outline, mirror back, on fluted turned supports.
£1,000-1,200 *RPI*

A Victorian mahogany four-tier whatnot, with a gallery and a drawer, 25.5in (65cm).
£1,200-1,500 *S(S)*

A Victorian burr walnut whatnot, with pierced fret gallery and turned finials, the lower part with fret-carved fall enclosing shelves flanked by spiral twist uprights, on turned legs, with drawer in the apron, 26.5in (67cm).
£1,700-2,000 *CSK*

An early Victorian rosewood whatnot, supported on baluster turned peg feet, 42in (107cm).
£900-1,000 *HSS*

An early Victorian mahogany reading whatnot, with hinged adjustable reading top flanked by hinged flaps fitted with 2 double sided frieze drawers, on turned uprights and 2 rectangular tiers, 30in (76cm).
£1,000-1,200 *CSK*

A late George III rosewood whatnot, with 4 tiers above a base drawer between baluster turned tapering finialled supports, on turned feet and brass casters, 17in (43cm).
£1,500-2,000 *C*

A William IV whatnot.
£1,200-1,500 *RBB*

The original purchase price of this item in the 1950's was £1!

A late George III mahogany whatnot, with 4 tiers, the second tier fitted with drawer, between baluster turned finialled supports, 18in (46cm).
£500-1,000 *CSK*

A Victorian walnut three-tier serpentine fronted whatnot, with pierced gallery, turned finials, wrythen fluted supports, plain shelves, single drawer to the base, on turned legs, 22in (55.5cm).
£950-1,200 *DDM*

A mid-Victorian mahogany whatnot, on ring turned tapering supports, 18in (46cm).
£1,200-1,700 *C(S)*

A Regency mahogany three-tier lectern whatnot, the top above a finialled base with drawer, joined by turned supports and vertical cross stretchers, on baluster turned legs and brass casters, 19.5in (50cm).
£2,000-2,500 *C*

l. A Victorian three-tier walnut graduating whatnot, with shaped outline.
£850-1,000
r. A Victorian walnut Canterbury with fretted sides and drawer under.
£1,200-1,500 *RPI*

A mahogany butler's tray, with folding sides and collapsable stand, mid-19thC.
£800-1,000 *WIL*

Miscellaneous

A Regency painted towel rail, 25in (64cm).
£100-120 *JAC*

A Black Forest carved and stained hat and umbrella stand, in the form of a large bear and 2 cubs, around a tree, 82in (208cm) high.
£3,000-3,500 *Bea*

An Edwardian mahogany three-tier cakestand, 36in (92cm) high.
£170-200 *GH*

A Victorian mahogany boot rack, supported between 2 turned uprights and trestle base, terminating in bun feet, c1880, 38in (97cm).
£250-400 *WIL*

A walnut butter cooler, the oval brass banded sides with heart pierced lifts and 2 hinged covers, 18thC, 13.5in (34cm).
£2,000-2,500 *WW*

PINE FURNITURE
Chairs

A church pew.
£180-200 *WEL*

A high/low chair, c1880.
£150-200 *AL*

A child's rocker.   **£35-45** *AL*

A school chair.
£15-20 *WEL*

A side chair, with a new seat,
31in (79cm) high.
£95-100 *AL*

A high/low rocking chair, c1890.
£185-200 *AL*

Chests

An English plan chest, c1880,
48in (122cm).
£375-400 *RK*

An English chest of drawers,
c1890, 36in (92cm).
£275-300 *RK*

A chest of drawers, c1840.
£300-350 *CPA*

A chest of drawers, 19thC, 36in
(92cm).
£150-155 *TRU*

A chest of drawers, c1820.
£450-550 *CPA*

A miniature waxed chest of
drawers, 11in (28cm).
£50-70 *TRU*

An Austrian mule chest, totally original, including lock and key, 48in (122cm).
£425-450 *CHA*

A chest of drawers, c1870, 32in (81cm) high.
£250-280 *AL*

Commodes

A miniature chest of spice drawers, c1890, 18in (46cm) high.
£250-280 *AL*

A Scandinavian or South German chest of drawers, 44in (112cm).
£200-225 *CHA*

A chest of drawers, 40in (102cm).
£275-300 *CHA*

A chest of drawers, with ply drawer bottoms, c1900, 45in (114cm) high.
£600-650 *AL*

A child's painted commode, 24in (61cm) high.
£75-100 *CHA*

An English bank of drawers, c1890, 89in (226cm).
£675-700 *RK*

Cupboards

A wall cupboard.
£45-60 *WEL*

A two-door glazed cupboard, originally with metal mesh, c1825, 72.5in (183cm) high.
£900-1,000 *AL*

A glazed cupboard with enclosed drawers, c1870, 15in (38cm) high.
£280-350 *AL*

A step commode, c1860, 18in (46cm).   **£160-170** *AL*

A corner cupboard, with key, c1830, 41in (104cm) high.
£440-500 *AL*

A four-door cupboard, c1850.
£700-750 *HON*

A pot cupboard.
£65-80 *WEL*

A two-door hanging corner cupboard, c1850, 32in (81cm).
£450-500 *AL*

A Georgian bowfront cupboard, 35in (89cm) high.
£300-350 *JAC*

A Danish bedside cupboard, c1870, 25in (64cm).
£175-200 *RK*

A glazed two-piece bookcase, c1880.
£900-920
CPA

A German bedside cupboard.
£100-150 *CPA*

An English corner cupboard, c1870, 27in (69cm).
£275-300 *RK*

A late George III standing corner cupboard, the moulded cornice with foliate carved frieze above a central lion's head and spandrels with paterae and trailing husks, single arched astragal glazed door between reeded uprights, with a panelled door below between similar uprights, 32.5in (82cm).
£1,200-1,700 *CSK*

A pot cupboard, c1860, 21.5in (54cm) high.
£200-250 *AL*

A mid-Georgian corner cupboard, with breakfront moulded cornice above a recess with open shelves and semi-domed top, flanked by moulded uprights, 48in (122cm).
£850-900 *CSK*

A German bedside cupboard.
£100-150 *CPA*

A pair of Continental waxed bedside cupboards, c1920.
£200-220 *TRU*

Desks

A Scandinavian pine desk, with oak top, c1910, 51in (130cm).
£350-400 *BEL*

An English twin pedestal desk, c1880, 57in (145cm). **£600-650** *RK*

A three-piece partners' desk, 51in (130cm) long. **£900-1,000** *AL*

A Regency simulated bamboo desk, with new leather top, c1820, 45in (114cm).
£1,200-1,400 *AL*

A fitted desk, with new sledge feet, c1870, 48in (122cm) high.
£900-1,000 *AL*

A desk, with black china knob handles, new leather top, c1860, 47in (119cm) long. **£900-950** *AL*

Dressers

A painted pine low dresser, c1700, 60in (152cm).
£1,500-1,800 *OSc*

A Welsh glazed dresser, c1880, 39in (99cm).
£600-650 *RK*

A Scottish dresser, c1880, 49in (125cm).
£500-550 *RK*

A Danish dresser base, c1895, 40in (102cm).
£375-425 *RK*

Stools

A two drawer sycamore dresser base, 63in (160cm) long.   **£400-500** *AL*

A pine stool.
£30-50 *WEL*

Tables

A Welsh drop-leaf table, c1865, 34in (86cm).
£150-170 *RK*

An oval table, c1860.
£200-250 *AL*

A cheese table, with turned legs, 18 by 18in (46 by 46cm).
£45-65 *WEL*

A three drawer writing table, c1820, 31.5in (79cm) high.
£600-650 *AL*

A beech piano stool, c1890, 22.5in (57cm) high.   **£70-80** *AL*

A two drawer work table, c1850,
72in (183cm).
£600-700 *AL*

A grained pine extending table,
on dual scroll carved supports
joined by lion's mask stretchers
and iron cross struts, possibly
Spanish, includes 2 extra leaves,
122.5in (310cm) extended.
£2,700-3,000 *CSK*

A table, 58in (147cm).
£230-240 *CHA*

A German shoemaker's bench,
47in (119cm) long.
£75-100 *CHA*

A shaped side table,
51in (130cm)long.
£200-300 *AL*

A cricket table, c1860.
£350-450 *AL*

A Danish side table, c1890, 31in (79cm) high.
£120-140 *RK*

A table, 52in (132cm).
£170-200 *CHA*

A North Wales baker's table, with lift-off lid revealing a dough trough, 56in (142cm).
£250-300 *CHA*

A cricket table, with bobbin turned legs.
£200-250 *AL*

Wardrobes

A Danish wardrobe, with pagoda top, c1880, 38in (97cm).
£375-400 *RK*

A pine wardrobe, c1875, 84.5in (214cm) high.
£450-500 *BEL*

A Danish wardrobe, with one door and one drawer, c1860, 37in (94cm).
£375-400 *RK*

Locate the Source

The source of each illustration in Miller's can be found by checking the code letters below each caption with the list of contributors.

A Danish wardrobe, c1860, 37in (94cm).
£275-300 *BEL*

A German wardrobe, with 2 panelled doors.
£400-450 *CPA*

Washstands

A washstand, with one door and one drawer, c1880, 40in (102cm) high.
£400-450 *AL*

A dressing table/washstand, c1870, 55in (140cm) high.
£400-450 *AL*

An original painted washstand, 36.5in (93cm) high.   **£200-250** *AL*

A washstand with marble top, c1880, 42in (107cm) long.
£300-400 *AL*

A pine washstand.
£55-80 *WEL*

A washstand and shelf, c1860, 35in (89cm) high.
£145-155 *AL*

Miscellaneous

A pine tub, 27in (69cm) diam.
£150-170 *AL*

Pine shelves, 21in (53cm).
£60-70 *AL*

A pine box c1880, on a new stand,
22in (56cm) high.
£85-95 *AL*

A German painted and decorated
pine marriage bedstead, the
shaped headboard painted with a
lady and a gentleman standing in
a landscape, with floral and leaf
motifs in polychrome, and
an inscription 'Johann and Maria
Katharina' and the date '1824',
with turned footposts, the tester
panel overhead painted with
bucolic landscapes within
medallions in polychrome, 50.5in
(128cm) wide.
£3,000-3,500 *S(NY)*

A Scandinavian painted beech
spinning wheel, c1860, 37in
(94cm) high.
£170-190 *RK*

A well used butcher's block.
£200-250 *WEL*

A display cabinet made from an
old meat safe, metal mesh sides
replaced by glass, on a new pine
stand, 30in (76cm).
£300-400 *AL*

A church hymn board.
£25-30 *WEL*

Horseshoe shaped coat pegs,
c1920, 17.5in (44cm) high.
£65-75 *AL*

A Danish dome-top box,
c1860, 43in (109cm).
£160-180 *RK*

A pine box, with candle box,
c1860, 42in (107cm) long.
£250-300 *AL*

A pair of carved pillars, with tops,
95in (241cm) high.
£1,200-1,500 *GRF*

A Victorian shop counter.
£950-1,100 *WEL*

A butcher's block with shelf,
c1850, 48in (122cm) long.
£450-550 *AL*

A set of West Country stocks, mid-19thC.
£700-800 *RP*

A German dome-top box.
£150-200 *CPA*

A fitted tool box, c1850, 33in (84cm) long.
£250-300 *AL*

A pair of George II style carved open wall shelves, with egg-and-tongue borders, each arched pediment centred by a female mask, with adjustable shelves, c1930 possibly incorporating 18thC components, by Callow of Mount Street, 38in (97cm).
£2,500-3,000 *S(S)*

A 3 tier stand, 33.5in (84cm) high.
£220-250 *AL*

A German dome-top box.
£150-200 *CPA*

An early pine overmantel, 27in (69cm). **£60-70** *AL*

A pine, glass and brass towel rail shelf, with hooks, 27in (69cm).
£35-40 *CHA*

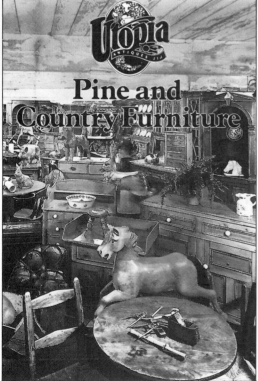

A hallstand, c1890, 71in (180cm) high.
£200-300 *AL*

A German cupboard, with interior shelves.
£375-400 *CPA*

A pine tray, on a new stand, 22in (56cm) high.   **£90-100** *AL*

A plant stand, 28in (71cm) high.
£80-85 *AL*

A pine easel, 43in (109cm) high.
£45-55 *AL*

IRISH FURNITURE

A glazed pine bookcase, c1870, 49in (124cm). **£475-500** *RK*

A pine chiffonier, c1870.
£270-295 *CPA*

A bed-settee, unrestored, c1800.
£500-550 *CPA*

A Co. Galway pine cottage
dresser, c1840.
£600-650 *HON*

A pine dresser, c1870.
£840-860 *CPA*

A chest of drawers, unrestored,
c1835.
£750-800 *CPA*

A glazed cupboard,
unrestored, c1840.
£450-480 *CPA*

A dresser, c1890.
£740-760 *CPA*

A Co. Galway pine cupboard,
c1840.   **£750-800** *HON*

A glazed two-piece
dresser, unrestored,
c1850.
£620-640 *CPA*

A glazed two-piece dresser,
unrestored, c1860.
£520-540 *CPA*

A dresser, c1880.
£800-840 *CPA*

354

A pine glazed two-piece dresser, c1840.
£870-890 *CPA*

A George II mahogany centre table, with later red walnut top, shaped moulded frieze carved with shells, on cabriole legs with paw feet, 33in (84cm).
£2,000-3,000 *Bea*

A fool's chair.
£120-140 *CPA*

A washstand, c1890.
£100-120 *CPA*

A pair of mid-Victorian mahogany hanging wall shelves, with shaped toprails, the rectangular shelves divided by turned baluster columns, 39in (99cm)
£750-850 *C(S)*

A washstand, c1890.
£140-165 *CPA*

A serving table, c1840.
£270-290 *CPA*

A farmhouse table, with sycamore top, c1880.
£670-690 *CPA*

WHAT IS AN ARCHITECTURAL ANTIQUE?

Broadly speaking, antique architectural elements fall into two categories; architectural salvage which covers reclaimed building materials, such as bricks, paving stones, roof tiles and balustrading, and architectural antiques which covers statuary, garden ornaments and chimneypieces.

BUYING AND SELLING ARCHITECTURAL ANTIQUES

Despite the enormous increase of interest in architectural antiques in recent years it is not an easy area for collectors. Unlike other specialist fields, such as porcelain or clocks where a massive amount of information on individual items and their values is readily available, there are only a small number of books currently in print on the subject, and few of these give even rudimentary advice on prices.

The first and most important rule for collecting architectural antiques is 'buy what you like'. There are two main reasons for this: First because you can live happily with your purchases even if they do not prove to be a good investment in financial terms. Secondly, you are unlikely to be misled by fashion. In recent years certain materials and manufacturers have drastically increased in price, only to fall rapidly back to more sensible levels. An example of this are the products of the Coalbrookdale foundry in Shropshire - notably cast iron garden seats and fountains - which, after a boom in prices in the mid 1980s, are now so debased by later copies that only the very rarest pieces achieve even moderate results at auction.

The second rule is to pay as much as you can reasonably afford. As in other fields of collecting you will, on the whole, get what you pay for and you are unlikely to buy good pieces at very low prices.

With reasonable luck and good judgement, however, it is perfectly possible to buy pieces which will not only enhance the appearance of your house and garden but may, in a few years time, provide a good return on your investment.

There are four main choices when buying and selling; auctions, specialist dealers, general dealers and demolition yards. The classic argument in favour of buying at auction goes as follows:- dealers buy at auction. When a dealer sells he must be charging the auction price plus his profit margin, therefore it must be cheaper to buy at auction.

The specialist dealer does at least deal in the goods 365 days a year, as opposed to 2 or 3 days for the auctioneer. Although the price he offers the vendor may be below an auctioneer's estimate, the seller has the certainty of a sale at a fixed price with no hidden charges. For the buyer, provided he takes the precaution of obtaining an invoice with a full description of the piece, including date of manufacture, material and any known provenance, he secures himself against most eventualities.

Many general dealers also carry architectural antiques in their stock. The advantage and disadvantage of buying from general dealers is the same. They may not know exactly what they have. Thus, whilst it is possible that a bargain may be secured, the reverse may also be true. Again it is important that the item is described fully on the invoice.

Demolition yards are theoretically most likely to yield bargains for the purchaser. Their stock-in-trade is usually architectural salvage, but they do occasionally deal in antique garden ornaments and fireplaces. A vendor may recognise the value of a piece even though it is tucked away in a dusty corner, and many an unsuspecting buyer has been fooled by dirt and disorder.

MATERIALS

Broadly speaking, the materials most commonly encountered fall into two categories; the carved and the moulded, or cast. The carved category includes marble and stone (but beware of the term bonded marble, which is cement made from marble dust and then cast). The cast and moulded materials include cast and wrought iron, bronze, brass, lead, spelter (a cheaper and lighter alloy), terracotta and cement, or reconstituted stone.

A decorative cast iron fountain, 42in (107cm) high.
£800-1,100 *DRU*

Because it is relatively cheap to cast items, they are far more likely to be modern reproductions than carved pieces. Indeed, the only substantial source of carved reproduction pieces is Northern Italy, where vast quantities of relatively high quality limestone pieces are still produced. Cast materials, on the other hand, have all been reproduced with varying degrees of success in recent years. Lead pieces are mostly produced in England, bronzes in Italy and the Far East, terracotta in Italy and Spain, and cast stone almost everywhere.

There is, of course, nothing wrong with modern reproductions, provided they are correctly described, but they may not appreciate in value and cannot reasonably be described as architectural antiques.

ARCHITECTURAL ANTIQUES
Bathroom Ware

A baby's W.C., 10.5in (46cm) high.
£120-150 *DRU*

A Rufford & Co, stoneware bath, complete with mahogany surround and mahogany encased thunderbox, restored, c1890, 90in (229cm) long.
£5,000-6,000 *DRU*

Provenance: Knowsley Hall, Knowsley, Lancashire, the residence of the Earl of Derby.

A copper bath, 65in (165cm) long.
£1,500-2,000 *DRU*

A copper bath, 54in (137cm) long.
£500-525 *DRU*

A French 3 bowl hairdressers' shop fitting, 168in (427cm) long.
£800-1,000 *ARC*

An Edwardian porcelain wash basin, T.C. Brown, Westhead, Moore & Co., of Stoke-on-Trent, with Queen Alexandra's Royal Warrant, 19in (48cm).
£300-350 *CHA*

A blue and white Trent Sanitary Closet, 18.5in (47cm) high.
£150-180 *GRF*

A bathroom chrome radiator towel rail, 37.5in (95cm) high.
£125-150 *GRF*

A Victorian mop sink.
£65-80 *WEL*

A Victorian scalloped basin, with brass taps, plug and chain.
£475-500 *DRU*

357

Bird Baths

A carved sandstone bird bath, 30in (76cm) high.
£600-650 *DRU*

A Yorkshire carved stone bird bath, 37.5in (95cm) high.
£550-575 *DRU*

A granite bird bath, 19thC, 39in (99cm) high.
£725-750 *DRU*

Chimney Pots

A chimney pot, 39in (99cm) high.
£55-65 *GRF*

Chimney pot, 42in (107cm) high.
£55-65 *GRF*

A chimney pot, with crown top and square base, 24in (61cm) high.
£45-55 *GRF*

Doors & Gates

A chimney pot, 29in (74cm) high.
£55-65 *GRF*

A square chimney pot, 37in (94cm) high.
£35-45 *GRF*

A pair of church doors.
£300-320 *WEL*

A pub door, with leaded glass panel, 80in (203cm) high.
£150-180 *GRF*

A pair of Gothic doors, with glass panels, 96in (244cm) high.
£150-180 *GRF*

A painted door, with stained glass insert, 80in (203cm) high.
£130-150 *GRF*

A painted wood door, with glass panels, porcelain handle and metal letterbox, knocker missing, 105in (267cm) high.
£150-180 *GRF*

A Tudor elm door.
£120-140 *WEL*

Terracotta gate caps.
£90-120 per pair *WEL*

Two pairs of cast and wrought iron doors, each with central roundel applied with a bronze, late 19thC, 119 by 34in (302 by 86cm).
£1,700-2,500 *S(S)*

Removed from the old Lloyds Building in London.

A pair of doors with glass inserts, 80in (203cm) high.
£150-200 *GRF*

A pair of cast and wrought iron gates, mid-19thC, each gate 58 by 58in (147 by 147cm).
£750-1,000 *S(S)*

ARCHITECTURAL ANTIQUES

WHAT TO LOOK FOR

* LEAD

Lead is one the most difficult materials to identify. After a few years exposure to the elements and a little judicious waxing, new lead and old are visually indistinguishable. However, early leadwork was primarily of very high quality and the finish and detail on 18thC figures is very good, whereas modern pieces suffer by comparison. Fingers are often clumsy, hair badly detailed and faces expressionless. Also, figures in reduced scale (i.e. less than lifesize) are almost certainly late, although often misleadingly described as 18thC. Genuine 18thC lead cistern tanks which make delightful planters, should have some evidence of having been used as cisterns, usually signs of an inlet pipe around the top rim and a tap hole at the lower edge.

An original mahogany lead-lined cistern.
£125-150 *GRF*

* BRONZE

Contrary to popular opinion, it is possible to produce virtually perfect copies of antique originals and green patination, which many take to be a sign of age, is easily applied. The underside of the piece should be examined and not look too clean and if there is wear in the patination it should be in places where it would occur naturally as the piece was handled over the years. Remember that signatures and foundry marks are as easy to fake as the piece itself.

* CAST IRON

Probably the most widely reproduced of all materials. If you are buying garden ornaments or furniture purported to be antique, first lift them. If they are light they are probably aluminium. If they are heavy, look at the finish. Casting marks, the little protruding spots of metal, were carefully removed in Victorian castings and any that were not would long since have been worn away. As with bronze, foundry marks are commonly faked.

* STONE

The two stones most commonly encountered are limestone and sandstone. Common types of limestone include Portland stone (grey/white) and Bathstone (yellow). Common sandstones include York stone (dark yellow weathering to black/green) and red sandstone. Broadly speaking, limestone is preferred for statuary and sandstone for architectural elements. Beware of pieces where the surface has broken down, as they may be beyond restoration. Limestone is generally more popular than sandstone because many people do not like the black and green colour of weathered sandstone. Sandstone is also more brittle and although it will take fine detail, it is susceptible to damage.

* MARBLE

There are many native British marbles, but the white marbles used in sculpture are mostly Italian. True statuary marble, the most highly prized and now virtually unobtainable, is a creamy white colour and has little or no veining. Carrara, or second statuary, is a bluer white with some degree of veining and is harder and thus more resistant to the British weather. Once the surface of the marble has broken down and become sugary, it is often beyond restoration.

Modern marbles, often dazzlingly white and imported from India, can be readily identified by their crystalline nature.

A weathered marble statue of a seated wounded cupid working on his net, late 19thC, 26in (66cm) wide. **£600-700** *MJB*

When buying marble statuary look for signs of quality carving in high relief, arms and hair carved away from the body and true proportions.

* TERRACOTTA

Terracotta (red earth in Latin) has been used since pre-classical times. It is resistant to weathering and thus ideal for exterior statuary and planters. The most desirable colour is yellow and the least, brick red. Oil jars have become a highly popular decorative feature in gardens in recent years, but because terracotta is a fragile material, genuine ones are rare and they are still produced in considerable quantities in Southern Europe. Genuine oil jars will probably have some signs of glazing on the interior.

A terracotta urn, 28in (71cm) high. **£180-200** *GRF*

* RECONSTITUTED STONE

Although debased by inferior modern castings, reconstituted stone has a long and honourable history. One of the earliest types used in England was Coadestone (named after Eleanor Coade, its inventor). Starting in 1769, the Coade factory produced an enormous number of pieces of the highest quality, and signed pieces fetch high prices.

Look for the same signs of quality as in marble carvings. The lines of cast pieces should be crisp and the material free from aggregate and air holes. As with carving, the casting should be free and confident.

A French cast iron fountain figure of a putto seated on an upturned ewer, late 19thC, 28in (71cm) high.
£750-1,000 *S(S)*

From an original model by Mathurian Moreau, 1821-1912.

A pair of wrought iron gates, early 20thC, each gate 90.5 by 59in (229 by 150cm). **£600-1,000** *S(S)*

A pair of wrought iron gates, each of arched rectangular form, early 20thC, each gate 86 by 54in (173 by 137cm).
£700-1,000 *S(S)*

Fountains

An original Victorian cast iron fountain, in tazza form with egg-and-dart mouldings, 38in (97cm) high.
£750-1,000 *DRU*

A composition stone fountain, with circular bowl surmounted by an associated lead figure of a putto, early 20thC, 115in (292cm) high.
£1,500-2,000 *S(S)*

> **Miller's is a price GUIDE not a price LIST**

An Italian rosso Verona marble fountain, in the form of a stylised dolphin with raised tail, 19thC, 31in (79cm) high.
£2,100-2,500 *S(S)*

A Vicenza stone lion fountain mask, mid-20thC, 28in (71cm).
£600-800 *S(S)*

Fireplaces

A Louis XVI style white marble chimneypiece, mid-19thC, 51 by 71in (130 by 180cm).
£3,000-5,000 *S(S)*

A cast iron fireplace, with tile decoration, 38in (97cm) square.
£300-400 *GRF*

A cast iron fireplace, 38 by 30in (97 by 76cm).
£300-350 *GRF*

A Victorian carved oak chimneypiece with overmantel, c1880, 97 by 102.5in (246 by 260cm).
£650-900 *S(S)*

A cast iron fireplace, with inlaid tiles and brass hood, 38in (97cm) square.
£350-385 *GRF*

A painted wood fire surround, 54 by 70in (137 by 178cm).
£400-450 *GRF*

A duck's nest hob grate, 23 by 31in (59 by 79cm).
£500-550 *DRU*

A cast iron fireplace, converted from coal to gas, 42 by 39in (107 by 99cm).
£225-285 *GRF*

A cast iron fireplace, 36 by 38in (92 by 97cm).
£250-275 *GRF*

A pair of Louis XV style bronze and gilt bronze chenets, in the form of scantily draped children warming themselves at flaming braziers, c1900, 14in (35cm) high.
£1,200-1,700 *S*

A pair of Louis XV style gilt bronze chenets, each with a small bronze urn supported on bold scrollwork, c1900, 14in (35cm) high.
£720-760 *S*

A French steel and brass adjustable fender, the ends with lions reclining on stepped spreading plinths with foliate mounts, joined by a foliage centred bar and stepped plinth base, 19thC, 46.5in (117cm) long when closed.
£2,000-2,500 *C*

A Georgian brass and steel fender, 11in (28cm) high. **£200-250** *JAC*

A Victorian brass and cast iron fire grate, the railed front above a fret pierced frieze, flanked by stepped square sectional uprights with urn finials and splayed legs, 35in (89cm).
£720-900 *C*

A pair of Louis XV style bronze chenet terminals, each in the form of a seated sphinx draped with fleur-de-lys, mid-brown patination, 19thC, 13in (33cm) high.
£1,200-1,500 *S(S)*

A Victorian cast iron fire basket.
£130-170 *WEL*

A pair of brass andirons, each with fluted ball finial above a gadrooned bulb and spirally twisted shaft, on hipped scroll legs and claw-and-ball feet, 19thC, 21.5in (54cm) high.
£800-1,200 *C*

A set of polished steel fire irons, with faceted pommels, comprising: a pierced shovel, a pair of tongs, a poker and a pair of fire iron supports, with scrolling arms, fluted and spirally turned knopped shafts and scrolling pierced trefoil bases, 26in (66cm) high.
£1,000-1,200   *C(S)*

A set of 6 fireplace tiles.
£40-60   *GRF*

A pair of seamed brass andirons, each with ring turned shaft and hipped downswept legs with ball feet, restored, possibly American, early 19thC, 16in (40cm) high.
£1,200-1,700   *C*

Garden Furniture

A pair of carved stone benches, early 18thC, 73in (185cm).
£3,000-3,500   *DRU*

A Coalbrookdale Rustic pattern cast iron seat, with diamond stamp for 7th April, 1851, and numbered 78766, c1860, 50in (127cm).
£1,000-1,500   *S(S)*

A carved stone garden seat, with high back and lion's feet, 65in (165cm).
£2,000-2,400   *DRU*

A Coalbrookdale Gothic pattern cast iron seat, stamped C. B. Dale Co., number 99277, with diamond registration stamp for 5th February 1854, and numbered 22, c1860, 72in (182.5cm).
£1,500-2,000   *S(S)*

This design registered in the 1875 Coalbrookdale catalogue.

An Italian rosso Verona marble chair, the arms in the form of winged lions, the front carved with anthemion and scrolls, late 19thC.
£4,000-5,000   *S(S)*

A pair of reeded wrought iron garden seats, early 19thC, 61in (155cm).   **£3,200-3,700**   *S(S)*

A wrought iron garden seat, the curved low back with 3 lyre shaped splats, with slat seat, on spade feet, 19thC, 84in (213cm).
£1,500-2,000   *RBB*

A Regency wrought iron garden seat, the back with latticework decoration, early 19thC, 43.5in (110cm).
£2,000-2,500 *(S(S)*

A reeded wrought iron chair, and a later wrought iron bench, early 19thC, 48in (122cm).
£700-1,000 *S(S)*

A Regency Coalbrookdale cast iron garden seat, with twig and laurel cast decoration, wooden slat seat, grotesque arm terminals, winged cabriole legs, indistinctly stamped on back, 47in (119cm).
£2,200-2,700 *SWO*

A reeded wrought iron games seat, with hinged foot rest, wheels missing, early 19thC, 61in (155cm).
£800-1,200 *S(S)*

A wrought iron garden seat, with cabriole legs, c1850, 48in (122cm).
£500-550 *DRU*

A late Victorian white painted cast iron garden bench, with oak leaves and branches, 46in (116.5cm).
£650-800 *C(S)*

A Coalbrookdale Horse Chestnut pattern cast iron seat, stamped Coalbrookdale Co., numbered 217568, and with registration stamps for 1868, 73in (185cm).
£2,500-3,500 *S(S)*

A Coalbrookdale Convolvulus pattern cast iron seat, numbered 2286, and with diamond registration stamp for 12th November 1842, 74in (188cm).
£1,500-1,800 *S(S)*

A pair of wrought iron benches, mid-19thC, 122in (310cm).
£4,000-4,500 *S(S)*

A pair of Regency wrought iron garden seats, with reeded scrolled frame and rosette finials, 72in (182.5cm).
£9,000-11,000 *RBB*

A garden table, with marble top, 50in (127cm) long.
£300-350 *DRU*

A carved stone garden table, with baluster leg, 36in (92cm) diam.
£800-850 *DRU*

A Coalbrookdale cast iron table, stamped C. B. Dale Co., and with diamond registration stamp for 15th February 1854, and numbered 186025, 44in (111.5cm).
£1,500-2,000 *S(S)*

This design was registered in the 1875 Coalbrookdale catalogue.

A pair of cast iron tables, each with oak top, on foliate and winged griffin supports with indistinct registration stamps, c1860, 47in (119cm).
£1,800-2,200 *S(S)*

A wrought and cast iron bridge, made-up, incorporating Victorian cast iron staircase uprights, 236in (600cm).
£4,000-4,500 *S(S)*

Pedestals, Posts & Finials

A pair of Italian rosso Verona marble gate pier lions, each seated on haunches, late l9thC, 20in (50cm).
£800-1,200 *S(S)*

A cast and wrought iron gazebo, made-up, the sides incorporating Victorian panels and with wooden and tiled roof.
£3,000-3,500 *S(S)*

A terracotta finial.
£90-120 *WEL*

A white marble Corinthian capital, early 20thC, 28in (71cm) high.   **£1,000-2,000** *S(S)*

A pair of composition stone finials, mid-20thC, 42in (106.5cm).
£2,000-3,000 *S(S)*

A set of 4 carved stone columns, English, c1800.
£5,900-6,200 *DRU*

A pair of French carved stone finials, c1870, 51in (129.5cm).
£1,500-2,000 *S(S)*

A Roman marble capital, carved in relief with acanthus, probably 2nd Century A.D., 31in (79cm), and another smaller, 20in (50.5cm).
£1,200-1,700 *S(S)*

A pair of rosso Verona marble gate pier lions, each seated on haunches, looking down, late 19thC, 33in (84cm).
£1,500-2,000 *S(S)*

A carved stone pedestal, 36in (92cm), and a Portland stone sundial column pedestal, 48in (122cm).
£1,500-2,000 *S(S)*

367

Pumps

A cast iron pump, 61in (155cm). **£90-120** *GRF*

A cast iron water pump, early 19thC, 57in (144.5cm). **£650-675** *DRU*

An Irish cast iron pump, A. Clyde, Ballymena, 51in (129.5cm). **£160-190** *GRF*

A small cast iron water pump, 27in (68cm). **£80-90** *GRF*

Roof Tiles

Hand made plain clay tiles. **£55-60 per hundred** *WEL*

Hand cut stone tiles. **£500-600 per tonne** *WEL*

An iron water pump. **£80-100** *WEL*

Hand made clay roof tiles. **£105-115 per hundred** *WEL*

A pair of early stone griffin ridge tiles, 25in (63.5cm) high. **£1,000-1,200** *DRU*

Staddle Stones

A staddle stone. **£100-130** *WEL*

A matched set of six staddle stones, 18th/19thC, 31.5in (80cm) high. **£1,000-1,200** *S(S)*

A staddle stone, 28in (71cm) high. **£150-170** *GRF*

Stands

A Coalbrookdale cast iron hall table, inlaid with marble top and with indistinct registration stamp, the backplate stamped No. 49 and centred with a mirror, 86in (218cm) high.
£1,500-2,000 *S(S)*

This design is registered in the 1875 Coalbrookdale Catalogue.

A cast iron hall stand, with registration stamp for 20th July 1846, 114in (290cm) high.
£1,000-1,500 *S(S)*

A lead head of a classical woman, mid-18thC, 14in (36cm) high.
£1,000-1,200 *S(S)*

Statues

A lead garden figure of a nymph, lacking attributes, 60in (152cm) high.
£2,800-3,000 *C(S)*

A lead statue of Father Time with flowing beard and moustache, lacking scythe, 56in (142cm).
£3,500-4,000 *C(S)*

A terracotta group, 18thC, 39in (99cm) high.
£7,000-7,500 *DRU*

A pair of Italian composition stone figures of putti musicians, modern, 59in (150cm).
£900-1,200 *S(S)*

A pair of Italian terracotta busts of Dante and Petrarch, the poets both crowned with laurel, 19thC, 29in (74cm) high.
£2,600-3,000 *S(S)*

A sandstone group of putti at play, with a dog, 19thC, 32in (81cm) high.
£4,000-4,300 *DRU*

A pair of recumbent stone lions, mid-18thC, 38in (96.5cm) long.
£2,700-2,900 *DRU*

A pair of stone eagles, 32in (81cm) high.
£350-450 *GRF*

A pair of Portland stone lions, each reclining on shaped rectangular base, 18thC, 30in (76cm) long.
£2,500-3,000 *S(S)*

A carved sandstone figure of Flora, 72in (182.5cm) high.
£3,000-3,300 *DRU*

A composition stone figure of Bacchus, on associated sandstone pedestal, late 19th/early 20thC, 96in (244cm) high.
£8,000-10,000 *S(S)*

This statue was removed from Ecclesgreig Castle, Angus, Scotland.

A Low Countries white marble figure of a woman standing next to a tree stump, early 18thC, 35.5in (90cm) high.
£1,700-2,000 *S(S)*

A lead figure of Mercury after Giambologna, the winged figure supported by an allegory of the North Wind, 72in (182.5cm).
£2,000-2,500 *S(S)*

A statue of an Oriental woman, 64in (162.5cm) high.
£500-600 *GRF*

A lead figure of a musician standing playing a violin, in 18thC dress, on a square base, 50.5in (128cm) high.
£1,500-2,000 *S(S)*

A marble statue of a lady, early 19thC, 58in (147cm) high.
£9,000-9,500 *DRU*

A pair of naively carved stone figures, mid-19thC.
£1,000-1,200 *DRU*

Make the Most of Miller's

In Miller's we do NOT just reprint saleroom estimates. We work from realised prices either from an auction room or a dealer. Our consultants then work out a realistic price range for a similar piece. This is to try to avoid repeating freak results - either low or high.

Sundials

Troughs & Planters

A pair of lead planters, the sides cast with a band of cherubs below ropework edges and rams' mask terminals, 32in (81cm) wide.
£1,300-1,700 *S(S)*

A pair of lead garden flower tubs, the bodies with rams' heads and decorated with a frieze of cherubs beneath rope edges, on bun feet, 18in (46cm) diam.
£700-900 *S(S)*

A sandstone sundial, with square column, the vertical dial with bronze gnomon beneath a pyramid top, on a stepped square base, early 20thC, 91in (230cm).high.
£800-1,200 *S(S)*

An Italian rosso Verona marble jardinière, late 17thC, 126in (320cm) long.
£6,250-7,000 *S(S)*

A Georgian sundial, 39in (99cm) high.
£2,500-3,000 *DRU*

A pair of marble mortars, 22in (55.5cm) wide.
£300-350 *DRU*

A stone water trough, marked Horses 1813.
£325-350 *WEL*

A marble sarcophagus trough, 3rd/4thC, 74in (188cm) wide.
£12,000-12,500
DRU

An Italian grey and white marble jardinière, late 18thC, 34in(86cm) wide.
£6,000-6,500 *S(S)*

A hand hewn stone trough.
£400-450 *GRF*

Urns

A Coadestone memorial urn, with plaque inscribed Ann Finch, O.B., 21 Sept. 1792, on a square foot stamped Coade London 1793, 30in (77cm) high, on a panelled pedestal inscribed with a funerary verse, 24in (61cm).
£3,200-3,500 *S(S)*

A white painted cast iron garden urn, on a separate square stepped plinth, 52in (132cm) high.
£550-600 *DDM*

A pair of carved stone urns, each on associated square plinth, late 17th/early 18thC, 27in (69cm) high.
£2,000-2,500 *S(S)*
Formerly at Newby Hall, Yorkshire.

A Medici reconstituted stone vase, early 19thC, 45in (114cm) high.
£4,000-4,200 *DRU*

A pair of composition fruit filled campana urns, on square bases, 28in (68.5cm) high.
£800-1,000 *C(S)*

A pair of white marble urns, mid-19thC, 29.5in (75cm) wide.
£1,800-2,200 *S(S)*

A pair of composition urns, with everted lips, the baluster bodies decorated with drapery swags upon spreading socles and square plinths, 24in (61cm) high.
£1,000-1,250 *C(S)*

A pair of Victorian cast iron urns, 27in (69cm) high.
£550-650 *GRF*

An Italian white marble model of the Warwick urn, on associated plinth, early 19thC, 27in (68cm) high.
£1,300-1,700 *S(S)*

A pair of cast iron urns, with egg-and-dart rims, fluted sides and socles, on square plinths, 19thC, 50in (127cm) high overall.
£900-1,200 *DN*

Originally from Syerston Hall, Newark.

A Victorian cast iron dish urn, 40in (101.5cm) diam.
£350-375 *DRU*

A pair of terracotta urns, 18in (46cm) high.
£300-350 *GRF*

A pair of Victorian cast iron garden urns, damaged.
£750-850 *SWO*

A pair of terracotta garden urns, 25in (64cm) high.
£700-750 *DRU*

Windows

A pair of composition garden urns, 53in (134.5cm) high.
£700-900 *Bea*

A pair of lead urns, 28in (71cm) high.
£1,000-1,500 *DRU*

A circular window.
£150-180 *GRF*

A pair of coloured church windows, c1870.
£100-120 *WEL*

Two stained glass windows
£300-350 each *GRF*

A stained glass panel.
£100-200 *GRF*

A stained glass window.
£250-300 *GRF*

A stained glass panel, 18 by 10.5in (46 by 25cm).
£85-95 *GRF*

Two stained glass religious scenes, 28 by 16.5in (71 by 42cm).
£300-375 *GRF*

A stained glass window, with City of London crest, 21 by 25in (53 by 64cm).
£100-130 *GRF*

A stained glass window, 23in (59cm) square.
£300-350 *GRF*

A stained glass panel, 18 by 10.5in (46 by 25cm).
£85-95 *GRF*

A stained glass panel, with grapes, 12in (30.5cm).
£65-85 *GRF*

A stained glass window, with Newcastle crest, 21 by 25in (53 by 64cm).
£100-130 *GRF*

A stained glass framed panel.
£100-150 *GRF*

Miscellaneous

A decorative radiator, c1890.
£175-200 *WEL*

A Stuart lead cistern, dated 1666 and initials I.F., 47in (119cm) wide.   **£2,000-2,500** *S(S)*

A decorative radiator, 38in (96.5cm).
£160-180 *GRF*

An owl nest opening, for building into a barn or house gable end, 6in (15cm).
£115-125 *WEL*

A copper roof vent, 75in (190cm) high.
£400-450 *GRF*

A clock tower, not in working order, 60in (152cm) square.
£550-600 *GRF*

A safe.
£120-130 *WEL*

A bell tower, with weather vane.
£1,800-2,000 *GRF*

A George II lead garden cistern.
£2,000-2,500 *P(S)*

An aluminium, copper and galvanized weather vane, c1930. 114in (290cm) high.
£1,500-2,000 *S(S)*
Removed from Southampton Ocean Terminal.

A post box.
£260-280 *WEL*

A set of 6 cast painted aluminium hoppers.
£200-250 *GRF*

CLOCKS

Prices and the recession

Oddly enough, the prices for good 'honest' clocks have not been too badly affected by the recession. On the contrary, prices for clocks in the lower and middle price bands have continued to rise. More expensive clocks have not always reached their estimated value but this could, in part, be due to the fact that higher priced 'top of the range' clocks are a highly specialised area.

A late Victorian ebonised chiming bracket clock, with arched brass dial signed on shield John Jackson, Portsea, triple-train fusee movement, striking on 8 bells and a gong, with matching bracket.
£1,200-1,700 *S(S)*

Makers

The great majority of British clocks made before about 1820 were actually made by the man whose name appears on the dial (except of course that the 'white' dial on those types of clocks was bought from a specialist dial maker). After 1820 an increasing number of clocks were bought pre-made by specialists with just the finishing touches being carried out by the local retailers. Bracket and other spring driven clocks pre-1850 are also slightly different. Certain makers specialised in this area and supplied both the engraved and white dial form of bracket clocks to retailers. Even famous

London clockmakers bought in spring clocks in this way, making them little more than retailers as far as spring clocks were concerned.

For famous makers and retailers the name will have a considerable bearing on price, especially with London makers. With provincial clocks the name is not nearly as important in affecting price, with the exception that in each county there was a handful or so of makers who were particularly skilled, famous or highly reputed within their own areas. Clocks by such makers, and especially early ones before about 1750, will carry a premium because of the name. Makers are still coming to light today, whose work is little known but may be of exceptionally high quality, and buyers who can learn to recognise features indicative of high quality may be fortunate in locating a clock where the maker's name has not yet attracted this quality premium in price. Many makers, including a few of exceptional ability, have escaped being recorded in the standard reference texts, so a clock might still be a very fine one even if by a maker as yet unrecorded.

A French ivory mantel clock, with a 2.5in (6.5cm) enamel dial, movement No. 4153, with platform cylinder escapement, outside countwheel striking on a bell, fluted half column case surmounted by a tazza, raised on scroll feet, 11in (28cm).
£3,200-3,700 *S*

A mahogany longcase clock, the 12in (31cm) arched and silvered the dial signed Graham, Grafton Street, Soho, 94in (238cm).
£2,500-3,500 *S(S)*

Special and Complicated Clocks

The field of musical and quarter-chiming clocks can be a difficult one for the unwary. Such a clock in fine mechanical condition and expertly restored will cost considerably more than a simple hourly-striking version. But beware of such clocks in <u>un</u>restored condition, as the restoration of these can be very difficult and costly - this applies especially in the case of musical clocks, some of which once may have played tunes which are now unrecognisable and therefore may be impossible to restore. Any clocks with missing trains (sets of gears) may well appear to be bargains, but even when restored such clocks will not rival in price a complete original one of the same type. Again, a highly-complex or unusual clock with vital parts missing may prove impossible to restore. Remember with any British clock before about 1850 parts are not interchangeable and anything missing has to be purpose-made. With imported clocks after about 1850 there is a greater chance that a restorer may have spare parts which can be used, <u>if</u> you can locate a restorer with enough spares.

Bracket Clocks

An English bracket clock, the enamel dial with Roman numerals and inscribed Thos. W. Field, Aylesbury, the 8-day 'A' plate timepiece movement with fusee drive, the inlaid mahogany case with domed pediment, open brass fishscale sideplate and fan form inlaid reserves, on brass ball feet, 18in (46cm).
£700-900   *OL*

A walnut cased bracket clock, by Garrard, Westminster chimes movement, the dial with silvered chapter ring and gilt metal mask spandrels, 15.5in (39cm).
£350-400   *GAK*

An ebonised bracket clock, signed James Chater, London, with rococo spandrels and date aperture, the movement formerly with a third musical train and a foliate engraved and signed backplate, in an associated black painted oak case carved with a dragon surmount and caryatid columns, with nest of bells, 27in (68cm).
£900-1,200   *S(S)*

A carved oak bracket clock, with German movement and Westminster chimes, early 20thC, 18in (46cm).
£200-250   *TRU*

A George II ebonised bracket clock, the 7in (18cm) dial signed in the stopped pendulum aperture Geo Hide, with calendar aperture, the 5-pillar movement with rack and bell striking and now with anchor escapement, in an inverted bell top case with carrying handle, shell and leaf cast brass door frets and ball-and-claw feet, one pillar missing, c1740, 19in (48cm).
£1,000-1,500   S(S)

A mahogany bracket clock, in mid-18thC style, with a broken arch brass dial and gong striking movement, c1920, 9.5in (24cm).
£500-550   *S(S)*

A William & Mary ebonised striking bracket clock, with foliate handle to basket top, later finials, cast gilt mask and foliate sound frets to the sides, on later turned brass feet, the 8in (20cm) square dial signed Al: Irving London, 16.5in (42cm).
£2,000-2,500   *C*

A Regency mahogany bracket clock, the painted convex dial signed Jas McCabe, Royal Exchange, London, No. 881, strike/silent lever above, reverse of dial scratched James McCabe, Royal Exchange, 881, 6084, similarly signed fusee and chain movement No. 6084, anchor escapement, bell-striking, pull repeat, c1820, 16in (41cm).
£1,700-2,000   S

A William III composed ebony veneered musical bracket clock, by Jonathan Lowndes, London, restored, c1695, 14in (36cm).
£10,000-15,000 *S*

A Regency bracket clock, by Perigal and Duterrau, Bond Street, London, the twin fusee repeating movement striking on a bell, circular painted dial with Roman numerals, in brass mounted mahogany case, on ball feet, 16in (41cm).
£850-950 *Bea*

A mahogany bracket clock, the 9.5in (24cm) silvered dial signed James McCabe, Royal Exchange, London, with moon hands and strike/silent at XII, the twin-chain fusee movement gong striking and with signed backplate, the case with outline leafy scrolls and pierced foliate rear door, early 19thC, 22in (56cm).
£1,500-2,000 *ALL*

A Regency mahogany bracket clock, inlaid brass detail to the case, the 8in (20cm) face inscribed T Verley, Fakenham, c1825.
£700-900 *GAK*

An early Victorian mahogany bracket timepiece, signed Wm. Johnson, 4 Hercules Passage, Stock Exchange, London, within foliate engraving with Roman chapter ring, 10.5in (26cm).
£500-700 *C*

A George II ebonised striking bracket clock, with 6-pillar twin fusee movement with verge escapement, pull quarter repeat on 6 bells, repeat pulley to foliate engraved backplate, securing brackets to case, 17in (44cm).
£4,500-5,500 *C*

The dial lay-out for this clock is similar to work by William Scafe, 1749-64.

A mahogany repeater bracket clock, the white painted dial with Roman numerals, enclosing an 8-day double fusee repeater movement striking on a single bell, early 19thC, 16in (41cm).
£900-1,200 *DDM*

An Italian mulberrywood quarter repeating bracket clock, the 6.5in (16cm) dial with central alarm and foliate spandrels, the square plated movement with baluster pillars, verge escapement and pull wound quarter repeating on 2 bells, key wound alarm, in a moulded domed case with carrying handle and ball finials, early 18thC, 17in (43cm).
£3,000-4,000 *S*

A Georgian bracket clock, with silvered dial, date dial and phases of the moon to the arch, decorated with applied gilt spandrels, fitted 8-day movement striking on 7 bells with repeat mechanism, the engraved backplate inscribed W. Tomlinson, London, the mahogany case surmounted by a brass carrying handle, with engraved brass ball feet, 15in (38cm).
£1,300-1,600 *AG*

An Italian ebony veneered quarter repeating bracket clock, the dial signed by Ganzinotto Genoua, with verge escapement, silk suspension and cycloidal cheeks, pull wind quarter repeat on 2 bells, key wound alarm, the case with a domed cresting and key drawer, late 17th/early18thC, 15in (38cm).
£3,000-4,000 *S*

A mahogany bracket clock, the 7in (18cm) arched brass dial signed on a shield Widenham, London, scroll spandrels, twin fusee bell striking movement, the case in the style of the late 18thC, c1850, 15in (38cm).
£900-1,200 *S(S)*

A mahogany bracket clock, with 7in (18cm) arched brass dial, triple-train fusee movement quarter chiming on coil gongs, the case carved with leafy scrolls, fluted columns and ovolos, c1900, 21in (53cm), with matching bracket.
£1,500-2,000 *S(S)*

A French Louis XV style green lacquered bracket clock, the waisted case surmounted by an allegorical figure and outlined with gilt metal mounts, the gilt dial inscribed Balthasard, Paris, late 19thC, 38in (97cm).
£800-1,200 *S(S)*

A Neuchatel bracket clock, with 9in (23cm) enamelled dial painted with putti at a fountain, the movement rack striking now on 2 gongs, the waisted case with verre eglomisé panels and painted with garlands, 28in (71cm).
£900-1,200 *S(S)*

A late Victorian chiming bracket clock, the arched brass and silvered dial with subsidiary dials for chime/silent and chime on 8-bells/Cambridge chimes, the repeating movement chiming on the quarter hours, in gilt brass mounted ebonised case, 24in (61cm).
£900-1,200 *Bea*

A late Victorian chiming bracket clock, with 7.5in (19cm) dial and subsidiary dials for chime/silent and chime selection for Westminster 8-bells/10-bells, the movement with a further 4 gongs and one other for the hour, the ebonised and imitation tortoiseshell case set with ornate gilt brass mounts, 28in (71cm).
£2,000-2,500 *Bea*

Carriage Clocks

A brass grande sonnerie carriage clock, the white enamelled dial and backplate signed C.J. Klaftenberger, with subsidiary alarm dial, the gorge case with bevelled glasses, the rear glass engraved Presented to Surgeon Major Logie, M.D., Royal Horse Guards by L. Wickham Esq., Feb. 1874, 5.5in (14cm), in leather travelling case.
£3,000-3,500 *S(S)*

A silver cased carriage clock, with a plain white enamel dial, platform lever escapement, the case of large size die-struck with masks and leafy scrolls, with carrying handle and resting on knurled bun feet, London 1891, 4.5in (11cm).
£600-800 *S(S)*

An 8-day repeating carriage clock, with alarm, No. 187, the white enamel dial signed Chas. Frodsham, Clockmaker to the Queen, 84 Strand London, the chapter ring with Roman numerals and alarm dial below, the lever movement striking the hour and half-hour on a bell, in gilt brass gorge case, 6in (15cm), and outer travelling case.
£800-1,000 *Bea*

A French brass carriage clock, inscribed Dent 61 Strand London, enclosing an 8-day movement, striking with 2 hammers on a single gong, 7in (18cm), and contemporary leather travelling case with brass key.
£500-600 *DDM*

A French gilt brass carriage clock, with a white enamelled dial and bell striking movement, in a one-piece case with bevelled glasses and moulded pillars, 5in (13cm).
£600-800 *S(S)*

A French carriage clock, with hour repeater and alarm, on bell, white enamel dial, retailed by Hall & Co., Manchester, movement stamped 'B' within a circle, c1900, 6in (15cm), and case with key. **£1,000-1,500** *McC*

A French gilt brass repeating carriage clock, with cream enamel chapter ring, leaf scroll engraved mask, gong striking movement, the case with upper and lower pierced friezes and with fluted columns and bail handle, 6in (15cm), and leather travelling case.
£600-700 *S(S)*

A brass carriage clock, with a white enamel dial and engine turned frost gilt mask, the movement numbered 4451, the case plain, on bracket feet, with bail handle, 3in (8cm).
£350-450 *S(S)*

Garnitures

A gilt metal mounted veined cream and brown marble clock garniture, the movement numbered 8608 and striking on a bell, some damage to eagle, clock 20in (50cm) high overall, urns 17in (42.5cm). **£550-650** *HSS*

A French clock garniture, the clock with an enamelled dial, signed T. Simpson et Cie, Paris, with blue Roman numerals and regulator square above XII, the centre painted with military trophies, the 8-day movement by Japy Frères, striking on a bell, the gilt metal case cast overall with diaper and scrollwork, incorporating 3 small enamel panels, the finial in the form of an armoured bust, 12in (31cm), with accompanying candelabra, all on giltwood stands and under glass domes.
£950-1,500 *Bea*

A French white marble and gilt brass clock garniture, the four-glass clock gong striking, the bevelled glasses mounted with garlands and with a vase surmount, c1800, clock 18.5in (47cm) high. **£2,200-2,700** *S(S)*

A French boulle clock garniture, with a 5.5in (14cm) cartouche dial, bell striking movement, in a waisted case with gilt brass scroll mounts and putto finial, 17in (43cm), and a pair of 4-light candelabra.
£1,200-1,700 *S(S)*

> **Miller's is a price GUIDE not a price LIST**

A clock garniture, the 8-day movement by Marti & Cie, in parcel gilt bronze mounted black marble case, surmounted by a bronze model of the Warwick vase, 19thC, 19in (48cm), the side pieces in the form of Medici vases, 18in (46cm).
£1,200-1,700 *Bea*

Lantern

A George I miniature brass lantern timepiece with alarm, the arched dial signed Massey London, with brass chapter ring, central alarm disc, pierced single steel hand, the movement with verge escapement and bob pendulum, alarm on bell above, lacking gallery frets and one side door, 8in (25cm) high.
£1,500-2,000 *C*

A brass striking lantern clock, with pierced blued hand, the movement with anchor escapement and countwheel strike on bell above, enclosed within pierced brass frets, 15in (38cm) high.
£800-1,000 *C*

A George III lantern clock for the Turkish market, with a 9in (22.5cm) dial with scroll and flower spandrels and signed Isaac Rogers London in the arch above, the posted movement with verge and short pendulum escapement and countwheel bell striking, c1770, 14in (35.5cm) high.
£1,500-2,000 *S*

A brass winged lantern clock, with a 6.5in (16.5cm) chapter ring, engraved dial, and central alarm disc, the central fret signed Peter Closon at London fecit, the movement now with verge escapement, outside countwheel and with central anchor pendulum, with an oak bracket and weight, with alterations and replacements.
£1,700-2,200 *S(S)*

A George II lantern timepiece with alarm, the dial signed John Belling Bodmyn 1753 beneath the chapter ring with central alarm disc, pierced blued single hand, the movement with verge escapement and alarm striking on bell above within engraved pierced gallery frets, spurs to back feet, 9in (23cm) high.
£4,000-4,500 *C*

A brass lantern clock, in 17thC style, with central alarm disc, verge escapement and bob pendulum, 8in (20cm), on a stained oak bracket.
£1,000-1,200 *S(S)*

Longcase

A George III mahogany longcase clock, with an 8-day movement striking on a bell with a chime of 8 bells, the chapter ring inscribed Rd. Bullock Ellesmere, 91in (231cm).
£3,500-4,000 *WW*

An oak longcase clock, the 11in (28cm) brass dial signed Gilbert Bullock, BPS. Castles, with date sector and 8-day bell-striking movement signed on the false plate Osborne, the case of good colour inlaid with chequerboard stringing and the trunk with parquetry panels, 81in (206cm).
£1,200-1,700 *S(S)*

An oak and mahogany longcase cock, with 8-day movement, and rack striking, signed D. Bowen, Alfreton, 90in (228.5cm).
£1,200-1,700 *L*

A George II walnut longcase clock, by John Benning, Windsor, the brass dial with ringed winding holes and date aperture, the lunar feature in the arch having a wheatear engraved border, the moon disc with starry sky background, c1730, 80in (203cm).
£8,000-8,250 *ALS*

An oak longcase clock, the brass dial with pierced spandrels enclosing an 8-day movement with seconds and date dials, the face inscribed, the rear of the movement marked W. Barnard Newark, number 473, 18thC, 78in (198cm). **£900-1,000** *DDM*

A George III red walnut longcase clock, the 13in (33cm) dial with calendar aperture, seconds dial, mask and leaf spandrels and signed Richard Corless Stockport, with rack and bell striking movement, c1770, 99in (251.5cm).
£2,500-3,000 *S*

An oak longcase clock, the brass dial with black Roman numerals and engraved decoration, by Thos. Brown, Birmingham, altered.
£350-450 *BWe*

An inlaid mahogany longcase clock, the painted arch dial by Blurton of Stourbridge, restored 8-day bell striking movement, early 19thC, 93in (236cm).
£1,300-1,600 *MJB*

A mahogany grandmother clock in the style of Dr. B. Franklin, by G. H. Bell, Winchester, with customary arched silvered dial with spiral scale, the 3-wheel movement with massive tapered plates and screwed pillars, the hood with broken arch, conforming trunk door and moulded plinth, c1971, 75.5in (192cm).
£900-1,500 *S(S)*

A George II blue japanned longcase clock, the 12in (31cm) dial signed Thomas Atherton, London, the 5-pillar movement with rack and bell striking, silvered wood finials and decorated throughout in gilt chinoiseries against a blue ground, 95in (241cm).
£2,000-2,500 *S*

A George III longcase clock, by Joseph Denton of Hull, with brass dial, moon phase and tidal indicators.
£4,000-4,500 *SWO*

A William III walnut and floral marquetry longcase clock, the 10in (25cm) brass dial signed Humphry Adamson, London, the 8-day bell striking movement with outside countwheel, with restoration and replacements, the formerly rising hood with plain pilasters, convex shoulder moulding, skirt replaced, 78.5in (199cm). **£12,000-15,000** *S(S)*

An oak longcase clock, with 8-day rack striking 4-pillar movement, with 12in (31cm) brass dial, the chapter with inner calendar ring, the circular boss in the arch signed R. Holborn, Tadcaster, 89in (226cm). **£800-1,000** *L*

A carved oak 8-day striking longcase clock, by Ben Kimberly, Catshill, 18thC, 90in (228.5cm). **£800-1,000** *GH*

A William IV automaton mahogany longcase clock, the 12in (31cm) dial signed And'w Rich, Bridgwater, with seconds dial, calendar sector, and an automaton scene in the arch of Adam and Eve, with rack and bell striking movement, the trunk door crossbanded with rosewood and flanked by similar pillars, 91.5in (232.5cm). **£1,500-2,000** *S*

A mahogany longcase clock, the 13in (33cm) dial signed S. Newnes, Whitchurch, the 8-day bell striking movement with false plate, 88in (223cm). **£3,200-3,800** *S(S)*

A George II burr walnut longcase clock, the 12in (31cm) dial signed Jn°. Berry, London, with seconds dial, calendar aperture, mask and leaf spandrels and a strike/silent dial in the arch, the movement with rack and bell striking in a flat top case with brass capped hood pilasters, some pieces replaced, 84.5in (215cm). **£2,000-2,800** *S*

An 8-day longcase clock, the white dial with a blue ground colour, by Samuel Deacon of Barton, in original oak case, 1806, 87in (221cm). **£2,800-3,500** *BL*

A Queen Anne japanned longcase clock, the 12in (31cm) dial signed Wm. Grimes, Hatton Garden fecit, with 6-pillar latched movement with inside countwheel, in a flat topped case with hood pilasters, rectangular trunk door with a lenticle and altered plinth, the whole decorated with gilt choinoiserie against a black ground, c1705, 84in (213cm).
£2,500-3,000 S

A George III mahogany longcase clock, the 14in (36cm) painted dial indistinctly signed Jnº Houghton, Chorley, the false plate signed Walker & Finnemore, the movement with rack and bell striking, in a well figured case with swan neck cresting and inlaid throughout with shells, fans and flowerheads, 87.5in (222cm).
£900-1,200 S(S)

A mahogany longcase clock, the 12in (31cm) arched brass dial signed on a plate Warburton, W. Hampton, with 8-day bell striking movement, 92.5in (234cm).
£1,500-2,000 S(S)

A George II longcase clock, with brass dial, silvered strike/silent, dial and chapter ring inscribed Christopher Harris, Leadenhall Street, London, in burr walnut case with feather inlay, base reduced, 82in (208cm).
£1,500-2,000 GSP

A longcase clock, by Denton Northgraves of Hull, with 8-day movement, in inlaid mahogany case, 96in (243.5cm).
£5,500-6,000 AH

A George II black japanned longcase clock, the dial signed Thomas Johnson, Richmond, with subsidiary seconds ring and calendar aperture, pierced blued hands, mask and foliate spandrels, the 5-pillar rack striking movement with anchor escapement, 88in (224cm).
£1,500-2,000 C

A longcase clock in early 18thC style, the brass dial with silvered chapter ring inscribed Tho. Lee, London, calendar aperture, the 4-pillar 8-day movement striking on a bell, in walnut veneered case, 69.5in (176cm).
£800-1,000 Bea

An exceptionally small 8-day white dial longcase clock, by McGregor of Ayton, Scotland, in original oak case, c1810, 79in (200.5cm).
£2,000-2,500 BL

A Scottish mahogany longcase clock, the 13in (33cm) silvered dial signed Chas. Merrilies, Edinburgh, subsidiary seconds and date dials, 8-day bell striking movement, the drum hood with concave brass bezel, 80.5in (204cm).
£1,200-1,700 S(S)

A George III satinwood and mahogany pedestal clock, the 13.5in (34cm) silvered dial signed Haswall London, with subsidiary regulation and calendar dials and a strike/not strike lever above XII, the 5-pillar bell striking fusee movement with anchor escapement, in a drum case with moulded wood bezel supported by a concave sided socle, inlaid with a fan on a satinwood ground within a border of ebony and box stringing, the whole standing on a later moulded satinwood pedestal, c1800, 66.5in (169cm).
£2,200-2,700 *S*

A mahogany 8-day longcase clock, by John Fladgate, London, c1775, 85in (216cm).
£5,500-7,000 *BL*

A mahogany longcase clock, the 12in (31cm) brass dial with silvered chapter ring, mask and scroll spandrels, signed in the arch Zak Mountford, London, 8-day bell striking movement, the hood with broken arch, pilasters lacking, conforming trunk door and moulded plinth, 86in (219cm).
£1,800-2,100 *S(S)*

An 8-day longcase clock with white dial, by Denton Northgraves of Hull, in original oak case of pagoda style, c1825, 88in (223cm).
£2,500-3,000 *BL*

A rare 8-day single handed longcase clock, by John Taylor of Ashton-under-Lyne, in its original very small oak case, 76in (193cm).
£3,500-4,500
BL

A William III ebonised longcase clock, the 11in (28cm) dial signed Charles Lowndes, Pall Mall London, the 5-pillar movement with inside countwheel and external detent, the case with domed caddy cresting, gilt wood finials and lenticle to the trunk door, 91in (231cm).
£5,000-7,000 *S*

A George III inlaid mahogany longcase clock, by Thomas, Millsom, the brass dial showing seconds, date, moon phase, and high water at Bristol, c1780, 91in (230cm).
£6,000-6,250 *ALS*

A George II oak longcase clock, with 6in (15cm) arch top dial, central alarm disc, single hand, scroll spandrels, signed on a disc in the arch Payne London, posted movement with anchor escapement, alarm bell above, 60in (152.5cm).
£2,500-3,000 *S*

A Queen Anne black lacquer longcase clock, the 11in (28cm) dial signed Brounker Watts, London, with silvered chapter ring, pierced blued hands, mask and foliate spandrels, the 5-pillar movement with anchor escapement and inside countwheel strike on bell, 76in (192cm).
£1,500-2,000 *C*

An oak and mahogany crossbanded 8-day longcase clock, by John Parton, Worksop, with white enamelled arched dial with hand painted floral spandrels and vignette scene in arch, second hand, date aperture, original minute and hour hands, 18thC, 90in (228.5cm).
£900-1,200 *GH*

A William and Mary chinoiserie decorated longcase clock, by John Wise, London, the 8-day movement with split winding barrels, outside countwheel striking, c1690, 94.5in (239cm).
£6,000-6,250 *ALS*

A George III oak and crossbanded longcase clock, the 13in (33cm) brass dial signed John Smith, Chester, with 8-day bell striking movement, 91in (232cm).
£3,500-4,000 *S(S)*

388

A George IV mahogany quarter striking longcase clock, the 14in (36cm) painted convex dial signed J. Summers, Bristol, with subsidiary calendar and strike silent dials, the curious movement composed of a Tavern clock movement with tapered plates and 5-wheel train, with an additional quarter striking movement mounted to the side sounding on 2 bells, the case with swan neck cresting and turned wood finial, rectangular trunk door flanked by canted corners inlaid with ebony stringing, plain plinth, feet missing, c1825, 84.5in (214.5cm).
£900-1,200 *S(S)*

An 8-day brass dial longcase clock, in original oak case with starburst inlay, by Tantum of Loscoe, c1730, 87in (221cm).
£2,800-3,500 *BL*

A George III green chinoiserie decorated longcase clock, by Vidion, Faversham, in pagoda top case, c1780, 96in (244cm).
£4,750-5,000 *ALS*

An 8-day longcase clock, by Richards of Uttoxeter, in original oak and mahogany case, c1830, 86in (218.5cm).
£1,800-2,500 *BL*

An 8-day longcase clock by Vurley of Wisbech, with a white dial, in original oak and mahogany case, 80in (203cm).
£2,000-2,500 *BL*

A George III mahogany longcase clock, the painted dial signed Jas. Troup, Stonehaven, with subsidiary seconds and calendar rings, pierced hands, foliate spandrels, the 4-pillar rack striking movement with anchor escapement, the case on ball feet, 76in (194cm).
£1,700-2,000 *C*

A George III Scottish mahogany longcase clock, the arch inscribed Turnbull and Aitchison, Edinburgh, the trunk with 2 panels veneered in burrwood, Corinthian columns at the corners, allover string lines and decorative bands, 8-day bell striking movement, 89in (226cm).
£1,300-1,800 *P(S)*

An oak longcase clock, the 11in (28cm) brass dial signed at the centre Peter Selby, Wareham, the 30-hour bell striking movement with outside countwheel, the hood with baluster columns, plain trunk and plinth.
£1,000-1,500 *S(S)*

A mahogany inlaid longcase clock, with a 14in (36cm) painted dial, signed M. Walker, Bolton, with 8-day bell striking movement, the case inlaid with shell and fan medallions and borders with stringing.
£1,500-2,000 *S(S)*

An Edwardian oak longcase clock, the projecting cornice above a brass face, with cast foliate spandrels and Roman numerals, case damaged.
£500-600 *BWe*

A mahogany chiming longcase clock, the 13in (33cm) dial signed John Smith Chester, the silvered chapter ring engraved 'Our days on earth are as a shadow and there is no abiding', chime control levers at IX and III, the 3-train movement chiming on 8 bells or 4 gongs with a further massive bell for the hour, and with wood rod pendulum, late 19thC incorporating some 18thC components, 97in (246cm).
£5,000-6,000 *S*

A green lacquer longcase clock, by Luke Thorowgood of London, the 12in (31cm) brass dial with strike/silent dial to arch, 8-day striking 5-pillar movement, the case decorated in gilt with chinoiserie, slight damage, 18thC, 88in (223.5cm).
£1,200-1,700 *CAG*

A George III mahogany musical longcase clock, the 14in (36cm) painted dial with seconds dial, subsidiary dials in the arch for chime/silent and tune selection, the 6-pillar bell striking movement playing one of 6 tunes on 12 bells at every hour, 91.5in (232cm).
£5,000-5,500 *S(S)*

This clock is in good original condition, but requires cleaning.

A rare English mahogany synchronome longcase clock, with 7in (18cm) skeleton chapter ring, pierced scroll hands, bell striking movement in two sections, the upper mechanism with two front mounted solenoids, one activating a sprung lever and pawl to operate the hands, the other similarly operating the striking by an electrically impulsed countwheel system, lower section with free mounted steel rod pendulum impulsing the detached gravity escapement, case with glazed door, moulded top and plinth with battery housing, early 20thC, 81in (205.5cm).
£1,800-2,200 *S*

A William and Mary walnut marquetry longcase clock, by Thomas Wheeler, London, the 11in (28cm) dial signed Tho. Wheeler Londini fecit, the movement with inside countwheel, flat top case with spiral hood pillars and long trunk door decorated with shaped panels of bird and flower marquetry with a lenticle, similarly decorated plinth with later apron, c1690, 84in (212.5cm).
£8,000-10,000 *S*

Thomas Wheeler was apprenticed in 1647, Free of the Clockmakers' Company from 1655 and served as Master in 1684. He died in 1694.

A George III longcase clock, by Radford of Leeds, with 8-day movement, subsidiary hand indicating date of the month, in oak crossbanded and inlaid case with brass ball surmounts, Corinthian column hood supports, and arched door with ivory escutcheon, 92in (233.5cm).
£2,000-2,500 *AH*

A mahogany granddaughter clock, with an 8in (20cm) brass dial, foliate spandrels, 8-day bell striking movement, the case with swan-neck pediment, fluted pilasters, chamfered trunk and plinth, inlaid with stringing, shells and floral motifs, c1900, 73.5in (186cm).
£1,700-2,200 *S(S)*

A mahogany longcase clock, the 12in (31cm) brass dial signed Joseph Smith, Chester on the chapter ring, with associated movement, the hood with broken arch, verre eglomisé frieze, trunk with shaped door and chamfered plinth, 83.5in (211cm).
£2,000-3,000 *S(S)*

An oak and crossbanded longcase clock, the 13in (33cm) arched brass dial indistinctly signed, 8-day bell striking movement, 86in (219cm).
£800-1,000 *S(S)*

An Edwardian mahogany chiming longcase clock, with a 12in (31cm) arched brass dial, triple-train movement, chiming on tubular gongs, 90.5in (230cm).
£2,200-2,500 *S(S)*

A mahogany granddaughter clock, the 6in (15cm) brass dial signed on the chapter ring Jan de Groot, 1751, with 8-day bell striking movement with rolling moon, restored, 52in (132cm).
£1,500-2,000 *S(S)*

A George III mahogany chiming longcase clock, the 13in (33cm) dial signed Robt. Welsh, Dalkeith, the substantial 3-train movement with anchor escapement, chiming the quarters on 6 bells with a further bell for the hour, 91in (228cm).
£2,500-3,000 *S*

A bleached and carved oak longcase clock, with a 14in (36cm) square painted dial, indistinctly signed, 8-day bell striking movement, 19thC, 83.5in (212cm).
£900-1,200 *S(S)*

An oak and mahogany longcase clock, the dial painted with a castle, 8-day movement, swan-neck pediment and brass eagle finial, early 19thC.
£600-700 *M*

A mahogany longcase clock, by Samuel Stephens of London, the 12in (31cm) brass dial with silvered nameplate to arch, 8-day striking 5-pillar movement, the figured case with turned and fluted pillars, the arched trunk door with moulded edges and with conforming panelled plinth, 18thC, 92in (233.5cm).
£2,000-3,000 *CAG*

An oak longcase clock, with 12in (31cm) arched brass dial, the painted arch with an automaton man-o'-war, silvered chapter ring, foliate scroll spandrels, date aperture and seconds dial, the hood with broken arch and brass ball finials, plain trunk and plinth, 88in (223cm).
£1,600-2,000 *S(S)*

An Edwardian mahogany chiming longcase clock, the 8-day movement with tubular chimes and an arched brass and silvered dial, with regulator to the lunette, gilt leaf spray spandrels, 86in (218.5cm).
£1,200-1,700 *WW*

A Scottish mahogany longcase clock, the 14in (36cm) dial signed J. Wiseman, Hamilton, with 8-day bell striking movement, arched hood with baluster columns, c1840, 83.5in (212cm).
£550-650 *S(S)*

A George III longcase clock, the painted dial decorated with flowers and Britannia in an oval, the 8-day movement with calendar and seconds dials and striking on a bell, the inlaid mahogany case with carved swan neck pediment and corner columns, 82in (208cm).
£1,700-2,000 *Bea*

A Victorian mahogany longcase clock, with painted figurative spandrels representing the seasons, the centre with Christ in the Wilderness, white chapter ring inscribed Blackhurst Over, subsidiary seconds dial, the well-figured trunk and inspection door with inlaid string lines, 8-day bell striking movment, 90in (228.5cm).
£1,200-1,500 *P(S)*

A Yorkshire longcase clock by James Whitworth, Lussley, the 12in (31cm) arched brass dial with rolling moon in the arch, subsidiary seconds and date pointer, 8-day 4-pillar rack striking movement with anchor escapement, 82.5in (209cm).
£1,200-1,700 *P(M)*

A mahogany longcase clock, the painted dial indistinctly inscribed, enclosing an 8-day movement with seconds and date dials, 19thC, 88in (223.5cm).
£800-1,000 *DDM*

Mantel Clocks

A French ormolu mantel clock, the 5in (12.5cm) white enamelled dial signed Perache à Paris, the drum movement with signed backplate, silk suspension and outside countwheel and with bell striking, 16.5in (42cm).
£1,800-2,000 *S(S)*

A French champlevé enamel and gilt metal mantel clock of lyre form with Japy Frères movement striking on a bell, the base set with two putti, late 19thC, 13in (33cm). **£1,200-1,500** *Bea*

A mahogany and brass inlaid mantel clock, the 6in (15cm) cream dial signed Catchpool, Bishopsgate St., London, twin fusee movement, with pull repeat, the backplate with engraved border, c1820, 16.5in (42cm).
£1,000-1,200 *S(S)*

An Empire bronze and ormolu mantel clock, the twin train movement with bell strike, the white enamel dial with Roman and Arabic chapter ring, inscribed Le Sieur à Paris, with engine turned bezel, 14in (5.5cm).
£2,500-3,000 *CSK*

A late Victorian chiming mantel clock, the dial with 3 subsidiaries, the substantial triple-train fusee movement chiming on 8 bells and striking on gongs, the architectural case inlaid with swags and scrolls, gilt brass mounts, 23.5in (60cm).
£1,500-2,000 *S(S)*

A gilt brass perpetual calendar mantel clock, the 3in (7.5cm) white enamelled dial signed Cotonie, Paris, and with subsidiary dials for day, date and month, with silk suspension and Japy Frères movement, the associated case with leaf engraved and pierced mask, 8.5in (21cm).
£700-900 *S(S)*

A Regency brass inlaid mahogany mantel clock, the painted dial with regulation and strike/silent dials, the movement with engraved backplate signed John Moore, Clerkenwell, pull repeat, the arched case with fishscale frets and moulded lower frieze, 20in (51cm).
£900-1,200 *S(S)*

A Louis Philippe ormolu automaton mantel clock, with an enamel dial and a silk suspension movement signed Guyerdet & Bouilly à Paris, striking on a gong in the base, the case in the form of a fortified chateau with a ship and a rowing boat rolling realistically on the choppy 'water' below, the automaton movement with 3 cams and mounted in an inlaid rosewood plinth, dome cracked, c1840, 25in (64cm).
£5,000-5,500 *S*

A French gilt mantel clock, the 3in (7.5cm) dial painted and signed Achille Brocot, bell striking, the case with pink porcelain panels and lion's masks, 14.5in (37cm), with dome and plinths.
£900-1,200 *S(S)*

A Napoleon III oval 4-glass perpetual calendar mantel clock, the bell striking Marti movement No. 6635 with Brocot escapement and mercury pendulum, the 2-piece enamel dial centred by a colourful calendar indicating date, day of the week and month, an aperture above showing moon phases, in a gilt brass oval four-glass moulded case, c1870, 15in (39cm).
£2,700-3,200 *S*

A small French gilded case mantel clock, with small drum case striking movement, with a silvered Roman numeral dial, 19thC, 5in (13cm).
£450-500 *GAK*

A Louis XV style bronze elephant
mantel clock.
£650-750 *P(S)*

A French pale rosewood and brass
inlaid mantel clock, the drum
movement stamped Jules à Paris,
the case with engraved gilt mask
and brass wire inlay, bell
striking, 6.5in (17cm).
£550-600 *S(S)*

A French mantel clock, the 8-day
movement by Vincenti & Cie and
striking on a bell, the ornate gilt
bronze and ormolu case set with
Sèvres style porcelain plaques
painted with portraits, cherubs
and gilt foliage on a turquoise
ground, mid-19thC, 14.5in
(36cm).
£1,500-2,000 *Bea*

A French ormolu mantel clock,
with a 4in (10cm) chased dial and
bell striking movement, 14in
(36cm).
£400-500 *S(S)*

A French ormolu
mantel clock,
surmounted by a
figure of Molière
seated at a table
with manuscripts,
19thC.
£550-750 *LRG*

A French ormolu
mantel clock,
the circular
exposed dial with
enamelled
numerals
inscribed Silvany
à Paris, enclosing
a brass 8-day
movement
inscribed Raingo
Frères Paris, with
silk suspension
pendulum and
strike on a single
bell, case and
movement
numbered 2393,
late 19thC, 20in
(51cm).
£750-850 *DDM*

A French black marble and inlaid perpetual calendar mantel clock, with exposed Brocot escapement, the subsidiary dial for calendar, in a shaped rectangular case, c1880, 18.5in (47cm).
£900-1,000 *S(S)*

A Louis Philippe lacquered brass case mantel clock, with gilt bronze neo-classical style mounts, the 8-day movement striking on a bell, the dial with an engine turned centre and enamel chapter ring. **£450-550** *WW*

An Austrian bronze and gilt bronze mantel clock, with 3.5in (9cm) enamel dial, circular movement with silk suspension, chalet case flanked by a recumbent ram and a putto carrying a lamb, 12in (30.5cm).
£700-1,000 *S*

A George IV mahogany and brass inlaid mantel clock, the 8in (20cm) convex cream dial and twin fusee movement with pull repeat, bell striking and shaped rectangular plates, 18in (46cm).
£900-1,200 *S(S)*

A French brass and boulle cased mantel clock, with a brass dial, the case mounted and surmounted with cherubs and having a drum case striking movement, 18in (46cm).
£350-650 *GAK*

A French gilt mantel clock, c1860, 16in (41cm), on giltwood plinth.
£450-550 *S(S)*

An Austrian carved walnut mantel clock, with a 4.5in (11.5cm) cartuche dial, now with a French bell striking movement, the case carved with deer climbing on a rocky mound, c1900, 27in (69cm).
£650-750 *S(S)*

A French brass mantel clock, in late 18thC style, the case cast in the form of the Chariot of Diomedes, the dial forming the wheel, c1880, 20.5in (52cm).
£1,500-2,000 *S(S)*

A French gilt mantel clock, with drum cased bell striking movement, on scroll supports and shaped plinth, c1870, 15in (38cm).
£500-600 *S(S)*

An Austrian Grande Sonnerie automaton mantel clock, the 7in (18cm) annular enamel chapter ring enclosing automaton cupids grinding and hammering arrows and connected to the striking trains, the 3-train movement with standing barrels, anchor escapement, silk suspension and gong striking, the shaped drum case supported by alabaster columns enclosing a mirrored recess below with a parquetry floor and applied with repoussé gilt brass and giltwood mounts, c1825, 25in (63.5cm).
£1,500-1,800 *S*

A French gilt brass mantel clock, with a 3.5in (9cm) cartouche dial, bell striking, the waisted case mounted with putti and goats at play, 17.5in (44cm).
£650-750 *S(S)*

An American 4-glass mantel clock, with a 4in (10cm) cream stepped dial signed for Ansonia, with exposed Brocot gong striking movement, the case cast with leafy scrolls and floral clusters, 15.5in (39cm).   **£500-600** *S(S)*

A French gilt brass mounted mantel clock, the bell striking movement in a spherical case painted with Zodiacal devices and supported on a winged eagle, on a white marble base, c1880, 13.5in (34cm).   **£500-700** *S(S)*

A French ormolu and enamel panel mantel clock, with striking gong, the case with musical trophy surmount, c1890, 10.5in (27cm).
£650-750 *S(S)*

An Empire ormolu mounted white marble mantel clock of obelisk form, surmounted by an inset plaque cast in relief with nymphs and Cupid, the top with an armillary globe, the black slate plinth on toupé feet, 24in (61cm).
£2,500-3,000 *CSK*

Regulators

A mahogany Vienna regulator, the 7in (18cm) 2-piece enamel dial indistinctly signed, the movement with arch top square plates, deadbeat escapement, ebonised wood rod pendulum with brass bob, dial cracked, c1845, 37in (94cm). **£800-1,000** *S(S)*

A month going mahogany Vienna regulator, the 8in (20cm) 2-piece enamel dial signed Adolf Hradetzkn in Brünn, flower and scroll cast bezel, movement with wide tapering plates, deadbeat escapement, micrometer adjustment to the crutch, ebonised wood rod pendulum with brass bob, c1850, 49in (125cm). **£4,000-5,000** *S*

A mahogany and ebonised wall regulator, the 7in (18cm) silvered dial with subsidiary seconds and hour dials, scroll pierced mask in a plain arched case with scroll shoulders, 39in (99cm). **£720-800** *S(S)*

An Austrian walnut Grande Sonnerie wall regulator, with a 2-piece enamel dial and finely pierced hands, the 3-train weight driven movement striking on 2 gongs with deadbeat escapement and wood rod pendulum, c1880, 52.5in (133.5cm). **£1,800-2,200** *S*

A French mahogany electric master wall regulator, the 7in (18cm) white enamel dial signed Henry Lepaute, Paris, Régulator Electrique, the similarly stamped movement No. 6116 with square brass plates, and deadbeat Brocot escapement sending periodic electrical pulses by the action of springs on staggered cams mounted on the third wheel arbor, wood rod pendulum with brass lenticular bob, c1905, 39in (99cm). **£1,200-1,500** *S*

A Victorian mahogany longcase regulator, by S. Bloomfield & Co. of London, the 12.5in (32cm) circular silvered dial inscribed with maker's name, the 8-day movement with deadbeat escapement and maintaining power, 72in (182cm). **£3,500-4,000** *HSS*

A mahogany Vienna regulator, with 7in (18cm) milk glass dial, cast and chased bezel, movement with square plates, deadbeat escapement, micrometer adjustment to the crutch, ebonised wood rod pendulum with brass bob, case lacking cresting, 37.5in (95cm).
£1,300-1,500 *S*

A mahogany Vienna regulator, with 7in (18cm) enamel dial, engine turned bezel, movement with square plates, c1830, 43in (110cm).
£2,800-3,200 *S*

A Victorian Vienna regulator with walnut and beech case, decorated with typical split turnings, unusual keyhole shaped glass covering white enamel dial, 8-day movement striking on single gong, 57in (145cm). **£550-750** *WIL*

A mahogany Vienna regulator, with 7in (18cm) 2-piece enamel dial indistinctly signed, florally cast bezel, movement with arch top square plates, deadbeat escapement, ebonised wood rod pendulum with brass bob, dial cracked, c1845, 37in (94cm).
£1,000-1,500 *S(S)*

Skeleton Clocks

A brass York Minster skeleton clock, by Alfred Smith of Huddersfield, with an 8in (20cm) skeletonised silvered chapter ring, 6-spoke wheels, twin fusee movement, rack and snail strike on a gong and bell pull repeat, stamped on base and on an ebonised plinth, c1860, 21in (53cm).
£2,000-2,500 *S(S)*

A Victorian balance wheel skeleton clock, with 4.5in (11.5cm) chapter ring, fusee movement with 6-spoke wheels, pierced barrel covers, maintaining power and deadbeat escapement with vertical balance and lever, in a scroll frame on a stepped rosewood plinth, c1850, with later glazed cover, 12.5in (32cm).
£1,500-2,000 *S*

A brass skeleton clock, the frame of scroll form, the 2-train fusee movement with bell striking and pull repeat,5-spoke wheels, the 5.5in (14cm) silvered chapter ring inscribed J. D. Taylor, Liverpool, wood base, 19thC, 13in (33cm), on an ebonised stand with glass dome. **£600-700** *P(S)*

An early Victorian month going skeleton clock, attributed to Parker and Pace, Bury St Edmunds, with 8.5in (21.5cm) silvered chapter ring, twin fusee movement driving the intermediate pinion and a 4-wheel train with deadbeat escapement and cylindrical bob pendulum, the backplate of solid arched form, the frontplate consisting of interlocking scrolls, marble base with glass dome, c1850, 11.5in (29cm).
£1,700-2,200 *S*

Table Clocks

A George III mahogany table clock, the 8in (20cm) silvered dial signed William Lindsey, London, central calendar, strike/silent in the arch, engraved flower spandrels, 5-pillar bell striking fusee movement, verge escapement and well engraved backplate, c1790, 17in (44cm).
£500-2,000 *S*

William Lindsey was apprenticed in 1759.

A Charles II ebony veneered table clock, with 6.5in (16.5cm) dial, calendar aperture, cherub spandrels, 5-pillar bell striking movement signed Henry Younge in ye Strand, verge escapement, formerly quarter repeating with unusual circular rack mounted on the front plate, well moulded case with small domed top, brass carrying handle and claw feet, verge rebuilt, c1680, 12in (30cm).
£7,000-9,000 *S*

Henry Younge was apprenticed in 1659 to Thomas Taylor and Free of the Clockmakers' Company from 1672; he worked in London until c1685. This clock was made soon after the introduction of rack striking and has a most unusual and efficient form of circular rack. Although the quarter repeating work has been entirely removed the 3-stepped quarters snail can still be seen on the minute wheel.

A Germanic striking table clock with alarm, the gilt movement signed Kriedel London on the top plate, with foliate pierced and chased footed lock, chain fusee for the gong, resting barrel for the bell in hinged base, pull wind alarm from the central disc in the silver champlevé arcaded dial, with blued steel hour hand and later minute hand, and similarly signed on the outer concentric alarm ring, c1700, 4in (10cm) dial diam.
£4,000-5,000 *CSK*

A Swiss cylinder paperweight table clock, the three-quarter plate keywind movement with going barrel, plain cock with steel regulator, plain 3-arm gilt balance with blue steel spiral hairspring, white enamel dial with subsidiary seconds, Roman numerals, blue steel hands, domed gunmetal case with silver bezel and a folding strut for use as a desk clock, c1870.
£50-90 *PT*

Wall Clocks

A George IV mahogany wall clock, the 15in (36cm) painted dial signed J. R. Parker, Walsingham, weight driven movement with tapered plates, 5 wheels in the train and anchor escapement, the case with moulded wood bezel, c1830, 53.5in (136cm).
£1,400-1,800 *S*

A mahogany and boxwood gaming wall clock, with framed and glazed baize lined dial, the frame surmounted by turned boxwood chess pieces, the twin going barrel movement with anchor escapement and strike on gong, frame 20in (51cm) square. **£800-1,200** *C*

Samuel Orr
The Clock Shop

36 High Street, Hurstpierpoint
West Sussex BN6 9RG

Telephone:
Hurstpierpoint (0273) 832081
(24 Hour Answerphone)

The Pantiles Spa Antiques
Tunbridge Wells
(0892) 541377
Car Phone: 0860 230888

ANTIQUE CLOCKS · BAROMETERS
RESTORATION CLOCKS PURCHASED

**FINE SELECTION OF ANTIQUE CLOCKS
FOR SALE**

Exhibitor at Olympia

A Dutch Zaandam striking and alarm wall clock.
£2,000-2,500 *P(S)*

A mahogany drop dial wall clock, the 12in (31cm) brass dial signed Thos. Pierce, Jnr., Bristol, twin fusee movement, bell striking, trunk with glazed lenticle, 27.5in (70cm).
£550-700 *S(S)*

A German Black Forest wall clock, with strike and alarm, the 3.5in (9cm) enamel dial with central alarm disc and set on a colourfully decorated porcelain surround, the wood plated weight driven movement with outside countwheel, gong striking and top mounted alarm bell, the frame with the original side doors, gong missing, c1860, 8in (21cm).
£550-750 *S*

A Victorian Gothic quarter chiming wall clock, signed W. Potts & Sons, Leeds, with blued spade hands, the massive 5-pillar triple chain fusee movement with anchor escapement chiming on 8 bells via 8 hammers and striking on gong on backboard, 35in (89cm) high.
£2,000-2,500 *C*

A French picture wall clock, with silvered dial enclosing an engine turned panel, the movement striking the quarters on 2 graduated bells, and with sunburst pendulum, 19thC, 21in (53cm).
£650-750 *HSS*

A George III mahogany wall clock, the 13in (33cm) painted dial signed T. Banks, Preston, the false plate signed Finnemore, 2-train rack and bell striking weight driven movement, teardrop case outlined with ebony and box stringing, veneered in well figured wood, c1800, 62in (157.5cm).
£1,200-1,800 *S*

> Miller's is a price GUIDE not a price LIST

Miscellaneous

A Continental walnut and boxwood strung cuckoo clock, the alabaster dial with cartouche chapter ring and enamel Roman numerals, the twin train movement striking on a gong, with bellow mechanism, 19thC, 19in (48cm).
£500-700 *CSK*

WATCHES

A Thomas Earnshaw 18ct. gold hunter cased half quarter repeating watch, hallmarked 1847, case maker's mark AC, 2 small chips around the edge, 4.9cm.
£1,200-1,500 *L*

A gold open faced keyless lever watch, by Patek Philippe, Geneve, with short length of 18ct. gold chain, 5.3cm.
£800-1,000 *L*

An 18ct. gold open faced key wind watch, the full plate fusee movement with lever escapement, plain gold 3 arm balance and signed French, Royal Exchange, London, hallmarked 1826, hinge to back cover defective, 4.2cm.
£300-350 *L*

A Swiss yellow metal hunter cased quarter repeating key wind pocket watch, the movement with compensated lever movement, repeating on 2 gongs with 2 hammers, white enamel dial with gold hands and subsidiary seconds dial, in an engine turned case with repeating slide in the band, with gold 'tipsy' key, 5cm.
£900-1,000 *L*

An 18ct gold open faced key wind watch, the full plate fusee movement with lever escapement, compensated balance, engraved cock and signed Wm. Simcock, Warrington, with small inspection on cover and hallmarked 1872, 4.6cm.
£200-250 *L*

A pink gold hunter cased keyless lever watch, No. 57032, matt gilded movement signed Deutsche Uhrenfabrikation Glashütte, gold escape wheel and pallets, compensation balance, blued steel spiral spring and regulator with micrometer adjustment, white enamel dial, signed Deutsche Uhrenfabrikation Glashütte I/S, Lange & Söhne, plain Louis XVI-type case, the three covers with the Lange stamp, c1910, 5.5cm.
£1,700-2,000 *S*

A spherical glass magnifying paperweight deck watch, by the New Haven Clock Co., 19thC, 7.5cm.
£200-220 *TRU*

A lady's silver and enamel cased fob watch, enamel chipped to rear.
£80-95 *TRU*

An 18ct. gold cased quarter repeating keyless lever pocket watch, with unsigned movement, white enamel dial with Arabic numerals and subsidiary seconds, the minutes divided into fifths, the back inner case engraved 'A Happy New Era, 1901', the outer case with monogram inlaid with blue enamel, some damage.
£900-1,100 *WIL*

A gentleman's pocket watch by Record, with nickel case and Swiss lever movement, with GWR insignia on the reverse.
£75-100 *TRU*

A gentleman's silver cased keyless chronograph pocket watch, with Swiss lever movement. **£80-95** *TRU*

A Swiss lever deck watch, in a nickelled open faced case, nickel split three-quarter plate keyless movement with going barrel, plain cock with polished steel regulator, uncut bimetallic balance with overcoil hairspring, signed white enamel dial with Arabic numerals, the quarter numerals luminous, subsidiary seconds, luminous hands, open face nickelled case with clip on back and bezel, Ministry of Defence broad arrow on the back cover above the letters GSTP, signed General Watch Co., Switzerland Helvetia, c1845, 5.2cm.
£100-120 *PT*

A Waltham, U.S.A., nickel cased lever deck watch, the grained nickel split three-quarter plate keyless movement with going barrel, plain cock with polished steel regulator, uncut bimetallic balance with overcoil hairspring, black dial with luminous Arabic numerals, subsidiary seconds, luminous hands, c1942, 5cm.
£100-120 *PT*

An 18ct. gold half hunter cased keyless lever watch, the three-quarter plate movement with compensated balance, and inscribed The Field, By Warrant to H. M. the Late Queen, and signed J. W. Benson, Ludgate Hill, London, the turned case hallmarked Birmingham 1922, and with push-piece in the band, 5.2cm.
£450-500 *L*

A silver rack lever pair cased watch, by Tobias, with full plate gilt keywind fusee movement with dust cover, Harrison's maintaining power, chased and engraved cock inscribed Patent on the foot, diamond endstone, signed M l Tobias & Co Liverpool 5090, hallmarked Chester 1818, maker's mark ITE, inner case and underside of the dust cover stamped T & Co. and numbered in accordance with the movement, 5.7cm.
£500-550 *PT*

A Swiss lever watch in an open face silver and niello case, plain cock with polished steel regulator, club foot lever escapement, signed engine turned silver dial with Roman numerals, blue steel hands, slim open face silver case decorated with a geometric design in niello, signed Fresard Watch Lucerne & Lausanne, c1890, 5cm.
£400-450 *PT*

A Rolex pendant watch, the circular stepped case enclosing a glazed Rolex Extra Prima 15 jewel movement, timed 6 positions for all climates, suspended from a suede fob.
£550-750 *CSK*

A Masonic silver watch, with indistinct Edinburgh import mark, the case back and sides decorated with Masonic symbols, the triangular mother-of-pearl dial with polychrome Masonic symbol numeral indicators and blued steel hands.
£1,200-1,700 *S(S)*

An 18ct. white gold purse-shaped cased pendant fob watch, by Rolex, the jewelled movement signed Rolex Observatory, 1000947, Swiss Made, Rolex Officially Tested in Eight Ways, the dial signed Rolex Prince Imperial, together with a dress Albert chain with swivel and a bolt ring as fitted.
£1,500-2,000 *S(S)*

A Swiss lever watch, by Patek Philippe, in a brass drum case, compensation balance with blue steel spiral hairspring, the lever with counterbalance extensions to the arms, signed white enamel dial with subsidiary seconds, blue steel hands, fitted in a brass case with screw back which is contained in a deep brass drum with glazed screw on bezel, 3 holes in the base, c1890, 5.5cm
£500-600 *PT*

A Swiss 8-day lever watch, with gilt keyless movement, compensation balance with blue steel overcoil hairspring, patent no. 6279+497 on the bridge, plain silver open face case with gilt winding crown, the back opening to form an easel stand, c1890.
£500-600 *PT*

An American gold plated hunter cased fob watch, with gold plated fob.
£50-60 *TRU*

A rare George III watch alarm, by W. Gossage.
£560-600 *RBB*

An 18ct. gold minute repeating pocket watch. **£2,200-2,700** *HSS*

An 18ct gold open faced key wind watch, signed Jas. Whitlaw, Edinburgh, hallmarked 1826, 5.3cm.
£300-350 *L*

A silver hunter cased verge watch, for the Turkish market, the full plate fusee movement with pierced and engraved cock, Turkish signature, and silvered regulator dial, the white enamel dial with Turkish numerals, unmatched hands and signed Ralph Gout, London, case hinge defective, hallmarked 1834, 4.9cm.
£250-300 *L*

Wristwatches

A gentleman's silver cased wristwatch, with jewelled Swiss lever movement, finished and retailed by Benson, c1930.
£95-120 *TRU*

A gentleman's wristwatch, by Longines, in a gold case, c1930.
£95-120 *TRU*

A Massey lever in a silver open face case, full plate gilt keywind fusee movement with signed and numbered dust cover, Harrison's maintaining power, engraved cock with diamond endstone, polished steel Bosley regulator, signed Hunt & Son Yarmouth 39248, hallmarked London 1825, maker's mark IHM, 5.3cm.
£280-320 *PT*

A lady's stainless steel cased Rolex Oyster Perpetual wristwatch, the silvered dial with applied gilt metal line batons with aperture for date, in a case of plain form on articulated stainless steel Rolex bracelet strap.
£350-400 *CSK*

A paste set metal wristwatch, by the Aircraft Watch Co., with Swiss cylinder movement, c1930.
£35-55 *TRU*

A gentleman's 9ct. gold cased wristwatch, signed Rolex, Observatory Quality, the signed silvered dial with black Arabic numerals, subsidiary seconds and gilt hands, the case back engraved 6 May 1929, import mark Glasgow, 1928, with a black strap.
£700-900 *S(S)*

An early white gold wristwatch, by Gruen, with a brushed silvered dial, the snap-on back with maker's mark, numbered 1240221, the signed lozenge shaped frosted gilt movement with unusual engraved scroll decoration, 17 jewels and numbered 700861, 2.4cm wide.
£450-500 *C*

An 18ct. gold Rolex Oyster Perpetual Day Date wristwatch, the reverse with engraved initials, on a plated strap.
£800-1,000 *MJB*

A gentleman's steel Rolex Oyster date precision wristwatch, the black dial with baton markers and sweep centre seconds, with maker's steel bracelet attached.
£150-175 *CSK*

A white gold Precision wristwatch, by Gruen, Anniversary model with silvered dial, the snap-on back with maker's signature, numbered 1111999, the signed lozenge shaped frosted gilt movement with unusual engraved scroll decoration, 17 jewels and numbered 702053, 2.4cm wide.
£450-500 *C*

A gold asymmetric wristwatch, by Hamilton, in a shield shaped case with stepped lugs, the snap-on back with maker's mark, the signed working movement with battery, 3.1cm wide.
£800-1,000 *C*

A 9ct. gold wristwatch by Zenith, c1930.
£150-170 *TRU*

A gentleman's 9ct. gold cased Rolex Oyster Perpetual chronometer, with Rolex 9ct. gold gate link style bracelet.
£1,500-2,000 *GAK*

A gentleman's steel Rolex Oyster chronometer wristwatch, with polished yellow bezel, the white dial with baton markers and sweep centre seconds, on leather strap.
£300-400 *CSK*

A battery operated advertising display in the form of a wristwatch, in a gilt case with milled bezel, the white dial with raised baton numerals and sweep centre seconds, with leather strap and gilt buckle, 11.5cm.
£120-170 *C*

A gun metal fob watch, with a Swiss lever movement, now converted to a wristwatch.
£22-30 *TRU*

A gentleman's steel and gilt Rolex Oyster perpetual wristwatch, the silvered dial with dot markers and sweep centre seconds, with maker's matching expanding bracelet attached.
£450-500 *CSK*

A gentleman's Continental Rolex Oyster Royal Precision wristwatch, the silvered dial with Arabic and dart markers, the movement inscribed Rolex Chronometer timed 6 positions, patented super balance, on leather strap.
£500-700 *CSK*

A chrome cased digital wristwatch, with Swiss lever movement, 15 jewels, c1930.
£95-120 *TRU*

A lady's Tudor wristwatch, with a 9ct. gold case and bracelet, c1930.
£65-80 *TRU*

A gentleman's steel Rolex Oyster perpetual wristwatch, with yellow bezel, the white dial with baton markers, sweep centre seconds, the date aperture, the bezel with hour markings, on maker's steel bracelet.
£450-550 *CSK*

A gentleman's yellow gold oyster perpetual wristwatch, the movement stamped Rolex Perpetual, Trigger Screw, Vis. Tirette 000, the silvered dial inscribed Rolex Perpetual, Chronometer, import mark for Glasgow 1937, on 9ct. expanding bracelet.
£1,500-2,000 *L*

A gentleman's silver wristwatch in a cushion shaped case, c1925.
£55-70 *TRU*

A Tourneau gold calendar and moonphase chronograph wristwatch, the matt silvered dial with outer date ring and central date hand, dagger 5-minute marks, subsidiary dials for running seconds, elapsed minutes and hours combined with phases of the moon, apertures for day and month, sweep centre seconds operated by two buttons in the band, the case with screwed back and maker's mark, numbered 1024324, the signed movement jewelled to the centre, 3.5cm.
£1,000-1,500 *C*

A collection of 46 steel watch keys, one in the form of a pipe, another a pistol, on a green cloth mount.
£1,700-2,000 *S*

BAROMETERS
Chronometers

A 2-day marine chronometer, by Victor Kullberg, No. 6357, the 4in (10cm) silvered dial signed and numbered, the movement with Earnshaw spring detent, escapement, palladium spring, compensated balance, spotted movement, gold hands and fully numbered, with brass gimbal and box, in a 3-tier mahogany case.
£1,500-2,000 *S(S)*

An 8-day marine chronometer, originally made for use with vacuum, glass and pump now missing, unsigned movement with reversed fusee, Earnshaw spring detent escapement, Z-balance, free sprung, 4in (10cm) silvered dial, the whole gimballed in mahogany carrying case with door at the front for access, c1800.
£6,500-7,500 *S*

A 2-day marine chronometer with integral balance, with later unsigned spotted movement with Earnshaw spring detent escapement, Guillaume integral compensated balance, blued steel helical spring, free sprung, restored silvered dial signed A. Lange & Söhne, Glashütte B/Dresden No. 79, Roman numerals, subsidiary dials for seconds and up-and-down, in brass box also numbered, stamped 671E and with crowned M, in brass bound rosewood box with flush handles, later key, diameter of bezel 5in (12cm).
£3,500-4,500 *S*

Stick Barometers

A Regency mahogany bowfront stick barometer, with ogee top, glazed vernier scale signed G. C. Dixey, London, moulded ebonised cistern cover to shaped base, restored, 38.5in (97cm).
£1,800-2,200 *C*

A mahogany stick barometer, the bone plates signed H. Hughes, 59 Fenchurch Street, London, with mercury thermometer, the case with arched top and turned cistern cover, 36.5in (93cm).
£700-900 *S(S)*

A mahogany bowfronted stick barometer, with step pediment and bowfronted thermometer to main trunk, with original ebony urn cistern cover to the base, c1835.
£2,800-3,800 *W&W*

A George I walnut barometer, by J Halifax of Barnsley, 6in (15cm) dial with mask spandrels, finely engraved centre scrolling leaves, the richly coloured chevron veneered trunk outlined in stringing and set with engraved recording dial, c1720.
£45,000-50,000 *MERT*

A Victorian rosewood mercury stick barometer, ivorine inner plates, thermometer, vernier reading scale, by J Gargory, Bull Street, Birmingham, 36in (92cm).
£750-850 *GH*

A mahogany stick barometer, the paper plates signed Manticha Fecit, the case with exposed tube, fluted corners and rectangular cistern cover, 38.5in (97cm).
£600-700 *S(S)*

A mahogany stick barometer, with silvered brass dials and long thermometer to the front of case, c1790.
£1,800-2,400 *W&W*

A mahogany stick barometer, with round top, glazed door to main dial, exposed tube on front of case and hemispherical cistern cover, c1800.
£1,600-2,300 *W&W*

A George II mahogany stick barometer, with later wood finial to cavetto arched top, the dial with foliate border engraving, moulded cistern cover, 38in (97cm).
£500-800 *C*

A Queen Anne walnut stick barometer, with concealed tube, brass register calibrated between 28 and 31 and signed John Williamson, adjustable pointer, arch top moulded cresting, barley sugar twist columns beneath, flanking a shaped splat, shaped base, turned cistern cover, c1700, 49in (125cm). **£3,000-5,000** *S*

An English mahogany stick barometer, with shaped brass plates, adjustable pointer, concealed tube with turned cistern cover, on a moulded backboard with broken arch top and base, late 18thC, 38in (97cm). **£400-600** *S*

A mahogany bowfront stick barometer, with original ebony urn cistern cover, c1790. **£3,800-4,500** *W&W*

A mahogany stick barometer, with break arch pediment, thermometer to main dial and exposed mercury tube to front of case, with original round cistern cover, c1800. **£1,200-1,800** *W&W*

A mahogany bowfronted stick barometer, early 19thC. **£3,000-4,000** *P(S)*

Wheel Barometers

A flight of 3 walnut barometers, by C. H. Chadburn & Son, with 8, 10 and 12in (20, 25 and 31cm) dials, with patented rack and pinion movement, dated 1861.
£4,000-4,500 the set *MERT*

An Edwardian Regency style mahogany aneroid wall barometer, crossbanded with satinwood, with thermometer box, 8in (20cm) silvered dial, J. Lucking & Co., Birmingham, 34in (86cm).
£300-400 *GH*

A Sheraton design mahogany banjo shaped barometer, by Catelly & Co, Hereford, the case inlaid with shells and chequered stringing.
£700-900 *LRG*

An oak cased aneroid barometer, in Art Nouveau design, by Negretti & Zambra, London, 11.5in (29cm).
£80-140 *MERT*

A carved oak aneroid barometer, with printed 8in (20cm) dial, by Coombes of Davenport, unrestored, c1910, 33in (84cm).
£100-150 *MERT*

An oak cased combination clock and barometer, in anchor design with rope carved pattern around bezels, 8-day clock movement, 21in (53cm).
£300-425 *MERT*

A mahogany and inlaid wheel barometer, with 8in (20cm) silvered dial, signed Josh. Frigerio, 281 High Holborn, and alcohol thermometer, the case with architectural pediment inlaid with shells and stringing, 38.5in (98cm). **£470-500** *S(S)*

An oak aneroid barometer, with thermometer, white glass dials, unrestored, c1930, 33in (84cm).
£60-120 *MERT*

A mahogany round top wheel barometer, the case inlaid with fan motif, c1785.
£1,500-2,000 *W&W*

A Cuban mahogany wheel barometer, with break arch pediment, the case inlaid with fan motifs, c1795.
£900-1,400 *W&W*

A mahogany wheel barometer, with break arch pediment, the case set with hygrometer, thermometer and 8in (20cm) main dial, the case inlaid with fan motifs, c1800.
£900-1,200 *W&W*

A flame mahogany wheel barometer, with a swan neck pediment, the case set with a hygrometer, thermometer, 8in (20cm) main dial and signed on round level, c1840.
£550-700 *W&W*

An oak cased aneroid combination clock and barometer, of Continental influence, 8-day clock with enamel face, 6in (15cm) barometer dial and porcelain thermometer scale, c1875, 28in (71cm).
£350-500 *MERT*

A mahogany wheel barometer, with hygrometer, bowfront thermometer, 6in (15cm) main dial and signed on spirit level, with a square base, c1840.
£900-1,500 *W&W*

An oak cased aneroid barometer, with thermometer, 4.5in (11cm) card dial, c1875, 26in (66cm).
£145-245 *MERT*

An unusual French bronze aneroid barometer, depicting foliage and ribbons, castings marked FW, 33in (84cm).
£650-850 *MERT*

A George III wheel barometer/thermometer, the silvered scale plates inscribed Manticha Fecit, 39in (99cm).
£2,000-2,500 *HSS*

A Louis XVI parcel gilt wheel barometer, with painted dial, thermometer above with painted register signed Philippe, Opticien, 59 Rue des Crois Cailloux, Amiens, c1780, 41in (104cm).
£1,000-1,500 *S*

A carved rope effect oak cased aneroid barometer, with 7.5in (19cm) dial and curved thermometer, c1900.
£150-225 *MERT*

An aneroid ship's barometer, with white glass 5in (13cm) dial, printed in fine filigree pattern, cast iron case, c1880..
£110-195 *MERT*

A Victorian moulded copper mounted aneroid barometer, with 5in (13cm) dial, unrestored, c1890.
£60-90 *MERT*

Miller's is a price GUIDE not a price LIST

A mahogany wheel barometer, the case inlaid with shell and floral motifs and strung in satinwood and ebony, c1815.
£600-900 *W&W*

An English walnut pillar barometer, in the manner of Daniel Quare, concealed tube with silvered scales contained within a glazed rectangular engraved gilt brass frame surmounted by finials controlling the pointers, the 3-stage column with plain, spiral and square sections divided by brass collars, on folding gilt brass cherub and leaf feet, 39in (99cm).
£3,000-4,000 *S*

An 8in (20cm) wheel barometer, by B Cantoni of Horsham, in distressed condition, c1830.
£100-150 *MERT*

An oak cased Admiral Fitzroy Improved Barometer, in Gothic style case, complete with thermometer.
£400-450 *GAK*

Miscellaneous

A Dutch inlaid walnut barometer, the pewter plates signed Joseph Brenta fec: Amsterd., with mercury 'U' tube, central tube and alcohol thermometer, the typical case inlaid with contrasting wood, late 18thC, 49.5in (125cm).
£1,500-2,000 *S*

A mahogany marine barometer, with ivory dials, original brass cistern, replacement gimbals, c1820.
£2,000-2,800 *W&W*

A mahogany ship's barometer, by Agusti of Falmouth, case in original polish with large brass cistern cover at base, restored, gimbal replaced, c1860.
£2,500-2,700 *MERT*

A George III mahogany and boxwood angle barometer, with moulded cistern cover, the thermometer scale signed Josho. Knight Fecit, the angle with rubbed silvered barometer scale, 32in (81cm).
£3,500-5,500 *C*

A rosewood marine barometer, with ivory main dial and silvered brass sympiesometer to the trunk, original brass cistern, replacement gimbals, c1840.
£1,800-2,500 *W&W*

A clock/barometer, the dial with Harrods & Co., a compass set above the barometer dial, early 20thC, 6in (15cm).
£460-520 *MJB*

SCIENTIFIC INSTRUMENTS

Dials

A brass miner's dial, the silvered dial engraved Francis Thomas, Engineer, Marazion, Cornwall, in brass box with spirit level and hinged sight enclosed by a hinged lid with integral sight, with engraved scale plates to the sides, on a tripod fitment with pinion 2-way revolutionary movement and clamping screw, small crack to glass, 18thC.
£150-250 *HSS*

An ivory and enamel compass dial barometer, signed Abraham Optician Cheltenham, with graduated mercury thermometer, compass needle, carved border decoration, in plush lined leather case, enamel cracked, 4.5in (11cm) diam.
£320-400 *CSK*

An English brass universal equinoctial dial, signed Thos Rubergall, Optician to the King, 27 Coventry Str.t, London, with silvered brass hour ring, hinged latitude arc and gnomon, compass rose inset with spirit levels, on 3 levelling screws, in original sharkskin covered and velvet lined case, c1830, 5in (13cm) wide.
£1,500-2,000 *S*

An Andreas Vogler brass universal equinoctial dial, engraved with foliage, inset compass with hinged latitude arc, hour ring and gnomon, 2in (5cm) with original printed list of cities and latitudes, in leather and card case, distressed, 18thC.   **£400-600** *Bea*

A German silvered brass horizontal sundial, unsigned, the plate engraved with hour scales and minute divisions, decorated with scrolls, incorporating a compass with iron needle and brass cap, a folding string gnomon and 3 adjustable levelling screws, in original chamois leather lined shaped case, the cover with traces of embossed decoration, 18thC, 7.5in (19cm) long.   **£1,500-2,000** *C*

A Continental universal equinoctial ring, c1740, 4.5in (11.5cm) high.
£600-750 *DHO*

A brass universal equinoctial ring dial, unsigned but engraved on the equinoctial ring James Heron's Present to W. Campbell at Rosemount April 3 1769, and an hour scale III-XII-IX, the meridian ring calibrated on one side with 0°-90° scale, the other side with a quadrant scale, the pivoted bridge with sliding pin-hole sight calendar and declination scales, 18thC, 3in (8cm) diam.
£800-1,000 *C*

A horizontal sundial, probably English, the brass plate engraved with hour scale, scrolling decoration and monogram, mounted with sliding gnomon and rotating above shaped brass plate engraved with 4 quadrants, late 18thC, 7in (18cm).
£1,500-2,000 *S*

Globes

A lacquered and silvered brass universal equinoctial compass dial, signed on the hour ring Je Ramsden London, the hour scale divided IIII-IIX-VIII with minute sub-divisions and scrollwork decoration, with spring loaded gnomon, the silvered latitude arc engraved 0°-60°, the silvered compass dial with level and cross bubble, engraved in 4 quadrants, with needle on jewelled pivot with clamp, on 3 adjustable screw feet, damaged, in shaped fishskin covered case, late 18thC, 7in (18cm) wide.
£1,500-2,000   *C*

An 18in (46cm) terrestrial globe, by Blades, East and Blades, 22 Abchurch Lane, London, mounted in brass meridian within horizontal ring of calendar and zodiac scales, on mahogany stand with stretcher, inset with a silvered dial compass, 41.5in (114cm) high.
£3,800-4,200   *AG*

A terrestrial globe, by W. & A. K. Johnston Ltd, early 20thC.
£4,000-4,500   *HSS*

A Charler Bloud ivory diptych dial, the upper outer face with equinoctial pin-gnomon dial with decorative geometric engraved decoration, upper inner face with silver volvelle, mis-shaped, lower inner face with analemmatic magnetic dial, lacking magnetic needle, glass cover and hinged latitude arm, the base with rotating silver disc engraved with calendar and operating the analemma, signed Fait et Jnue par Charles Bloud Dieppe, late 17thC.
£900-1,200   *S*

A 2in (5cm) terrestrial globe, the maker's label inscribed MALBY & Co Houghton Str. Newcastle St. Strand, dated 1842, the paper gores delicately coloured, the globe with steel axis pin, in a mahogany case with domed cover, mid-19thC, 3in (8cm) high.
£1,500-1,800   *C*

A Malby 18in (46cm) terrestrial globe, published by Edward Stanford , 55 Charing Cross, London, Jan. 1st 1883, the gores with analemma and lines of variation, the engraved brass meridian circle divided in 4 quadrants, with hour ring, the printed horizon circle with zodiac and calendar scales supported on an oak tripod stand with compass, needle and glass missing, late 19thC, 45in (114cm).
£3,000-3,500   *C*

A G. M. Lowitz 5in (13cm) celestial globe on stand, the sphere applied with well engraved and hand coloured gores, mounted in brass meridian and horizontal ring applied with coloured print of calendar and zodiac scales, on 4 turned and ebonised wood legs, on oak base, 1747.
£3,000-3,500   *S*

A terrestrial pocket globe, with 12 hand coloured gores, prime meridian of London, printed within cartouche 'A New Globe of the Earth by R Cushee 1731', in fishskin covered case with print of celestial globe applied to inner surface, 3in (8cm) diam.
£2,500-3,000 *S*

Richard Cushee was a surveyor and globe maker at the sign of the Globe and Sun in London.

A pair of 8in (20cm) Camille Flammarien globe de la Lune, by C. M. Gaudibert, the gores printed with a list of 343 lunar craters, mountains and sea, on ebonised baluster turned support and base, 19thC, 12in (31cm), and the companion Mars globe by E. Antoniadi.
£4,500-5,500 *C*

A pair of English Dudley Adams 9in (23cm) terrestrial and celestial globes, each sphere mounted in brass meridian, on ebonised wood stand with horizontal ring applied with print of calendar and zodiac scales, restored, early 19thC, 13in (33cm) high. **£2,000-2,500** *S*

A pocket terrestrial globe, 3in (8cm), with label inscribed 'A Correct Globe with the New Discoveries', hand coloured and showing the tracks of Captain Cook, in fishskin covered case with coloured print of the constellations, labelled 'A Correct Globe with ye New Constellations of Dr. Halley and Co'., late 18thC.
£1,500-2,000 *P(S)*

A 1.5in (4cm) terrestrial globe, the maker's label inscribed 'NEWTON & SON'S New Terrestrial Globe', 1842, the paper gores delineated with the tracks of Capt. Cook and Clarke & Gore, East Africa labelled Caffereria and Alaska as Russian Settle, with steel axis pin, in plush lined leather covered drum shaped case, mid-19thC, 2in (5cm) high. **£1,200-1,700** *C*

A 2in (5cm) Newton terrestrial pocket globe, the sphere with hand coloured gores, contained in fishskin covered case with print of the moon phases and terrestrial seasons applied to the inner surfaces, mid-19thC. **£1,400-2,000** *S*

A pair of early Victorian celestial and terrestrial table globes, published by C. Woodward, London 1845, on mahogany triform bases with turned stems and bun feet, some damage, 10.5in (26cm).
£1,700-2,000 *WW*

Surveying

A lacquered brass surveying level, signed on the finely engraved compass dial Cole Fecit, the compass star engraved with scrolls, the dial with 2 scales, one in 4 quadrants, the other 0°-360°, with maker's trade label, in fitted oak carrying case, late 18thC, 25.5in (65cm).
£1,500-2,000 *C*

A set of drawing instruments, by Elliott Brothers, The Strand, London, in a purple velvet lined 3-tiered rosewood box with plaque inscribed Elliott Smith, 13.5in (35cm).
£2,000-2,500 *HSS*

An octant, by H. Hughes, Fenchurch Street, London, in original fitted case, early 19thC.
£450-550 *LRG*

A part set of W. & S. Jones drawing instruments, with nickel silver instruments, including triangular compasses, proportional compasses, wheel pen, beam compasses, miniature compasses, ivory and ebony parallel rule, in mahogany case, early 19thC, 13in (33cm).
£1,000-1,500 *S*

A lacquered brass level, by Thos. Cooke, York, with inserted bubble level, draw tube focusing, 1.25in (3cm) lens, limb attached to body tube by fixed column and levelling screw on bayonet tripod mount with screw adjustment, in fitted mahogany case with trade label.
£300-350 *CSK*

Thomas Cooke 1807-68.

A gunner's quadrant, the brass base frame stamped C.T.D.E.M and dated 1612, engraved with flower and foliate decoration, the quadrant with stamped numerals with scale 45°-0°-45° each end of the quadrant terminating with the head of a mythical beast, with plummet indicator, and fitted to base frame by twin screws and lugs, the base drilled and tapped at each end, early 17thC, 5in (13cm) wide.
£1,700-2,200 *C*

A lacquered brass part surveying level, telescope missing, signed on the silvered compass rose, Martin London, with fine blued steel needle on agate pivot, with rack adjustment, silvered vernier with folding magnifier, telescope mounting and staff socket, in fishskin covered fitted case, 18thC, 5in (13cm).
£320-400 *C*

A E. & G .W. Blunt ebony octant, with ivory scale, vernier and maker's plaque, brass index arm, peep-hole sight and set of coloured filters, American, c1835, 10.5in (26cm) radius.
£350-500 *S*

A Hadley's quadrant, signed on ivory plaque MADE BY BOTT and WARDELL 1766 for Andw. Stevenson LONDON, ebony frame with ivory scale and vernier, brass index arm engraved with flowers and arms, peep-hole sight and one set of coloured filters, in pine case, dated 1766, 17.5in (45cm) radius.
£1,200-1,700 *S*

A lacquered brass miniature sextant, signed on the index arm Dollond London, the frame with folding handle, pin-hole sight with shade, glass missing, single deep red shade and mirrors, the index arm with vernier and magnifier, the arc with engraved scale, late 18thC, 2in (5cm) radius.
£1,500-2,000 *C*

An English brass ladder-frame sextant, indistinctly signed under the silver scale, complete with vernier, magnifier and 2 sets of coloured filters, 7in (18cm) radius, in shaped mahogany case with 5 telescopes, together with a 2in (5cm) brass refracting telescope, with rack and pinion focusing and leather covered tube, mid-19thC.
£600-700 *S*

A miniature brass sextant, signed Harris and Son, London, with peep-hole eyepiece and sun filter, scale with vernier, ivory handle, early 19thC, 2.5in (6cm) radius, with morocco covered case.
£900-1,200 *P(S)*

A brass sextant, signed Gambey à Paris, with silver scale and vernier, 2 sets of coloured filters, mahogany handle and magnifier, 7.5in (19cm) radius, in mahogany case with one telescope, mirror missing, tangent screw assembly now detached, mid-19thC.
£700-800 *S*

A lacquered and polished brass theodolite, signed on the base plate Andrew Yeates, 12 Brighton Place, New Kent Road, London, the telescope with rack and pinion focusing, ray-shade, dust slide and graduated bubble level, the 7in (18cm) vertical circle with silvered scale divided in 4 quadrants, the limb with 2 verniers, supplementary level and magnifiers, fine adjustment by tangent screw and clamp, the axis on massive U-shaped support over the horizontal circle with silvered scale and 3 verniers labelled A.B. and C, with single magnifier, the verniers and horizontal circle with independent tangent screw fine adjustment, on tripod stand with 3 adjustable screw feet, 19thC, 15.5in (39cm).
£900-1,500 *C*

A brass transit theodolite, signed T. Street, Comml. Rd., Lambeth, the telescope mounted in a trunion with silver scales and verniers, magnetic compass, tangental screws, on 4 levelling screws and tripod base, 15in (39cm), in mahogany case.
£600-700 *S*

A brass theodolite, signed J. King & Son, Bristol, the telescope mounted in a trunion with altitude adjustment by rack and pinion, magnetic compass, spirit level and tangental screw adjustment to the horizontal circle of degrees, c1830, 9.5in (24cm).
£500-600 *S*

Locate the Source

The source of each illustration in Miller's can be found by checking the code letters below each caption with the list of contributors.

Telescopes

A 4in (10cm) brass reflecting telescope on stand, signed G. Adams at No 60, Fleet Street, London, Instrut. Maker to his MAJESTY K. G. III, late 18thC, 27in (69cm), together with a spare reflector and fragment of Dixey trade label.
£1,200-1,800 *S*

A 4in (10cm) Broadhurst Clarkson & Co. brass refracting telescope on stand, 55in (140cm) tube, in pine case, with 5 eyepieces including a prismatic lens, late 19thC.
£1,700-2,500 *S*

A 2in (5cm) brass refracting telescope on stand, the tube with rack and pinion focusing, mounted on bracket above tapering column and folding tripod base, signed R. & J. Beck, 31 Cornhill, London, c1880, 33in (84cm).
£600-900 *S*

A 3in (8cm) brass refracting telescope on stand, signed on tube Newton & Co, Opticians to the Queen, 3 Fleet Street, London, mid-19thC, 41in (104cm) tube, in mahogany case, with 3 oculars.
£1,200-1,500 *S*

A brass refracting telescope on stand, by G. Carter, Exeter, the 3in (8cm) tube with rack and pinion focusing, on turned brass column and folding tripod base, early 19thC, 41in (104cm), in fitted wood case with additional eyepieces.
£450-600 *Bea*

A brass 2in (5cm) 5-draw refracting telescope, signed James Jeffreys, St. Johns Street, London, with lens cap and eyepiece, dust slide and mahogany outer body tube, with associated folding tripod and accessories, in fitted mahogany case, 19thC, 13in (33cm).
£800-1,200 *C*

A 4.5in (11cm) refracting telescope, signed T. Cooke & Sons, York, the 64in (163cm) long body tube with rack and pinion focusing, lens hood and star finder, mounted on a trunion with geared azimuth motion, the centre column supported from the mahogany tripod by folding locking arms, the steadying bar with later body tube attachment, late 19thC.
£1,500-2,000 *C*

A 4in (10cm) reflecting telescope, signed on the backplate, JAMES SHORT LONDON, the 24in (61cm) long tube with screw-rod focusing, lens cap and star finder telescope, with fine gear alt-azimuth mounting with tangent screw fine adjustment, on pillar support and folding tripod stand, the cabriole legs terminating in pad feet, 18thC. **£1,700-2,200** *C*

A vellum pressed card and lignum vitae telescope, unsigned, the object glass 2.5in (6cm) diam, the outer body tube with gilt embossed decoration, the 3 body tubes inscribed in ink B1, B2, B3, late 17thC, 48.5in (123cm) long fully extended.
£800-1,000 *C*

A refracting telescope nécessaire, probably French, the green painted wood tube with gold and silver mounts, fitted with tweezers, spatula, needle and pricker, late 18thC, 3.5in (9cm) long.
£1,200-1,500 *S*

A brass 3.5in (9cm) refracting telescope, signed on the backplate NEGRETTI & ZAMBRA LONDON, the 49in (125cm) long body tube with rack and pinion focusing, star finder and lens cap raised on a tapering pillar support, with solar filters, in fitted mahogany carrying case, with brass drop handles, late 19thC, 52in (132cm) long.
£1,500-2,000 *C*

A 3-draw vellum and paper card telescope, unsigned, with 1in (3cm) object glass, 'Augsburg' type paper covered draw tubes, leather outer cover, horn and mahogany fittings, 18thC, 56in (142cm) fully extended.
£1,200-1,500 *C*

A Steward 3in (8cm) brass refracting telescope, the tube with rack and pinion focusing, mounted on bracket above tapering column and supporting strut, folding tripod base, 37.5in (95cm) long tube, late 19thC.
£550-650 *S*

Microscopes

A refracting and reflecting brass telescope, the tube inscribed Newton and Co., Opticians, 3 Fleet St., Temple Bar, London, together with original mahogany box with Newton and Co. paper label, 7 alternative eyepieces, 62in (157cm) long.
£3,000-3,500 *P(S)*

A lacquered brass 'Culpeper' type miscroscope, unsigned, simple draw tube focusing, the stage signed Adams London and united with the mahogany plinth base by scroll supports, with diamond shaped feet, the plinth base with accessory drawer, pyramid shaped mahogany case, with further accessory drawer, early 19thC, 18in (46cm).
£1,200-1,700 *C*

A compound monocular miscroscope, signed on the trade card E. Culpeper Sculp. London, with brass eyepiece and turned lignum vitae mount, single draw applied with green vellum, the wooden tube with grey rayskin cover, circular stage raised on 3 brass columns above reflector and lignum vitae base, in original oak pillar case with drawer of accessories including 5 objectives, stage condensor, fishplate, live box and large glass stage plate, 1730, 14in (36cm) high.
£5,200-6,200 *S*

A brass binocular microscope, by Baker, 244 High Holborn, London, in fitted mahogany case, with many accessories including objectives, oculars and condenser. **£600-800** *Bea*

A binocular microscope, by C. Collins, 157 Great Portland Street, London, with accessories, in mahogany case, 18.5in (47cm). **£450-500** *MJB*

An English brass Cary type botanical microscope, the mahogany case containing compound tube, racked supporting column, side reflector, c1830. **£250-350** *AG*

A compound monocular microscope, with turned lignum vitae eye piece, pasteboard tube with grey rayskin covered binding, shaped brass stage on wooden base of later date, together with 2 objectives, fishplate, reflector and wheel of specimen mounts, mid-18thC, 13.6in (34cm) high. **£2,500-3,000** *S*

A brass compound monocular microscope, with sliders and some accessories, 18thC, 11in (28cm) high, and a small pocket telescope by Ramsden. **£1,500-2,000** *C*

A brass monocular compound microscope, signed Baker, 244 High Holborn, London, the bar limb construction with rack and pinion focusing, mechanical stage and sub-stage, large plano/concave mirror, the tube engraved 'Presented to Thomas Hodge by the Honourable the Commissioners of Inland Revenue for proficiency in Chemistry shown at the Examinations held by Professor Frankland at the close of the session 1871-72', 19in (48cm) high, together with 3 objectives, 2 oculars and live box. **£600-800** *S*

A lacquered brass compound monocular microscope, unsigned, probably Dutch, late 18thC, 9in (22cm) long. **£1,200-1,800** *C*

A binocular compound microscope, signed Ross London 5303, with A-shaped base mounted with 2 columns supporting sub-stage, circular stage and binocular tubes, in mahogany case with bench condenser, c1885, 16in (41cm) high. **£750-850** *S*

A brass compound monocular microscope, signed Thos. D. King Optician Bristol, No 203, Paris 1855, on tripod base, in mahogany case with 6 oculars, camera lucida, bench condenser and separate 2 cases of specimen slides, 18in (46cm) high. **£1,200-1,500** *S*

A brass compound binocular microscope, signed Negretti & Zambra, of Ross-type design with fine focusing by calibrated milled screw, mechanical stage and sub-stage and large plano-concave reflector, in mahogany case with monocular tube, 6 oculars, 4 objectives, analyser, polariser and live box, late 19thC, 19.5in (49cm) high.
£1,000-1,500 *S*

A compound binocular microscope, signed Ross London 5394, focusing by micrometer screw and rack and pinion, rotating circular stage with sub-stage assembly and plano-concave mirror, on A-shaped base, 20in (51cm) high, together with 5 oculars, 4 objectives, Lieberkuhn, live box, dark ground condenser, other accessories and 3 boxes of specimen slides, c1885.
£800-1,200 *S*

A brass monocular microscope, on a shaped base inscribed Nachet et Fils, 17 Rue St. Severin, Paris, in a fitted mahogany carrying case with 2 spare oculars, 2 objectives by R. and J. Beck, an R. and J. Beck objective case and 2 boxes of tiny glass specimen slides.
£200-300 *HSS*

A brass compound monocular microscope, signed on the folding tripod stand Dollond London, with accessories, incomplete, in fitted mahogany case, mid-19thC, 11in (28cm) wide.   **£1,000-1,200** *C*

A screw barrel microscope, signed E. Culpeper Fecit on the screw barrel, turned ivory handle, 7 numbered objectives, ivory talc box, black/white disc and stage forceps, set of ivory and brass specimen slides and a small booklet of instructions, in green velvet lined fishskin covered case, early 18thC, 5in (13cm) wide.
£2,200-2,700 *S*

A lacquered brass 'Jones's Most Improved' type compound monocular microscope, signed on the folding tripod stand Cary London, in baize lined and fitted mahogany case, 19thC, 11in (28cm) wide.
£1,500-2,000 *C*

A polished and lacquered brass solar microscope, signed on the base plate DOLLOND. LONDON, with Wilson screw-barrel extension, brass slide and other accessories, in fitted mahogany case, 12in (31cm) wide.
£1,200-1,500 *C*

An oxidised and lacquered brass binocular microscope signed Henry Crouch, London, No. 722, with draw tube eye piece adjustment, rack and pinion focusing, nose piece fine focusing screw, prism, double nosepiece, limb with central axis, circular stage, detachable sub-stage condenser, plano-concave mirror, on jointed arm on 'Y' shaped foot, in fitted mahogany case, with accessories, late 19thC, 15.5in (39cm) high. **£450-550** *CSK*

A lacquered brass compound binocular microscope, signed on the stand Smith & Beck, 6 Coleman St, LONDON, No. 1885, with rack and pinion coarse and micrometer fine focusing, prism, mechanical stage, sub-stage wheel condenser, plano-concave mirror and an extensive range of accessories in supplementary case including double nosepiece, 3 objectives, Abbe condenser and other items, with a bull's-eye condenser, in mahogany carrying case with brass handle, 19thC, 20in (51cm) high.
£2,700-3,000 *C*

A brass binocular compound aquarium microscope, signed on the base Ross, London 3227, c1875, 16in (40cm) high, in original mahogany case with Ross Ltd documentation and original catalogue, pricing the microscope at £21 and the case with accessories at £2.10s., accessories include 4 oculars and 3 objectives. **£2,500-3,500** *S*

A lacquered brass compound binocular microscope, signed on the Y-shaped stand ROSS London No. 3701, with rack and pinion coarse and fine focusing, micrometer differential screw extra fine adjustment, the base of the body tubes engraved Wenham's Binocular by Ross, London, 19thC, 25.5in (65cm) high.
£1,800-2,000 *C*

A Cuff type compound monocular microscope, unsigned, the body tube located on a limb from the rectangular section vertical pillar, with internal rack and pinion adjustment to the stage, bull's-eye condenser and plano-concave mirror, with scroll support on mahogany veneered oak plinth base, with accessory drawer containing a numbered set of 6 objectives, ivory sliders, sprung stage and other items, in pyramid shaped mahogany case, with supplementary drawer, early 19thC, 19.5in (49cm) high.
£2,000-2,500 *C*

A lacquered brass Martin's type drum microscope, with draw tube and rack and pinion focusing, rack work mounted to outer body tube, circular 2-tier stage with internal spring to stage, concave mirror on circular foot, in fitted case with accessories, 11in (28cm) wide. **£600-900** *CSK*

A lacquered and oxidised brass compound binocular microscope, signed on the horseshoe stand Swift & Son, 81 Tottenham Court Rd., London W., 19thC.
£1,000-1,200 *C*

MEDICAL INSTRUMENTS

An English mahogany medicine chest, with brass carrying handles, early 19thC, 9in (23cm) wide.
£1,500-2,000 *S*

A set of 25 eyes varying in sizes, iris and scleral colouring, in a fitted case with 25 sub-divisions, box clasp signed L.Z. PARIS, 6.5in (16cm).
£250-300 *CSK*

A pair of Benjamin Martin type iron Martins Margins, with large ring ends, counter sunk non-slotted screws, inserted horn visuals, repaired, c1750, lenses 1in (3cm) diam.
£200-250 *CSK*

An apothecary's mahogany travelling medicine chest, with brass carrying handles, the lid opening to reveal a fitted compartmented interior, early 19thC, 10in (25cm) wide.
£500-600 *HSS*

A pair of spring framed spectacles, inset into the inner cover of the book Breviarium Theologicum, published 1702, pigskin binding with tooled decoration, probably German.
£5,000-6,000 *S*

It is extremely rare to find a book used as a housing or case for a pair of spectacles.

A pair of 'Nuremberg' single wire rim nose spectacles, in flat edged grooved copper wire, German c1670, 1.5in (4cm) diam. lenses.
£1,200-1,500 *CSK*

An English trephine set, the brass mounted and fishskin covered case fitted with 2 Hay's saws, elevator, crown saw, tweezers, case restored, late 18thC, 9in (23cm) wide. **£1,200-1,700** *S*

An English leather reading glass, with thumb extension, lens with grey colouration, 3in (8cm) diam., chipped, c1650, 5in (13cm) long.
£1,500-2,000 *CSK*

A pair of Martin's Margins rivet nose spectacles, from the circle of James Ayscough, horn frame, horn insert, with a steel folding bridge, reduced aperture lenses, 1in (2cm) diam, power of +2 on each, invented by Benjamin Martin, in original fitted papier mâché case, c1760, 3in (8cm) high.
£2,700-3,000 *CSK*

A pair of steel surgical forceps, with join and parallel action jaws, a knuckle triangular blade with serrated face, signed blade 'Plum' with flat smooth horn face, central parallel plate lock, 18thC, 6.5in (16cm) wide.
£320-370 *CSK*

A home medicine chest by Springweiler and Co., London, the mahogany case with sunken brass handle and hinged front, the interior fitted with glass bottles, balance scales and a glass pestle and mortar, early 19thC, 8.5in (21cm) high.
£700-900 *Bea*

A Dr Butcher's bone saw, with ebony handle and steel frame with screw tension, English mid-19thC, 13in (33cm) long, and a monaural stethoscope, in turned beech, 5.5in (14cm) high.   **£500-700** *S*

An amputation bone saw, signed W. & H. HUTCHINSON, SHEFFIELD, Instrument Makers to the Royal Navy, with carved lion, crown and unicorn on shaped ebony handle, 15in (38cm) long.
£100-150 *CSK*

A pair of folding eyeglasses, with riveted steel bridge engraved 6, leather rims, English, c1750, 1.5in (4cm) diam.
£2,200-2,700 *CSK*

The style is depicted on the trade card attributed to James Ayscough of London.

A Weiss set of surgeon's amputation instruments, the brass bound mahogany case with badge engraved Dr. Settle, fitted interior with bone saw, 2 Hay's saws, set of liston knives, 2 tourniquets, tweezers, ligatures and needles, signed along the lock mounting Weiss's Improved Air Tight Case, 62 Strand, London, c1840, 15in (39cm) wide.
£1,700-2,000 *S*

An English cased trephine set, in fishskin covered case with red velvet lining, fitted with hand drill with 2 crown heads and an arrowhead, ivory handled brush, bone remover and 2 lenticulars with rosewood handles, late 18thC, 9 by 7in (23 by 18cm).
£1,200-1,800 *S*

A silver nipple shield, hallmarked London 1801, together with a silver pap boat hallmarked 1769, with beaded rim, 4.5in (11cm) long.
£550-650 *S*

An English carved ivory phrenology head cane handle, the head engraved with numbered sections of the skull, with corresponding characteristics including 'Indivuality, Wonder, Ideality and Imitation', the base with screw thread, mid-19thC, 3in (7cm) high.
£1,200-1,500 *S*

A John Weiss & Sons cased surgical instrument set, the brass bound oak case fitted with 2 lift-out trays, containing dental instruments, trepanning set, Liston knives, scalpels, bone saws, bullet extractors, clamps and others, c1900, 18in (46cm) wide.
£900-1,200 *S*

An amputation set, by S. MAW Son & THOMPSON LONDON, ALDERSGATE St. LONDON, and MAW LONDON, with bone saw, finger saw, tourniquet, 3 liston knives and other items, with chequered grip ebony handles, in a velvet lined brass bound mahogany case, c1870, 14.5in (37cm).
£800-900 *CSK*

A tracheotomy set, signed Mathieu, with lift-out tray containing 4 silver graduated tracheotomy cannulae, folding tongue depressor, 2 retractors, a hooked spreader with ebony chequer grip handle, 2 forceps and 2 ivory handled lancets, in mahogany case with brass fittings, brass plate inscribed Dr. Mauricel, with suede interior and accessories, 10in (25cm) wide.
£900-1,200 *CSK*

A surgeon's pocket set, signed Manufactured by H. Schively at his Surgical Instrument Manufactury No 75 Chestnut St Philadelphia, with 6 smooth ivory handled lancets, in velvet lined paper covered wooden case, 19thC, 7in (17cm) wide.
£150-200 *CSK*

A similar set is displayed at the Virginia Apothecary Shop, Williamsburg U.S.A.

An English surgeon's pocket instrument set, in red leather case fitted with a variety of instruments including a silver tongue depressor, hallmarked London 1802, a number of scalpels with tortoiseshell guards, scissors, probes, early 19thC, 6in (15cm) wide.   **£500-700** *S*

A Fowler's ceramic phrenology head, lettered with transfers and with underglaze blue lining, late 19thC, 12in (31cm) high.
£900-1,200 *S*

A set of French scalpels, in steel with ivory handles, in original leather case with cloth and metal braid, c1800, 9in (23cm) wide.
£450-650 *CSK*

A pair of French obstetric forceps, indistinctly signed LS EI and stamped with maker's symbol, with central locking pin, straight limbs and flat cross shaped ends, late 18thC, 18in (46cm) long.
£400-500 *CSK*

A brass enema, by Salt & Son, cutlers to the Queen and surgical instrument manufacturers, Birmingham, with cord attachment, ivory handled plunger and nozzles, in velvet lined fitted mahogany case, 11in (28cm).
£200-250 *CSK*

A fruitwood 2-part monaural stethoscope, with removable bell, 19thC, 7in (18cm) high.
£400-450 *CSK*

External aspect nerves, arteries, veins and muscles of the head, with maker's label Lehrmittelwerke Berlinische Verlagsanstalt GmbH. Berlin N.W.87, with descriptions of the various numbered areas in both Latin and English, study in wax, in black painted glazed case, 9.5in (24cm) high, and another study of the diseases of the teeth, 12.5in (31cm) wide.
£400-500 *CSK*

A field surgeon's amputation set, signed Young Edin. and Evans and Co. London, the instruments with smooth ebony handles, including a large bone saw, small bone saw with hinged back, trephine with chequer grip handle, silver tracheotomy tube, cross legged forceps, trocar and cannulae, Liston knives, in velvet lined fitted brass bound mahogany case, 17.5in (45cm) wide.
£1,200-1,700 *CSK*

An ebony monaural stethoscope, with student's listening outlet, c1870, 8in (20cm) high.
£600-650 *CSK*

A black painted tin ear trumpet, 4in (10cm) diam. **£100-150** *CSK*

A French plaster ecorché, after Bouchardon, the figure with various muscles and tendons named in ink, on oval base, 19thC, 23in (59cm) high.
£1,200-1,500 *S*

A Rein & Son silver plated ear trumpet, with scrolling decoration and simulated ivory earpiece, mid-19thC, 6in (15cm) high, together with a silver shaving cream warmer, hallmarked London 1900, with cylindrical container mounted above burner, 6in (15cm) extended.
£700-900 *S*

A set of male urethral sounds, with 4 graduated sounds and an adjustable urethral dilator with ivory handles and chrome rod, in satin lined case, 15in (38cm) wide.
£300-400 *CSK*

A plaster anatomical male demonstration model, each piece numbered in order of assembly, with an additional section for female uterus.
£300-400 *CSK*

An English Adam, Rouilly & Co painted plaster anatomical model of the human torso, with removable organs, on baseboard, early 20thC, 30in (76cm) high.
£500-700 *S*

A Dr. D'Odredanne's patent ether apparatus, the brass and copper instrument with paper exhalation bag, marked Collin, French, c1906, 9in (23cm) long.
£400-600 *S*

A double leg amputee's hardwood crutch with arm rest, spirally reeded stem with brass stringing and bone ferrule, early 19thC, 24in (61cm) high.
£200-300 *CSK*

A Rein brass 'London Dome' ear trumpet, with floral engraving to the surface and pierced cover to the trumpet opening, c1865, 6in (15cm) long.
£400-500 *S*

A black painted tin ear trumpet, with wooden earpiece, 6.5in (16cm).
£120-170 *CSK*

Dental Instruments

A leather and iron surgical corset and neck brace, with metal strapwork to spine, hips and neck, cloth shoulder straps and front tying bodice, WWI.
£100-150 *CSK*

An English carved ivory phrenology head handle, of dark yellow patina with head inscribed with numbered segments and corresponding characteristics listed around the base, mid-19thC, 4in (10cm) high, on mounting pin.
£1,700-2,000 *S*

A silver toothbrush, hallmarked 1801, in leather case with powder holder, 5in (13cm) long, together with a silver tongue scraper hallmarked London 1813, 4in (10cm) long, and a tongue depressor 5in (13cm) long.
£600-800 *S*

A set of dental instruments, signed Read with maker's label for Thomas Read & Co., manufacturers of Chirugical Instruments, Parliament St. Dublin, with octagonal ivory handles, steel instruments including 2 steel tooth keys with fluted cranked shafts, smooth ivory handles with removable claws, 4 steel forceps, pull-out tray with part set of steel shaft and smooth ivory handled scalers with 2 replacement instruments, including small finger saw, in mahogany brass bound case, early 19thC, 9in (23cm) wide.
£1,200-1,700 *CSK*

A set of 5 educational dental views, Made for the Dental Board of the United Kingdom by Educational & Scientific Plastics Ltd., Croydon, Surrey, in clear plastic and wood display cases, 13 by 18in (33 by 46cm). **£200-300** *CSK*

A dentist's surgery suite, comprising DMC Ltd leather upholstered adjustable chair with footrest, spittoon on stand, mouthwash stand, cases of dentures, c1900, approx. height of chair 47in (120cm). **£700-750** *ALL*

CAMERAS

An Eastman Ordinary Kodak camera, No. 1218, the film back stamped 1800, with lens and string set shutter, rollfilm polished wood body.
£1,000-1,200 *CSK*

A metal body hanging advertising sign in the shape of a film box, with hanging panel and mounting bracket, with cream, orange and blue painted text 'Made in Great Britain Ensign Film. Films Developed and Printed', Houghton-Butcher Mfg. Co. Ltd., London.
£175-250 *CSK*

This sign dates from the 1920s and features the Ensign house colours and design of the period.

An Eastman Kodak 35mm Ektra camera, No. 3363, with a magazine back No. C-4758 and a Kodak Ektra 50mm f/1.9 lens, Kodak rangefinder, Kodak right angle viewfinder, a Kodak waistlevel finder and a copy instruction booklet, in maker's fitted leather case.
£600-800 *CSK*

A 5 by 4in (13 by 10cm) wet-plate sliding box portrait camera, No. 676, with a brass bound J.H. Dallmeyer lens No. 5729, inset label J.H Dallmeyer, Optician, London, a brass bound lens with flange.
£800-1,200 *CSK*

A 3.5 by 4.5in (9 by 12cm) Ernoflex folding reflex model II camera, No. 1094064, with a Carl Zeiss Jena Tessar f/4.5 18cm lens no. 563546, film pack adapter and 3 double darkslides, in a fitted metal case, Ernemann-Werke, Dresden.
£250-300 *CSK*

A brass mounted mahogany plate view camera, by J.H. Dallmeyer of London, with rack and pinion focusing, fine focusing adjustment by rack and pinion on the lens, and individual slide aperture control, applied with a mahogany plaque inscribed J.H. Dallmeyer, Optician, London, together with 3 double and 2 single dark slides and a viewing screen, slight damage, c1861.
£1,700-2,200 *HSS*

A Jahagee Kine Exakta camera, No.484441, with round magnifier in hood and Jahagee Anastigmat Exakta f/3.5-5.4cm lens, No. 751738, in a brown leather carrying case, together with 3 instruction booklets, an extension tube, an Adon patent telephoto lens by J.H. Dallmeyer, London, No. 67349, an Ilford photo electric light meter and lens hood.
£300-500 *HSS*

A Jos-Pe 3 colour camera, No. 585, with top mounted sportsfinder, 3 backs, a Steinheil Quinar anastigmat f/2.5 10.5cm lens No. 165091 in a dial set compound shutter and 6 single metal slides, in maker's fitted leather case.
£1,200-1,700 *CSK*

A quarter plate mahogany body pinhole camera, with removable back panel and a brass bound lens section with screw lens cap with pinhole, pivoting shutter and engraved James Dixon & Sons, Sheffield.
£350-400 *CSK*

A Leitz screw-fit Elmar f/4.5 135mm lens, with barrel engraved 573, a FODIS rangefinder, early black WINKO right angle viewfinder and 3 Leitz filters, in a Leitz leather outfit case.
£350-400 *CSK*

A W. Kunik Petie Vanity outfit, comprising a 16mm Petie camera in a red leather covered vanity case, with powder compact, lipstick holder, spare film holder and instruction sheet, in maker's box, W. Kunik, West Germany.
£350-500 *CSK*

A Kern-Paillard Bolex stereo outfit, comprising a Kern stereo f/1.6 20mm lens No. 212972 lens hood, viewfinder stereo masks, viewfinder mounting bar, a Kern Yvar stereo 12.5mm f/2.8 lens No. 210441, instruction booklet Bolex Stereo Movies and polarising glasses, in maker's fitted box.
£100-150 *CSK*

A single speed Leica Motor, No. 911, with fixed 2-speed button.
£750-1,000 *CSK*

A Leitz 35mm restored grey Leica IIIc camera, No. 390330K, with a Leitz Elmar f/3.5 50mm lens, No. 93147, in maker's leather ever ready case.
£650-700 *CSK*

A Ross 3 by 3in (8 by 8cm) twin lens reflex camera, with a brass bound Ross, London, Rapid Symmetrical 5in (13cm) viewing lens, a brass bound taking lens in a Koilo shutter and 2 double darkslides.
£500-700 *CSK*

A Leitz screw-fit non standardised Elmar f/4.5 135mm lens, with barrel numbered 359.
£150-200 *CSK*

A 35mm Red Flag 20 camera, No. 770184, with a Red Flag 20 f/1.4 50mm lens, No. 770015, in ever ready case, a Red Flag 20 f/1.4 35mm lens, No. 77140, in maker's plastic keeper and a Red Flag 20 f/2 90mm lens, No. 760037, in maker's plastic keeper.
£1,800-2,000 *CSK*

A Nikon outfit, comprising a 45mm Nikon S3 camera, No. 6304070, with a Nippon-Kogaku Nikkor-S.C f/1.4 5cm lens, No. 387998, in maker's ever ready case, Nikon S3 instruction booklet, a Nikon leather outfit case containing a Nippon Kogaku Nikkor-P f/2.5 10.5cm lens, No. 925644, aperture defective, in leather case, a W-Nikkor.C f/3.5 2.8cm lens, No. 716580, in leather case, a Nikon 2.8 optical finder in leather case, a Nippon Kogaku, Tokyo, Universal finder, No. 545235, engraved Nikon in leather case and lens hoods.
£1,700-2,000 *CSK*

A Leitz 35mm Leica MDa camera, No. 1254651, in maker's leather ever ready case, a Leitz Super-Angulon 21mm f/4 lens No. 1646648 and lens hood, in maker's plastic keeper, 21mm SBKOO finder in leather case.
£900-1,200 *CSK*

A tropical folding plate camera, with retailer's plaque A Stegemann, Berlin, the brass reinforced teak body with double extension, rack and pinion focusing, red morocco bellows, Tessar 18cm f/6.3 lens, shutter 1/150 to 1 sec. 3 by 4in (8 by 10cm) in ground glass screen, together with 3 double plate holders.
£300-500 *S*

A Newman & Sinclair 35mm NS cinematographic camera, No. 761, with polished duraluminium body, built in recording watch mounted on front panel and marked 761 PATT 5875, a Ross, London Xpres 2in (5cm) f/3.5 lens No. 195469 a Ross, London Xpres 4in (10cm) f/3.5 lens, No. 177106, a Ross, London Xpres 6in (15cm) f/3.5 lens, No. 177153, each panel engraved 761, and a film magazine marked 761, in maker's fitted leather case.
£750-850 *CSK*

A Voigtländer Bijou camera, with a Voigtländer Heliar 10cm f/4.5 lens, No. 98607, focal plane shutter, focusing screen missing, and retailer's plate The Westminster Photographic Company Ltd., 119 Victoria St., S.W.
£500-600 *CSK*

A Newman & Guardia quarter plate Reflex camera, No. SR.1838, with rising focusing hood, a Carl Zeiss Jena Tessar f/4.5 150mm lens, No. 91868, a Carl Zeiss Distar lens 3/IV, No. 4209, instruction booklet The Newman & Guardia Reflex Self focusing cameras, 3 N & G double darkslides and a film pack adapter, in a fitted pigskin case.
£350-500 *CSK*

A Marion & Co., quarter plate tropical reflex camera, No. M.1596, with polished teak and lacquered brass fitted body, a Carl Zeiss Jena Tessar f/4.5 15cm lens, No. 204595, a Carl Zeiss Jena Magnar f/10 45cm lens, No. 218422a (sic) and 6 tropical double darkslides, in a fitted leather case.
£3,000-5,000 *CSK*

HANSA Canon NEW MODEL
MINIATURE CAMERAS

HANSA CANON is a miniature camera of unique design fitted with Nikkor Anastigmat lens and range finder. It takes 36 pictures of 24 × 36 mm. with standard Cine film. **Shutter speed** ranges from 1/1, 1/2, 1/4, 1/8, 1/20 up to 1/500th of a second. **Lenses** F/2, F/2.8, F/3.5 and F/4.5 are available. **Sold** complete with spare magazines, sky-shade and ever-ready case.

A complete run of 6 volumes of British Journal Photographic Almanac 1917-1963, Henry Greenwood and Co in yellow paper wrappers, the remainder in green cloth.   **£400-500** *CSK*

A 7 by 3.5in (18 by 9cm) boxform detective stereoscopic camera, with rack and pinion focusing, a pair of lacquered brass barrel Wray, London, 5in (13cm) stereo lenses Nos. 6542 and 6543, set in a roller blind shutter.
£250-300 *CSK*

A camera obscura, probably French, the walnut case with iron hinged lid opening to shaped folding panel inset with projection lens and folding mirror, the base with 3 folding sides opening to receive drawing paper, c1800, 23in (59cm) sq. **£1,000-1,500** *S*

A 7 by 3.5in (18 by 9cm) brass and mahogany stereoscopic tailboard camera, with a pair of Wray, London, 5in (13cm) Stereo lenses, Nos. 9284 and 9285, in a roller blind shutter and 3 double darkslides, in maker's fitted canvas case.
£600-700 *CSK*

An ebonised wood pedestal stereoscope, with decorated gilded designs, a pair of focusing eye pieces, hinged lid and internally contained stereocards.
£420-500 *CSK*

A Leitz Fiman Leica developing drum outfit, comprising a metal stand with handle and attached 6in (15cm) diam. glass drum and a 6 by 8in (15 by 20cm) glass chemical dish. **£100-150** *CSK*

A 7 by 3.5in (18 by 9cm) brass and mahogany hand and stand camera, with red leather bellows and a pair of Wray, London, 5.5in (14cm) Rapid Rectalinear lenses, Nos. 7043 and 7044, set in an integral sliding shutter and internal self-collapsing septum.
£450-550 *CSK*

A Newman & Guardia quarter plate Nydia collapsable camera, No. 1064, with a Ross, London Homocentric 5.5in (14cm) f/6.3 lens, No. 66322 and Newman & Guardia changing back, in maker's leather case.
£400-600 *CSK*

SILVER

Baskets

A George II bread basket, engraved with a coat-of-arms within a rococo cartouche, by Edward Aldridge, 1759, with blue glass liner, 17in (43cm) wide, 52oz.
£7,500-8,000 *C*

A set of 4 William Pitts II dessert baskets, on cast leaf scroll feet, the centres engraved with contemporary coats-of-arms, one piece of foliage missing, London 1821, 12.5in (32cm) wide, 143oz.
£8,000-8,500 *WW*

A William IV sweetmeat basket, chased and embossed with scrolling foliage, the centre with a relief view of Abbotsford, chased swing handle, maker's Taylor & Perry, Birmingham 1836, 5in (13cm), 3oz.
£350-450 *WW*

A Georgian silver boat shaped fruit basket, with engraved handle, pierced rim and matching foot, maker JS, London 1909, 5in (13cm) high, 22oz.
£900-1,200 *GH*

A George V basket, the pierced scalloped bowl with gadroon edging, scrolling mermaid handle, and 3 dolphin supports, maker's mark indistinct, London 1912, 10in (25cm) wide, 38oz.
£2,000-2,500 *Bea*

A George V bread basket, engraved with a presentation inscription, raised on 4 acanthus leaf, cabochon and C-scroll supports, terminating in stylised hoof feet, maker's mark rubbed, London 1924, 13in (34cm) wide, 1278gr.
£1,000-1,500 *HSS*

A Victorian cake basket, by Robinson, Edkins & Aston, Birmingham 1843, 12in (30cm) diam., 795gr.
£650-750 *HSS*

A George III sugar basket, faceted boat shaped with formal bright cut band, crested and initialled below a scalloped rim, spreading foot and swing handle, London 1787, 7in (18cm), 6oz.
£450-550 *S(S)*

A George IV cake basket, by Robert Garrard, in mid-18thC style, the centre engraved with the Haddington family armorials, London 1823, 14in (36cm) diam., 62oz.
£4,000-5,000 *Bea*

A cake basket, the body embossed with wrythen scrolls and chased flowerheads and foliage, engraved crest to centre, folding handle, entwined with foliage, London 1832, 14in (36cm) diam., 41oz.
£1,200-1,500 *WIL*

A mid-Victorian cake basket, maker's mark A.C. over T.P., London 1867, 11.5in (30cm), 1,115gr.
£600-800 *HSS*

A Victorian dessert basket, oval shaped on a spreading foot, scroll and flower embossed and lattice pierced, London 1890, 12in (31cm), 23oz.
£700-800 *S(S)*

A mid-Victorian sugar basket, by Joseph Angell, allover pierced and engraved with strapwork, with frosted glass liner, slight splitting, Birmingham 1875, 6in (16.5cm) high including handle, 145gr.
£250-350 *HSS*

A Victorian boat shaped cake basket, with gadroon edging above pierced and bright cut sides, on spreading pedestal base, by Thomas Bradbury and Sons, Sheffield 1900, 12 .2oz.
£350-400 *Bea*

A Victorian shell shaped basket, the pierced scalloped bowl with gadroon edging, scrolling mermaid handle and on 3 dolphin supports, by Goldsmiths and Silversmiths Co. Ltd., London 1900, 35.4oz.
£2,500-3,000 *Bea*

A late Victorian quatrefoil pierced cake basket, on applied shell and scrolling foliate feet joined by scrolling mounts with ball finial, the basket die-stamped with rococo flowers, shells, scrolling foliage and beading, by James Dixon & Son, Sheffield 1900, 12in (31cm), 20.25oz.
£700-800 *CSK*

A Victorian silver sugar basket, in neo-classical style, boat shaped with rope twist edges and swing handle, bright cut and pierced body and oval foot, Birmingham 1861, 8.5oz.
£350-450 *GAK*

A Victorian silver gilt dessert basket by George Fox, in the manner of Paul de Lamerie, crest engraved on the underside, London 1874, 14in (36cm) wide, 62oz.
£5,000-6,000 *S(S)*

A Victorian bread basket, with pierced and embossed floral and trellis decoration to border, London 1898, 11in (29cm) diam, 9oz.   **£250-350** *WIL*

A late Victorian silver cake basket, with heavy embossed and chased decoration, pierced detail, double rope twist swing handle, Birmingham 1899, 16oz.
£300-350 *GAK*

An oval cake basket, by S. J. Phillips, the pierced sides applied with ribbon tied husk swags centred by a pair of oval cartouches cast with profile portraits, beaded borders, pierced loop handles and 4 panel feet, London 1907, 11.5in (29.5cm), 23oz. 9dwt.   **£1,200-1,500** *S(C)*

A cake basket, part scroll pierced shaped oval, with ribbon tied reeded rim, spreading foot, swing handle, Sheffield 1912, 12in (31cm), 24oz.
£500-600 *S(S)*

Make the Most of Miller's

CONDITION is absolutely vital when assessing the value of an antique. Damaged pieces on the whole appreciate much less than perfect examples. However a rare, desirable piece may command a high price even when damaged.

A pair of Victorian baskets, each on 3 dolphin feet, by William Gibson and John Langman, 1895, 11in (28.5cm) wide, 83oz. **£7,000-8,000** *C*

A pair of pierced circular silver comports, with flower decorated rims, leaf surmounted and flower decorated bases, London 1909, 6in (15cm) wide, 19oz. 15dwts. **£550-700** *AH*

A pair of Edwardian oval dessert baskets, embossed and pierced fret decorated with beaded foliage borders and cartouche shape panels, with spray lifts, on chased cast rococo legs with shell feet, and scroll stretchers, maker's James Dixon & Sons, Sheffield 1908, 9.5in (24cm), 23.5oz. **£850-950** *WW*

l. and r. A pair of late Victorian baskets, the central oval panels engraved with an initial, London 1900, 9in (23cm) wide, 820gr. **£750-800**
c. A late Victorian bowl, of lobed quatrefoil form, stamped and pierced with scrolls, foliage and flowerheads, on a similar openwork foot, Sheffield 1898, 10in (25cm) wide, 309gr. **£350-400** *HSS*

Beakers

A French bell shaped beaker, engraved with foliage and shells and with 3 oval panels depicting a water well, a fountain and a windmill, by Louis-Jacques Berger, Paris 1798/1809, 5in (13cm), 5.75oz. **£350-400** *CSK*

A Russian parcel gilt beaker, chased with a pair of oval cartouches centred by a bird and running beast, within scrolling foliate and fish scale mantling, maker's mark GG in Cyrillic, Moscow 1778, 3in (8cm), 2oz. 10dwt. **£600-650** *S(C)*

Bowls

A George II Irish bowl, on spreading foot and with moulded rim, by Peter Racine, Dublin 1734, 7.5in (19cm) diam., 19oz. **£3,250-3,750** *C*

A George III two-handled bowl with monteith rim, engraved with armorials within a frame of scrollwork, with devil's mask drop ring handles and notched, pierced rim on spreading base, maker's mark W. B., London 1817, 11in (28cm), 100.8oz. **£5,000-6,000** *Bea*

A George II sugar bowl with detachable cover, the body engraved with a crest, by John Le Sage, 1730, 4in (10cm) high, 17oz. **£9,000-11,000** *C*

The arms are those of Perkins quartering another, with another in pretence.

A Victorian silver rose bowl, London 1891, 8.5in (21.5cm) wide. **£800-900** *TVA*

A set of 4 silver pedestal bon bon dishes, Chester/Birmingham 1928, 2.5in (6.5cm) high.
£650-750 *TVA*

A pair of silver punch bowls, with half-fluted design, London 1896, 10in (25cm) diam.
£1,500-2,000 *McC*

A late Victorian punch bowl, by Martin Hall & Co., London 1889, 13.5in (34.5cm) diam., 2,530gr., and an Edwardian Old English pattern ladle engraved with crests, London 1909, 311gr.
£3,000-4,000 *HSS*

A pair of French silver gilt finger bowls, each chased with a single foliate band incorporating a monogrammed cartouche below an applied gadroon rim, c1880, 5.5in (14cm), 16oz.
£400-500 *S(S)*

A heavy silver bowl, decorated with embossed sea creatures on dolphin supports, London 1899, 36oz. **£1,500-2,000** *N(A)*

A circular footed punch bowl, with shaped floral rim, 13in (33.5cm) diam., and 12 matching cups, 3in (7.5cm), silver embossed with floral decoration, maker WAH, Birmingham 1952, bowl 76oz, cups 54oz. **£1,500-2,000** *GH*

A late Victorian floral and foliate-chased two-handled christening bowl, with a pierced rising shaped circular foot and applied with a pierced rim, engraved with a crest, Wakely and Wheeler, London 1897, 8in (20cm), 10.25oz.
£400-450 *CSK*

Boxes

An Edwardian silver foliate engraved card case, Birmingham 1902, 3in (8cm) wide.
£90-125 *TVA*

An American fruit bowl, chased in high relief with a frieze of acanthus leaves with various flowers and foliage above, applied with a floral and foliate scroll rim and on a shallow rising circular, Jacobi & Jenkins, Baltimore, Maryland, c1898, 8in (20cm), 23oz.
£600-700 *CSK*

A Victorian jewel casket, by George Edwards & Son, Edinburgh, bombé oblong, embossed with putti and arabesque panels above baluster supports, ovolo, stiff leaf and mask borders, the hinged domed cover with recumbent classical maiden within a lattice and shell border, velvet lined, lock and key, 1887, 7in (18cm) wide.
£1,200-1,500 *S(S)*

A silver trinket box, with finely inlaid tortoiseshell lid, Birmingham 1919, 5in (13cm) diam.
£400-500 *TVA*

A biscuit barrel, with hinged cover and integral stand, on 4 paw and rosette feet, Sheffield 1898, 8in (21cm), 968gr.
£1,200-1,700 *HSS*

A George II toilet box and cover, the detachable slightly domed cover engraved with a coat-of-arms, the base later engraved with a crest, by Charles Kandler, 1727, 3in (8cm) diam., 6oz.
£2,500-3,000 *S*

A Charles II plain tobacco box, the detachable cover engraved with a coat-of-arms, the base engraved with a monogram, maker's mark indistinct, 1671, 4in (10cm) high.
£1,500-2,000 *C*

A casket, Dutch or German, the body embossed with tavern and coaching scenes between mask headed corner volute supports, the cover with scene of Napoleon greeting Josephine with attendant officers and ladies in waiting, gilt interior with inscription, fitted lock, import mark Chester 1905, 9.5in (24cm) wide, 43oz. **£1,800-2,200** *S(S)*

A card case, die struck with a bagpiper playing for his ladies, London 1897, 4in (10cm), and 2 other boxes.
£450-500 *S(S)*

An Edwardian silver embossed pill box, Birmingham 1901, 1in (3cm) diam.
£40-60 *TVA*

A Victorian silver box, embossed with hunting scenes, Schoonhoven, Netherlands, 1887, 1.5in (4cm) high.
£80-110 *TVA*

A Norwich silver 2 sectioned box, with cut corners, central hinge, the lid engraved with shells and acanthus scrolls, each base of the interior marked with the maker's mark of Elizabeth Haselwood, c1700, 3 by 2in (8 by 5cm).
£4,500-5,000 *GAK*

A Continental silver tobacco box, the cover chased with putti at play, the sides flat chased with shells and scrolls, 4.5in (12cm).
£350-400 *S(S)*

A Scottish silver gilt double snuff box, with cut corners, bright cut with foliage borders and engraved with military trophies, thistles, roses and Royal Crown, the cover and base with presentation inscription, maker's mark RH, probably for R. Hexton, Edinburgh, c1800, 3.5in (9cm) long, 6oz.
£3,000-3,500 *S*

The inscription on the lid reads 'A Testimony of Gratitude, Esteem & Attachment from the OFFICERS of the MID LOTHIAN REGIMENT to their Much Respected Friend and Lieut. Coll. SIR JAMES FOULIS BARt, Drogheda Septr 22nd 1800'. The base is engraved with the name of the Colonel, The Earl of Ancram, together with further names of Captains, Lieutenants and Cornets.

A Continental fan shaped box, decorated all over with cherubs, flowers and scrolling foliage, import mark for London 1913, 7in (18cm) wide, 7.9oz.
£450-550 *Bea*

Candelabra

A George II candlestick, matching snuffers and tray, each engraved with a coat-of-arms, by James Gould, 1729, candlestick 6in (15cm) high, tray 6.5in (17cm) long, 22oz.
£11,000-15,000 *C*

The arms are those of Newman.

An early Victorian four-branch, five-light candelabrum, the fluted bell shaped sockets with detachable circular sconces, one matched, on concave drip pans issuing from scrolled branches on a single stick of flared cylindrical form and on a lobed shaped circular foot, possibly Dixon & Co., 22in (56cm) high.
£650-750 *HSS*

A pair of George II table candlesticks, one engraved with an earl's arms, crest and initial below similar knopped stems and lapped shell moulded sconces, detachable stiff leaf nozzles, William Gould, London 1751, 10in (25cm) high, 48oz.
£2,700-3,000 *S(S)*

A pair of Continental six-light candelabra, engraved with coats-of-arms and an inscription, one defective, c1880, 29in (74cm) high, 8,571gr.
£9,500-11,000 *S*

A pair of George III square based candlesticks, having leaf decorated corners, with baluster stems with spool shape candle holders, detachable nozzles, by William Cafe, London 1770, 9in (23cm), 27oz. **£2,000-2,500** *WW*

A pair of George III candlesticks, engraved with a coat-of-arms and crest, by John Lloyd, Dublin, c1770, 12in (31cm), 52oz.
£3,500-4,500 *S*

Candlesticks

A pair of Queen Anne candlesticks, engraved with a coat-of-arms within a scalework cartouche, by William Denny, 1702, 8in (20cm) high, 18oz.
£2,500-3,000 *S*

A pair of George III candlesticks, with corded border and flower and foliage decoration engraved with a coronet and initial B, by Joseph Craddock and William Reid, 1819, 12in (31cm), 107oz.
£4,500-5,500 *C*

A pair of George IV table candlesticks, engraved with a crest, marked on bases and extension nozzles, by Samuel Whitford, London 1852, 8in (20cm), 32oz.
£2,000-2,500 *S(S)*

A set of 4 George II cast silver candlesticks, by John Cafe, marked on bases, 1745, 7in (18cm), 61oz.
£7,500-8,000 *GSP*

A set of 4 table candlesticks, 8in (20cm). **£850-900**
and a pair of candlesticks, 4in (10cm).
£300-350 *P(S)*

A set of 4 George IV silver gilt candlesticks, engraved twice with crest and Earl's coronet, by Robert Garrard, 1823, one nozzle 1825, 13in (33cm), 180oz.
£10,000-12,000 *S*

Four George II candlesticks, with detachable nozzle and ovolo borders, engraved with a crest, by John Cafe, one 1752, one 1754 and two 1755, 9.5in (24cm) high, 81oz.
£9,000-10,000 *C*

A pair of cast desk-top candlesticks, with shaped square bases and knopped stems, by Asprey, London 1962, and a pair of detachable Britannia Standard circular nozzles, 27.81oz.
£300-400 *Bea*

A George II plain taperstick, on spreading hexagonal base and with baluster stem and spool shaped socket, engraved with a crest, the base with later initials, by Gawen Nash, 1728, 4in (10cm), 3oz.
£1,500-2,000 *S*

A pair of German candlesticks, of hollow seam construction and octagonal knopped form, on square bases with ogee moulded corners, 18thC, 7in (18cm), 15.5oz.
£3,500-4,000 *P(O)*

A pair of William IV chamber candlesticks, by Paul Storr, London 1832, the bases inscribed Storr & Mortimore 88, 6.5in (16cm) diam. 28.9oz.
£3,500-4,000 *Bea*

The crest is that of the Earls of Cork, probably for Edmund, 8th Earl of Cork 1767-1856.

A William IV chamber candlestick, with reeded edging, detachable nozzle and conical extinguisher, by Henry Wilkinson and Co., Sheffield, 1835, 6in (15cm) diam. 11.2oz.
£400-500 *Bea*

Casters

A pair of sugar casters, by Walker & Hall, Sheffield 1931.
£300-350 *GIL*

A Victorian sugar caster, of urn form, with 2 curved side handles, gadrooned rim, ornate chased and pierced concave sided top with boss finial, London 1891, 8.5in (21cm), 13oz. **£400-500** *GAK*

A George I silver sugar caster, with inset restricting sleeve to the pierced top, maker's mark WE, London 1718, 6in (15cm), 7oz. **£500-600** *GAK*

Centrepieces

A Victorian dessert stand, the circular base applied with beading, and cast in high relief with entwined scaly dolphins and putti holding reins, the dolphins tails supporting a large gilt lined shell shaped bowl, by Frederick Elkington, 1875, 12.5in (32cm), 84oz.
£5,500-6,500 *C*

A George V dessert stand centrepiece, the central bowl with pierced decoration, supported on a panelled tapering stem with 3 scroll branches, with similarly decorated swing handled baskets, on a monogrammed shaped circular base, by Walker & Hall, Sheffield 1920, 13in (33cm), 43.7oz.
£900-1,200 *Bea*

A table centrepiece, the central boat shaped bowl issuing from a foliate sheathed baluster stem flanked by 2 similar smaller bowls, issuing from foliate sheathed scrolling branches, on a lobed quatrefoil base raised upon 4 acanthus leaf, scroll and shell feet, with cast scroll and foliate angles, 15in (38cm).
£550-650 *HSS*

An early George V three-piece table suite, comprising an èpergne, the central trumpet vase with pie crust rim enclosing foliate piercing, flanked by 3 smaller trumpet vases, the 3 scroll branches hung with shallow baskets, one handle missing, each raised on 3 lion paw feet, from a high domed base, engraved with a monogram, and a pair of trumpet shaped posy vases, by Walker & Hall, Sheffield 1910, 2931gr.
£2,500-3,000 *HSS*

An early George V small èpergne, the central trumpet shaped posy vase surmounted by a basket, stamped and pierced with flowerheads and pendant husks, flanked by 2 similar smaller bowls on scroll branches, on a swept circular foot, London 1910, 10.5in (26cm), loaded.
£350-550 *HSS*

Cups

A Charles II plain wine cup, the bowl with slightly everted rim, pricked with initials and dated 1671, maker's mark PD, pellets above, cinquefoil below, 6in (15cm), 7oz.
£8,000-9,000 *S*

A George II silver gilt inverted bell shaped cup and cover, later applied with a drapery cartouche enclosing a crest, the cover later engraved with an inscription, by John Tuite, 1730, the cover with maker's mark struck twice only, 12in (31cm), 83oz.
£3,000-3,500 *S*

The inscription reads 'Presented to John Nash Esqr. by LADY GREY EGERTON, in testimony of the sincere esteem and regard of his departed friend SIR JOHN GREY EGERTON BART. 1825.'

A Victorian cup and cover, with two handles in griffin and scroll form, embossed and chased with decorative cartouches, female masks, bands of ribbon tied oak foliage and other formal designs, inscribed 'Debrooghur Races 1872, Presented by Wm. Minto', lacking finial, maker's mark JD and S, Sheffield 1870, 13.5in (34cm), 35.25oz.
£700-900 *P(S)*

A Scottish Victorian cup and cover, engraved with a coat-of-arms within a strapwork and ribbon cartouche, the detachable cover chased and engraved with strapwork, foliage and grotesque masks and with pointed finial, the base engraved with a presentation inscription, by Rait, Glasgow, 1888, 29in (74cm), 177oz.
£2,700-3,200 *S*

A Victorian loving cup, of tapering cylindrical form with C-scroll handles, inscribed 'Jhansie Sky Races, 1879, Jhansie Cup', possibly by Robert Pringle, Sheffield 1878, 6.5in (16cm), 29.75oz.
£400-500 *P(S)*

A three-handled trophy cup, chased with a band of matted acanthus leaves and mounted with three scroll handles with leaf-capped leopard's head terminals, on a spreading foliate chased circular foot, by Walker & Hall, Sheffield 1905, 17in (43cm), 97oz.
£1,700-2,000 *S(C)*

'The Calcutta Cup', a Victorian cup and cover of campana shape, the two handles in the form of elaborate swans' heads with outstretched wings, the ovoid knop to the stem embossed and chased with masks, the domed cover surmounted by a figure of a horse and rider, inscribed 'The Calcutta Cup, Jorrhant Races, 1878 won by', maker's mark C and W, Birmingham 1869, 25in (64cm), 132.5oz.
£2,000-3,000 *P(S)*

Coffee and Chocolate Pots

A George II pear shaped coffee pot, cast with rocaille ornament, the body chased with flowers, foliage and scrolls, the curved leaf-capped spout with vacant rococo cartouche, the domed cover with flower finial, the body engraved with 2 vacant foliate cartouches, by Thomas Whipham, 1757, 10in (25cm), 32oz.
£3,000-3,500 *C*

A George III baluster coffee pot, husk swag and paterae chased incorporating engraved armorials, similarly chased spreading foot and domed cover, stylised bud finial, leaf capped curved spout, wood scroll handle, by Charles Wright, London 1776, 12in (31cm), 30oz.
£2,500-3,000 *S(S)*

A George III coffee pot, with later composition double scroll handle, marked on base and cover, Courtauld & Cowles, London 1769, 12.5in (32cm), 33oz.
£2,200-2,700 *S(S)*

A George IV coffee pot, with inverted pear shaped baluster body, flower cluster chased and ribbed at intervals incorporating armorials, above a spreading foot, loop handle, domed cover with flower finial, London 1824, 10in (25cm), 33oz.
£800-1,000 *S(S)*

A George III plain vase shaped coffee jug, stand and lamp, engraved with a crest, by Paul Storr, 1801, 13in (33cm), 48oz.
£3,000-4,000 *S*

A Maltese coffee pot, with wood scroll handle, Rosso, c1840, 9.5in (24cm), 29oz. **£1,800-2,000** *S(S)*

A matched pair of café au lait pots.
£200-250 *HSS*

A Continental plain bellied coffee pot, with scroll handle and leaf and bud finial, early 19thC, 6in (15cm).
£400-500 *CSK*

A George III coffee pot, monogrammed, crested and decorated with scrolls, flowers and foliage, with wood handle, on spreading base, maker's mark W.C., London 1762, 10in (25cm), 22.9oz. **£900-1,200** *Bea*

A George III coffee pot, with baluster body, later armorial engraved, above a spreading foot, with leaf wrapped curved spout, ivory scroll handle and stepped domed cover, with stylised bud finial, gadroon borders, marked on body and cover, W. & R. Peaston, London 1771, 11.5in (29cm), 28oz. **£2,200-2,700** *S(S)*

A George II chocolate pot, engraved with a crest, swan neck spout, flat domed hinged cover with detachable turned finial and ivory scroll handle, on spreading base, Isaac Cookson, Newcastle 1732, 10in (25cm), 29.2oz. **£4,500-5,500** *Bea*

A George III beaded vase shaped coffee pot, later chased with drapery swags and arabesques, with a later added scroll handle and domed hinged cover with stylised artichoke finial, engraved with a crest, the pot London 1778, the handle with Victorian hallmarks, 12.5in (32cm), 31.75oz. **£1,200-1,500** *CSK*

Cutlery

A George III silver shovel caddy spoon, by Joseph Taylor, Birmingham 1810, 2in (5cm). **£100-120** *TVA*

A Victorian Old English beaded pattern cutlery service. **£4,000-4,500** *P(S)*

A pair of cased silver fruit spoons, the bowls and stems finely chased with flowers and foliage, scrolled terminals to handles, London 1885/6. **£200-250** *GAK*

A fiddle and thread table service comprising: 12 table spoons, 12 table forks, 12 dessert spoons, 12 dessert forks, 12 teaspoons, a pair of sauce ladles and a fish slice with pierced blade, the majority by William Eaton, 1826, 1834, 1837, 131oz. **£4,500-5,500** *C*

A Victorian Old English beaded pattern part flatware service, each piece engraved with a monogram, comprising: 9 tablespoons, 20 table forks, 19 dessert spoons, 23 dessert forks, 12 teaspoons, a basting spoon and a set of 4 fruit spoons with gilt lined shell fluted bowls, George Adams, London 1878 and 1879, 195oz, and a pair of plated Old English pattern beaded basting spoons, each engraved with an initial, Mappin and Webb. **£8,000-9,000** *CSK*

A George III Old English pattern table service, comprising: 24 spoons and forks, 12 teaspoons, by Richard Crossley, 1798, 1801/2/3, with 12 table and cheese knives, and 2 carving knives and forks, with steel blades and prongs, 1964 and 12 fish knives and forks with silver blades and prongs, Sheffield 1965, in fitted wood case, 113oz. **£4,500-5,500** *C*

A 185 piece Kings pattern silver dinner service. **£3,000-3,500** *CoH*

A mid-Victorian travelling apple corer, the tapering cylindrical hollow handle enclosing the screw action blade, engraved E.B.N., by George Unite, Birmingham 1875, 5.5in (14cm), 30gr.
£250-300 *HSS*

A George II silver serving spoon, used for hash or stew, finial split, the base of the bowl engraved with initials I.W.I.,by Mary Lofthouse, London 1732, 186gr.
£1,300-1,700 *HSS*

A French silver gilt table service, comprising: 60 spoons, 84 forks, 12 fish knives and forks, 12 dessert knives and forks, a soup ladle, 20 various serving spoons and forks, a ham bone holder, 12 table knives with steel blades, 12 each pineapple, cheese and caviar knives, the majority with maker's mark HS, late 19thC, 8,150gr.
£7,000-9,000 *C*

Dishes

A William IV soup plate, the edges decorated with moulded flowers and scrolls, by W. K. Reid, London 1835, 30.5oz.
£300-400 *P(S)*

Two George I meat dishes, each with ovolo border, engraved with a coat-of-arms, by David Willaume I, 1725, Britannia Standard, 13 and 14in (33 and 36cm) long, 75oz.
£3,200-3,700 *C*

A Victorian butter dish, cover and stand, of dairy bucket shape, the cover in the form of a roof with eagle finial, the banded body with two handles, London 1855, 5in (13cm) diam.
£120-170 *McC*

A pair of entrée dishes and covers, with gadrooned borders, detachable handles, Sheffield 1933, 101oz.
£1,000-1,200 *DN*

A pair of George IV entrée dishes and covers, with gadrooned borders and engraved with armorials, detachable handles missing, by Joseph Craddock and William Reid, London 1823, 11in (28cm), 120oz.
£2,200-2,700 *DN*

A Continental dish, chased with a seraphim surrounded by symbols of the Evangelists, the underside nielloed with birds, letters and a date 1777, 4in (10cm), and a Continental circular dish chased with flowers and foliage, 5in (13cm). **£1,500-2,000** *CSK*

An early George III silver meat dish, of shaped oval design, with gadrooned edge, by Sebastian and James Crespell, London 1764, 21oz.
£350-400 *GAK*

A pair of George III entrée dishes and covers, with loop handles, the domed covers with turned finials, by M. Fenton and Co., Sheffield 1791, 15in (38cm), 52.75oz.
£1,700-2,000 *P(S)*

Inkstands

A Scottish silver and hardstone inkwell, by Aitchisons, Edinburgh 1855, 5.5in (14cm).
£1,500-2,000 *S(S)*

A Victorian inkstand, with applied shell punctuated gadroon border and pierced corner panel supports, complete with two silver capped glass wells, extinguisher and nozzle, fully marked, Charles Stuart Harris, London 1898, 10.5in (26cm), 32oz.
£2,100-2,700 *S(S)*

A partners' inkstand, the 2 glass wells with silver mounts, a taperstick with nozzle and extinguisher, with shaped moulded borders, on 4 hoof feet, by Goldsmiths and Silversmiths Co., London 1904, 62.5oz.
£1,700-2,000 *WW*

The taper holder frame inscribed to The Rev. Charles L. Lovett-Cameron, M.A. Vicar of Mortimer.

A silver novelty inkwell-cum-vesta case, in the form of a starboard ship's lantern, London 1894, 2in (6cm).
£550-600 *S(S)*

A silver lantern inkwell, with red lens, the hinged cover with stamp recess, by S.J., London 1894, 2in (6cm).
£350-450 *S(S)*

A Victorian cast inkwell, the canted sides decorated with leafy panels below a Celtic frieze, the platform with cast gallery of entwined sea nymphs and shells, the plain faceted glass bottle with silver mounts and mermaid cover, on 6 foliate paw feet, by Robert Garrard, London 1870, 5in (13cm) wide, 19oz 13dwt.
£900-1,200 *S(C)*

A Victorian inkstand, with presentation inscription, beaded edging, central rectangular reservoir with dog finial, 2 cut glass wells, Birmingham 1890, 10in (25cm) long, 11.3oz.
£800-900 *Bea*

An Edwardian inkwell, the single girdled cylindrical pot centred by a hinged domed cover, enclosing pottery liner, flanked by 5 pen apertures, on a circular reeded flange foot, by R. & S. Garrard and Co., London 1904, 5in (13cm) diam., 285gr.
£300-350 *HSS*

447

An Italian inkstand, chased with rococo scroll and rocaille borders, enclosing a central pomegranate finial and 2 detachable cylindrical wells, similarly chased and pierced and with hinged covers, pad supports, Turin c1770, liners, the wells unmarked and possibly later, 10.5in (26cm) wide.
£4,000-4,500 *S(S)*

Jugs

A George II plain beer jug, on spreading moulded foot, with leaf-capped double scroll handle and moulded rim and spout, by Fuller White, 1748, 7in (18cm), 29oz.
£4,500-6,500 *C*

An early Victorian covered jug, the pear shaped body embossed with panels of foliage, engraved with a crest, the moulded border with floral sprays, rococo moulded hinged cover with cast flower finial, leaf-capped engraved scroll handle, on floral leaf spray scroll feet, by Mortimer & Hunt, London 1843, 7in (18cm), 17oz.
£700-900 *WW*

A Charles II plain inkstand, maker's mark on base, IM between pellets, c1680, 5.5in (13cm) wide, 18oz.
£3,500-5,500 *C*

A silver and tortoiseshell mounted leather blotter, with reed and tie border, by John Collard Vickery, London 1912, 11.5 by 8.5in (29 by 21cm).
£400-500 *Bon*

A George III cream jug, with undulating border, acanthus leaf sheathed double C-scroll handle, on 3 trefoil feet, base engraved with initials, London probably 1762, 4in (10cm), 87gr.
£180-250 *HSS*

A George III hot water jug, with coronet and crest engraved baluster body, gadroon ring foot and rim, domed cover with turned finial, raffia covered loop handle, by John Barbe, London 1763, 10in (25cm), 17oz.
£700-800 *S(S)*

A Victorian ewer, the plain bellied body with narrow cylindrical neck and beaded border, the cover with coronet finial above a Staffordshire knot, simple handle, on spreading foot, by Stephen Smith, London 1864, 9.5in (24cm), 19oz 16dwt.
£700-900 *S(C)*

Locate the Source

The source of each illustration in Miller's can be found by checking the code letters below each caption with the list of contributors.

An Armada pattern claret jug, richly chased with blooms, scrolls and rocaille framing vacant cartouches and applied with winged figures, self opening cover, on spreading base, by Elkington & Co., London 1896, 12.5in (32cm), 28oz 18dwt.
£1,000-1,200 *S(C)*

Mugs & Tankards

A Charles II tankard, with scroll handle and dolphin thumbpiece, engraved with a later coat-of-arms, crest and motto, maker's mark C over W, 1680, 8in (20cm), 38oz. **£5,500-6,500** *C*

A Charles II tankard, the front engraved later with the coat-of-arms of Smythe of Elkington, maker's mark I.A., in a shield with fleur-de-lys below, London 1681, 7in (18cm), 27oz.
£7,000-9,000 *Bon*

A Charles II plain tankard, the cover engraved with a coat-of-arms within foliate scroll mantling, the body with the inscription Edm-Jennings Junior/Donum aviae meae Domae-Frances Barkam de Tottenham high-crosse in Comitatu Middle, quae obijt-9 diae July Anno Domi- 1667, maker's mark DR, c1667, 6in (15cm), 19oz.
£5,500-6,500 *C*

A George I mug, engraved with armorials and crested, on scroll handle, with spreading base, by Edward Vincent, London 1723, 3.5in (9cm), 8.4oz.
£650-750 *Bea*

A Queen Anne Scottish cylindrical mug, engraved with a coat-of-arms within foliate scroll mantling, by William Ged, Edinburgh, c1710, 3in (8cm), 8oz.
£1,200-1,700 *S*

A George II baluster tankard, engraved with a presentation inscription within a rocaille cartouche hung with swags of fruit and flowers, by William Shaw & William Priest, London 1752, 8in (20cm), 24oz. 10dwts.
£1,700-2,000 *S(C)*

The inscription reads 'The gift of Susannah Hacking 50 years a faithful servant to the Rossell family.'

Two Georgian pint mugs, both later foliate scroll chased baluster above spreading bases, leaf-capped double scroll handles, London 1798 and Newcastle 1744, 5in (13cm), 20oz.
£550-600 *S(S)*

A George II tankard, by Robert Williams, 1728, 7in (18cm), 24oz.
£2,500-3,500 *C*

A George II pint mug, on a rising foot, the underside scratch engraved with contemporary initials, probably Samuel Welles, London 1749, 5in (13cm), 12.5oz.
£600-700 *CSK*

A George II plain mug, the base engraved with initials, by Humphrey Payne, 1744, 5in (13cm), 12oz.
£800-900 *S*

A pair of George III mugs, engraved with armorial crests, 3.5in (9cm).
£2,000-2,500 *Bon*

A George II pint mug, with double scroll handle, inscribed beneath 'Given by Chas Chetwynd, Earl Talbot 1807', by Samuel Welles, London 1756, 5in (13cm), 11oz.
£800-1,000 *DN*

A pair of George III mugs, engraved with coat-of-arms, crest and initial between reeded bands and with leaf-capped handles, maker's mark worn, possibly C.F. for Charles Fox, London 1815, 5in (13cm), 23.8oz.
£750-950 *Bea*

A George III tankard, engraved with an armorial crest, the hinged flat cover engraved with monogram, bracket handle with bar pierced thumbpiece, by Henry Chawner, London 1787, 7in (18cm), 47.5oz.
£2,200-2,700 *Bon*

A George III pint mug, with double scroll handle, inscribed beneath 'Trav'ling o'er we now thank Heaven, Are arrived at Thirty Seven, and may no bitter cup reach thee, unless that cup resembles me', by Samuel Welles, London 1760, 5in (13cm), 11oz.
£800-1,000 *DN*

A Victorian plain waisted christening mug, on a skirted foot, with a moulded rim and leaf-capped scroll handle, the underside with later presentation inscription, by Messrs. Barnard, London 1845, 4in (10cm), 7oz.
£200-300 *CSK*

A pair of George III salt cellars, by Robert and David Hennell, London 1798, 5in (13cm), and a pair of closely matching Victorian salt cellars, by Edward and John Barnard, London 1861, 14oz. **£550-650** *P(S)*

A Victorian trophy in the form of a covered tankard, with mask spout, the body embossed and chased, inscribed 'Jorehant Races 1877-78' and 'Mouse Cup won by', by Frederick Elkington, London 1874, 12in (31cm), 45oz.
£2,500-3,000 *P(S)*

Salts

A set of 4 Irish William IV heavy cast salt cellars, on lion mask and paw feet, maker's mark WN, marks rubbed, blue glass liners, one replaced, 4in (10cm) diam. 33oz.
£700-900
and a Victorian mustard pot en suite, London 1840, 10.5oz.
£300-350 *P(S)*

Four George IV silver gilt salts, the everted rims chased in high relief, with flowers and foliage, on spreading bases, by Charles Fox, London 1828, 4in (10cm) diam., 22oz.
£900-1,400 *Bea*

A pair of Victorian salts, with shell, flower and mask chased borders, on mask and scroll feet, by Joseph Angell, London 1829, 4in (10cm), and a pair of King's pattern crested salt spoons, London 1829, 12oz.
£300-350 *DN*

Salvers

A George I Britannia Standard small pedestal salver, with raised reeded edge, raised upon a waisted socle and stepped circular foot, the underside engraved E * P, by David Hennell, London 1718, 6.5in (17cm) diam., 269gr.
£1,500-1,700 *HSS*

A George II salver by John Tuite, on 4 scroll feet, with moulded border, engraved with a coat-of-arms and motto, by John Tuite, 1733, 13in (32.5cm), 30oz.
£2,200-2,700 *C*

The arms are those of Cowper, presumably for William, 2nd Earl Cowper, died 1764.

A George III salver, the borders moulded with a band of roses and other flowers, maker's mark W S, 1817, 11in (28cm), 40oz.
£1,200-1,700 *P(S)*

A George II waiter on hoof feet, with applied shell and scroll rim and plain ground, maker's initials I.M., in script, London 1751, 6in (15cm), 7oz.
£500-600 *CSK*

An early George II pie crust salver, the central panel probably later, flat chased with rococo scrolls, foliage and scallop shell enclosing an engraved crest, raised on 4 acanthus leaf sheathed knurl feet, by John Tuite.
£650-850 *HSS*

A pair of George II Irish waiters, the serpentine moulded borders with leaf scrolls, centred by cartouches with a boar crest, on cast scroll pad feet, by William Williamson, Dublin, c1750, 6.25in (16cm), 16.5oz.
£1,500-1,700 *WW*

A Queen Anne Britannia standard pedestal salver, on a waisted socle and stepped foot, the underside engraved ICF, by Jno Read, London 1707, 7.5in (19.5cm) diam., 289gr.
£1,000-1,200 *HSS*

A small silver card salver, with wavy edge and standing on 3 cast feet, Sheffield 1915, 11oz.
£200-250 *GAK*

A George III salver, the moulded border with a florette and bead edge, 3 claw and ball feet, maker's mark R I, London 1780, 9in (22.5cm), 14oz.
£300-400 *P(S)*

A George III salver, engraved with initials within a shell and scroll border, on 3 pad feet, maker's mark R.R. possibly for Robert Rew, London 1762, 8in (20cm) diam., 11.5oz.
£300-400 *Bea*

A George IV salver by William Eley, in the mid-18thC taste, on hoof feet and with an applied shell and scroll rim, the ground engraved with a crest, London 1824, 8in (20cm), 10.5oz.
£500-600 *CSK*

A late George III salver, the gadrooned border with acanthus leaf angles, raised on 4 stiff leaf and rosette feet, by Paul Storr, London 1814, 12in (30.5cm) diam., 949gr.   **£1,500-1,700** *HSS*

A Victorian waiter by George Richard Elkington, London 1867, 8in (20cm), 10.5oz.
£250-350 *P(S)*

A George III oval waiter, 9in (22.5cm) wide.
£500-600 *P(S)*

An early George V presentation salver, with pie crust border, raised on 4 stepped hoof feet, centrally bright cut engraved with the coat-of-arms of George Nathaniel Curzon, First Marquess Curzon Kedleston and the facsimile signatures of the Cabinet of 1916/17, including Lloyd George, Austen Chamberlain, Bonar Law, Lord Derby, Balfour and other members, maker's mark C.S. & H.S., London 1916, 20in (51.5cm) diam., 3,500gr.
£1,500-2,500 *HSS*

A Victorian salver by John Harris, on 4 openwork scroll feet and with cast Bacchanalian mask and trailing vine border, engraved with a band of demi-putti, vines and scrolling foliage, the centre engraved with a coat-of-arms, 1840, 25in (63.5cm) diam., 187oz.
£6,000-8,000 *S*

A George IV salver by John Mewburn, armorial engraved within a broad band of flat chased scrolls, vine and lattice, raised and applied scroll and shell border, on volute supports, 23in (59cm) diam., 138oz.
£3,200-3,700 *S(S)*

Sauceboats

A pair of George II sauceboats by J. S. Harman, each on spreading moulded foot and with shaped rim and double scroll handle, 8.5in (21.5cm), 30oz.
£1,000-1,500 *S*

A Victorian salver by Robert Harper, the centre engraved with floral festoons, scrolling foliage and monogram above the date 1878, bead edge, claw and ball feet, London 1876, 8.5oz.
£200-300 *P(S)*

A William IV Scottish salver by J. McKay, on foliate and shell feet, with an applied foliate, shell and floral rim, the ground chased with a frieze of arabesques and with contemporary presentation inscription, 1830, 12in (31cm), 29.75oz. **£500-600** *CSK*

A late George III pap boat by Crespin Fuller, the plain oval bowl with applied double reeded border, London 1808, 4.5in (11cm), 55gr.
£170-200 *HSS*

A French two-handled double lipped oval sauceboat with shaped reeded border and fitted oval stand, late 19thC, 10in (25cm).
£320-370 *CSK*

A late Victorian sauceboat and cover by Walker & Hall, the boat with beaded border, acanthus leaf sheathed double C scroll handle, raised upon 3 stepped hoof feet with scallop shell terminals, the lift-off cover with ivory finials, Sheffield 1899, 560gr.
£450-550 *HSS*

A pair of George III sauceboats with punched bead rims and leaf capped flying scroll handles, each on 3 pad feet, maker's mark W.S. possibly that of William Skeen, London 1768, 20.1oz.
£1,000-1,500 *Bea*

A pair of silver sauceboats in George III style, by the Goldsmiths and Silversmiths Company, on oval stepped bases, London 1931, 18oz.
£400-450 *GAK*

A pair of George III sauceboats, by Daniel Piers with shaped rim, leaf capped scroll handles, 3 short shell and scroll feet, initialled and crested, London 1749, 25.5oz.
£800-900 *P(S)*

Services

A George IV three-piece tea set by Joseph Angell, the basin and jug with gilt interiors, fully marked, London 1823, 50oz.
£1,500-2,000 *S(S)*

A William IV four-piece tea and coffee set by Edward Barnard & Sons, the basin and jug with gilt interiors, fully marked, London 1836, 79oz.
£3,000-4,000 *S(S)*

A Victorian silver gilt tea service, in the German taste, by William Cooper, comprising: a teapot with curved spout and hinged domed cover, a two-handled sugar basin and a cream jug, 1842, teapot 5in (12.5cm) high, 25oz.
£2,000-2,500 *C*

Miller's is a price GUIDE not a price LIST

An early Victorian Scottish three-piece tea service by Mackay & Chisholm, Edinburgh, the milk jug and sugar basin gilded inside, all with leaf scroll handles and leaf panel feet, 1840, and a pair of matching sugar tongs, 1839, 50oz, with a fitted wooden case.
£1,500-2,000 *WW*

A Victorian four-piece tea and coffee set, by Edward Barnard & Sons, London, the basin and jug with gilt interiors, fully marked, 1850, 68oz.
£2,000-2,500 *S(S)*

A Victorian four-piece tea and coffee set by Frederick Francis, London, fully marked, 1852, 78oz.
£2,200-2,700 *S(S)*

A Victorian three-piece silver tea service, the sugar basin and cream jug with gilt interiors, London marks for 1857, 47oz.
£1,200-1,700 *MJB*

A Victorian tea service by John Tapley, comprising: teapot, sugar basin and cream jug, each on 4 acorn and foliage feet and chased with panels of farmyard scenes, with tendril handles, the teapot with similar spout and acorn finial, 1843, teapot 6.5in (16.5cm) high, 53oz.
£2,000-2,500 *S*

A Victorian three-piece tea set by John Samuel Hunt, the pot with facetted curved spout, flat cover and ivory button the basin and jug with gilt interiors, fully marked, 1860, 49oz.
£1,500-2,000 *S(S)*

A Victorian three-piece tea set by John Sherwood & Sons, Birmingham, the basin and jug with gilt interiors, fully marked, 1862, 45oz.
£1,200-1,700 *S(S)*

A William IV four-piece tea and coffee service by Jonathan Haynes, 1831 and 1833, coffee pot 9.5in (24cm) high., 82oz.
£2,000-2,500 *S*

A Victorian four-piece tea and coffee set by H. W. Curry, the pots with rocaille scroll moulded curved spouts, domed covers and convolvulus finials, the basin and jug with gilt interiors, fully marked, London 1868, 82oz.
£2,000-2,500 *S(S)*

A Victorian four-piece tea and coffee service by George Richard Elkington, 1856, coffee pot 10in (25cm) high, 84oz.
£3,000-4,000 *C*

A Victorian silver gilt punch set by Martin Hall and Co. Ltd., the jug and beakers on 3 ball feet and engraved with a band of trailing vines, 1872, jug 10in (26cm), 177oz. **£3,500-5,500** *S*

A Victorian four-piece tea and coffee set, the pots with wood handles and buttons, Birmingham, 1897, 76oz.
£1,000-1,500 *S(S)*

455

A Victorian silver presentation tea set by G. Martin Hall & Co. Sheffield, comprising: an ovoid teapot with flattened loop handle, domed hinged lid with urn finial, pedestal base and allover chased leaf, flower and geometric decoration, 8.5in (21cm), matching cream jug and sugar bowl, London 1874, and a matching coffee pot, London 1872, 11in (28cm) high, 71oz. 5dwts.
£2,000-2,500 *AH*

A Victorian four-piece tea and coffee set by Edward Charles Brown, each piece engraved with ornate cartouches, the scrolled handles moulded foliage, inscribed Debrooghur Races 1877-78, Presented by J. Berry White Esqr and Cunningham Hudson Esqr, and Jokai Plate won by, London 1876, 81oz.
£2,200-2,700 *P(S)*

A four-piece tea set of oblong form, by Nathan and Hayes, the teapot and hot water jug with wood handles and finials, Chester 1904 and 1906, the hot water jug with maker's mark DandH, Birmingham 1934, 56oz.
£700-900 *P(S)*

A silver tea service by James Dixon & Sons, executed in the Waterloo pattern after a Paul Storr original of 1815, comprising: a spirit kettle, teapot, hot water jug, sugar bowl, milk jug, slop basin, 2 stands and an oval serving tray, Sheffield 1925, 350oz., in original oak chest. **£7,500-8,000** *GIL*

An Edward VII three-piece tea service, with reeded girdles above lower bodies, applied decoration and scroll handles on spreading bases, London 1904, 41.6oz. **£500-700** *Bea*

A Victorian three-piece tea service by E. J. & E. Barnard, the ogee panelled bodies with engraving, moulded borders and handles, the teapot with a swan neck spout finial to the domed hinged cover, the milk jug and sugar basin with gilded interiors, on cartouche appliqué scroll feet, London 1852, 45.5oz.
£1,500-2,000 *WW*

A four-piece tea and coffee set, the pots with composition handles and buttons, Sheffield, 1932/33, 52oz. **£800-1,000** *S(S)*

A Victorian five-piece tea and coffee set.
£3,000-3,500 *P(S)*

A Victorian silver gilt three-piece Bachelor's tea set by Finnegan's Ltd., initial engraved, with loop handles, the pot with straight spout and domed cover with flower finial, fully marked, Dublin 1898, 30oz. **£1,700-2,000** *S(S)*

A silver tea service by Walker & Hall, Sheffield 1959, 53oz.
£500-600 *GIL*

A Victorian four-piece tea and coffee set.
£1,000-1,500 *P(S)*

Tea Kettles

A William IV tea kettle-on-stand, by J. C. Edington, engraved with crests and coat-of-arms within rococo cartouches, with a turned ivory swing handle, fully marked, London 1831, 14in (36cm) high, 100oz.
£2,500-3,500 *Bon*

A George IV tea kettle and stand, by John Edward Terrey, with plain detachable lamp, the kettle with curved spout and partly wicker-covered swing handle, the cover with shell and foliage finial, chased overall with shells, scrolls, foliage and scrollwork on a matted ground the kettle and burner engraved with a crest, 1829, 14in (36.5cm) high, 81oz.
£2,000-2,500 *S*

A Victorian embossed plated tea urn with chrome lid, scrolled handles and tap to front, on dome stem to a square base with ogee feet, embossed detail over, 17in (43cm) high.
£200-250 *GAK*

An early George V small tea kettle on a stand, London 1913, and a burner, London 1896, 1,302gr.
£500-550 *HSS*

Make the most of Miller's

Unless otherwise stated, any description which refers to 'a set' or 'a pair' includes a valuation for the entire set or the pair, even though the illustration may show only a single item.

A mid-Victorian tea kettle-on-stand with burner, probably by Stephen Smith, engraved with a continuous band of ivy and a crest, with fixed overhead handle and hinged domed cover, the fluted domed stand with cast acanthus leaf apron raised upon 3 double C scroll supports on leaf feet, London 1867, 2,239gr.
£1,200-1,700 *HSS*

A late Victorian tea kettle on a stand with burner, with fixed overhead acanthus leaf sheathed handle, raised on an arcaded and rosette pierced cylindrical stand on 3 lion paw feet with mask terminals, hinge damaged, 17.5in (45cm) high. **£400-600** *HSS*

A mid-Georgian silver tea kettle on a stand by Thomas Whipham, with part wicker covered swing loop handle, cone finial on hinged lid and allover embossed rococo decoration, the stand with similar pierced decoration, on 3 scrolled supports, London 1739, 15.5in (39cm), 78.25oz.
£3,200-3,700 *AH*

Tea Caddies

A pair of George II vase shaped tea caddies and sugar box, by Samuel Taylor, engraved with a coat-of-arms, 1753, in fitted silver mounted wood case, sugar box 6in (14.5cm) high, 31oz.
£5,000-6,000 *C*

A pair of early George III vase shaped tea caddies, by Samuel Taylor, London 1764, and Benjamin Brewood, London 1763, the slightly domed covers with cast flowerhead finials, one engraved G, one cover with lion passant only, 5.5in (14cm) high.
£1,200-1,700 *HSS*

A George III tea caddy, by Thomas Chawner, the domed cover with ivory finial, engraved with a coat-of-arms and monogram within bright cut escutcheons, the base with the inscription 'The Gift of Maria Blizard to her Niece and God-daughter Hester Carter Smith', 1786, 6in (14.5cm) high, 12oz.
£2,000-2,500 *C*

A George III tea caddy by Hester Bateman, the domed cover with urn finial, London 1789, 5in (13cm) wide, 10.25oz.
£1,500-2,000 *P(S)*

A pair of George II tea caddies, by William Soloman, each chased with bands of scrolls, foliage and rocaille ornament and engraved with initials, 1758, each with original lead lining, 4.5in (11.5cm) high, 46oz.
£5,000-6,000 *C*

A tea caddy with repoussé decoration of rococo design, London 1893, 6in (15cm) high, 8oz. **£450-550** *WIL*

A pair of George III tea caddies and matching sugar box, by William Vincent, with detachable domed covers and rose finials, each later engraved with a crest and initials within a ribbon tied foliage cartouche,1769, and a pair of sugar tongs, c1770, contained in a silver mounted japanned oblong case with lock plate and key, sugar box 5in (13.5cm) high, 28oz.
£4,500-5,500 *S*

Teapots

A George I teapot by John Gorsuch, with curved decagonal spout, hinged domed cover and baluster finial, engraved with a crest, 1726, 6in (15.5cm), 19oz.
£11,000-13,000 *C*

A late George III teapot by Joseph Craddock and William Reid, with melon fluted ivory finial and with polished fruitwood scroll handle, London 1813, 565gr.
£450-550 *HSS*

A George IV Bachelor's teapot by Rebecca Emes and Edward Barnard, the hinged domed cover with mushroom finial and with acanthus leaf sheathed loop handle, London 1823, 411gr.
£300-500 *HSS*

A George IV melon shaped silver teapot by the Barnards, with bud and leaf finial to lid, scrolled handle, cast 4-footed base, London 1842, 26oz.
£550-650 *GAK*

A George III teapot and stand by Robert Hennell, the teapot engraved with a coat-of-arms, 7in (17.5cm) high, the stand conforming in outline and similarly engraved with armorials within a foliate band, and on 4 ball feet, 7in (17.5cm) long, 19oz. 17dwt.   **£1,500-2,000** *S(C)*

A George III teapot by Robert and David Hennell, with straight spout, domed cover, wooden handle and finial, bright cut with 2 vacant cartouches and formal bands, London 1796, 13.25oz.
£900-950 *P(S)*

A George III teapot by Robert and David Hennell, engraved crest and initials within shield shaped cartouches, engraved wrigglework and reeded borders, tapering spout, scroll wood handle, London 1796, 11.5oz.
£750-850 *WW*

A George III teapot by Thomas Robins, with bright cut band above crests and initials within wreaths, with ivory finial and angular handle on 4 ball feet, London 1805, 7in (18cm) high, 19.2oz.
£350-450 *Bea*

A George III teapot and stand by Crispin Fuller, the pot with straight spout, domed cover with green stained ivory finial and later wood loop handle, the stand with reeded border and panel supports, London 1794, fully marked, 6.5in (16.5cm) high, 21oz.
£2,200-2,700 *S(S)*

A William IV compressed melon fluted teapot by Edward, Edward Jnr., John and William Barnard, London 1834, 9.5in (24cm), 17oz.
£700-800 *TVA*

A George III teapot, festoon bright cut and crest engraved compressed vase shaped, ring foot, everted collar, wood loop handle and button, London 1805, 5in (12.5cm), 21oz.
£500-600 *S(S)*

459

A Victorian silver teapot with fluted base rising curved spout, hallmark 1899.
£150-180 *LF*

A late George III teapot probably by Thomas Wallis, with ivory finial, ebonised reeded angular handle and raised upon 4 spherical feet, the shield shaped panel later engraved with a presentation inscription, London 1806, 796gr.
£500-600 *HSS*

Trays

A George III tray by John Crouch, on 4 foliate feet, and with shell, oak leaf, acorn and gadrooned border, with similar scroll handles, engraved with a coat-of-arms, 1808, 29.5in (75cm) wide, 195oz. **£6,000-9,000** *S*

A tea tray by James Dixon & Sons, centred by a presentation inscription, gadrooned borders interrupted by foliate shells, on 4 openwork supports, Sheffield 1909, 29.5in (75cm), 6,760gr.
£2,500-3,500 *S(Ch)*

A George III tea tray, engraved with scrolling flowers and foliage with a gadrooned border and reeded handles, maker's mark I.M. possibly for John Mewburn, London 1818, 26in (66cm) wide, 118.6oz.
£1,500-2,000 *Bea*

Miller's is a price GUIDE not a price LIST

A George III tray by Thomas Hannam and John Crouch, on 4 feet, with gardrooned border and fadrooned and foliage handles, engraved with a later crest and coronet within a wreath, 1801, 22.5in (56.5cm) wide, 93oz.
£3,200-4,000 *C*

A Victorian silver engraved two-handled footed gallery tray, with pierced rim, London 1898, 22in (55.5cm) long, 70oz.
£1,400-2,000 *GH*

Tureens

A late Victorian tureen, cover and liner, of inverted baluster oval form richly repoussé with flowerheads and scrolls, maker's mark W.W. over BT, London 1900, 2,910gr. **£3,500-4,500** *HSS*

A soup tureen and cover by James Dixon & Sons, engraved with a crest and presentation inscription below the gadroon border, reeded loop handles and pedestal base, Sheffield 1909, 15.5in (39.5cm) wide, 2,103gr. **£2,000-2,500** *S(Ch)*

Two two-handled soup tureens and covers, one tureen Dublin, perhaps John Gumley, c1760, the other tureen and the 2 covers E. J. & W. Barnard, 1840, 15in (38cm) wide, 163oz.
£7,500-9,500 *S*

Four George III sauce tureens and covers by Henry Chawner, engraved either side with a coat-of-arms and motto below reeded borders, similar loop handles and pedestal bases, the crested covers with urn finials, 9in (22.5cm) 2,122gr.
£7,500-8,500 *S(Ch)*

A pair of William IV entree dishes by William Bateman, with covers and handles, each with gadrooned borders and detachable foliate scroll handle, the covers engraved with a coat-of-arms and plumed helmet, 1830, 11.5in (29cm) wide, 114oz.
£3,000-4,000 *S*

A Regence ormolu mounted boulle bracket clock and bracket, signed Mynuel à Paris.
£2,800-3,200 *C*

A Louis XIV ormolu mounted brass inlaid tortoiseshell boulle marquetry bracket clock, 39in (99cm).
£3,500-4,000 *C*

An English repeating carriage clock, by James McCabe, London, c1860, 8.5in (21cm).
£5,000-6,000 *S*

A gilt brass mounted ebonised musical and chiming bracket clock, by Higgs & Evans, London, c1780, 26in (66cm) high.
£10,500-12,500 *S*

A Regency mahogany bracket clock, with brass stringing. **£2,500-3,200** *CLC*

A 6 bell quarter pull repeat bracket clock, with original verge escapement, London, c1760.
£5,500-6,500 *CLC*

A bronze and cut glass mounted japanned musical bracket clock, by George Prior, London, c1770, 32in (81cm).
£12,000-15,000 *S(NY)*

A Regency bracket clock, London.
£3,000-3,500 *CLC*

A French Napoleon III boulle bracket clock and bracket, Paris, 1850.
£4,000-4,500 *S*

A Louis XV ormolu mounted brass inlaid rosewood and tortoiseshell boulle marquetry bracket clock, by François Clement, 18thC.
£2,500-3,000 *C*

A French carriage clock in an ornamental brass case, with enamel chapter ring, 5.5in (13.5cm).
£280-300 *PCh*

An 8-day striking ebony veneered bracket clock, with 6.25in silvered chapter ring, by John Bushman, London, works restored, c1695.
£10,000-12,000 *S(NY)*

461

A Scottish, mahogany longcase clock, 13.5in dial signed John Johnson, Galway. **£4,500-5,000** *S*

A mahogany electric longcase clock, by Alexander Bain, London, c1845, 82.5in (209cm). **£38,000-40,000** *S*

A walnut musical longcase clock, by Nicholas Lambert, c1730. **£10,000-11,000** *S*

A quarter striking calendar and tidal longcase clock, Isaac Nickals Wells, c1750. **£18,000-22,000** *S*

A lacquered longcase clock, 18thC. **£10,000-11,000** *S(NY)*

l. A walnut marquetry longcase clock, c1695. **£8,500-9,000** *S*

A three-train longcase clock, 18thC. **£3,500-4,000** *Bea*

A chiming and musical longcase clock, by Claudius de Chesne, c1720. **£6,500-7,000** *S(NY)*

l. A Regency mahogany longcase clock, dial signed Massey, 1803. **£9,000-10,000** *CLC*

Derek Roberts Antiques

25 Shipbourne Road
Tonbridge, Kent TN10 3DN
Telephone: (0732) 358986
Fax: (0732) 770637

FINE ANTIQUE CLOCKS FOR SALE AND WANTED

We carry a very extensive range of clocks of all types including longcase, bracket, mantel, wall, skeleton, carriage clocks and longcase regulators and can arrange delivery virtually anywhere in the world. Stock Lists are available but should you have any specific enquiries let us know. We have written the following books: The British Longcase Clock; British Skeleton Clocks and European and American Skeleton Clocks. *We also wrote the horological section of* Millers Understanding Antiques *and our book,* Collectors Guide to Antique Clocks *should be published in October 1991.*

COLOUR REVIEW

A German neo-classical ormolu-mounted longcase clock, late 18thC. **£16,500-17,500** *S(NY)*

l. An oak longcase clock, the brass dial with moonphase, c1770. **£4,200-4,800** *CLC*

l. A mahogany longcase clock, with moon-phase and calendar, c1770. **£7,500-8,500** *CLC*

l. A burr yew longcase clock, London, c1695. **£15,000-16,000** *CLC*

A small Scottish longcase clock, c1810. **£2,500-3,500** *CLC*

A gilt bronze mounted and brass inlaid rose-wood longcase clock, signed John Jones, London, 18thC. **£11,000-12,000** *S(NY)*

An oak painted dial longcase clock, c1810. **£2,500-3,200** *CLC*

A burr walnut month going longcase clock, Daniel Quare, London, c1705. **£25,000-35,000** *S*

l. A mahogany longcase clock, London, c1790. **£8,000-10,000** *CLC*

An olivewood marquetry longcase clock, by Thomas Tompion, London, c1680. **£70,000-90,000** *S*

An olivewood month going striking longcase clock, by Joseph Knibb, London, c1680. **£60,000-80,000** *S*

An ebonised longcase clock, by Thomas Tompion, London, No. 533, c1710. **£60,000-80,000** *S*

464

l. A olivewood and walnut longcase clock, Fromanteel & Clarke, c1700.
£14,500-15,500 *S*

l. A mahogany longcase clock, with Battledore & Shuttlecock automata, c1810.
£4,750-4,950 *ALS*

l. A mahogany, boxwood strung and inlaid 8-day longcase clock, by Garland, Plymouth, c1830.
£4,750-5,000 *ALS*

l. A Dutch mahogany musical automaton longcase clock, dial signed Cs. Both, late 19thC.
£5,000-6,000 *S(NY)*

A small oak and mahogany longcase clock, c1840.
£3,000-3,500 *CLC*

A walnut longcase clock, 11in latched dial signed Fromanteel and Clarke, c1700.
£9,500-10,500 *S*

A Charles X ormolu and bronzed mantel clock, Thomire & Ce, 19thC.
£8,000-9,000 *C*

An Empire ormolu and bronze mantel clock, the dial signed Le Paute à Paris, 21.5in (54.5cm).
£6,250-6,750 *C*

A Louis Philippe ormolu and Baccarat mantel clock, 16in (41cm).
£1,500-2,000 *C*

A bronze mantel clock, with twin fusee movement signed by Webster, London, c1850.
£4,000-4,500 *CLC*

A Charles X ormolu and bronze mantel clock, 21.5in (55cm).
£2,000-2,500 *C*

A Louis XV ormolu mounted corne verte mantel clock, signed Martin à Paris, 43in (109.5cm).
£9,000-9,500 *C*

465

An Empire ormolu mantel clock, the 4.75in enamel dial signed Jean Perin à Paris, c1810, 19.5in (49.5cm).
£3,500-4,000 *S*

A Louis XVI ormolu mantel clock, the dial inscribed Petitdant à Paris, late 18thC, 14.5in (36.5cm).
£10,500-12,000 *S(NY)*

An ormolu and white marble Directoire mantel clock, the 4.75in enamel dial signed Coteau, c1795, 15in (38cm).
£3,500-4,000 *S*

A Regency ormolu mounted griotte marble striking mantel clock, by Benjamin Vulliamy, 12in (30.5cm).
£7,500-8,000 *C*

A Revolutionary ormolu and marble mantel clock, 4in enamel dial signed Duval à Paris, c1795, 17in (43cm).
£7,000-8,000 *S*

A Second Republic silvered and gilt brass mantel clock, Japy Frères bell striking movement and Brocot escapement, c1850, 29in (73cm).
£3,500-4,000 *S*

A Louis XVI ormolu and marble mantel clock, the enamel dial inscribed Lepaute H. Du Roi, late 18thC, 23in (58.5cm).
£9,500-10,000 *S(NY)*

A French bow-sided porcelain mounted ormolu mantel clock, the movement with maker's stamp of J.B. Delettrez, c1870.
£2,500-3,000 *S*

l. A Louis XVI ormolu mounted marble mantel clock, the dial signed Le Pareur, c1790, 22in (55cm).
£3,000-3,500 *S*

An electrically wound wall
regulator with Riefler deadbeat
escapement, c1905.
£26,000-28,000 *S*

An Austrian rosewood
regulator, c1850.
£6,000-7,000 *S(NY)*

A Louis XIV ormolu mounted brass
inlaid tortoiseshell and ebony mantel
clock, 20in (50cm). **£5,000-5,500** *C*

A mahogany month
going wall regulator, by
Charles Frodsham, late
19thC. **£13,000-14,000**
S

A gilt bronze 4-glass
mantel clock, 11in
(28cm). **£350-450** *E*

A Louis XV ormolu and
Meissen mantel clock,
c1750. **£4,250-4,750** *C*

An Austrian mahogany
regulator clock, by Gustaf
Becher. **£300-360** *JH*

An English mahogany regulator,
with jewelled dead beat
escapement, 71in (180cm), c1860.
£7,000-7,500 *CLC*

r. A mahogany weight driven
table regulator, by Benjamin
Martin, c1775, 25in (64cm).
£18,500-19,500 *S*

A French bow-sided porcelain
mounted mantel clock, c1870,
20in (51cm).
£2,000-2,500 *S*

467

A mahogany quarter striking table clock, by Francis Perigal, London, c1800, 18in (46cm). **£4,250-4,750** *S*

An ebony veneered basket top table clock, by Johannes Fromanteel, c1690, 13in (33cm). **£6,500-7,500** *S*

A walnut grande sonnerie table clock, by Edward Bird, c1685, 21.5in (55cm). **£20,000-25,000** *S*

A silver mounted quarter repeating walnut table clock, c1690. **£9,500-10,000** *S*

An ebony veneered table clock, by Joseph Knibb, c1680, 13in (33cm). **£20,000-25,000** *S*

An ebony veneered quarter repeating and alarm basket top table clock, by Henry Jones, c1690, 12in (31cm). **£10,000-15,000** *S*

An Arabesque marquetry table clock, by George Etherington, c1695. **£14,000-18,000** *S*

An ebony veneered quarter repeating table clock, by Jonathan Lowndes, c1690. **£5,000-7,000** *S*

A mahogany musical table clock, by Eardley Norton, c1780, 29in (74cm). **£10,000-14,000** *S*

An ebonised quarter repeating table clock, dial signed Ja. Boyce London, c1700. **£5,500-6,500** *S*

A brass bound ebonised, chiming table clock, c1785. **£6,000-6,500** *S*

A French inlaid
striking balloon
clock, c1900.
£900-1,100 *CLC*

An ebonised brass bound
chiming table clock, by
William Webster, c1765.
£6,500-7,000 *S*

A night clock,
early 20thC, 10in
(25cm). **£140-175**
BWA

An ormolu mounted ebonised
musical clock, 7in enamel dial
signed George Prior, c1780.
£18,000-22,000 *S*

A Gothic oak
quarter chiming
clock, by William
Roskell, c1880.
£700-900 *BWA*

An American ship's striking
clock, The Goldsmiths &
Silversmiths Co., in heavy
brass case, 9in (23cm) wide.
£150-200 *PCh*

A Victorian brass skeleton
clock, with a single fusee
movement, inscribed
Widenham, London.
£600-650 *SWO*

A Louis XVI ormolu
mounted Paris
porcelain musical
automaton clock, the
dial signed Ardiot.
£12,000-12,500 *C*

An American inlaid
rosewood 8-day wall
clock, late 19thC.
£345-365 *ALS*

A japanned clock with
wood dial, by John
Longhurst, Kingston.
£2,800-3,000 *JH*

A black and gilt japanned
tavern clock, by John Wright
of Dorking, c1790.
£4,500-5,000 *S*

An iron chamber
clock, South German/
Swiss, dated 1693.
£8,500-9,000 *S*

A repoussé gold verge watch, by Thomas Cartwright, c1725. **£3,750-4,000** *S*

A stainless steel split second chronograph deck watch with register, by Ulysse Nardin, Locle, c1900. **£1,700-1,900** *S(NY)*

A gold hunter cased watch, by A. Lange & Söhne Glashütte, no. 42532, c1900, 5.2cm. **£3,500-4,000** *S(NY)*

A gold chronograph watch, c1900. **£1,600-1,800** *S(NY)*

A gold 'Montre Humide', c1890. **£2,500-3,000** *S(NY)*

Three gold lapel watches, by Ulysse Nardin, Locle, c1900. **£1,500-2,000** *S(NY)*

An 18ct gold hunter cased box hinge watch, by Picard & Cie, Geneve, c1890. **£1,500-2,000** *S(NY)*

A gold hunter watch, by Js. Calame Robert, c1890. **£1,600-2,000** *S(NY)*

A gold and enamel watch, by Gregson à Paris, c1790. **£1,600-2,000** *S(NY)*

A lady's gold and diamond lapel watch, by Vacheron & Constantin, c1900. **£1,500-2,000** *S(NY)*

l. A gold hunter minute repeating watch, by C. J. & A. Perrenoud & Cie, Le Locle, white enamel dial, Roman numcrals, 5.6cm. **£3,000-3,500** *S(NY)*

A gold hunter watch, by Perrez y Martin, Assuncion, c1890. **£2,000-2,500** *S(NY)*

A gold hermetic Movado watch, 18k, silvered matte dial, luminescent Arabic numerals and hands, c1940.
£2,300-3,000 *S(NY)*

A gold and enamel hunter cased minute repeating watch, c1890.
£6,200-7,000 *S(NY)*

A Viennese gilt metal and enamel watch, with scent compartment, late 19thC.
£1,200-1,500 *S(NY)*

A gold and enamel hunter cased watch, Le Roy à Paris, c1830.
£1,200-1,700 *S(NY)*

A gold open faced dress watch, signed Breguet, c1930. **£1,800-2,200** *S(NY)*

Two gold open faced watches, Universal Geneve, c1930 and Piguet & Co., c1920.
£1,500-2,000 *S(NY)*

A lady's gold, enamel and diamond open faced lapel watch, c1900.
£1,700-2,000 *S(NY)*

A gold, enamel and pearl lapel watch, Patek Philippe & Co., c1900, 2.7cm.
£1,700-2,200 *S(NY)*

A gold hunter cased pocket chronometer, Dent no. 26605, London c1860.
£2,800-3,200 *S(NY)*

A gold and enamel hermetic Movado watch, c1945, 2in (4.7cm) long.
£2,500-3,000 *S(NY)*

A gold open faced watch, Patek Philippe & Co., no. 121841, c1905, 5.6cm.
£1,800-2,200 *S(NY)*

A gold open faced watch with Guillaume balance, Patek Philippe & Co., no. 162718, extra, 23 jewels, dial and movement signed, c1915.
£2,800-3,500 *S(NY)*

A gold hunter cased watch, J. Assmann, Dresden, no. 3223, c1880, 5.1cm.
£3,200-3,800 *S(NY)*

A gold Rolex Oyster Perpetual calendar watch, c1949.
£16,000-17,000 *S(NY)*

A gold Rolex Oyster Perpetual calendar watch, c1950.
£1,900-2,200 *S(NY)*

A white gold self winding watch by Patek Philippe & Co., 1965. **£1,300-1,500** *S(NY)*

A gold watch, by Patek Philippe & Co., c1925. **£4,500-5,000** *S(NY)*

A stainless steel watch, by Ulysse Nardin, Locle, c1945. **£1,200-1,500** *S(NY)*

A Rolex Oyster cosmograph, Daytona, c1970.
£3,000-3,500 *S(NY)*

A stainless steel chronograph watch, by Gallet.
£1,300-1,500 *S(NY)*

A gold jump hour watch, with moon phases, dial signed DF.
£19,000-21,000 *S(NY)*

A cushion calendar watch, by Patek Philippe & Co., c1928.
£180,000 -200,000 *S(NY)*

A gold watch, by E. Gübelin, c1950.
£1,500-2,000 *S(NY)*

A stainless steel and gold watch, by Movado, c1945.
£1,300-1,500 *S(NY)*

A gold 'Helm' watch, by Cartier, c1935.
£32,000-35,000 *S(NY)*

A stainless steel watch, by Universal Geneve, Aero-Compax, c1940.
£2,500-3,000 *S(NY)*

A gold and enamel automatic 'bridge' watch, by Cartier.
£12,000-13,000 *S*

A stainless steel and gold watch, by Vacheron & Constantin, c1950.
£1,400-1,600 *S(NY)*

A silver 'Mother and Child' terrestrial/celestial globe couplet, early 19thC, unsigned, 2in (5cm) diam. **£3,000-4,000** *C*

A Regency inlaid barometer. **£750-800** *CLC*

A mahogany stick barometer, by Tangate, 18thC. **£1,100-1,250** *ALS*

A mahogany wheel barometer, by Levy & Co., Bristol, c1845. **£550-650** *ALS*

A pair of miniature table globes, by J. Wyld, c1840, 10in (25cm) high. **£4,750-5,000** *S*

A silver miniature armillary sphere, signed J. Chapotot, 18thC. **£2,500-3,000** *C*

A metal celestial globe, possibly Persian, 13in (33cm) high. **£4,500-5,000** *C*

A Regency bowfront mahogany stick barometer, by Bate. **£3,300-3,500** *ALS*

l. A mahogany stick barometer, by J. M. Ronkett, 19thC. **£1,300-1,500** *E*

A 12in time globe, by Juvet & Co., late 19thC. **£800-1,200** *C*

A pair of Cary's celestial and terrestrial library globes, each in a William IV mahogany stand, 1820 and 1836. **£20,000-25,000** *S(NY)*

A Ross Wenham's binocular compound microscope, c1865. **£2,400-3,000** *S*

A brass 4in refracting telescope, by Ross London, 19thC, 67in (107cm) long. **£3,600-4,600** *C*

A brass horological compendium, dated 1605. **£11,500-12,500** *C*

A Stegmann solar microscope, by Cassel, dated 1759, 9.5in (24cm) long. **£2,500-3,000** *S*

A brass Ottoman equatorial dial, signed Abu l-Fath Ali, dated 1161H (AD 1748). **£7,500-8,000** *C*

A brass 5in reflecting telescope, signed Thomas Morton, 19thC. **£5,000-6,000** *C*

A sundial and nocturnal, dated 1650, 4in (10cm) long. **£3,500-4,000** *C*

A boxed Wilson Screw microscope set, c1920. **£350-450** *BWA*

A lacquered brass compound binocular microscope, signed Powell & Lealand, dated 1895. **£4,000-5,000** *C*

The 'Berselius' astrolabe, with dedication dated 1522. **£50,000-55,000** *C*

A combination microscope and 3-draw telescope. **£1,800-2,200** *BWA*

A brass refracting telescope, by J. H. Steward, body 41in (104cm). **£550-600** *WW*

The Globe typewriter, by The American Typewriter Co., with original tin cover, c1893. **£100-150** *BWA*

An exhibition multi-blade knife with 32 blades, stamped Wlaszlovits Stos, inlaid with mother-of-pearl, 8in (20cm) long. **£1,200-1,500** *CSK*

A set of Boullay amputation instruments, French, late 18thC, case 22.5in (57cm) long. **£4,000-4,500** *S*

An Animatographe No. 4 cinematic projector, by R. W. Paul, c1900. **£400-600** *BWA*

A Phrenology head by L. N. Fowler, early 20thC, 18in (46cm) high. **£600-800** *BWA*

An x-ray tube, early 20thC. **£60-80** *BWA*

A marine chronometer, by Thomas Earnshaw, London, No.724, c1800, in gimballed mahogany carrying case, with brass plaque inscribed John S. Buckwell, Brighton. **£15,500-18,000** *S*

A large slide rule calculator, c1920. **£120-160** *BWA*

A clockwork telegraph receiver, by Elliott Bros, c1870. **£200-250** *BWA*

A Dutch pierced silver bread basket, by Dirk Blom, Amsterdam 1767, 10in (25cm) long, 1,581.5gr. **£28,750-40,000** *S(Am)*

A Scottish George II silver bread basket, the base engraved with a coat-of-arms, by James Ker, Edinburgh 1745, 13in (33cm) long, 61oz. **£21,000-25,000** *S*

A silver centrepiece, by Robert Garrard, 1861, 18in (46cm). **£4,000-5,000** *S*

A George III seven-light silver candelabrum centrepiece, by Paul Storr, 1817, 18in (46cm) high, 447oz. **£20,000-23,000** *S*

A silver gilt centrepiece, by Brahmfeld & Gutruf, Hamburg, c1860, 39in (99cm) high. **£17,000-20,000** *S*

Six Victorian silver candlesticks, 4 by John Hunt and Robert Roskell, 1886, 2 by Robert Garrard, 1874, one nozzle by Craddock and Reid, 1820, 12in (30cm) high, 208oz. **£11,000-15,000** *S*

A James II silver gilt two-handled porringer and cover, by Robert Cooper, 1688, 7.5in (19cm) high. **£5,000-8,000** *S*

A silver oil and vinegar frame, by Paul de Lamerie, 1723, 8in (20cm) high, 18oz. **£11,500-14,000** *C*

A silver gilt two-handled cup, engraved with inscription and date 1844, by Paul Storr, 1821, 15.5in (39cm) high, 114oz. **£7,000-10,000** *S*

A silver sugar box and 2 tea caddies, by Edward Cornelius Farrell, London 1817, 6 and 6.5in (15 and 17cm) high, 87oz. **£7,000-9,000** *S*

Twenty George III silver soup plates, by John Houle, engraved with armorials and crests, 1818, 10.5in (26.5cm) diam, 491oz. **£11,500-13,500** *S*

An inverted helmet-shaped ewer, by John Bodington, 1712, 10in (26cm). **£11,500-13,500** *C*

A George III silver-gilt tray, by Benjamin & James Smith, London, 1810, 30in (77cm) long, 237oz. **£61,000-65,000** *S*

A George IV silver presentation tea tray, by Benjamin Smith, London, 1827, 31in (79cm) long, 203oz 12dwt. **£6,100-6,500** *S*

A set of 12 George III dinner plates, 1768, 9.5in (24cm) diam, 153oz. **£9,000-11,000** *S*

A set of 4 George III silver gilt wine coasters, Robert Garrard, 1818. **£21,000-25,000** *S*

A 4-piece silver tea set, Birmingham 1920, 47oz. **£400-500** *PCh*

A George II silver cream boat, Paul de Lamerie, London, 1744, 4.5in (12cm) long, 5oz 6dwt. **£6,000-8,000** *S(NY)*

A silver jardinière, by Robert Garrard, London, 1863. **£16,000-17,000** *S*

A pear-shaped teapot, stand and lamp, 1713. **£17,000-18,000** *C*

Two George III sauce tureens, c1805, 11in (28cm) wide. **£4,500-5,500** *DN*

COLOUR REVIEW

A set of 4 silver salt cellars, by John Hunt and Robert Roskell, 1852, each base stamped Hunt & Roskell late Storr & Mortimer, 7in (18cm) high, 108oz. **£15,500-20,000** *S*

A set of 4 silver salt cellars, with hooved stems and gilt interiors, by Robert Hennell, London 1776, 4.5in (11cm), 22oz 3dwt. **£4,500-5,500** *S*

A silver mounted mirror plateau, by Paul Storr for Storr & Mortimer, London 1826, 14 by 18in (36 by 46cm). **£38,000-42,000** *S*

A silver ginger jar and 2 similar vases, the jar and one vase by W.W. Williams, 1869, the other by William Mann, 1856, 224oz. **£10,500-12,000** *S*

A silver wine cooler or tureen and cover, The Goldsmiths & Silversmiths Co. Ltd., London 1912, 20in (50cm) long. **£12,500-15,000** *S*

A George III tureen, cover and liner, engraved twice with a coat-of-arms, by Paul Storr, 1805, the liner 1834, 16in (40cm) long, 158oz. **£10,000-12,000** *S*

A silver soup tureen, stand, cover and liner, by Paul Storr, 1819, 352oz. **£35,000-50,000** *S*

A silver and cut glass épergne, 1807, 58oz. **£5,000-7,000** *S(NY)*

l. An Irish ten-branch épergne, by Thomas Jones, 1789. **£13,500-18,000** *S*

A silver vase, by Paul Storr, 1838, 235oz 2dwt. **£11,000-13,000** *S*

A bronze figure of Lord
Kitchener, signed Sydney
March, 1911.
£7,000-9,000 *C*

A pair of bronze and gilt bronze chenets, mid-
19thC, 23in (58cm) wide.
£11,000-12,000 *S*

A bronze of 'Teucer',
signed Hamo
Thornycroft, c1900.
£13,500-15,000 *C*

A bronze of Penelope,
stamped J. Cavelier, 19thC.
£2,500-3,500 *C*

A Florentine bronze of a pacing horse,
from the workshop of Pietro Tacca,
17thC, 9in (23cm) high.
£16,500-20,000 *S(NY)*

A bronze of a girl,
'La Toilette', signed
Pradier, c1860.
£5,000-7,000 *C*

A bronze of a mower, signed Hamo
Thornycroft R.A., early 20thC, 25in
(64cm) high. **£11,500-14,000** *C*

A bronze of Pandora,
signed Pradier Scpt.,
mid-19thC.
£3,250-4,000 *C*

A bronze of
Nature, signed E.
Barrias, late
19thC.
£7,250-8,000 *C*

A group, 'Children watching Punch
and Judy Show', by Juan Clara.
£700-1,000 *SWO*

A bronze of Diana
Victorious, signed Carrier
Belleuse, late 19thC.
£13,500-15,000 *C*

A cock and hen pheasant, Viennese,
with Bergman monogram, late 19thC.
£1,500-2,000 *CSK*

A French gold and enamel étui, each piece enamelled with flowers, in original fitted leather case, c1830.
£500-600 *S(NY)*

An Empire gilt bronze table centrepiece, signed Thomire à Paris, c1815, 27.5in (70cm) high.
£25,500-30,000 *S*

An Italo-Flemish bronze wine cooler, with scroll handles and paw feet, 17thC, 37in (94cm) diam.
£7,000-9,000 *S*

A steel and brass model of the Arc de Triomphe in Paris, on a grey painted wooden base and block feet, c1920, 19in (48cm) high. **£3,500-6,000** *C*

A pair of French bronze models of the Medici vase, on square stepped Siena marble plinths, mid-19thC, 17.5in (44cm) high. **£4,500-5,500** *CSK*

An 18ct gold and enamel City of London freedom casket, maker's mark A.P., Chester 1888, 8in (20cm) wide, in original silk-lined case.
£15,500-20,000 *S*

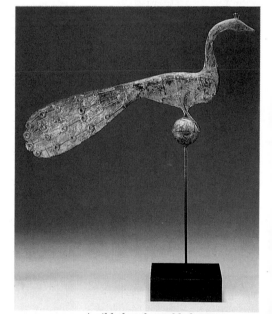

A gilded and moulded copper peacock weathervane, possibly A.L. Jewell, Massachusetts, c1860.
£10,000-12,000 *CNY*

l. A French model of a bull, the head to sinister, on oval base signed I. BONHEUR, 19thC, 8in (20cm) wide.
£2,000-2,500 *CSK*

r. A Dutch or Flemish oval brass wine cooler, with lion's mask handles and paw feet, 33in (84cm) wide.
£7,500-8,500 *S*

A pair of Siena marble and bronze jardinières, trough shaped, with tapering sides centred by Bacchic masks, on scroll legs, 18in (46.5cm).
£6,250-7,000 *C*

An Italian marble figure of a fisherboy, by Bazzanti, late 19thC,
£10,000-14,000 *C*

A marble head of an emperor, Italian, 17thC, 32in (81cm) high.
£26,000-28,000 *S*

An Italian white marble bust, mid-19thC, 27in (69cm) high. **£4,500-5,500** *S(S)*

A white marble vase, c1760, 38in (96cm) high.
£3,750-5,000 *S*

A marble bust of Lady Ribblesdale, 1804, 29.5in (75cm) high. **£6,000-7,000** *S*

A Napoleon III ormolu-mounted griotte marble urn, 21in (53cm) high.
£2,000-3,000 *C*

A pair of Italian marble busts after Bernini.
£4,750-5,500 *C(S)*

A pair of ormolu-mounted Porphyry urns, late 19thC, 12in (30.5cm) high. **£18,000-19,000** *C*

A pair of marble busts of Roman emperors.
£4,750-5,500 *C(S)*

A pair of Italian marble plinths, mid-19thC, 43.5in (110cm).
£14,500-15,500 *C(S)*

A Neapolitan carved giltwood and polychrome group of the Virgin and Child, 18thC, 17.5in (44cm) high. **£1,500-2,000** Two others. **£400-800 each** *CSK*

A pair of ivory reliefs of the Flagellation and the Mocking of Christ, within gilt and eboinised wood frameworks, Austrian or North Italian, late 17thC. **£11,000-16,000** *S(NY)*

A French terracotta bust of a lady, signed A. CARRIER, 19thC, 26in (66cm). **£4,500-6,000** *C*

A gilt and painted wood group of St. George and the Dragon, restored, c1480. **£23,000-25,000** *S(NY)*

An Upper Rhenish painted lindenwood figure of St. Cecilia, c1480, 28in (71cm) high. **£40,000-50,000** *S(NY)*

An Upper Rhine polychrome and giltwood figure of St. John, some damage and restoration, c1485, 61.5in (156cm). **£20,000-30,000** *C*

A late Elizabeth I pearwood cup and cover, 11in (28cm) high. **£10,000-12,000** *C*

An Upper Rhine painted wood group of Adam and Eve, comprising 3 separate carvings, early 17thC, figures 28 and 29in (71 and 74cm), tree 47in (119cm) high. **£25,500-30,000** *S(NY)*

A Dieppe ivory architectural cabinet-on-stand, carved and engraved, with 7 concealed drawers, mid-19thC, 66in (168cm) high overall. **£19,500-23,000** *C*

A Dieppe ivory carved centre table, mid-19thC, 36.5in (93cm) wide. **£5,000-7,000** *C*

A Swiss singing bird box, in white metal serpentine shaped case, 4in (10cm) wide. **£900-1,100** *DN*

A gold and agate vinaigrette, early 19thC. **£2,500-3,000** *Bon*

A gold snuff box, interior inscribed 'Mrs Ann Lind to John Gray 1793', 3in (8cm). **£2,500-3,000** *S*

A Staffordshire enamel patch box, late 18thC, 1.5in (4.5cm). **£2,250-2,750** *Bon*

A Staffordshire enamel patch box, late 18thC, 1.5in (4.5cm). **£3,250-3,750** *Bon*

A Staffordshire enamel patch box, late 18thC, 2in (4.5cm). **£650-800** *Bon*

A 2-colour gold snuff box, engine turned, with engraved roundels, French, c1870, 3in (7cm). **£2,000-3,000** *Bon*

A 2-colour gold snuff box, by C. M. Weishaupt, Hanau, the lid with an oval chased floral flourish, c1825, 3in (8cm). **£2,000-2,500** *S*

A silver-gilt and enamel snuff box, Birmingham, 1825. **£1,250-1,500** *S(Ch)*

An enamelled cigarette case, with secret compartment, c1910, 3.5in (9cm) long. **£900-1,100** *S*

A Staffordshire enamel patch box, titled R. McGuire, late 18thC, 1.5in (4cm). **£1,750-2,250** *Bon*

A silver box with enamel-inset screw-on cover, probably South German, mid-18thC, 2in (5cm). **£600-700** *S*

A gold and enamel Swiss snuff box, by Rémond, Lamy & Co., Geneva, with painted lid by Jean-Louis Richter, c1802, 3in (8.5cm). **£5,250-5,750** *S*

A 2-colour gold, tortoiseshell and enamel powder box, Paris, 1789. **£2,750-3,250** *S*

A painted and carved cedar box, probably American Indian, 19thC, 23.5in (60cm) long. **£3,250-3,750** *CNY*

A Swiss snuff box, by Jean-George Rémond & Co., c1810, 3in (8cm). **£800-900** *S*

l. A French lacquer travelling necessaire and bodkin case, with silver mounts, c1790, 6.5in (16.5cm). **£3,500-4,000** *Bon*

A Victorian calamander toilet box, makers G.B., G.W.B. and J.B. & S. Mordan & Co. **£12,000-14,000** *P(O)*

A tortoiseshell piqué toilet box, Naples, c1740, 6in (15.5cm). **£2,000-3,000** *S*

A gilt-bronze surtout, c1820, 9.5in (23cm). **£1,775-2,250** *S*

A tortoiseshell and jewelled gold piqué snuff box, c1750, 2in (5cm). **£1,500-2,000** *S*

A Restauration gilt-bronze lion, the plinth concealing a well, c1825, 10in (25cm). **£2,500-3,500** *S*

A French bodkin case, late 18thC, 6in (15cm) long. **£5,000-5,500** *Bon*

A lapis lazuli snuff box, with silver gilt mounts, by Luigi Mascelli, Rome, c1815. **£2,500-3,500** *S*

A French gilt and embossed leather playing card case, c1780, 3in (7.5cm) square. **£500-600** *Bon*

Miscellaneous

A George V dressing table mirror, monogrammed, with bevelled glass within a frame of scrolling foliage and flowers, Birmingham 1911, 14.5in (35.5cm) high.
£300-400 *Bea*

A pepperette, cast in the form of a spaniel's head, Birmingham 1905, 2in (4.5cm) high.
£170-200 *WIL*

A George III barrel shaped silver nutmet grater crested at each end, maker's mark S.M.
£200-250 *LAY*

A silver novelty propelling pencil, by Sampson Mordan, in the form of a rowing boat with well modelled planking, oars and rigging, c1890, 2.5in (6cm).
£350-400 *S(S)*

A late Victorian wafer holder of escallop shell form, opening to reveal pierced hinged grilles, and with rustic cast stand and overhead handle, 10in (25cm) high.
£200-250 *HSS*

A pin cushion in the form of a jockey's cap, with 3 ribbed segments and brim, Birmingham 1891.
£170-200 *WIL*

A George III large plain circular saucepan, the body of shaped outline and with turned wood handle, engraved with a crest, maker's mark worn, presumably Benjamin Gignac, 1769, 6in (15cm) high, 32oz.
£4,000-4,500 *S*

An Edwardian silver child's rattle, Birmingham, 1902, 5in (12.5cm) long.
£100-160 *TVA*

A pair of late Victorian ribbon threaders or sugar nips, in the form of a running stork, with one blue stone eye, the body enclosing a baby wrapped in swaddling bands and the stork raised on the back of a tortoise, London import marks 1890, 40gr.
£300-350 *HSS*

Although these items are often called ribbon threaders, this pair has no eyelet in the beak.

A late Victorian silver novelty pepperette in the form of a fish, maker's mark indistinct, London 1884, 4.5in (11cm) long, 82gr.
£200-250 *HSS*

A pair of Victorian harlequin sugar nips, maker's mark indistinct, Birmingham 1872, 63gr.
£250-300 *HSS*

A George IV presentation trowel with inscription, used by Frederick, Duke of York, with a turned ivory handle, maker's mark W.K., London 1823, 15in (38cm) long. **£750-850** *Bea*

A model of a milkmaid, with detailed costume, holding 2 jugs and a basket of fruit above a stepped oval base of 17thC style, detachable head, German, 19thC, 11.5in (29.5cm) high, 18oz. **£950-1,000** *S(S)*

A silver gilt sewing necessaire, comprising: a needle case, scissors, bodkin, needle and associated thimble, in a green leather case with embossed gilt chinoiserie decoration, French, c1880. **£470-520** *S(S)*

SILVER PLATE
Candlesticks

A pair of electroplated Corinthian column five-light candelabra, the stepped square bases, drip pans and detachable nozzles with beaded edging, 20.5in (52cm) high. **£1,500-2,000** *Bea*

A pair of Sheffield plate candelabra, the shaped circular bases, knopped tapering stems, drip pans and detachable nozzles with scroll reeded edging, 20in (51cm) high. **£650-750** *Bea*

A set of 4 Sheffield plate table candlesticks, the circular bases, fluted tapering stems and detachable nozzles with beaded edging, 11.5in (29cm) high. **£650-750** *Bea*

A pair of electroplated three-light candelabra, with detachable nozzles and stepped square bases with gadrooned edging, 18.5in (47cm) high. **£750-850** *Bea*

A pair of Old Sheffield plate candelabra, the tapering vase form stems on spreading circular bases, with reeded borders, the 2 scrolling branches supporting circular drip pans, campana shaped sockets with detachable nozzles and urn finials, c1790, 15in (38cm) high. **£550-650** *Bon*

Services

An electroplated four-piece tea and coffee service, engraved with scrolling acanthus and with scroll handles on spreading bases, the teapot and coffee pot with strawberry finials.
£400-500 *Bea*

A plated oval shaped four-piece tea service, by Mappin & Webb, comprising: a teapot, hot water jug, milk jug and sugar basin, on 4 claw feet, together with a plated tray by Mappin & Webb, 25in (63.5cm), and a pair of sugar tongs.
£350-400 *GAK*

Tureens

A pair of electroplated rounded entrée dishes with detachable acanthus handles and gadroon edging, on 2 warming bases with 4 acanthus supports, 14in (36cm).
£500-600 *Bea*

A Sheffield plate oval soup tureen, by Matthew Boulton & Co., c1825, 15.5in (40cm) wide.
£1,200-1,500 *S(C)*

A plated bacon dish with revolving lid, decorative cast rams' head legs, late 19thC.
£400-450 *GAK*

Miscellaneous

An electroplated two-division oil lamp with revolving boat-shaped reservoir, supporting 2 burners, decorated with masks and scrolling acanthus and with central carrying handle, on spreading pedestal base with reeded edging, together with 2 glass funnels, shades missing, stamped Patent Wild & Wessel Berlin, 25.5in (65cm) high.
£600-700 *Bea*

A plated two-handled floral patterned tray with vine decorated rim, 25in (64cm) long.
£150-200 *GH*

An Old Sheffield plate kettle-on-stand, the kettle with repoussé foliate scroll decoration and engraved with a coat-of-arms and crest, the stand with burner and raised on scroll feet, 15in (38cm) high overall.
£300-400 *P(O)*

A Victorian parcel gilt and silver electro-type tankard.
£1,000-1,200 *P(S)*

A graduated matched set of 5 electroplated salvers, each engraved with a vacant circular panel within a frame of Greek key pattern and within a pierced border with beaded edging, small salver 12in (31cm) diam. **£950-1,200** *Bea*

A plated near complete canteen, by Walker & Hall, comprising: a 12 place setting including ivory hafted fish and dessert services, together with a pair of entrée dishes, a four-piece tea and coffee set, toast rack, butter dish, a pair of cruet stands, and accessories, in a carved oak cabinet-on-stand with cabriole legs and casters, 31.5in (80cm) wide. **£2,500-3,000** *AH*

An electroplated two-division biscuitière, with hinged scalloped bowls each with a pierced retaining grille on a stand with chased decoration and central carrying handle, 11in (28cm) high. **£400-450** *Bea*

A Sheffield plate argyle, of cylindrical form, engraved with crest within a wreath and with engraved ribbon-tied festoons and fronds, with beaded edging, detachable cover and wood scroll handle, 5in (13cm) high. **£600-650** *Bea*

WINE ANTIQUES

A wagon-form double wine coaster, the circular coasters with pierced sides, with shaped square join between, on 4 wagon wheels, with swivelling reeded pull and baluster handle, c1810, 16in (40.5cm) long. **£560-600** *CNY*

A pair of George III silver wine coasters, probably by Robert Hennell, pierced with bright cut decoration enclosing crested cartouche, with turned mahogany bases, marks rubbed, London 1792. **£900-1,100** *GIL*

Two silver crested, pierced and bright cut wine coasters, London 1777, 4.5in (11.5cm) diam. **£1,200-1,500** *TVA*

A pair of Regency red lacquer ribbed wine coasters, with Sheffield plated rim and ring handles, 5.5in (14cm) diam. **£700-750** *CSK*

A pair of George III wine coasters, by J. W. Story & William Elliott, with wooden bases centred by a circular boss engraved with a crest, London 1809, 7in (17.5cm) diam. **£1,000-1,500** *S(C)*

A selection of Victorian pottery cellar bin labels, with black enamel lettering, impressed with Farrow & Jackson, Wedgwood, Minton, Copeland and Spode. **£20-60 each** *CS*

A composite set of 5 William IV bottle tickets, of shaped rounded rectangular form, the borders stamped with rosettes and acanthus leaves, engraved 'Noyeau' and 'Shrub,' Sheffield 1836, maker's mark S.W. and Co, and 'Rum', 'Hollands' and 'Whisky', Sheffield 1830, by S. C. Younge and Co., on belcher link chains, some damage. **£300-350** *HSS*

A selection of silver or enamel decanter labels, 18th and 19thC. **£20-180 each** *CS*

A walnut tantalus, supporting 4 square decanters with faceted stoppers, in a case with hinged lid, 20thC. **£500-600** *WIL*

A set of 3 George III Scottish silver labels, by Matthew Crow, Edinburgh, c1805, 1.5in (4cm) wide. **£200-260** *TVA*

A silver decanter label of goblet and festoon shape, engraved with rare name 'CARLOWITZ', London 1880, maker's initials JA over JS. **£100-120** *CS*

A Victorian engraved and shaped silver wine label, Birmingham 1847, 2in (5cm). **£70-85** *TVA*

A Derby porcelain wine taster's tastevin, the bowl decorated with sprigs of blue flowers, c1770. **£450-550** *CS*

A multi-tool with spoon and fork, including a small corkscrew, with a plastic handle simulating a stag's antler, c1920. **£20-40** *CS*

Five antique corkscrews, including a Thomason type, **£120-140,** lady's legs, **£70-90,** Heeley A1 Double Lever, **£40-50,** an all steel bone handled King's Screw, **£150-200,** and an iron open frame corkscrew, **£200-220** *CS*

A George III all steel pocket picnic corkscrew, the sheath inserts through the ring to form a handle, c1790.
£60-90 *CS*

A French pinion assisted side wind corkscrew, open framed nickel plated, c1880.
£80-120 *CS*

A George III silver and ivory handled pocket corkscrew with silver sheath, stamped with maker's initials.
£140-180 *CS*

A German 'Naughty Nineties' corkscrew, in celluloid and nickel silver, the lady's legs flesh with pink and white striped stockings.
£80-120 *CS*

A cast steel side lever corkscrew, known as the 'Royal Club', with brass oval plaque, Charles Hull's Patent of 1864.
£450-550 *CS*

An all steel with gilt/bronze finish lever corkscrew named THE EMPIRE, by James Heeley & Sons, c1884.
£200-250 *CS*

A cast iron bar corkscrew, named the 'Original Safety', 19thC.
£70-75 *CS*

A Victorian turned wood handle double helix corkscrew, stamped on steel stem S Pat, patented by James Wilson in 1877.
£80-100 *CS*

An all steel concertina corkscrew with copper finish, stamped The Pullezi, Heeley's Original Patent.
£40-60 *CS*

An all steel double concertina corkscrew with copper finish, Weir's patent by J. Heeley & Sons, c1880.
£200-250 *CS*

An all steel concertina corkscrew, stamped H. D. Armstrong's Patent, c1902.
£30-40 *CS*

An all brass bar corkscrew, named 'The Rotary Eclipse', c1880.
£350-450 *CS*

A selection of Victorian Champagne taps.
£30-70 each *CS*

A German open frame all steel corkscrew, named Monopol Universal, with ball bearing collar.
£70-80 *CS*

A selection of corkscrews, late 19thC, *top to bottom*: cast iron cork drawer in 2 parts by Lund, **£30-60**, a French Zig Zag concertina, **£20-30**, a Spanish BOJ 2 lever, **£15-20**, a Heeley A1, **£35-65**, a French Perille, **£15-25**, a Concertina, **£25-35**, and a German open frame, **£15-20** *CS*

A brass bar cork drawer, named 'The Slam', with cast iron adjustable clamp, c1890.
£100-140 *CS*

An all steel four-pillar King's Screw, with turned bone handle, c1820.
£250-350 *CS*

A turned bone handled corkscrew with dusting brush, known as the 'King's Screw', with brass barrel and steel side wind, with applied oval Royal coat-of-arms, by Heeley & Sons.
£180-240 *CS*

A Victorian champagne tap, by S. Maw & Son, London, c1880, 4.5in (11.5cm) long.
£60-75 *TVA*

A champagne dispensing tap, in brass with ebonised turned wood handle, with Archemedian steel worm, by Edwin Wolverson, c1877.
£50-70 *CS*

A double action brass barrel Thomason type corkscrew, with bone handle and applied brass plaque showing the Royal coat-of-arms, c1840.
£100-140 *CS*

A George III 2-part silver wine funnel of plain design with reeded edges, by Peter & William Bateman, London 1813, slightly damaged.
£300-350 *GAK*

A George III wine funnel with reeded rim, part fluted spout, London 1803, 5.5in (14cm), 4oz.
£200-300 *P(S)*

A silver wine funnel by Samuel Meriton II, London 1782, 18thC, 5in (12.5cm).
£700-800 *TVA*

A liqueur set in the form of a bird cage, with carrying handle, opening to release a moulded glass decanter in the form of a cockatoo, with electroplate head and glass eyes, with 8 glasses, Austrian, 18.5in (47cm) high.
£1,200-1,500 *WIL*

A George III wine funnel with gadrooned rim and shaped tapering spout, maker's mark S H, London 1815, 5.5in (14cm).
£300-400 *P(S)*

A George III silver 2-piece wine funnel with gadrooned edge and tab to fit over the rim of a punch bowl to filter fruit juices, hall-marked, c1790.
£200-300 *CS*

A silver wine funnel with fluted spout, plain strainer, marked on both pieces, London 1799.
£350-400 *GAK*

A Victorian brandy bowl with a flared rim and pouring lip, turned wood handle, maker's mark C S, London 1889, 4in (10cm).
£330-380 *P(S)*

A parcel gilt wine jug, with later wood handle, the cover with bayonet fitting, formed as the head of a sphinx, with foliage finial, by Jacques Louis Clement, Kassel, German, 1793, 12in (11.5in (29.5cm) high, 915gr.
£4,250-5,000 *C*

A George IV shaped wine funnel, by Emes & Barnard, in 2 parts, the detachable simply pierced bowl with an overhanging cast fruiting vine border and vine leaf clip, the lobed body engraved with the initial S above a chased band of flowers and acanthus leaves, on a matted ground, London 1827, 6in (15cm) long, 6oz. 2dwt.
£600-650 *S(C)*

A baluster shaped wine measure of gallon capacity, the flat circular cover inscribed Ryde Chapel and having a double-volute thumbpiece, 18thC, 12.5in (32cm).
£800-1,000 *S(S)*

A mid-Victorian wine ewer, and matching goblets.
£2,200-2,500 *HSS*

A George III brass-bound mahogany wine cooler, with hinged lid and lead-lined interior, with slightly tapering body, the stand with associated canted tapering legs, the sides with ring and foliate carrying handles, tap missing, 17in (43cm) wide.
£2,200-2,500 *C(S)*

A George III mahogany and brass-bound wine cooler, the hinged top above sides fitted with carrying handles, enclosing a lined interior, on square splayed legs, the stand restored, 20in (51cm) wide.
£1,500-2,000 *CSK*

A George III mahogany wine cooler on stand, the brass-bound octagonal body with crossbanded segmentally veneered hinged top inlaid with chevron lines and a star medallion, the stand with fluted frieze and conforming square legs with brass casters, 19in (48cm) wide.
£4,000-4,500 *Bea*

A George III mahogany cellaret, brass-bound and with leaded interior divisions, on stand with squared supports, brass side handles, 15.5in (39.5cm) wide.
£1,900-2,500 *GSP*

A George III mahogany wine cooler, inlaid with neo-classical marquetry and banded in satinwood, the lid with laurel decoration, the fluted frieze with an ornate brass ring handle above a panel with swags, paterae capped reeded pilasters, the sides with later brass swag handles, formerly on a stand, the present square tapering legs with brass casters, 25in (64cm).
£4,500-5,000 *WW*

A George III mahogany and brass-bound oval wine cooler, with lined interior and lion's mask and ring carrying handles on later square tapered legs and casters, 26in (66cm) wide.
£3,000-3,500 *CSK*

A George III mahogany wine cooler with canted rectangular hinged top and green baize lined interior, the sides with brass carrying handles, on angled square legs with later base and restorations to legs, 24.5in (62cm) wide.
£1,500-2,000 *C*

A Georgian brass bound mahogany wine cooler. **£1,000-1,500** *LRG*

A late George III mahogany and brass bound octagonal wine cooler, the hinged lid enclosing a later fitted interior and lining, flanked by brass lion's mask handles, on turned tapering legs, 10in (51cm) wide.
£1,700-2,500 *C*

A George III mahogany wine cooler with 2 brass bands, having hinged lid with internal lead lining and brass drain tap, supported on matching stand with 4 square tapering legs and brass casters, 18in (46cm) wide.
£3,000-3,500 *GH*

A Regency mahogany wine cooler with brass banding, original lead lined interior, and tap to drain melting ice.
£2,200-2,700 *HSS*

An Irish Regency plum-pudding mahogany wine cooler, with coffered canted rectangular hinged top enclosing a lead lined divided interior, the tapering sides with brass lion mask and ring handles, one ring missing, on later paw feet, 26.5in (67cm) wide.
£1,200-1,800 *C*

A William IV oak and ebonised wine cooler with moulded circular top and lead lined interior, above a gadrooned body and on spreading fluted shaft and square base, 26in (66cm) diam.
£2,500-3,500 *C*

A Victorian tôle pcintc wine cooler, rectangular with canted corners, repainted with flower borders and stylised flowerheads, with removeable liner, twin scroll handles and on 4 spoked wheels, 24.5in (62cm) long.
£400-500 *ALL*

An early Victorian mahogany sarcophagus shaped wine cooler, with raised tambour style domed top, swivel lead lined cellarette, supported on hairy lion paw feet, 31in (78.5cm) wide.
£1,000-1,500 *GH*

A William IV Old Sheffield plate wine cooler, of loosely Warwick form, the detachable rim engraved with a crest, in a bead and ovolo border, with twin entwined handles, the sides with acanthus leaf decoration, on a square base, 10in (26cm) high.
£900-1,000 *P(O)*

A pair of Victorian fluted campana shaped wine coolers on rising foliate cast shaped square bases, applied with cast body bands with trailing vines incorporating crossed tendril handles, each engraved with an armorial, 12in (30.5cm).
£3,500-4,000 *C*

A pair of William IV Sheffield plate wine coolers, the campana shape bodies with melon panelling and a band of grape vines, gadroon shell leaf borders, detachable rims to the liners, moulded leaf appliqué handles on knopped circular feet, 10.5in (26.5cm).   **£1,500-2,000** *WW*

Make the most of Miller's

Unless otherwise stated, any description which refers to 'a set' or 'a pair' includes a valuation for the entire set or the pair, even though the illustration may show only a single item.

A pair of openwork wine coolers, applied with a grape vine, with short tendril stem, the sides composed of open work reeded trelliswork, liners missing, 10.5in (26.5cm) high.
£2,200-2,500 *CNY*

METALWARE

Gold

A 9ct gold liqueur set, by Wakeley & Wheeler, comprising: a waiter, with reeded mount, on hoof feet, 8in (20cm), a set of 4 goblets, 3.5in (8.5cm), and a single goblet, 5in (12.5cm), all initialled B and engraved Cartier, London, 1967.
£1,800-2,200   *S(S)*

A Charles I pewter flagon, with knopped cover, erect heart- pierced thumbpiece, indistinct touch mark to handle, on a domed foot, c1625, 12in (30cm).
£1,700-2,200   *S(S)*

A pewter 3-pint tappit hen, the shouldered body with bands of reeding.
£300-400   *P(O)*

A 9ct gold cigarette box, the interior of the hinged cover engraved with a inscription 'From The Directors of Thomas W. Ward Ltd., to Arnold Carr. On completion of Fifty Years Service. 1st November, 1965', wood lined, Birmingham 1965, 8in (20cm) wide.
£1,500-2,000   *HSS*

A pewter half gallon measure, by Richard Dunne, late 17thC, 11in (28cm).
£1,200-1,700   *HSS*

A pewter lidded flagon of Beefeater type, the muffin knopped cover with twin cusp thumbpiece stamped with a row of 4 hallmarks, the plain drum above ovolo moulded foot, c1670, 10in (25.5cm).
£900-1,500   *S(S)*

The flat lid appears to be later inset. The paper label under the lid is inscribed A.W. T79, c1670.

Pewter

A James I pewter flagon, with knopped bun cover and erect ridged thumbpiece, the plain drum on raised ovolo moulded foot, some surface pitting, c1615, 11.5in (29cm). **£1,000-1,500**   *S(S)*

A pewter half gallon flagon, the domed lid with wrythen thumbpiece and shaped flange, the slightly tapering cylindrical body with bands of stringing, early 18thC, 11.5in (29cm).
£1,500-2,000   *P(O)*

A pewter wrigglework pint tankard, with voluted handle terminal and splayed foot, late 17thC, 6.5in (16cm).
£2,500-2,700   *P(O)*

A collection of pewter chargers, 18in (46cm) diam., **£120-200**, and plates, 9in (23cm) diam. **£30-40** *KEY*

A Normandy pewter flagon, 18thC, 12.5in (32cm) high. **£300-350** *KEY*

A pewter lidded flagon, by Terry of York, the domed cover with fretted brim stamped S.S. and with Yorkscroll thumbpiece, the tapering drum with hooped bands around base, touchmark ? T in base, c1700, 11.5in (29cm). **£800-1,200** *S(S)*

An English pewter charger, c1790, 20in (51cm) long. **£200-225** *KEY*
front: A pewter porringer, 18thC, 5in (12cm). **£160-190** *KEY*

l. An English pewter barrel shaped tankard, c1790, 5in (14cm) high. **£120-150** *KEY*
r. A Swiss pewter wall cistern, 18thC, 9.5in (24cm) high. **£200-225** *KEY*

A Guernsey pewter measure, 18thC, 11.5in (29cm) high. **£440-500** *KEY*

A Jersey pewter measure, 18thC, 8in (21cm) high. **£280-320** *KEY*

A Scottish pewter tappit hen, 18thC, 11in (27cm) high. **£400-440** *KEY*

A pewter spire flagon, 1763, 11in (28cm) high. **£400-450** *KEY*

A pair of pewter and brass table
candlesticks.
£200-300 *HCH*

A French armorial pewter
jardinière, by Louis Alegre,
Angers, with moulded rim, the
front cast with the arms of the
City of Angers, the back with
Christopher Columbus, the side
ring handles suspended through
the mouths of lion masks,
underside marked, c1820, 9in
(23cm) diam.
£1,100-1,300 *CNY*

A German pewter soup tureen
and cover, by A.M., with circular
foot and stem supporting the
globular body with moulded
banding and square side handles,
the fitted domed cover with urn
finial, underside marked, early
19thC, 12.5in (32cm) wide.
£3,250-3,500 *CNY*

A pair of French pewter sconces,
each with cartouche shaped back
plate terminating in a flame
finial, the pierced scroll arm with
spiral fluted drip pan and
campana shaped socket with
everted rim, probably 18thC, 14in
(35.5cm).
£3,000-3,250 *CNY*

A French pewter armorial ewer,
by Laurent Morant, Lyon, the
reeded foot supporting a knopped
stem and helmet shaped body
with moulded banding centering
an engraved coat-of-arms, the
double scroll handle with shell
finial, underside marked, 1711,
10in (26cm).
£1,000-1,500 *CNY*

*The arms are those of Delglat de
La Tour du Bost.*

A French armorial
pewter platter, cast
with the French Royal
arms enclosed within
floral garlands, the
sloping rim engraved
with scrolling vines
within a moulded
scallop edge, underside
indistinctly marked,
19thC, 20in (50cm)
long.
£1,300-1,500 *CNY*

A French pewter cistern and
basin, the cistern formed as a
dolphin, a spigot in its mouth, the
basin formed as a scallop shell
raised on tripod feet cast with
masks, the splash plate cast in
relief with Diana and Acteon, one
fin missing, probably 18thC, 23in
(59cm).
£1,100-1,500 *CNY*

Brass

A Turkish brass pear shaped
ewer and hinged domed cover on
4 feet with scrolling mythical
head handle and tapering lobed
spout, the lobed body with single
leaf petals on each section, 18thC,
13in (33cm).
£600-800 *CSK*

A George III brass and silvered
travelling coin balance, by V.
Anscheutz and J. Schlaff,
Denmark Street, Soho, London,
the scale from 0-36 and signed
Anscheutz & Co., No. 1620, with
original instructions, in
mahogany shaped case.
£700-800 *DN*

A Flemish brass inkstand in the form of a lion, the hinged head with stylised mane, his body with stamped disc decoration, his rear leg pierced for the quill, liner missing, probably 15thC, 3.5in (8.5cm) wide.
£1,700-2,200 *C*

A Victorian coromandel brass mounted inkstand, with domed hinged superstructure, above 2 inkwells and base fitted with a single drawer, on bun feet, 11.5in (29cm) wide.
£300-350 *P(M)*

A Regency style brass jardinière, with lobed and embossed body, lion's mask ring handles, paw feet, 11in (28cm).
£150-200 *GAK*

An Italian brass and pietra dura clock garniture, the pierced case and three-light candelabra inset with circular pietra dura plaques decorated with flowers and birds, the dial signed H. Bosi, Firenze, with French 8-day movement, late 19thC, 17in (43cm) high.
£2,000-2,500 *P(O)*

A pair of Adam style gilt brass coal vases and covers of oval fluted and reeded form with pineapple finials, 16.5in (42cm) high.
£1,700-2,000 *Bea*

Bronze

A three-quarter life size bronze head of an elderly woman, wearing a scarf, by W. Reynolds-Stephens, on a dark marble base, 22in (56cm).
£650-750 *L&E*

A French bronze of Clytie, by Pierre Charles Eugène Delpech, with rich dark brown patination, on a black marble plinth, signed and inscribed London, early 20thC, 15.5in (39.5cm) high.
£800-900 *S*

A pair of English bronze busts of Byron and Scott, rich mid and dark brown patination, on black marble plinths, c1830, 13.5in (34cm).
£1,700-2,000 *S*

A French bronze bust of Minerva, with a helmet and aegis over her robe, cast from a model by Albert-Ernest Carrier-Belleuse, signed A. Carrier-Belleuse and with Valsuani Cire Perdue stamp, on mottled green marble socle, 19thC, 15.5in (39.5cm) high.
£1,200-1,700 *C*

A bronze bust of a girl with one hand to her mouth, by George van der Straeten, red/brown patination, signed and with foundry stamp, on an alabaster plinth, 7.5in (19cm) high.
£450-550 *S(S)*

An Italian bronze bust of a gentleman with a moustache, from a model by Giuseppe Renda, on a moulded socle, signed and dated G. Renda settembre '94, late 19thC, 20in (51cm).
£1,500-2,500 *C*

A Belgian bronze bust of a young Bacchante woman, by Jef Lambeaux, with rich green patination, slight rubbing, 25in (63.5cm) high.
£1,300-1,900 *S*

A bronze bust of a girl holding cherries in her mouth, by George van der Straeten, red/brown patination, signed and with foundry stamp, on an alabaster base, c1910, 9in (23cm) high.
£400-500 *S(S)*

Giuseppe Renda (1862-1939) studied under Toma, Lista and Solari. He executed monuments and portrait busts, but specialised primarily in bronze statuettes in an Art Nouveau style. He exhibited internationally, winning prizes and acclaim for his images of sensuous maidens, though these were later considered licentious by the Fascist regime. This bust reveals Renda's taste for the Continental Belle Epoque, with its stylish treatment of the moustache, summary and asymmetric shoulder and elegant moulded socle. Though a fashionable bronze, Renda has skilfully combined sensitive portraiture with the decorative, particularly in the delicately lined eyes, strong nose and upward tilt to the head.

A bronze figure of a fisher boy, signed on the base Lavergne, 7in (18cm) high.
£150-200 *GAK*

A French bronze bust of Diana, after Jean-Antoine Houdon, on waisted socle with laurel wreath moulded base, inscribed HOUDON sculpt., 19thC, 29in (73cm) high.
£2,000-3,000 *C*

A copper electrotype figure of a Nubian slave girl, by John Bell, with brown patination, signed and inscribed Elkington & Co., Founders, c1880, 21in (55cm) high.
£600-800 *S(S)*

A bronze figure of a Grenadier Guardsman, inscribed 'J. E. Boehm Scr.', stamped Elkington, on an ebonised plinth, 1815, 23in (59cm) high.
£1,500-2,000 *P(S)*

A pair of Italian bronze figures of Roman warriors in elaborate battledress, on square bases, on ebonised stands, 19thC, 17in (43.5cm) high.
£1,500-2,000 *Bea*

A bronze figure of the Dancing Pan with cymbals, after the Antique, on a square base, 12in (31cm) high.
£250-350 *CSK*

An English 'New Sculpture' bronze figure of an allegorical maiden, possibly Justice, on a stained wood socle, early 20thC, 11.5in (29.5cm) high.
£2,000-2,500 *C*

A bronze figure of a young gentleman wearing a doublet and hose, carrying a sword,19thC, 48in (122cm) high.
£4,500-5,000 *B*

A bronze figure of St Michael and Satan, by Edward William Wyon, with rich dark green/brown patination, inscribed 'Executed by E. W. Wyon after the original of Flaxman for the Art Union of London, 1842,' 20in (51cm) high.
£1,500-2,000 *S*

An English Art Union bronze figure of a boy at a stream, cast from a model by John Henry Foley, the base stamped J. H. Foley, mid-19thC, 21.5in (54.5cm) high.
£2,000-2,500 *C*

John Henry Foley R.A., 1818-1874, rose from humble origins to become one of the foremost sculptors of the Victorian era. He designed the figure of the Prince Consort and the group of 'Asia' for the Albert Memorial. He was born in Dublin, and on his death left his casts to the Schools of the Royal Dublin Society.

The Art Union of London was founded in 1837 with the high ideals of promoting the appreciation of British sculpture. The Committee decided to commission reductions of monumental sculpture, stipulating 'that the pieces should be of moderate expense and of a convenient size ... fitted for a drawing room table'. The Art Union's selection for 1846 was the present model by Foley, the monumental plaster of which had enjoyed great acclaim at the Westminster Hall Exhibition of 1844, and is now preserved by the Royal Dublin Society.

A bronze figure of a naked Bacchanalian youth, pouring wine from a skin, 9in (23cm) high.   **£200-250** *P(O)*

A bronze figure of a young male hunter, holding a bow and horn, wearing a loin cloth with a dead deer at his feet, after Marioton, inscribed 'Eug. Marioton, Hallalt', 27in (69cm) high.
£320-370 *DDM*

A bronze group of a young girl, restraining a setter from a game bird, with brown/black patination, by Engelbert Joseph Peiffer, signed, c1860, 14in (35cm).
£1,000-1,200 *S(S)*

A bronze female torso, by Karin Jonzen, pale green patination, indistinctly signed, 16.5in (42cm) high.
£900-1,200 *S(S)*

A bronze statuette of Bacchus and child.
£400-450 *SIM*

A bronze figure by James Butler, R.A., entitled Little Dancer Holding Her Skirt, limited edition of 12, signed, 14.5in (37cm) high.
£1,000-1,500 *GC*

A bronze figure of Joan of Arc, by Henri Michel Chapu, signed F. Barbedienne Fondeur, and with the Collas reduction seal, mid-brown patination, mid-19thC, 18in (46cm).
£1,000-1,200 *S*

A bronze figure of the Farnese Hercules, standing by a tree stump, with black patination, on a rectangular base, 19thC, 15.5in (41cm) high.
£500-700 *S(S)*

A bronze figurine of a girl, in a flowing dress and plumed hat, on a shaped plinth, signed 'C. Ceribelle', 19thC, 31in (78.5cm).
£2,500-3,000 *GH*

A pair of French School bronze cherubs, on red marble socles, with rich brown patination, mid-19thC, 33in and 34in (84cm and 87cm).
£3,500-5,500 *S*

These bronze figures are mid-19thC casts of the 1768 models by Jean Baptiste Pigalle.

A bronze figure, by Hippolyte Moreau.
£3,500-4,000 *SWO*

An Austrian cold painted bronze figure of a young negro, 15.5in (40cm) high.
£1,000-1,500 *HSS*

A bronze figure entitled 'The Juggling Clown', signed by Francesco de Matteis, c1880.
£1,500-2,000 *GIL*

A bronze figurine of a young boy, standing playing a mandolin, on a plinth, stamped 'Reduction mecanique F. Barbe Dienne Fondeur', signed P. Dubois, dated 1865, 30in (76.5cm).
£2,000-3,000 *GH*

A bronze figure of Mephistopheles, by Jacques Louis Gautier, signed and inscribed Duplan et Salles Ft. de Bronze, with dark brown/black patination, mid-19thC, 26in (66cm).
£900-1,200 *S*

Gautier was a pupil of Rude and made his debut at the Salon of 1850. Mephistopheles was first modelled in the early 1850's and was produced in several variants by the foundry Duplan et Salles, c1855.

A bronze figure of a young girl wearing a flowing dress and holding a garland of flowers, standing on a rocky circular base, inscribed 'S. Kinsburger', 25in (64cm) high.
£400-450 *DDM*

A bronze figure entitled 'La Glaneuse, by Henri Godet, with green and light brown patination, signed and stamped A1989 and with the Bronze Garanti au Titre seal, c1900, 30in (76cm).
£2,000-2,500 *S*

A French bronze figure of Henri IV, cast from a model by Baron François-Joseph Bosio, shown as a child, dressed contemporary breeches and doublet, signed B. ON BOSIO, sword blade missing, mid-19thC, 49in (125cm) high.
£3,200-4,200 *C*

François-Joseph, Baron Bosio, 1768-1845, studied under Pajou in France and Canova in Rome. He was widely patronised, in particular by Bonaparte, the Bourbons and Louis Philippe. Bosio's Henri IV Enfant was originally executed in marble, commissioned by the ministre de L'Interieur for the town of Pau. It was exhibited at the Salon of 1824 and with the King's permission Bosio had a limited edition of reductions cast in bronze. A silver version was also cast, it was listed in the Cabinet du Roi in 1824, and is now in the Louvre.

A French bronze figure of a muse, cast from a model by Etienne-Henri Dumaige, signed H. Dumaige, 19thC, 13in (33cm) high.
£1,000-1,500 *C*

A bronze figure of David with the head of Goliath, by Jean Antoinne Mercié, signed, inscribed F. Barbedienne Fondeur, stamped with the Collas reduction seal and numbered 82, with brown patination, 29in (74cm) high.
£2,000-2,500 *S*

A French School bronze, entitled 'The Wishing Well', with a rich dark brown patination, on a marble plinth, signed, late 19thC, 17in (43cm).
£2,000-2,500 *S*

A French School bronze of a child offering Cupid a drink of wine, with a rich dark brown patination, on a marble base, 17in (43cm).
£1,500-2,000 *S*

A bronze figure entitled 'Une Fille D'Eve', by Alfred Grévin, with pale brown patination, signed Grévin & Beer, with founder's mark E. Tassel, c1880, 23in (60cm) high.
£2,000-2,500 *S(S)*

A French bronze figure entitled 'Soldat Spartiate', by Jean Pierre Cortot, signed and inscribed F. Barbedienne Fondeur Paris, with bronze, dark brown and green patination, 15in (38.5cm).
£1,200-1,700 *S*

Jean Pierre Cortot studied at the Ecole des Beaux Arts and won the Prix de Rome in 1809. Soldat Spartiate is a reduction cast of the marble group now in the Louvre, sometimes known as 'Soldat de Marathon', exhibited at the Salon of 1834 and cast posthumously in an edition by Ferdinand Barbedienne.

A French School bronze of Cupid stringing his bow, with a dark brown patination, on a marble plinth, late 19thC, 21in (53cm) high.
£1,500-2,000 *S*

A French School bronze of two young Bacchante women, with green/brown patination, late 19thC, 19in (48cm).
£2,000-2,500 *S*

A bronze figure, entitled Fascinator, by Eugène Marioton, with mid-brown patination, signed, 33in (84cm) high.
£2,500-3,000 *S*

Two French School bronze figures of Giuliano de Medici and Lorenzo de Medici, with rich dark brown patination, 16in (40.5cm) high.
£2,500-3,000 *S*

These bronze figures are reductions after the original marble statues in the Medici Chapel in Florence, made by the Italian master Michelangelo Buonarroti, 1475-1564. They portray the Duke of Nemours and the Duke of Urbino and are situated in the chapel above the figures of Night and Day.

A bronze figure entitled 'The Family', by Henry Etienne Dumaige, signed, with rich mid-brown patination, c1850, 21in (53cm) high.
£1,500-2,000 *S*

A bronze group of 2 putti and a young faun, signed Clodion, on green marble oval base, with dark green patination, late 19thC, 11in (28cm) high.
£600-800 *S(S)*

A bronze figure of a Japanese geisha girl, by Eugène Laurent, with variegated patination, signed E. Laurent and Raingo Fes, c1880, 17in (43cm) high.
£1,000-1,500 *S(S)*

Eugène Laurent was born in Gray on 29th April 1832, he died in Paris in 1898. He studied under Coinchon and exhibited at the Salon from 1861. He specialised in portrait busts and figures of contemporary and historical French celebrities. He sculpted the monument of Jacques Callot in Nancy and the statue of François Boucher in the Paris town hall.

A bronze figure, entitled 'The Successful Hunter', by Marcel Début, with dark brown/green patination, signed, c1900, 35in (88cm) high.
£2,500-3,500 *S*

A bronze figure, entitled 'L'amour enchainant La Fortune', by Auguste Moreau, signed, stripped patination, c1900, 20in (51cm) high.
£1,500-2,000 *S*

A bronze figure of Pan, seated, by Jacques Antoine Theodore Coinchon, with green patination, signed, c1870, 17in (43cm).
£1,000-1,500 *S(S)*

A bronze figure of 'The Blacksmith', by Edouard Drouot, signed, with mid-brown patination, on a naturalistic base mounted on a red marble plinth, 25in (64cm) high.
£900-1,200 *S(S)*

A bronze figure entitled 'Young Hunter', by Marcel Début, with rich chocolate brown patination, c1900, 26.5in (67cm) high.
£1,500-2,000 *S*

A French revolving bronze group, entitled 'Devoir, Present, Prepare, L'Avenir', of a seated man on an anvil with a woman and child holding a sword, signed Rancouler, repair to arm, 31in (79cm) high.
£3,200-3,700 *GH*

A French bronze figure of a judge, cast from a model by R. Colombo, signed R. Colombo and with Bronze Garanti stamp, on a rouge marble stepped base, with bronze trim and cartouche inscribed JUGE AU CONSEIL DES DIX VENISE, late 19thC, 21.5in (54.5cm) high.
£1,000-1,500 *C*

A pair of French bronze and ivory figures of a musician and a poet, by Eustache Bernard, on onyx plinths, 19thC, 10.5in (27cm) high.
£900-1,200 *S*

A pair of cold painted bronze figures of Arabs, by Franz Bergman, each with Bergman stamp, on green marble plinths, tallest 15in (38cm) high.
£4,000-4,500 *S(S)*

An Italian bronze figure of a reclining maiden, cast from a model by Vittorio Caradossi, on a green marble socle with cartouche inscribed DOLCE FAR NIENTE, PROF. V. CARADOSSI, on green marble fluted columnar pedestal, c1900, 24in (61cm).
£4,000-5,000 *C*

A German bronze figure of the nightwatchman, signed F. Bernaver, Munchen, on a mottled black circular plinth, 27in (69cm) high.
£700-1,000 *P(S)*

A bronze figure of Caesar Augustus, after the Antique, standing by a putto on a dolphin, on a circular base inscribed A. MESSINA ROMA, black/green patination, 19thC, 28in (71cm) high. **£1,500-2,000** *S(S)*

A French bronze figure, entitled 'La Danseuse Nattova', by Serge Yourievitch, with brown patination, on a marble plinth, early 20thC, 15.5in (39.5cm) high. **£2,500-3,000** *S*

A Hungarian bronze group of Adam and Eve, by Mark Weinberger Vedres, on a marble plinth, signed, 19thC, 16in (41cm) high. **£2,000-2,200** *S*

An Armenian bronze figure of Isadora Duncan, by Akop Gurdjan, with brown patination, signed and stamped with foundry seal Le Blanc Barbedienne, Cire Perdue, à Paris, 20thC, 18in (45cm) high. **£1,200-1,700** *S*

An Italian bronze figure of Spring Awakening, by Amadeo Gennarelli, signed and stamped, 20thC, 18.5in (47cm) high. **£1,800-2,000** *S*

A bronze figure of Martha Graham, by George Aarons, rich mid-brown patination, signed and dated 1941, No. 4/12 and inscribed Modern Art Fdry. N.Y., 14in (35cm) high. **£2,000-2,500** *S*

George Aarons was born in Lithuania and moved to the United States at the age of 10. His work is in the collections of the Museum of Art, Ein Harod, Israel; the Fitchburg Art Museum, Massachussetts and the Musée de St Denis, France.

Gurdjan exhibited in Paris in 1945 at the Salon des Artistes Libres Arméniens. His known works include a bust of the architect, Houspian.

A bronze model of a First World War Cavalryman, by Pierre-Robert Christophe, signed, with rich mid-brown patination, on a mottled marble plinth, 21in (52.5cm). **£1,500-1,800** *S*

A Norwegian bronze figure of Brunhilda on horseback, on a rocky incline, cast from a model by Stephan Sinding, signed, with founder's inscription AKT. GES. GLADENBECK-BERLIN D964, sword replaced, late 19thC, 20.5in (52cm) high. **£2,000-2,500** *C*

A bronze figure of a cloaked medieval warrior riding a galloping horse, by Attino Prendoni, 24in (61.5cm) high. **£700-900** *GAK*

An Austrian School cold painted bronze of a clown and a donkey, c1900, 10in (26cm) wide. **£700-900** *S(S)*

A bronze study for Europa and the Bull, by Sydney March, with dark brown patination, signed, English School, 20thC, 11.5in (29cm).
£900-1,200 *S*

A bronze figure of a seated bear holding a table lighter in the form of an oil lamp, after Christophe Fratin, underside of base soldered, signed with reverse 'N', 5.5in (13.5cm) high.
£200-250 *HSS*

A French bronze equestrian figure of Charles V, on a rouge marble base, late 19thC, 21.5in (54cm) high.
£1,500-2,000 *C*

A French bronze equestrian figure of a hussar, cast from a model by Pierre-Nicholas Tourgueneff, the hussar in First Empire uniform, signed P. Tourgueneff and inscribed Susse F. es. Ed.rs., with Susse Frères foundary stamp, plume missing, late 19thC , 22in (56cm) high.
£2,000-2,500 *C*

Pierre-Nicholas Tourgueneff, 1853 -1912, was a French sculptor of Russian extraction. He trained under the celebrated animalier and historical sculptor Fremiet.

An Austrian School cold painted bronze of an elephant tiger hunt, on a marble plinth, c1900, 12in (30.5cm).
£1,200-1,700 *S*

A bronze group of children playing with a tortoise, by Louis Ernest Barrias, signed and dated 1877, inscribed F. Barbedienne, with rich mid and dark brown patination, 5.5in (13.5cm).
£1,700-2,000 *S*

A bronze figure of an eagle, by Antoine Louis Barye, signed, with rich dark brown patination, 11in (28cm).
£2,500-3,000 *S*

A bronze figure of 2 eagles attacking a goat, by Christophe Fratin, signed, with gold and red/brown patination, 19.5in (49.5cm).
£1,500-2,000 *S*

A French bronze animalier group of a monkey jockey astride a racehorse, on a naturalistic rectangular base signed J. GECHTER, 19thC, 5.5in (14cm) high.
£300-400 *CSK*

A bronzed and parcel-gilt Napoleonic eagle, with outstretched wings and clutching a ribbon-tied laurel wreath, 19thC, 38.5in (98cm) wingspan.
£2,500-3,000 *C*

A bronze group of two birds courting, by Jules Moigniez, signed, on an oval reeded base, with black patination, 8in (20cm).
£500-700 *S(S)*

A bronze retriever with pheasant, by Jules Moigniez, with rich dark brown patination, 12in (30cm).
£1,000-1,500 *S*

An American bronze group of 3 terriers, cast from a model by C. Mackarness, on naturalistic ground, signed and dated C. Mackarness 1912, with Roman bronze works N-Y- stamp, 8.5in (21cm) high.
£1,600-2,000 *C*

A bronze and parcel-gilt eagle with outstretched wings and clutching a ring, 19thC, 37.5in (95.5cm) wingspan.
£1,500-2,000 *C*

A bronze group of a bird protecting its chick from a snake, by Jules Moigniez, on a reeded base, signed, with black patination, c1870, 12.5in (32cm).
£500-700 *S(S)*

A bronze retriever and pheasant, by Lambert Leonard, signed, with rubbed dark brown patination, 8.5in (22cm).
£600-900 *S*

A bronze figure of a pointer dog, on a mottled black marble base, 12in (31cm) long.
£200-300 *GAK*

A bronze figure of a dachshund, entitled C. H. Wiseacre, signed Percy Taylor, c1920, 35.5in (90.5cm) long.
£2,500-3,000 *SWO*

A bronze figure of an emu, by Franz Bergman, signed Nam Greb and with seal, brown patination, c1900, 6in (16cm).
£400-600 *S(S)*

A bronze group entitled Chiens Braque et Epagneau sur Faisan, by Paul Edouard Delabrierre, with green/dark brown patination, 11in (28cm).
£900-1,200 *S*

A cold-painted bronze model of an ibex, standing on a naturalistic rocky base, by Franz Bergman, stamped 294 Gesch and with Bergman seal, 11in (28cm).
£400-600 *S(S)*

A bronze figure of a mare and foal, by Christopher Fratin, on a naturalistic base, signed, mid brown patination, c1850, 8in (20cm).
£1,200-1,700 *S(S)*

A French bronze model of the racehorse 'Prestige', cast from a model by Henri-Louis Cordier, signed, inscribed 'Prestige', c1900, 17in (43.5cm) high.
£1,700-2,200 *C*

A bronze model of a goat, by P. J. Mêne, standing on an oval naturalistic base signed P. J. Mêne, with gold, brown and black patination, c1870, 5in (13cm).
£500-700 *S(S)*

A Viennese School bronze figure of a kangaroo, with brown patination, c1900, 6in (15cm).
£350-450 *S(S)*

Henri-Louis Cordier, 1853-1926, studied both under his father, the celebrated 'ethnographic' sculptor, and under Frémiet, Gérôme and Mercié. He exhibited at the Salon from 1877, and specialised in equestrian figures and studies of animals, though he did execute some ethnographic subjects. He was awarded several medals and was made a Chevalier of the Légion d'Honneur in 1903.

A bronze model of an Asian elephant, by Antoine-Louis Barye, base signed Barye and stamped 'H', with green/black patination, slightly rubbed, 19thC, 6in (15cm).
£900-1,200 *S(S)*

A Italian bronze figure of a lioness on a rock, by Giacomo Merculiano, with green patination, and marble base, 15in (38cm).
£1,700-2,000 *S*

A bronze figure of a walking lion, by R*** Thomas, signed and stamped C. H. Gautier Bronzier, with rich dark green/brown patination, on a wooden plinth, 14in (37.5cm) long.
£1,500-2,500 *S*

A Regency Gothic bronze standish, the plateau with 4 ink and pounce pots, nib holders and dished pen tray, the frieze with arcaded niches above bands of conforming ornament, twin handles on the sides, on foliate scroll feet, 13in (33cm) wide.
£2,000-2,500 *C*

A Paduan bronze triangular inkwell, the sides with friezes of scrolling foliate pattern, on 3 lion's paw feet, the lid with acanthus decoration, and a putto finial, 5.5in (14cm) wide.
£1,700-2,000 *S*

A pair of Viennese cold-painted bronze models of penguins, on square onyx plinths with chamfered edges, 19thC, 5in (12cm) high.
£700-900 *C*

A bronze figure of 2 stags, by Charles Valton, signed, 21in (53cm) high.
£1,700-2,000 *S*

A bronze inkstand in the Grecian manner, with central herm figure, on a breccia marble socle, 19thC.
£400-500 *LRG*

An Empire bronze inkwell, in the form of a boat, on a rouge marble platform base.
£100-180 *LRG*

A bronze figure of The Stag Hunt, by Pierre Jules Mêne, signed and inscribed Susse Frs Edts, with red/brown and dark brown patination, 15in (38cm) high.
£3,000-5,000 *S*

A bronze figure of a stag and doe beside a stream, by Pierre-Albert Laplanche, signed, with brown and green patination, on a green marble plinth, 18in (45cm).
£1,800-2,200 *S*

A bronze figure of a stag and doe, by Alfred Dubucand, with rich mid and green/brown patination, 11in (28.5cm).
£800-1,200 *S*

A Netherlands bronze snail head oil lamp, with bulbous eyes and wick emerging from trunk-shaped smiling jaws, with pale gold patina, c1600, 6.5in (16.5cm).
£2,500-3,500 *S*

An Italian bronze mortar dedicated to Pietro Bono of Perugia, inscribed around the rim in two bands PETRVS. BONVS. CANCS. GNLIS. PERVSIE. ET. VMBRIE, his coat-of-arms on one side and decorative cartouche on the other, 1618, 5in (13cm) high.
£2,500-3,000 *S*

A bronze figure of a doe, early 20thC.
£600-800 *SWO*

A bronzed standard lamp, in the form of an Egyptian woman, the base stamped Miroy Frères, Paris, 19thC.
£2,000-2,500 *LRG*

A pair of bronze game vases and covers, by Pierre Jules Mêne, signed, with brown patination, 17in (44cm) high.
£2,500-3,000 *S*

A pair of French gilt-bronze vases in the manner of Clodion, each cast with grotesque mask handles, swags and numerous playing putti, on octagonal black marble bases, 16in (41cm) high.
£900-1,200 *Bea*

A pair of French bronze models of the Medici and Borghese urns, each on square marble base, gilt patination, c1870, 14in (36cm) high.
£1,000-1,200 *S(S)*

A pair of bronze vases, with twin handles and swan neck terminals, the bodies with raised classical friezes, on stepped bases with square plinths, 19thC, 15.5in (39.5cm) high.
£700-1,000 *CSK*

A bronze table centrepiece, by Frederic Auguste Bartholdi, of two fauns holding a basket, signed, with brown patination, 8in (20cm).
£900-1,200 *S(S)*

A French bronze vase, by Léon Aimé Joachim Lecointe, the body cast in relief with Bacchante and other classical figures amongst foliage, with vine entwined handles, signed L. Lecointe, on foliate cast rising circular foot, lid missing, dated 1775, 38in (97cm) high.
£1,500-2,500 *S(S)*

An Austrian cold-painted bronze lamp, modelled as a semi-clad lady lying on a couch smoking a cigarette, being served a drink and fanned with a palm, signed on the carpet base Chotha or Chotka, 19thC, 15in (38cm) high.
£500-700 *GSP*

A bronze mortar, with waisted body cast with heraldic devices and ring handles, possibly German, 16thC, 10in (25cm) wide. **£800-1,000** *Bon*

Copper

A Netherlands repoussé copper wine cooler, the body with lion's masks at each end and gadrooned decoration, on paw feet, rings missing from handles, 17th/18thC, 30in (76cm) wide.
£3,000-3,500 *C*

A French bronze vase, with ovoid body, stylised bird twin handles, flaring neck with everted rim, Greek key pattern border above bands of stylised Oriental ornament, the base inscribed CHRISTOFLE & CIE, late 19thC, 10in (25cm) high.
£350-550 *CSK*

A copper kettle, the lid with finial.
£70-100 *GAK*

l. A copper lidded saucepan, c1800, 4.5in (11cm). **£70-80**

r. A copper coffee pot, c1790, 7.5in (19cm). **£140-160** *KEY*

A red patinated copper and white metal teapot, stand and burner, the teapot with ebonised turned bar handle, the body applied with white metal flowers, blossom and butterflies, the stand on 4 claw-and-ball feet, both teapot and stand stamped Gorham & Co. Y85, Cuivre, 10.5in (26.5cm) high. **£1,700-2,200** *C*

Firemarks

l. Phoenix, copper firemark, c1865-75, 9.5in (24cm) high. **£70-90**

r. Salop Fire Office, lead, c1785, 7.5in (19cm). **£150-180** *KEY*

Iron

Sun Fire Office, lead, c1797, 6.5in (16cm). **£80-100** *KEY*

> **Miller's is a price GUIDE not a price LIST**

A pair of damascened iron profile reliefs of Henri II and Catherine de Medici, the queen richly bejewelled, highlighted with silvering and gilding, in painted wood frames, French, early 17thC, 7.5in (19cm) high. **£2,000-2,500** *C*

An iron door knocker, c1800. **£60-80** *KEY*

A set of 4 French cast iron models of owls, late 19thC, 16.5in (42cm). **£800-1,200** *S(S)*

A pair of cast iron classical columns, each with square top on fluted stem, with paw feet, 19thC, 51in (129.5cm). **£3,000-3,500** *S*

A pair of cast iron Nubian torchères, each classically draped woman holding a lamp aloft, with later light fittings, stamped Miroy Frères, Paris, on ebonised wood bases, 70.5in (178cm). **£5,000-8,000** *S*

Ormolu

An iron eagle door knocker, c1830. **£60-80** *KEY*

A pair of Empire style ormolu candlesticks, each with bead-and-reel drip pan, on a reeded columnar shaft above tripartite monopodia and canted incurved triangular plinth banded with leaf tips, 13in (33cm). **£1,600-1,800** *CNY*

An ormolu inkstand, in the form of a cherub playing drums, 19thC, 8in (20cm). **£600-700** *RID*

An Empire ormolu brûle parfum, the dish with pierced cover, on tripod ram's head monopodiae support, on concave griotte marble plinth, 8.5in (21cm) high. **£250-350** *CSK*

A Charles X ormolu encrier, the globular well with bands of engine turned decoration, on tripod ram's head monopodiae and concave base, 6.5in (16cm). high. **£600-700** *CSK*

A French ormolu encrier, in the form of a cockerel's head, with inset glass eyes, 19thC, 4.5in (11cm) high. **£200-250** *CSK*

Ivory

A French ivory and gilt copper casket, with roof shaped lid, the ivory veneer bound by gilt copper straps engraved with zig-zag decoration, baluster knopped swing handle, lockplate engraved with arabesques, the lid with sliding drawer at the side, 4 sections of copper banding at one end lacking, ivory cracked, 16thC, 8in (20cm) wide. **£5,000-6,000** *C*

A South German ivory high relief allegorical figure group of Charity, the classically draped female figure with elaborately coiffed hair, some minor losses, late 17thC, 4in (10cm) high. **£4,500-5,500** *S*

A Siculo-Arabic ivory and silver mounted pyx, with central silver ringed knop, the central section with 4 double splayed mounts and hinged lockplate, the body with conforming silver mounts, some replacements to mounts, some warping to ivory, 12th/13thC, 3in (7.5cm) diam. **£4,000-5,000** *C*

Turned ivory boxes and pyxes of this type were mostly produced in Sicily by Islamic artisans, during the Norman rule. The ivory was sometimes painted with decoration, and at other times as this case, was enriched with stylish metalwork. A very similar pyx is now in the Museo d'Arti Applicate del Castello Sforzesco, Milan.

An ivory baton, German or French, carved with portrait medallions and the crowned arms of France below spiral lobing, fleur-de-lys terminal, one break restored, 24in (61cm).
£600-800 *S(S)*

The portraits shown are named as those of François II, Henry (sic) II, Charles IX and Henry III, dated 1574.

A North Italian ivory portrait medallion of Don Juan of Austria, his head crowned with a laurel wreath, in elaborate armour and with the Order of the Golden Fleece, inscribed 'Giovanni D'Austria', in gilt bronze frame with suspension loop, late 18th/early 19thC, 4in (10cm) high.
£900-1,200 *C*

A Goan carved ivory group of The Virgin and Child, the babe with fingers raised in benediction, the orb base with cherub heads, traces of polychrome, 18thC, 9in (23cm) high.
£900-1,000 *C*

A Continental bas relief ivory figure group, 7.5in (19cm) high.
£1,700-2,000 *HSS*

A Dieppe ivory dressing glass, applied with a bust portrait of Louis XIV, inscribed 'Ludovicus XIV Rex', with 2 small drawers to the frieze with lion mask and ring handles, and raised on lion's paw feet, 19thC, 35in (89cm) high.
£2,500-3,500 *HSS*

An Italian ivory relief of Cupid, as 'Love the Conqueror', with label on the reverse inscribed Omnia Vincit Amor, background partially broken, in Venetian parcel gilt wood frame, 17thC, 3in (7.5cm) high.
£1,200-1,700 *C*

A Spanish ivory crucifix figure, damage to fingers and crown of thorns, early 18thC, 9in (23cm), in modern velvet lined glazed case, together with ivory inscription plaque.
£600-900 *S(S)*

A German ivory memento Mori skull, one side of the skull covered with decomposing flesh being eaten by worms, the other revealing the skull, pierced as a rosary bead, early 17thC, 2in (5cm).
£1,500-2,000 *S*

A carved ivory open twist tapering column, with fluted spear surmount, on a stepped cylindrical hardwood socle, 11in (28cm) high.
£700-800 *CSK*

A South German silver gilt mounted ivory tankard, the drum finely carved in high relief with the Triumph of Bacchus, his chariot drawn by 2 galloping stallions, late 17th/early 18thC, 7in (17.5cm) high.
£8,000-10,000 *S*

514

Marble

A pair of alabaster portrait busts of Brutus and Marcus Agrippa, in draped armour, on integral socles, 19thC.   **£1,700-2,000** *LRG*

A French marble bust of a satyr, shown with leering expression and short curled hair, horns repaired, 13in (33cm), on grey marble socle.
£2,500-3,000 *S*

An Italian marble bust of Emperor Augustus, after the antique, with breastplate carved with confronting horsemen, 23.5in (60cm).
£6,000-7,000 *S*

A Victorian white marble portrait bust of a woman, mid-19thC, 28in (71cm) high.
£800-1,000 *S(S)*

A Victorian marble bust of a girl, her hair tied up, raised on a low pedestal, unsigned, 23in (59cm) high.
£650-700 *SWO*

A Victorian white marble portrait bust of a woman, mid-19thC, 28.5in (72cm).
£900-1,200
S(S)

A pair of Flemish marble busts of children, 18thC, 12in (31cm) high, on socles.
£1,200-1,700 *S*

An Italian white marble figure of a girl, standing semi-naked wearing a dress and patterned robe, holding a bunch of flowers, on circular base, 34.5in (87cm) high.
£2,200-2,700 *S(S)*

A pair of marble busts of Mars and Minerva, perhaps South German, 18thC, 24in (61cm) high, on socles.
£4,200-4,600 *S*

An Italian white marble bust of a maiden, signed G. Verona, late 19thC, 20in (50cm) high.
£1,700-2,000 *C*

A white marble bust of La Frileuse, after Houdon, c1880, 27.5in (70cm).
£1,200-1,700 *S(S)*

A sculpted white marble bust of the young Caesar Augustus, on an integral socle, 19thC, 21in (53cm) high.
£1,200-1,700 *C*

A marble group of 2 putti, allegorical of Winter, in the style of Giuseppe Sanmartino, Naples, the pedestal inlaid with mottled greenish grey marble panels, 4 fingers missing, late 18thC, 26in (66cm) high.
£6,000-7,000 *S*

A white marble figure of a child, holding her dress over her head, the base signed P. Dal Negro F. Milano 1878, 37in (94cm) high.
£3,000-4,000 *S(S)*

An Italian white marble group of a mother and child, late 19thC, 33in (83cm) high, on composition stone vermiculated pedestal, 24in (60cm) high.
£2,000-2,500 S(S)

An Italian white marble group, of a young man seated on a tree trunk kissing a girl, on oval base, 19thC, 42.5in (106.5cm) high.
£1,700-2,500 *S(S)*

An Italian white marble and alabaster figure of Beatrice, in early Renaissance costume, her alabaster robe richly decorated with foliate arabesques, the book inscribed with the initials 'PB', on striated green marble base, with cartouche inscribed 'Beatrice', late 19thC, 41in (104cm). high.
£3,000-4,000 *C*

The initials 'PB' on the book cover may refer to Beatrice's family name, Beatrice Portinari, but are more likely to relate to the initials of the sculptor.

An English white marble figure of a nude woman, signed and dated E. Roscoe Mullins 1891, on grey onyx socle, late 19thC, 33in (84cm) high.
£2,500-3,000 *C*

An English white marble figure of Young Romilly, by Alexander Munro, the young boy shown embracing his hound, wearing medieval tunic and breeches, damages and repairs to front paws and tail of dog, with interlaced AM monogram, c1863, 37in (94cm) high.
£5,000-8,000 *C*

Alexander Munro (1825-1871) was born in Scotland, but through the patronage of Harriet, 2nd Duchess of Sutherland, studied in London and worked for Sir Charles Barry on the sculpture for the Houses of Parliament.

An Italian veined red marble column pedestal, late 19th/early 20thC, 40in (102cm) high.
£700-900 *S(S)*

A mottled purple marble jar, of tapering cylindrical form, 10in (25cm).
£500-600 *S(S)*

A pair of Italian marble reliefs of angels, one swinging a censer, the other with an incense boat, within plain borders, late 17th/early 18thC, 31 by 26in (79 by 65.5cm).
£4,000-6,000 *S*

An Italian inlaid marble table top, depicting the Doves of Pliny within concentric coloured marble frames, on slate base, 19thC, 25in (64cm) diam.
£1,000-1,700 *S(S)*

A green marble kylix, of shallow form with loop side handles, on black marble socle, 21in (53cm) wide.
£6,000-6,500 *S(S)*

Terracotta

A pair of French cast terracotta busts of courtesans, in 18thC style, with décolleté dresses and ribbons around their necks and at their shoulders, on wood socles, 24in (61cm) high.
£3,500-4,500 *S*

A pair of serpentine marble tazzas, each on waisted socle and square base, one with broken and restored top, the other with chipped rim, late 19thC, 9.5in (24cm).   **£400-600** *S(S)*

A pair of terracotta busts of a boy and girl, by Karin Jonzen, mounted on wooden plinths,15in (38cm) high.
£300-400 *GAK*

An Anglo-Flemish terracotta statuette of an allegorical female figure, in the style of Scheemakers, holding poppies or pomegranates in her left hand, 18thC, 21in (54cm) high. **£5,000-6,000** *S*

A terracotta group of a bacchante riding a satyr, after Clodion, the nymph grasping a horn in her right hand and carrying a thyrsus over her shoulder, bearing signature of Clodion, on gilt stand, repaired, 14in (36cm). **£1,500-2,000** *S*

A French terracotta bust of a young girl, after Jacques Saly, said to be La Boudeuse, cast with a socle, 16.5in (42cm). **£2,500-3,000** *S*

A marble version of around 1750 is in the Victoria & Albert Museum. The subject is thought to be the daughter of de Troy, Director of the French Academy in Rome.

A Spanish polychrome wood male reliquary bust, perhaps St. Lawrence, with fringed collar of silver gilt thread to his gilded cope, a tassel decorating the reliquary niche with gilt metal frame, much original colour and gilding, 16thC, 23in (59cm). **£3,200-4,000** *S*

A terracotta high relief of the Baptism of Christ, attributed to Angelo Pio, Emilia, the dove of the Holy Spirit appearing above surrounded by angels, to the right dancing angels, to the left of partly draped men, in wood frame, 18thC, 19 by 26in (48 by 66cm). **£7,000-9,000** *S*

A polychrome and giltwood figure of the Virgin and Child, in the manner of Hans van Judenburg, late 15thC, 12in (31cm). **£7,500-8,500** *S*

Woodcarvings

A German limewood Corpus, with traces of red polychromy on the perizonium, arms and part legs missing, worming, 15thC, 22in (56cm) high. **£1,700-2,200** *C*

A polychrome limewood group of the Virgin and Child, probably Austrian, the Schöne Madonna with hips swung to the left in an almost S shape curve holding the Child in her left arm, some original colour beneath later overpainting, damage and restoration, c1430, 36in (92cm) high. **£8,500-9,500** *S*

A Spanish polychrome and giltwood statue of the Virgin and Child, the Virgin standing holding the Christ Child within her left arm, some damage, 17thC, 17.5in (44cm) high. **£1,700-2,200** *C*

A set of 3 Italian giltwood statues of children, depicting Summer, Autumn and Winter, mid-19thC, 18in (46cm) high.
£1,500-2,000 *C(S)*

A walnut figure of Atlas, formerly a chimneypiece jamb, Continental, late 19thC, 44in (111cm).
£1,200-1,500 *S(S)*

A South German polychrome and giltwood figure of a male saint, his arms gesturing outwards, wearing a robe, cloak and boots, on a square wood base, some chips and restorations, late 17thC, 41in (104cm) high.
£6,000-7,000 *C*

Two polychrome and giltwood angel candlesticks, with candlesticks resting on their knees, gilding worn, Tyrol, 16thC, 17 and 18.5in (43 and 47cm).
£10,000-15,000 *S*

A pair of giltwood brackets, carved as eagles, 19thC, 15in (38cm) high.
£1,500-2,000 *S*

A Flemish walnut relief of Mary Magdalene renouncing her wordly goods, damaged, late 17thC, 23.5 by 15in (60 by 38cm).
£700-1,000 *C*

A Netherlands oak group of the seated Virgin and Child, the Madonna holding the sandalled Child with an orb standing on her knees, restored, late 15thC, 30.5in (77cm).
£6,200-7,200 *S*

An Italian polychrome wood figure of a candle bearing angel, wearing gilt drapery with crosses painted on sash, bearing a candle holder, with base decorated with border of foliate design, on material covered base, early 16thC, 19in (49cm) high.
£5,000-6,000 *S*

A carved wood and polychrome corbel figure of a tonsured monk, a shield emblazoned on his breast, 15in (38cm) high, mounted in a frame.
£600-700 *C*

A Spanish wood relief of the Mocking of Christ, the slumped figure of Christ before Caiaphas and a soldier standing on a raised dais, surrounded on each side by a crowd of jeering Jews and soldiers, St. John in the background and other figures watching from the windows behind, traces of original colour, on a wood stand, early 16thC, 18in (46cm).
£4,500-6,000 *S*

An English carved and painted wood Royal coat-of-arms, mid-19thC, 70 by 73in (178 by 185cm).
£2,500-3,000 *S*

A carved wood and polychrome panel of the Royal Arms, as used by King George V, 32 by 33.5in (81 by 85cm). **£500-600** *CSK*

A pair of carved giltwood brackets, in the form of owls with outstretched wings, 19thC, 13in (33cm) high. **£2,000-2,500** *S*

A pair of South German giltwood statuettes of angels, kneeling in prayer on voluted pediments, wormed, 18thC, 10in (25cm) high.
£2,500-3,500 *S*

A Georgian carved wooden money box, as a Toby Jug figure of a seated auctioneer holding a gavel, some damage, 14in (36cm).
£2,700-3,200 *RHE*

ANTIQUITIES

Marble

A Roman marble relief fragment, probably from a sarcophagus, carved in high relief with a fruiting garland and a bucranium, foliate and tongue motifs above and below, 23 by 29in (59 by 74cm).
£8,000-9,000 *S*

A fragmentary Roman marble male torso, probably from a figure of Herakles, the lionskin knotted around his neck, circa 1st-2nd Century A.D.
£12,000-15,000 *S*

A Roman marble head of a young woman, circa 120-20 B.C. after an original of the 4th Century B.C., 9in (23cm).
£7,000-9,000 *S*

A Roman marble sandalled foot, circa 2nd Century A.D., 10in (25cm).
£3,200-4,000 *S*

A Roman marble head of the young Dionysus, wearing a garland of vine leaves, berries and bunches of grapes, with centrally parted hair, a fillet around his head, circa 2nd Century A.D., 12in (31cm).
£6,000-8,000 *S*

A Roman marble male portrait head, originally from a portrait bust, 2nd-3rd Century A.D., 13.5in (34cm).
£7,500-10,000 *S*

A Roman marble figure of Hermes, with drapery over his left arm, restored, circa 1st-2nd Century A.D., 52.5in (133cm).
£25,000-30,000 *S*

A Roman marble male head, the irises and pupils of the eyes incised, circa 1st Century B.C./1st Century A.D., 15.5in (39cm).
£16,000-18,000 *S*

A Luristan bronze axehead, the shaft decorated on both sides with the figure of an animal in relief, depicted holding the blade in its open mouth, 8th-7th Century B.C., 2 by 6in (5 by 15cm).
£2,000-2,500 *S*

A Roman bronze appliqué in the form of the hollow bust of Dionysus as a child, the pupils of the eyes recessed, circa 1st Century B.C/1st Century A.D., 3.5in (9cm).
£3,000-4,000 *S*

Metalware

A Roman bronze arm, circa 1st-2nd Century A.D., 11in (28cm).
£2,000-3,000 *S*

A fragmentary Roman bronze left hand and foot, the hand wearing a ring with a large oval bezel, both circa 1st-2nd Century A.D., 8in (20cm).
£2,000-2,500 *S*

An Etruscan bronze stamnos, from the Weiskirchen Group, probably made in Vulci, with tongue and bead motifs around the overhanging rim, the handles attached to 4 oval handle attachments decorated with satyr masks, each surmounted by a pair of eyes and set in a frame of stacked ivy leaves, circa 430-400 B.C., 14in (36cm).
£4,500-6,500 *S*

A Roman or early Byzantine bronze steelyard weight, probably representing Athena, the whole filled with lead, 4th-5th Century A.D., 8in (20cm).
£1,700-2,000 *S*

An Early Christian bronze right hand, holding an orb surmounted by a cross, a cross in relief on its wrist, circa 6th-7th Century A.D., 14in (36cm).
£6,000-8,000 *S*

These hands holding an orb and cross clearly derive from the hollow cast hands associated with the Phrygian God Sabazios. It is difficult to be certain about their functions. They may have been mounted on staffs as votive offerings perhaps to be paraded before the faithful when the healing powers of hands were needed.

Two Scythian bronze axeheads, with animal heads projecting from one side of the shafts, 7th-6th Century B.C., 5 and 5.5in (12 and 14cm) long. **£4,500-5,000** *S*

An Egyptian bronze figure of a cat, seated, with its tail curling round towards the right, restored, 26th Dynasty, circa 664-525 B.C., 7in (18cm).
£10,000-12,000 *S*

An Egyptian bronze figure of Harpocrates, wearing the Lock of Eternal Youth and the Crown of Upper and Lower Egypt, 30th Dynasty-Ptolemaic Period, circa 380-30 B.C., 13in (33cm).
£6,000-8,000 *S*

An Egyptian bronze figure of a cat, seated, with its tail curling round its body towards its forepaws, Saite Period, circa 664-525 B.C., 7in (18cm).
£17,000-20,000 *S*

A bronze vessel, in the form of a male bust, probably representing the God Dionysus, on stemmed foot, Roman Provinces, circa 3rd Century A.D., 9in (23cm).
£7,000-8,000 *S*

The flask-like mouth opening is unusual. The use of these vessels is not absolutely clear. They may have been used as an unguent vase, (balsamarium), or as a censer.

> **Miller's is a price GUIDE not a price LIST**

Four Scythian bronze stags, Black Sea area, 7th-6th Century B.C., 1.5 by 3.5in (4 by 9cm) each.
£6,000-7,000 *S*

Pottery

A Mycenaean pottery hydria, decorated with an octopus with long tentacles, Greece, circa 1200 B.C., 5.5in (14cm).
£6,000-6,500 *S*

A South Italian Greek pottery trefoil oinochoe, the decoration in white and yellow slip, Apulia, 4th Century B.C., 19in (48cm).
£3,000-3,500 *S*

A pottery bowl, the decoration in light and dark brown slip on a cream ground, 2nd Millennium B.C., 18.6in (47cm).
£10,000-12,000 *S*

A Canosan pottery pyxis and cover, polychrome painted, chiefly in pink, blue, red and white, the cover with a pair of embracing lovers, a figure of Eros to the right, all in relief, South Italy, circa 3rd Century B.C., 5 by 11.5in (13 by 29cm).
£3,500-5,500 *S*

An Etruscan pottery panel amphora, from the La Tolfa Group, on one side a monstrous spirit, with wings on his back and feet, on the other 2 companions or followers of the spirit, the decoration with touches of applied white paint, with lid not belonging, circa 530 B.C., 13.5in (34cm).
£4,000-6,000 *S*

Miscellaneous

An Egyptian wood mask, from a sarcophagus, with traces of polychrome painting to the left and upper side of the face, Late New Kingdom, 19th Dynasty, 5.5in (14cm). **£4,000-5,000** *S*

A Roman iridescent green glass trefoil jug, standing on a splayed pedestal foot, with rounded body, cylindrical neck and trefoil lip, a single trail encircling the neck and another running around the base of the neck, a vertically ribbed handle attached to the shoulder and folded on to the rim, circa 4th Century A.D., 9.5in (24cm). **£2,500-3,000** *S*

A Roman green glass twin-handled flask, the neck with fine horizontal spiral trailing, the indented base with pontil mark, circa 4th Century A.D., 6in (15cm). **£1,500-2,000** *S*

The smooth chin bears no trace of a beard attachment which suggests that the mask is a female depiction. The large, widely spaced eyes with the gentle curvature of the eyebrows and exotic lips are stylistically typical of funerary art of the Ramesside era, a period when form, decoration and colour took on a more naturalistic appearance. Often the inner cover of the sarcophagus represented the owner as seen in real life and here the beautifully carved features show a young high-born woman.

Four Minoan and Mycenaean terracotta vessels, of varying types, all circa 1400 B.C., 3 to 6in (8 to 15cm).
£3,500-4,000 *S*

SEWING

A Roman green glass wheel engraved bottle, with pear shaped body standing on a stemmed foot, funnel shaped neck and ground rim, the body with the remains of a Greek inscription, wheel cut decoration above and below, with some light weathering, repaired, 4th-5th Century A.D., 8in (20cm).
£1,200-1,500 *S*

The lid from an Egyptian anthropoid wood coffin, with yellow face and the body with polychrome painted decoration, the text, flanked by the four Sons of Horus, has a standard funerary text for a man called Irt-Hor-Rw, son of Djehutyirdis, born to Saas, Late Dynastic Period, circa 716-332 B.C., 65in (165cm).
£6,500-7,500 *S*

A tortoiseshell étui, inlaid with mother-of-pearl, c1820, 4in (10cm) high.
£600-800 *RdeR*

A horn sewing box, c1820, 14in (36cm) wide.
£400-500 *JAC*

A Bilston pink enamel étui, c1780, 3.5in (8.5cm) high.
£800-1,000 *RdeR*

A gold mounted Continental porcelain needle case, painted with gilt flowers in white reserves and on a blue ground, 19thC, 4in (10.5cm) high.
£700-900 *S(S)*

A Newton Wilson Princess of Wales lockstitch hand sewing machine, with gilt decoration and wood carrying case.
£250-300 *CSK*

A French opaline and ormolu sewing nest, 6.5in (16.5cm).
£500-600 *RdeR*

A home shuttle lockstitch sewing machine. **£150-200** *CSK*

A Regency boxwood model of the Royal Pavilion, with detachable sections enclosing a pin cushion and needlework implements including a thimble, 8.5in (21.5cm) high. **£1,500-2,000** *GSP*

A Cookson's lockstitch sewing machine with part-plated mechanism on cast iron base and wood cover, damaged. **£1,000-1,500** *CSK*

A Florence Sewing Machine Co. treadle sewing machine, with black painted frame and gilt and floral decoration, in mahogany cabinet with hinged lid and double door at the front opening to treadle, American, c1870, 30in (66cm) wide. **£1,500-2,000** *S*

A Regency rosewood bobbin winder, with 2 drawers mounted overall with bone bobbin winders, wool winders, pin cushions and thimble stand, on bone feet, 17in (43cm) wide. **£1,200-1,500** *S(S)*

A Weir chain-stitch sewing machine with gilt transfers, table clamp and original instructions. **£170-200** *CSK*

A Beckwith portable sewing machine, with geared crank drive, nickel-plated frame and stitchplate, stamped Beckwith S.M. Co. N.Y. Apr. 1871, by Wm. G. Beckwith and G.W. Bacon & Co. London, Eng., with table clamp. **£700-900** *CSK*

A French gilt metal mounted étui case, with green ground reserved with riverscapes and foliate motifs within gilt cartouches, 4in (10cm) high, **£200-225** *CSK*

A Mme. Demorest 'Fairy' sewing or running-stitch machine, the ornamentally cast iron base marked twice Patented May 13 1862, with hand-cranked gear cloth-feed and stop screw for stitch length, 5.5in (14cm) wide. **£500-700** *CSK*

TEXTILES
Costume

A baby's bonnet with hollie point panel worked with a monogramme SB(?) and (17)83, another bonnet with asymmetric hollie point flowerspray and 2 under bonnets, all 18thC.
£200-400 *CSK*

A dress of blue and white striped satin, the cuffs and front trimmed with ivory satin and blue satin ribbons, with pleated train, c1870.
£400-500 *CSK*

A christening set of linen, trimmed with pleated applied linen, comprising: bonnet, bib, a pair of mittens, sleeves, 2 head bands and 2 triangular forehead panels, late 17thC, a linen square with appliqué trim.
£500-700 *CSK*

A cocktail dress of black chiffon, the front pink panel embroidered with pink, black and opalescent beads with flowers and geometric patterns, c1923.
£150-200 *CSK*

A child's linen suit, comprising: chemise and pantaloons, early 19thC.
£450-500 *CSK*

A French Au-Louvre scarlet full length dolman cape, embroidered in Turkish moresque patterns with coral, scarlet and gold thread, some discolouration to lining, one small hole, with black and scarlet woven label bearing a lion, the letter L and numbered 58030, c1895.
£1,300-1,700 *S(NY)*

A Victorian linen smock, the bodice, sleeves, collar, cuffs and pockets embroidered with blue cotton.
£200-300 *Bon*

A Redfern brocaded evening jacket, labelled Redfern Scte. Francais, numbered 174339, the black, ivory and gold fabric covered with ferns and snakeshead lilies, brown fur shawl collar and cuffs lined in gold velvet, label slightly frayed small stain to lining, c1928.
£800-900 *S(NY)*

A Castillo for Elizabeth Arden black satin evening mantle, labelled Elizabeth Arden, New York, lined with rose pink satin, the shoulders applied with a fichu of black satin petals, American late 1950's.
£500-550 *S(NY)*

A red ground silk kossu robe, the bright red ground worked with eight dragons pursuing 'flaming pearls' amidst clouds scattered with bats and Precious Objects, above the wide lishui band, the arms and neck bordered with a dragon band, all in brightly coloured silk, 19thC, 57in (145cm).
£1,200-1,700 *S*

Two Salon Moderne silk chiffon evening gowns, one red, the other blue, boned strapless bodices, the skirts polonaises caught by 2 velvet bows to the rear, American, 1961.
£250-300 *S(NY)*

Sophie Gimbel was married to Adam Gimbel, owner of Sak's Fifth Avenue. She opened her own couture department in 1931 which she named Salon Moderne. In addition to her own designs she sold dresses by the major French fashion houses on a made-to-order system.

A Michel Goma embroidered oyster pink satin ballgown, unlabelled, together with a pair of Delicata shoes, and stiffened petticoat gown shortened slightly, French, c1959.
£350-400 *S(NY)*

A gown of ivory satin, printed with undulating bands of pink columbines against sea green and lilac heart shaped leaves, the sleeves and hem trimmed with lilac ruched ribbon in the Regency manner, labelled Paul Poiret à Paris, the reverse with canvas tag inscribed Mad. Saxton-Noble, 20133, the boned deep waistband inscribed Vanessa Jebb, waist sash missing, damage to underarm.
£4,000-6,000 *CSK*

Michel Goma was born in Montpellier France in 1932 and moved to Paris at the age of 19 where he tried to sell his fashion designs. He received encouragement from Christian Dior but was employed first of all by Lafaurie (1950-1958) when he bought the company and renamed it Michel Goma. He closed in 1963 and moved to Patou where he stayed until 1973.

A pair of George III shoes of blue silk and brocade, with fitted clogs.
£500-700 *WW*

A Salon Moderne Chantilly lace evening gown, the oyster satin strapless sheath entirely covered with tiers of navy Chantilly lace, American, 1964; together with a Salon Moderne scarlet satin ball gown, with stylised scooped neckline, elbow length sleeves, full skirt falling in gathers from the hips, separate petticoat, American, 1963.
£175-225 *S(NY)*

A collection of hats, including a black silk hat with horsehair overlay, black lace bow to the front, c1914; a rust velour with feather trim, c1918, and a black velvet Jacques Fath with plumes, c1950.
£1,000-1,500 *S(NY)*

A lace and rose trimmed bonnet, by Donnell and Davis Artistic Millinery, Brattleboro, VT, the wired brim and crown covered with ivory satin roses, ribbons and burgundy foliage, American, c1905.
£250-300 *S(NY)*

A blue sequined sheath, with blue silk underpinning overlaid with tulle, entirely covered with iridescent blue sequins, spangled tulle fichu to shoulders, probably French, c1930.
£350-400 *S(NY)*

527

A dress of fine wool, printed with stripes of slate grey alternating with striped cones, the V-shaped bodice trimmed with pleating and piping, c1840.
£300-350 *CSK*

A pair of bathing boots, the white rubber soles moulded 'Hood Seaview Bathing Made in U.S.A., size 4,' bright green satin with white trim, slight damage, c1910.
£900-1,000 *S(NY)*

A wide brimmed straw hat with shallow crown, lined with red silk, brocaded with flowers, with original green silk ribbons woven with garlands of flowers, c1770.
£2,000-3,000 *CSK*

A Bob Bugnand black satin evening coat, embroidered, beaded, jewelled Paisley botehs overall, slits to each side, Paris, 1960.
£200-250 *S(NY)*

A North American Indian seed beaded bandoleer bag, decorated with stylised geometric patterns on black and red fabric, the shoulder strap with black and patterned red fabric, probably late 19thC.
£450-550 *LAY*

Three Maison Lewis straw hats, labelled Maison Lewis, 16 Rue Royale Paris, comprising ivory straw applied with outsized daisy, ribbon streamers; a black silk and velvet with 'shaving brush' quill of feathers and white ribbon rose; another with silvered Art Deco pierced metal sunburst medallion and on ivory band, French, c1922. **£350-400** *S(NY)*

A linen coif, embroidered in black work and gilt threads, with tightly coiling stems bearing small flowerheads with various infilling patterns, English, c1600, 16in (41cm) wide.
£3,250-4,000 *CSK*

A cut steel and glass bead bag, English, c1850, 11.5in (29.5cm) long. **£50-150** *CB*

A French ivory silk wallet, embroidered in tambour stitch with coloured silks, the front, back and inside worked with sprays of roses and pansies within a leaf border, embellished with coloured spangles, lined with green silk, late 18thC.
£200-250 *CSK*

A cut steel miser's purse, 24in (61.5cm) long.
£50-100 *CB*

An English bead bag, c1850, 8in (20cm) long.
£50-150 *CB*

A Paisley shawl, woven with an unusual rectangular centre, the end borders woven with the initials JC, c1855, 74in (188cm) wide.
£1,500-2,000 *CSK*

An English glass bead and cut steel bag, c1860, 8in (20cm) long.
£50-150 *CB*

A wool Paisley throw, woven in shades of blue, green and maroon centred by a cream and crimson foliate panel.
£170-200 *HSS*

An Austrian parasol shaft, with enamelled vinaigrette finial in the shape of a sedan chair, with mirror windows, the door opening to reveal a chased and pierced vinaigrette, c1914.
£1,800-2,200 *CSK*

An English purse in the form of a bunch of grapes, the grapes worked in coloured silks and silver gilt threads, in padded detached buttonhole stitch embellished with seed pearls, with 3 similar pendants, the vine leaves in green silks and gilt threads, the concertina purse lined with salmon pink silk, with a pink silk and silver gilt thread plaited drawstring and handle, early 17thC, 3in (7.5cm) long.
£3,000-3,500 *CSK*

A Paisley shawl, woven in 9 colours, with 2 central palmette tipped columns flanking a black cruciform medallion, the harlequin shawl ends woven and over-embroidered with the crest of Napoleon III above the words BIETRY in one corner and CACHEMIRE in the other, c1855, 64in (162.5cm) wide.
£8,500-9,500 *CSK*

At the 1855 Universal Exhibition in Paris, Anthony Berrus displayed a pivoting shawl woven by Bietry with the arms of Napoleon III woven in to the corner. The Empress Eugenie attended the Exhibition and is said to have ordered a shawl by Berrus to be woven by Bietry.

A silk shawl, woven with a blue field, the ends woven with snaking intertwined cones in pairs between green and blue columns, in the manner of Clabburn Son & Crisp, mid-19thC, 70in (177.5cm) wide.
£500-700 *CSK*

A parasol, the stained wood shaft tipped with an elephant's head finial of carved horn, the shade of ivory silk with black Maltese lace overlay, one tusk missing, c1916.
£150-200 *CSK*

A parasol, the folding ivory shaft inset with coral knots, the finial and handle of coral carved with a putto against a leafy base, the spoke guards also coral in the form of hands with a coral drop, the shade of French black lace, late 19thC.
£400-600 *CSK*

A lawyer's wig, labelled 'J. K. Methirell, Maker, 14 Bell Yard, Temple Bar, London', also with inscription 'W. J. Johnson Esq', in original tin, the name painted on the outside, and the original padlock.
£650-700 *CSK*

Embroidery

An English needlework picture, embroidered in coloured silks and metal threads, embellished with beads, spangles and mica strips, with a lady and gentleman in the centre standing above a pond and flanked by 2 houses, the corners each with busts within raised work frames, c1660, 17in (43.5cm) wide, framed and glazed.
£1,700-3,000 *CSK*

A pair of needlework maps of the continents of Africa and America, each worked with country borders and oceans in black on a plain linen ground, early 19thC, 13in (33cm) diam, in ebonised frames.
£500-600 *S(S)*

A pair of needlework seat covers, worked in coloured wools, one worked with a dog, the other with a cat against a black ground, the borders of roses and other flowers, mid-19thC, 18in (46cm) wide.
£500-600 *CSK*

A French letter case, of brown silk, woven with gilt threads and coloured silks with episodes from the Fables de la Fontaine including the fox and the crow with the piece of cheese, lined with pale pink silk, late 17thC, 7in (17.5cm) wide.
£1,200-1,700 *CSK*

A pair of English needlework pictures, worked in coloured silks, each with a medallion of a figure seated in front of a window, surrounded by a floral border, one worked with a King, the other with a Queen, mid-17thC, 8in (20cm) wide, framed and glazed.
£850-1,000 *CSK*

An English embroidered picture, worked in coloured wools, mid-18thC, 17in (43.5cm) wide, framed and glazed.
£1,700-2,000 *CSK*

Lace

An English needlework picture, embroidered in coloured wools, highlighted with silks, with a spray of tulips, carnations, roses and other wild flowers, fastened by a ribbon, mid-18thC, 22in (55.5cm) high, in a carved walnut frame.
£1,500-2,000 *CSK*

A needlework top for a card table, probably French, embroidered in coloured wools with trompe l'oeil playing cards, counters, coins and gaming purse against a blue ground, within a border of strapwork, c1730, 27in (69cm) wide. **£1,500-2,000** *CSK*

A collection of lace, including a pair of Alençon lappets, late 18thC, 4in (10cm) deep, a single Mechlin lappet, 4in (10cm) deep, and a single Brussels lappet, mid-18thC, 3in (7.5cm) deep.
£250-350 *CSK*

A flounce of point de gaze lace, worked with a border of flowers beneath an undulating ribbon with posies of flowers and raised petals above, c1860, 9in (22.5cm) deep, and a separate matching fragment.
£1,200-1,700 *CSK*

A pair of Mechlin bobbin lace cravat ends, worked with classical motifs of elegant leaves and urns, c1720.
£3,500-4,000 *CSK*

A deep flounce of Brussels mixed lace, worked with a border of needle lace roses among bobbin lace leaves, point de neige spotted net, late 19thC, 23in (58.5cm) deep.
£500-600 *CSK*

A flounce of Alençon lace, worked with a border of flowers and ivy leaves beneath oval medallions with needle lace fillings, alternating with flowersprays, in two pieces, 7in (17.5cm) deep.
£400-600 *CSK*

A flounce of Italian needle lace, worked with scrolling vines with pomegranates and flowers, 17thC, edged with 16thC vandyking, 5in (12.5cm) deep.
£300-400 *CSK*

A pair of Brussels lace lappets, worked with baskets of flowers, c1740, 4in (10cm) deep.
£450-550 *CSK*

A flounce of point de gaze lace, worked with a scalloped edge of roses with raised petals with patterns worked in, the flounce worked with convolvulus, lilacs and iris, many with raised petals, late 19thC, 14in (35.5cm) deep.
£2,500-3,000 *CSK*

Samplers

A sampler by Hannah Mills, 'aged 12, April the 30, 1818', worked in silks with a verse 'Teach me to feel Another's Woe to hide the fault I see that Mercy I to others shew that Mercy shew to me', damaged, 13in (33.5cm) wide.
£450-500 *DN*

An early Victorian silk needlework sampler, 1848, 25in (64cm) wide.
£300-350 *HSS*

A needlework sampler, in colourful silks, by Elizabeth Taylor, 'in the eleventh year of her age', dated 1748, 13in (33cm) wide, unframed.
£500-800 *Bon*

A sampler by Jane Thompson, probably American, worked in coloured silks on linen gauze, 1824, 25in (64cm) wide.
£2,000-2,500 *CSK*

A child's needlework sampler, inscribed 'Elizabeth Barclay her work finished 25th day of the seventh month 1725', slight damage, 12in (31cm) high, in maple frame.
£700-900 *Bea*

A sampler by Jane Mesman, worked in coloured silks with a verse 'See how the lillies', 1735, 16in (40.5cm) long, framed and glazed.
£1,000-1,200 *CSK*

A silk worked sampler, repaired, dated 1788, 12in (31cm) wide, framed and glazed.
£650-750 *S*

A sampler by Amelia Pewiner, worked in brightly coloured silks with a verse 'Misfortunes Advantageous', 18thC, 12in (31cm) wide, framed and glazed.
£450-550 *CSK*

A band sampler by Elizabeth Hoskins, aged 12 in 1799, 12in (31cm) wide.
£300-400 *DN*

A silkwork sampler by Sarah Johnson, aged 10 in 1843, with 2 figures, a house, baskets of flowers and trees, within a meandering border of carnations, slight damage, 12in (31cm) wide.
£300-350 *DN*

Tapestries

A George IV needlework sampler, 1820, 48in (122cm) wide.
£400-450 *HSS*

A Brussels tapestry fragment woven in wools and silks, on a brown ground, previously the border of a tapestry, reduced in size, mid-17thC, 123.5in (314cm) wide.
£5,500-6,000 *C*

A tapestry picture, woven in coloured wools and silks depicting an urn of roses, carnations and honeysuckle resting on a plinth, mid-18thC, 12in (31cm) wide, framed.
£750-850 *CSK*

A Flemish tapestry covered cushion, woven in many colours with a double headed female figure, possibly Prudence, holding two goblets, late 16thC, 21in (53cm) wide; and another cushion.
£700-900 *CSK*

A group of 3 Aubusson tapestry portières, each depicting a ribbon-tied floral spray above flowers and foliage on a scrolling support, on an ivory ground with wide red border, 19thC, 113in (287cm) long.
£2,000-2,500 *Bea*

A tapestry panel for a bed head, probably Beauvais, woven in colours with 2 coats-of-arms surmounted by a coronet, each side with a monogram CB and coronet, the border of scrolling acanthus leaves and ribbons, against a dark pink ground, late 18thC, 53in (134.5cm) wide.
£700-1,200 *CSK*

An Aubusson tapestry panel for a chair seat, within a wreath frame, the border of écru, late 19thC, 29in (74cm) square.
£400-500 *CSK*

An Aubusson tapestry fragment woven in wools and silks, with a thin brown border, 116in (295cm) long.
£1,500-2,000 *C*

Miscellaneous

A pair of silk needlework pictures, 18thC, 7in (18cm) wide. **£500-700** *RdeR*

A pair of beadwork covered footstools, 12in (31cm) diam.
£400-500 *CB*

A woolwork picture of a ship, c1840, 21.5in (54.5cm) wide.
£700-800 *RdeR*

A collage of seaweed with baby crabs, inscribed 'Call us not weeds, we are flowers of the sea', c1850, 10in (25cm) wide.
£300-400 *RdeR*

A petit point picture of a tabby cat, 15in (38cm) wide.
£400-450 *RdeR*

A patchwork coverlet, composed of red, blue and sand coloured felt patches, probably from uniforms, the borders with applied felt spot motifs, including animals, canon, flowers, the royal coat-of-arms and the date 1859 with the initials FB and a heart beneath, with vandyked edges, c1859, 56in (142cm) square.
£200-400 *CSK*

A padded woolwork collage of strawberries in a basket, 18thC, 9.5in (24cm) wide.
£700-900 *RdeR*

A set of 4 blue velvet hangings, with applied embroidery in silver gilt and gilt threads, 35in (89cm) wide; a panel worked with an urn with a castle motif, 45in (114cm) wide; and another with a crowned orb, 74in (188cm) wide, late 19thC.
£2,200-4,200 *CSK*

A pair of English crewelwork curtains, embroidered in shades of green, blue, yellow and red, with a phoenix amongst flowering trees growing from small hillocks, distressed, c1700, 40in (101.5cm) wide. **£3,000-3,500** *CSK*

A Italian crimson silk border applied with yellow silk outlined with couched cord, with a central crown linking curling leaves, flanked by clumps of lilies and other flowers, c1800, 12in (31cm) deep.
£250-350 *CSK*

Locate the Source

The source of each illustration in Miller's can be found by checking the code letters below each caption with the list of contributors.

A brocatelle hanging, probably French, woven in ivory and crimson silk with a large scale 18thC style design of formalised flowers and scrolling leaves, late 19thC, 51in (129.5cm) wide.
£900-1,200 *CSK*

A pair of Morris and Company wool curtains, woven with a repeating floral Tulip and Rose pattern in shades of blue, cream and rust, late 19thC, 62in (157cm) wide.
£1,000-1,500 *CSK*

Tulip and Rose was designed by William Morris and registered as a fabric on 20 January 1876.

A length of crimson and white silk damask, woven with a repeating pattern of urns flanked by exotic flowers and strapwork, c1835, 21in (53.5cm) wide.
£450-550 *CSK*

FANS

A fan, the leaf painted with a classical scene, the ivory sticks pierced and painted with a couple dining under a vine, the narrow guardsticks stained red and green and pique with silver, slight damage, c1700, 11in (28cm).
£1,700-2,000 *CSK*

A marriage fan, the leaf painted with an allegory of love, the reverse with putti, the mother-of-pearl sticks carved, pierced, gilt and backed with mother-of-pearl, repaired, c1760, 12in (31cm).
£600-800 *CSK*

A Canton brisé fan, painted and lacquered against a gold ground, with an upper border of animals against a black ground, the reverse with a tiger hunt against a silver ground, rubbed, c1820, 7.5in (19cm), and a Canton lacquer fan box.
£900-1,200 *CSK*

A Japanese ivory brisé fan, with pierced oval panels and lacquered in gold with figures and buildings, the guardsticks decorated with shibyama work, slight damage, c1880, 10in (25cm), in a Canton lacquer box.
£2,500-3,000 *CSK*

A Chinese lacquer fan of 'A Thousand Faces', the leaf painted with groups of ivory-faced figures, the guards and sticks of yellow, cream, grey, red and brown with silver and gilt painted scenes, in a lacquered case, mid-19thC.
£400-500 *ALL*

A French fan, the silk leaf painted with cherry pickers and 2 still lives of flowers, the mother-of-pearl sticks carved, pierced and gilt, repaired, c1775, 11in (28cm).
£1,800-2,200 *CSK*

An ivory brisé fan, painted and lacquered with a classical scene, possibly Jason, the reverse with ruins in a landscape, slight damage, c1890, 9in (23cm).
£700-800 *CSK*

A leaf painted fan with 2 asymmetrical vignette of villages, the reverse with farm buildings, the ivory sticks carved, pierced and painted with rabbits and birds amongst ferns and flowers, repaired, c1750, 11in (28cm).
£900-1,200 *CSK*

A fan, possibly South German, the leaf painted with a king watching a harvest, the mother-of-pearl sticks carved, pierced and gilt, c1770, in contemporary shagreen box, 10.5in (26.5cm).
£1,700-2,000 *CSK*

A fan, the leaf painted with a classical scene, the reverse with lovers in a landscape, the mother-of-pearl sticks carved with figures, pierced, gilt and backed with mother-of-pearl, damaged, c1750, 11.5in (29.5cm).
£1,000-1,500 *CSK*

A French fan, with ivory battoire sticks, carved, pierced and gilt, for the Spanish market, c1760, 10in (25cm).
£1,000-1,500 *CSK*

A fan, the leaf painted with chinoiserie figures in a garden, the sticks lacquered in red and gold, repaired, c1780, 12in (31cm), in a 19thC Chinese embroidered fan case.
£500-700 *CSK*

A handscreen, the satin leaf printed with a bird's-eye view of The Royal Victoria Infirmary, Newcastle-upon-Tyne, the metal mount set with 2 enamelled escutcheons with The Prince of Wales' crest and the arms of Newcastle, the handle set with peridots, one missing, leaf worn.
£550-850 *CSK*

A fan, the canepin leaf painted, signed Adrien-Moreau, the verso inscribed Voisin Richard, the ivory sticks finely carved and pierced, the guardsticks carved with monograms L.L., slight damage, late 19thC, 12in (31.5cm).
£2,500-3,000 *CSK*

A lace trimmed fan, the gauze leaf painted with a girl catching butterflies, signed F. Houghton, on curved mother-of-pearl sticks, late 19thC, 13.5in (34cm).
£350-400 *DN*

A fan, with mother-of-pearl sticks carved and pierced with figures and backed with mother-of-pearl, rubbed, c1840, 11in (28cm).
£800-900 *CSK*

A fan, the ivory guards carved with statues and stylised dolphins, plain shaped sticks, the leaf painted with a classical scene, 11in (28cm).
£650-750 *S(S)*

A Canton brisé fan, painted and lacquered with figures in a garden against a red lacquer ground, the reverse similarly lacquered with figures in a boat, rubbed, c1820, 8in (20cm).
£1,200-1,700 *CSK*

A French fan, the leaf painted with a maiden by a lakeside scene attended by putti, the reverse painted with a scene of San Gregorio in a central panel, with mother-of-pearl sticks decorated with gilt putti and flowers, the gilt metal guards applied with coral busts, some missing.
£350-450 *S(S)*

An Edwardian painted fan, 12in (30cm) long.
£80-120 *HSS*

A pair of papier mâché handscreens, decorated with Turkish style street scenes, on turned giltwood handles, mid 19thC.
£300-350 *DN*

An ivory brisé fan, carved in romantic style, 10in (25cm) long.
£250-350 *HSS*

A gold mounted and gem set tortoiseshell fan, the single guard mounted with textured gold sheath and applied with rose diamonds and cabochons in a floral design, plain, tortoiseshell sticks and ostrich feather leaf.
£420-520 *S(S)*

RUGS & CARPETS

A Kazak rug, woven in traditional colours, with 2 rows of 10 octagons filled with hooked and geometric motifs, on a blue ground, 95 by 58.5in (241 by 148cm).
£1,200-1,700 *P(S)*

A Caucasian runner, the field with green, ivory, red, blue, brown and yellow diagonal rows of boteh, in a red border of stylised floral motifs, between yellow and blue floral stripes, worn and repaired, 141 by 44in (358 by 112cm).
£2,000-2,500 *C*

A Feraghan rug, the dark blue field woven with an herati design, the dark red main border with a palmette meander, in good condition, 64 by 43in (163 by 109cm). **£700-750** *L*

A large Tibetan rug, the shaded brick red field with 2 large lotus flowerheads with key pattern centres issuing leafy tendrils and flanking a stylised Chinese character, in a narrow plain brown border with inner plain ivory and light blue stripes, slight wear and repair, 119 by 64in (302 by 163cm).
£4,000-4,500 *C*

A Bakhtiari carpet, the mustard yellow field with 2 stepped pink panels, plain outer yellow stripe, one border damaged, 132 by 82in (335 by 208cm).
£2,500-3,000 *C*

A Daghestan prayer rug, the white ground decorated with a floral motif within a lattice design, in a multiple border, magenta silk pile in some of the flowers, the rug bears the date 1221 A.H. (for A.D. 1809), 56in by 49in (142 by 125cm).
£2,500-3,000 *P(O)*

A Heriz carpet, with an ivory vine trellis design on a blue field, with green, ivory, blue and pink, 285 by 177in (724 by 450cm).
£30,000-35,000 *DN*

A Caucasian runner, possibly kuba, the red field woven with a florette trellis pattern, the cream main border with linked star florettes, in good condition, 104 by 45in (264 by 114cm).
£1,700-2,000 *L*

A Kashan silk prayer rug, the ivory field with a vase of flowers flanked by trailing vines, deep crimson mihrab with trailing flowers, one bright blue border with leaves and flowers and several narrow borders, ends missing, 78 by 53in (198 by 135cm).
£3,000-3,500 *DN*

A Beshir carpet, the dark blue field woven with a palmette trellis within multiple borders, in fair condition, 145 by 71in (369 by 180cm).
£500-600 *L*

A Karabagh runner, the indigo field with a rococo European design within scrolling golden frames divided by similar motifs and surrounded by floral sprays, in a narrow reciprocal Y-pattern border, minor damage, 234 by 42in (594 by 107cm).
£7,000-8,000 *C*

A Kazak rug, with red pointed ground, azure surround and central medallion with floral decoration within stylised border, 71 by 53in (180 by 135cm).
£200-300 *LRG*

A Chondzorek rug, the shaded brick-red field with 2 large indigo and sea-green panels in a shaded light blue border, corrosion and repair, 101 by 56in (256 by 142cm).
£1,500-2,000 *C*

A Karabagh kelleh, in indigo, blackcurrant red and light blue, slight wear and repair, 218 by 79in (553 by 201cm).
£2,500-3,500 *C*

A Qashqa'i rug, in blue with red and white, the liver main border with stylised flowering plants, good condition, 81 by 58in (206 by 147cm).
£750-850 *L*

A Kirman rug, the dark blue field closely woven with floral and palmette tendrils, small cream spandrels and lobed medallion, the blue main border with a palmette meander, in good condition, 82 by 49in (208 by 125cm).
£1,200-1,700 *L*

A Sarouk rug, the cream field woven with floral tendrils, red spandrels and a blue lobed pole medallion, the red main border with a palmette meander, in good condition, 81 by 57in (106 by 145cm).
£700-900 *L*

A Turkoman wool rug, 126 by 81.5in (318 by 207cm).
£650-750 *HSS*

A Magri rug, worked in bottle green, rust red, golden yellow, and ivory, some wear and repair, 94 by 65in (238 by 165cm).
£1,500-2,000 *C*

A Serapi runner, the indigo field with small floral motifs around 2 large tracery vine panels with open central indigo pole medallions containing floral motifs, in a broad ivory crab rosette border between reciprocal trefoil stripes, a few knots repiled, 160 by 45in (406 by 114cm).
£1,000-1,200 *C*

A pair of Serapi runners, the pale camel field of each with angular motifs around a string of 3 shaped ivory panels, each containing narrow diagonal stripes around a red floral pole medallion, in an ivory border of chequered and serrated motifs between spiralling ribbon and reciprocal skittle pattern stripes, one end braided, slight wear and damage, 180 by 36in (457 by 92cm). **£2,500-3,000** *C*

A pair of Senneh kilims, the ivory field of each with angular floral sprays around a large serrated indigo lozenge medallion containing similar motifs radiating from a similar central ivory floral lozenge, the red spandrels similar, in a narrow rust red lozenge border between medium blue similar stripes, 87 by 48in (221 by 122cm) and 85 by 52in (216 by 132cm).
£1,500-2,000 *C*

A Qashqa'i rug, in plum red, ivory and orange, with brief inscription and the date 1319 (1901 A.D.), between orange flowerhead and serrated leaf stripes, various minor stripes, a panelled skirt and kilim strip at each end, 77 by 48in (196 by 122cm).
£1,500-2,000 *C*

A Persian rug, the shaded brick field woven with floral tendrils, the dark blue main border with a palmette meander, in good condition, 78 by 48in (198 by 122cm).
£2,000-2,500 *L*

A Sewan Kazak rug, the shaded brick red field in a brown border of angular rectangular panels containing stylised flowerheads and the Christian date 1916, between zig-zag stripes, slight wear, 103 by 71in (262 by 180cm).
£1,500-2,000 *C*

A North West Persian kelleh, the shaded indigo field with staggered rows of polychrome boteh, in a broad shaded light blue angular flowerhead and serrated leaf border, dated 1333 (1914-5 A.D.) in one corner, between brown floral and barber pole stripes, a short kilim strip at each end, 216 by 86in (549 by 218cm).
£3,500-4,500 *C*

A Ziegler carpet, the charcoal grey field with a counterposed design in a rust red flowerhead and palmette vine border between minor ivory and golden yellow floral stripes, some damage, 180 by 158in (457 by 401cm).   **£5,500-6,500** *C*

An East Turkestan rug, the shaded brick red field with a pictorial design of perching water fowl and a cockerel amongst flowering lotus below a large flowering tree with perching birds, repaired, 105 by 70in (271 by 178cm).
£1,500-2,000 *C*

DOLLS

Nothing in life is static and the doll market is no exception. Although prices have not risen at the very top end of the market, largely due to the lack of Japanese buyers, there have been some interesting developments, particularly in the middle of the price range. A charming Bru Jne, size 9 in original pale blue satin dress fetched £15,400 in September and in the same sale the only known example of Steiner's last patent drawing was sold for £3,200. This was of a clockwork Zouave Soldier who knelt down and fired his rifle. The curious thing about this patent is its remarkable similarity to an earlier clockwork toy produced by Theroude.

Automata also sold well in the sale, £31,900 being paid for a Vichy model of 'Pierrot Serenading the Moon', a European record price, and £27,500 for a jokey 'Peasant and Baby' also by Vichy. This was in fact of a Bohemian young man irritatedly feeding a piglet on his lap.

Wax dolls, particularly wax over composition, after being unfashionable for many years, have seen some high prices paid for those in good condition and original clothes. A beautiful large poured wax English doll of 1860 in a pretty original spotted muslin frock with blue silk sash and matching decoration on the skirt and sleeves fetched £1,980 at Christie's last year against an estimate of £500-600. This May £880 was paid for a pair of late 19thC wax over composition dolls in high quality original 18thC style fancy dress, the woman with fan and pearls, the man with tricorn hat and knee breeches. It is so unusual to find toys in an unplayed with condition, that collectors will always pay a premium for them.

Other factors that contribute to a high price are rare marks, original boxes or labels. An interesting high quality English poured wax doll we sold in May had a hitherto unknown shop stamp on its body. After extensive research we discovered that the shop stamp belonged to a fancy jeweller in Sloane Street, known to have been in business at least from 1886-1908. In spite of damaged limbs, its serenely pretty face meant it sold for £462. A pretty Pierrotti baby in good condition and attractive clothes now fetches over £500.

In the past few years we have seen a sharp rise in interest for 20thC English cloth dolls. A surprising £495 was paid for a pretty 1950s Chad Valley baby doll with sleeping eyes. In pristine condition, original knitted sewn-on clothes and tied into its labelled box, it represented a good return on its original price tag of 5/6 (27p). A couple of pairs of dolls in original boxes modelled as the Bisto Kids sold for £500 and £480. Those were cheap quality composition-headed advertising dolls again still tied in their boxes, perhaps over production accounted for them not being named on the lids, or perhaps they were such well known characters, that it was not deemed necessary.

Another curiously high price was paid for an unusually voluptuous celluloid lady doll complete with just visible painted flesh coloured stockings and high heels. Made by the Rheinische Gummi and Celluloid Fabrik and from a private collection it realised £660, probably a record for a celluloid doll. The same collector also sold a doll complete with original trousseau and a pretty paper covered wardrobe. These early 20thC French sets were normally not of very high quality but still a delightfully fascinating toy. Although the doll was only approximately 7 inches high, the complete wardrobe and doll with some additions sold for £770.

Collecting early Barbie dolls has been a new field at Christie's South Kensington. Here the appeal is equally in the boxed doll, her friends and relations as well as in their sets of lined clothes and accessories, e.g. a group of four boxed dolls with a selection of clothes fetched £1,000.

The dolls house market has remained strong throughout the year. Enormous interest was shown in the sale of the Camme Bache dolls house collection and catalogues were sold out before the sale. Although there were very few manufactured houses, all of them were fully furnished and inhabited, many with good quality pieces and unusual half-bisque doll people. Collectors were particularly interested as they came from Scandinavia, and there were many items that were typical of the Danish lifestyle but are not found in English houses. The biggest price of the sale was for an English butchers shop, once used by a 'flesher' of Dumfries. It was sold for £9,900. The dolls house and chattels sections continued to be strong throughout the year, Christie's having been building up this area; we now offer a larger selection and wider range of periods than any other auction house.

Whereas the higher priced French bébés and rare characters have tended to hold or slightly decline in price, middle and lower price range dolls in immaculate condition have been strongly sought after. The message for the recession seems to be if it's pretty and perfect in its own field then it's worth buying. The emotions are often uppermost in the decision to buy a doll, so the love affair between the collector and the doll has never been more important than now. A doll has to have the right look in order to appeal to a prospective owner and not remain on the shelf. Dealers are therefore becoming more cautious in their purchases and are only buying what they know they will have a ready market for.

DOLLS
Wooden

A George II wooden doll, with painted gesso covered face, nailed flax wig, legs jointed at hip and knee, block feet, cloth upper and wooden lower arms, dressed in green, pink, cream and blue, fragments of brocaded and ribbed silk and satin, lined with paper, silk stockings and boots, c1740, together with an English waxed shoulder papier mâché doll, with black glass eyes, dark real hair, cloth body and legs, and leather arms, wearing Chinese style coat, c1830, 14 and 14.5in (36 and 37cm).
£3,000-4,000 *S*

An early German carved wooden doll, with painted hair and features, jointed body with painted yellow shoes, wearing original gold silk fringed dress and pantaloons, c1800, 6in (15cm) high.
£600-800 *CSK*

A George III wooden doll, with painted features, inserted blue eyes with dotted lashes and brows, white blonde real hair, squared hips peg jointed to straight tapering legs ending in block feet, cloth upper arms with blue kid forearms, in pink beige silk dress, restored, c1790, 13in (33cm).
£700-900 *S*

This doll is reputed to have belonged to Queen Victoria who gave it to her maid-in-waiting the Hon. Caroline Cavendish who in turn gave the doll to the aunt of the present owner.

A Grödnertal painted wooden headed doll, with yellow comb, jointed wooden body and contemporary clothes, damaged, c1820, 9in (23cm) high.
£400-500 *CSK*

A Grödnertal painted wooden headed doll, with moulded yellow comb, jointed wooden body, Welsh tweed clothes and basket, c1820, 11in (28cm) high.
£800-1,000 *CSK*

A George III wooden doll, with gessoed face, inset black enamelled eyes, brown ringlet wig, brown leather arms, articulated wooden legs, wearing a muslin skirt, voile apron, cotton underclothes, damaged, early 19thC, 18in (46cm).
£600-1,000 *S*

A pair of carved and painted wooden nodding figures, probably South German, with moving lower jaws, damaged, c1850, 8in (20cm) high.
£200-250 *CSK*

Wax

An English Pierotti wax shoulder head, with fixed blue glass eyes, closed painted mouth, inserted blonde hair, eyebrows and eyelashes, 5in (13cm). **£600-800** *S*

This shoulder head comes from a direct descendant of the Pierotti family.

A Charles Marsh poured wax shoulder doll, with inserted blonde hair, blue lashed eyes, wax lower limbs, maker's stamp on cloth torso, damaged and restored, c1878, 18.5in (47cm). **£500-700** *S*

A pair of wax over composition headed dolls, dressed in 18thC style, with blue eyes, blonde mohair wigs, stuffed bodies, waxed arms and composition lower legs, the man wearing black silk knee breeches, red velvet, silver braided jacket, tricorn hat, heeled shoes, the lady with open/closed mouth showing teeth, dressed in ruby pleated silk skirt with floral overdress trimmed with lace, heeled shoes and fan, damage to toe of man, 17in (43cm) high. **£800-1,000** *CSK*

A poured wax head and shoulder doll, 19thC, 17.5in (44cm) high. **£300-400** *HSS*

A wax over composition headed doll, with blue eyes, blonde inset mohair, stuffed body with composition limbs, moulded shoes and socks, wearing original blue silk lace and flower trimmed dress with train, posy and fan, cracks to face, c1888, 18in (46cm) high.   **£350-450** *CSK*

A poured wax child doll, with fixed blue eyes, short brown inset hair, downturned mouth, stuffed body, wax limbs and contemporary blue wool dress, late 19thC, 23in (59cm) high. **£350-550** *CSK*

A poured wax headed child doll, with blue eyes, downturned mouth, remains of inset hair, stuffed body, wax limbs, metal eyelets and baby robe, body stamped W.J. Weedon, Importer & Manufacturer of British & Foreign Goods, 164 Sloane Street, Belgravia S.W., damaged, 23in (59cm) high. **£450-550** *CSK*

William J. Weedon is listed in Kelly's Street Directory of Chelsea, Pimlico and Belgravia as a fancy jeweller in 1886-7, 1890, 1900 and 1909.

A Lucy Peck poured wax doll, wearing original bonnet, c1900, 27in (69cm) high. **£1,200-1,500** *DOL*

Bisque

A brown bisque headed character doll, with brown eyes, dark wig and bent limbed composition body, impressed Heubach Koppelsdorf 344 3/0, replaced eyes and wig, 13in (33cm) high. **£400-600** *CSK*

A bisque headed jester doll, the wire spring and wood body with squeaker, wearing original clothes, 10.5in (26cm) high. **£250-300** *CSK*

A bisque headed musical poupée, with fixed blue eyes, blonde wig, original pink and white streamers with pompoms, covering a bonbon box, 12.5in (32cm) high. **£300-400** *CSK*

A bisque headed child doll, with blue lashed sleeping eyes, moulded and feathered brows, pierced ears, auburn wig, jointed wood and composition body, voice box and walking and kiss throwing mechanism, wearing red wool dress, coat and cape, straw bonnet and leather shoes with bee mark, impressed DEP 10, 24in (61cm) high. **£600-800** *CSK*

A bisque headed character doll, modelled as H.R.H. Princess Elizabeth, with blue lashed sleeping eyes, brown wig and composition toddler body, impressed Porzellanfabrik Burggrub Princess Elizabeth D.R.G.M., firing crack at neck. **£650-750** *CSK*

Two German shoulder parian bisque dolls, with blonde moulded hair, painted faces, cloth bodies and lower parian limbs, c1870, 16 and 17in (41 to 44cm). **£700-800** *S*

A Bähr & Pröschild bisque Oriental doll, with fixed blue glass eyes, closed mouth, black mohair wig, pierced ears, jointed wood and composition, impressed 220/3, re-dressed, eyes replaced retouching to fingers, 15in (38cm). **£900-1,200** *S*

A bisque headed character doll, modelled as Father Christmas, with inset eyes, original clothes and beard, impressed with an ogee curve and 6/o, 8.5in (21cm) high. **£170-250** *CSK*

A French shoulder bisque swivel head fashion doll, with fixed blue glass eyes, closed mouth, remnants of blonde real hair wig over cork pate, Gesland type body, bisque lower arm, re-dressed, one upper and lower arm missing, one foot damaged, unmarked, c1885, 10.5in (26cm). **£400-600** *S*

A bisque shoulder fashion doll, 19thC.
£650-700 *HCH*

Three all bisque Bye-Lo baby dolls and an all bisque Kewpie doll, all impressed to backs, with jointed arms and legs, early 1920s, 4 to 5in (10 to 13cm).
£750-850 *S*

A domed bisque swivel-headed doll, with feathered brows, pierced ears, blonde mohair wig, stuffed body, bisque arms, wearing original regional costume, impressed S H 905, 13.5in (34cm) high.
£900-1,200 *CSK*

A French bisque doll, with fixed spiralled blue glass eyes, closed mouth, Belton type head with long real hair wig, pierced ears, jointed wood and composition body, wearing blue lawn pleated lace trimmed dress and later bonnet, impressed 13/1 4, slight damage, 11in (28cm).
£550-650 *S*

A bisque headed character doll, modelled as an Oriental, with brown sleeping eyes, pierced ears, black mohair wig, jointed body and original red embroidered clothes, impressed SH 1199 DEP, 15in (38cm) high.
£1,600-2,000 *CSK*

An early bisque headed bébé, with brown yeux fibres, shaded lids, pierced ears, fair mohair wig, jointed wood and papier mâché body, fixed wrists, original red hat and contemporary cotton print frock, impressed and body stamped with Schmitt & Fils shield, 16in (41cm) high.
£5,000-7,000 *CSK*

A bisque headed character doll, with brown sleeping eyes, moulded blonde hair and bent limbed composition body and jointed wrists, dressed in whitework dress and cape, one broken finger, impressed 2048 5, by Bruno Schmidt, 18in (46cm) high.
£1,200-1,500 *CSK*

A bisque headed character baby doll, with blue sleeping eyes, feathered brows, brown mohair wig and bent limbed composition body, dressed in white velvet coat, marked 10 BSW, 18in (46cm) high.
£300-500 *CSK*

A group of 51 dolls house and all bisque dolls, German and French, some distressed, late 19th/early 20thC, from 1.5 to 6in (4 to 13cm).　**£3,000-4,000** *S*

A bisque headed character doll, modelled as an Oriental, with pierced ears, black wig and jointed wood and composition body, damaged, impressed SH 1199 DEP 8, 20in (51cm) high.
£2,000-2,500 *CSK*

A bisque headed child doll, with feathered brows, pierced ears, blonde mohair wig, cloth covered jointed body with fixed wrists, dressed in beige silk, 11.5in (29cm) high. **£1,700-2,000** *CSK*

A bisque headed child doll, with blue sleeping eyes, pierced ears, jointed body, wearing a green dress and coat, impressed S & H 1249 DEP 6, 16.5in (42cm) high.
£350-450 *CSK*

Bru

A Bru pressed bisque swivel-head fashion doll, the closed smiling mouth, fixed blue glass eyes, pierced ears, auburn mohair wig over cork pate, gusseted kid body with jointed wooden arms and hands, wearing original clothes and shoes, together with her trunk containing accessories, c1872.
£3,500-4,500 *S*

A bisque headed character doll, with blue sleeping eyes, moulded brows, pierced ears, blonde mohair wig, jointed body and red check wool dress, impressed 1339 S & H L.L. & S. 8., 19in (48cm) high.
£600-700 *CSK*

François Gaultier

A bisque swivel-necked doll, gusseted white kid leather body, original blonde wig, underwear, modern turquoise brocade gown, probably F. Gaultier, impressed 4, c1875, 18in (46cm) high, together with a velvet pouch.
£1,200-1,700 *S*

A Bru jeune R bisque head, with open mouth, upper teeth, weighted brown glass eyes, pierced ears, damaged, impressed BRU Jne R 9, c1892, 5in (13cm).
£600-800 *S*

A moulded bisque doll, with fixed blue glass eyes, red-blonde real hair wig, jointed papier mâché and wood body with straight legs, in original cream wool dress, paint scuffed, impressed 7 4. F.G. in a scroll. **£1,500-2,000** *S*

Gebrüder Heubach

A swivel-head pressed bisque doll, with closed mouth, fixed blue glass eyes, fair mohair wig over cork pate, kid covered wooden body with vertically jointed swivelling hips, tenon joints at knees, shoulders and elbows, bisque forearms, wearing silk and satin dress, straw bonnet and brown leather heeled boots, impressed on the shoulder F 4 G, damaged, c1865, 18in (46cm).
£4,000-4,500 *S*

A bisque socket head baby boy doll, 14in (37cm) high.
£500-600 *HSS*

A shoulder bisque character crying doll, with open/closed mouth and simulated tongue, intaglio eyes, cloth body with composition forearms, wearing original embroidered cream silk long robe, net cape and lacy bonnet, fingers chipped, impressed 3, c1912.
£700-800 *S*

A bisque character doll, with blue intaglio eyes, moulded light brown hair, curved limb composition body, in a whitework embroidered dress, some damage and repair, impressed with sunburst mark, 76 04, 6, c1910, 15in (38cm).
£700-800 *S*

A flirty-eyed toddler character doll, Heubach 267, c1920, 28in (71cm) high.
£600-700 *DOL*

Jumeau

A Jumeau bisque headed bébé, with blue yeux fibres, pierced ears, brown wig, the jointed wood and papier mâché body dressed in cream silk, original cotton print shift with Bébé Jumeau ribbon, underwear, shoes and socks, stamped in red Tête Jumeau and on body in blue Jumeau Medaille d'Or, in original Jumeau box, 28in (71cm) high, with additional pair of slippers and petticoat.
£2,000-2,500 *CSK*

A Jumeau triste pressed bisque doll, with fixed brown glass paperweight eyes, applied and pierced ears, brown real hair over cork pate, jointed wood and composition body, wearing pink dress, stringing loose, impressed 15, c1875, 31.5in (80cm).
£8,000-10,000 *S*

An Emile Jumeau doll, wearing original clothes, c1870, 23.5in (60cm) high.
£6,000-7,000 *DOL*

A Jumeau bisque doll, with fixed blue glass eyes, blonde wig, jointed wood and composition body, white bonnet, chipped and cracked, stamped in red Deposé Tête Jumeau Bte S.G.D.G., c1885, 17in (43cm).
£2,200-2,700 *S*

A Jumeau bisque doll, with brown paperweight eyes, long brown wig, jointed wood and composition body, with label to buttock, in printed floral dress and bonnet, leather pumps, paint scuffed, chipped hands, unmarked head but impressed 5, c1890, 16in (41cm). **£800-1,000** *S*

J.D. Kestner

A J.D. Kestner Bru-type bisque doll, with open/closed mouth, simulated teeth, fixed blue glass eyes, pierced ears, flattened domed head, jointed wood and composition body, wearing a cream lacy dress, impressed 121 0, c1897, 7.5in (19cm).
£800-1,000 *S*

An all bisque doll, probably Kestner, 'The Wrestler', c1890, 10.5in (26cm) high.
£1,500-1,600 *DOL*

A bisque character doll, with large weighted blue glass eyes, open mouth with upper teeth, original brown mohair wig, curved limb baby body, wearing later knitted pink dress and cap, arms and legs rubbed, impressed 257/64, c1916, 25in (64cm).
£800-1,000 *S*

A bisque headed character baby doll with brown lashed sleeping eyes, short wig and baby's body, impressed J.D.K. 257 51, 19in (48cm) high.
£400-600 *CSK*

A bisque doll, probably by Kestner, with open mouth and upper teeth, weighted blue glass eyes, pierced ears, fair mohair wig over original plaster pate and jointed wood and composition body, wearing cream silk dress and red wool coat and bonnet, impressed 192 4, c1910, 15in (38cm), together with her trunk, containing brush, comb and hand mirror, 2 jackets, 2 skirts, 4 items of underwear, purse bonnet and parasol, trunk 12.5in (31cm) wide.
£1,700-2,200 *S*

A bisque character doll, with sleeping blue eyes, open mouth with moulded upper teeth, curved limb body, wearing original dress and kid shoes, replaced wig, c1915, 13in (33cm).
£350-450 *S*

A bisque Oriental doll, with open mouth and 2 upper teeth, fixed brown glass eyes, black moulded hair and curved limb composition body, wearing yellow and white tunic, cracked, impressed 14, 16in (41cm).
£1,500-2,000 *S*

A bisque headed character doll, with blue sleeping and flirting eyes, brown mohair wig, the bent limbed composition body dressed in knitted suit, impressed J.D.K. 257, 18in (45.5cm) high.
£700-800 *CSK*

A bisque headed character baby doll, with open/closed mouth, blue sleeping eyes, baby's body and blue rompers, impressed F 10 211 J.D.K., 12in (31cm) high.
£800-1,000 *CSK*

A bisque headed character doll, with blue sleeping eyes, brown wig and bent limbed composition body dressed in turquoise blue cotton, impressed P.M. 914, 14in (36cm) high.
£150-200
A bisque headed character doll, with water melon mouth, sleeping side glancing googlie eyes, plaster pate, composition toddler body, starfish hands and original boots and socks, impressed J.D.K. 221, fingers damaged, 10in (25cm) high.
£2,000-3,000 *CSK*

An all bisque child doll, with brown eyes, blonde mohair wig, shoulder and hip joints, moulded peach coloured socks and black two-bar shoes with bow, original blue silk lace trimmed frock and underwear, probably by Kestner, chipped and unstrung, 8in (20cm) high. **£800-1,000** *CSK*

An all bisque googlie-eyed character doll, with blue sleeping eyes, jointed body with moulded and painted shoes and socks, impressed 112 2, by Kestner, 5.5in (13cm) high.
£900-1,200 *CSK*

A bisque turned shoulder headed doll, with closed mouth, blue inset eyes, feathered brows, blonde mohair wig, the stuffed body with bisque limbs, dressed in underwear, impressed 8, by Kling, damaged, 18in (46cm) high.
£1,200-1,700 *CSK*

Use the Index

Because certain items might fit easily into any number of categories, the quickest and surest method of locating any entry is by reference to the index at the back of the book.
This has been fully cross-referenced for absolute simplicity.

A bisque headed bébé, with closed mouth, blue yeux fibres, feathered brows, pierced ears, cork pate, blonde mohair wig, the jointed wood and composition body dressed in white shift and bonnet, impressed Déposé E 12 J, slight damage, 25in (64cm) high.
£3,700-4,200 *CSK*

Lenci

A Lenci painted felt doll, with brown eyes glancing to the left, blonde curly wig and original pink and white check felt clothes, Series 111, 12in (31cm) high.
£450-650 *CSK*

A pair of Lenci felt dolls, with original card and woven tags to backs, he dressed in plaid kilt, green jacket, maroon waistcoat and undershorts, white shirt, sporran, tartan socks and black shoes, tartan wool scarf, brown cap, face painted with blue eyes looking left, blonde hair, 14.5in (37cm), she with Lenci card and woven tags to back of skirt, painted face with brown eyes looking right, black hair, layered dress of net applied with cut-out felt flowers and vines in pink, red and black, black lace mantilla and red painted wood comb to hair, white socks and black shoes, 14.5in (37cm). **£800-1,000** *S*

Armand Marseille

An Armand Marseille bisque headed doll, with blue sleeping eyes, open mouth, brown hair wig, composition body, in knitted shorts and top, impressed Germany 971 A5M, 16in (41cm) high.
£400-500 *HCH*

An Armand Marseille bisque doll, with cropped black wig, jointed wood and composition body in contemporary red and white striped dress, impressed 1894 AM 8, one finger restored, c1894, 23in (59cm) high.
£900-1,200 *S*

A bisque headed character baby doll, with blue lashed sleeping eyes, brown mohair wig and toddler body, dressed as a boy, impressed 971 A 8 M, 18in (46cm) high.
£300-350 *CSK*

An Armand Marseille bisque socket-head girl doll, 23in (59cm) high.
£280-350 *HSS*

An Armand Marseille bisque socket head doll, 23in (59cm) high.
£200-300 *HSS*

l. An Armand Marseille bisque socket head character doll, 17in (43cm) high.
£350-400
r. An Armand Marseille/ Koppelsdorf bisque socket head doll, 19in (48cm).
£250-300 *HSS*

An Armand Marseille howling doll, cloth body with squeaker, No. AM 347, c1929, 15in (38cm) high.
£1,100-1,200 *DOL*

An Armand Marseille bisque socket head girl doll, 20.5in (52cm).
£200-250 *HSS*

S.F.B.J.

A character doll with bisque head with raised brows, pierced ears, long hair wig, sleeping dark French eyes and jointed composition body, impressed 10, with S.F.B.J. sticker on the body, the head probably by Simon and Halbig, similar to mould No. 1159, 23in (59cm) high.
£300-400 *CSK*

An Armand Marseille jointed doll, with sleeping eyes, No. AM 390, c1900, 13in (33cm) high.
£190-200 *PSA*

Simon & Halbig/Kammer & Reinhardt

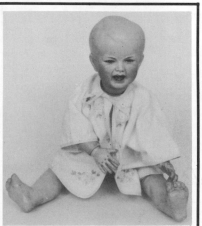

An S.F.B.J. boy doll, The Screamer, with jointed toddler body, impressed No. 233, 20in (51cm) high.
£3,000-3,500 *DOL*

A bisque headed character doll, with open/closed mouth, blue sleeping eyes, brown mohair wig and bent limbed composition body, impressed R SFBJ 236 Paris, body marked with SFBJ label, 19in (48cm) high.
£500-650 *CSK*

A Simon & Halbig bisque 'Santa' doll, with weighted blue glass eyes, pierced ears, blonde mohair wig, ball jointed wood and composition body, with several items of clothing, impressed 1249 DEP SANTA 8, stringing perished, unclothed, 19in (48cm) high.   **£600-800** *S*

A Simon & Halbig bisque character doll, the long face with fixed pale blue paperweight eyes, closed mouth, long brown ringletted wig, jointed wood and composition toddler body, cream silk dress, pale aquamarine coat, cape and bonnet, impressed S 12 H, 939, restored, 19.5in (50cm) high.
£2,000-2,500   *S*

A Simon & Halbig shoulder bisque doll, with fixed spiralled brown glass eyes, closed mouth, pierced ears, moulded curly blonde hair, leather body with leather upper arms, in underskirt, cream raw silk gown, lace cap, knitted gloves, three-button brown leather boots, impressed S12H, c1890, 24.5in (62cm) high.
£1,000-1,500   *S*

A bisque headed character doll, with blue sleeping, flirting eyes, fair mohair wig, jointed wood and composition body, rubber hands and original underclothes, impressed K*R Simon & Halbig 117N 53, 20in (51cm) high.
£1,000-1,500   *CSK*

An Oriental bisque doll, with almond shaped fixed brown eyes, closed mouth, black wig with pigtail, on straight limbed composition body, moulded red shoes, in contemporary gold and blue printed gown and a cardboard hat, head probably by Simon & Halbig, impressed 3/0, 12in (30cm) high.
£500-700   *S*

A Kammer & Reinhardt bisque doll, with brown eyes, blonde curly wig, jointed wood and composition body, in original broderie anglaise dress, ivory silk coat and wired bonnet, knitted silk socks and white leather shoes, impressed 73, 29in (73cm) high.
£800-1,200   *S*

A bisque headed character baby doll, with brown lashed sleeping and flirting eyes, brown mohair wig and bent limbed composition body, marked K*R Simon & Halbig 121 56, 21in (53cm) high.
£350-500   *CSK*

Did you know

MILLER'S Antiques Price Guide builds up year by year to form the most comprehensive photo-reference system available.

A bisque headed character doll, with open/closed mouth, blue sleeping eyes, fair mohair wig and bent limbed composition body, impressed K*R Simon & Halbig 116/A 42, 16in (41cm) high.
£1,200-1,500   *CSK*

A Simon & Halbig bisque swivel-necked doll, with brown eyes, short blonde wig, closed mouth, applied pierced ears, jointed German style pink kid leather body, bisque lower arms, dressed in a pink taffeta 1880's style gown, trimmed with ribbon and tulle, impressed 13 719 DEP, the breastplate impressed S 13 H 720, damaged, c1885, 29in (74cm) high.   **£1,800-2,500**   *S*

A bisque headed character doll, with blue sleeping, flirting eyes, brown wig, the jointed wood and composition body with voice box, dressed in knitted outfit and brown leather shoes, impressed K*R Simon & Halbig 117N , 24.5in (62cm) high.
£1,000-1,500 *CSK*

Jules Steiner

A bisque headed doll, with blue sleeping eyes, moulded brows, flapper knees with short upper leg sections and rigid arms, impressed 1159 SIMON 7 HALBIG S & H 6, 14in (36cm) high.
£650-750 *CSK*

A Jules Steiner walking/crying doll, the pale bisque head with fixed blue glass eyes, brown wig over domed head, the fabric covered papier mâché body encasing the clockwork mechanism, with winding key and start/stop lever which causes the doll to agitate its arms and legs and to emit cries, damaged, c1880, 20in (51cm) high.
£1,200-1,700 *S*

Miscellaneous

A limited edition Princess Elizabeth doll, 20.5in (52cm) high.
£1,350-1,500 *DOL*

A composition Topsy doll, c1940, 12.5in (32cm) high.
£65-80 *DOL*

A German three-faced doll depicting Red Riding Hood, the Wolf and the Grandmother, one bisque head showing Red Riding Hood with open/closed mouth, fixed blue glass eyes, the grandmother's lined face with smiling closed mouth and fixed blue glass eyes, the brown bisque wolf with painted slanting eyes and red moulded tongue, all under a cardboard cowl and central turning knob, the jointed wood and composition body in blue dress, white apron and top and red waistcoat, cape and lace edged red bonnet, a finely woven basket in her hand, probably by Bergner, c1895, 12.5in (32cm) high.   **£3,500-4,500** *S*

A German doll, with a five-piece body, and original clothes, 11.5in (29cm) high.
£120-150 *PSA*

A painted cloth headed boy doll, with blue-grey eyes with white highlights, separate thumb section and wide hips with five-piece legs, by Kathe Kruse, Doll No. 1, no. on foot 23715, c1920, 17in (43.5cm) high.
£1,200-1,700 *CSK*

A mask headed character doll, modelled as Snow White with black mohair wig, cloth body and original velvet and rayon dress printed 'Snow White and the Seven Dwarfs', 15in (38cm) high, and the Seven Dwarfs, in original outfits, 6.5in (16.5cm) high, all by Chad Valley.
£450-650 *CSK*

A Steiff felt soldier doll, the face with centre seam, glass eyes, painted mouth, with jointed limbs, in felt uniform and cap numbered 28, with iron cross, and sword, c1915, 14in (35cm) high.
£800-1,000 *S*

A Steiff felt soldier doll, the face with glass eyes, painted mouth, cap numbered 28, oilskin boots, swivel limbs, c1915, 14in (35cm) high.
£800-1,000 *S*

A pottery shoulder headed doll, with painted brown eyes, open/closed mouth with teeth, moulded hair, stuffed body, pottery arms and original Scottish solder's uniform, impressed G 7, by Goss, stamped on the body British Toy Company, and with swing ticket reading Trade Mark 'WARDOL' Registration applied for, 1915, 13.5in (34.5cm) high.
£500-700 *CSK*

Dolls House

An open pine shooting lodge, with galleried attic of 2 rooms, fully furnished, 28.5in (72.5cm) wide.
£600-800 *CSK*

'The Skelskoer House', with 5 bays, opening central front door with porch and balcony above, fully furnished, c1900, 39in (99cm) wide, and 2 bisque headed women with moulded hair, one in original maid's clothes.   **£1,500-2,000** *CSK*

A doll's open room, probably Italian, c1770, 18in (46cm) wide.
£3,000-4,000 *S*

A German group of 'satinwood' dolls house furniture, with blue silk upholstery, including an elaborate curtained dressing table, a wardrobe with curved doors and drawers and a half-tester bed, c1870, dressing table 6.5in (16.5cm) high.
£800-1,000 *CSK*

'Patricia's House', a painted wooden open dolls house, the roof simulating red tiles, with bedroom, nursery, living room and kitchen, including furnishings, 1865, 39in (99cm) wide, and a bisque headed doll with moulded fair hair and circular hairband, 8in (20cm) high.
£1,500-2,000 *CSK*

A pink painted wooden dolls house, with mansard roof, the open back showing 4 rooms, and 3 bisque headed dolls and a bonnet-head baby, 29in (74cm) wide.
£1,300-1,500 *CSK*

'Edith's House', a painted open wooden dolls house with original wallpapers, 4 rooms, and 5 bisque dolls.
£1,700-2,000 *CSK*

A painted wooden two-storey dolls house, with simulated lift-off blue slate roof, and elaborate pink transfer decoration to façade, each section opening and with original striped wallpapers, embossed friezes, paper covered pelmets, net curtains, embossed gilt paper tie-backs with red cotton ribbons, and a set of printed card furniture and dolls, with Christian Hacker printed label on base and pencilled number 138/4 5, c1890, 16.5in (42cm) wide, and a bisque headed doll with high piled hair.
£1,500-2,000 *CSK*

'Anna's Pleasure' a painted wooden house of simulated stone with coining and sand finish, fretted window and door pediments, slate roof and wood grained door, the front removing to reveal one room, the roof lifting to show three attic rooms, furnished as a sitting room, c1860, 38in (96.5cm) wide.
£1,800-2,500 *CSK*

A Regency yew-wood table, 4in (10cm) diam, **£20-30**, and a Wedgwood dinner service, **£12-40 each piece** *CD*

A painted tinplate kitchen, the corner stove with hood, a painted glass window at the back, and utensils including a copper hot water bottle, possibly Märklin, late 19thC, 11.5in (29cm) wide.
£620-670 *CSK*

A wooden dolls house of 5 bays and 2 storeys, painted brown and grey to simulate stone with slate roof, with castellated central tower, dormer windows, hinged front, attic, windows at the sides and remains of furniture including a gilt metal fireplace, early 20thC, 47.5in (120cm) wide.
£600-800 *CSK*

A J. & G. Lines painted wooden dolls house, No.24, c1909, with 3 bays and 2 storeys, 32.5in (82.5cm) wide, 4 dolls house people, and 3 other dolls.
£4,000-5,000 *CSK*

'Lise's House', a wooden open roomed, separate storey house, painted to simulate brickwork, with elaborate semi-circular decorations above the windows, 37in (94cm) wide, and a Grödnertal doll.
£3,000-4,000 *CSK*

'Villa Gurre', a painted wooden dolls house with 2 bays and 2 storeys, fully furnished, c1920, 32.5in (82.5cm) wide, and 2 bisque headed dolls.
£1,600-2,000 *CSK*

A group of English dolls house furniture, the piano inscribed Samuel Adams, West Bromwich.
£500-600 *CSK*

Samuel Adams was a leading musical figure in West Bromwich, being both a piano tuner and dealer, and the owner of St George's Hall, where numerous concerts were held.

A selection of dolls house furniture, c1900.
£1,200-1,700 *S*

A painted wooden toy grocer's shop, with named drawers, fitted counter, bell, windows, mirror and stock, including bolts of cloth, sugar cones, food on plates, barrels, steps, baskets and items of pottery, 34in (86cm) wide. **£450-550** *CSK*

A collection of European and English dolls house metal and beadwork furniture, damaged, c1900, fire surround 5in (12cm) wide. **£500-700** *S*

A group of German dolls house furniture, c1900.
£500-700 *S*

A group of tinplate dolls house drawing room furniture, painted to simulate wood grain and upholstered in blue silk, by Rock and Graner, c1870, some damage, sofa 7in (18cm) long. **£500-700** *CSK*

A painted wooden toy kitchen, with furnishings including tinplate kitchen range, water holder, cupboard, saucepans, and pottery jugs and bowls, 33in (84cm) wide. **£350-550** *CSK*

A selection of ladies leather shoes and boots, with flower decoration. **£15-30 each** *CD*

A group of painted soft metal dolls house furniture, corner table 4in (10cm) high. **£400-600** *CSK*

Two bronze blackamoor statues, by John Hodgson, 4.5in (11.5cm) high. **£180-190** *CD*

A Georgian yew-wood dresser, by Escutcheon, 11in (28cm) wide. **£130-150** *CD*

TOYS
Automata

A French musical rabbit in a cabbage automaton, the white fur rabbit pricking up his ears and rising from inside a fabric cabbage, key wind and stop/start mechanism and with battery compartment to illuminate the eyes, c1890. **£500-700** *Bea*

A French musical automated scene of a carpenter, the papier mâché headed carpenter hammering at his bench in an open room, the pull-string musical and mechanical movement activated by continuously pushing the start knob, under a glass dome, dome missing, 12.5in (32cm) high. **£1,200-1,800** *S*

A French rabbit in a lettuce automaton, the white fur covered animal with glass eyes, within lettuce leaves in a basket, clockwork movement causing him to rise pricking up his ears, movement defective, 6in (15cm) high. **£300-500** *S*

A French Lambert automaton of a lady with a fan, the seated figure with a bisque Jumeau head with blue paperweight eyes, bisque lower arms and hands, dressed in exotic Oriental style outfit, when activated she fans herself and moves her left hand and head in time to the music contained in the green velvet covered base, repaired, 17.5in (45cm) high.
£2,500-3,500 *S*

A Roullet et Decamps musical drinking bear, the fur covered bear with glass eyes, lifting and pouring liquid from a metal bottle in his right hand into a beaker which he lifts to his mouth while tilting his head back and lowering his jaw, the keywind stop/start musical movement contained within the body, c1910, 16in (40cm) high.
£1,700-2,000 *S*

A Roullet et Decamps drinking bear automaton, the red fur covered glass eyed bear seated on his hind legs pouring liquid from a metal bottle into a beaker, lifting it to his face, tilting his head back and lowering his jaw, with keywind stop/start movement, 14in (36cm) high.
£1,500-2,000 *S*

A French walking pig automaton, covered in leather with amber and black glass eyes, wheels to feet, curled tail, clockwork mechanism driving legs and bellows within operating 'oink', 10in (25.5cm) long.
£600-800 *S*

A Roullet et Decamps musical automaton of a rabbit in a tree trunk, the white fur rabbit pops out of a papier mâché tree trunk decorated with leaves and grass, c1900, 9in (23cm) high.
£750-1,000 *S(NY)*

An automated display figure, possibly French, with a composition head and fixed blue glass eyes, open/closed mouth, on felt covered base with clockwork motors to base and figure's torso, 27in (69cm) high.
£2,000-3,000 *S*

A Decamps jumping lion automaton, early 20thC, 14in (36cm) long, and a nodding peasant on donkey figure, possibly by Roullet, with clockwork mechanism, some damage, 21in (54cm) high.
£550-750 *S*

A hand-operated musical automaton of 3 bisque headed dolls in original clothes playing instruments, with wooden hands and composition painted boots, impressed 52 10/0, 15in (38cm) wide.
£1,500-2,000 *CSK*

TEDDY BEARS

When Christie's held the world's first all Teddy Bear and Soft Toy sale in December 1985, I said during an interview that I felt the teddy bear craze would be short-lived and that I did not think that prices being achieved then would hold up over a number of years. How nice it is to be wrong.

During this recessionary period it is interesting to note that one of the most healthy areas in the toy collecting field has been in teddy bears and soft toys. Indeed, London appears to be the centre of the trade, dealers coming from Europe and particularly North America and paying bullish prices for good quality teddy bears in good condition, of all colours, makes and styles.

At the end of 1991 £1,540 was paid for a 29in 1908 white Steiff bear as the thighs were worn and it was rather dusty. Compare this price to the £2,090 paid seven months later for a normal pale gold 28in Steiff of 1906, with worn muzzle, recovered pads and no button. These two bears were both large, but we have seen similar increases in tiny ones.

A spray scent bottle inside a red 3in Schuco fetched £550 in May. These dual purpose animals were popular in the twenties; others were made as compacts, purses, lipsticks, lighters, hot water bottles and manicure sets.

A marvellous 33in Jester bear in fine condition, with pointed cap and bell-trimmed ruff over his blue and yellow parti-coloured body fetched £3,300. There was some discussion as to his manufacture, but the probability was that he was made by Bing.

English bears, if by good makers such as Farnell, Chad Valley, Chiltern, Merrythought or Deans, sell well if in good condition. An incredibly appealing late 1930's, 20in Farnell was sold for £880.

German bears are still at the top of the market. A 28in Steiff of 1906 in almost perfect condition fetched £3,520, and a rare pink musical 14in Schuco of the 1920's sold for £1,045 during 1992.

As one would expect, age, quality and condition are all important, but added to these three, rarity of colour and unusual designs are also major factors in determining the price of a bear. Although loved and battered teddies are still bought for sentimental reasons, investment money is being placed in fine and rare bears.

a. An American golden plush covered teddy bear, with hump and growler, pads recovered, 32in (81cm) high. **£400-600**
b. 'Billy Winky', a Deans golden plush covered teddy bear, with brown glass eyes and jointed limbs, pads missing, 17in (43cm) high. **£350-450**
c. A Steiff golden plush covered teddy bear, with elongated jointed limbs, cardboard-lined feet and hump, worn, c1907, 28in (71cm) high. **£2,000-2,500**

d. A wicker pram with hood, 2 turned wooden handles and iron rimmed wheels, 29in (73.5cm) high, and a doll's wicker chair. **£150-200**
e. A light brown plush covered teddy bear, with boot button eyes, black stitched nose and claws, felt pads, jointed limbs and slight hump, 15in (38cm) high. **£150-200**

f. Two English golden plush covered teddy bears, with brown glass eyes, cloth pads and growler, one growler inoperative, pre-War, 20in (51cm) high. **£500-600**
g. A golden plush covered teddy bear, with black stitched nose, glass eyes, elongated limbs, joined claws, stitched across pads and slight hump, probably by Farnell, pads replaced, growler inoperative, c1925, 22in (56cm). **£300-400** *CSK*

A golden plush covered teddy bear with elongated limbs, boot button eyes, wide apart ears, felt pads, pronounced snout, hump, growler and Steiff button in ear, c1907, 28in (71cm) high.
£4,000-4,500 *CSK*

A German Schuco yes/no bellboy teddy bear, with orange plush head, hands and feet, amber and black glass eyes, black stitched nose and snout, in red felt jacket and black trousers as torso and limbs, red felt cap at rakish angle, tail operating turning and nodding of head, 15in (38cm) high. **£1,500-2,000** *S*

A brown plush Steiff teddy bear, with black stitched snout, black button eyes and swivel jointed body with excelsior filling, button missing, c1908, 24.5in (62cm) high.
£4,000-5,000 *S(S)*

A Steiff teddy bear, blonde plush with black button eyes, with button in ear, worn, 26in (66cm) high.
£1,500-2,000 *S*

'Ted' originally belonged to Miss Rosa Florella Schmidt who was the daughter of an English mother and German father. In 1914 her father left the family home in Berkshire to return to Germany whilst his wife and daughter remained in England. Unfortunately Herr Schmidt never returned (presumably killed in the war) and this bear, his parting gift to his daughter, became immensely important to the little girl as this was all she had to remember him by. The bear stayed with Rosa all her life apart from a period during World War II when she was teaching in London and decided that he would be safer if he was evacuated to the countryside.

A teddy bear, c1920, 10in (25cm) high.
£100-150 *PC*

A teddy bear, 18in (46cm) high. **£100-150** *PC*

A teddy bear, 15in (38cm) high.
£100-150 *PC*

A mid brown plush Steiff teddy bear, early 20thC, 23.5in (60cm) high.
£1,500-2,000 *HSS*

A Steiff teddy bear, c1915, 29in (74cm) high.
£1,200-1,500 *PC*

A Hygienic Toys teddy bear, made for Peacock stores, 18thC.
£220-270 *PC*

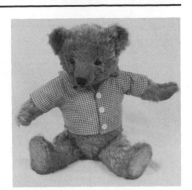

A teddy bear with a check jacket, 18in (46cm) high.
£140-180 *PC*

A German brown plush covered 'Circus Bear', possibly by Bing, with short fawn plush muzzle, one glass eye, down-turned paws, enlarged feet, with neck mechanism operated by lever in tail and flexible snap joints in hips, Steiff button in ear, slight hump, felt pads, stuffed with excelsior, 33in (84cm) high.
£1,500-2,000 *CSK*

A teddy bear, possibly Pedigree, with squeaker, 17in (43cm) high, c1950.
£120-140 *PC*

A Chad Valley teddy bear, 20in (51cm) high.
£90-110 *PC*

A Schuco yes/no brown plush teddy bear, with glass button eyes, felt pads on feet, turning the tail activates the bear's head, and the button on his chest activates the musical box within his body that plays 'Rock-A-By-Baby', 17in (43cm) high.
£300-500 *S(NY)*

'The Dancing Bears', a rare joined couple, the white plush lady bear with elongated limbs, brown glass eyes, brown stitched nose and claws, felt pads and cut muzzle, wearing striped cotton skirt, 10in (25cm) high, dancing with a golden plush covered gentleman bear with elongated limbs, brown glass eyes, black stitched nose and claws, felt pads and cut muzzle, wearing turquoise felt jacket and orange felt trousers, 12in (31cm) high, both with Steiff buttons in ears, c1910.   **£4,000-4,500** *CSK*

Lead Soldiers & Figures

A boxed set of W. Britains Bedouin Arabs.
£120-170 *HSS*

A Britains King's Troop Royal Horse Artillery gun team, boxed, incomplete.
£250-300 *HSS*

A Britains mounted gun team of The Royal Artillery.
£150-200 *HSS*

A Britains part set of The Knights of Agincourt, comprising a herald, 2 attendants, a tournament marshal and 3 mounted knights, 5 similar mounted knights, and 19 foot knights, various conditions.
£60-80 *HSS*

A Britains King's Troop Royal Artillery trotting gun team, together with an outrider at full gallop, boxed.
£250-300 *HSS*

A Britains set of 6 pipers from the Drum and Pipe Band of the Irish Guards, 4 11th Hussars, dismounted with horses,
£150-200 *HSS*

A Britains Coronation set, with box.
£350-450 *HSS*

An imported wooden play box, containing 12 model legionnaires and triple-barrel cannon with lead shot, the box when opened depicts a fort under attack, marked J. Robinson & Son, 172 Regent Street, London, Importers of Scientific Novelties, Opticians and Photographers, c1900.
£250-300 *RID*

A Britains Royal Navy landing party.
£150-170 *HSS*

A Britains collection of 15 painted lead anthropomorphic animals.
£70-100 *HSS*

A Britains collection of 18 mounted soldiers.
£200-250 *HSS*

Money Banks

An American cast iron Paddy and the Pig mechanical bank, by J. & E. Stevens, the figure with a blue jacket, the pig kicks the coin placed on his snout into Paddy's mouth, the base with patent date and coin trap, c1885, 7in (18cm).
£1,200-1,700 *S*

A painted cast iron 'Paddy and the Pig' mechanical bank, by J. & E. Stevens, designed by James H. Bowen, the pig's forepaw striking a coin into the figure's mouth, dark blue coat variant, with coin trap, 7in (18cm) long.
£1,500-2,000 *CSK*

An American Shepherd Hardware Company Stump Speaker cast iron mechanical bank, patent date on base, some paint chipping, c1880, 10in (25cm) high.
£3,000-3,500 *S*

'Magie Bank', a German lithographed tinplate mechanical bank of a wizard, with lever operated arms, standing behind a brightly decorated table, tray missing, 7in (18cm) high.
£600-700 *CSK*

A German tinplate sentry bank, for Lyon's toffee, the articulated figure raises his gun to present position, moves his eyes and accepts coin when the top lever is pressed, the back with cartoon figures, minor surface wear, 9in (22cm) high.   **£600-800** *S*

A German lithographed tinplate 'Saluting Sailor' money bank, possibly by Saalheimer and Strauss, the sailor standing in front of the gun breech, with spring-loaded saluting action, coin slot 'hidden' by his left elbow and key, c1920, 7in (18cm) high.
£700-900 *CSK*

Tinplate

A collection of Dinky diecast toys, comprising 20 boxed and 35 unboxed cars, mixed conditions, 1945-52.
£1,500-2,000 *S*

A Tippco clockwork tinplate Mercedes 770K 'Wagen des Führers' staff car with electrically lit headlights, in black and blued steel finish, 1939, some damage, 9in (23cm) long.
£600-800 *CSK*

A Karl Bub clockwork lithographed tinplate four-door limousine, with chauffeur in open-front compartment, opening side doors, tinplate artillery wheels, side lamps and headlamps, finished in lined red over black, c1912, 14in (36cm) long.   **£1,500-2,000** *CSK*

A Corgi Batmobile, No. 267, boxed.
£100-120 *HCH*

A Hessmobil 1024 lithographed
tinplate limousine, c1920, 10in
(25cm) long. **£500-600** *CSK*

A French wood and tinplate four-
seat open touring car, probably by
Jouets de Paris, with mahogany
and unpainted tin, the seats
covered in maroon silk, with cast
steering wheel and red painted
spoked wheels, and white rubber
tyres, 11.5in (29cm) long.
£1,000-1,200 *S*

A Schuco Studio 1050 tinplate
clockwork model driving school
racing car, boxed.
£100-120 *HCH*

A Bing lithographed tinplate
clockwork four-seat open tourer,
Cat. Ref. 10480/2, finished in
maroon with dark red and cream
lining, brake, steering front
wheels and tan 'buttoned' seats,
chauffeur missing, c1914, 10.5in
(26.5cm) long.
£1,000-1,200 *CSK*

A Distler lithographed tinplate
clockwork six-light saloon car
with electrically lit front indicator
and brake light, chauffeur,
opening windscreen and opening
rear doors, Cat. Ref. 667, finished
in blue over black with red lining,
one door and mascot missing,
c1920, 14in (36cm) long.
£500-600 *CSK*

A Märklin 'Der Kleine Spediteur'
clockwork cart, carrying 3 milk
churns, 3 wooden crates, paper
and string wrapped parcel, and 3
cotton sacks, 8in (21cm) long.
£1,500-2,000 *S*

A Rossignol clockwork
lithographed tinplate two-door
two-tone green roadster, with
Peugeot-style grille, registration
91-CR-921, front wheel drive and
rear wheel steering, 13in (33cm)
long.
£400-450 *CSK*

A French JEP tinplate Bugatti
racing car, finished in white,
numbered 4 and detailed in red,
with pressed tin wheels small
lithographed driver, adjustable
front axle, clockwork motor
driving rear wheels with integral
key, 16.5in 42cm) long.
£700-900 *S*

A Lehmann clockwork
lithographed tinplate EPL No.
760, racing car, finished in blue
and yellow, 6in (15cm) long.
£450-550 *CSK*

A Distler clockwork lithographed
tinplate four-light limousine,
finished in blue over black, with
artillery wheels folding bevelled
glass windscreen, chauffeur,
steering, opening doors and 2
boxes on running-boards, c1920,
12in (31cm) long.
£1,500-2,000 *CSK*

A Bing tinplate taxi, finished in
scarlet and maroon, with black
roof, hinged rear doors, adjustable
front wheels, handbrake, white
rubber tyres on spoked wheels,
clockwork motor driving rear
wheels, applied lithographed
maker's plaque to rear, worn,
c1909, 10in (26cm) long.
£2,500-3,500 *S*

A Distler tinplate limousine, the clockwork vehicle lithographed in dark blue with pastel blue lining, light green spoked wheels and finished in thick lacquer in parts, uniformed chauffeur, front lamps, glazed front windscreen and opening rear doors, damaged, c1920, 12in (30.5cm) long.
£650-900 *S*

A tinplate clockwork open top double decker Electric Omnibus Company bus, early 20thC.
£350-400 *HSS*

A Buick tinplate police car by Ichiko of Japan, with push-and-go mechanism, rotating roof lights and retractable roof radar, with original box.
£70-90 *WAL*

A Chad Valley lithographed tinplate single deck Greenline bus, finished in green, as a Windsor service, with hollow tin wheels, clockwork motor driving rear wheels, 12in (30cm) long.
£800-1,000 *S*

An André Citroen clockwork painted tinplate B2 10hp Torpedo four-seat tourer, finished in blue, with leathercloth seats and folded hood, windscreen, steering and brake, in original box inscribed 'Noel 1925', box repaired, 15in (38cm) long.
£1,200-1,500 *CSK*

A Minic tinplate double decker London Transport bus, in red and cream with 'Ovaltine' and 'Bovril' advertisements, and a Minic tinplate single deck Greenline bus with 'Bisto' advertisement on the back and Dorking destination board.
£100-120 *WAL*

A Hans Eberl tinplate clockwork limousine, lithographed in red, black and yellow, with 'pyjama' striping to rear coachwork, grey roof, running boards and mudguards, complete with driver, opening doors, glass windscreen, removable lights and key, 14in (35.5cm) long.
£1,100-1,500 *S*

A Japanese tinplate 1950 type Cadillac saloon, finished in 2-tone blue with push-and-go mechanism, in original box.
£30-40 *WAL*

A 'Rico' (Richards & Co) lithographed tinplate novelty turnover clown car, with 'patchwork' surface in red, blue, and yellow, pressed tin wheels with clown faces to hubs, pressed tin clown driver, clockwork motor driving rear wheels, damaged, 10.5in (26.5cm) long.
£1,500-2,000 *S*

A Bing clockwork painted tinplate two-seat motor car, Cat. Ref. 14138/4, finished in yellow with red lining and red 'buttoned' seats, with single headlamp, full-length mudguards, steering and hollow rubber tyres, c1906, 8.5in (21.5cm) long.
£1,200-1,500 *CSK*

A Märklin painted tin train station, with a red mansard roof, pierced windows, a hinged door, and outdoor passenger covered waiting area, a bench and a ticket office, finished in yellow on a green base, c1920, 18in (46cm) long.
£1,300-1,500 *S(NY)*

A Märklin painted tin Central Station, the central tower with hipped roof, flag, foliate eaves, and arched pierced glazed windows, with a waiting room and telegraph room, 2 hinged doors revealing candles, 14in (36cm) long.
£2,000-2,500 *S(NY)*

A Bing painted tin train station, with 6 pierced windows, a central entrance hall, a textured tiled roof and the walls painted to simulate brick, c1905, 14in (36cm) long.
£400-500 *S(NY)*

A Bing painted tin train station 'Central Bahnhof', with a double mansard roof, 4 hinged doors and a pierced railing surrounding the whole station, finished in cream with grey trim on a green base, 13in (33cm) long.
£1,200-1,500 *S(NY)*

A Lehmann 'Mars' No. 825 tank, in lithographed grey tinplate, with clockwork mechanism and rubber tyres, marked Jane, driver missing, c1940, 5.5in (14cm) long.
£400-600 *CSK*

A Doll & Co. tinplate rope railway, with 2 hand painted tin cars running on metal chains between ground level and mountain huts, turning handle on the side, 14in (36cm) wide.
£750-800 *S*

A Lehmann tinplate novelty 'Ski Rolf' toy, marked EPL 781, the figure dressed in blue, on mustard yellow skis, clockwork mechanism to torso, 7.5in (19cm) high, together with a Mickey Mouse clockwork handcar, with 4 wheels, lithographed red with image of Goofy running, and painted composition figures of Mickey and Minnie, 7in (18cm) long.
£1,700-2,000 *S*

A Roullet et Decamps clockwork acrobat on a tricycle, the figure with a bisque head and brown glass eyes balances on his hands on his bike, wearing a red and white silk clown costume, the clockwork mechanism activates his hands on the front wheels and the bike to move and his head moves side to side, 11in (28cm) long.   **£1,500-1,700** *S(NY)*

A French tinplate clockwork model speedboat.
£120-170 *HCH*

An American Lionel painted tin clockwork 'Speed Craft' No. 44, with driver and passenger, finished in white and red, complete with a stand and instructions, in its original box, 17in (43cm) long.
£500-1,000 *S(NY)*

A German painted tin clockwork bicyclist toy, the mechanism activates the rear tyre and the legs, one leg missing, 8in (20cm) long.
£500-700 *S(NY)*

A Japanese Nomura 'Mechanised Robot', 'Robby', battery operated tinplate toy, with silver finish, perspex dome to head covering mechanism with 4 working pistons, antennae to sides to dome, black rubber hands, black painted feet, legs with battery compartments, start/stop lever to chest, in original cardboard box, 12.5in (32cm) high, together with a Masudaya Radicon Radio Remote Control bus, with silver finish, black rubber tyres, in original cardboard box, with control unit and instructions, 14in (36cm) long. **£3,500-4,000** *S*

A German tinplate clockwork motorcycle and rider, by Arnold, the side mounting rider seated on a Mac 700 bike with coloured lithographed details, 8in (20cm) long.
£250-300 *HSS*

A Danish hand painted tinplate fire pumper toy, finished in red, gold, and black, with pressed tin wheels and 2 figures, pulled by a white horse, some paint loss, 14in (35cm) long.
£800-1,200 *S*

A Wolverine painted and lithographed tinplate clockwork No. 48 'Zilotone', with clown musician playing xylophone, controlled by cam-action tune disc, with discs for Silent Night, The Farmer in the Dell, and Listen to the Mocking Bird, c1920, 7in (18cm) high.
£500-800 *CSK*

A hand painted tinplate horse drawn carriage, possibly by Buchner, the body finished in cream lined blue and orange, with opening doors, grey lined white undercarriage and suspension, spoked cast wheels, pulled by 2 brown painted carved wood horses, mid-19thC.
£800-1,200 *S*

A Lehmann clockwork tinplate tricycle, 20thC, 5in (13cm) long. **£80-120** *HSS*

An American clockwork velocipede, possibly by George Hawkins and William Farr Goodwin, the tricycle decorated in red with floral stencil work and blue cast iron wheels, 9in (23cm) long.
£650-850 *S(NY)*

A German tinplate clockwork 'Mickey Mouse' organ grinder toy, probably Distler, Mickey as grinder to side, miniature Minnie to top dancing to accompany him, clockwork mechanism within bright hurdy-gurdy organ, pressed tin wheels, damaged, 8in (20cm) high.
£2,000-2,500 *S*

Miscellaneous

A painted tinplate horse drawn cabriolet, probably French, finished in yellow with black lining, with silk lined folding leathercloth hood, blue buttoned silk upholstery, rein rail, 2 whip sockets, rubber tyres and C-springs, c1890, 14in (36cm) long.
£350-450 *CSK*

A French pink suede covered clockwork walking pig, 11.5in (30cm) long.
£170-220 *HSS*

'Negro', a felt-covered clockwork walking figure by Schuco, dressed as a bell-hop, with on/off switch on his back, some damage, c1920, 10in (25cm) high.
£1,700-2,000 *CSK*

A painted wooden frog, with glass eyes, tin flippers and clockwork swimming mechanism.
£200-250 *CSK*

A Merrythought orange and cream velvet stuffed figure of Bonzo the dog, 22in (56cm) high.
£200-300 *HSS*

A painted papier mâché Mickey Mouse display, probably English, the cartoon figure in characteristic pose, some paint loss to ears, c1950, 36in (92cm) high.
£800-1,000 *S*

A painted papier mâché Donald Duck display, probably English, c1950, slight paint loss, 26in (66cm) high. **£300-500** *S*

A matchstick construction model of an Austin Seven touring motor car, made by the late Alec Sales of Hull, reputedly using in excess of 40,000 matches to complete over a period of 18 months, 35in (89cm) long. **£100-120** *DDM*

A carved painted wooden rocking horse, probably by G. & J. Lines, on a safety stand with shaped stretchers, glass eyes, remains of padded saddle, pommel holes and distressed chairs at either end, late 19thC, 70in (177.5cm) long. **£1,500-2,000** *CSK*

A child's carved wooden horse, painted in naturalistic colours and wearing a red fabric bridle and saddle, standing on a platform and 4 wheels, 20.5in (52cm) high. **£200-250** *WIL*

A French wood and metal pull-along child's car, dark green with red and yellow striped panels, red undercarriage, wooden spoked wheels with iron rims, leather trim with brass beading, ceramic handle to draw bar, restored, c1903, 26in (66.5cm) wide. **£3,000-5,000** *S(S)*

An American Gendron Packard twin six pedal car, original red with black and yellow lining and black wings, wooden chassis, pressed steel body and wings, opening door, cast iron steps, bell-type headlamps, drum rear lights, opening boot, imitation dashboard, side-mounted spare wheel with cover, adjustable windscreen, imitation ignition control to wood-rimmed steering wheel, solid rubber tyres, unrestored, c1927, 65.5in (166cm) long. **£4,200-6,000** *S(S)*

An Italian Giordini Indianapolis pedal car, in Italian racing red with cream vinyl upholstery, pressed steel construction, chromium plated external exhausts, windscreen, imitation brake drums, electric horn, one rear view mirror, racing number 6, solid tyres, c1950, 50.5in (128cm) long. **£800-1,000** *S(S)*

A French veteran pedal car, dark blue with light blue panels and cream lining, with wooden body, steel undercarriage, radially spoked wheels with solid rubber tyres, wood rimmed steering wheel, steps, oil lamps, deep buttoned upholstery, restored, 1905, 49in (124.5cm) long. **£5,000-6,500** *S(S)*

A child's pedal sports car, probably by Lines Brothers, c1950. **£700-900** *LRG*

An H. J. Mulliner MG two-door drophead pedal car, maroon with beige, coachbuilt with hand made aluminium panels, opening bonnet, near side door and boot, removable spats, electric lights and horn, internal handbrake, perspex windscreen, ace-type rear number plate box, chromium-plated bumber bars with overriders, solid rubber tyres, c1939, 56in (142cm) long. **£6,500-9,500** *S(S)*

A scratch-built Ferrari Testarossa 250 child's sports car, yellow, welded box-section steel chassis, fibreglass body, polished alloy wood-rimmed steering wheel, working lights and brakes, tonneau cover, clutchless transmission, pneumatic tyres, unused, 1958, 74in (188cm) long. **£2,000-3,000** *S(S)*

A Phillips 4.5 litre supercharged Bentley child's electric car, British racing green, fibreglass body with wood and steel strengthening, 4-wheel cable operated drum brakes, cast aluminium dummy supercharger, electric lights, external handbrake, foot accelerator and brake pedals, gear change lever, side-mounted spare wheel, tonneau cover, pneumatic tyres, wire spoked wheels, 12-volt electric motor with belt drive to lay shaft and chain drive to back axle, c1965, 76in (193cm) long. **£3,000-4,000** *S(S)*

A scratch built Bentley 3 litre pedal car, British racing green, pressed steel, part fabric covered, opening bonnet with leather strap, external handbrake lever, bucket seat, perspex windscreen, spare wheel mounted at the rear, wire spoked wheels, pneumatic tyres, c1980, 56in (142cm) long.
£2,500-3,500 *S(S)*

An Austin J40 pedal car, red with black upholstery, heavy gauge pressed steel, dummy engine, opening boot and bonnet, handbrake, lights, pneumatic tyres, restored, c1955, 60in (152cm) long. **£700-1,200** *S(S)*

A Lines Brothers Bullnose Morris pedal car, field grey with black mudguards, wooden chassis and wood and metal body, opening door, fold-back windscreen, adjustable seat, pressed steel wheels, rubber tyres, in original condition, c1927, 42in (107cm) long. **£3,500-4,500** *S(S)*

A German painted wooden Noah's Ark, with about 100 pairs of animals and 8 figures, Noah with a beard, together with a framed and glazed printed list of the contents, and a baby ark, with 22 animals and 4 figures, mid-19thC, large ark 18in (46cm) long.
£2,000-2,500 *S*

A German carved and painted wood hunting set, comprising 5 mounted figures and 10 hounds, some woodworm, c1920, figures 7in (18cm) high.
£1,000-1,500 *S*

A coloured straw-work Noah's Ark, with sliding panel and a quantity of painted wooden animals including Noah's family, damaged, 13in (33cm) long. **£1,000-1,200** *CSK*

A German painted wooden Noah's Ark, finished in cream and brown, with hollow bottom, lower storey fitted with three fenced stables, falling front, upper storey with removable front, sloping half hinged roof, with about 35 painted animals, worn, late 19thC, 22in (55cm) long.
£800-1,200 *S*

A flying model of the Westland Lysander, Serial No. V 9350, with fabric covered wooden airframe, glow-plug engine, carburettor and fuel tank removed, rubber tyred undercarriage and finished in RAF camouflage, 59in (150cm) wingspan.
£350-450 *CSK*

Models

A detailed model of the Focke-Wulf Fw 190-A6 single-seater fighter, serial No. 1-5, finished in camouflage and mounted on an airstrip plinth, glazed case, 6in (15.5cm) wide.
£220-270 *C*

A large scale flying model of a Messerschmitt Me 323 'Gigant', with provision for 6 engines, 72in (183cm) long.
£450-550 *CSK*

A flying model of a Curtiss Tomahawk, engine removed, 60in (152.5cm) wingspan.
£350-450 *CSK*

A flying model of the Fokker D VIII parasol monoplane, Serial No. 238, with glow-plug engine, finished in green, red and yellow with Maltese crosses, 52in (132cm) wingspan.
£200-300 *CSK*

A detailed 1:24 scale static display model of the Supermarine Spitfire Mk. IX, Serial No. MH486, in the camouflage and markings of 132 Sqn., RAF, built by T. Scott, c1944, 19in (48cm) wingspan.
£350-550 *CSK*

A detailed flying model of the Fokker DR1, Serial No. 152/17, with glow-plug engine, finished in red, red and white stripes, and green, with Maltese crosses, 46in (117cm) wingspan.
£450-550 *CSK*

A flying model of the Supermarine Seagull prototype, finished in green and cream with RAF markings, 57in (145cm) wingspan.   **£350-450** *CSK*

A detailed flying model of the Sopwith Camel, C1701, Fiji 19 glow-plug engine, 56in (142.5cm) wingspan.
£500-600 *CSK*

'Battle of Britain Flypast', a 1:144 scale aluminium model of the RAF Memorial Flight Lancaster, Spitfire and Hurricane, by Doug Vaan, 9.5in (24cm) wide.
£350-450 *C*

A Karl Bub 0-4-0 O gauge electric locomotive, No. 1-48, in green, red and pale green livery, some damage, 10.5in (26cm) long. **£90-120** *HCH*

A Lionel 2-4-0 'Bild-a-Loco' electric locomotive No. 384, in black livery with brass mounts, 12in (31cm) long. **£80-120** *HCH*

A German Doll et Cie tinplate model steam engine, with vertical boiler and horizontal engine, dummy boiler and mounted on a 4-wheel chassis, altered, 12.5in (32cm) wide. **£200-300** *Bea*

A Bassett Lowke Gauge I electric 2-6-0 locomotive, finished in LMS maroon and black, with matching 6-wheeled tender numbered 13000 in gold, some damage, 25in (63cm) long. **£600-900** *S*

A model of an English 1830 stagecoach, in black, blue and red livery and brass mounts, supported on a wooden plinth, 20thC, 10in (25.5cm) high. **£200-300** *WIL*

A Hornby 0-Gauge 'Princess Elizabeth' 20-volt 4-6-2 locomotive and tender with original presentation box, complete with illustrated details inside lid, c1937. **£3,000-3,500** *DDM*

A model of a cargo vessel, Lexden Hall, the wooden hull painted black and salmon pink, uncased, early 20thC, 102in (259cm) long. **£2,200-2,700** *HSS*

A Continental model hull of a Fourth Rater, painted planked construction, carved and gilded stern, part of the figurehead missing, c1660, 29in (74cm) long. **£2,500-3,000** *WW*

GAMES
Chess Sets

A Cantonese red and natural ivory chess set, each carved piece on pierced concentric ball pedestal bases, kings 7in (17cm) high, together with a highly decorated lacquered chess/backgammon board with mother-of-pearl white squares, and a vellum-covered carrying case, late 19thC. **£450-550** *S*

A four-handed chess set, comprising 4 tournament sized sets of Staunton pattern, one of natural ivory, one red stained ivory, one boxwood, and one ebony, with a booklet containing 'Rules and a List of Members of the London Four-Handed Chess Club', and another blue covered booklet with gold lettering 'Rules of the Game of Four-Handed Chess', and with large folding chess board of mahogany with satinwood and ebony squares, in an oak case with brass handles, some damage, c1880, kings 4.5in (11.5cm) high. **£3,000-5,000** *S*

Miscellaneous Games

A 'Novelty Merchantman' Crane by the Exhibit Supply Co. Chicago, the crane takes the form of the bow end of a merchant ship with the grab as a derrick mounted on the foredeck, contained in glazed wood and cast iron case, 71in (180cm) high.
£400-700 *Bon*

A JEP platform car racing game, with circular track around which 5 small cast racers spin by lever mechanism, with lid, box base covered in black textured paper, 10.5in (27cm) wide.
£300-400 *S*

A Bryans Quadmatic Allwin, with 2 Elevenses Allwins, a 7-cup Allwin with 5 winning and 2 losing cups, and a U-Win Allwin with one large U-shaped winning cup and 2 smaller losing cups, 66in (167.5cm) high.
£600-1,000 *Bon*

MUSIC
Musical Instruments

A Bundfrei clavichord, by Pehr Lindholm, Stockholm, the facia board of mahogany with boxwood stringing, the case of mahogany, the four and a half octave keyboard with ebony naturals and bone overlaid accidentals, on frame stand with square tapered legs, labelled on the soundboard Förfardigadt af Pehr Lindholm, Instrumentmakare Stockholm ar 1792, 64in (163.5cm) long.
£5,000-6,000 *S(S)*

Clavichords were the first stringed instruments with keyboards, the predecessor of the piano.

A Bundfrei clavichord, probably Danish, the interior and the keyboard surround painted red, the 5 octave keyboard with ebony naturals and ivory overlaid accidentals, bistrung throughout and with additional 4ft. stringing in the bass up to f, on 4 cabriole legs carved with gilded acanthus leaves on the knees, inscribed Factum Anno 1768, Rep. 1918 Hockauf, 69in (175cm) long, c1770.
£8,000-9,000 *S(S)*

A mahogany cased baby grand piano, by Bechstein with plain repolished case, no. 240228, 59in (149.5cm) wide, together with a mahogany duet stool.
£1,500-2,000 *DDM*

A walnut cased baby grand piano by Hagspiel, Dresden, with ripple mouldings and 2 brass pedals on a lyre-shaped support, raised on 3 tapered octagonal legs with brass casters, 70in (177cm) long.
£1,500-2,000 *S(S)*

An English chamber barrel organ, on a stand containing spare barrel, c1800, 51in (130cm) high.
£1,200-1,700 *CSK*

A grand piano, by Bechstein, model B, no. 105019, the ebonised case with tapering octagonal legs and brass casters, 80in (203cm) long.
£800-1,200 *Bea*

A boudoir grand piano, by Bechstein, the walnut case on 3 pairs of tapering square legs with brass casters, 81in (205.5cm) long.
£2,000-2,500 *Bea*

A grand piano, by John Broadwood & Son, in a crossbanded mahogany case with satinwood interior and inscribed nameboard, on a mahogany trestle stand with brass casters, c1806, 89.5in (227cm) long.
£4,000-5,000 *C*

An Art Deco style walnut cased baby grand piano, by Monington & Veston of London, on inlaid block supports, with iron frame overstrung movement, no. 60013, 50in (127cm) long.
£1,600-2,000 *DDM*

A rare German 32in Polyphon Concerto orchestrion, the coin-operated 101 key movement playing on side and bass drums, cymbals, 10 tubular bells and symmetrical piano, driven by massive spring, contained in stained wood case with double doors at the front with etched glass panels, pediment above with trade name, on matching base with drop front for disc storage together with 10 metal discs, restored, c1905, 103.5in (262cm) high.
£20,000-25,000 *S*

The Polyphon Concerto was the largest of the Polyphon disc machines and was only produced in very limited numbers. Regina imported the Polyphon Concerto and sold it in the U.S.A. as the Regina Sublims.

A square piano, by Frederic Beck of Broad Street, Soho, with mahogany and inlaid case-on-stand, with square tapering supports and brass paterae headers, dated 1790.
£1,100-1,500 *LRG*

A Gothic revival straight strung piano, by Gebruder Knake, Munster, the oak case pierced and carved, with brass candle arms and side handles, 64in (162.5cm) wide.
£1,000-1,500 *Bea*

An orchestrion, with piano, xylophone, base and snare drums, cymbal, tambourine and wood block housed in an oak case with 2 leaded coloured glass panels, the piano movement with metal frame 'Wellington No. 211511' by the Cable Co., Chicago, coin slot to take American quarters, 61.5in (156cm) long, with 2 'O' ten-tune Play-rite rolls and transformer.
£4,000-5,000   *ALL*

A George III mahogany cased chamber barrel organ, playing 15in cylinders and with a range of 45 pipes, coronet-applied gilt metal rose spray and square legs, 58in (148cm) high, and 2 barrels from another organ, 19in (48cm).
£1,500-2,000   *P(O)*

A chamber barrel organ, playing 8 airs with 62 keys and stoppered wooden pipes, in a walnut veneered cabinet with fabric front, side and cornice panels, 68in (172.5cm) high.
£250-300   *Bea*

A Regina Sublima piano, with 73-note roll-operated mechanism, electric motor drive, coin mechanism with mercury switch, printed instruction sheet and oak case, no. 3040666, suppliers label Barney, Newport R.I., 70in (170cm) high, with 4 rolls.
£2,500-3,000   *CSK*

A Seybold & Hohner 'Magic Organa' automatic accordian, the paper roll mechanism operated by foot pedal, contained in original case with separate case for foot pedal and with 7 paper rolls.
£3,000-4,000 *S*

The foot operated vacuum pump was designed to be operated unobtrusively. The vacuum supply tube could be connected from the separate foot pump to the accordian by running the tube up the operator's trouser leg, through his shirt, and out through his shirt sleeve, at which point it was connected to the accordian.

A Tanzbar automatic concertina, by A. Zuleger of Leipzig, the paper roll mechanism operated by crank lever mounted on the side in conjunction with bellows, complete with rewind handle, and 12 paper rolls, 10in (26cm) wide.
£700-900 *S*

An Italian violin, school of Gabrielli, attributed to Pier Lorenzo Vangelisti, the 2-piece back of broad figure, similar ribs, the scroll of plain wood, the table of medium to open grain, dark golden varnish over a lighter ground, the back 14in (36cm) long, with a letter from W. E. Hill & Sons dated 18 May 1953.
£8,500-9,500 *C*

A violin, by Sebastian Vuillaume, Paris, labelled Jean Baptiste Vuillaume à Paris, 3 rue Demours-Ternes JBV 1965, with the certificate of Hulmuth A. Keller, Philadelphia, 7th April 1969, the one-piece back of medium curl descending from left to right, the ribs of similar curl, the head of faint narrow curl, the table of fine grain in the centre opening out towards the flanks, the varnish of a red brown colour, the back 14in (36cm) long, in a case with outer canvas cover.
£7,200-8,000 *S*

A violin, by Emile Laurent, labelled Fait par Emile Laurent/à Paris l'an 1928, inscribed by the maker, the 2-piece back of medium curl, the ribs and scroll similar, the table of open grain, red colour varnish over a golden ground, the back 14in (36cm) long.
£3,500-4,000 *C*

A gold mounted violin bow, by François Nicolas Voirin, branded F. N. Voirin à Paris, the round stick mounted with a gold and ebony frog with Paris eye and gold-sheathed adjuster, 60.5gr.
£8,500-9,000 *C*

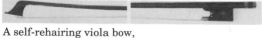

A self-rehairing viola bow, Pajeot/Maire style, unbranded, the round stick mounted with a nickel and ebony frog and adjuster, 64gr.
£1,700-2,000 *C*

A Cremona school violin, with exceptionally wide lower bouts, the 2-piece back of wood cut on the slab of narrow horizontal curl, the ribs of similar wood, the head probably later of medium curl, the table of medium to fine grain, golden brown varnish, c1700, the back 14.5in (36cm).
£2,000-4,000 *S(S)*

An English seven-keyed Serpent, the body of leather bound wood, brass mounts, brass keys with circular covers, ivory bushed fingerholes, one missing, brass crook, ivory and brass mouthpiece from another instrument, c1835, 102in (259cm) long.
£2,000-2,500 *S(S)*

A six-course guitar, ascribed to Francesco Sanguino, the table with extensive inlays in mother-of-pearl and various woods both around the sound hole, c1780, 18.5in (47cm) long.
£6,500-7,500 *S(S)*

A guitar, with rosewood back and sides, boxwood inlay and stringing, mother-of-pearl bands and insets, c1900, 37in (94cm) long, in a plush lined burr walnut veneered case.
£300-350 *GAK*

A walnut and giltwood harp, by Jackson, 7 Molesworth Street, Dublin, with 8 foot pedals, the maker's name inscribed on the brass harmonica curve, 66in (167.5cm) high.
£850-900 *GH*

A Regency bird's-eye maple harp, by I. & I. Erat, with gilt-gesso neo-Grecque mouldings, the brass plate engraved I. & I. Erat, patent Harp Manufacturers, 23 Berners Street, London, No. 2217, 68in (172.5cm) high.
£15,000-17,000 *S(S)*

A cross strung harp, inscribed Harpe S** G Lyon B**, Pleyel Wolff Lyon & Cie, Paris, 73in (185cm) high.
£5,000-5,500 *S(S)*

An 11-keyed boxwood oboe, probably German, with detachable top finial, ivory mounts, brass keys with circular covers, c1860, 21.5in (55cm) long.
£1,000-1,200 *S(S)*

Musical Boxes

A 10-keyed boxwood oboe, by Jacques Nonon, Paris, with onion and cotton reel finial, brass mounts, brass keys including the Brille key, the Eflat key with duplicate touchpiece, stamped Nonon, Paris, with the device of a treble clef, 22in (56cm) long.
£1,500-2,000 *S(S)*

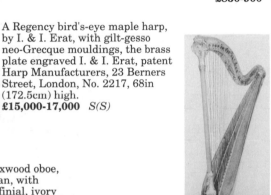

A Swiss orchestral cylinder musical box, with 16in (41cm) cylinder playing 8 airs, with snare drum, 8 bells and castanets in sight by Nicole Frères, No. 43590, retailed by John A. Mills, London, in floral marquetry rosewood case with gilt brass side handles, 19thC, 26in (66cm) wide.
£2,000-2,500 *GSP*

A Swiss Sublime Harmony interchangeable cylinder musical box-on-stand, each of the six 39cm cylinders playing a selection of 8 popular airs, raised on 4 ebonised wood cabriole legs, 50in (127cm) long.
£10,000-12,000 *S*

A Grand Format musical box, by Nicole Frères, No. 32027, playing 4 overtures (Freischutz, Robert le Diable, William Tell and La Fille du Regiment), Gamme No. 1500, with lever wind, 3-wing governor, engraved tune sheet, Imhof & Mukle instructions for key-wind boxes, and label on base, the rosewood veneered case inlaid on front and lid in brass, enamel and mother-of-pearl, 28.5in (72cm) wide, on a later fitted walnut stand with turned legs.
£17,000-20,000 *CSK*

A Polyphon disc musical box, the coin-operated movement with periphery drive and twin combs, contained in upright wood case with glazed door at the front, and sides with coin chute and winding handle, surmounted by shaped pediment, c1900, 48in (122cm) high, and 12 metal discs.
£5,000-6,000 *S*

A German Symphonion 'rococo' disc musical box, the sublime harmonie comb arrangement contained in ornately mounded wood case with velvet lined lid interior inset with coloured silk print of an amorous couple, c1905, 19in (48cm) wide, with approximately 38 metal discs.
£3,000-3,500 *S*

A Swiss figured walnut, amboyna and ebonised cased Sublime Harmony musical box, the 13in (33cm) interchangeable brass cylinder and 2 comb movement playing 6 airs, with butterfly shaped fly wheel, no. 15976, the case inlaid with mother-of-pearl and brass, with kingwood banding and strung with ebony and box, and with gilt brass foliate cast fixed handles to the sides, 19thC, 40in (102cm) long.
£2,000-3,000 *HSS*

Phonographs

A 'Puck' type phonograph, with green and gold painted base cast as a mermaid, floating reproducer, flower horn, maker's carton, instruction sheet and dealer's letter dated 1908.
£900-1,200 *CSK*

The letter, sent out by the United Phonograph Co., of 5 Helmet Row, E.C., indicates that the phonograph was being offered as a promotional scheme, for 5s. 11d. to cover postage and packing, with an option to 12 cylinders at 11d. each. A circular on the instruction sheet offers a free gramophone to the purchaser of 50 cylinders, or to a customer selling 8 phonographs among friends. By July 1908, a company with large stocks of Puck phonographs would have been very anxious to dispose of them by any means.

A Swiss and English Bremond mandoline, interchangeable cylinder musical box-on-stand, each of the six 33cm cylinders playing 6 airs as indicated by pointer and listed on tune sheet, contained in walnut veneered case and mounted on non-original aesthetic movement mahogany table with 2 cylinder storage drawers in the front, c1880, 41in (104cm) wide.
£3,000-5,000 *S*

A cabinet phonograph, incorporating a Model A Edison Triumph mechanism 45035 with 2-speed pulley and Diamond C reproducer connected via telescopic tapered brass arm to a flower horn within the cabinet, with approximately 24 two minute and four minute cylinders, 49in (124.5cm) high.
£1,500-2,000 *CSK*

An Edison 'Red Gem' phonograph, model D, no. 359142, with Model K reproducer, on an oak plinth beneath a bentwood cover with carrying handle, together with a red painted 'Fireside' horn and horn crane.
£500-600 *HSS*

An Edison 'Gem' phonograph, cased with aluminium horn and 12 rolls, winding handle missing.
£300-350 *WIL*

An Edison Fireside phonograph, Model A, no. 93470, with Model R large diaphragm reproducer, no. 10 Cygnet horn, now with Music Master style transfer, substitute crane, repolished pale oak case and replica Model K reproducer, gear cover missing.
£900-1,200 *CSK*

An Edison Concert phonograph, Model A No. C6840, now with combination pulley, standard and slip-on Concert mandrel, C reproducer with adapter, Triton motor, Edison Bell plaque, oak case with banner transfer and brass carrying handles, and large brass horn with folding tripod stand, 40in (102cm) long.
£1,200-1,700 *CSK*

Gramophones

A Dulcephone horn gramophone, with Dulcephone single-spring motor in walnut case with carved mouldings, Dulcephone (Lindstroem 'Reform') soundbox on ball-jointed arm and green flower horn.
£400-600 *CSK*

Dulcephone was the main brand name of Barnett Samuel up to 1914. Although both motor and back bracket are cast with the name this machine is clearly of Lindstroem manufacture.

A Monarch Senior gramophone by Gramophone & Typewriter Co., with original brass horn, c1904.
£1,000-1,200 *BTA*

An 'Academy' mahogany gramophone, the cabinet decorated with white string inlay and transferred urn and swags, hinged lid opening to reveal turn table, with 2 doors which open to reveal speakers, supported on 4 square tapered splay legs and circular platform, 20thC.
£350-400 *WIL*

A Peter Pan alarm clock gramophone, c1925.
£800-1,200 *BTA*

An HMV Model 510 cabinet gramophone, with Lumière pleated diaphragm, quadruple spring motor and quarter veneered oak case with ebony stringing to doors, horizontally divided record compartment, and cabriole legs, c1924, 43.5in (110cm) high.
£1,500-2,000 *CSK*

A 'Trade Mark' gramophone, by the Gramophone Company, no. 5219, with March '98 Patent date, Clark-Johnson soundbox no. J19297, lacquered brass horn, leather elbow, record clamp, winding crank and cam-and-spring brake, the oak case with Gramophone Co. and Wallace Ash, Southsea transfers, c1898, a teak carrying case, a 7in Berliner record of God Save the Queen, and 4 other Berliner records, 2 cracked.
£2,500-3,000 *CSK*

A Cliftophone bijou grand gramophone, in oak cabinet on twist turned legs, with Cliftophone horizontal soundbox, internal wood horn with transfer enclosing panelled doors and gilt fittings, c1924, 32.5in (82cm) high.
£450-500 *CSK*

An EMG handmade gramophone, the papier-mâché horn with 28in (71cm) diameter mouth, and an oak case with 12in (31cm) turntable, c1930.
£2,500-3,000 *S*

A German double spring gramophone, with Art Nouveau light oak case and painted tin horn, 23in (59cm) diam.
£450-500 *WIL*

A Columbia disc gramophone, with original brass horn, c1912.
£1,000-1,200 *BTA*

A Klingsor gramophone, in oak case with pierced door to upper compartment containing horn aperture and strings and Klingsor soundbox in lower compartment with sloping flap, 27in (69cm) high.
£800-900 *CSK*

A horn gramophone, by H.M.V., with 12in turntable, Exhibition soundbox, mahogany horn and base with trade transfers, together with needle tin and accredited dealer enamelled badge, c1912. **£600-800** *S*

A Mark XB 'Tropical' handmade gramophone, by EMG Handmade Gramophones Ltd., 6 Newman St., with four-spring soundbox, Paillard GGR double-spring motor, crossbanded oak case and two-piece papier-mâché horn, 29.5in (75cm) diam.
£2,700-3,000 *CSK*

A 'His Master's Voice' horn gramophone, with patent dates for 1905 and examination date for 1913, 28in (71cm) high.
£800-1,000 *DDM*

A Victorian penny-in-the-slot type Polyphon, by Nicole Frères, the twin combs playing 15.5in (39cm) discs, in an upright walnut cabinet with architectural features, 34in (86cm) high, and 30 discs of popular songs, etc., in an oak case.
£6,000-7,000 *RBB*

A walnut cased wall mounted penny-in-slot Polyphon disc player, playing discs of 20in (50cm) diam., with a plaque on the side inscribed 'Drop A Penny In The Slot - Nicole Frères - Leipzig', the base set with a drawer, and on baluster turned and tapering front supports, 51in (130cm) high, together with 24 discs. **£2,500-4,500** *HSS*

Miscellaneous

A William and Mary silver mounted shagreen instrument case, with shallow drawer and narrow silver borders, the elaborate hinges and lockplate engraved with stylised flowers and pierced with kidney shaped motifs, the slightly raised cover with applied oval plaque engraved with the arms of the Barber Surgeons' Company and with the initials ME and dated 1695, the mounts unmarked, the interior inscribed indistinctly in ink 'This Box with Instruments Bought June 9th, 1695'.
£3,500-4,500 *C*

Without doubt the most important instrument case to have survived is that applied with the enamelled coat-of-arms of King Henry VIII, now in the collection of The Worshipful Company of Barbers, and given to them by the King, probably in 1512. The case also bears the arms of the Barbers' Company and below it the badge of the Fellowship of Surgeons. During the reign of Henry VIII the two were incorporated becoming the Barber-Surgeons' Company in 1540.

A similar instrument case to the present shagreen example, also engraved with the Barber-Surgeon's Arms and with the intials IK, possibly for John Knight, sergeant-surgeon to King Charles II in 1661, is also in the collection of the The Worshipful Company of Barbers.

An Ami Continental II two hundred selection jukebox, with traditional domed glass cover, c1962.
£1,500-2,000 *Bon*

A German 19.5in (49cm) Polyphon disc musical box, 19thC, 48in (122cm) high, together with 10in discs.
£3,000-4,000 *AG*

BOXES

A mahogany and marquetry tea caddy, with a hinged brass handle, c1790, 8in (20cm) wide.
£400-500 *S(S)*

A George III mahogany tea caddy, with folding brass handle, interior with 3 compartments and pen tray, on bun feet, 9.5in (24cm).
£200-250 *WIL*

A Queen Anne walnut tea caddy, inlaid with geometric fruitwood banding, the interior with 2 divisions, with waved apron, on shaped bracket feet, the right side rising to reveal secret drawer, the base inscribed in pencil JBG twice, 11in (28cm) wide.
£1,000-1,500 *C*

A George III tea caddy, the interior with hinged lid, plush velvet and 2 lidded compartments, 5in (13cm) high.
£550-650 *WW*

A late George III tortoiseshell tea caddy, with canted angles, on silver plated ball feet, one replaced, 6in (16cm).
£400-500 *P(O)*

A Georgian fruitwood tea caddy, in the form of an apple, the stalk forming the handle 5in (13cm) high.
£1,000-1,200 *CSK*

A George III mirror panelled diamond shaped tea caddy, with interior lid, small crack, 7.5in (19cm).
£450-550 *WW*

A George III burr yew and boxwood banded tea caddy, with ivory escutcheon, 5in (13cm) high.
£70-80 *CSK*

A Regency amboyna and ebony 3 division tea caddy, of sarcophagus outline, the interior with cut glass mixing bowl, flanked by sliding canisters, ring handles to the sides, 15.5in (37cm) wide.
£350-450 *CSK*

A Regency rosewood tea caddy, with sarcophagus formed lid, box string inlaid, 2 sectioned interior, metal handles and feet, inscribed to the inner 'In the memory of the late William Foster Esquire'.
£150-200 *GAK*

A George III harewood tea caddy, the cover with floral patera, the front with ivory escutcheon and sprays of lily of the valley and mysotis, 6.5in (16cm) wide.
£550-600 *CSK*

A Regency penwork tea caddy.
£700-800 *JAC*

A Regency tortoiseshell tea caddy, with moulded 'starburst' front, the interior with 2 lidded compartments, 6.5in (16cm) wide.
£800-900 *Bea*

A tortoiseshell veneered hexagonal tea caddy, the domed top surmounted by a button finial, with a plinth base, veneer chipped, c1810, 5in (13cm) wide.
£600-800 *S(S)*

A rosewood tea caddy, with sarcophagus formed lid, squat circular feet, with 2 interior sections plus cut glass mixing bowl, early 19thC.
£350-400 *GAK*

A pair of George III mahogany knife boxes, crossbanded and with chequer stringing, with serpentine fronts and fitted interiors, on ogee bracket feet, 15.5in (39cm) high.
£1,500-2,000 *S(S)*

A pair of George III mahogany knife boxes, painted in polychrome with river landscapes, urns, flowerheads, foliage and lambrequin swags, with later converted interiors, 14.5in (37cm) high.
£2,000-2,500 *CSK*

A pair of Georgian mahogany serpentine front knife boxes, the hinged sloping covers having brass lion's mask ring handles, enclosing fitted interiors with boxwood stringing, 15in (39cm) high.   **£1,700-2,000** *RAG*

A Georgian mahogany knife box, with serpentine front, the top with shell inlay, converted for stationery.   **£400-500** *LRG*

A pair of George III inlaid mahogany cutlery boxes, each with serpentine fronts and fitted interiors, late 18thC, 14.5in (37cm) high.
£2,500-3,000 *S(NY)*

A Sheraton inlaid and crossbanded knife box, with fitted interior. the sloping lift-up lid with shell inlay patera, 9in (23cm) wide.   **£500-700** *HCH*

A 4 compartment smoker's box, on 4 elaborate scroll feet, the centre with matchbox holder on pedestal base, the interior of the compartments with grille between, 11.5in (29cm) long.
£1,000-1,500 *CNY*

A mahogany studded shoe snuff box, c1840, 5.5in (14cm) wide.
£200-350 *RdeR*

Two similar shagreen mounted knife boxes, with plush lined fitted interiors, containing 12 Hanoverian pattern table spoons, John Gorham, London, 1750, 24 steel bladed knives, with indistinct maker's mark and lion passant, all crested and with shell capped handles and wave mouldings, mid-18thC.
£6,200-7,000 *S(Ch)*

A late Victorian biscuit box, with straight fluted panels alternating with stamped foliage, fruit and scroll panels, the hinged domed cover with rounded rectangular finial, on an integral stand with 4 bun feet, maker's mark B.G. & Co. Ltd., Sheffield 1897, 7.5 by 5.5in (19 by 14cm), 1120gr.
£1,000-1,200 *HSS*

A smoker's box, carved in the form of a cabin trunk, with twin handles, the interior fitted with 2 trays, one with a canister and cigar holders, the top tray fitted with a meerschaum pipe bowl, a vesta case and 2 further cigar cases, 19thC, 14in (36cm) wide.
£1,500-2,000 *P(O)*

An early 19thC mahogany decanter box, 11in (28cm) wide.
£500-600 *HSS*

A mother-of-pearl and silver inlaid tortoiseshell snuff box, probably French, damaged, c1780, 3in (8cm) long, together with another mother-of-pearl inlaid and silver piquet point tortoiseshell snuff box, probably French, silver gilt mounts, damaged, mid-18thC, 3in (8cm) wide. £500-600 *S(C)*

A German silver mounted snuff box, painted with a goldfinch, a great tit, 2 bullfinches and a shrike attacking a fledgling, chipped and cracked, perhaps Höchst, c1770, 3.5in (9cm) wide.
£1,800-2,200 *C*

A French enamel double snuff box, waisted, one cover painted with the bust of a lady, the other with a farming scene, 19thC, 3.5in (9cm).
£550-650 *S(S)*

A rococo gold mounted hardstone snuff box, of cartouche form, with figured agate panels, the sides chased with scrolls and flowers on a stippled ground, maker's initials P.V., 3in (8cm). £800-1,000 *GSP*

A Mauchline ware cheroot box, signed, c1840, 3in (8cm) wide.
£150-250 *RdeR*

A monkey snuff box, 18thC, 3.5in (9cm) wide.
£200-400 *RdeR*

A Mauchline ware snuff box, pen worked and painted, 3in (8cm) wide.
£150-250 *RdeR*

A 19thC Continental micro-mosaic and gilt metal snuff box, the lid with finely detailed plaque of the Pliny doves, within engine turned panels with foliate angles, 3in (8cm), pseudo hallmarks,
£1,000-1,200 *GSP*

A French snuff box, overlaid with gilt on a maroon ground, the cover centred by a medallion of a classical scene, 19thC, 3in (8cm).
£350-450 *S(S)*

A coquilla nut snuff man, 18thC, 3in (8cm) high.
£300-400 *RdeR*

A Victorian trinket box, the front applied with a well cut and enamelled reverse crystal intaglio of a bulldog, the back sliding to reveal a gilt lined drawer, Thomas Johnson, London 1881, 3.5in (9cm).
£2,000-2,500 *CSK*

A yew wood stationery casket, in the form of a house, with hinged lid and architectural windows fitted with painted glass panes, worn, 19thC, 7.5in (19cm) high.
£1,000-1,200 *S(S)*

A Charles II blue grey and red painted boarded box, with hinged top, the panelled front carved with tulips amidst scrolling foliage, repair to top, partially redecorated, the right side later incised CF 1691, 24in (61cm) wide.
£2,000-2,500 *C*

The carving is similar to that on a chest of c1660 from Ottery St. Mary, Devon, and closely related to a group of chests, chairs and other items made in Ipswich, Massachusetts by William Searle, who was born and trained in Ottery St. Mary and moved to Ipswich by 1663; and Thomas Dennis (working in Ipswich 1668-1706). These English examples seem to represent a prototype for the Massachusetts style.

An enamel box, possibly Limoges, with allegorical scenes and The Rape of Europa on the lid, early 19thC.
£1,200-1,500 *LRG*

A fruitwood casket, inlaid with brass piqué work, inscribed Mary Bales, James Bales, January 17th 1826, Massingham, Norfolk, John Bales, and Jane Bales, 5.5in (14cm) wide.
£400-500 *S(S)*

An articulated fish shaped box, with red stone eyes, unmarked, early 19thC, 5in (13cm), in a fish shaped sharkskin covered box.
£200-250 *DN*

A walnut and brass bound stationery cabinet, enclosing a leather covered writing surface and an arrangement of pigeon-holes, with 3 small drawers and a pair of glass ink bottles, c1880, 16.5in (42cm) wide.
£800-1,200 *S(S)*

A Nuremburg steel miniature strong box, engraved with figures amidst formal scrolling foliage, lid mounted lock and with ball feet, 4.5in (11cm) long.
£1,200-1,500 *P(O)*

A gilt mounted tortoiseshell portrait box, with carved basketwork design and mounted on the inside cover with a portrait miniature of a gentleman wearing a scarlet waistcoat, c1760, 2.5in (6cm). **£400-600** *S(S)*

Did you know

MILLER'S Antiques Price Guide builds up year by year to form the most comprehensive photo-reference system available.

TRANSPORT
Vehicles

A Starley and Jeffries 'Ariel' Ordinary bicycle, all metal with large main wheel, 45in (114cm) diam, fitted inside with eye-holes threaded with spokes attached to central hub, central tension bar, metal spine attached to small wheel, 22in (56cm) diam, simple wooden handles linked to central steering head and simple metal pedals, detached, c1872.
£1,500-2,000 *S*

A vintage Dursley Pederson lady's bicycle, with original overpainted frame, wheels 26in (66cm) diam.
£1,400-1,800 *RBB*

A gentleman's cross frame safety bicycle, with solid tyres, adjustable pedals with replaced rubbers, foot rests on front forks, leather sprung saddle and mudguard to rear wheel, c1870, wheel 28in (71cm) diam.
£1,700-2,000 *S*

An English child's tricycle, the cast iron frame stamped Hughes Birm., with shaped handlebars, solid rubber tyres and shaped metal seat, the pedals acting on the front axle, early 20thC.
£350-550 *S*

A Victorian tricycle, pedal and chain drive, foot rests on front forks, lever band brake to rear axle, also activated by left foot pedal on frame, adjustable pedals, sprung saddle and turned wooden handlebar grips, with 24in (61cm) front wheel, 40in (102cm) rear wheels.
£4,000-5,000 *S*

An 'Open Lot' gipsy caravan, with canvas external cover, fixed back with single window and an open frame front, with additional decorated side panels and crown board, mounted on 2 pairs of 36in (92cm) wheels with contemporary shafts, the interior with individual panels, rear mounted bed with under cupboards and drawers, painted in typical fashion, 138in (336cm) long.
£2,000-3,000 *DDM*

A Canadian clinker built canoe, of copper pinned mahogany planks over oak frames, 168in (427cm) long.
£900-1,100 *CSK*

Built at Peterborough, Victoria, c1906, with 7 planks a side and frames at 6in (15cm) spacing, this canoe has been rescued and restored, (some frames require replacing) and has original metal work, the gunwale information plate is missing.

An 1885 Wagonette, by Woodall & Son of London, with detachable saloon top, finished in black livery with red coachlining and navy blue upholstery.
£4,500-5,500 *S*

Originally the property of Squire Carter, High Sheriff of Hampshire and acquired from the coach house of the family home.

An 1886 dog cart, by Morgan & Co. Ltd., of Longacre, with leaf springs, iron tyres and wooden wheels, 54in (137cm) diam.
£1,000-2,000 *S*

A popular vehicle in the late 19thC, with back-to-back seating designed to allow sportsmen to carry their dogs beneath the seats and much used on country estates.

Leather and Luggage

A Scandinavian 2-man racing sledge, with painted pine body, metal mounts and runners, 84in (213cm).
£220-270 *DDM*

A horsedrawn landau, by Woodall & Son, of Orchard Street, London, mounted on rubber tyres and equipped with skimpy flared mudguards with spoon brakes to the rear tyres, c1860.
£6,500-8,000 *S*

This well preserved Landau from London coachbuilders Woodall & Son was originally the property of Squire Carter, High Sheriff of Hampshire and came from the coach house of the family home. It still carries the family crest of the Red Lion on the doors.

A Louis Vuitton double opening office trunk, covered in LV monogram material, brass and leather bound, leather carrying handle, with key, interior with fitted sliding tray for typewriter, brown felt covered compartments with straps for files, paper and envelopes, labelled LV Paris, London No. 811908, 26in (66cm) high.
£1,500-2,000 *ONS*

A Louis Vuitton cabin trunk, the monogrammed cloth covered case with brass and leather mounts, fitted with 6 drawers, hanging compartment and shoe box, 1930s.
£1,500-2,000 *S*

A Japanese double foliot travelling alarm clock and case, posted lacquered iron movement with fusees for the gong and strike and spring barrel for the alarm, verge escapement with 2 foliots, engraved brass case with a fixed silvered chapter ring, on a wood stand with key drawer and a glazed wood travelling case with sliding front panel, 18thC, 8in (20cm) high.   **£5,500-6,500** *S*

Leather & Luggage

The condition of luggage is very important, as with most things, and items must be very fine in order to achieve top prices. Dressing cases and other items with fittings must be complete.

The highest demand continues to be for fine quality luggage by the top makers and unusual items for a particular function such as the office trunk, fishing rod box and drinks cases.

A Louis Vuitton gentleman's fitted dressing case, covered in brown leather with matching carrying handle, brass lock and catches, interior lined with black morocco, fully fitted interior with lift-out manicure set complete, each item stamped LV, the case stamped in gold LV, Paris London No. 736272, lock No. 047814, 17.5in (44cm) long.
£3,000-3,500 *ONS*

A Continental tortoiseshell and silver travelling inkstand, the exterior with sloping hinged lid, side carrying handles, on circular feet, the front with 2 hinged doors concealing 2 trays, the interior with mirrored lid, 2 glass bottles, folding pencil, tweezers, funnel, etc., 19thC, 4in (10cm).
£550-600 *DDM*

A Louis Vuitton lady's fitted dressing case, covered in red grained leather with matching carrying handle, brass lock and catches, interior lined in fine red leather fitted with 8 silver topped crystal containers each stamped LV and engraved monogram GM, 11 tortoiseshell fittings, 2 small circular containers each with gold inlaid monogram GM, 7 fitted matching red leather boxes, standing mirror and incomplete manicure set, the case stamped Louis Vuitton, Made in France 820176, lock No 053221, 21in (53cm) long.
£3,500-4,000 *ONS*

A Louis Vuitton cabin trunk, the interior with a removable tray, 44in (111cm) wide.
£1,000-1,200 *S(S)*

> Miller's is a price
> **GUIDE** not a price
> **LIST**

SPORT
Cricket

A cast iron slot machine, pre-WWI, 68in (173cm) high.
£800-1,200 *BWA*

A pair of M.C.C. white metal and enamelled cufflinks, engraved 'West Indies 1948' and 'G.O.A.'
£250-270 *DN*

These cufflinks belonged to Gubby Allen.

A group of 9 posters produced by various newspapers in the 1930s, printed in red and black with banner headlines such as 'G.O. Allen Sensational Bowling', 'Allen's Mistake' and 'Allen made no Mistake', some tears and wear at folds, one with printed date, 18th August 1936, all from the M.C.C. Australasian Tour 1936-37.
£1,700-2,000 *DN*

Football

A maroon Scotland -v- England International cap, 1893.
£500-550 *C(S)*

A collection of Gubby Allen's detailed engagement diaries from 1925-88, including 2 with presentation inscriptions from Pelham Warner, 1945 and 1946, together with an autograph notebook detailing Allen's play from 1914-21, whilst at Eton, and 5 fixture notebooks from Eton, 71 in all, including a diary of the Australian tour, 1936-37.
£3,000-3,500 *DN*

A blue Scotland -v- Wales International cap, 1889, a blue Scottish Football League cap 1893, a purple Glasgow -v- Sheffield cap, 1891, a brown Glasgow -v- Edinburgh cap, 1892, a Scotland -v- Ireland 1886 embroidered cloth jersey badge, 5 various Renfrewshire F.A. embroidered jersey badges, 1885-1888, and a silver medal, the obverse engraved with a scene of a footballer, the reverse inscribed Thompson, 1887.
£900-1,200 *C(S)*

A blue Scotland International cap, awarded for games against England, Ireland and Wales, 1947-48.
£450-500 *C(S)*

A blue Scotland -v- England International cap, 1923.
£300-350 *C(S)*
The above cap was awarded to Denis Lawson, St. Mirren. It was his only appearance in the International arena. An outside right by nature, his professional career started with St. Mirren in 1920, thereafter Cardiff City in 1923, Springfield F.C., U.S.A., 1926 Wigan Borough, 1927, and Clyde 1928-29.

A 15ct gold and enamel medal, the obverse inscribed 'From Aston Villa F.C. Presented to James Cowan', the reverse inscribed 'Presented to James Cowan by the Directors of The Aston Villa Football Club, in Recognition of His Long and Valued Services, 1890-1903', with ring suspension.
£400-600 *C(S)*

Two commemorative postal covers and a team photograph celebrating the 25th Anniversary of the European Cup, 1980-81, Liverpool 1 - Real Madrid 0, autographed by Liverpool players and officials, framed and glazed, 22 by 15in (56 by 39cm).
£720-780 *C(S)*

A bronze figure of a footballer, in aggressive pose, inscribed E. Drouot, early 20thC, 13in (33cm) high.
£900-1,200 *C(S)*

F.A. Cup Final, 18.4.23, first Wembley Final, Royal Box edition programme, bound in gilt tooled blue morocco.
£1,000-1,200 *C(S)*

A Scotland -v- England International jersey, 1907, primrose and yellow, with white cotton collar, and a blue Scotland -v- England International cap, 1907.
£2,100-2,500 *C(S)*

A maroon Manchester City jersey, bearing embroidered badge inscribed 1934, with button-up white cotton collar.
£1,200-1,500
With a blue and white Ipswich Town jersey, bearing embroidered cloth badge, with button-up collar.
£300-500 *C(S)*

A 10ct gold and enamel medal, the obverse inscribed 'U.S.F.A.' the reverse inscribed 'Dr. I. Schriecker, Vice-Pres. Federation Internationale De Football Assn.', with ring suspension and brooch ribbon, in original case. A.A.S., won by A.
£350-450 *S(C)*

Fishing

The thumb magnifier, by Fosters of Ashbourne, to fix on the thumb and to help tying flies, as shown in 1921 catalogue.
£15-20 *JMG*

A 5in unnamed sea reel, probably designed and made by Slater, 1930s. **£40-50** *JMG*

A Shaw's fly-fishing knife, Fred Shaw was the fly-fishing winner in 1905.
£70-90 *JMG*

An Allcocks Silver Superb reel, c1953. **£30-40** *JMG*

A 3in Hardy Perfect, with ivorine handle, c1917.
£70-80 *JMG*

A 4.5in wide drum salmon reel, marked and sold by Harrods, 1920s. **£50-65** *JMG*

A 4.25in Hardy Silex No. 2, c1911.
£70-90 *JMG*

A 3in Hardy Perfect, narrow drum reel, with ivorine handle, 1912.
£140-170 *JMG*

A 4.25in Hardy Perfect reel, brass faced, brass rimmed unperforated back, 1900.
£150-220 *JMG*

A 3in Hardy Perfect narrow drum reel, with no ball bearings, Eunoch model, agate lineguard, c1918.
£90-120 *JMG*

A 2.5in Hardy Uniqua, Spitfire model from WWII, manufactured by Jimmy Smith.
£60-95 *JMG*

A 3.5in Hardy Bros.
Perfect fly reel, mark II.
£75-90 *Bea*

A 3in Hardy Bros.
Perfect fly reel.
£70-80 *Bea*

A 4in Hardy The Goodwin sea
reel, c1920. **£60-75** *JMG*

A 4in Hardy Bros. Silex Major
spinning reel.
£80-120 *Bea*

An Illingworth casting reel, with
1905 patent no. 9388, in red
velvet lined green leather covered
case.
£450-500 *HSS*

A 3in Hardy
Perfect, with
narrow drum, left
handed, 1906.
£110-160 *JMG*

A 3.25in Hardy Silex Major,
1925-28. **£50-60** *JMG*

A 3.5in Hardy Perfect reel,
with wide drum, and nickel
silver lineguard, 1940s.
£110-150 *JMG*

A rare Scottish vintage fishing
tackle dealer, c. 1924, with a deep
knowledge of old reels, grey beard,
ruddy-ish patina, and a most
generous nature towards owners of
fine tackle; buys up to £1000 *JMG*

A 3.25in Hardy The
Lightweight reel,
1936. **£60-85** *JMG*

A 2.5in Hardy Perfect,
with small but wide
drum, 1896.
£210-260 *JMG*

A 4in Hardy Silex No. 2, with
brass brake on rim, c1915.
£90-120 *JMG*

A 3.25in Hardy Silex No. 2 reel, with red
handle on the edge, c1919.   **£60-85** *JMG*

A 3.5in brass faced Hardy Perfect, c1900.
£250-300 *JMG*

A 4in Wallace & Watson of Hexham reel,
with elaborate mechanism.   **£40-60** *JMG*

l. A Julius Vom Hofe ebonite and
nickel muliplier reel, with
counterbalanced crank, sliding
click and insciption 'Julius Vom
Hofe, pat. Nov. 17 '85, Oct. 8
1889', the foot stamped 3.5,
2.25in.
£150-200
r. A Julius Vom Hofe ebonite and
plated multiplier reel, with
counterbalanced crank, sliding
click, raised pillars and
inscription 'Julius Vom Hofe pat.
June 15 '86, October 5th 1889',
the foot stamped 4, 2.25in.
£200-250 *EP*

A 3in Hardy Uniqua reel, with
ivorine handle and horseshoe
latch, c1905.   **£50-70** *JMG*

A 3in Hardy Perfect, reel in
superb condition, with box, c1960.
£40-50 *JMG*

A 4.25in Hardy Perfect salmon fly
reel, with circular revolving line
guide, ivorine handle and alloy
foot, 1917 check.   **£150-200** *EP*

A 2.75in Hardy Silex Multiplier
casting reel, with ebonite handle
ivorine thumb bar, knurled rim
check with brass brake indicator
and brass foot.
£400-450 *EP*

A 2.5in Hardy brass crankwind
fly reel, with tapered horn handle
on curved crank arm stamped
'Hardy's Alnwick', fixed check,
brass foot, 1890s.
£240-270 *EP*

A 2.5in Hardy platewind
gunmetal reel, with enclosed oval
logo, horn handle and fixed check.
£120-170 *EP*

A 4.25in Hardy Perfect salmon fly reel, with fat black handle, grooved brass foot, drum with turned rim for fitted optional auxiliary brass rim brake, the face engraved H.H.L -G, Captain Henry Herbert Liddel-Grainger, Scots Guards of Ayton Castle, Eyemouth, Berwickshire 1886-1935, duplicated Mark II check, revolving patent nickel silver line guide, in Hardy leather case, c1930.   **£550-600** *EP*

A 3.75in Hardy Perfect brass faced salmon fly reel, with rod and hand trademark and straightline logo, strapped tension screw with turks head locking nut, circular nickel revolving line guide in brass frame, ivorine hand and brass foot, 1905 check. **£300-350** *EP*

A Farlow Billiken multiplier reel, with counterbalanced crank with lever in slot, push button release to free spool, rim check lever, vane with cover having 4 spokes inscribed Farlows Patent, holdfast logo and C Farlow & Co. Ltd, London, with most original finish, in maker's fitted wooden box with nameplate inside lid, together with leather strap holding 2 spare vanes, and oil bottle with dipper. **£1,500-1,800** *EP*

A 4in Coxon Aerial reel, optional check and Bickerdyke line guide. **£300-350** *EP*

A 3.75in Hardy Silent St George trout fly reel, with ivorine handle, brass foot, agate line guide, cracked, strapped tension screw, 3 screw drum latch and silent check. **£220-270** *EP*

A 3.75in Hardy Perfect reel, with nickel silver lineguard, 1906. **£120-160** *JMG*

A 3.5in Hardy Perfect reel, with agate lineguard, 1930s. **£50-70** *JMG*

Miscellaneous

An East European huntsman's trophy, mounted on a mahogany shield, 16in (40.5cm) high.
£1,200-1,700 *WW*

The bow section of a racing boat, built by George Simms of Putney, in the livery of the City of London, 'Henry Beaufoy', with shelves inserted for use as a bookcase, 69in (175cm) high.
£350-500 *Bon*

A full-size mahogany billiard table, by Burroughes and Watts, c1900. **£5,500-6,500** *FB*

A full-size mahogany billiard table, by Burroughes and Watts, c1880.
£8,000-12,000 *FB*

A three-quarter size mahogany billiard dining table, by George Wright, with clockwork rise and fall mechanism, c1880.
£5,500-6,000 *FB*

A half-size mahogany billiard dining table, by E. J. Riley, with dining leaves removed, and raised ready for play, c1900. **£2,000-3,000** *FB*

A mahogany revolving billiard dining table, the flip-over middle section with dining surface on one side and billiard table on the other, c1900.
£5,000-5,500 *FB*

LIGHTING

A pair of Meissen figure candlesticks, raised on a scroll moulded base picked out in turquoise, puce and gilt, crossed swords mark in underglaze blue, incised and impressed numbers, late 19thC, 11in (28cm) high.
£1,500-2,000 *S(S)*

A pair of Bilston enamelled candlesticks, c1780.
£600-650 *GIL*

A pair of Derby candlestick figures of cherubs, restored, c1770, 7in (17.5cm).
£750-800 *S(S)*

Three English wooden based rushlight holders, c1760, 9in (22.5cm) high.
£120-140 each *KEY*

Two English porcelain lamp bases, decorated with gilding, with later matched baluster columns painted with either bands or sprays of flowers, fitted for electricity, some damage, c1830, 23in (58cm) high.
£1,000-1,200 *S(S)*

A Doulton Lambeth glazed stoneware oil lamp, all raised on a black glazed circular base, fitted with brass burner and opaline glass shade, chipped, impressed marks, late 19thC, 26.5in (67cm) high.
£400-500 *S(S)*

A matched pair of Victorian steel lamps, with modern pale yellow cloth shades with tasselled fringes, fitted for electricity, 59.5in (151cm) high, excluding fittings and shades.
£900-1,200 *C*

A wrought iron rushlight holder, 18thC.
£350-450 *KEY*

A metalware tin lantern, c1800, 10in (26cm) high.
£120-140 *KEY*

A porcelain Pierrot night light, c1920, 7.5in (18.5cm) high.
£200-250 *ML*

A Victorian giltmetal 18-light chandelier, with foliate corona sexpartite rigid spirally twisted shaft supports, the circlet with scrolling foliate branches above a cast boss, the central section possibly replaced, 38in (97cm) high.
£900-1,200 *C*

A cut crystal electric table lamp, with cut crystal shade, c1920.
£190-220 *LF*

A chrome and glass table lamp, on a black base, c1930, 24in (61.5cm) high.
£250-300 *GAZ*

A heavy cut glass mushroom shaped electric table lamp, on a plated base with 2 bulb sockets and chain pulls, c1920, 18in (46cm) high.
£300-320 *LF*

A pair of cut glass and giltmetal candlesticks, each with beaded circular base and faceted cylindrical plinth supporting baluster stem and lobed drip-pan hung with glass lustres, c1780, 13.5in (35cm) high.
£1,500-2,000 *S(S)*

A brass table lamp with original beaded shade, c1920, 19.5in (49.5cm) high.
£100-130 *ML*

An Edwardian spelter lamp, with flambeau glass shade, probably gas originally, 22in (56cm) high.
£150-170 *ML*

A Continental bronze table lamp, formed as a tree trunk, modelled with a figure of a bare-footed young girl in pensive mood, the naturalistic base indistinctly signed, possibly by A. E. Crick of Antwerp, on a verde antico marble stand, c1900, 27in (69cm) high.
£300-400 *CSK*

A pair of Georgian style candlestick lamps, with original painted glass shades, c1920, 14.5in (37cm) high.
£180-200 *ML*

A dentist's lamp, 38in (96.5cm) high.
£210-270 *WAR*

A French carved wood classical revival lamp, c1910, 27.5in (70cm) high, with French shade.
£100-125 *ML*

An Art Deco plaster cat lamp, with lined black and white silk shade, 30in (76cm) high.
£160-180 *ML*

A Victorian Arts and Crafts iron candle lamp and shade, 9.5in (24cm) high.
£70-130 *ML*

An Ediswan original wall light and shade, c1900, one glass panel replaced. **£100-110** *ML*

An original brass doctor's lamp, with metal shade, c1920, 13.5in (35cm) high.
£170-200 *ML*

A brass Art Nouveau angel lamp, with lace shade, originally gas, 21in (53.5cm) high.
£170-200 *ML*

A brass table light, with scrimshaw type decoration on the shell shade, the base of the shell lined with metal, c1920, 11in (28cm) high. **£80-90** *ML*

A French original Art Nouveau iron dragon table lamp, 12in (31cm) high. **£170-200** *ML*

A brass banker's lamp, with steel shade, c1920, 11in (28cm) high.
£170-200 *ML*

A Victorian spelter cherub lamp, with flambeau shade, 12in (31cm) high.
£150-165 *ML*

A pair of Art Nouveau iron lily candlesticks, 9in (23cm) high.
£100-125 *ML*

Miller's is a price GUIDE not a price LIST

A pair of Victorian Kashmiri brass figures made into lamps, with pagoda silk shades, 17in (43.5cm) high.
£220-270 *ML*

An Art Nouveau bronzed iron lamp, with beaded shade made of original celluloid plastic, 25in (64cm) high.
£150-180 *ML*

A pair of French bronze and parcel gilt candlestick bases, the columns with winged caryatid figures and foliage, the tripod concave bases modelled with wolves' heads, on paw feet, with acanthus leaf chased stand, 19thC, 15in (38cm) high.
£600-650 *CSK*

A French pink glass table light, with painted enamelled scenes, with a pleated silk shade.
£120-140 *ML*

A pair of bronze candelabra of mermen, probably English, each kneeling bearded figure set on a rocky outcrop supporting scrolled foliate branches, brown patination, finely chased surface and detail, late 19thC, 15in (37cm) high.
£3,500-4,000 *S(S)*

A gilt bronze hall lantern, the engraved panes with anthemion crestings, with foliate scroll corona, late 19thC, 33in (83.5cm) high.
£800-1,000 *CSK*

A pair of French gilt bronze six-light candelabra, of Empire design, each formed as a winged putto, holding aloft the branches, standing on a sphere and laurel wreath-mounted plinth, 27in (69cm) high.
£4,500-5,500 *S*

A pair of Edwardian brass candlesticks, 8in (20cm) high.
£40-60 *ML*

A set of 3 Harrods copper lily wall lights, with a hanging centre light, c1901, centre light 14in (36cm) diam.
£275-300 *ML*

A pair of French chandeliers, probably Paris, in Louis XV manner, each for 24 lights, with moulded glass balusters and a gilt bronze cage, hung with drops, c1885, 66in (167.5cm) high.
£10,000-15,000 *S*

A pair of Art Nouveau brass wall lights, with milk glass shades, 15in (38cm) wide.
£425-550 *ML*

A Continental five-light chandelier, with a gilt metal frame adorned with numerous graduated chains of cut glass beads and prism drops, bordered with curving leaf shape mounts, 34in (86cm) high.
£650-700 *DDM*

A pair of Second Empire ormolu three-light wall appliqué, each with a pierced foliate backplate, the scrolling branches supported by a wreath emanating from a lion's mask with foliate drilled nozzles, 10in (25cm) high.
£1,200-1,700 *C*

A pair of brass piano candle holders, to screw on to the piano, 9in (23cm) high.
£55-75 *ML*

A pair of Arts and Crafts polished steel wall lights, 11.5in (29.5cm) high.   **£200-235** *ML*

A French Art Nouveau ironwork lantern, with replacement glass, 15.5in (40cm) high.
£170-190 *ML*

A pair of brass piano candle holders, weighted at the base, 7in (17.5cm) high.
£85-120 *ML*

A brass gas pole, with original transfer printed pink shade.
£70-100 *ML*

A pair of Art Deco chrome and glass wall lights, 9.5in (24cm) high.   **£70-100** *ML*

An Art Deco original leaded glass, iron and brass hall lantern, 19in (48cm) high.
£160-190 *ML*

A French cream painted brass hall lantern, the bulbous tapering body with 6 glass panels in a beaded bell husk cast frame, c1900, 37in (94cm) high.
£3,700-4,000 *S*

A pair of giltwood twin branch wall lights, each carved with a dove and scallop shell on a ribbon tied backplate, 53in (134cm) high.
£2,000-2,500 *S*

A pair of brass candle sconces, signed, c1900.
£200-250 *ML*

A pair of leaded glass ceiling lights, c1920, 22in (56cm) wide.
£350-400 *GAZ*

A brass hanging lantern, the sides with arched bevelled glass panels centred by a star burst below an acanthus scroll cresting, suspended by 6 scrolled supports, 28in (71cm) high.
£1,500-2,000 *C*

A Georgian design gilt bronze cylindrical hall lantern, the glazed body with beaded rims and ribs, hung with flower swags, 31in (78cm) high.
£1,200-1,500 *S(S)*

A bronzed plaster cherub with beaded shades, cherub 11in (28cm).
£170-200 *ML*

A gilt metal and glass light, 15.5in (39cm) high.
£300-500 *HSS*

A pair of the Empire style gilt brass candelabra, 19thC, slight damage, 22.5in (57.5cm) high.
£600-700 *Bea*

A pair of oak barley twist candlesticks, c1930, 14.5in (37cm) high.
£75-95 *ML*

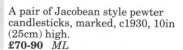

A pair of Empire style gilt metal five-branch candelabra, 30in (76cm) high.
£1,200-1,700 *HSS*

An oviform grey veined onyx column lamp, on a square base, c1920.
£300-400 *LRG*

A pair of Jacobean style pewter candlesticks, marked, c1930, 10in (25cm) high.
£70-90 *ML*

CRAFTS

A stoneware coiled and pinched vase, by Betty Blandino, oxide painted with ochre, brown and grey sponged glazes, impressed BB seal, c1991, 10.5in (26cm) high.
£250-300 *C*

An Abuja Pottery stoneware plate, by Michael Cardew, with everted rim, incised linear decoration, brown glazed body beneath cream details, impressed MC with Abuja Pottery seal, 10in (25cm) high.
£160-200 *C*

A Kingwood earthenware baluster vase, by Michael Cardew, the upper section covered in a grey-brown glaze with cream brushwork and incised decoration, beneath a fine translucent cream glaze, impressed with MC and Kingwood Pottery seals.
£700-900 *C*

A Michael Cardew bowl, painted with fish in brown reserved against an olive green ground, impressed Wenford Bridge seal and MC mark, c1970, 10in (25cm) diam.
£600-700 *S*

A stoneware slab built vase, by Ian Ault, with combed textured sides and applied wide collar, covered in an olive green and mushroom coloured pink tinted glaze, impressed IA seal, 12in (30cm) high.
£400-600 *C*

An earthenware bowl, by Michael Cardew, on a short foot, the interior covered in a mottled yellow ochre and olive green glaze, the exterior dark brown over yellow, with yellow brushwork, minor chips to rim, impressed MC with Winchcombe Pottery seal, 11.5in (29cm) diam.
£800-900 *C*

A porcelain 'Pot with Wave' vase, by Joanna Constantinidis, the foot with horizontal combed decoration, covered in a matt saggar fired pale brown glaze, impressed C seal, 1981, 17in (43.5cm) high.
£600-800 *C*

A stoneware coffee pot, by Michael Cardew, covered in a dark green glaze, incised through to body with cross-hatching and linear decoration, impressed MC and Wenford Bridge seals, 10in (25cm) high. **£300-400** *C*

A stoneware bowl, by Hans Coper, the interior covered in a matt manganese slip pooling to reveal translucent white glaze beneath, the buff coloured exterior burnished and textured, impressed with HC seal, 6in (15cm) diam.
£800-900 *C*

A stoneware bowl, by Hans Coper, the interior with matt manganese running and pooling glaze revealing translucent white glaze beneath, the matt buff-coloured exterior burnished and textured, minor chips to rim, impressed with HC seal, 7in (18cm) diam.
£900-1,200 *C*

A stoneware vase, by Joanna Constantinidis, covered in a yellow ochre and mottled brown glaze with iron-brown speckles, impressed C seal, 20in (51cm) high.
£300-500   *C*

A stoneware jug, by Ray Finch, with yellow and black speckled body beneath metallic brown, impressed seal, 11in (27.5cm) high.
£100-120   *C*

'The Rose and Crown', a stoneware slab built pub, by Ian Gregory, applied with elaborate architectural and figurative motifs, salt glazed in beige and brown with green, blue and yellow highlights, 27in (89cm) high.
£300-400   *C*

A stoneware 'Body Pot', by Joanna Constantinidis, covered in a saggar fired pitted metallic glaze, impressed C seal, 1974, 21.5in (55cm) high.
£900-1,200

A stoneware vase, by Joanna Constantinidis, with irregular rim, with incised spiralling decoration, covered in a mottled iron-brown glaze, impressed C seal, 19in (49cm) high.
£400-600   *C*

A tea bowl, by Ewen Henderson, of various laminated clays textured with pink, brown, green and ochre slips, glazes and oxides, 1991, 4in (10.5cm) high.
£200-250   *C*

A raku water container, by Keiko Hasegawa, with iron grey body covered in a mottled mushroom-coloured crackled and pitted glaze with lustrous metallic splashes, impressed potter's seal, 6in (15.5cm) high.   **£200-300**   *C*

A stoneware bowl, speckled grey with a rust brown rim, impressed HH seal, 6in (15.5cm) diam.
£120-160   *Bon*

A porcelain bowl, by Marian Gaunce, laminated in green, purple and blue clays, the rim with purple laminated chequered pattern, 5in (12cm) high.
£250-350   *C*

A stoneware bowl, olive green, the interior with bird design, glaze flakes to rim, impressed HH seal, 11in (28cm) diam.
£300-350   *Bon*

A stoneware bowl, speckled green-grey with a brown circular motif, impressed HH seal, 6in (15cm) diam.
£200-250   *Bon*

An earthenware bowl, decorated with 3 engraved fishes, brown and green, impressed HH seal, 7in (18.5cm) diam.
£400-600   *Bon*

A porcellaneous beaker, with pale grey glaze, decorated with a band of brown and blue lines, impressed HH seal, 4in (10.5cm) high.   **£100-120**   *Bon*

A stoneware vase, by Janet Leach, covered in a speckled oatmeal run and pooled glaze, impressed JL with St. Ives Pottery seal, 5in (12cm) high.
£110-150 *C*

An inlaid stoneware plate, by Tatsuo Shimaok, the interior inlaid in pale green slip with herringbone pattern and stylised with iron brown rim, the underside covered in a mottled brown and olive green glaze, impressed seal, 12in (31cm) diam.
£400-600 *C*

A stoneware vase, by William Staite Murray, covered in a pitted mottled olive green glaze stopping short of the foot, with iron brown details, impressed M seal, 7.5in (19cm) high.
£200-300 *C*

A stoneware cut-sided vase, by Malcolm Pepper, covered in a thick crackled pale grey glaze, impressed seal obscured by glaze, 10.5in (26cm) high.
£80-120 *C*

A large stoneware oviform vase, by Malcolm Pepper, covered in a finely crackled grey glaze beneath a brushed white glaze with cobalt blue brushwork, with impressed seal, 11.5in (29cm) high.
£140-160 *C*

A thickly potted cylindrical stoneware vase, by Alan Wallwork, covered in an oatmeal and lavender grey glaze, 19.5in (50cm) high.
£100-200 *C*

A stoneware bowl, by Takeshi Yasuda, green with raised white decoration and some running brown glaze, c1980, 6in (15cm) diam.
£170-200 *Bon*

A stoneware vase, by Alan Wallwork, with uneven V-shaped rim, covered in a mottled pale olive green glaze with large iron brown flecks, inscribed AW, 15.5in (39cm) high.
£200-350 *C*

An earthenware water pot, with textured vertical bands, 12in (31cm).
£180-250 *Bon*

A stoneware vase, by William Staite Murray, with prominent potting rings, the interior covered in a crackled brown glaze, the exterior in a crackled mushroom coloured glaze with olive green and blue decoration, impressed M seal, 6in (15cm) high.
£180-220 *C*

ORIENTAL
Bamboo & Wood

A sagemono, in the form of wood rolled makimono, inlaid with takaramono, in wood and stag antler, damaged, Asakusa School, unsigned, 19thC, 5in (12cm).
£300-500 *S(S)*

A Japanese giltwood and lacquer figure of a Buddha, seated in dhyanasana, the hair dressed in tight knots, the overlapping robes falling over his legs and forming the base, cracked, chipped and worn, 15in (38cm) high.
£800-900 *CSK*

A wood carving of a horse, with a blanket tied to its girth, nicks to top of tail and himotoshi, unsigned, 19thC, 2in (5cm).
£1,300-1,500 *S(NY)*

A boxwood okimono of a snake and turtle, the turtle emerging from its shell as the snake winds around it, the wood lightly stained and the eyes inlaid, signed in an oval reserve Shomin, late 19thC, 2.5in (6cm).
£1,800-2,200 *S*

A boxwood group of 5 turtles, in the style of Chuichi (Tadakazu), one forming a base for the others to clamber upon, their eyes inlaid, unsigned, late 19thC, 2in (5cm).
£700-900 *S*

A Chinese lacquered and painted wood figure of a seated multi-armed Buddha, wearing a hat with hanging masks at the back, 3 arms broken and repaired, 17th/18thC, 7.5in (19cm) high.
£350-450 *CSK*

Two bamboo carvings, one comprising a group of 2 happy figures holding auspicious attributes including a double gourd, a turtle and a lotus stem, small chip, 18/19thC, 7.5in (19cm) high, the other carved as a mythical treetrunk raft, with an openwork fruiting and flowering branch growing from the gunwales of the hull, and small figures standing on the deck, small loss, 18thC, 8.5in (21cm) long.
£1,300-1,900 *C*

A Japanese wood, lacquer and gilt carving of a reclining Buddha, resting his head on his right arm, wearing long flowing robe over one shoulder, the hair worn in tight curls, chipped and worn, 18th/19thC, 20.5in (52cm) long. **£500-600** *CSK*

A wood okimono of shibunkin, by Chikuju, the group of long tailed goldfish naturalistically carved, the eyes inlaid in horn, signed on a horn tablet, Meiji period, 10in (25cm).   **£2,600-3,000** *S*

A Chinese bamboo brush pot, carved to the exterior with a panel of sages being entertained by musicians in a garden landscape, the reverse with birds perched among flowering prunus and bamboo, cracked, Daoguang mark and of the period, 3in (8cm) diam.   **£420-500** *CSK*

Cloisonné & Enamel

A Japanese cloisonné enamel plaque, showing irises in colours, on black ground, Meiji period, 9 by 7in (23 by 18cm), the hardwood frame relief carved with dragons amongst waves.
£400-600 *P(S)*

A pair of cloisonné enamel vases, decorated with panels of irises and baskets of flowers on each of the 4 raised panels, against the dark blue ground, small blisters, impressed Daikoku's head rebus, Meiji period, 6in (15cm).
£750-850 *S(S)*

A pair of cloisonné vases, decorated in musen-jippo with irises on a pale cream ground, the rims mounted in shakudo, inlaid mark of Ando Jubei, Meiji period, 9.5in (24cm).
£900-1,200 *S*

A pair of blue and white cloisonné enamel and gilt bronze jardinières, decorated on either side, a ruyi collar at the shoulder, applied at either side with loose-ring double animal head handles, pitted, late Qing Dynasty, 22in (56cm) diam. **£3,200-3,600** *C*

A cloisonné enamel meiping, decorated with red, pink, yellow, blue, white and green stylised lotus flowers among scrolling foliage, on a blue ground with ruyi heads around the short neck, 18th/19thC, 12in (30.5cm) high.
£1,000-1,500 *C*

A pair of cloisonné vases, decorated in musen-jippo with irises on a pale cream ground, the rims mounted in shakudo, inlaid mark of Ando Jubei, Meiji period, 9.5in (24cm).

A cloisonné enamel dish, decorated in gold and silver wire with a central landscape panel, inlaid lozenge mark of Hayashi Kodenji, Meiji period, with original fitted wood box, 7in (18cm).
£3,700-4,000 *S*

A Canton enamel supper set, the central dish painted in famille rose enamels, with Shou-hsing and other figures in a landscape, the 8 fan shaped subsidiary dishes with similar decoration, 18thC, 17in (43cm).
£220-260 *ALL*

A Chinese cloisonné vase, mid-19thC, 14in (36cm) high.
£500-600 *Wai*

Furniture

A Chinese export padouk wood bureau, enclosing a fitted interior, on later shaped bracket feet, the base incised SDR 42, mid-18thC, 37in (94cm) wide.
£1,500-2,000 *CSK*

A Japanese carved hardwood and lacquer side cabinet, with a pagoda pediment, numerous galleried shelves, cupboards and drawers each with a lacquer panel and mounted carved ivory, allover decorated with open carved phoenix and flowering branches, 84in (213cm) high.
£600-800 *P(S)*

A Chinese export black lacquer and lac burgaute brass cabinet, enclosing shelves and a pair of drawers, c1800, 40in (102cm) wide.
£1,200-1,700 *CSK*

A Chinese Export black lacquer small secrétaire cabinet, gilt decorated with shell and scroll cornice above a pair of panel doors enclosing shelves and 2 short drawers, the base with hinged writing surface and pen rest, on stand with 4 turned supports, 61in (155cm).
£900-1,200 *ALL*

A Chinese export black and gilt lacquered chest-on-stand, the stand with acanthus scroll carved X-shaped supports joined by stretchers, early 19thC.
£600-800 *S(S)*

A Chinese black lacquer cabinet, set with hardstones and mother-of-pearl, 38.5in (97cm) square, with later ebonised stand.
£600-800 *Bea*

A Chinese ebonised padouk wood side cabinet, inlaid in copper wire, mother-of-pearl, ivory and bone, with brass flat hinges and door plates, on key pattern carved bracket feet, door set with white metal plaque inscribed 'Lock Hing Curios & Arts, Hong Kong. Established 1870', 46in (117cm) wide. **£700-800** *HSS*

A nest of 4 Chinese hardwood occasional tables.
£450-650 *Bea*

A Japanese parquetry and lacquer table cabinet, late 19thC, 18in (46cm) wide.
£400-600 *HSS*

A Chinese huang huali altar table, the cleated top above a stylised pierced and carved frieze, on square legs with scroll feet, late 19thC, 53.5in (136cm) wide.
£600-800 *S(S)*

A Chinese huang huali davenport, profusely carved, the top revealing 3 small drawers, the sides with a pen drawer above 8 opposing drawers and pierced dragon brackets, on a platform base with claw-and-ball feet, some damage, late 19thC, 33in (84cm) wide. **£450-650** *S(S)*

A Chinese four-fold painted hide screen, with pagodas, figures, boats and floral vase motifs, within a nailed gilt hide border, distressed, 19thC, each fold 75 by 23in (191 by 59cm). **£1,500-2,000** *S(S)*

A Chinese brown lacquer six-fold screen, late 19thC, 78in by 15in (198 by 38cm). **£1,000-1,200** *CSK*

A nest of 4 Chinese hardwood tea tables, the borders and legs carved as bamboo, the aprons pierced and carved with scrolling fruiting foliage, 15 to 8.5in (38 to 21cm). **£500-600** *P(S)*

An inlaid hardwood screen, carved with lotus and inlaid in bone and mother-of-pearl, with numerous fighting frogs, Meiji period, 70.5 by 67in (178 by 170cm). **£4,500-6,500** *S*

A Chinese two-fold screen, each panel decorated with onlaid cloisonné vases and censers containing flowers and fruiting sprays, on a coral coloured lacquer ground, within a hardwood frame decorated with a band of key-pattern, 69.5in (178cm) high. **£1,000-1,200** *CSK*

A Chinese huang huali centre table, the top with a burr wood panel within concentric bandings, the carved and pierced frieze above 6 supports, joined by pierced stretchers, on stylised carved feet, 19thC, 53.5in (135cm) diam. **£1,200-1,700** *S(S)*

An Oriental carved hardwood jardinière stand, with inset rouge marble top, pierced side aprons, shaped legs and cross stretcher, 19thC, 10in (25cm) diam. **£150-200** *GH*

An Anglo-Chinese rosewood hall table, with pink veined marble inset top, on cabriole front supports, with carved shell and leafage ornament and scroll toes, on serpentine fronted plinth base, 19thC, 50in (127cm) long. **£1,500-2,000** *CAG*

A black and gold lacquer painting table, braced at each end by twin stretchers, decorated by an allover design of gold lacquer scrolling stylised lotus, Wanli, 36in (91cm). **£3,500-4,500** *C*

An Oriental carved hardwood jardinière stand, with inset rouge marble top, pierced side aprons, under gallery, supported on circular legs with claw and ball feet, 16in (41cm) square.
£300-400 *GH*

A pair of Chinese 2-tier hardwood urn stands, the aprons, legs and edges all carved to simulate bamboo, 18in (46cm) square.
£700-900 *P(S)*

A Chinese Export black lacquer work table, decorated in gilt throughout in traditional manner, 25in (64cm) wide.
£650-850 *Bea*

An Oriental carved hardwood plant stand, with inset marble panel, on 4 cabriole legs, 19in (48cm) high.
£200-250 *GAK*

An Oriental carved hardwood jardinière stand, with inset rouge marble top, floral carved side apron, shaped legs and pierced floral under gallery, 19thC, 36in (92cm) high.   **£300-350** *GH*

Two lacquered armchairs, and a lacquered square table, each decorated in gilding with figures and flowers on a black lacquer ground.
£800-1,500 *CAm*

Inros

A three-case wood inro, decorated in relief and lacquered with an eagle perched on rocks, damaged, 19thC, 3.5in (8cm).
£400-450 *S(S)*

A two-case wood inro, decorated in gold, silver and black hiramakie with tigers among bamboo, late 19thC, 2.5in (7cm) and an attached ivory netsuke of karashishi, cracked, 18thC.
£600-800 *CAm*

A five-case lacquer inro, bearing a kinji ground, decorated in gold and silver takamakie, hiramakie, gold foil and kirigane with a flowercart filled with cherry blossoms and camelia, scratches, with coral bead ojime, and guri lacquer manju netsuke, chipped, 19thC, 3.5in (9cm).
£850-1,000 *S(NY)*

A four-case inro, decorated in gold togidashi, takamakie, kirigane and gold leaf, with a flight of cranes above a ship, signed Kajikawa saku, 19thC, 3.5in (9cm), with a lacquer hako-netsuke showing a ferry boat.
£2,500-3,000 *S*

A three-case inro, decorated in gold hiramakie and nashiji, on a roi ronuri ground with characters, and a wood netsuke of a seated figure, 19thC, 2.5in (7cm).
£600-800 *CAm*

A Japanese ivory okimono of Tenku emerging from an egg, 4in (10cm) wide.
£200-300 *HSS*

Ivory

A pair of ivory tusk vases, carved in relief with a monkey trainer, musicians and dancers beneath cherry blossom, mounted on wood bases, Meiji period, 10.5in (26cm).
£1,700-2,000 *S*

An ivory tusk vase and cover, carved overall in high relief with quail and millet, the quail with stained plumage, some cracks, signed on a mother-of-pearl tablet Yoshikazu, Meiji period, 7in (18cm).   **£2,500-3,000** *S*

A Japanese ivory group, of a standing sage holding a staff in one hand and stroking his beard with the other while looking at a butterfly perched on the frond of a palm tree issuing from rockwork, the details stained black, on oval base, minor damage, signed on red lacquer reserve Kogyoku, 5.5in (14cm) high.
£600-700 *CSK*

A Japanese carved ivory group of 3 figures on a log raft, one with an oar and a bundle of sticks, one seated, and a child with gourd, late 19thC, 10in (25cm) high, with plinth.
£550-650 *CAG*

A Japanese ivory carving of a warrior, mounted on the back of a rearing stallion, both horse and rider with heads turned to the right, the warrior with his right arm raised above his head, the details stained black, sword missing, old damage, 5in (13cm) long, with stand. **£700-800** *CSK*

A Japanese wood and ivory group, of a street entertainer with his assistant, red lacquered signature to base, Meiji, 9in (23cm) high.
£1,200-1,700 *WW*

An ivory group of bananas, by Banshu, the fruit attached to a stem, naturalistically carved and stained, signed, Meiji period, 7in (18cm).
£1,200-1,700 *S*

An ivory study of a rabbit, seated facing ahead and with its ears drawn back for compactness, the ivory bearing a good colour and the eyes inlaid, chipped, Kyoto, late 18thC, 2in (5cm). **£1,700-2,000** *S*

An ivory tusk carving of a kneeling man struggling with an octopus, a woman and child escaping behind his back, Meiji period, 10in (25cm) long, on wood stand.
£800-900 *S(S)*

A large ivory okimono of a man and two boys, the man standing with one child holding a rabbit at his feet, the other boy on his back, with an elaborate revolving wood stand, the figure signed Atsumochi, Meiji period, 31in (79cm) overall height.
£3,500-4,500 *S*

A Japanese ivory carving of a kangaroo, carrying her young in her pouch, inlaid eyes, set on a wood stand, 6in (15cm) high.
£350-450 *CSK*

An ivory and lacquerwork carving of a leaping carp, the fish flexed upon its tail, the ivory head, gills and fins finely rendered, its body painted to simulate scales, repaired, Meiji period, 6in (15cm), on wood stand.
£900-1,200 *S(S)*

An ivory model of a Kakemono, by Hidemasa of Osaka, opening to reveal Okame seated, throwing beans to exorcise an oni who climbs over the top of the scroll, a hanging pole at the base, the ivory is slightly worn and of a good colour, signed, early 19thC, 2.5in (6cm).
£620-800 *S*

A pair of Japanese ivory bezique counters, both carved in sunken low relief with monkeys playing with crab and toad, the tabs with further apes, Meiji period, signed, 4in (10cm).
£350-450 *S(S)*

Three Chinese ivory seals, 2 surmounted by Buddhistic lions, one by a mythical animal with a bifurcated tail, on rectangular or oval bases, and an oval soapstone seal surmounted by a rabbit beside a cabbage, 18thC and later, 2in (5cm) high.
£400-600 *CSK*

Jade & Agate

A carved jade dragon plaque, of domed oval form, carved in relief with a dragon amidst lotus, mounted as a table screen, in a well carved pierced wood stand, Kangxi, 12in (31cm).
£900-1,200 *S(S)*

A white jade deer cup, the scallop shaped cup resting on a short foliate foot, a deer's head with delicate pointed ears and short beard carved at the pointed end, chipped, 18thC, 3.5in (9cm) wide, with padded box.
£2,200-2,700 *C*

A pale celadon jade pierced censer and cover, the body and domed cover crisply carved and incised in openwork with scrolling peony flowers and 3 peony stem handles, on a flaring openwork base, 18thC, 5in (13cm), with wood stand.
£4,000-5,000 *C*

Lacquer

A speckled burnt jade figure of an elephant, draped with a decorative tasselled howdah, surmounted by a young boy grasping a lotus stem, and another standing at its rear holding a vase, the pale cream jade richly speckled with black flecks, repaired, probably Ming Dynasty, 7.5in (19cm) long.
£1,500-2,500 *C*

A Chinese moss agate peach shaped libation cup, with chilong handle, carved to the exterior with leafy tendrils, 4.5in (11cm) wide.
£200-300 *CSK*

A lacquer coffer, decorated in gold and black and mother-of-pearl with foliate panels, flaked, c1600, 9in (23cm). **£1,700-2,000** *S*

A lacquer comb and hairpin, signed Ryushin Sei, Meiji period, the pin 6.5in (16cm).
£750-1,000 *CNY*

A Japanese lacquer picnic set, comprising 3 flat square boxes and covers and 4 triangular trays, each decorated to simulate different wood samples, in a fitted lacquer casket of hinged vertical square section, covered in herringbone pattern and coloured raffia, with open side panels, early 20thC, 10in (25cm) high.
£200-250 *HSS*

A japanese gold lacquer figure of Hotei, seated on his sack holding a peach in one hand, his robes decorated in hiramakie and black, on a gilt metal base, damaged, 8in (20cm) high. **£150-200** *CSK*

An Export lacquer coffer, decorated in gold takamakie, hiramakie, kirigane and inlaid mother-of-pearl, with shaped panels showing palaces and gardens, birds and flowers reserved on a nashiji ground, chipped, mid-17thC, 52in (132cm) long, on a later English stand. **£9,000-12,000** *S*

A Chinese red lacquer sewing box and cover, incised with figures in a landscape of trees, 13in (33cm) diam.
£350-400 *RBB*

A pair of red lacquer drums and stands, the drums painted and gilt with lotus scrolls, the stands with dragon head terminals, drums 26.5in (67cm) wide.
£1,000-2,000 *CAm*

A gold lacquer saddle, decorated on the nashiji ground in gold takamakie, hiramakie and foil with ho-o, chipped, 18th/19thC, 15in (38cm) long.
£3,500-4,000 *S*

Metal

A bronze study of a lion, its teeth bared in a roar, impressed seal Seiya saku, Meiji period, 20in (51cm), with wood base.
£1,000-1,200 *S*

Two bronze figures of a warrior and a falconer, each in flowing robes with floral medallions, the warrior brandishing a drawn sword, the other holding a hawk balanced on a perch, gilt details, bearing a rich dark patina, on wood stands, one missing a weapon, both signed Gyoko, Meiji period.
£4,200-5,000 *S*

A Japanese bronze model of a walking camel, signed, 12in (31cm) high.
£1,500-2,000 *CSK*

An Oriental bronze cauldron, decorated with figures and clouds, having elephant mask and trunk handles, 18in (46cm) diam.
£200-250 *RBB*

A Japanese bronze group of a seated monkey gazing at a lotus bud held in one hand, the fur markings well defined, 7in (18cm) high.
£350-450 *CSK*

A Japanese inlaid bronze bowl, of flower form, the exterior decorated in low relief with crested water birds wading among lotus, heightened in gilt, signed, Meiji period, 8in (20cm) diam.
£600-700 *S(S)*

A bronze elephant, cast with wrinkled skin, the trunk raised with a pair of ivory tusks, impressed seal Seiya saku, Meiji period, 17.5in (44cm) long.
£500-700 *S(S)*

COLOUR REVIEW

A Clarice Cliff Tankard shaped coffee set, in Gay Day
pattern.
£650-750 *RIC*

A Clarice Cliff
Solitude pattern
sugar sifter, 5.5in
(14cm) high.
£500-575 *RIC*

A pair of Clarice Cliff
Autumn design vases,
8.5in (21cm) high.
£1,500-1,800 *HEW*

A Clarice Cliff My Garden pattern bowl, 12in
(31cm) diam.
£250-350 *ADC*

A Clarice Cliff bowl, Devon pattern, Daffodil shape
475, 13in (33cm) long.
£650-750 *ADC*

A Clarice Cliff Orange House pattern,
5in (13cm) high.
£425-475 *RIC*

A Clarice Cliff Isis vase, in
Woodland design, 9.5in (24cm)
high.
£450-550 *RIC*

A Clarice Cliff baluster vase,
Sliced Fruit pattern, 15in
(38cm) high.
£1,000-1,200 *RIC*

A Clarice Cliff bowl footed,
c1930, 9in (23cm) diam.
£2,000-2,200 *HEW*

A Clarice Cliff stepped
vase, in Latona Red
Rose pattern, 6in
(15cm) high.
£450-550 *RIC*

A Clarice Cliff large Athens shape teapot,
Diamonds pattern
£450-550 *ADC*

614

A Clarice Cliff Nuage bowl, shape No.33, 13in (33cm) wide.
£450-550 *ADC*

A Clarice Cliff Bizarre vase, c1930.
£600-700 *HEW*

A Clarice Cliff Bizarre model of a pig, after a model by Louis Wain, 4.5in (11cm) high.
£500-600 *RIC*

A Clarice Cliff Inspiration Bizarre Conical vase, restored, 7in (18cm).
£600-700 *HEW*

A Clarice Cliff floral Nuage Stamford shape biscuit barrel with lid.
£275-325 *RIC*

A pair of Clarice Cliff Geometric vases, 7in (17.5cm).
£1,200-1,400 *HEW*

A Clarice Cliff Inspiration vase, 10in (25.5cm).
£1,200-1,500 *HEW*

A Clarice Cliff Orange Roof Cottage, 7in (17.5cm).
£400-450 *HEW*

A Clarice Cliff umbrella stand.
£3,500-4,000 *RIC*

A Clarice Cliff mask, 7in (17.5cm).
£450-500 *HEW*

A Clarice Cliff Sunburst design coffee set, coffee pot 7in (17.5cm) high.
£1,000-1,200 *HEW*

A Clarice Cliff basket vase, Bridgewater design, 13in (33cm) wide.
£600-650 *HEW*

A Moorcroft Leaf and Berry design flambé squat vase, c1932, 6in (15cm) high.
£550-650 *LIO*

A Moorcroft baraware design vase, made for Liberty, restored, c1908, 3.5in (9cm) high.
£250-350 *LIO*

A Moorcroft Anemone design lustre vase, made for Liberty c1909, 8in (20cm) high.
£800-1,200 *LIO*

A Walter Moorcroft yellow Hibiscus design vase, c1960, 6in (15cm) high.
£130-170 *LIO*

A MacIntyre Moorcroft salmon and green Carnation design vase, c1898, 12in (31cm) high.
£1,000-1,500 *LIO*

A Moorcroft flambé Waratah design vase, 1939, 17in (43cm) high.
£7,000-9,000 *LIO*

A Moorcroft saltglaze Fish design vase, dated 1931, 14in (36cm) high.
£2,200-3,200 *LIO*

A Moorcroft matt glaze ochre Leaf and Berry design vase, c1936, 4in (10cm) high.
£350-450 *LIO*

A Minton stick stand, 23in (58cm) high.
£400-500 *CAR*

A MacIntyre Moorcroft Florian ware Blue Tree design vase, c1902.
£1,500-2,500 *LIO*

A MacIntyre Moorcroft Pansy design vase, restored, c1912, 10.5in (26cm) high.
£400-600 *LIO*

A Charlotte Rhead Rhodian pattern bowl, 10in (25.5cm). **£90-100** *HEW*

An Art Deco group, by Lobel Riche, c1925, 14in (35.5cm) high. **£600-650** *POW*

A Charlotte Rhead posy bowl, 6in (15cm) diam. **£40-45** *HEW*

A Goldscheider ceramic figure, c1930, 14in (35.5cm) high. **£500-700** *ASA*

An Austrian porcelain figure of a girl, by Lenst Waliliss, c1910, 17.5in (44cm) high. **£900-1,200** *HOW*

A Royal Dux porcelain female figure, Bohemian, c1910, 15.5in (39cm) high. **£900-1,200** *HOW*

A pair of Katshütte figures of skiers, 11.5in (29cm) high. **£1,000-1,500** *ASA*

'The Hornpipe', a Royal Doulton figure, HN2161, 10in (25.5cm). **£300-350** *PCh*

A Royal Dux porcelain bust of a young woman, minor losses, impressed factory marks, c1900. **£1,500-2,000** *S(NY)*

An Austrian porcelain figure, c1900. **£900-1,200** *HOW*

A Rosenthal porcelain figure of a snake charmer, c1920. **£350-550** *ASA*

A Royal Doulton wall plaque, by Frank Brangwyn, in Harvest pattern, decorated by hand, 13in (33cm).
£250-350 *ADC*

A Martin Brothers salt glazed porcelain Love Birds group, dated 1902. **£4,600-5,000** *S(NY)*

A Royal Dux two-handled vase, 16in (41cm) high.
£350-450 *PCh*

A Gray's Pottery Art Deco eight-piece coffee set, in yellow and black geometric pattern.
£90-150 *PCh*

A Susie Cooper charger, signed and dated 1934.
£1,500-1,800 *CAR*

A Martin Brothers bird and cover, c1913.
£1,500-2,500 *S*

A pair of Mettlach vases, 1904, 14.5in (37cm) high.
£700-750 *POW*

A pair of Bermantofts vases, by V. Kremer, 11in (28cm) high.
£1,800-2,000 *NCA*

A figure of Bat Girl, 8.5in (21cm) high.
£350-500 *ASA*

A Bursley Ware tray, TL43, in shades of blue on grey, 9in (23cm) long.
£75-85 *ADC*

A Charlotte Rhead vase, 7in (18cm) high.
£100-120 *HEW*

A Royal Doulton vase, by Frank Butler, c1906, 19in (48cm) high.
£1,000-1,250 *POW*

A Ferdinand Preiss cold painted bronze, tinted ivory, marble and onyx figure, 'Ecstasy', c1930, 22in (56cm). **£4,000-6,000** *S*

A Pierre le Faguays cold painted bronze and marble figure, 'Dancer with Thyrsus', 1920s, 22in (56cm). **£3,000-4,000** *S*

A Chiparus silvered, cold painted bronze, ivory, marble and onyx figure, 'Antinea', c1925. **£54,000-58,000** *S*

A Ferdinand Preiss cold painted bronze, ivory and onyx figure, 1930s. **£1,800-2,000** *S*

A Chiparus bronze and ivory 'Pierrot', with silver/grey patina, 1920s. **£3,000-5,000** *S(S)*

A Morante bronze figure of a dancer, 16in (41cm) high. **£1,000-1,500** *ASA*

A cold painted bronze, ivory and onyx 'Dancer', c1925, 10in (25cm). **£700-1,000** *S*

A Fredy Stoll silvered bronze, and marble figure, 'Daphne', c1925. **£10,000-12,000** *S*

A Pierre Le Faguay bronze figure, 'Bacchante'. **£7,000-9,000** *C*

'.A Ferdinand Preiss bronze and ivory 'Autumn Dancer'. **£8,000-10,000** *C*

A Joe Descamp bronze and ivory figure, 15in (38cm) high. **£4,000-5,000** *ASA*

r. A Ferdinand Preiss cold painted bronze and ivory 'Grecian with Torch'. **£3,000-4,000** *S*

Two René Lalique drinking services: *l.* 18 pieces, after 1934. **£1,000-1,200** *r.* 29 pieces, after 1924. **£2,500-3,000** *S*

A René Lalique opalescent glass vase, 'Orleans', marked, 8in (20cm). **£1,700-2,000** *S*

A René Lalique opalescent glass clock, 'Inseparables', after 1926, 4.5in (12cm). **£1,400-1,600 S**

A Lalique moulded, frosted and enamelled glass vase, model introduced 1926, inscribed R. Lalique, 7in (18cm). **£5,000-6,000** *S(NY)*

A René Lalique opalescent glass plate, 'Assiette Calypso', stencilled mark, after 1930. **£2,500-3,500** *S*

l. A Lalique glass vase, 'Tournesol' after 1927. **£1,500-1,800** *r.* A Lalique perfume bottle. **£600-800** *S*

A René Lalique table decoration, 'Faisans', comprising: 2 glass candelabra and a serving dish, dish with engraved mark, chips to dish, after 1942. **£2,500-3,000** *S*

A René Lalique glass and nickel plated metal plaque, moulded mark, slightly polished, c1925, 16in (40cm). **£6,000-7,000** *S*

A Lalique moulded and frosted glass vase, 1914 model, moulded and inscribed. **£1,500-2,000** *S(NY)*

A René Lalique glass vase, 'Aras', moulded mark R. Lalique, after 1924, 9in (23cm). **£5,000-6,000** *S*

A Lalique moulded glass perfume bottle, 1926 model, 3in (7.5cm). **£5,500-6,500** *S(NY)*

A René Lalique black enamelled clear glass vase, wheel cut R. Lalique and engraved France No.970, 8in (20cm) high. **£6,500-7,500** *CNY*

A Daum etched and wheel carved glass vase, 12in (31cm) high.
£14,500-20,000 *CNY*

An Emile Gallé carved vase, c1902, 11in (28cm).
£41,000-45,000 *S*

A Daum purple tinted cameo glass vase, decorated with iris, on round base, signed Daum, Nancy, 16in (41cm) high.
£2,500-3,000 *E*

A stained glass window, 'Minstrel with Cymbals' designed by William Morris, 25.5 by 19in (65 by 48cm). **£10,000-12,000** *C*

A Morris & Co. stained glass window, designed by Edward Burne-Jones, 41in (105cm) high.
£10,500-15,000 *C*

A Sabino opalescent glass lamp, 'Suzanne Au Bain', chipped, c1930, 10in (25cm).
£1,500-2,000 *S*

A Gallé enamelled glass liquor set, inscribed E. Gallé, c1890, decanter 8.5in (21cm), stand 12.5in (32cm).
£10,500-12,000 *S(NY)*

A Gallé cameo glass vase, minor fleck at base, c1900, 13.5in (34cm) high.
£4,700-5,500 *S(NY)*

A Gallé cameo glass pilgrim vase, signed in cameo, c1900, 17in (43cm) high. **£6,000-8,000** *S(NY)*

A Koloman Moser for E. Bakalowits & Söhne sherry jug, in dimpled glass with electroplated metal mounts c1900, 10in (25cm). **£5,000-6,000** *S*

A 'Dragonfly' leaded glass and gilt bronze table lamp, stamped Tiffany Studios New York, 23in (59cm) high. **£17,000-20,000** *CNY*

A Handel reverse painted glass and cold painted metal lamp, c1920. **£9,500-11,000** *S(NY)*

A Handel reverse painted glass and patinated metal lamp, c1915. **£3,500-4,500** *S(NY)*

A leaded glass and bronze floor lamp, by Tiffany Studios. **£5,500-7,000** *CNY*

A leaded glass and bronze table lamp 'Favrile Fabrique', by Tiffany Studios. **£5,500-7,000** *CNY*

A Tiffany Favrile glass and bronze peony lamp, c1910, 23in (58cm) high. **£20,000-22,000** *S(NY)*

A Tiffany Favrile and bronze poinsettia border lamp shade and base, c1910. **£15,000-17,000** *S(NY)*

A Tiffany Favrile glass and gilt bronze poppy filigree lamp, c1920. **£20,000-22,000** *S(NY)*

A Handel reverse painted glass and patinated metal lamp, c1920. **£9,000-10,000** *S(NY)*

A Pairpoint reverse painted glass scenic sea gull lamp, c1915, 25in (64cm). **£3,500-5,000** *S(NY)*

An Emile Gallé double
overlaid and etched glass
table lamp, 11in (28cm)
high. **£7,500-10,000** *CNY*

A Daum etched glass table
lamp, 15in (38cm) high.
£11,000-13,000 *CNY*

An Emile Gallé glass and
wrought iron table lamp,
with cameo signature,
20.5in (52cm) high.
£12,500-14,000 *CNY*

A Daum etched and
enamelled glass 'Rain' table
lamp, 14in (36cm) high.
£17,000-20,000 *CNY*

A Daum etched and enamelled
table lamp, signed on base
Daum Nancy, 14in (36cm) high.
£12,000-14,000 *CNY*

An Edgar Brandt gilt
bronze table lamp,
20in (51cm) high.
£4,500-6,000 *CNY*

A Daum etched and
enamelled glass vase, signed
Daum Nancy, 28in (71cm)
high. **£13,000-15,000** *CNY*

l. A Gallé cameo
glass plafonnier,
signed in cameo
Gallé, c1900, 16in
(41cm) diam.
£5,000-6,000
S(NY)

A Pairpoint reverse painted
blown-out glass and patinated
metal lamp, unsigned, c1915,
17.5in (45cm) high.
£3,000-4,000 *S(NY)*

l. A Gallé cameo glass and bronze
boudoir lamp, shade and base
signed, c1900, 10.5in (26cm)
high. **£5,500-7,000** *S(NY)*

A Daum etched glass and copper lamp, shade and base engraved Daum Nancy France, 1920s, 16.5in (42cm). **£5,500-7,000** *S*

A G. Argy-Rousseau pâte-de-verre and wrought iron lamp, base and shade signed, 1926, 14.5in (37cm) high. **£23,000-25,000** *S(NY)*

A Favrile ten-light glass and bronze table lamp, by Tiffany Studios. **£14,000-16,000** *CNY*

A Daum etched and enamelled glass table lamp, signed on base, 12.5in (32cm) high. **£6,500-9,000** *CNY*

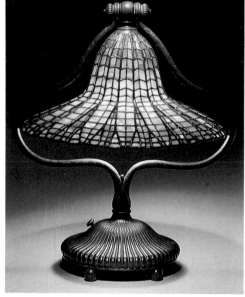

A Tiffany Studios 'Lotus' leaded glass and bronze table lamp, base stamped Tiffany Studios New York 6874, 18in (46cm) high. **£14,500-18,000** *CNY*

A Le Verre Français, cameo glass and wrought iron mushroom lamp, 1920s. **£3,500-4,000** *S*

A Daum etched glass and wrought iron chevron lamp, shade and base with engraved mark Daum Nancy France, 1920s, 12in (31cm). **£3,000-3,500** *S*

A pair of Albert Cheuret gilt bronze and alabaster tulip lamps, each inscribed Albert Cheuret, c1925. **£6,500-7,500** *S(NY)*

A Pairpoint reverse painted blown-out and patinated metal boudoir lamp, c1920. **£2,500-3,500** *S(NY)*

A Daum etched, applied and wheel carved glass vase, 10.5in (26cm) high. **£10,000-12,000** *CNY*

A silver plated brass tea infuser, by Christian Dell, 1924, 5in (13cm).
£2,000-2,500 *S*

A pair of Austrian silver table lamps, F. & D. Maly, marked and stamped with coat-of-arms, c1910.
£6,000-7,000 *S(NY)*

An Austrian brass lamp, c1920
£11,000-13,000 *S(NY)*

A Walker & Tolhurst silver bowl, designed by Gilbert Marks, maker's marks and London hallmarks for 1902, 2248.3gr.
£6,000-7,000 *C*

A Charles Rennie Mackintosh fish knife and fork and dessert spoon, c1905.
£600-900 *S*

An Austrian dessert knife and fork and table fork, c1906.
£3,000-4,000 *S*

A black painted nickel plated metal and plastic table lamp, Gae Aulenti for Martinelli Luce, c1960.
£300-400 *S*

A Georg Jensen silver coffee pot, marked, c1925.
£1,300-1,500 *S(NY)*

An Artificers Guild hammered silver bowl, London 1912.
£2,500-3,000 *C*

A pair of Renner and Maras wrought iron torchères, c1934.
£10,500-11,500 *S(NY)*

A pair of WMF electroplated metal candelabra and a dressing table mirror, stamped factory marks, c1900.
l. & r. **£5,000-6,000** *c.* **£1,200-1,500** *S*

A silver, lapis lazuli and glass cigarette box, stamped Cartier and importer's mark J.C., 1930, 7in (18cm) wide. **£2,000-2,500** *S*

An Otto Prutscher tea and coffee service, executed by Eduard Friedmann, each piece with maker's mark, c1913. **£60,000-70,000** *S*

A Georg Jensen silver four-piece tea and coffee set, numbered 71 and 181A, marked on bases, c1930. **£5,500-6,500** *S(NY)*

A Georg Jensen silver four-piece tea and coffee set, c1940. **£6,250-7,000** *S(NY)*

A Frans Zwollo Snr. Art Nouveau vase, finely engraved, signed, 1899. **£6,000-7,000** *S(Am)*

A Dagobert Peche silver coloured metal and ivory coffee pot, for the Wiener Werkstätte of 1922. **£14,000-16,000** *S*

A pair of Georg Jensen silver two-light candelabra, each marked 324, c1938, 9in (22cm) high, 73.5oz. **£11,000-13,000** *CNY*

A Josef Hoffmann silver coloured metal and ivory teapot, with hinged cover, for the Wiener Werkstätte, c1924. **£5,000-7,000** *S*

A Christopher Dresser, for Hukin & Heath, Aesthetic Movement electroplated sugar basin, c1880, **£600-1,000** and 7 cruet sets, c1880. **£2,700-3,500** *S*

A pair of Limoges Art Nouveau enamelled copper vases, restored, c1900, 12in (31cm) high. **£3,250-4,000** *S(NY)*

An aluminium, Bakelite and brass lamp. **£2,000-3,000** *S(NY)*

A patinated silvered bronze vase, stamped Christofle B63G, c1925. **£600-700** *S*

A gilded rosewood mirror, Wiener Werkstätte, c1925. **£12,000-14,000** *S*

A patinated and silvered bronze fish, marked E. M. Sandoz and initialled E.R., c1920. **£6,000-8,000** *S*

A silver coloured metal box and cover, with WW monograms and trademark, c1904. **£36,000-38,000** *S*

A brass jar and cover, Dagobert Peche for the Wiener Werkstätte, c1920. **£7,000-8,000** *S*

A silver coloured metal, coral and glass cruet set, marked, WW monogram, c1905. **£24,000-25,000** *S*

A parcel gilt silver vase, maker's mark of Tiffany & Co., New York, c1885, 6.5in (16.5cm), 16oz. **£13,000-15,000** *CNY*

Two Christofle electroplate champagne buckets, c1935. **£1,200-1,500** *S*

A silver coloured metal dish, Josef Hoffmann for the Wiener Werkstätte, marked, 1927. **£3,600-4,000** *S*

A pair of WMF Art Nouveau decanters and a visiting card tray, with factory marks, c1905. *l. & r.* **£1,800-2,000** *c.* **£1,300-1,500** *S*

A Georg Jensen silver vase, signed Arno Malinowski, 7in (18cm). **£2,300-2,600** *S(NY)*

A Georg Jensen silver coloured metal inkwell, with glass liner, 1919. **£1,700-2,000** *S*

W.E.J. Benson copper and brass entrée and muffin dishes, on a large tray, signed. **£600-800** *ASA*

A Hugo Leven electroplated metal tazza, impressed twice with facsimile signature 'H. Leven', c1900, 12in (31cm). **£900-1,200** *S*

An Edgar Brandt wrought iron grille, impressed E. Brandt, c1925, 33in (84cm) high. **£2,600-3,600** *S(NY)*

A Koch & Bergfeld, Bremen, silver and ivory covered cup, c1930, 11in (28cm) high, 23oz 10dwt. **£1,000-1,500** *S(NY)*

A set of 6 W.H. Haseler silver and enamel coffee spoons, for G.L. Connell, in original fitted case, 1906. **£950-1,500** *S*

A Tiffany Studios seventeen-piece bronze desk set, in the Zodiac pattern, all impressed Tiffany Studios/ New York and numbered, lamp shade cracked and repaired, c1920. **£3,000-3,500** *S(NY)*

A Dagobert Peche for the Wiener Werkstätte brass coupe, stamped with designer's monogram, 6in (15cm). **£2,000-3,000** *S*

A Josef Hoffmann vase, for the Wiener Werkstätte, c1910, 6.5in (16cm). **£3,000-4,000** *S*

A Maurice Bouval Art Nouveau bronze figural tray, inscribed M. Bouval, c1900, 16in (41cm) long. **£2,000-2,500** *S(NY)*

An Edgar Brandt wrought iron snake paperweight and geometric frame, stamped,1920s. **£1,500-2,000** *S*

A Jean Goulden champlevé enamelled silver box, the interior of the lid mottled turquoise, inscribed Jean Goulden, dated 1928. **£10,000-12,000** *S(NY)*

An Archibald Knox silver and turquoise vase, for Liberty & Co. 1902. **£3,500-4,000** *S*

A George Ellwood mahogany and stained glass cabinet, for J.S. Henry, c1900, 77.5in (197cm) high. **£2,000-2,500** *S*

A pair of Art Deco stained oak bergéres, re-upholstered, c1925, 33in (85cm). **£3,500-4,000** *S*

A Shapland and Petter oak dresser, inlaid with pewter, mother-of-pearl and brass, possibly designed by Baillie-Scott, c1890. **£1,700-2,200** *S*

An ebonized and painted corner cabinet, designed by Charles Rennie Mackintosh, with painted panel by Margaret Macdonald Mackintosh, c1897, 72.5in (183cm) high. **£13,500-15,000** *C*

A double door oak and brass cabinet, attributed to Leon Jallot, c1907, 76in (193cm) high. **£1,700-2,200** *S*

A pair of Heal's oak and rush ladderback armchairs, c1905, 48in (122cm). **£2,200-2,500** *S*

A Paul Poiret lacquered, gilt and silvered wood double bed, with nightstands and stools, c1929, 82in (208cm) long. **£4,500-6,000** *S(NY)*

A thuya wood side cabinet, c1870, 40in (102cm) high. **£2,000-2,500** *S*

An oak and rush high back armchair, c1907, 51in (130cm). **£2,500-3,000** *S*

An oak and brass buffet, attributed to Leon Jallot, c1907, 52in (132cm) high. **£1,700-2,500** *S*

A mahogany Art Nouveau hall stand, c1900, 104in (264cm) high.
£3,500-4,500 *S*

A Frank Lloyd Wright oak and leather chair, c1904.
£14,000-15,000 *S*

Two Alvar Aalto for Finmar Ltd., armchairs, maker's stamps, c1931.
£2,000-5,000 each *S*

Four Joubert et Petit mahogany and rosewood barrel chairs, c1930.
£3,500-4,500 *S(NY)*

A pair of leather and wood 'cloud' armchairs, some wear, c1930.
£700-800 *S*

A Charles Rohlfs oak drop front desk, with stylised monogram, maker's logo and date 1902, 36in (92cm).
£10,500-12,000 *CNY*

An Armand-Albert Rateau bronze and marble low table, raised on bird form supports, 40in (101.5cm).
£120,000-140,000 *S(NY)*

A chromium plated steel and glass table, 'B 19', by Marcel Breuer for Thonet, original label, c1928, 55in (140cm).
£5,000-6,000 *S*

A mirrored glass and pale wood laminate coffee table, c1930.
£900-1,200 *S*

An oak settle, by Gustav Stickley, model No. 291, with firm's red decal, c1908, 78in (198cm). **£7,500-8,500** *CNY*

A pair of cantilever nickel plated steel, leather and glass armchairs and a coffee table, by Josef Müller, Berlin, glass replaced, table 24in (61cm) diam. **£95,000-100,000** *S*

An Eavestaff 6-octave mini piano in Art Deco walnut case, 51in (130cm) wide, and matching stool. **£400-600** *PCh*

A Gillow & Co. 'Stafford' satinwood and walnut wardrobe, in 3 sections, stamped Gillow & Co L5778, 87.5in (223cm) high. **£5,000-6,000** *C*

An inlaid mahogany, writing bureau, with metal attachments, c1903. **£6,000-7,000** *S*

An Edgar Brandt wrought iron and gilt bronze firescreen, c1925, 33in (84cm) high. **£9,000-10,000** *S(NY)*

A Gio Ponti rosewood, parchment and marble dining room suite, c1935, table 87.5in (223cm) long. **£13,000-15,000** *S(NY)*

A Brandt firescreen. **£10,500-12,000** *S(NY)*

A wrought iron hall stand, attributed to Paul Kiss, c1925. **£7,250-8,500** *S(NY)*

A carved mahogany dining table and 18 dining chairs, with carved foliate frames and upholstered in tooled leather, c1910. **£12,000-15,000** *CNY*

A wrought iron firescreen, c1925, 31in (79cm). **£3,000-4,000** *S*

An Atelier Martine Art Deco wool carpet, signed Martine, c1923, 113 by 76in (287 by 193cm). **£3,000-4,000** *S*

A Wilton hand-knotted woollen carpet, by Edward McKnight Kauffer, c1929, 83 by 46.5in (210 by 117cm). **£5,500-6,500** *C*

An Art Deco wool carpet, c1923, 119 by 69in (302 by 175cm). **£1,500-2,000** *S*

A Liberty & Co. pewter and enamel clock, designed by Archibald Knox, 8in (20cm) high. **£2,500-3,500** *C*

An Adolf Loos brass and bevelled glass clock for J Heeg, with original movement, c1898, 19in (48cm). **£28,000-30,000** *S*

A Liberty & Co. pewter clock, with copper numerals and inset with abalone shells, 18in (46cm) high. **£3,000-4,000** *ASA*

An Art Deco diamond and black onyx desk clock, signed Cartier, Paris, No. 502, 769, 3416. **£6,500-7,500** *CNY*

A Liberty & Co. mantel clock, 1903. **£3,000-5,000** *S*

l. A Max Bill kitchen clock, with timer, for Gebrüder Junghans, Schramberg, 1951. **£1,000-1,200** *S*

A Martin Brothers salt glazed stoneware clock case, a fantastic creature crouched beneath clock face, damage, 1874. **£2,600-3,500** *S(NY)*

An Albin Müller patinated brass serpentine clock, designer's monogram on pendulum, c1906, 12.5in (32cm), with 2 keys. **£7,000-8,000** *S*

An Art Deco diamond, ruby, emerald and cultured pearl clip, mounted in platinum.
£13,000-15,000 *CNY*

A pair of Art Deco diamond clips, set with square, baguette, bullet and old European cut diamonds, mounted in platinum.
£5,000-7,000 *CNY*

An Archibald Knox for Liberty pendant, c1902.
£4,000-5,000 *S*

An Art Deco diamond double clip brooch, set with pavé and round diamonds, enhanced by an old European cut diamond, mounted in platinum. **£10,500-12,000** *CNY*

A silver coloured metal brooch, by Harry Bertoia, c1945.
£5,500-6,500 *S*

A silver coloured metal and coral pendant, stamped Stüber, c1908.
£900-1,200 *S*

An Art Deco emerald and diamond set platinum ring, 2.5ct.
£4,500-5,500 *MJB*

A silver coloured metal and enamel buckle, by Albrecht Holbein, c1900.
£1,400-1,600 *S*

An Art Deco diamond and gem set double clip brooch, mounted in platinum.
£5,500-6,500 *CNY*

A gold and rose quartz pendant, c1905.
£1,200-1,500 *S*

A silver, enamel and chalcedony stylised bird pin, Theodor Fahrner for Murrle, Bennett & Co., c1900.
£600-800 *S*

An Art Deco diamond, emerald and black onyx bracelet, mounted in platinum, 7in (18cm) long.
£10,000-12,000 *CNY*

Below An Art Deco ruby and diamond bracelet, mounted in platinum, 7in (18cm).
£12,000-14,000 *CNY*

Below An Art Deco diamond and emerald bracelet, mounted in platinum, 7.5in (19cm).
£8,500-10,000 *CNY*

An Art Deco cabochon ruby and diamond bracelet, 7in (18cm).
£15,000-18,000 *CNY*

An Art Deco diamond and emerald bracelet.
£10,000-11,000 *CNY*

An Art Deco diamond bracelet, mounted in platinum, 7in (18cm).
£12,000-14,000 *CNY*

l. An Art Deco emerald and diamond bracelet, mounted in platinum, signed Tiffany & Co, 7in (18cm).
£14,500-15,500 *CNY*

A silver coloured metal abstract brooch, stamped Ed Wiener, c1955, 3in (7.5cm).
£1,000-1,200 *S*

An Art Deco diamond dress clip, mounted in platinum, signed by Van Cleef & Arpels, No. 37.383.
£8,500-9,500 *CNY*

r. A silver coloured metal bracelet and earrings, the bracelet and one earring stamped Ed Wiener, c1947, bracelet 3in (7.5cm) max width.
£900-1,200 *S*

A Paolo de Poli enamelled copper and wood peacock. **£1,200-1,800** *S*

A funerary vase, by Elizabeth Fritsch, 1991. **£5,000-6,000** *C*

A stoneware footed bowl, by Dame Lucie Rie, with a golden bronze band at the rim, impressed LR seal, c1978, 7in (18cm) diam. **£1,800-2,200** *Bon*

A Shino stoneware teabowl, by Toyozo Arakawa, incised signature, c1950, 5in (12.5cm) diam. **£7,000-8,000** *Bon*

A stoneware vase, by Dame Lucie Rie, impressed LR seal, c1978, 9in (23cm). **£3,500-4,500** *Bon*

An earthenware vase, stamped Teco twice, model 85, 12in (30cm). **£4,000-4,500** *CNY*

'River and Moon Pot', by Elizabeth Fritsch, 1991. **£3,500-5,000** *C*

A stoneware inlaid sgraffito bowl, by Dame Lucie Rie, impressed LR, c1980. **£4,000-4,500** *C*

A stoneware bottle form vase, by Bernard Leach, impressed BL and St. Ives seals, c1965, 14in (35cm). **£1,800-2,200** *Bon*

A porcelain bowl, by Dame Lucie Rie, impressed LR seal, c1982, 6in (15cm). **£7,500-8,500** *Bon*

A stoneware vase, by Hans Coper. **£3,000-5,000** *C*

A Japanese bronze lobed
jardinière, on 8 elephant head
feet, inscribed Dai Nippon,
Bunsei Nensei, Sei Minju, 24.5in
(62cm) diam.
£3,500-4,000 *CSK*

A Japanese silver coloured metal
and shibyama two-handled vase,
cover and liner, the body inlaid in
mother-of-pearl and polished
hardstones, on a gold lacquered
ground applied with two dragon
shaped metal handles, the white
metal shoulders, domed quatrefoil
foot and domed cover decorated
with champlevé enamelled sprays
of flowers, the cover with hawk
shaped knop, indistinct seal mark
to base, damaged, 10.5in (26cm)
high.
£2,500-3,000 *HSS*

A bronze two-handled vase, cast with archaic
designs below central roundels of kylins,
with gilt details, 19thC, 16in (41cm).
£850-1,000 *S(S)*

Two Japanese bronze models of crayfish,
realistically modelled with their tails
tucked under their bodies, their
antennae slightly raised, old wear, 8.5in
(21cm) long.   **£350-450** *CSK*

A Japanese inlaid bronze vase,
the exterior decorated with a
continuous panel of a pagoda
among pine trees below a key-fret
style border and above 3 lotus
flowerheads and scrolling foliage,
on tripod feet, signed, Meiji
period, 3in (8cm).   **£450-600** *S(S)*

A Japanese patinated bronze
group of quail, coloured in copper,
shakudo and gilt, mounted on a
carved wood base, signed
Yoshitani sei, late 19thC, 14in
(35cm) long.
£1,700-2,000 *S*

A Japanese bronze articulated model of a crab,
the details of claws and body naturalistically
rendered, 4in (10cm) wide.   **£620-700** *CSK*

An inlaid iron tetsubin,
19thC, 7in (18cm).
£400-600 *S(S)*

A Japanese silver coloured
metal and shibayama tray,
10in (25cm) wide.
£2,500-3,000 *HSS*

A Japanese bronze model of a warrior, dressed in robes decorated in relief with dragons among clouds, with a long and short sword to his side, pole missing, 24in (61cm) high.
£550-650 *CSK*

A Japanese bronze model of a swimming carp, supported on its fins, the head turned slightly to the left, gilt inlaid eyes, signed, 8in (20cm) long. **£1,500-2,000** *CSK*

Netsuke

Two ivory netsuke, the first being a Manju, carved in relief with Konoha Tengu balancing a spinning top on his nose, signed Gyokugi, the second is a fishergirl with a large octopus on her back, signed Gyokkosai, both 19thC, 1.5 and 2in (4 and 5cm).
£1,000-1,200 *S*

A wood and ivory nesuke of a skull, thigh bone and lotus bud resting on a large lotus leaf, 1.5in (4cm) wide.
£300-400 *CSK*

An ivory netsuke of a spider on a melon, with a vine leaf and bud, 19thC, 1.5in (4cm).
£200-250 *S(S)*

An ivory netsuke of Onna Daruma, seated on a removable circular mat, signed Mitsutsugu, 19thC, 1.5in (4cm).
£420-500 *S(S)*

A marine ivory netsuke of coiled snake resting on a skull, 1.5in (4cm) long. **£250-300** *CSK*

A set of 3 boxwood mask netsuke, representing Okame, Usofuki and Kannon, each crisply carved in lightly stained and patinated wood, a bar on the back forming the himotoshi, signed Sogaku to, c1900, 1.5in (4cm).
£800-1,200 *S*

Snuff Bottles

An agate thumbprint snuff bottle, of pebble shape, the stone with grey and white bands, c1800.
£300-400 *S(S)*

A macaroni agate snuff bottle, of flattened ovoid form, on an oval foot rim. **£300-350** *S(S)*

An agate snuff bottle, the smoky grey stone carved with vertical reeding, gilt metal mounted stopper. **£350-500** *S(S)*

An agate snuff bottle, carved with a sage beneath a willow tree, the reverse with figures and peaches, mask and ring handles carved in low relief.
£600-700 *S(S)*

A coloured ivory snuff bottle, carved in relief with a figure on a rearing horse, colleagues standing back in alarm under plantain and willow branches, incised Qianlong mark, 20thC.
£700-800 *S(S)*

A puddingstone snuff bottle, the mottled stone with circular inclusions, c1800.
£400-450 *S(S)*

A cinnabar lacquer snuff bottle, carved with Shou Lao standing beneath a pine tree, the reverse with a maiden, restored, c1800.
£240-300 *S(S)*

A lacquer burgauté snuff bottle, of flattened pear form, decorated using minute chips of gilt metal and mother-of-pearl, in shades of blue and green, with circular flower panels reserved against a diaper pattern ground.
£250-350 *S(S)*

A moulded porcelain snuff bottle, finely modelled with 9 dogs-of-Fo gambolling with brocade balls, against a cloud pierced ground, all coloured cinnabar red with gilt detail, mark and period of Jiaqing.
£400-600 *S(S)*

A red overlay glass snuff bottle, carved with animals of the Zodiac over a bubble suffused ground, c1780.
£450-550 *S(S)*

A porcelain snuff bottle, formed as a folded lotus leaf with reeds and birds, c1850.
£200-300 *S(S)*

A puddingstone snuff bottle, of stout squared form, the stone with mottled light and dark inclusions.
£300-350 *S(S)*

A blue overlay glass snuff bottle, decorated with figures beneath bamboo and prunus over a bubble suffused ground, c1800.
£450-550 *S(S)*

A porcelain snuff bottle, enamelled with 2 dragons chasing a flaming pearl amidst clouds and waves, silver coloured metal mount and stopper, the six-character mark painted in iron red on base, mark and period of Guangxu. **£500-600** *S(S)*

An agate snuff bottle, of flattened stout ovoid form, carved using speckled brown and ochre inclusions in the pale grey stone with various animal subjects, c1800. **£400-600** *S(S)*

A Peking glass snuff bottle, imitation nephrite, finely polished discoidal form, 18thC. **£200-400** *S(S)*

Tsuba

An iron tsuba, carved in relief with the large head of a nio expelling a wasp from his nose, his scarf of inlaid brass and other details gilt, the reverse with 3 birds in shishiaibori, inscribed on 2 inlaid silver tablets Hamano Noriyuki, 19thC, 3.5in (9cm). **£1,700-2,000** *S*

A copper tsuba, carved in relief with Daruma floating on waves, his hossu floating on the reverse, beneath gouged clouds, details in shibuichi, signed with a kakihan, early 19thC, 3in (8cm). **£700-900** *S*

An associated pair of sukashi tsuba for a daisho, each in the form of 2 encircling oxen, their tails curling to form a rim, one with a rope halter, 18thC, 3in (8cm). **£700-1,000** *S*

A ko-kinko yamagane sukashi tsuba, of mokko form, carved and pierced as a stylised flower, with tomobako and certificate, Muromachi period, 16thC, 2.5in (6cm). **£600-700** *S*

The certificate describes the tsuba as tachi-shi and dates it 1470-1570.

Miscellaneous

A Japanese embroidered silk picture, very finely worked with a study of a peasant woman carrying a bundle of reeds, Meiji/Taisho period, 19 by 12in (48 by 31cm) framed and glazed. **£400-600** *S(S)*

A Chinese red, green and cream 3-tiered box with canted corners, containing shaped smaller boxes and covers, decorated within red lacquer pierced container modelled as a table, the cover carved in relief with figures in pavillion gardens in a mountainous river landscape, within a band of key and cell-pattern, old damage and restoration, Qianlong, 7in (18cm) high. **£900-1,200** *CSK*

TRIBAL ART

Although during the past year the percentage of unsold lots in tribal art sales has on average increased, this has for the most part been due to the reluctance of sellers to part with good quality material rather than a real decline in auction values or interest from buyers. When top quality lots have appeared in the salerooms they have still commanded very high prices, particularly if they have not been seen on the market before. For example, a Songye stool which surfaced from the collection of a Belgian colonial family sold at Christie's in the last few months for £110,000, against an estimate of £60,000-80,000, more than had been realised for a similar stool sold during the 'peak' of the market in 1987. The McCarty-Cooper tribal sale at Christie's New York was a great test of the market as almost every item had been purchased during the past seven years, many having been bought for sums which, even at the peak of the market, had caused quite a stir. In the event, the sale result came as a great relief to dealers and collectors, several lots exceeding expectations and exceeding the prices McCarty-Cooper had paid for them at the peak of the market. A Fang figure purchased in New York for $71,500 in November 1984 sold for $440,000.

There has been no reduction in the number of fakes appearing in the auction rooms during the past year and rumours have been rife at the auction views. This has meant those lots with a good provenance have been at a premium, sometimes commanding several times the price of a lot without history; for example, the Ashanti pottery lamp known to have been in the Pitt Rivers Museum at the beginning of the century realised £4,180 against an estimate of £2,000-3,000.

Stories of important tribal artefacts turning up in the country and being bought for a song have been circulating for many years but the current scarcity of good quality material has also led to the phenomenon of extraordinary excitement being generated when a piece, even of mediocre quality, turns up at a provincial saleroom, often realising several times its likely auction price at a specialised sale in London. A Maori bowl for which a dealer is reputed to have paid £9,000 in a country sale was sold in London for £2,000 recently, a cautionary tale for would-be bargain hunters.

African art has been the most difficult area during the past year. It has always accounted for 50% or more of the lots in tribal sales and despite the scarcity of top quality material in the sales there has been no shortage of mediocre or bad African art. Zaire and Gabon have continued to command the highest prices but again only for the very best material. The market for Yoruba art has suffered more than most with no shortage of material, even the very best examples having met with little interest from buyers. By contrast, the art of South Africa has increased dramatically in value with a number of long standing collectors recently turning their attention to this area; consequently today headrests, snuff bottles and unusual knobkerries are frequently fetching four figure sums which, a few years ago, could have been bought for a few hundred pounds or less.

The demand for American Indian and Eskimo art has not diminished and competition between serious American collectors is often fierce. A pair of Seminole moccasins estimated at £1,000-1,500 were sold in London recently for £20,000 after a battle between telephone bidders. Artefacts from the turn of the century have become more acceptable to the modest collector, with items made for 'Wild West' shows early this century being in demand.

The market for Pre-Columbian material is still poor in London with the majority of material available being heavily restored or simply fake. Many of the fakes are themselves now antique and whilst buyers exist prepared to pay modest sums for decorative pots, prices rarely exceed a few hundred pounds.

Polynesian art has remained popular with record breaking prices for top lots. A Fiji headrest from the Methodist Missionary Society which had sold for £6,500 in June 1987 was sold recently for $77,000. Such high prices have led to an increase in the number of high quality Polynesian fakes appearing on the market though this is by no means a new phenomenon. A Hawaiian style figure thought to be the work of the famous carver James Little who worked at the beginning of this century and which was published as genuine as recently as 1967 sold this year for £1,100.

New Guinea art has not been in short supply, the vast majority dating from the 1960's or later, and whilst there are still buyers interested for its decorative quality, prices rarely exceed £500, though carvings with a provenance going back to the early years of this century, or even later for more remote areas of the island, can still bring several thousand pounds.

With very few named carvers and many objects which defy classification, tribal art has never been a field for the investor. Its relatively small group of enthusiastic collectors frequently pay far in excess of what might be considered a reasonable sum for a fine and rare carving in the not unreasonable belief that they may not get another chance to buy such a piece again. As a result tribal art has remained relatively unaffected by the recent decline in prices seen in the Impressionist and Contemporary Art markets.

Tribal Art

A Sierre Leone soapstone figure, nomoli, forearms missing, 16thC, 6in (15cm) high.
£650-750 *C*

A Maori feather box, carved at each end in high relief with a tiki figure, the remaining surface covered with notched scrolls, concentric circles and linked chain ornament, dark patina, cracked and repaired, 18.5in (47cm) wide.
£1,700-2,000 *C*

A Krinjabo terracotta funerary head, blackish patina, minor damage, 9in (23cm) high.
£1,000-1,500 *C*

A Yoruba bowl, for ifa divination, agere ifa, crusty patina, from Iseyin, 8in (20cm) high.
£500-600 *C*

An Ashanti pottery lamp, modelled as a maternity figure, the mother seated on a large stool which forms the lamp, her large flat head with features modelled in relief, holding the child who stands between her legs, neck repaired, 9in (23cm) high.
£4,200-4,700 *C*

A group of 7 ibeji from Abeokuta, 2 pairs of females, another pair, male and female, wearing various coloured bead and coconut shell ornaments, and a male with incised apron, all on square bases, 8.5 to 9in (21 to 22cm) high.
£400-500 *CSK*

Birds appear to be a popular motif for the supports of agere ifa in the Iseyin area, carved in various modes from realistic to the stylised. Our example is conceived as a series of triangular forms, the wings to tail tip as the central triangle with 2 smaller triangles to complete the tail.

A Californian basket, woven with 7 cactus-like motifs in dark fibre on a pale ground, plaited rim, perhaps Washo, 9.5in (23cm) diam.
£600-900 *C*

A Lulua figure, crouched with the hands placed behind the ears, the arms and legs forming a continuous curve, 3 horns carved about the coiffure, the narrow face with open mouth and spectacle type eyes, glossy dark brown patina, c1890, 9in (22cm) high.
£4,500-6,000 *C*

A rare Nilotic fibre doll, the elaborate coiffure formed as 2 large wings of plaited fibre, 4 strands of pink and blue beads above the carved wooden breasts set in gum, knotted fibre buttocks, multiple strands of red and white striped beads retaining a skin loin cloth, reddish patina, 8.5in (21cm) high.
£600-700 *CSK*

A Rotse bowl and cover, the handle carved as a leopard, a band of notched ornament below the rim of the bowl, ribbed panel to one end, scorched patina, lid chipped, 16in (40cm) long.　**£500-600**　*C*

A Haida argillite carving of 2 figures in a canoe, the female with inset ivory labret and seated behind the male who wears a hat, their cloaks and the sides of the canoe have carved bear features and heads of bears each end, the female's left arm missing, damaged, 19thC, 10.5in (26cm) long.　**£2,500-4,000**　*C*

An Ngala executioner's sword, the birfurcated blade incised on each side with a band of notched ornament, the base of the blade bound with metal wire, the double flanged hilt with inset upholstery nails, 27in (68cm) long.
£150-200　*C*

Three Maori Kauri gum heads, each with painted moko ornament to the face, 2 with black painted hair, the third with yellow hair and moustache, inscribed on the reverse Kauri gum head of King Tawhiao, damaged and repaired, each 13.5in (34cm) high.　**£1,300-1,700**　*C*

A Samoan bowl, for kava, carved as a turtle, the flippers with notched triangles about the border, the head with shell inlay eyes, on 8 legs, dark glossy patina, 21.5in (54cm) long.
£2,300-3,000　*C*

An Ashanti display figure, for the ntan dance group, representing a seated District Officer, carved wearing uniform, pith helmet and watch, his feet resting on a chief's palace, painted black, damaged, 19in (48cm) high.
£250-650　*C*

A Bobo antelope mask, with triangular snout, the tip of one horn with native mend, the whole painted with red, white and black pigments, minor damages, 19in (48cm) long.
£250-300　*C*

A Mangaia turret adze, the basalt blade secured with finely plaited coir, the broad shaft and base of oval section, the latter pierced with 28 square apertures, carved allover with chevrons and crosses, damaged, 21in (53cm) high.
£900-1,200 *CSK*

An Anyi pottery vessel, the 2 spouts each modelled in relief with a head, one with lobed coiffure the other ridged, raised scarification to the necks and faces, the spherical body modelled in relief with 2 splayed recumbent figures, old label, 13in (33cm) high.
£250-350 *C*

A rare documented carving, by James Little, the standing figure carved in the Kona style, with hands on the hips, the forked head, lateral panels and teeth each with serrated edges and showing extensive traces of blue paint, 20in (51cm) high.
£1,500-2,500 *CSK*

A Maori post figure, standing with the arms carved in relief and hands placed on the abdomen, the face with engraved and blackened tattoo ornament, the body with notched scrolls, 3 sides of the tall base with carved scrolls, notched edges along 2 corners, mid-19thC, 36in (91cm) high.
£1,200-2,000 *C*

Two Maori figures, one standing with the arms free of the body and the hands on the abdomen, the other with elongated head, the arms in relief, each with the surface carved extensively with notched bands, each with old label with monogram AEC damaged, 21.5 and 27in (54 and 67.5cm) long.
£1,800-2,200 *C*

A Canadian Indian beaded birchbark vase, of hexagonal section and baluster form, the silk covered bark sewn with various foliate and geometric motifs in coloured beads incorporating the date 1888, in fine condition, with glass dome, 7in (17.5cm) high.
£500-600 *C*

Three Letti figures, each crouching with the arms folded across the knees, the 2 largest each with forked headdress carved with scrolls, the rectangular bases similarly carved, the smallest with tuft to the top of the head, 4 to 7.5in (10 to 18.5cm) high.
£900-1,200 *C*

A Bobo animal mask, with concentric circular eyes, long ears and pierced triangular mouth, painted in black, red and white, minor damage, 16in (40cm) long.
£200-300 *C*

A Tonga basket, of compressed spherical form, ornamented with cross hatched triangles in plaited coir, damaged, 18in (45cm) diam.
£3,000-3,500 *C*

A Colima pottery dog, standing with pierced open mouth showing many teeth, pierced nostrils, the ears pinched and pierced, the tail curved over the plump body, restored, 14.5in (37cm) long.
£1,000-1,500 *C*

A brass presentation 'King Plate' of crescent form, a pierced circle at each end with an emu and a kangaroo respectively, inscribed 'Presented to Queen Grace Of The Nyungar 11th May. 1881. Tamulgani Outstation', the border with stamped crescents and circlets, pierced twice for suspension, 9in (22cm) wide.
£500-700 *C*

A New Caledonia ceremonial axe, the rectangular nephrite blade secured to the wood head with finely bound plaited coir, 2 bands of woven flying fox fur about the top of the shaft, dark glossy patina, 25.5in (65cm) long.
£1,000-1,200 *C*

A roll of Santa Cruz feather money, tavau, the long band of fibre sewn with the brilliant red feathers of the small honey bird, Myzomela cardinalis, suspending clusters of Job's tears and fibre tassels. **£920-1,200** *C*

A Haida mountain goat horn spoon, the handle carved as a bear, a mask on its abdomen, its ears flanking the bird head finial, 19thC, 8in (20cm) long.
£800-900 *C*

A Solomon Islands ceremonial paddle, the blade carved as a bonito, the open mouth with carved teeth grasping the shaft, the eyes and body with inset fretted pearl shell inlay, similar shell inlay to the tapered finial and crescent crossbar, black painted embellishments, 6 inlays missing, 59in (150cm) long.
£2,000-3,000 *C*

A Mangaia adze, the small stone blade lashed with plaited coconut fibre to the cylindrical shaft which is carved with 39 bands of stylised figures, damaged finial, 28in (71cm) long.
£500-700 *C*

A brass presentation 'King Plate' of crescent form, 8.5in (21cm) wide.
£900-1,200 *C*

A Haida mountain goat horn spoon, the handle carved as a chief wearing ceremonial hat in the jaws of a killer whale whose body is incised on the back of the bowl, 8in (20cm) high.
£1,300-1,700 *C*

A Maori quarter staff, taiaha, the head finial with haliotis shell inlay eyes, 2 deficient, woven flax collar below the head with red yarn, attached feathers and flax tassels, dark glossy patina, 54.5in (138cm) long.
£600-800 *C*

A Marquesas pipe, the bowl carved as a stylised figure, his hands before him flanking a panel carved with angular geometric motifs, the stem carved with a stylised supine figure, dark glossy patina, crack to stem, 6.5in (15.5cm) long.
£1,700-2,200 *C*

A rare Easter Island club, ua, the Janus head finial with eyes recessed for inlay, grooved coiffure, slightly flared shaft, 44in (111cm) long.
£4,000-4,500 *C*

A Fiji kava bowl, on 11 tapered cylindrical legs, pierced triangular lug to underside, glossy patina, 27in (69cm) diam.
£800-1,200 *C*

Two nautilus shell vessels, each covered with hatched triangles and other geometric designs in brown resin, each pierced twice for twisted fibre cord, inscribed on the inside 52/11935, with old museum label Nicobar or Andaman Islands, 8 and 7.5in (20 and 18cm) long.
£800-900 *C*

An Anang (Ibibio) mask, of oval form, with twisted features, a crooked nose, the mouth to one side, pierced oval eyes below the domed forehead, the crescent coiffure with outer notched edge, some fibre about the pierced border, black patina, minor restorations and eroded border, 12in (30cm) high.
£400-600 *C*

A rare Tetela-Sungu Janus helmet mask, each face with small features carved in relief, rectangular eye holes flanking the mouth, the median crest with 3 rows of holes for insertion of feathers, missing, the whole painted reddish brown with bold geometric design in white, native hide repair to the rim, pierced about the border, 12.5in (32cm) high.   **£1,000-1,200** *C*

A Yoruba headdress, for the Egungun masquerade, with a hare carved behind the large ears and a waisted ornament in front, medicine bottles carved on the forehead of the bearded face, the whole painted in colours, by the Eshubiyi household of Abeokuto, damaged, 18.5in (47cm) high.
£450-500 *CSK*

A North West Coast mountain sheep horn spoon, the flat handle with applied white metal panel with engraved creature, beaver's tail and a plaque below, some unfinished carving to the underside, c1900, 10.5in (26cm) high.
£300-400 *C*

A Luba shankadi axe, the metal blade inset in the mouth of the carved head which has an elaborate coiffure embellished with inset brass upholstery nails, 16in (40cm) high.
£1,200-1,700 *C*

An Ekoi Janus headdress, each skin covered face pierced for the eyes and mouth and coloured a reddish orange, applied above with 4 carved figures, and 2 inset mirrors, each figure with articulated arms and painted in colours, the flared circular base pierced 4 times, 19.5in (49cm) high.   **£600-700** *C*

Two New Ireland bird finials, for dance staffs, each carved as the head of a hornbill with some red and black painted motifs and panel at the rear, inset shell-opercula eyes, one with cassowary feathers bound at the next with twisted fibre, also suspending shells and feathers on strands of beads, the other with fibre bound with barkcloth, 7 and 10.5in (18 and 26cm) long. **£1,800-2,200** *C*

A Fang staff, with standing figure finial, the face with applied circular metal eyes and tall brass collar, the shaft of square section below 4 flared knops, dark glossy patina, 27.5in (70cm) high.
£800-1,200 *C*

A Vanuatu head, nambuci, the wood shaft with applied head of mud, fibre and cobwebs, coloured black, white and orange, the fibre top knot blackened, 2 inset curved boar's tusks flanking the mouth, from the Small Nambas of South Central Malekula, 27in (68cm) long.
£900-1,500 *C*

A Bijugo buffalo mask headdress, the face pierced horizontally at the jaws to show the inset tongue, the nose and eyes encrusted with mud, the flared base with wing like ears and attached plaited and twisted fibre binding, painted red triangles within black borders about the jaws and back of head, the remainder painted black and white, minor old damage, 23in (58cm) high.   **£350-450** *C*

Part of a New Ireland mask, carved as a squatting figure with shell opercula inlay eyes, the jowls encrusted with fibre and mud, the limbs spread eagled flanked by 2 wing like panels, pierced at the centre, the base with old label, various deficiencies, 20.5in (52cm) wide.
£800-1,200 *C*

A Tonga 'Paddle' club, culacula, the broad blade and upper shaft carved allover with asymmetric design with panels of triangles, lozenges, rectangles, a zigzag spiral and other motifs, raised transverse ridge to each side, the grip carved with bands of zigzags above the flared butt, fine dark glossy patina, minor repair, 47in (118cm) long.   **£5,000-5,500** *C*

A pair of Eastern Great Lakes moccasins, of smoked buckskin, the uppers embroidered with curved motif in red and blue dyed porcupine quill.
£4,000-4,500 *C*

An Athapaskan beaded cloth octopus bag, red wool tassels on triple green glass bead fringe, plaited fibre carrying strap, c1880, 21in (53cm) long.
£1,800-2,000 *C*

A Huron birchbark dish, with oblong centre and flared sides with shaped borders, the whole embroidered in coloured moosehair with exotic flowersprays, minor damage, 10.5in (26cm) long.
£150-200 *C*

A Senufo helmet mask, the carved horns each with 4 applied white metal bands, a female figure seated upon a crescent each side obscuring part of the serrated median crest, cloth panel with sewn cowrie shells pendant at the back, from the Boundiali region, 13.5in (35cm) high without attachments.
£2,000-3,000 *C*

ISLAMIC WORKS OF ART

A Mamluk Pottery baluster vase, the white exterior painted with a broad band of Mamluk 'thuluth' inscription, the gaps between the letters painted black, a band of roundels around the shoulder and stripes around the neck, restored, 14thC, 6in (16cm) high.
£1,500-2,500 *C*

The inscription reads 'al-'izz al-da'im wa'l-iqbal' (perpetual glory and good fortune).

A Mamluk brass gulla tray, with pierced floral decoration, the interstices filled with palmettes and flowering vine around engraved roundels with birds flying around rosettes, the central sunken roundel surrounded by a 'thuluth' honorific inscription interrupted by rosette roundels, outer lobed motif stripe, rubbed, 15thC, 17.5in (45cm) diam. **£5,000-6,000** *C*

An Ottoman mother-of-pearl and tortoiseshell veneered pen box, the upper edge with zigzag motifs made from rhino horn and walrus ivory, the lower edge similar with ebony and bone, the top of the lower section with silver and hardwood banding, later silver hinges and hooks, velvet lining, damaged, 17thC, 12.5in (31.5cm) long. **£2,000-2,500** *C*

An Herati silver inlaid bronze stem, heavily cast with medial ridge, the upper section with a repeating lozenge lattice of palmettes, rubbed, 13thC, 14in (35.5cm) high. **£1,700-2,000** *C*

An early Safavid tinned copper Dervish's bowl (kashkul), with inscription, each side carved with a panel of elaborate palmettes, the rim with similar minor band, associated tinned brass complex link chain with swivelling attachments, rubbed, late 15thC, 8in (20.5cm) long. **£4,500-5,500** *C*

An Ottoman enamelled copper jar and cover, imitating the Continental porcelain original, the jar of broad baluster form on spreading foot, the cover of shallow double domed form, 'tombak' floral knop, the green sides painted with gold scrolling leafy vine around white cusped cartouches with floral sprays, the interior plain white, slight damage, c1850, 7in (18cm) high. **£1,300-1,700** *C*

Three Turkish brass candlesticks, the centre of which rises to a faceted stem with plain and tulip-shaped bosses below the similarly shaped mouth with flared serrated rim, slight damage, 17thC, largest 15in (37.5cm) high. **£2,000-2,500** *C*

The personal seal of Major General Sir Willoughby Keane of Ghuznee (sic) and Cappoquin, the pale yellow agate finely carved with scrolling vine around the elegant 'nasta'liq' inscription, in original gold mount with repoussé dense foliage and walrus ivory round handle with waisted shaft, dated AD 1839, 4in (10.5cm) high. **£1,700-2,200** *C*

An East Persian pierced bronze jardinière, the sides with a broad band of pierced interlaced arabesques enclosing stylised knotted roundels, an arcaded band below, a band of 'kufic' inscription around the mouth with inner linked roundel band, slight damage, 13thC, 5in (12.5cm) diam. **£900-1,200** *C*

Did you know

MILLER'S Antiques Price Guide builds up year by year to form the most comprehensive photo-reference system available.

RUSSIAN WORKS OF ART

A Russian porcelain egg, painted within a gilt frame joined by a turquoise ground and gilt diaper band, 3.5in (9cm) high, with a cover and stand; and a Russian porcelain egg, painted with Christ's ascension from the grave, reserved on a gold ground, 3in (7.5cm) high, on a stand.
£500-550 *C(S)*

A Russian pottery egg, painted with Christ holding the cross, enamelled in colours on a gold ground, the reverse with a monogram X.L., ring mount, 4.5in (11.5cm) high.
£400-500 *C(S)*

Mother of God Vladimirskaia, realistically painted, with parcel gilt oklad, repoussé and engraved with stylised foliage scrolls and arabesques, maker's mark illegible, in a glazed kiot, Moscow, 1892, 12in (31cm) high.
£2,000-2,200 *C*

A Russian Imperial Glass Factory engraved and cut glass goblet, the bowl engraved with a profile portrait of Tzarina Elizabeth Petrovna, 9in (22.5cm) high.
£1,100-1,200 *C(S)*

A Russian cut glass mug, with gilt rim and handle, 4in (10cm) high.
£1,500-2,000 *C(S)*

A pair of Russian engraved wine glasses, each decorated with a crowned shield medallion with an eagle divided by a chevron, the reverse with ribbon tied foliage on a spiral stem on a domed foot, 9in (22.5cm) high.
£650-700 *C(S)*

A Russian cut glass wine glass, gilt with a profile portrait of Marshal Kukuzov, beneath a gilt key pattern band above a fluted lower part and on a faceted knop and fluted stem, 7.5in (19cm) high.
£1,600-1,700 *C(S)*

A silver trompe l'oeil cigar box, engraved and chased overall to simulate tobacco tax bands and brand name with seals, by Petr Miliukov, Moscow 1896, 5.5in (14cm) long.
£2,300-3,000 *C*

A Russian icon of the Mother of God of the Burning Bush, 12in (31cm) high.
£400-500 *CSK*

A composite 12-piece silver toilette set, comprising: a dish and beaker with gilt interiors, a covered powder box with original puff, 2 patch boxes, 2 candlesticks, a silver covered pentray, and 4 silver mounted perfume bottles, all with the engraved initials JC, the beaker by Efim Siderov, St Petersburg, one patch box Moscow 1852, unknown maker's Cyrillic initals FV, the remainder St Petersburg, various makers, various later years, in a lined fitted wooden case, the hinged lid stamped in Russian 'Vladimirov, SPB, Nevskii prospekt no. 31', with brass handles and catches, on a stand, dish 8in (20.5cm) long.
£3,500-4,500 *C*

ART NOUVEAU

DECORATIVE ARTS

It is generally accepted that Art Nouveau was born out of the Arts and Crafts Movement and peaked during the late 1890s and 1900s. By the onset of WWI, its demise was certain, but during this very short span of time a revolution in design had taken place. Artists and designers were inspired by the free forms and sinuous lines which were to become synonymous with the Art Nouveau style. Having discovered a new found freedom from the ordered but over fussy Victorian ideas of decoration they set out to explore and exploit this freedom.

In France Emile Gallé and Daum were the leading exponents of the art of cameo glass. Many of their designs were inspired by the delicate plant form motifs found in Japanese art. Whilst the asymmetrical inlaid and marquetry furniture designs of Louis Marjorelle display a totally new and uninhibited approach.

Credit must be given to Arthur Lasenby Liberty, the creator of the famous London store whose far-sighted approach to retailing led him to commission the work of individual artists, the most notable of whom is Archibald Knox, whose fluid, though more restrained work in silver, pewter and jewellery has come to epitomise the English style of Art Nouveau.

The semi-clad, slightly innocent but teasingly erotic portrayal of the female form was surely the most oft-repeated image of the era, whether captured on the canvas by Toulouse Lautrec, incorporated in poster designs by Alphonse Mucha or cast with free flowing hair amidst floral motifs in the pewter designs of the German company W.M.F. Though today we may find Art Nouveau charming and almost coquettish, there is no doubt that at the time the Art Nouveau style appealed largely to the Bohemian and avant garde. One cannot help but imagine that amongst polite post-Victorian society the portrayal of sensuously half-clad females may have 'sat' rather uncomfortably.

It was impossible for the gently poetic forms of Art Nouveau to survive alongside the horror of war. The Art Deco artists emerging after WWI eschewed the romantic forms of Art Nouveau, preferring the sharper angles, straighter lines and more austere materials which reflected the machine age fast growing up around them. They looked to, and were influenced by, Hollywood and its stars. In Egypt, the discovery of Tutankhamen's tomb explains the strong Egyptian forms seen in the sculpture and ceramics of the period. Sometimes called 'The Jazz Age' , it was certainly 'Art imitating life' - with an immediacy as never before. The tantalus was replaced by the cocktail shaker. Ladies danced The Charleston in revealing beaded dresses. Fashionable society travelled in limousines adorned with the stylised mascots designed by René Lalique. The mass production techniques he employed in his glass making allow today's collectors the opportunity to build collections of his work. His jewellery designs though were unique. He combined the use of non-precious materials with the rarest of gems to produce what can only be described as sculpture to adorn the body. His work, and the work of many contemporary artists, was displayed at the Paris Exhibition of 1926 from whence the term 'Style Moderne' evolved.

Whether one's passion is for Jungenstil from Germany, Art Nouveau from France, style Liberty from England or Art Deco, described through a myriad of terms which evoke the style, there is no doubting the immense appeal of the artifacts of these times to today's collectors.

Arts and Crafts furniture has for some time been emerging as a major interest to collectors. Individually designed and made, it is

A Clarice Cliff Fern pot, decorated with swirls, 3.5in (9cm) high.
£325-360 *RIC*

almost always of fine quality and if unsigned can often be attributed to the artist responsible.

Bronze and bronze and ivory figures by Preiss, Chiparus, Colinet, Lorenzl, Zack and others have a sustaining appeal. The hand finishing techniques involved make them prohibitively expensive to reproduce today and although copies do exist, it is rarely without some sacrifice to quality.

Whilst the work of the larger pottery companies such as Moorcroft and Doulton have always found a ready market, the smaller ones have sometimes struggled to achieve the same level of interest. I am pleased and not a bit surprised to see a resurgence of interest in the Royal Lancastrian lustre wares produced by the Pilkington Co., the Isnic inspired designs of the Burmantofts factory and the scraffito decorated wares of Della Robia, amongst others.

It is not surprising that the output of the Art Nouveau and Deco Movements was so finite when one considers the very short time span involved. Whilst the finest examples of work by the major artists are out of reach of the average buyer, it is still possible for a discerning novice with modest resources to acquire good examples of the work of the less famous designers. Examples across the spectrum are available to the new collector, who would be well advised to seek the assistance of a reputable dealer whose stock is sympathetic to their taste and who can guide them at their pace.

ART NOUVEAU

Arts and Crafts Furniture

A Scottish Arts & Crafts oak bureau bookcase, by G. Laird, Glasgow.
£720-800 *GIL*

An Arts & Crafts buffet, 55in (139.5cm) wide.
£450-575 *APO*

An Arts & Crafts oak bureau, standing on 4 reeded legs, 27in (68.5cm) wide.
£220-250 *GAK*

An oak bureau by Sidney Barnsley, with a fitted interior, with frieze drawer and 2 panelled cupboard doors, on moulded trestle ends with arched apron, 34in (86cm) wide.
£2,500-3,500 *C*

A Neo-Gothic carved and inlaid oak hanging cabinet, 41in (104cm) wide.
£3,200-3,700 *C*

A pair of oak side cabinets, with parquetry decoration, stamped Gillow & Co. 2344, 65in (164.5cm) wide, with single pedestal en suite stamped Gillow & Co. 2343.
£5,000-6,000 *C*

An Arts & Crafts oak bureau, with a fitted interior of pigeon-holes and 2 drawers, above 3 long similarly panelled drawers, on bracket feet, 36in (91.5cm) wide.
£1,000-1,200 *C*

An oak inlaid dwarf cabinet, by J. P. White, designed by M. H. Baillie-Scott, the cupboard door with pewter and fruitwood inlay, c1904, 20in (51cm) wide.
£1,700-2,000 *C*

A mahogany and satinwood breakfront cabinet, the design attributed to Thomas E. Collcutt, the marquetry to Stephen Webb, with original red velvet interior, stamped Collinson & Lock, 900, c1885, 65in (165cm) wide.
£2,000-2,500 *C*

A corner cabinet, by Heal & Son, on a plinth base, 21.5in (54cm) wide.
£400-500 *C*

Four dining chairs and one carver, by George Walton, 40in (101.5cm) high.
£250-300 *APO*

An Arts & Crafts high backed elbow chair in dark oak, with solid seat.
£100-120 *LF*

A pair of oak side chairs, designed by J. P. Seddon, the moulded arched backs with carved leaf motifs, upholstered backs and seats, stamped Seddon, New Bond Street, 9969.
£2,000-2,500 *C*

An oak low chair, by Arthur Simpson of Kendal, the curving arched back with pierced motif, with similarly curved seat on square section arched legs, damaged.
£500-600 *C*

A set of 7 oak Arts & Crafts dining chairs, including an open armchair. **£1,000-1,200** *CSK*

A set of 6 oak side chairs, designed by A. W. N. Pugin, on turned and chamfered legs joined by chamfered stretchers, upholstered in brown hide, with casters on front legs.
£1,500-2,000 *C*

An oak adjustable open armchair, upholstered in embroidered fabric, supported by Y-shaped arm and legs sections carved and pierced, on brass casters, late 19thC.
£1,000-1,200 *C*

A set of 8 chairs, including 2 carvers, by Ernest Gimson, with barber's pole inlay, tapering grille backs and upholstered drop-in seats, 38in (96cm) high.
£3,200-4,200 *Bon*

An oak 'Manxman' piano, by John Broadway & Sons, designed by M. H. Baillie-Scott, with wrought iron hinge plates and drop handles, brass and wrought iron candle brackets, panelled base, the case inscribed J. B. & Sons, movement no. 95972, c1899, 56.5in (142.5cm) wide.
£6,700-7,200 *C*

A walnut occasional table with ebony feet, by Gordon Russell, 23in (58cm) wide.
£600-700 *C*

GEORGE HENRY WALTON (1867-1933)

Closely associated with the Arts & Crafts movement, George Walton spent the first ten years of his career in Glasgow. In 1888, after little formal training, he established retail premises and workshop for his own business, 'George Walton & Co., Ecclesiastical and House Decorators'.

Design commissions from this period included Clutha glass for James Couper & Son, stained glass panels for William Burrell, furniture and interiors for Liberty & Co. and the refurbishment of Miss Cranston's Argyll and Buchanan Street Tearooms.

In 1898 Walton moved to London and concurrently set up business in York. He received a major commission to redesign a series of interiors for Kodak in Glasgow, Brussels, Vienna, Milan, Moscow, Leningrad and London, and later widened his range of activities by turning his hand to architecture, designing and building houses in Wales, London, France and Oxfordshire.

A pine wardrobe, designed by E. W. Godwin, the panelled front with 2 studded brass bands and central cupboard door enclosing a single fitted shelf, above a long drawer with central circular escutcheon and drop ring handles on channelled square section legs and casters, 60in (152.5cm) wide.
£13,500-15,000 *C*

This wardrobe was probably designed for Castle Dromore, County Limerick, Ireland. The door fittings are identical to those illustrated in the drawings of Godwin's door furniture for Dromore in the Drawings Collection at the Royal Institute of British Architects.

An Arts & Crafts mahogany framed four-fold draught screen, with embossed board panels decorated and gilt with pomegranates and meandering foliage, 75in (190.5cm) wide.
£600-650 *C(S)*

An Arts & Crafts oak sideboard, the finialled ledge back with copper panel, quadrant tiers and slatted sides above a rectangular top and 2 frieze drawers and arched recess below, flanked by 2 panelled doors with carved tree motifs, on block feet, stamped Maple & Co. Ltd. in drawer and Nos. 4053, 2547, 1, design, to the reverse.
£800-1,000 *CSK*

An Arts & Crafts oak smoking cupboard with coppered hinges, marked Rd 39192, c1885, 12in (30.5cm) wide.
£40-50   *ROW*

A mahogany gateleg table, by Kenton & Co., designed by Ernest Gimson, the sides with Rose and Briar palmwood inlay, c1891, 32in (81.5cm) wide extended.
£3,500-4,000   *C*

An Arts & Crafts ebonised card table, 36in (91.5cm) wide.
£450-500   *APO*

An oak writing desk, designed by George Walton, the rectangular top above 3 drawers, on square tapering supports, c1900, 37in (94cm) high.
£650-700   *C(S)*

A Thebes mahogany stool, 17in (43cm) square.
£275-325   *APO*

A pair of highback ash armchairs, by Clisset, designed by Ernest Gimson, with ladderbacks above rush seats, on turned tapering legs joined with turned stretchers.
£700-850   *C*

An oak side table, designed by Gordon Russell, 33.5in (85cm) wide.
£250-350   *C*

An Arts & Crafts hall table/bureau, in the manner of Gustav Stickley, the 2 drawers with copper handles, 49in (124.5cm) wide.   **£600-700**   *APO*

An oak chequered inlaid wardrobe, possibly designed by M. H. Baillie-Scott, 85in (216cm) wide, and a matching chest with 2 hinged lids above a pair of doors and 3 drawers, on octagonal supports, 55in (139.5cm) high, both with copper curved handles.
£1,800-2,200   *C(S)*

A mahogany and cane newspaper basket, designed by Sir Edwin Lutyens, with carved 'rope' decoration and cane panels, the rectangular basket on 4 square section legs, each pair joined with single plain stetcher, on casters, 32in (81cm) wide.
£1,500-5,000   *C*

This newspaper basket was designed by Sir Edwin Lutyens for his own use, certainly at 13 Mansfield Street, where he lived from September 1919, however it may have been designed earlier while he was living in Bedford Square. His daughter, Mary Lutyens, remembers the piece being in constant use.

English Furniture

A marquetry cabinet, profusely decorated.
£4,500-5,500 *ASA*

An inlaid armchair, 22in (55.5cm) wide. **£450-500** *APO*

A Glasgow-style mahogany display cabinet, with a pair of stained and leaded glass doors, 69in (175cm) high.
£1,200-1,500 *C(S)*

A breakfront cabinet, on arched trestle ends, with metal plaque Liberty & Co., London, 48in (122.5cm) wide.
£600-800 *C*

Continental Furniture

A polished mahogany bedroom suite, designed by Carlo Zen, comprising:
A pair of bedside cabinets, each set with marble plaque, and shaped panelled cupboard door carved with stylised floral motifs, on arched bracket feet, with original labels, Carlo Zen, Milano, 17in (43.5cm) wide. **£2,000-2,500**
A matching double bed, the front panel elaborately carved with a flowerspray, the back panel with original label, Carlo Zen, Milano, 46in (117cm) wide. **£3,000-3,500**
A large matching wardrobe, with floral brass lock-plates, 77in (196cm) wide. **£3,000-3,500** *C*

A carved mahogany mirror, by V. Epeaux, the glass enclosed in a curvilinear framework of apple blossom, 63.5in (161cm) high. **£3,500-4,500** *C*

A black and white painted cabinet, by Wiener Werkstätte, designed by Josef Hoffmann, c1910, 34in (86cm) wide.
£1,200-1,400 *C*

This piece is part of a suite of furniture designed for the home of Heinrich Bohler, Vienna.

Textiles

Three curtains, by Morris & Co., 'Violet & Columbine' design, woven wool and mohair in a repeating design of pink and red flowerheads amid entwined green foliage on dark blue ground, 67in (170cm) wide.
£2,000-2,500 *C*

A curtain, by Morris & Co., 'Daffodil', designed by J. H. Dearle, in printed cotton with braid border, with repeating pattern of daffodils and wild flowers between waved stylised vines in various greens, yellows and pinks, on smoke blue ground, 18in (45cm) wide.
£400-600 *C*

A wall hanging designed by Walter Crane, 'The Four Seasons', in woven silk on cotton, with repeating design of roundels enclosing classical figures, surrounded by figures representing the four seasons, c1893, 44in (111cm) wide.
£3,700-4,200 *C*

Glass

A Gallé vase, overlaid in green and brown and etched with seed pods and leaves, cameo signature, c1900, 5in (13cm) high.
£300-500 *S(S)*

A woven wool curtain, the design attributed to B. J. Talbert, with repeating floral design, dark olive green ground with sage green, rust and beige, 49in (125cm) wide.
£600-650 *C*

A French cameo glass vase, with a lustrous pink and green ground, overlaid and etched in green with pendant fuchsias and foliage, indecipherable incised mark, c1900, 16in (40cm) high.
£650-700 *S(S)*

A green glass vase, attributed to Bakalowitz, with 2 lug handles, the body enamelled in green with stylised berried branches, 8in (20cm) high.
£100-150 *Bon*

A Gallé bottle and stopper, enamelled with small polychrome flowers on gilt stems, repeated on the button stopper, crack to neck, painted mark Emile Gallé, c1900, 4in (10cm) high.
£500-600 *S(S)*

A Daum, Nancy, cameo pedestal bowl, decorated with flowers and foliage in shades of red on an amber ground, 4.5in (11cm) high.
£750-1,000 *Bea*

A Le Verre Français cameo glass goblet, in a yellow glass overlaid in orange and green, etched with fruits, raised on a purple veined stem and flared foot, applied millefiori cane, c1920, 13.5in (34.5cm) high.
£300-400 S(S)

A Gallé cameo glass vase, overlaid in yellow, lilac and mauve, etched with a lakeside landscape, incised signature, c1900, 7in (17.5cm) high.
£620-800 S(S)

A Gallé cameo glass vase, in a grey and pink glass overlaid in green and etched with sycamore seeds and foliage, minor chips, cameo mark Gallé, 8in (20cm) high.   £400-500 S(S)

A Legras acid-etched glass vase, decorated with leafy boughs in purple coloured glass against a frosted ground, signed 'Legras', 12in (30cm) high.
£250-350 P

A Daum applied vase, the clear glass with air inclusions and areas of mottled grey towards base, applied with trailed purple glass and small yellow globules in the form of stylised thorns and berries, with wheel-carved signature Daum Nancy with the Cross of Lorraine, 11.5in (28.5cm) high.
£3,000-3,500 C

A Legras enamelled glass vase, decorated with tall trees in a snowy winter landscape, with a woman depicted collecting logs on a mountain path, in brown, white and mauve on a frosted ground, signed 'Legras', 10in (25cm) high.
£300-350 P

A Legras glass vase, internally decorated with red and orange coloured feathering, with yellow tendril-like bands to the exterior, signed 'Legras', 13in (33.5cm) high.
£120-160 P

A Legras glass vase, enamelled with blackberry clusters with large orange leaves and tendrils against a yellow and orange ground, signed, 9.5in (24cm) high.
£220-260 P

Iridescent Glass

Two Austrian iridescent glass inkwells, with brass stylised decoration on the lids, c1900, 2in (5cm) high.
£200-400 each *ASA*

An iridescent glass vase, probably Austrian, of Persian inspiration, decorated with a band of gilt calligraphy on a vermiculé ground, divided by 3 lugs, the short trumpet neck gilt with scrolls, painted mark 515/2, late 19thC, 6in (15cm) high.
£350-500 *S(S)*

A Loetz-style iridescent glass compôte with a metal stand.
£200-250 *JL*

A Loetz-style iridescent glass vase, applied with a dot and thin line pattern in a deep blue on a mottled green ground, slight rubbing to neck, unmarked, 5in (13.3cm) high. **£575-675** *S(S)*

A miniature Tiffany Favrile iridescent glass vase, in a pale amber glass decorated with millefiori cane flowers amongst green lily pads and trails, on a gilt ground, engraved L.C.T., 8429A, c1906, 1.5in (4cm) high.
£350-450 *S(S)*

A Tiffany-style iridescent glass vase, with green shading to blue iridescence, with Sterling silver mounts to the rim pendant with stylised droplets, mount stamped L. Sterling, glass unmarked, 6in (15cm) high.
£400-600 *HSS*

Lighting

A copper, brass and coloured glass lamp, 37in (94cm) high.
£300-450 *ASA*

A bronze table lamp, by Thomas Elsely, designed by C.F.A. Voysey, the base incorporating a heart-shaped lever switch with inverted collar, the tulip-shaped stem with central disc knop, the hemispherical shaped shade supported on scrolling brackets, fitted for electricity, c1904, 19.5in (49cm) high.
£1,900-2,200 *C*

A W.M.F. pewter lamp, fitted with an onion-shaped purple, blue and green iridescent glass shade, base stamped W.M.F., c1905, 20.5in (52cm) high.
£700-900 *S(S)*

A cantilevered brass desk lamp, 15.5in (39cm) high.
£150-200 *ASA*

A French glass lamp, signed, c1900.
£400-600 *ASA*

A copper and brass oil lamp, by W. A. S. Benson, supported on 3 high looped handles extending to the base, raised on a tripod stand, with overlapping copper shaped sheets forming the shade, slight damage, unmarked, c1890, 12in (31cm) high.
£400-450 *S(S)*

Silver

A silver handled brush.
£60-100 *ASA*

A Hukin & Heath sugar scoop, 5in (13cm) long.   **£70-80** *NCA*

A Liberty & Co. lightly hammered silver four-handled bowl, attributed to Rex Silver, stamped L&Co., with Birmingham hallmarks for 1900, 5.5in (14cm) high, 910gr.
£1,200-1,500 *C*

A silver and enamel jewellery box, 11in (28cm) long.   **£900-1,200** *ASA*

A pair of candlesticks, hallmark 1910, 5.5in (14cm) high.
£400-450 *NCA*

A William Hutton & Sons Ltd., silver and enamel frame, embossed with typical Art Nouveau motifs, the recesses above filled with green and blue enamel, wood back, stamped factory marks, damaged, Rd: 404508, London 1902.
£1,200-1,600 *S(S)*

A Hukin & Heath silver sugar bowl, designed by Dr. Christopher Dresser, with engraved crest, stamped with maker's marks JWH, JTH and London hallmarks for 1881, 5.5in (14cm) 195gr.
£500-700 *C*

A silver mounted glass jug.
£500-550 *GIL*

A pair of Art Nouveau silver photograph frames, Birmingham 1903, 12 by 10in (31 by 25cm).
£1,400-1,700 *MAT*

A Guild of Handicraft silver toast rack, on bun feet, the end panels with repoussé decoration of stylised fish and cabochon turquoises, stamped maker's marks G of H Ltd., with London hallmarks for 1904, 5in (13cm) high, 230gr.
£1,500-2,000 *C*

A pair of silver novelty pepperettes, by Goldsmiths & Silversmiths Company, in the form of champagne bottles, the corks engraved as smiling faces, on vestigial feet and circular bases, London 1908, 3.5in (9cm).
£350-400 *S(S)*

Miller's is a price
GUIDE not a price
LIST

A Georg Jensen fruit dish, on short cylindrical foot, with 2 cast and applied stylised floral handles, with stamped marks GJ No. 618 and Denmark Sterling, 12.5in (32cm) wide, 1,240gr.
£3,000-3,500 *C*

A Tiffany and Co. Japanesque jug, the copper body applied with 3 Sterling silver fish, one swimming amongst silver fronds, the others amongst engraved fronds, above a lobster and below 2 dragonflies, stamped Tiffany and Co., 8844 Makers 2678 Sterling Silver, Other Metals 925-1000 over T, 5.5 pints, 8.5in (21cm high.
£11,000-13,000 *HSS*

A set of 6 Liberty & Co. silver coffee spoons, the terminal of each decorated with stylised honesty, stamped maker's mark L&Co., with Birmingham hallmarks for 1907, in fitted case, 80gr.
£300-400 *C*

A set of 6 Liberty Cymric spoons, with heart shaped bowls, reeded stems and pierced oval terminals enamelled with foliage, in original fitted case, stamped maker's marks, Birmingham 1902, 4in (10cm) long.
£180-250 *CSK*

A Tiffany & Co. silver repoussé and chased rococo style coffee pot, of Turkish form, marked beneath Tiffany & Co. 5401 M 4145 Sterling silver, 9in (23cm) high, 15oz.
£600-650 *HSS*

An Art Nouveau ten-piece silver backed dressing table set, in original leatherbound velvet and satin lined fitted case, stamped maker's marks, London 1901/2.
£900-1,200 *CSK*

An H.G. Murphy silver tazza, the base applied with 2 shields bearing coats-of-arms and the inscription 'From Colfes Grammar School to Sir Lulham and Lady Pound on the opening of the New Science Building, Founders Day 1929', stamped with maker's marks HGM, with London hallmarks for 1929, 6.5in (17cm) high, 875gr.
£1,000-1,200 *C*

A four-piece tea and coffee set, Arts and crafts style, with bulbous cylindrical hammered finish, with applied rosettes, pad supports, the pots with composition handles and buttons, Birmingham 1925/26, 46oz.
£600-800 *S(S)*

A Walker & Hall four-piece electroplated tea service, designed by David Mellor, the base stamped Walker & Hall, 53722 with flag monogram, 6.5in (16cm) high. **£500-600** *C*

A preserve jar and cover, the frosted glass body decorated to simulate a drum, the elecroplate lid surmounted by a drummer boy, all supported on a bright cut stand terminating in 3 bun feet, together with a spoon, 6.5in (16cm) high. **£120-150** *WIL*

A Guild of Handicraft hammered silver inkwell, 3.5in (9cm) high.
£300-400 *ASA*

A Hukin & Heath electroplated tankard designed by Dr. Christopher Dresser, with ebonised bar handle, stamped maker's marks H&H 2089.
£420-500 *C*

Silver Plate

A James Dixon & Sons electroplated toast rack, designed by Dr. Christopher Dresser, stamped with James Dixon & Sons marks and facsimile signature Chr. Dresser, 68, 6.5in (17cm) long. **£3,500-4,500** *C*

A white metal and copper jardinière, designed by Oliver Baker, 13.5in (35cm) long.
£1,500-2,000 *C*

A Hukin & Heath silver mounted claret jug, designed by Dr. Christopher Dresser, with ebonised bar handle, stamped maker's marks JWH, JTH with London hallmarks for 1881, and date registration lozenge for 9th May 1881, 8.5in (21cm) high.
£1,300-1,700 *C*

A Hukin & Heath electroplated double bonbon dish, designed by Dr. Christopher Dresser, stamped H&H 2223, c1881, 5.5in (14cm) high. **£500-600** *C*

A Hukin & Heath electroplated toast rack, designed by Christopher Dresser, stamped maker's mark, signs of wear, H&H 2555, 1880s, 5in (13cm).
£350-500 *S(S)*

A Hukin & Heath electroplated twin sweetmeat bowl, designed by Dr. Christopher Dresser, on 4 spike feet, stamped with maker's mark H&H 2523, 10.5in (27cm) long. **£600-700** *C*

Pewter

A W.M.F. round silver box, 5in (13cm) diam.
£300-400 *ASA*

A W.M.F. silvered pewter bowl, with swing handle, and green glass liner, stamped marks, 10in (25cm) wide.
£500-550 *CSK*

A W.M.F. silver plated pewter champagne bucket, signed and dated 1906.
£1,000-1,500 *ASA*

A pewter bowl, modelled with female heads and swirling draperies and cut glass liner.
£250-300 *LRG*

A Liberty & Co., Tudric pewter clock, the arched top cast with heart shaped leaves, their stems flanking the tapering rectangular body, the copper dial above 2 blue enamelled cabochons, stamped marks, 8in (20cm).
£1,000-1,200 *Bon*

A pair of Tudric candlesticks, attributed to Archibald Knox, 5.5in (14cm) high.
£100-180 *NCA*

A Liberty & Co., pewter and enamel clock, c1900, 7.5in (19cm) high.
£1,800-2,200 *ASA*

A Liberty & Co. pewter and enamel clock, 4.5in (11cm) high.
£700-1,000 *ASA*

A Tudric pewter picture frame, with stylised honesty decoration, 10in (25cm) high.
£800-1,000 *C*

A Liberty & Co., pewter and enamel clock, 8in (20cm) high.
£1,500-2,500 *ASA*

A German pewter top claret jug, 11.5in (29cm) high.
£300-500 *ASA*

A Liberty & Co. hammered pewter rose bowl, the design attributed to Oliver Baker, set with 5 green glass studs, on 5 curved legs and trefoil feet, stamped English Pewter made by Liberty & Co, 01130, 6.6in (16cm) high.
£420-500 *C*

A W.M.F. pewter dressing table mirror, 12.5in (32cm) high.
£250-300 *APO*

A W.M.F. pewter inkstand, 8in (20cm) wide.
£300-500 *ASA*

A W.M.F. pewter jug, 12in (31cm) high.
£80-150 *ASA*

A German green glass and pewter claret jug, 14in (36cm) high.
£250-300 *ASA*

A Tudric pewter tea set, tray 18.5 by 11.5in (47 by 29cm).
£350-400 *APO*

A Continental pewter plaque, with central dished panel chased with the head of pre-Raphaelite maiden, flanked by curved uprights pendant with husks with stepped cresting, the reverse initialled EP and stamped 279, 8.5in (21cm) wide.
£100-150 *HSS*

A W.M.F. electroplated pewter tazza, 12.5in (32cm) high.
£400-450 *HEW*

A Tudric pewter vase, cast in relief with sprays of honesty and bearing the inscription 'For Old Times Sake', stamped marks, 8in (20cm) high. **£180-220** *CSK*

Miscellaneous Metalware

Two Art Nouveau gilt metal plaques, on wooden surrounds.
£300-500 *ASA*

A Benham & Froud copper coffee pot, designed by Dr. Christopher Dresser, with ebonised handle, stamped with maker's mark, c1884, 8.5in (22cm) high.
£800-900 *C*

An Art Nouveau two-handled French copper jug, 19.5in (50cm) high.
£250-300 *APO*

A copper box, with ship on lid, attributed to John Pearson, 8in (20cm) long.
£130-150 *NCA*

A copper charger, by John Pearson, 20in (51cm) diam.
£300-400 *ASA*

An Art Nouveau brass note pad holder, 7.5in (19cm) high.
£30-40 *ASA*

An Artificer's Guild hammered gilded copper bowl, designed by Edward Spencer, with inscription 'To Edward & Ellen Packard, Wedded 50 years, May 23rd 1917, with the love from their sons and daughters, Charles, Katherine, Winifred, Celia, Reginald, Nina, Walter, Sylvia, Phyllis, Harold', on 5 bun feet, numbered 891, 11in (28cm) diam.
£1,000-1,200 *C*

A Benham and Froud copper and brass kettle-on-stand, on domed tripartite foot, the scrolling openwork column arching over to form hooks from which the kettle is suspended, stamped maker's mark, 32in (81cm) high.
£200-300 *CSK*

A pair of polished steel twin branched candelabra, by Alfred Bucknell, c1920, 14in (35cm) high.
£2,000-2,500 *C*

A pair of Artificer's Guild wrought iron candelabra, designed by Edward Spencer, numbered 3009, 11in (28cm) high.
£1,400-1,700 *C*

A pair of polished steel firedogs, attributed to Alfred Bucknell, each bud finial above hammered and fluted perpendicular, on trestle feet, 22.5in (57cm) high.
£750-850 *C*

A pair of Arts and Crafts copper framed mirrors, the central plate flanked by twin Celtic style motifs, 19in (48cm) high.
£300-400 *P*

A set of polished steel fire irons, attributed to Thornton & Downer comprising: a poker, pair of tongs, a shovel, a brush, supported on square section stand with 3 arched legs, bands of engraved decoration, 25in (64cm) high.
£1,300-1,800 *C*

Two Talwin Morris embossed brass finger plates, each with a central motif of a heart imposed on a stylised foliate grid of blooming and budding roses, cracked, c1893, 11 by 15in (28 by 38cm).
£350-450 *C(S)*

Jewellery

A silver and enamel brooch, by Phoebe Anna Ramsay Traquair, the central plique à jour enamel panel with 2 lovers in medieval costume embracing, coloured in blue, green, pink, brown and yellow with touches of gold, enclosed within a silver mount with single bar pin, the enamel inscribed to the reverse 'The Kiss' and with P.R.T. monogram, the silver mount for Edinburgh 1935, 2in (5cm) diam.
£1,800-2,200 *C(S)*

Born in Dublin in 1852 and married in 1873 to Ramsay Traquair, the keeper of the National Gallery of Scotland, Phoebe Traquair was one of the most renowned enamelists of her time and possibly the best known after Alexander Fisher. Her work, often of a religious nature, was regularly featured in exhibitions and in 'The Studio' magazine. She carried out many important commissions including work for St. Mary's Cathedral in Edinburgh, the National Gallery of Scotland and for Sir Robert Lorimer. She may also have worked for Omar Ramsden. In 1883 she remarried, her full name becoming Phoebe Anna Traquair Reid. She died in 1936.

A citrine single stone and diamond pendant/brooch, with frosted crystal and diamond surround to a diamond and gem-set suspension, with detachable fittings for conversion to a clasp.
£800-1,000 *CSK*

An Arts & Crafts chalcedony, amethyst and mother-of-pearl openwork pendant with matching drop and neck chain; and a chalcedony, chrysoprase and marcasite articulated drop brooch/pendant.
£400-450 *CSK*

Continental Ceramics

An Amphora ware mirror, 12in (31cm) high. **£200-250** *HEW*

A ceramic figure with sea shells, by Ernst Whallis, 16.5in (42cm) high. **£600-900** *ASA*

An Austrian vase, 12.5in (32cm) high.
£100-200 *ASA*

A Royal Dux ceramic figure on a sea shell, 14in (36cm) high.
£350-500 *ASA*

A terracotta lamp by Goldscheider, 28in (71.5cm) high.
£1,500-2,000 *ASA*

A pair of German tiles, both depicting maidens with flowing hair in coloured glazes, the Muse of Music playing a harp, and the Muse of Dancing, having raised outlines, 5in (14cm) wide, framed.
£700-750 *P*

A pair of Zuid vases, Dutch, with 4 undercut edges and applied handles, painted with pendant stylised flowers on the neck, painted mark made in Zuid, Holland, J. H. and incised 213, 8.5in (22cm) high.
£300-350 *S(S)*

A Reps and Trinte pottery clock case, the base supporting a female bust flanked by 2 floral buttresses beneath triangular face, impressed marks and incised Shellmacher, damaged, early 20thC, 21in (53cm) high.
£720-800 *S(S)*

A Clement Massier turquoise glazed earthenware jardinière and stand, of organic design moulded in relief with leaves, flowers and branches, the oviform bowl on cylindrical stand, impressed factory marks, 37in (94cm) high.
£1,000-1,500 *CSK*

A Continental ceramic standing lamp, with 3 banana leaves each concealing a light fitting, painted in shades of green and buff, impressed AK Turn, E. Otto, chipped, 38in (96.5cm) high.
£1,500-2,000 *ASA*

A Rozenberg vase, painted in rich polychrome colours, black printed factory mark and year symbol of a flower, Rozenberg, den Haag, a cross in a square, 372, c1913, 6in (15.5cm) high.
£300-400 *S(S)*

A pair of Rozenberg vases, decorated in rich polychrome colours, black painted factory mark and year symbol of a flower, Rozenberg, den Haag, cross in a square, 472, c1913, 8.5in (21.5cm) high.
£300-400 *S(S)*

British Art Pottery

A vase by C. H. Brannam, c1885, 10in (25cm) high.
£160-180 *NCA*

A pair of spill vases, by C. H. Brannam, converting to candlesticks, 10in (25cm) high.
£300-350 *NCA*

A Bretby spill vase, decorated with a stork and bamboo, yellow coloured, 12in (31cm) high.
£70-80 *NCA*

A blue frog, by C. H. Brannam, 3in (7.5cm) high.
£50-60 *NCA*

A Bretby 'copperette' jug, 12in (31cm) high.
£140-150 *NCA*

A Watcombe cheese dish, attributed to Christopher Dresser, 6.5in (16.5cm) high.
£160-180 *NCA*

An early Burmantofts turquoise blue planter, No. 1082, 7in (18cm) high.
£150-190 *NCA*

A green vase by C. H. Brannam, with 6 handles, 1903, 6.5in (16cm) high.
£100-120 *NCA*

A Burmantofts vase, decorated with dragons, by V. Kremer, 9.5in (24cm) high.
£580-600 *NCA*

A figure of The Brighton Wet Nurse, with nodding head and suspended body, dressed in a cloak and gown baring a bosom to a babe in arms, standing on a circular base marked Rye B4, 6in (15cm) high. **£320-370** *RAG*

An Ault vase, by Christopher Dresser, 12in (31cm) high.
£180-200 *NCA*

A pair of Bretby pottery vases, with applied horn and insect decoration, No. 1470, 14in (35.5cm) high.
£350-380 *NCA*

A Burmantofts pottery ewer, 10in (25cm) high.
£150-180 *NCA*

A Burmantofts green pottery vase, with Gothic decoration, 9.5in (24cm) high.
£130-150 *NCA*

A vase by Thomas Forester, 8in (20cm) high.
£75-125 *AOS*

A Linthorpe pouring vessel, designed by Christopher Dresser, covered in a mottled and streaked green glaze, impressed Linthorpe, .312, facsimile signature Chr. Dresser with Linthorpe Pottery seal, 6.5in (16.5cm) high.
£800-1,000 *C*

A Linthorpe pottery vase, after a design by Christopher Dresser, in a streaked brown glaze, with a pierced flower and foliage in the centre in green, stamped Chr. Dresser, HT, c1880, 8.5in (21.5cm) high.
£450-600 *S(S)*

A Minton porcelain vase, designed by Christopher Dresser, painted in gold, green, yellow, blue, black and orange enamels, restored, 11.5in (29cm) high.
£2,000-2,500 *C*

A Linthorpe vase, by Clara Pringle, 9.5in (24cm) high.
£280-300 *NCA*

A Linthorpe vase, designed by Christopher Dresser, impressed with a spiralling feather design, covered in an olive green glaze, impressed Linthorpe with facsimile signature Chr. Dresser, 298 and HT monogram, 7.5in (19cm) high.
£350-550 *C*

A pair of Martin Brothers stoneware panels, the arched forms impressed and incised with profile images of Cower and Chaucer, each against a patterned background, covered in a salt glaze in shades of blue and brown, indistinct marks and date, 17in (43cm) long. **£500-700** *C*

A pair of Minton Art Pottery moon flasks, painted in blue with frogs and fish or birds and rabbits within chevron bands, the short cylindrical neck flanked by a pair of loop handles, impressed, printed and painted marks, c1870, 8.5in (21.5cm) high. **£620-700** *S(S)*

A Martin Brothers jug, in a mottled blue/green on a brown ground, the neck with a band of vertical incised lines, incised Martin Bros., London & Southall, 2-1894, chip to spout, c1894, 8.5in (21.5cm) high. **£300-500** *S(S)*

A Martin Brothers vase, painted with spiny fish and eels swimming amongst water weeds and other aquatic life, in shades of grey and brown on a buff ground, incised Martin Bros, London & Southall, 10-1891, repaired, 7.5in (19cm) high; and a miniature Martin Ware vase. **£400-600** *CSK*

A Linthorpe vase, by Christopher Dresser, shape No. 24, 12.5in (32cm) high. **£230-250** *NCA*

A Martin Brothers stoneware tobacco jar and cover, modelled as a comic bird with curly plumage, standing erect with eyes closed, glazed in shades of blue and buff, base incised Martin Bros London & Southall, cover incised Martin 30.8.81 London & Southall, repaired, 12in (31cm) high. **£1,200-1,700** *CSK*

A Minton Art Pottery studio moon flask, one side with painted head and shoulders portrait of a girl in the style of W. S. Coleman, framed by a band of holly, the reverse in dark blue, impressed Minton 1498 and printed mark Minton's Art Pottery Studio Kensington Gore, damaged, 14in (35cm) high. **£600-700** *P(S)*

A set of 20 Minton stoneware tiles, designed by A. W. N. Pugin, the ochre ground with brown and black glazed decoration of quatrefoil reserve with central flowerhead within foliate motifs, reverse with moulded marks Minton & Co., Stoke-upon-Trent, Patent, each tile 6in (15cm) square. **£600-800** *C*

A Minton Seccessionist jardinière, decorated in purple, turquoise and green, repeated around the body, impressed and printed factory marks, Mintons, No. 72, c1910, 13in (32.5cm) high.
£700-800 *S(S)*

A Minton stoneware bread plate, designed by A. W. N. Pugin, with inscription 'Waste Not, Want Not', covered in rust and blue encaustic glazes, stamped 430, 13in (33cm) diam. **£1,200-1,700** *C*

A William de Morgan two-tile panel of a manned galley within a classical harbour, with turquoise, green, amethyst and yellow glazes, c1880, 12in (31cm) long.
£900-1,200 *C*

A William de Morgan deep red lustre bowl, decorated by Fred Passenger, with decoration of an eagle attacking a grotesque lizard within a scrolling foliate border, painted FP initials, c1890, (25cm) diam.
£700-800 *C*

A Minton Seccessionist jardinière, after a design by Léon V. Solon and John W. Wadsworth, decorated in turquoise above printed scrolling green foliage, moulded Minton's, England, impressed factory marks and date cypher, damaged, 12.5in (32cm) high. **£300-400** *S(S)*

A William de Morgan oviform vase, painted in turquoise, tones of blue, grey, black, and dark red on a cream ground, damaged, unmarked, 16in (40cm) high.
£3,000-3,500 *C(S)*

A William de Morgan four-tile panel of 2 snakes amongst flowering foliage against turquoise ground, with green, puce and amethyst glazes, chipped, each impressed WM, Merton Abbey seal, c1882, 16in (41cm) square.
£1,400-1,700 *C*

A Pilkington's red vase, 5.5in (13.5cm) high.
£50-75 *AOS*

A Bernard Moore enamelled flambé plate, the centre painted and enamelled with the bust of a female figure, the face in profile, hands clasped in prayer, with an inscription in a halo, on a flambé ground, overpainted hands and face, painted monogram B.M., circular frame, 10in (25.5cm) diam. **£300-400** *S(S)*

A Pilkington's Royal Lancastrian lustre charger, by Mycock, inscribed on reverse, c1900, 11.5in (29cm) diam.
£800-1,200 *ASA*

A Pilkington's Royal Lancastrian vase, signed, 6.5in (16cm) high.
£75-100 *AOS*

A Pilkington's vase, 6in (15cm) high. **£50-75** *AOS*

A collection of William de Morgan tiles, decorated with a parrot, flowers, guinea fowl, great curassow, pelican with fish, and ships, some lustre and some polychrome, various marks, two 8in (20cm) square the others 6in (15cm) square. **£2,000-2,500** *CSK*

A Pilkington's Royal Lancastrian 'Vermillion' glaze vase, moulded with fish amongst waves on a green ground under a speckled orange glaze, impressed factory marks, c1920, 8in (20cm) high; and a similar vase, after a design by William S. Mycock and modelled by E. T. Radford, with a mottled green and speckled orange glaze, impressed factory marks E.T.R., painted monogram and year cypher, c1929, 7in (18cm) high. **£200-250** *S(S)*

A Royal Lancastrian uranium glazed vase, by Richard Joyce, 5in (13cm) high. **£400-440** *NCA*

'Ruskin Pottery' high-fired stoneware lettering, the speckled green glaze with areas of cloudy blue, mounted on copper panels, c1905, each letter 7in (18cm) high. **£3,500-4,500** *C*

These are the original letters used at the Ruskin Pottery factory.

A Ruskin plate, with incised mark, 6in (15cm) diam. **£25-38** *AOS*

A Ruskin lustre vase, dated 1922, 8in (20cm) high. **£50-95** *AOS*

A Ruskin blue vase, c1930, 5.5in (14cm) high. **£50-75** *AOS*

A Rye Pottery 'Sussex Pig', lead glazed mainly in blue, having a hook-on head inscribed with the motto 'Wun't be druv', 4.5in (11.5cm) long. **£200-240** *RAG*

A Wedgwood Fairyland lustre 'Elves and Bell Branch' bowl, after a design by Daisy Makeig'-Jones, decorated with elves and fairies dancing and amongst tall grass against a black ground with a gilt spider's web, printed Portland vase mark England, painted number Z4968, minor rubbing, c1920, 3in (7.5cm) high.
£550-650 *S(S)*

A pair of Shelley 'Intarsio' ware vases, after a design by Walter Slater, decorated with stylised pink flowerheads amongst interlinked foliage in green, brown, and blue, printed mark Late Foley, Shelley, England, Intarsio and painted number 544 3617, c1915, 6.5in (16cm) high.
£300-400 *S(S)*

A Rye Pottery vase, with flared neck, applied with daffodils and leaves, marked on base Sussex Ware Rye, 6in (15cm) high.
£120-170 *RAG*

A pair of Wedgwood Fairyland lustre vases, afer a design by Daisy Makeig-Jones, each decorated with the 'Imps on a Bridge and Tree House' pattern, against a flame red ground, Portland vase mark Wedgwood, Made In England and painted number Z5481, c1920, 10in (26cm) high.
£3,500-4,000 *S(S)*

A Pilkington's Royal Lancastrian lustre wall plaque, after a design by Walter Crane and painted by Charles E. Cundall, with a peacock standing with its tail displayed, in copper lustre with red details on a mauve ground, the reverse with 4 copper lustre floral motifs, damaged impressed factory 'P' and Bee mark, VII, and lustre monograms, c1907.
£550-750 *S(S)*

A Wileman & Co. 'Intarsio' jug, after a design by Frederick Rhead, modelled as the body of a bird with an Egyptian style head, in typical palette, raised on 3 feet, printed factory mark Intarsio, Registration No. 330274, painted No. 3076, c1900, 5in (13.5cm) high. **£320-400** *S(S)*

A Wedgwood Fairyland lustre 'Woodland Bridge' bowl, after a design by Daisy Makeig-Jones, decorated outside with orange, yellow, green and purple shrubs on a black ground, the interior with the 'Fairy with Large Hat' pattern, cobwebs in the trees, fairies and elves amongst the toadstools on the banks of a river, gilt printed factory mark and painted number Z4968, c1920, 6in (16cm) diam.
£2,000-2,500 *S(S)*

A tapering vase, the body applied with branches, acorns and oak leaves, marked on base S.R.W. Rye, 4in (10cm) high.
£70-90 *RAG*

A Wileman & Co. 'Intarsio' jardinière, after a design by Frederick Rhead, decorated with a frieze of geese between foliate bands, in typical colours printed factory mark Intarsio, Registration No. 330400, printed No. 3143, c1900, 7in (18cm) high.
£500-600 *S(S)*

A Rye Pottery bowl, the brown body profusely covered with applied green hops, the rim banded with petite leaves, marked on base Rye Sussex, dated 1919, 8in (20cm) diam.
£300-400 *RAG*

Moorcroft

Moorcroft pottery is very much in vogue at the moment. This British pottery was first made by William Moorcroft at the factory of James MacIntyre in 1898.

From the start it was important to Moorcroft that ornament was used to accentuate form. Each piece was thrown on the potters wheel to produce the forms and variety he wanted. William then drew each design himself. His drawings were outlined in slip and practically every piece was signed.

While at MacIntyre's William became known for his Florian ware. His recognition grew rapidly on both sides of the Atlantic and his work was sold at Tiffany of New York and Liberty of London. In 1904 he won his first gold medal at St. Louis.

In 1913 William left James MacIntyre to build his own workship at Cobridge and to found the private company of W. Moorcroft Ltd., which still flourishes today.

As you delve deeper into the history of this pottery you wonder just how many different shapes and designs there are, when you think, at last you've seen them all, low and behold you find another!

The quality of the workmanship is so precise, sharp, clear and distinct that, to the observer, other types of pottery look primitive by comparison. Each piece portrays a variety of pure colour. Design preference is of an individual taste, but the landscape, trees and toadstool outweigh most for popularity. For absolute brilliance the flambé pieces are unrivalled. The rare and exotic waratah and protea have much appeal, but probably the early wisteria on a white ground, because of its simplicity and incredible beauty, is a favourite with most people. Another popular choice is the pomegranate - this particular design is probably the one which is most associated with Moorcroft pottery, because it was in production continually between 1910 & 1940.

William Moorcroft's pottery has proved to be an extremely good investment from both a financial and collector's point of view. While the value of other potteries tend to rise and fall with current trends, Moorcroft has always risen steadily. With the prevalent strong market both here and abroad, past and present prices and performance point to a continued growth for the future.

In each category of art, great masters stand out in their field. In art pottery William Moorcroft stands alone with his genius as the consummate master potter.

His artistry will leave an everlasting legacy of beauty for the World to enjoy.

A Moorcroft two-handled Blue Pansy design biscuit barrel, c1929, 7in (17.5cm) high. **£550-750** *LIO*

A W. R. Jacobs & Co. biscuit tin , moulded in a Moorcroft shape and transfer decorated with the pomegranate design, 6in (16cm) high. **£50-70** *WIL*

A MacIntyre Moorcroft Blue Poppy design salad bowl and servers, c1902, 10in (25cm) diam. **£850-1,050** *LIO*

A MacIntyre Moorcroft Yellow Cornflower design tobacco jar, c1910, 6in (15cm) diam. **£600-700** *LIO*

A Moorcroft Pomegranate design octagonal bowl, c1925, 10in (25cm) diam. **£400-500** *LIO*

A Moorcroft exhibition pomegranate ginger jar, 1927, 12in (31cm) diam. **£3,000-4,000** *LIO*

A MacIntyre Moorcroft blue 18thC design teapot, c1906. **£450-550** *LIO*

A MacIntyre footed bowl, the exterior decorated with sprays of blue pansies on a green ground, impressed factory marks, signed in green, rim restored, 9in (22.5cm) diam. **£200-300** *CSK*

A Moorcroft yacht design meat dish, c1934, 16.5in (42cm) long. **£60-90** *LIO*

The yacht design was introduced by William Moorcroft in 1934, taken from an original sketch by his daughter, Beatrice Moorcroft.

A Moorcroft pottery jardinière, with Florian style daisy and poppy decoration in green, blue and yellow glazes, with two loop handles, impressed Cambridge factory mark, and green painted signature, c1916, 10in (25cm) wide. **£1,000-1,500** *AH*

A MacIntyre Moorcroft Florian ware blue on Blue Tulip design jug, c1901, 12in (31cm) high. **£800-1,000** *LIO*

A Moorcroft Claremont Toadstool design vase, decorated in shades of yellow, mauve and blue on a mottled green ground, impressed Moorcroft, Burslem, 1914, signed in green, 4.5in (11cm) high. **£500-600** *WIL*

A Lise B. Moorcroft Toadstool design plaque, dated 1990, 16in (41cm) diam. **£250-350** *LIO*

Lise B. Moorcroft is the daughter of Walter Moorcroft, who ran the factory from 1945-1986 and the granddaughter of the founder, William Moorcroft.

A Moorcroft small Blue Pansy design jardinière, c1928, 4in (10cm) high. **£200-300** *LIO*

A Moorcroft pink Flamminian design teapot with cup, saucer and plate, c1914. **£250-350** *LIO*

A Walter Moorcroft Caribbean design mug, c1962, 4.5in (11cm) high. **£180-250** *LIO*

A MacIntyre Moorcroft Aurelian design coffee pot, c1897, 7in (17.5cm) high. **£350-450** *LIO*

A Moorcroft blue teapot, c1918, 6in (15cm) high. **£50-80** *LIO*

A Moorcroft saltglaze pink waving corn landscape vase, c1934, 11in (28cm) high.
£2,500-3,000 *LIO*

A MacIntyre Moorcroft two-handled Tulip and Forget-me-not design vase, c1902, 9in (23cm) high.
£1,000-1,200 *LIO*

A Moorcroft Eventide tree design vase, c1928, 6in (15cm) high.
£850-1,050 *LIO*

A MacIntyre Moorcroft Alhambra design crocus vase, c1903, 6in (15cm) high.
£500-600 *LIO*

A Moorcroft ochre Spring Flower design vase, c1936, 9.5in (24cm) high.
£550-700 *LIO*

A Moorcroft Moonlight blue tree design vase, c1925, 9in (23cm) high.
£1,000-1,500 *LIO*

A MacIntyre Moorcroft Aurelian design vase, c1897, 12in (31cm) high.
£375-475 *LIO*

A Moorcroft two-handled inverted baluster shaped vase, painted with the Brown Chrysanthemum pattern on a green ground, with green W. Moorcroft signature, c1915, 9in (23cm) high.
£1,000-1,200 *C(S)*

A Moorcroft pomegranate design vase, c1928, 9.5in (24cm) high.
£350-400 *LIO*

A pair of Moorcroft MacIntyre double-gourd shaped vases painted with the Brown Chrysanthemum pattern on a green ground, printed marks and W. Moorcroft signature in green, impressed 166, 12in (31cm) high.
£1,800-2,000 *C(S)*

A Moorcroft Pomegranate design vase, c1930, 9in (23cm) high.
£300-500 *AOS*

A MacIntyre Moorcroft blue on blue Cornflower design vase, c1901, 5in (13cm) high.
£400-500 *LIO*

A Moorcroft saltglaze Spring Flower design vase, c1936, 6in (15cm) high.
£300-400 *LIO*

A Moorcroft MacIntyre Liberty smoker's set, damaged, c1903, 17in (43cm) wide.
£800-1,200 *LIO*

A Moorcroft blue panel saltglaze vase, dated 1941, 9in (23cm) high.
£900-1,100 *LIO*

A Walter Moorcroft Dahlia design vase, c1959, 8in (20cm) high.
£300-400 *LIO*

Doulton

Anthea, a Royal Doulton figure, HN 1526, green printed and painted marks, 1932-38, 7in (18cm) high.
£400-450 *S(S)*

A Marlene Dietrich wall mask, with brown eyes and hair, and pale pink lips, marked HN 1591, 8in (20cm) long.
£250-300 *WIL*

Autumn, HN 314, model number 222, introduced in 1918, withdrawn in 1938, 7.5in (19cm) high.
£320-500 *WIL*

A Royal Doulton figure, Lady Fayre, HN 1265, green printed and red painted marks, c1928-38, 5.5in (14cm) high.
£300-400 *S(S)*

A Doulton Burns punch bowl, 9in (23cm) diam.
£80-100 *OD*

Scotties, HN 1281, designed by L. Harradine, introduced in 1928, withdrawn in 1938, ear damaged, 5in (13cm) high.
£400-450 *WIL*

Easter Day, HN 2039, a Royal Doulton figure, designed by M. Davies, introduced in 1949, withdrawn in 1969.
£160-200 *WIL*

Griselda, a Royal Doulton figure, 1947-53, 6in (15cm) high.
£200-230 *TRU*

Memories, a Royal Doulton figure, 1949-59, 6in (15cm) high.
£150-165 *TRU*

Modena, HN 1846, a Royal Doulton figure, withdrawn 1949, cracked.
£120-180 *Bea*

Capt. Hook, D 6597, a Royal Doulton figure, designed by M. Henks and D. Biggs, introduced in 1965, withdrawn in 1971, 7in (18cm) high.
£200-220 *WIL*

The Laird, HN 2361, a Royal Doulton figure, designed by M. Nicoll, introduced in 1969.
£60-80 *WIL*

Coppelia, a Royal Doulton porcelain figurine, HN 2115, 7in (18cm) high.
£180-220 *GAK*

Francine, a Royal Doulton figure, designed by J. Bromley, introduced in 1922, discontinued in 1981, 5.5in (14cm) high.
£50-70 *TVA*

A Royal Doulton figure of a seated bulldog with a Union Jack draped over its back, printed factory marks, 4in (10cm) high.
£200-250 *CSK*

A Doulton Lambeth jug to commemorate Emin Pasha, Relief Expedition 1887-1889, with a portrait of H. M. Stanley, 8in (20cm) high.
£250-300 *WIL*

A Doulton Fishing plate, 10.5in (26cm) diam. **£80-100** *RP*

Little Boy Blue, a Royal Doulton figure, designed by Leslie Harradine, introduced in 1950, discontinued 1973, 6in (15cm) high. **£70-90** *TVA*

A flambé model of a leaping salmon, signed Noke, 12.5in (32cm) high. **£400-450** *WIL*

A part set of 6 Doulton ware dessert plates. **£50-75** *AOS*

A pair of Royal Doulton vases, light blue ground decorated with pink roses and green leaves, outlined in white piping, impressed mark, c1902, 14in (36cm) high. **£140-200** *WIL*

A pair of Doulton stoneware vases, decorated by Hannah Barlow, with bands of deer within stylised foliage borders, impressed mark and date 1885, 9.5in (24cm) high.
£720-760 *SWO*

A Royal Doulton Chang vase, covered in a thick crackled mottled white, black, red, ochre glaze running over mottled shades of ochre, red, blue and black, printed marks Chang, Royal Doulton, Noke, 4.5in (11cm) high.
£450-600 *C*

A pair of Royal Doulton baluster vases, with mottled green glaze and raised design of stylised flowers and foliage.
£300-350 *LRG*

A Royal Doulton teapot and cover commemorating Lord Nelson, blue ground with brown glazed rope twist handle and spout, with raised decoration of the head of the Admiral, the other side depicting the Victory, and inscribed around the neck, 'England Expects Every Man Will Do His Duty', monogrammed Ap., 5in (13cm) high.
£110-150 *RID*

A Royal Doulton urn with Grecian figures, 13in (33cm) high.
£250-380 *ASA*

A Doulton Studio ware vase, c1930, 7in (18cm) high.
£75-95 *AOS*

A pair of Royal Doulton toy vases, hand painted with a country scene, c1910, 1.5in (4cm) high.
£200-250 *TVA*

A pair of Lambeth Doulton stoneware vases, decorated by Florence Barlow in green slip with black grouse, incised marks, F.E.B., 14in (36cm) high.
£640-700 *MJB*

A Royal Doulton vase, decorated with a continuous floriate pattern in blue, white and gilt, against a shaded ground, 18.5in (47cm) high.
£220-270 *RID*

A pair of Doulton stoneware vases, 11in (28cm) high.
£200-300 *ASA*

ART DECO

Furniture

A Heal's oak cabinet, designed by Ambrose Heal, the drawers with heart shaped pulls, with inlaid plaque Heal & Son Makers, London W, 44.5in (113cm) wide.
£900-1,200 *C*

An upholstered 'shell' armchair, the padded back and seat in the form of a scallop shell, with scrolling 'nautilus shell' arms and with a fringe apron, c1930.
£500-700 *S(S)*

A Makers of Simple Furniture birchwood chest of drawers, designed by Gerald Summers, with retailer's label Bowmans Bros., Ltd., Complete House Furnishers, Camden Town, London N.W.1, 27in (69cm) wide.
£400-500 *C*

Four Isokon stacking plywood chairs and a table, designed by Marcel Breuer, c1936, table 54in (137cm) wide.
£3,000-3,500 *C*

A burr maple sideboard, the design attributed to Ray Hille, 44.5in (113cm) wide.
£620-700 *C*

A Hille sideboard, the design attributed to Ray Hille, the burr-veneer fronted sideboard with 4 short drawers flanked by single cupboard doors, each with stylised carved leaf handles and enclosing a single fitted shelf, on 4 bowed carved legs, stamped Hille, 66in (167.5cm) wide.
£620-800 *C*

A Makers of Simple Furniture birchwood millinery chest, designed by Gerald Summers, on platform base, with retailer's label Bowman Bros. Ltd., Complete House Furnishers, Camden Town, London N.W.1., 27in (69cm) wide.
£400-500 *C*

An ebonised and sycamore cheval glass-cum-dressing table, supported at the side by a bow-front cupboard inlaid with polka dots, 41in (102cm) wide; and a matching upholstered stool, the cupboard bearing the label of Marcus Adams, 6 Granville Place, Portman Square.
£600-700 *S(S)*

A French sideboard, 62in
(157cm) wide.
£500-600 *APO*

A burr maple sideboard, the
design attributed to Ray Hille,
54in (137cm) wide.
£700-900 *C*

A Heal's oak dining table,
designed by Ambrose Heal, 57in
(145cm) wide.
£1,800-2,000 *C*

Lalique Glass

A French daybed, with mattress covered in black
and white zebra skin with matching cylindrical
cushion, on 4 tapering fluted legs, 1930s, 74in
(188cm) long.   **£1,500-1,800** *C*

A Lalique 'Figurines et Voiles' box
and cover, moulded with a band
of classically draped figures
holding roses and swirling
lengths of material, heightened in
red, the lid with 2 similar figures,
damaged, moulded mark R.
Lalique, made in France, c1930,
3in (7.5cm) high.
£200-250 *S(S)*

A Lalique 'Filix' glass bowl, the
deep well moulded outside with a
band of large fern leaves picked
out with frosting, wheel engraved
R. Lalique, France, c1927, 13in
(33cm) diam.
£500-600 *S(S)*

An opalescent Lalique glass
ashtray, with beetle design, 5.5in
(14cm) diam.   **£200-250** *ASA*

A Lalique 'Medicis' glass ashtray,
with 2 pairs of naked female
figures amongst flowers, moulded
mark R. Lalique, engraved R.
Lalique, France, No. 280, c1925,
6in (15cm) long.
£300-400 *S(S)*

A Lalique 'Enfants' box and cover,
moulded outside with a band of
nude children holding a weight
above their heads on a blue
stained ground, the lid moulded
with 5 tiers of rose bands
similarly coloured, stencilled
mark R. Lalique, France, c1930,
3in (7.5cm) high.
£300-350 *S(S)*

A Lalique 'Ondines' opalescent
glass plate, moulded underneath
with 6 mermaids in swirling
water on the border, wheel
engraved R. Lalique, France,
engraved No. 3003, c1922, 11in
(28cm) diam.   **£600-800** *S(S)*

A Lalique 'Roger' box and cover,
moulded with long-tailed exotic
birds perched in branches
amongst clear glass discs,
engraved Lalique, France, c1927,
5in (13cm) diam.
£300-400 *S(S)*

A Lalique clock, the circular dial
with black enamelled chapters,
engraved 'R. Lalique, France',
with chrome base enclosing light
fitting, 7in (18cm) high.
£1,000-1,500 *C(S)*

A Lalique 'Prunes' glass vase, moulded in high relief with an opalescent band of rounded fruits on leafy branches, damaged, wheel engraved R. Lalique, France, c1930, 7in (18cm) high. **£2,600-3,000** *S(S)*

'Suzanne', a Rene Lalique opalescent figurine, of a naked maiden, her arms outstretched and holding her robes, chipped, moulded R. Lalique signature, 9in (23cm) high. **£7,000-8,000** *C(S)*

A Lalique amber moulded vase shaped table lamp, modelled as a stylised artichoke, engraved in script R. Lalique, France, 9in (23cm) high. **£1,500-1,800** *LRG*

A Lalique 'Ceylan' vase, moulded with opalescent pairs of budgerigars below foliage wheel, engraved mark R. Lalique, 9.5in (24cm) high. **£1,000-1,200** *WIL*

A Lalique 'Saint Francois' opalescent glass vase, moulded outside with birds perched in leafy branches, damaged, stencil mark R. Lalique, France, c1930, 7in (18cm) high. **£800-900** *S(S)*

A Lalique 'Epis No. 1' stained glass plate, the border moulded and stained in blue with a repeated band of wheatears, with a fluted radiating centre, moulded R. Lalique, engraved France, c1922, 12.5in (31.5cm) diam. **£100-200** *ASA*

Glass

An amber glass trinket set in the form of a butterfly, comprising: a tray, 3 boxes and lids, and 2 candlesticks. **£20-30** *GAK*

A pink frosted glass flower holder with a figure, 8.5in (21cm) diam. **£50-80** *ASA*

A Sabino blue glass vase, moulded with overlapping peacock feather motifs in low relief with slight frosting, incised Sabino, France, c1930, 8in (20cm) high. **£210-300** *S(S)*

A glass mascot, minor chips, unmarked, 1930s, 5.5in (14cm) high. **£300-400** *S(S)*

A Verlys frosted and opalescent glass plafonier, moulded with 3 large sunflowers and foliage, moulded mark Verly, France, 1930s, 14in (36cm) high. **£250-300** *S(S)*

A red glass Ashay car mascot, 5in (13cm) high.
£200-300 *ASA*

Three John Walsh engraved glass wares, after a design by Clyne Farquharson, each engraved with polished stylised leaf forms on sinuous stems, in a clear glass, comprising:
a gently tapering vase, a wide flared bowl, and a high sided bowl, the vase incised Clyne Farquharson, NRD, 8in (20cm) high; the flared bowl incised Clyne Farquharson and with a limited edition number 23/250, 36, 12in (31cm) diam., the other unmarked 8in (20cm) diam.
£450-550 *S(S)*

A Dubarry scent bottle and stopper, moulded in relief with sunburst motif, in original fitted box with lithographed interior, 4in (10cm) high.
£25-35 *CSK*

A Sabino iridescent moulded glass vase, modelled with classical Bacchic scene, chipped, engraved Sabino, Paris, 9in (23cm) diam.
£450-500 *LRG*

An Etling opalescent model of a Penguin, damaged, moulded Etling, 203, France, 5in (13cm) high.
£210-300 *S(S)*

A Continental glass vase, internally decorated with birds in flight in blue on a speckled white ground graduating to red at the neck, unmarked, 20thC, 7in (18cm) high.
£200-250 *S(S)*

An Orrefors 'Graal' vase, by E. Hald, internally decorated with scaly green and brown fish swimming amid reeds, etched to base Orrefors Sweden Graal 26416 Edward Hald, 5.5in (14cm) high.
£900-1,000 *P*

Metalware

A spelter figure lamp, c1930, 13.5in (34cm) high.
£300-350 *HEW*

A spelter figure holding a clock, c1930, 22in (56cm) high.
£350-400 *HEW*

A stylised figure of a deer, by Hagenauer, 14in (36cm) long. **£400-500** *CAR*

Jewellery

An aluminium and brass sailing ornament, with 3 graduated stylised sailing boats in aluminium, on a brass and wood base, 12in (30.5cm) high.
£270-350 *S(S)*

A spelter figure of a bird on a base, signed Rochard, 16in (41cm) wide.
£250-350 *ASA*

A chrome metal figure with a cigarette lighter, 9.5in (24cm) wide.
£80-130 *ASA*

A plated metal smoker's companion, in the form of an aeroplane, consisting of 2 cigarette cases, 4 ashtrays and a cigar cutter, 10in (25cm) wide.
£700-900 *Bon*

An Art Deco style diamond and ruby set cocktail bracelet, each link alternately set with brilliant cut diamonds and square cut rubies.
£3,000-3,500 *HSS*

A lady's Art Deco style platinum and diamond wristwatch, the jewelled lever movement inscribed 'Garrard', the case with diamond surround and diamond openwork panel shoulders, to cordette straps, in maker's stamped case.
£700-900 *CSK*

A pair of diamond set dress clips, each in a leafage and geometric pierced design, set with small cut and baguette diamonds with the principal diamonds mounted at the centre in the Art Deco taste.
£1,800-2,200 *S(S)*

An opal and diamond brooch, the cut opal stone set in a surround of cut diamonds, the mount in a fan pierced geometric design in the Art Deco taste, c1920.
£1,500-2,000 *S(S)*

A diamond set platinum cocktail watch, the silvered dial with black Arabic numerals inscribed 'Crusader Swiss Made', within a border pave set with numerous small diamonds, with pierced angular shaped shoulders set with further diamonds, on an articulated bracelet strap.
£850-950 *HSS*

A lady's pavé diamond wristwatch, with diamond graduated panel shoulders, to a 9ct. white gold Brazilian link bracelet, the rectangular dial with Arabic numerals.
£300-400 *CSK*

Locate the Source

The source of each illustration in Miller's can be found by checking the code letters below each caption with the list of contributors.

Bronze and Ivory

'One man and his lion', a green patinated spelter figure, cast from a model by M. Le Verrier, on a marble base, restored, with engraved signature M. Le Verrier, 20.5in (52cm) high.
£2,000-2,500 *C*

A Dutch brass model of a woman dancing, on an oval base, signed Th. A. Vos., and 'Kunst-Bronsgieterij 'De Kroon', Haarlem', 19in (48cm) high.
£250-350 *C(S)*

Thomas Vos was born in Groningen in the Netherlands in 1887. Having learnt to sculpt in Brussels, he worked principally on figures of women, animals and children until his death in Haarlem in 1948.

'Dancer', a bronze and ivory figure, cast and carved from a model by Gerdago, her costume with gold patination, and cold painted geometric decoration in red and shades of blue, on an oval green onyx base, decoration rubbed, signed in the bronze A. R. Gerdago, 13in (33cm) high.
£3,000-4,000 *C*

A Preiss bronze and ivory figure, on a stepped green and black onyx base, lacking hands, signed in the maquette, c1930, 5in (13cm) high.
£600-900 *S(S)*

A P. Tereszczuk bronze inkwell, with a young girl crossing a stream, a basket in each hand, signed, c1920, 12.5in (32cm) wide.
£100-200 *S(S)*

An ashtray with a figure of a boy, 6in (15cm) high. **£500-800** *ASA*

A silvered bronze figure, by Helène Grünne, indistinct foundry mark, 1920s, 11.5in (29cm) high.
£700-800 *S(S)*

An enamelled bronze and ivory dancer, in red and black shoes, her dress decorated in orange, red, blue, green, black and gilt flowerheads, a wide-brimmed hat similarly painted, raised on a stepped oval green onyx base, incised Austria on the base, 1920s, 12.5in (32cm) high.
£2,100-2,700 *S(S)*

A chrome plated sculpture of a reclining figure, worn, stamped A. Reimann, Ges Gesch, made in Germany, 5.5in (14cm) long.
£500-600 *S(S)*

A Lorenzl silvered bronze and ivory figure of a dancing girl, painted with bell-formed blue flowers and green foliage, raised on a green onyx base, damaged, moulded mark Lorenzl, painted Crejo, 1920s, 14.5in (37cm) high.
£2,000-3,000 *S(S)*

A silvered bronze figure, by P. Phillipe, 10.5in (26cm) high.
£1,500-2,000 *ASA*

A bronze figure of a mummy and case, by Bergman, 6in (15cm) high. **£400-600** *ASA*

A bronze sitting figure, by Lorenzl, 4in (10cm) high. **£200-300** *ASA*

A bronze figure, c1930, 7.5in (19cm) high. **£250-275** *HEW*

'L'inspiration', a French spelter figure, after T. H. Somme, on green marble base, early 20thC, 22.5in (57cm) high. **£350-400** *GAK*

'Goat Charmer', a silvered bronze figure signed by H. Fugere, 19.5in (19cm) wide. **£800-1,200** *ASA*

'Dagger Dancer', a bronze figure by Marquet, c1930, 19in (48cm) high. **£1,000-1,500** *ASA*

An ivory figure with roses by J. Descamp, 9.5in (24cm) high. **£1,500-2,000** *ASA*

'Innocence', a bronze and ivory figure by Chiparus, c1930, 9.5in (24cm) high. **£2,500-3,000** *ASA*

A pair of spelter figures by August Moreau, c1900, 30in (76cm) high. **£1,500-1,800** *ASA*

British Ceramics

A Burleigh jug with parrot
design, c1930, 8in (20cm) high.
£55-80 *AOS*

Two Carlton Ware dishes, with
Pink Daisy design, 4.5in (11cm)
wide. **£20-25 each** *ADC*

A Hancock vase, decorated with
Autumn design, 7in (18cm) high.
£100-150 *AOS*

A Burleigh jug with kingfisher
pattern, c1930.
£50-75 *AOS*

A Carlton Ware bowl, and a
drainer, with Water Lily design,
9.5in (24cm) and 8.5in (22cm)
wide.
£45-65 each *ADC*

A Hancock vase, with
pomegranate pattern, 10in (25cm)
high. **£95-145** *AOS*

A Carlton Ware vase, with
stylised flower heads in
polychrome enamels, c1930,
9in (23cm) high.
£300-350 *CAR*

A pair of Carlton Ware porcelain
vases, painted with pairs of
swallows and stylised foliage,
polychrome on pastel blue ground
with gilt details, the interior
covered in mauve glaze, printed
marks Carlton Ware, Made in
England, 'Trade Mark', 10in
(25cm) high. **£520-620** *C*

A Carlton Ware blue toilet jug
and bowl set, with chinoiserie
pattern, printed mark in blue.
£300-400 *HSS*

A Crown Ducal vegetable dish,
decorated in red trees pattern,
c1925.
£20-35 *AOS*

A Burleigh jug with fox and stork
design, 8in (20cm) high.
£75-125 *AOS*

A Royal Cauldron fruit bowl,
c1935, 9in (23cm) diam.
£65-95 *AOS*

A Carlton Ware teapot, milk jug and sugar bowl, in Water Lily pattern, c1930.
£100-150 *AOS*

Three Gray's Paris jugs, with geometric design by Susie Cooper.
£250-300 each *CAR*

A Hancock part coffee service. **£125-175** *AOS*

A Gray's Pottery plate and bowl, by Susie Cooper, bowl 5in (13cm) wide. **£250-300,** plate **£150-180** *CAR*

A pair of Compton Pottery stoneware bookends, each trefoil form with relief decoration of a butterfly, on semi-circular base, covered in a matt green glaze with black, ochre and yellow painted decoration, impressed seal Compton Pottery, Guildford, c1945, 5in (12cm) high.
£150-300 *C*

A Susie Cooper cased part coffee set, each piece painted with wash and solid bands in mixed grey, brown and blue, comprising: 6 coffee cans, 6 saucers and 6 electroplated shell moulded spoons with blue bead ends, in a fitted case, printed factory marks A. Susie Cooper Production, Crown Works, Burslem, England, cans 2in (5.5in) high.
£320-400 *S(S)*

A Carlton Ware blue coffee service, decorated in jewelled enamels and gilt with exotic birds and with wisteria, with gilt interiors, comprising: coffee pot and cover, two-handled sucrier and cover, cream jug and 6 coffee cups and saucers, printed mark in black.
£200-300 *ASA*

A Carlton Ware tête-à-tête, each piece with a speckled pale blue ground heightened with gilding, applied with solid gilt ribbed handles, comprising: teapot and cover, 2 cups and saucers, jug, sugar bowl, jam pot and cover, plate, and biscuit barrel and cover, printed marks, 1930s.
£450-550 *S(S)*

A Maling ware fruit bowl, 8.5in (21cm) diam.
£95-145 *AOS*

A Maling ware oval dish in the Stork design, decorated by Janet Taylor, c1932, 10in (25cm) wide.
£120-140 *IS*

A Hancock bowl, with Pomegranate pattern, 9in (23cm) diam.
£85-125 *AOS*

A pair of Hancock vases, in Cremorne pattern, 11in (28cm) high. **£175-275** *AOS*

A Gray's Pottery lamp base, painted with golfers, c1930, 6in (16cm) high.
£750-800 *CAR*

A Maling ware wall plaque, decorated in the Anemone pattern, c1936, 11in (28cm) diam.
£180-220 *IS*

A Gray's Pottery teapot, with Cubist face design, decorated with orange and yellow enamel, 4.5in (12cm) high.
£200-250 *CAR*

A Maling ware ginger jar, c1950, 8in (20cm) high.
£45-85 *AOS*

A Hancock bowl, with Water Lily pattern, 9in (23cm) diam.
£85-125 *AOS*

A Poole pottery jug, with geometric design, 6in (15cm) high.
£55-85 *AOS*

A Maling ware oval bread basket decorated in the Gladioli pattern, c1936, 11in (28cm) wide.
£150-180 *IS*

A Maling ware wall pocket in the Michaelmas Daisy pattern, c1938, 9in (23cm) high.
£180-200 *IS*

A Poole pottery bowl, 1960s.
£8-12 *AOS*

A Radford ware vase, with tree design, c1930, 10in (25cm) high.
£65-95 *AOS*

A Radford ware dish, 11in (28cm) diam.
£25-45 *AOS*

A Radford ware jug, decorated with carrots, c1930, 6.5in (16cm) high.   **£35-45** *AOS*

A Charlotte Rhead jug, 6in (15cm) high.   **£45-65** *AOS*

A Radford ware two-handled vase, 10in (25cm) high.
£50-75 *AOS*

Two Charlotte Rhead Crown Ducal vases, Nos. 5623 and 5983, 7in (18cm) high.
£95-135 each *ADC*

A pair of Charlotte Rhead vases, 7in (18cm) high. **£400-450** *HEW*

A Charlotte Rhead Crown Ducal plaque, decorated in light and dark pink and grey on a cream background, No. 6778, 12.5in (32cm) diam.
£220-280 *ADC*

A pair of banded Shelley vases, 8in (20cm) high.
£65-95 *AOS*

A Charlotte Rhead Crown Ducal jug, No. 5623, 9.5in (24cm) high.
£85-95 *ADC*

A Shelley tea set for two, Oxford shape, with green leaf motif, No. 12387, c1935.
£125-175 *AOS*

A Radford ware jug and vase, c1930.
£30-45 each *AOS*

'Travel', a Wedgwood 44 piece dinner service, designed by Eric Ravilious, grey ground transfer printed in black and heightened in blue enamel, printed marks Travel, designed by Ravilious, Wedgwood of Etruria & Barlaston, Made in England, c1953, dinner plate 10in (25cm) diam.
£2,500-3,000 *C*

A Shelley banded jam pot, 4.5in (11cm) high.
£20-30 *AOS*

A Shelley nursery plate, with Mabel Lucie Attwell design, printed in colours with a little girl standing with her doll beneath an umbrella, watching a parade of pixies, with inscription 'Fairy folk with tiny wings flying all over my plates and things', printed factory marks, 8in (20cm) diam.
£120-150 *CSK*

A Staffordshire model of a cat, after a design by Louis Wain, in green, yellow, red, blue and black, slight rubbing, impressed and overpainted facsimile signature on the back, stamped Made in England and impressed registration mark, 1920s, 5in (13cm) high.
£400-500 *S(S)*

A Poole pottery teapot stand, c1930.
£20-30 *AOS*

A Cszechoslovakian vase, 8in (20cm) high.
£45-75 *AOS*

A W. H. Grindley coffee service of 15 pieces.
£75-125 *AOS*

Clarice Cliff

A Clarice Cliff cup and saucer, in football pattern, c1929.
£140-190 *AOS*

A Clarice Cliff melon bowl, 8in (20cm) diam.
£200-250 *AOS*

Two Clarice Cliff grapefruit dishes, with daffodil shape and rainbow pattern, 6.5in (17cm) wide.
£65-75 each *ADC*

A Clarice Cliff basket, with Fragrance pattern, 13in (33cm) high.
£350-450 *AOS*

A Clarice Cliff plate, with Rudyard design, 9in (23cm) diam.
£325-375 *RIC*

A Clarice Cliff Chloris bowl, 9in (23cm) diam.
£100-150 *AOS*

A Clarice Cliff octagonal bowl, with Woodland pattern, 9in (23cm) diam.
£400-450 *ADC*

A Clarice Cliff plate, decorated in the Honolulu pattern, painted in colours with green and black striped rim, printed factory marks, 9in (23cm) diam.
£250-300 *CSK*

A Clarice Cliff Bizarre plate, painted in the Rudyard pattern, in pastel colours with striped rim, printed factory marks, 9in (23cm) diam.
£200-250 *CSK*

A Clarice Cliff plate by Graham Sutherland, impressed mark, 1934, 9in (23cm) diam.
£100-150 *AOS*

A Clarice Cliff Athens shaped jug, with Sliced Fruit pattern, 8in (20cm) high.
£200-245 *RIC*

A Clarice Cliff plate, with Laura Knight design, from the Artists in Industry range, 9in (23cm) diam.
£550-750 *RIC*

A Clarice Cliff jug, in Gibraltar pattern, 4in (10cm) high.
£500-550 *ADC*

A Clarice Cliff Newport Pottery Bizarre 'Inspiration-Persian' pottery charger, decorated with quatrefoil flowerhead within a border of scrolls in mottled blue, green, apricot and lilac glazes, inscribed in brown, 13in (34cm) diam.
£500-700 *HSS*

A set of 3 graduated Clarice Cliff meat plates, each designed by Ernest Proctor and painted in pink, green, black and blue with abstract waves and coils, printed and impressed marks, 1934, largest 18.5in (47cm) wide.
£600-700 *S(S)*

A Clarice Cliff Newport Pottery Fantasque Melon pattern Lotus jug, printed mark and facsimile signature in black, 11.5in (29cm) high.
£550-650 *HSS*

A Clarice Cliff Athens shape teapot, decorated with umbrellas and rain, 7in (18cm) high.
£425-475 *RIC*

A Clarice Cliff Oceanic jug, with Windbells pattern, 6in (15cm) high.   **£225-275** *RIC*

A Clarice Cliff Athens shape teapot, decorated with Berries, 4.5in (11cm) high.
£300-350 *ADC*

A Clarice Cliff Lotus pattern jug, Goldstone painted, 6.5in (16cm) high.
£120-140 *GAK*

A Clarice Cliff, Newport Pottery teapot in the form of a Teepee, by Betty Silvester, moulded with moose and leaves, the spout in the form of a Red Indian, the handle as a totem pole, inscribed under the base, Greetings from Canada, 7in (18cm) high.
£600-1,000 *Bea*

A Clarice Cliff cylindrical vase, decorated in geometrical pattern, 6in (15cm) high.
£325-375 *RIC*

A Clarice Cliff Dover shape jardinière, with Canterbury Bells pattern, 8in (20cm) high.
£380-425 *RIC*

A Clarice Cliff Alpine Lotus jug, c1932, 12in (31cm) high.
£1,000-1,500 *AOS*

A Clarice Cliff fish group, 10in (25cm) wide.
£750-850 *ADC*

A Clarice Cliff ribbed vase in Poplar pattern, 7in (18cm) high.
£700-750 *RIC*

A Clarice Cliff 'Inspiration' floral vase, decorated with flowers in typical underglaze shades of blue, pink and buff heightened in orange and green enamel, printed mark, c1931, 6in (16cm) high.
£680-750 *S(S)*

A Clarice Cliff vase, with Alpine pattern, c1932, 7in (18cm) high.
£220-270 *AOS*

A Clarice Cliff Tulip shape vase, No. 583, 5.5in (14cm) high.
£300-350 *ADC*

A Clarice Cliff Odillon coffee set, each piece painted overall in orange, green and with black handles, comprising: coffee pot and cover, 4 cups, 6 saucers, jug and sugar bowl, chipped, printed and impressed marks, 1930.   **£300-500** *S(S)*

A Clarice Cliff Newport Pottery Bizarre pattern globular shaped vase, decorated with a landscape, castle, flowers and leaves, banded, impressed number 370, 6in (15cm) diam.
£400-450 *L&E*

A Clarice Cliff 'Café au Lait' Bizarre vase, the brown speckled ground decorated with the Red Roofs pattern, Shape 358, printed marks, c1931, 8in (20cm) high.
£300-500 *S(S)*

A Clarice Cliff vase, decorated with umbrellas and rain, shape 342, 8in (20cm) high.
£750-800 *ADC*

A Clarice Cliff Newport Pottery Latona vase, the globular body with a graduated ringed neck, painted with blue, pink, green, yellow and black flowers above a yellow band, black printed factory mark, c1930, 8in (20cm) high.
£400-600 *S(S)*

A Clarice Cliff Flora pattern vase, shape No. 342, 7.5in (19cm) high.
£600-850 *AOS*

A Clarice Cliff Geometric Lotus vase, painted with a wide band of repeated angular shapes within rectangular panels, in purple, orange, brown and yellow betwen orange bands, black printed factory mark, c1930, 11in (28cm) high.
£500-600 *S(S)*

A Clarice Cliff geometric pattern vase, shape No. 355, 8in (20cm) high.
£300-500 *AOS*

A Clarice Cliff Newport Pottery, Latona candlestick, painted with stylised blue, pink, green, yellow and black flowers with a yellow band below, black printed factory mark, remains of paper label, c1930, 8in (20cm) high.
£200-300 *S(S)*

A Clarice Cliff sabot, c1932.
£165-225 *AOS*

A Clarice Cliff swan, 10.5in (26cm) wide.
£500-550 *ADC*

A Clarice Cliff conical pepper pot, decorated with pink pearls, 3in (8cm) high.
£20-25 *RIC*

A Clarice Cliff Newport Pottery Bizarre Sunray pattern confiture and cover of plain cylindrical form, printed mark in black, 3in (8cm) over knop.
£300-350 *HSS*

A Wilkinson & Sons Clarice Cliff Bizarre Gayday bowl, 5.5in (14cm) diam., and 3 Bizarre mugs, 2 decorated in Fantasque and Nasturtium pattern, 3.5in (9cm) high.
£300-400 *WIL*

A Clarice Cliff Sungleam handled pitcher, decorated with Yellow and Orange Crocus pattern, shape No. 634, 7in (18cm) high.
£300-350 *RIC*

Continental Ceramics

An Art Deco ceramic night light holder.
£30-50 *ASA*

A Goldscheider terracotta wall mask, with black printed marks, impressed 1107, 1930s, 8in (20cm) high.
£300-400 *S(S)*

A Goldscheider ashtray, formed of interlinked circles with a recess in the rim applied with a female head with orange curly hair on the edge, stamped Goldscheider Wien, c1925, 10in (25cm) wide.
£300-500 *S(S)*

A cat by Georges Jacques Adnet, c1930, 14in (36cm) high.
£300-345 *POW*

A French porcelain box and cover, signed, with 'France Editions Etling Paris' on base, 5in (13cm) diam.   **£80-120** *ASA*

A Goldscheider figure of a boy, c1920, 10in (25cm) high.
£250-280 *TVA*

A Royal Dux Ballet Russe figure, c1928, 12in (31cm) high.
£350-380 *CAR*

A Rosenthal porcelain figure, naturalistically modelled and coloured as a female nude reclining on a rock, green printed and painted marks, c1934, 16in (41cm) wide.
£900-1,200 *S(S)*

A Royal Dux porcelain group, in dark blue with gilt detailing, raised on a scallop edged circular base, applied pink triangular mark, stamped Made in Czechoslovakia, 2993 4, c1930, 12in (31cm) high.
£450-550 *S(S)*

A French white porcelain figure, signed, 13in (33cm) high.
£350-450 *ASA*

A Saint Clément Ged Condé polar bear, c1920, 11in (28cm) wide.
£240-265 *POW*

A Rosenthal porcelain figure of Pierrot, 12in (31cm) wide.
£800-1,200 *ASA*

A Saint Clément Ged Condé fish, with white crackle glaze, c1920, 10.5in (26cm) wide.
£170-185 *POW*

Miller's is a price GUIDE not a price LIST

A Boch Frères Keramis Ch. Catteau figure of 'The Skaters', 13in (33cm) high.
£250-285 *POW*

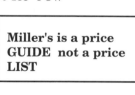

A Lenci earthenware group, modelled as a naked adolescent girl seated at the foot of a kneeling woman wearing a flowing blue robe and cream scarf spangled with gilt stars, minor glaze chips, painted factory mark, 1938, 16in (41cm) high.
£400-450 *CSK*

A Goebels Pottery set of ashtrays and a jockey cigarette box, decorated in orange and black, box 6in (15cm) high.   **£20-40 each** *ASA*

A Goldscheider Butterfly model of a figure, after a design by Lorenzl, incised marks Goldscheider, Wien, Lorenzl, 5917 515 4, facsimile signature on the base, 1930s, 10in (25cm) high.
£890-920 *S(S)*

PAPIER MACHE

A papier mâché pencil box, 8in (20cm) long.
£30-32 *AI*

A papier mâché box, inlaid with mother-of-pearl, 9.5in (24cm) long.
£30-36 *AI*

A mid-Victorian shell inlaid and parcel gilt papier mâché and iron bedstead, the uprights and foot uprights similarly decorated, restored, 60in (153cm) wide.
£3,000-3,500 *CSK*

A papier mâché box, 7in (17.5cm) wide.
£15-25 *AI*

A papier mâché shaped snuff box, 'The Ring Master', c1850, 3in (7cm) wide.
£250-300 *RdeR*

A papier mâché snuff box, c1840, 3in (7.5cm) wide.
£300-400 *RdeR*

A Victorian papier mâché table top, painted after Landseer's 'Dignity and Impudence'.
£150-200 *HSS*

A papier mâché snuff box, c1840, 3in (7.5cm) wide.
£300-400 *RdeR*

A papier mâché shaped snuff box, c1850, 3in (7.5cm) wide.
£300-400 *RdeR*

A papier mâché crumb scoop, 10.5in (26.5cm) wide.
£50-75 *AI*

A Victorian black lacquered papier mâché tilt-top table, probably Birmingham, 47.5in (120cm) diam.
£3,000-3,500 *MCA*

A pair of Victorian black lacquered papier mâché tilt-top tables, with mother-of-pearl, painted, and gilt floral decoration.
£1,000-1,500 *MJB*

A papier mâché blotter, 9in (22.5cm) high.
£80-85 *AI*

A Victorian green and gilt papier mâché cradle style planter, with a metal liner to the boat-shaped panel sides, on an open scroll base with gilt flowers.
£2,000-2,500 *WW*

A Victorian papier mâché tray, the centre painted with an extensive Italian landscape, in a gilt foliate and floral reserve border, the back signed indistinctly 'Mechi', 4 Leadenhall St., London, 32in (81cm) wide.
£900-1,200 *P(O)*

KITCHENALIA

A Georgian salt box, 17.5in (44.5cm) high.
£300-350 *JAC*

A Welsh spoon rack with spoons, in staircase form, with a shaped apron, 18thC.
£300-345 *CHA*

A pair of late Victorian Avery Pole Scales, in brass and cast blackened wrought metal, the centre stand supporting a brass balance rail with pans and holders.
£320-370 *GAK*

A pair of fruitwood nutcrackers, with printed label EVAN-THOMAS COLLECTION, numbered in ink 51, 18thC, 5in (12cm) long.
£300-350 *CSK*

A pair of Queen Anne yew nutcrackers, carved with a hare and incised with a shepherd, a fox, a cat and a seated bird, dated 1708, 8in (21cm) long.
£700-750 *CSK*

A pair of boxwood nutcrackers, modelled as a bishop's head and a stylised bird and animal, carved with the legend 'He that is willing/peace for to make/must be indifferent/and no partie take', the body bearing a fleur-de-lys below a coronet, c1600, 8in (21cm) long.
£1,600-2,000 *CSK*

A brass and glass wall mounted towel rail.
£50-58 *CHA*

An exhibition standard 7.25in gauge model of the Texas and Pacific Railroad 4-4-0 locomotive and tender, No.34, by M. Pavie, 84in (213cm) long. **£9,000-10,000** *C*

A Bing hand painted tinplate limousine, minor paint loss and over-varnishing, original cardboard box, c1908.
£11,000-12,000 *S*

A dolls perambulator, late 19thC.
£50-80 *PCh*

A German dolls open kitchen filled with accessories, mainly 19thC, 22.5in (57cm)wide.
£3,500-4,000 *S*

A Steiff white plush teddy bear,with blank metal button in left ear, 23in (59cm).
£2,000-2,500 flying a Steiff display aeroplane, canvas on wooden frame, 48in (122cm).
£500-1,000 *S*

A 5in gauge model of the Great Western Railway River Class 2-4-0 locomotive and tender, No.76, 'Wye' modelled as modified c1896 by R.F. Richards, Southsea, 54in (137cm) long. **£4,500-5,500** *C*

A scratch built model of an omnibus.
£60-80 *N(A)*

A child's pedal car, by Lines Bros (Tri-ang), 2-speed drive and solid rubber tyres, partially restored, 1950s. **£175-225** *JH*

An important Admiralty Dockyard model of a 96-Gun Second Rate Ship-of-the-Line, the fruitwood frame with exposed planking to hull and exposed plank deck, c1700, 33.5in (85cm) long.
£180,000-200,000 *S(NY)*

A 7.25in gauge model of the Great Western Railway 14XX Class 0-4-2 side tank locomotive, by I.R. Holder, 45in (114cm) long.
£9,000-12,000 *C*

A model First Rate Ship-of-the-Line, H.M.S. Majestic, late 18thC, 33in (84cm) long.
£30,000-35,000 *S(NY)*

A Gustave Vichy musical automaton of a negro fruit seller, c1870, in display case.
£20,000-22,000 *S*

A Jumeau bisque headed two-faced doll, wearing late 19thC clothes, 18in (46cm) high.
£5,000-6,000 *S(NY)*

A Roullet et Decamps musical automaton, c1880, 23in (59cm) high.
£8,000-10,000 *S*

A leather headed clockwork musical automaton, by Vichy.
£9,000-10,000 *CSK*

A German papier mâché doll, c1860, 15.5in (39cm).
£900-1,000 *DOL*

A European bisque headed lady doll, with poured head, wood and composition jointed body, unmarked, 22in (56cm) high.
£14,000-16,000 *S(NY)*

A composition headed clockwork musical automaton, by Vichy, 18in (46cm) high.
£3,000-5,000 *CSK*

An Armand Marseille 1920s flapper doll, No. 390, 18in (45cm) high.
£250-350 *DOL*

A Lenci boudoir doll, in original organza dress, garters with roses, stockings, shoes trimmed with roses, c1920, 28in (71cm) high, with original box. **£1,800-2,000** *DOL*

A Leopold Lambert musical automaton , with papier mâché head, c1890, 23in (59cm) high.
£11,000-14,000 *S*

An Emile Jumeau all original doll, c1870, 14.5in (37cm) high.
£2,200-2,500 *DOL*

A Jules Steiner Bourgoin pressed bisque doll, unstrung, replacement wig, incised Steiner, c1882.
£2,500-4,000 *S*

A Simon & Halbig bisque headed character doll. **£800-1,200** with accessories. **£400-600** *CSK*

A folding pine room box, representing a drawing, with original wooden set of furniture, German, c1880, 11in (28cm) wide.
£900-1,200 *CSK*

A Jumeau bisque doll, in muslin frock, some damage, impressed Depose, 10, 23in (59cm).
£6,000-7,000 *S*

A Kammer & Reinhardt bisque character doll, c1910.
£2,500-3,500 *S*

A Scandinavian painted wooden grocer's shop, dated 1883.
£600-800 *CSK*

A Simon & Halbig Mulatto bisque character doll, c1910.
£1,600-2,000 *S*

'Anna's Pleasure', a painted wooden dolls house, c1860, 38in (96.5cm) wide.
£1,800-2,500 *CSK*

A J.D. Kestner Oriental doll, impressed F.10, 243 JDK, c1914, 13in (33cm).
£2,000-2,500 *S*

'Villa Lily', a painted wooden dolls house, with Walterhausen furniture.
£3,500-4,000 *CSK*

A Kammer & Reinhardt character doll, damage to wig, impressed 101 K*R 46, c1910.
£2,500-3,000 *S*

'The Dennis House' a painted wooden dolls house, possibly American, c1880.
£3,500-4,000 *CSK*

A South Italian Greek pottery krater, Apulia, circa 4th Century B.C.
£6,000-8,000 *S*

An Hellenistic terracotta figure, 4th-3rd Century B.C., 7.5in (19cm).
£5,000-6,000 *S*

A Roman marble cinerarium, Italy, Tiberian or early Claudian period, circa 20-40 A.D., 16in (41cm) long.
£10,500-12,500 *S*

An Egyptian limestone relief fragment, depicting a retinue of musicians, Amarna Period, circa 1372-1355 B.C., 21in (53cm) long.
£10,000-12,000 *S*

A Greek red figure kalpis, probably by the Tithonos painter, Attic, early 5thCentury B.C. **£27,500-30,000** *S*

A Visigothic bronze buckle, circa 6th Century A.D., 4in (10cm) high.
£2,000-3,000 *S*

A Roman marble vase, with bell shaped lid, circa 1st Century A.D., 19.5in (50cm) high.
£15,500-17,500 *S*

A Roman ivory miniature Corinthian capital, circa 1st-2nd Century A.D., 2in (4.5cm).
£1,200-1,500 *S*

An Etruscan bronze figure of a kouros, circa 520-500 B.C., 4.5in (11.5cm).
£4,500-6,500 *S*

A Greek bronze peplophoros, circa 460 B.C., 4in (10cm).
£12,000-14,000 *S*

A Roman marble head of Eros.
£10,000-12,000 *S*

A young girl, by Richard
Schwager, signed and dated 1868,
4in (10cm) high.
£4,000-4,500 *C*

Colonel Black, by George
Engleheart, c1753-1829,
with plaited hair reverse,
2in (5cm).
£1,500-2,000 *C*

Charles and Samuel Black, by
Abraham Daniel, died 1806, 4in
(10cm) high. **£3,500-5,000** *C*

A lady, by John Smart,
dated 1788, 3in (8cm)
high.
£18,000-20,000 *C*

An Officer, by John
Smart.
£11,000-15,000 *C*

A lady, by John Smart, 1742-
1811, initialled and dated 1800,
3in (8cm). **£12,000-15,000** *C*

A lady, by Jeremiah Meyer,
R.A., 1735-1789, in a silver gilt
frame with enamel border, 2.5in
(6cm) high. **£2,500-3,000** *C*

An Officer, by Frederick
Buck, 1771-c1840, 2.5in
(6cm) high.
£650-800 *C*

A lady, by Dominicus du Caju,
1802-1867, signed on the obverse,
4in (10cm) diam.
£3,500-4,500 *C*

Two girls, in a double sided gold
locket, by George Engleheart, 1750-
1829, 1.5in (4cm) high.
£5,500-6,500 *C*

r. Frederica,
Duchess of
York, in a
gold frame,
by William
Grimaldi,
1751-1830,
3in (7cm)
high.
£3,000-3,500
C

Above An Officer,
wearing the uniform of
the 65th Foot, in gilt
metal frame, by
Abraham Daniel, died
1805, 3in (8cm) high.
£3,000-4,000 *C*

An early ivory study of a baku, unsigned, 18thC, 3in (7cm).
£14,000-16,000 *S*

A pair of Japanese wood vases, inlaid in ivory, horn, mother-of-pearl, ebony and with metal studs, minor cracks, 21in (53cm). **£2,000-3,000** *CSK*

A pair of inlaid and lacquered wood vases, on gilt wood stands, Meiji period, 25.5in (65cm).
£5,500-7,000 *S*

l. A wood kiseruzutsu, with Tomobako, by Hokkyo Sessai, late 19thC.
£7,000-8,000 *S*

An ivory study of a Dutchman, unsigned, 18thC, 4in (9.5cm).
£2,000-2,500 *S*

A cloisonné vase, by Namigawa Sosuke, the sides mounted in shakudo, signed in a silver wire seal, Meiji period, 8in (20cm).
£20,000-25,000 *S*

A recumbent jade horse, Ming Dynasty or later, 8in (20cm) long. **£3,000-5,000** *C*

A pair of Peking glass vases, Jiaqing.
£7,000-9,000 *S*

An ivory figure, 18thC.
£3,000-4,000 *S*

A jadeite bowl and cover, on 3 cabriole legs and crisply carved with mask handles suspending loose rings, the cover surmounted by a seated qilin finial, 5.5in (13.5cm) wide, on wood stand. **£7,000-8,000** *C*

An ivory tusk, carved in relief with monkeys dressed as shishimai and sambaso dancers, the reverse with lions and tiger fighting, carved wood stand, signed Kizawa, Meiji period, 36.5in (92cm). **£4,500-5,000** *S*

An ivory monkey, holding a fruit, signed in relief seal Ishikawa, Meiji period, 4.5in (11cm). **£5,500-7,000** *S*

A lacquer tobako-bon, decorated in gold, small chips, 19thC, 10in (25cm). **£3,500-4,500** *S*

A silver mounted ivory and shibayama tankard, Meiji period. **£2,500-3,000** *S*

An embellished gilt bronze vase, cast as 2 phoenix, Qianlong, 19.5in (49cm) high. **£12,000-14,000** *C*

A suzuribako, decorated in gold and silver, chipped, 18th/19thC. **£3,500-4,500** *S*

Above A gold lacquer, two-case inro, by Shiomi Masanari, 19thC. **£12,000-14,000** *S*

A pair of enamelled silver and shibayama vases, Meiji period, 13in (33cm). **£5,000-6,000** *S*

Below A lacquer kogo, 19thC, 3in (8cm). **£950-1,200** *S*

l. A gold lacquer box and cover, 19thC, 4in (10cm). **£11,000-12,000** *S*

An Imperial gilt bronze mirror, Qianlong. **£2,000-2,500** *S*

A komai style gilt bronze shrine, decorated in gold, base marked Kusa, Meiji period. **£5,000-6,000** *S*

An Export cabinet-on-stand,
elaborately decorated, 17thC, 32in
(82cm). **£30,000-40,000** *C*

A roironuri ground inro-dansu,
old damage, unsigned, 19thC.
£75,000-80,000 *C*

A composite lacquer sage-
jubako, some damage, 18thC,
12in (30.5cm) high.
£5,000-6,000 *C*

A lacquered palanquin, with gold hiramakie on
a roironuri ground, gilt fittings, 19thC, the case
41.5in (105cm) long. **£30,000-35,000** *C*

A shibayama style kodansu, the silver ground carved
in relief, minor restorations, signed on the nashiji
ground base Masayoshi, late 19thC, 12in (30.5cm)
high. **£25,000-30,000** *C*

A composite lacquer
sage-jubako, c1800,
9.5in (24.5cm) high.
£3,500-4,500 *C*

l. A satsuma vase, signed
Keishu ga, blue satsuma
mon, late 19thC, 24in
(61.5cm) high.
£22,000-25,000 *C*

A lacquer vase and cover, minor old
damage, signed Sadatoshi, late
19thC, 10.5in (26cm) high.
£20,000-30,000 *C*

A Continental neo-classical ormolu, blue glass and cut glass, twelve-light chandelier, early 19thC, 48in (122cm) high.
£11,000-13,000 *S(NY)*

A pair of gilt bronze wall lights, each with three-candle nozzles, supported by winged female terms from anthemion backplates, 9in (23cm).
£2,000-3000 *S*

A Restauration gilt bronze mounted etched glass hanging light, c1820, 13.5in (34cm) high.
£5,000-6,000 *S*

A painted glass and gilt bronze hanging light, with screw-in candle nozzle, mid-19thC, 13in (33cm) wide. **£7,000-7,500** *S*

A pair of Empire ormolu and marble seven-light candelabra, fitted for electricity, early 19thC, 44.5in (112cm) high. **£42,000-50,000** *S(NY)*

A pair of Regency gilt metal and tôle peinte chinoiserie decorated five-light candelabra, c1820, 22in (56cm) high.
£10,500-15,000 *S(NY)*

A pair of Restauration gilt bronze candlesticks, with anthemion cast nozzles, c1815, 8in (20cm) high.
£2,500-3,000 *S*

A pair of Empire bronze, gilt bronze and marble candlesticks, c1810, 17in (43cm) high.
£13,500-14,500 *S*

A French gilt brass twenty four-light chandelier, 19thC, 53in (135cm) high. **£9,000-10,000** *P(O)*

A pair of Empire gilt bronze wall lights, c1815, 7in (18cm).
£1,600-2,000 *S*

A set of 6 brass and glass wall lights, each with three nozzles, 19thC, 8in (20cm).
£2,500-3,000 *S*

A pair of gilt bronze table candelabra, each with a pair of detachable scrolling arms, mid-19thC, 16in (41cm) high.
£4,000-5,000 *S*

A pair of early Louis XVI gilt bronze wall lights, c1775, 18in (46cm) high.
£4,000-5,000 *S*

A Baltic glass and gilt bronze chandelier, part 1800, 50in (127cm) high.
£4,000-6,000 *S*

A George III cut glass mounted oval mirror, with two-light girandole.
£23,000-25,000 *S(NY)*

A pair of ormolu and bronze ten-light candelabra, with foliate nozzles and drip pans, wired for electricity, late 19thC, 43in (109cm) high.
£15,500-17,000 *C*

r. A set of 4 ormolu twin-light wall applique, 20thC, 16.5in (42cm) high.
£3,000-4,000 *C*

A pair of Napoleon III parcel gilt and silvered Egyptian revival bronze torchéres.
£4,000-5,000 *C*

A Louis XV gilt bronze and glass chandelier, mid-18thC, some restoration, 45in (115cm) high. **£3,500-5,000** *S*

l. A pair of Louis XV ormolu two-light candelabra, mid-18thC, 18in (46cm) high. **£8,500-10,000** *S(NY)*

r. An ormolu hall lantern, with four-branch light fitment and glazed panels, 41in (104cm) high.
£3,500-5,000 *C*

A New Hebrides wood
slit drum, 96in (244cm).
£5,000-6,000 *S(NY)*

A Kuba ceremonial
drinking cup, 7in
(18cm) high.
£2,500-3,000 *S(NY)*

A Mossi ivory
pendant, 8in (20cm)
high.
£2,000-3,000 *S(NY)*

A face mask, remains of red
and white pigment, 12.5in
(32cm) high.
£3,000-3,500 *S(NY)*

A Songe face mask, pierced
along the perimeter for
attachment, 20in (51cm)
high.
£4,500-5,500 *S(NY)*

An Easter
Island club,
£3,500-4,500
S(NY)

An anthropomorphic Kuba
cup, areas of encrustation.
£45,000-50,000 *S(NY)*

A fang spoon, aged
dark brown patina,
6in (15cm) long.
£20,000-22,000 *S(NY)*

A Fang male reliquary
guardian figure.
£27,000-30,000 *S(NY)*

A Lower Sepik river
male figure.
£26,000-30,000 *S(NY)*

A Senufo figure of a
hornbill.
£20,000-25,000 *S(NY)*

A Kuba cup.
£1,300-1,700 *S(NY)*

A German hunting trousse, c1750.
£11,000-13,000 *S(NY)*

l. An etched state glaive.
£11,000-13,000 *S(NY)*

Two German
officers' daggers,
WWII.
£80-150 each *ASB*

A German etched state
halberd, on original wooden
staff, c1625, head 23.5in
(60cm).
£13,000-15,000 *S(NY)*

A German etched comb morion,
Nuremberg, c1700, 10.5in (26cm).
£5,500-6,500 *S(NY)*

German hunting swords, c1740-
1800.
£100-700 each *ASB*

An early fluted blued steel close
helmet, some replacements, probably
Innsbruck, c1520, 11.5in (29cm) high.
£17,000-20,000 *S(NY)*

A French
hunting sword,
for exhibition,
c1860.
**£15,000-
18,000** *S(NY)*

A Chinese brass cannon, 25in (64cm) barrel.
£1,000-1,300 *ASB*

An English sabretache, 20th
Hussars. **£400-450** *ASB*

BOW-WELL ANTIQUES
EDINBURGH

WE BUY & SELL, EXPORT & IMPORT

**Scottish pebble jewellery, Scottish regalia,
early Scottish pottery, Scottish pictures and paintings,
silver and plate, clocks and scientific instruments,
furniture, light fittings and glass.**

103-105 WEST BOW, EDINBURGH EH1 2JP
(Between the Grassmarket and The Royal Mile)

Shop hours 10am-5pm Monday-Saturday

**Tel: 031-225 3335
Fax: 031-665 2839
Mobile: 0831 106768**

ALL CREDIT CARDS ACCEPTED

A brass barrelled flintlock blunderbuss pistol, c1780.
£1,250-1,500 *ASB*

A .400 self-opening sidelock ejector rifle, No. 25057, 25.5in (65cm) chopper-lump barrels, by J. Purdey & Sons, in its oak and leather case with canvas outer cover.
£15,000-20,000 *S(G)*

A pair of English flintlock blunderbuss coaching pistols, with crest of Baronet Hume-Purves Campbell, signed Joyner, London, c1765. **£2,000-3,000** *ASB*

A cased percussion pepperbox revolver, by Blissett, c1840.
£900-1,000 *ASB*

Three Japanese swords, with wakisashi blades, 19thC, 20 to 22in (51 to 56cm) long.
£300-450 each *ASB*

A .240 flanged 'Royal' model detachable sidelock ejector gun, No. 31445, 25in (64cm) chopper-lump barrels, by Holland & Holland. **£11,500-15,000** *S(G)*

Two English Transitional percussion revolvers, c1830.
£270-300 each *ASB*

A .318 'Royal' model detachable sidelock ejector rifle, No. 35011, 25in (64cm) chopper-lump barrels, with pistol grip and cheek piece, in its oak and leather case with canvas outer cover, by Holland & Holland. **£16,000-20,000** *S(G)*

An English double barrelled percussion pistol, in original case with accessories, in near mint condition, c1840. **£1,000-1,400** *ASB*

A Japanese lacquer saddle, a pair of iron abumi, stirrup leathers, a crupper, saddle flaps, felt and silk traces, bridle and bit, variously decorated.
£9,500-11,000 *CSK*

A pair of North American Indian beaded moccasins, in very good condition, 19thC, 10in (25cm). **£200-250** *ASB*

A silk work basket, late 18thC. **£1,500-1,800** *CSK*

An embroidered purse, re-lined, late 16thC. **£850-1,200** *S*

An Italian embroidered cushion cover, c1700. **£3,500-4,000** *S*

A French polychromatic beaded watch case, c1790. **£650-800** *Bon*

A painted fan, with mother-of-pearl sticks carved and pierced with dancing figures, c1760, 11in (28cm). **£2,500-3,000** *CSK*

A hand painted fan, early 20thC. **£170-200** *N(A)*

A French polychromatic beaded patch box, c1790. **£450-550** *Bon*

Three Flemish tapestry covered cushions, late 16thC. **£3,500-4,500** *S*

A French portrait miniature case, c1790, 3.5in (9cm). **£600-700** *Bon*

A French painted paper leaf fan, with ivory sticks carved and pierced with figures, c1784, 20.5in (52cm). **£5,500-6,000** *Bon*

A Beauvais tapestry covered cushion, early 18thC, 33in (84cm) square. **£6,500-7,000** *S*

l. A French painted silk leaf fan, with ivory sticks, 18thC, 20in (51cm). **£3,000-3,500** *Bon*

A Balenciaga chiné taffeta cocktail dress, with tie belt and matching stole, c1954. **£200-250** *S(NY)*

A Christian Dior faille dress, jacket and stole, c1956. **£1,700-2,000** *S(NY)*

A Christian Dior embroidered taffeta ball gown, c1954. **£250-350** *S(NY)*

A Christian Dior figured silk dress, c1957. **£400-450** *S(NY)*

A Christian Dior sequined cocktail dress, c1956. **£2,500-3,000** *S(NY)*

A French beaded court robe, c1926. **£5,000-6,000** *S(NY)*

A Christian Dior wool ensemble, with mink collar, c1953. **£2,000-2,500** *S(NY)*

A Christian Dior beaded silk faille dress, c1955. **£800-900** *S(NY)*

A Christian Dior organza strapless dress, with bolero jacket, c1956. **£600-700** *S(NY)*

A Doucet silk faille mantle, c1911. **£500-550** *S(NY)*

A Christian Dior embroidered organdie dress, c1953. **£900-950** *S(NY)*

l. A Michel Goma embroidered taffeta ball gown, c1960. **£400-450** *S(NY)*

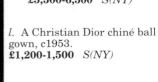

A Christian Dior tulle ball gown, c1954. **£5,500-6,500** *S(NY)*

l. A Christian Dior chiné ball gown, c1953. **£1,200-1,500** *S(NY)*

An Antwerp historical tapestry, depicting the story of Augustus sacrificing at an altar, inscribed IGNOTO DEO, late 17thC, 119 by 165in (302 by 419cm). **£12,000-14,000** *S(NY)*

A pair of Italian polychrome silk needlework and metal thread embroidered wall panels, both distressed, c1800. **£4,500-5,000** *S*

An English needlework picture, mid-17thC, 12 by 17in (31 by 43cm). **£3,000-4,000** *CSK*

A Brussels baroque biblical tapestry, depicting Gideon selecting his army to fight the Midianites, late 16th/early 17thC, 135 by 241in (343 by 612cm). **£25,000-30,000** *CNY*

An embroidered portrait miniature and mount, late 16th/early 17thC, wooden base and velvet possibly later, 9 by 8in (23 by 20cm). **£850-1,500** *S*

A Brussels silk and wool mythological tapestry, early 18thC, 178 by 129in (452 by 328cm). **£16,500-20,000** *CNY*

l. A woolwork picture of a ship, with cushion sails, c1840, in original frame, 20.5 by 16in (51 by 41cm). **£1,000-1,500** *RdeR*

An English needlework picture, framed and glazed, mid-17thC. **£7,500-9,000** *CSK*

A pin barrel organ, with fusee mechanism, early 19thC. **£800-1,200** *BWA*

A French 'overture' chamber barrel organ, mid-19thC.
£3,000-5,000 *S*

A 'Standard' 7in (17.5cm) gramophone, c1900.
£250-350 *BWA*

A German Komet penny-in-the-slot disc musical box, c1900.
£6,000-8,000 *Bea*

A pair of drawing room barrel pianos, with 10 tunes.
£1,500-3,000 each *BWA*

A musical game, by Ann Young of Edinburgh, patented 1801.
£800-900 *BWA*

An Italian violin, by Andrea Guarneri, Cremona, c1674.
£40,000-45,000 *S*

A German polyphon disc musical box, c1910.
£4,000-5,000 *S*

An Italian violin, by Enrico Rocca, Genoa, 1911.
£33,000-38,000 *S*

A Jacob Bertsche grand piano, with 6 pedals, 4 gilt Turkish headed monopodia, tapering to gilt feet, with music stand, c1815, 89 by 48in (226 by 122cm). **£20,000-25,000** *S(S)*

A two-keyed oboe, Dresden, 1798. **£1,500-2,500** *S(S)*

A Robert Woffington single manual harpsichord, Dublin, c1770, 88.5 by 39in (225 by 99cm). **£31,000-35,000** *S(S)*

A Jacob and Abraham Kirckman single manual harpsichord, London 1772, 99 by 39in (252 by 99cm). **£23,000-30,000** *S(S)*

A Conrad Graf grand piano, with labelled gilt metal frame, 4 pedals, and 3 baluster legs, c1835, 97 by 49.5in (246 by 125cm). **£13,500-20,000** *S(S)*

A Jacob & Abraham Kirckman, two manual harpsicord, London 1789, 94.5 by 39in (240 by 99cm). **£55,000-65,000** *S(S)*

A Noblet Frères two-keyed boxwood oboe, c1840. **£1,500-2,000** *S(S)*

A polygonal virginals, with four octave keyboard, possibly Venetian, 17thC, outer case with late 19thC painted decoration, 61.5 by 20in (156 by 51cm). **£12,000-15,000** *S(S)*

A Tabriz carpet, kilim strip at one end, 125 by 87in (317 by 221cm). **£2,500-3,000** *C*

A Kirman carpet, 163 by 124in (414 by 315cm). **£1,500-2,000** *C*

A Sarouk carpet, with scrolling vine around a concentric medallion, 124 by 85in (315 by 216cm). **£7,000-8,000** *C*

A Ziegler carpet, some wear, damage and repair. **£2,000-3,000** *C*

A Ziegler carpet, repairable splits, 100 by 93in (254 by 236cm). **£13,500-14,500** *C*

A Heriz carpet, restored, late 19thC, 201 by 142 in (510 by 360cm). **£22,000-25,000** *S(NY)*

A Dabir Kashan carpet, early 20thC, 212in (538cm). **£11,000-12,000** *S(NY)*

A Ziegler carpet, slightly stained, minute repairs, 199in (505cm). **£8,000-12,000** *C*

A silk and metallic thread brocade prayer rug, Isphahan or Kashan, 17thC.
£10,000-12,000   *S(NY)*

A Seychour runner, North East Caucasus, minor repairs, late 19thC, 120in (305cm) long.
£5,000-6,000   *S(NY)*

A silk and metallic thread velvet panel, Kashan or Isphahan, early 17thC, 78in (198cm).   **£130,000-140,000**   *S(NY)*

A Khotan rug, East Turkestan, early 19thC, 92in (234cm).
£5,500-6,500   *S(NY)*

An Armenian Kazak rug, some repairs, dated 1841. 113in (287cm) long.
£3,500-4,500   *S(NY)*

A Kazak prayer rug, South West Caucasus, late 19thC, 55in (140cm) long.   **£4,000-5,000**   *S(NY)*

A Shirvan prayer rug, dated 1306 (1888), repaired, 49in (125cm).
£8,500-10,000   *S(NY)*

A Mughal carpet fragment, early 17thC.
£35,000-40,000   *S(NY)*

A Directoire Aubusson carpet, restored and rewoven throughout, late 18thC, 116 by 113in (295 by 287cm). **£23,000-25,000** *S(NY)*

A Kazak rug, South West Caucasus, late 19thC, 59 by 49in (150 by 125cm). **£5,000-6,000** *S(NY)*

A Gabbeh rug, South Persia, late 19thC, 80 by 51in (203 by 130cm). **£3,500-4,000** *S(NY)*

A Perpedil prayer rug, North East Caucasus, worn with some holes, early 19thC, 92 by 43in (234 by 109cm). **£2,200-2,500** *S(NY)*

A Yomud Okbash, West Turkestan wool rug, c1800, 23 by 18in (59 by 46cm). **£24,000-26,000** *S(NY)*

A Karagashli rug, North East Caucasus, late 19thC. **£16,500-18,000** *S(NY)*

A Qashqa'i wool rug, South West Persia, worn, mid-19thC, 80 by 62in (203 by 157cm). **£5,000-6,000** *S(NY)*

l. An Anatolian kilim, rewoven areas, mid-19thC, 88in by 55in (224 by 140cm). **£5,000-7,000** *S(NY)*

An Aubusson rug, Napoléon III, 109 by 76in (276 by 194cm). **£5,500-8,000** *S*

A Kurdish woven carpet, from Khorassan area, Saumak and plain weave banding, c1940. **£1,300-1,600** *GRG*

A Charles X Aubusson carpet, restorations, c1825, 112 by 95in (285 by 241cm). **£25,000-30,000** *S(NY)*

A Shirvan runner, East Caucasus, 121in (307cm) long. **£3,000-4,000** *S*

An Aubusson carpet, early 20thC, 170in (432cm). **£15,000-17,000** *S(NY)*

A Khorassan carpet fragment, 17thC, 126in (320cm) long. **£30,000-35,000** *S*

l. A Kazak rug, West Caucasus, 41 by 33in (104 by 83cm). **£2,200-2,500** *S*

A title lobby card for the film The Mummy, Universal, 1932, in good condition, 11 by 14in (28 by 36cm).
£6,500-7,500 *CNY*

Orson Welles working scripts for Citizen Kane and The American, dated 4/30/40-5/9/40, together with another for The Magnificent Ambersons, 1942.
£6,500-8,000 *CNY*

A 'He Who Kills, Zuni Fetish Doll', 1975.
£2,700-3,700 *CNY*

The Poor Little Rich Girl, 20th Century Fox, 1936, linen backed, in good condition, 81in (206cm) square.
£2,500-3,500 *CNY*

l. A poster for The Oregon Trail, Republic, 1936, linen backed, in good condition, 41 by 27in (104 by 69cm).
£6,500-7,000 *CNY*

A 'Thing's Box' from TV's The Addams Family, 1964-66, together with 4 photographs and a letter from Mrs Jackie Coogan.
£13,000-15,000 *CNY*

A Bill Melendez celluloid from It was a Short Summer Charlie Brown, 1969. **£1,500-2,000** *S(NY)*

Below. A Walt Disney celluloid from Winnie the Pooh and the Blustery Day, 1968. **£3,000-4,000** *S(NY)*

r. A Bill Melendez celluloid from It's The Great Pumpkin Charlie Brown, 1966, 11 by 13.5in (28 by 34cm).
£3,000-4,000 *S(NY)*

TOOLS

A glazed wall display cabinet of I. Sorby's 'Punch' brand tools, including hand and tenon saw, turnscrews, chisels, gouges, pincers, secateurs, draw-knife, spirit level, adjustable spanner and ratchet brace, 43.5in (110cm) high.
£2,000-2,500   *CSK*

A carved wood moulding plane, 19thC, 18.5in (47cm) long.
£550-600   *HSS*

A universal cutting frame.
£200-300   *CSK*

This is of overhung pattern similar to Evans of Birch, but ungeared. The jockey pulleys are mounted on tubular supports through which the driving band runs. The object seems to be to prevent the band coming off, in which it succeeds. It is clearly by one of the professional makers. No other of this pattern has been recorded.

An epicycloidal cutting frame, with 17 change wheels and 11 cutters, in a fitted mahogany chest with drawer and brass drop handles at ends.
£1,000-1,500   *CSK*

A slope-top mahogany cabinet, with till top and 2 drawers, containing 151 O/T slide rest tools (mostly fancy forms), 8 various adaptors, 71 small and 78 large O/T drills.
£1,800-2,000   *CSK*

A Swedish brass plated plough, of composite beech, fruitwood and mahogany with brass screw stems and nuts, the full-length depth stop adjusted by key-operated rack and pinion, with compartment in fence for adjusting and locking keys, fence engraved C. G. Hermanson and C.G.H., 1883.
£300-500   *CSK*

A violin plane with plain and toothing cutters, another with plain cutter, both with Preston cutters, another with plain and toothing cutters, the lever and cutters with TZ monogram, longest 2in (5cm) long, and 5 various other cutters.
£450-500   *CSK*

A Norris A32 thumb plane, of steel-soled gunmetal with rosewood infill and wedge, twin-thread Patent Adjustment, Norris cutter, traces of lacquer on gunmetal and Buck & Ryan stamp on heel, 7in (17.5cm) long.
£1,800-2,000   *CSK*

A slope top mahogany chest, fitted for tools.
£2,200-2,700   *CSK*

ARTISTS' MATERIALS

A box of artist's pastels, by Henri Roche, comprising 5 trays of numerous individually numbered colour sticks.
£300-350 *CSK*

A pair of artist's treen hands, with articulated joints, 10in (25cm) high.
£400-450 *CSK*

A Winsor & Newton mahogany artist's box, the cover leather lined and gilt decorated, with remains of watercolour blocks, 3 ceramic slabs and drawer to base, 12in (31cm) wide.
£130-170 *ALL*

A late Victorian Arts & Crafts stained beech wood easel, 75.5in (192cm) high.
£800-900 *C(S)*

A box of Grumbacher artist's pastels, comprising 4 trays of numerous individually numbered colour sticks.
£250-350 *CSK*

An artist's oak studio easel, by Reeves & Sons, with winding mechanism, 19thC, 76in (193cm) high.
£500-550 *CSK*

An artist's oak studio easel, with winding mechanism, late 19thC, 77in (195cm) high.
£500-600 *CSK*

An artist's oak studio easel, with an adjustable shelf and winding mechanism, 19thC, 84in (213.5cm) high.
£400-600 *CSK*

An artist's oak studio easel, by J. Bryce Smith, with adjustable shelf above a materials shelf and winding mechanism, 19thC, 92in (234cm) high.
£350-550 *CSK*

An artist's oak studio easel, by Young & Co., with winding mechanism, 102in (259cm) high.
£400-600 *CSK*

Make the most of Miller's

Unless otherwise stated, any description which refers to 'a set' or 'a pair' includes a valuation for the entire set or the pair, even though the illustration may show only a single item.

PENS

A Swan 445/90 silver grey lizard skin effect leverless pen, c1938, and a Waterman's No. 92 brown lizard skin effect lever filled pen, with decorated cap and barrel bands, clip missing, c1933.
£100-150 *CSK*

A Conklin Endura Symetric green marble pen, with Toledo nib, c1930.
£80-90 *Bon*

A Mabie Todd gold plated eye dropper pen, with 'puffball' decoration and ladder-fed No. 2 nib, c1915.
£150-200 *Bon*

A lacquered Dunhill Namiki lever fill pen, with Maki-E design of 2 birds beside a wood fence and foliage, a similar scene without birds on the cap, lacquered ball clip, lever, nib section, cap band and original Dunhill Namiki No. 3 nib, cap cracked.
£450-600 *CSK*

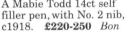

A Mabie Todd 14ct self filler pen, with No. 2 nib, c1918. **£220-250** *Bon*

A Conway-Stewart 22 Floral pen, with Conway-Stewart nib, c1955.
£120-170 *Bon*

A De la Rue lapis blue 5501-96 pen, with 3/81 nib, c1935, and a black/pearl 1743-22 lever filler pen, with No. 4 nib, clip missing, c1934.
£80-120 *Bon*

A lacquered Dunhill pyramid shaped pencil, with design of an ocean-going ship in full sail and metal lead surround, base with legend Dunhill-Paris-Fabrication-Japonaise.
£800-1,200 *CSK*

A Mabie Todd brown marble and white chased button fill L205/47 pen.
£40-50 *CSK*

A Parker 9ct. 61 Flammé pen, c1974.
£250-350 *Bon*

A Parker black and pearl Duofold pencil and a yellow-metal and black banded Fyne Point propelling pencil.
£50-100 *CSK*

A Parker gold plated lady's pen, with Parker fountain pen nib, c1921.
£80-100 *Bon*

A Mont Blanc black 6M safety pen, with No. 6 nib, c1922.
£400-450 *Bon*

A Mont Blanc black 1 EF safety pen, with No. 1 nib, c1922.
£200-250 *Bon*

A Parker black/pearl Lucky Curve Junior pen, with 18ct nib, c1924.
£50-60 *Bon*

A Waterman 9ct gold cased Line and Dot 52 pen and pencil set, with No. 2 nib, 1929 and 1930.
£250-350 *Bon*

A Waterman silver overlaid 52.5 Line and Dot pen, with No. 2 nib, 1922.
£200-250 *Bon*

A red Parker Lucky Curve Senior pen, with Duofold pen nib, c1927.
£100-120 *Bon*

A Waterman 13 Mottle Eye Dropper pen, with No. 3 nib, c1909.
£40-60 *Bon*

A Waterman 9ct gold overlaid 42 safety pen, with fluted decoration and No. 2 nib, damaged, 1924.
£200-400 *Bon*

A silver overlaid eye dropper fill pen, with ornate floral decoration on barrel, plain cap with one chased band, c1900.
£50-60 *CSK*

A Parker red button fill Duofold pen and a red button fill Duofold Junior pen.
£40-45 *CSK*

EPHEMERA

Pop Ephemera

A brooch of white and baguette white rhinestones, worn on stage by Marvin Gaye, 2in (5cm) wide; a black leather wallet made by Givenchy, with printed gilt inscription inside 'To Marvin With All My Love, Faith, 4-2-'83'; a printed handbill for Marvin Gaye and Tammi Terrell at the Cocoanut Grove, c1967-70; 2 tour jackets for the Marvin Gaye Concert Tour '83; a printed proclamation from the Mayor of Buffalo declaring Friday, May 13th, 1983 to be Marvin Gaye Day; a pair of brass goblets used on stage by Marvin Gaye during his last tour (one damaged); and a portrait of Marvin Gaye, signed A. Cross 5-21-83, mixed media, 20in (51cm) wide; and related material.
£400-600 *CSK*

A publicity photograph of The Beatles, in a recording studio, c1963, signed by each member of the group in blue biro, 11in (28cm) wide.
£750-850 *CSK*

An original sketch by Marvin Gaye for the album cover 'In Our Lifetime', 1980, in black and blue ink, 7in (18cm) wide, mounted together with a copy of the final album cover, an explanatory statement from the artist commissioned to design the sleeve and a colour picture of the singer, framed and glazed, 24in (61cm) wide.
£650-750 *S*

A black felt hat trimmed with an American Indian style band of leather and metal decorated with circular panels stamped with a star motif; and a matching belt, the buckle stamped with a steer-head motif, worn by Hendrix on stage, c1963.
£5,000-7,000 *CSK*

Mick Jagger's Victorian coat, in black cut velvet and red, brown and gold paisley design; and an affidavit confirming provenance. **£1,700-2,500** *S*

A Dezo Hoffmann publicity photograph, 1963, signed by each member of The Beatles in blue biro, 8 by 10in (20.5 by 25cm) wide. **£550-650** *CSK*

A Jimi Hendrix concert poster for Hastings Pier, Sunday 22nd October, 7.30-11, 1967, featuring Jimi Hendrix Experience plus full supporting program (sic), 20in (50.5cm) wide. **£2,000-2,200** *CSK*

An autographed slip of paper inscribed 'Thanks for the Roses, The Beatles, Paul, John, Ringo, George', 3 by 5in (7.5 by 12.5cm). **£220-260** *GIL*

A brown velvet stage jacket decorated at the shoulders with embroidered orange, yellow and green flowerheads and mirrored sequins; accompanied by a copy of Black Stars Magazine, January 1975, featuring several photographs of Gaye wearing a similar jacket on stage at Chicago's Amphitheatre; and a copy of Step News International, May 1976, featuring a photograph of Gaye on the front cover wearing this jacket at a Charity Concert in Radio City Music Hall, New York, where he was presented with a US State Department Ambassador of Good Will award by Shirley Temple Black. **£700-850** *CSK*

A bank cheque signed by Jimi Hendrix, 1968, together with 4 original colour slides of Jimi on stage, c1970. **£600-650** *S(NY)*

The Beatles E.P., Twist and Shout, 1963, signed on the back cover by all 4 members of the group. **£550-650** *CSK*

A piece of writing paper illustrated with a pencil portrait of Jimi Hendrix, signed and inscribed 'Love to you forever thank you - I wish you the Best of Love constantly Jimi Hendrix EXP', and 'Backwards Noel Redding xxx', and 'love Mitch xxx', 5.5in (14cm) wide. **£1,000-1,200** *CSK*

A black felt trilby, signed and inscribed on the underside of the brim 'All My Love Michael Jackson' and stamped with artist's name in gilt lettering on inside band; accompanied by a letter of authenticity from MJJ Productions and a colour photograph of Jackson wearing a similar hat.
£900-1,200 *CSK*

Michael Jackson's leather jacket, in black with matching quilted lining, fringes on arms and back, elaborately decorated overall with silver studs, with Maxfield Los Angeles label, size 42.
£7,500-12,000 *S*

Worn by the singer for the 'Moonwalker' video.

A Coral Records promotional postcard, 1958, signed by Buddy Holly, Joe Mauldin and Jerry Allison, 3.5in (8.5cm) wide; and a collection of promotional postcards and miniature publicity photographs of various recording artists and film stars, c1955, mounted in an album.
£700-900 *CSK*

The Isley Brothers' matching 2-piece Western-style stage suits in suede and leather, in 3 different colours of suede, burgundy, black and turquoise, each trimmed at the cuffs, shoulders and seams with gold or silver coloured leather; and one pair of corresponding gold and turquoise suede platform shoes; and 2 zebra-striped sleeveless stage tops, one with a matching scarf, worn on stage by Marvin, Kelly and Ronald Isley; and 2 photographs of Ronald Isley wearing the burgundy suit from the Isley Brothers Souvenir Book, 1976.
£620-820 *CSK*

A half length publicity photograph of Elvis Presley, signed and inscribed 'To Linda Best Wishes Elvis Presley', c1960, 4.5in (11cm) wide.
£250-300 *CSK*

A Michael Jackson phonograph, made by Vanity Fair, 1984, with instruction leaflet, in original box, 12.5in (32cm) wide.
£80-90 *CSK*

A complete stage outfit from the Purple Rain Tour, 1984, comprising: an ornate purple lurex coat, a pair of high-waisted trousers, a matching pair of high-heeled ankle boots, a white shirt with Prince label in purple stitched inside, and a gilt metal crucifix and chain, worn by Prince, and an illustrated souvenir concert programme from the same tour.
£10,000-14,000 *CSK*

A rhinestone stage glove, with Western Costume Co. Hollywood woven label, printed with the artist's name Michael Jackson and order number 2481-1, stitched inside, fastening at the cuff with a single hook, thought to have been worn by Michael Jackson at the 1984 Grammy Award ceremonies, February 28th 1984, where he won 8 Grammy Awards and to the USA For Africa We Are The World recording session, January 28th 1985; and a custom-made rotating display case of black and clear perspex, 59in (149.5cm) high.
£17,000-25,000 *CSK*

Michael Jackson's rhinestone glove is probably the most recognisable piece of Rock and Roll costume of the 1980s.

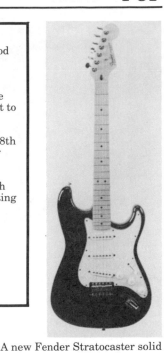

A new Fender Stratocaster solid body guitar, serial number MN006714, black, double cut-away body, 4 bolt maple neck, headstock face with Fender logo, 21 fret fingerboard with black dot marker inlays, 3 single coil pickups, selector switch, 3 controls, tremolo bridge/tailboard and white pickguard, signed and inscribed on the body Eric Clapton '91.
£1,200-1,700 *CSK*

A single-sided acetate for Black Star, 20th Century Fox Film Corp. white label with typescript details giving title of song by Elvis Presley and Orchestra, 78 rpm; accompanied by a letter from Sid King of Sid King & The Five Strings stating that Presley had given him this acetate in the 1960s.
£2,500-4,500 *CSK*

Sid King and his band were friends with Elvis and shared the billing at a number of venues in the 1950s.

Elvis Presley's custom made pendant with monogram T.C.B. (Taking Care of Business), set above a lightning bolt motif on a rope work chain; and a cloth concert banner from 'Elvis Summer Tour', Las Vegas, c1970.
£550-650 *CSK*

The bolt of lightning was taken from the comic strip Captain Marvel Jnr. Elvis gave T.C.B. necklaces to the male members of his entourage and T.L.C. necklaces (Tender Loving Care) to the female associates.

A black shirt worn by Prince on stage, 1986, with a postcard showing him wearing a similar garment.
£1,200-1,400 *S*

According to information supplied, this was obtained at a concert in the Sportpaleis Ahoy, Rotterdam on 19th August 1986, having been thrown into the audience by Prince.

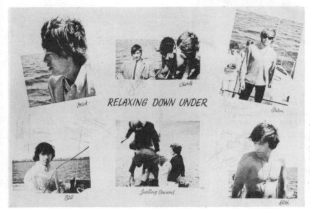

A Rolling Stones illustrated souvenir concert programme, 1965, signed by Mick Jagger, Brian Jones, Charlie Watts, Keith Richards and Bill Wyman, and 6 of the other performers; and a page from an autograph book signed by Brian Jones, 2 tickets for the Odeon Theatre, Southend-on-Sea; and related material.
£900-1,200 *CSK*

A drumskin, with Remo head signed and annotated by Phil Collins in black felt tip pen, 'As used on the 'Serious' album sessions. Thanks for your help!', and with cartoon self portrait, 8.5in (21.5cm) diam., with an accompanying signed letter from Phil Collins, framed and glazed, 12in (30cm) wide. **£600-700** *S*

Two printed rayon bandannas allegedly worn by Jimi Hendrix at the Isle of Wight Festival; accompanied by a letter of authenticity stating that Hendrix gave them away back stage; and a photograph of Hendrix wearing similar scarves on stage. **£1,200-1,700** *CSK*

A B.C. Rich Bich 10 string solid body electric guitar, serial No. 82011, red finish, c1980; and a letter stating that it was purchased from Jamie Crompton, a guitarist in Suzi Quatro's band, who was given the guitar by Suzi Quatro. **£1,400-1,800** *CSK*

A single-breasted multi-coloured striped jacket worn by Keith Richards, c1967, and a copy of a letter stating that Richards gave this jacket to his personal assistant Tony Sanchez in the early 1970s.
£1,200-1,700 *CSK*

A silk screen proof print of Elvis Presley by David Oxtoby, 'Golden Years - Elvis', titled and signed by the artist in pencil, 18in (46cm) wide, framed.
£320-400 *CSK*

Michael Jackson's sequined jacket, in black with matching lining, gold-coloured buttons decorated with the American eagle, the right shoulder embellished with chain and studded, black leather strap.
£12,000-15,000 *S*

Worn by the singer in the well-known cola commercial.

A 'gold' disc, 'Stuck On You', presented to Elvis Presley, the single mounted above a plaque bearing the R.I.A.A. Certified Sales Award and inscribed Presented to Elvis Presley to commemorate the sale of more than one million copies of the RCA Records single record 'Stuck On You', 13in (33cm) wide, framed. **£620-800** *CSK*

A signed and inscribed colour picture of Bruce Springsteen, used on the cover of the album 'Darkness on the Edge of Town'.
£60-80 *VS*

Three striped waistcoats worn by Keith Richards, c1967; and a copy of a letter stating that Richards gave these waistcoats to his personal assistant Tony Sanchez in the early 1970s. **£900-1,200** *CSK*

A Rolling Stones concert poster, The Sensational Rolling Stones at the Odeon, Southend, Saturday 10th October, 1964, signed by all 5 members of the group and 3 others including Simon Scott and Don Spencer, 12in (31cm) wide. **£1,200-1,500** *CSK*

Posters and Postcards

Amsterdam Olympics, 1928, including Marathon Nos. 100,101, 104, 105; Stadium No. 17; Swimming Ladies 400m No. 107; Mens Diving No. 106; 400m Track Semi-final, No. 94. **£40-60** *VS*

A vinyl portrait doll modelled as Diana Ross, made by Mego Corp, 1977, in original uncut box with stand, 12.5in (32cm) high. **£120-250** *CSK*

A complete stage outfit worn by Prince, comprising: an ornate black crepe coat with pink and brown net overlay, a pair of matching high-waisted stretch trousers, a pair of high-heeled ankle boots, and a white ruffled shirt with 'Prince' label in purple inside, worn by Prince during the 1984 Purple Rain concert tour. **£12,000-16,000** *CSK*

Tobacco, advertisements by Jasmatzi, advertising Unser Marine 2.5-pf cigarettes, with vignette of sailor smoking one to reverse, WWI Feldpost, front being coloured head and shoulders of General Von Mackensen, by Schneider and Renatus, one with pencil message to reverse. **£20-30** *VS*

Novelty, Opening Comedy Cards, all with double flap opening to show full picture, topics including Drinking, Romance, etc. published by W.S.S.B., Nos. 312, 314, 315, 317, 325-327.
£30-40 *VS*

Tom Browne, Davidson 2599 complete, Pa Learns To Ride A Horse.
£20-30 *VS*

Longley Chilton, Art Deco Girls, published by A. G. & Co., Series 442.
£30-40 *VS*

Cheshire, RP, unloading the electric car at Runcorn, by Hall, 1906.
£20-30 *VS*

Advertisements, chromo for Toni-Kola, showing people drinking with a negro tourist being surprised at finding the product, 1908.
£14-18 *VS*

Black and white advertisements, News of the World Bioscope Wagon with traction engine, published by Taunt's.
£20-25 *VS*

H-T-L Santa with 32 lights, pale purple robe.
£20-30 *VS*

Nazi, Unser Deutches Heer (Our German Forces), a card game for troops in the field exactly like Happy Families, consisting of 12 sets of 4 cards, comprising good action photos of infantry, cavalry, panzers, mountain troops, Hitler with soldiers etc., in original carton.
£45-55 *VS*

Exhibitions, a set of 6 Chromos for the 1897 Stockholm Exhibition, by Anna Palm, showing Industry Hall, Tourist Pavilion, Infantry, Old Ships etc.
£50-80 *VS*

Sarawak RP of Sir Charles Vyner Brooke, with block of 4 l-c purple, and special cachet Kuching 1938.
£14-18 *VS*

Disney

Pluto and a cat surprised, unknown production, c1940, 10in (25cm) wide.
£2,000-2,500 *CSK*

Bashful Playing An Accordian, from Snow White and the Seven Dwarfs, 1937, framed, 6in (15cm) wide.   **£700-1,200** *CSK*

Peter Pan, Captain Hook feels the tip of his hook and Tinkerbell points downwards as she flies along, 1953, largest 16in (41cm) wide. **£1,800-2,000** *CSK*

A sketch of Roger Rabbit, signed and inscribed 'From Roger Rabbit Via Richard Williams, May 18th 1990', coloured pencil on paper, unframed, 11.5in (29cm) wide.
£1,200-1,500 *CSK*

Doc talks to Snow White through the window, from Snow White and the Seven Dwarfs, 1937, 8in (20cm) wide.
£3,000-4,000 *CSK*

Peter Pan dressed in an Indian headdress, Wendy half-length, and Wendy three-quarter length, 1953, 12.5in (32cm) wide.
£1,400-1,700 *CSK*

Dopey looks bashful, from Snow White and the Seven Dwarfs, 1937, 5in (12.5cm) wide.
£1,400-1,700 *CSK*

An illustrated première programme for Walt Disney's Snow White and the Seven Dwarfs, Cathay Circle Theatre, Los Angeles, California, December 21st, 1937, with pull-out poster, illustrations, original wrappers.
£200-300 *CSK*

Grumpy plays the piano, from Snow White and the Seven Dwarfs, 1937, 7in (17.5cm) wide.
£1,500-2,000 *CSK*

Mickey Plays Papa, 1934, 11.5in (29cm) wide.
£2,500-3,000 *CSK*

A piece of card signed and inscribed To Marie Rose, Our Best Walt Disney, 5in (12.5cm) wide. **£220-270** *CSK*

Two celluloids for American TV each depicting Mickey Mouse as The Sorcerer's Apprentice, one of Mickey surrounded by brooms carrying pails of water, the other of Mickey being reprimanded by the sorcerer, both gouache on celluloid, 10.5in (26cm) square.
£400-450 *CSK*

Lady runs to the Tramp, from The Lady and the Tramp, 1955, 13in (33cm) wide.
£1,700-2,000 *CSK*

Mickey, Pluto and Donald, Studio Wartime Art, c1942, 7.5in (18.5cm) wide.
£2,500-3,300
CSK

A German lithographic tinplate mechanical bank with lever action eyes and extending tongue operated by pressing Mickey's right ear, probably made by Saalheimer & Strauss, c1930, 7in (17.5cm) high.
£8,500-9,500 *CSK*

Lady in a muzzle, Jock glaring, the Tramp digging and the Tramp standing with his head cocked to one side, from The Lady and the Tramp, 1955, 16in (41cm) wide.
£3,000-3,500 *CSK*

Cross Reference

For a further selection of money banks, see page 563

Mickey Mouse and Minnie, from The Klondike Kid, 1932, 9in (22.5cm) wide.
£2,500-3,000 *CSK*

Film and Theatre

A painted plaster portrait model of Christopher Reeve as Superman in a flying pose, 26in (66cm) long.
£300-400 *CSK*

A red and white striped cotton jacket, stamped MGM Wardrobe and inscribed Gene Kelly inside the collar, possibly worn by Kelly in the 1952 MGM film Singing in the Rain; and a still photograph of Kelly wearing a similar striped jacket in the film.
£200-300 *CSK*

A postcard of Charlie Chaplin, signed in white ink.
£100-120 *VS*

A printed souvenir menu for the Grand Order of Water Rats House Dinner, at the Savoy Hotel, London, September 21st 1947, with illustrated cover featuring guests of honour, Laurel and Hardy, autographed in blue ink; and 2 group photographs of the occasion, and similar souvenir menus.
£1,200-1,700 *CSK*

A signed and inscribed postcard of Robert Ryan.
£30-40 *VS*

A signed sepia photograph of Laurel and Hardy, 1930, 10in (25cm) wide.
£750-850 *S*

An American one sheet poster for The Empire Strikes Back, 20th Century Fox, 1981, signed by Harrison Ford, Dave Prowse, Billy Dee Williams, Carrie Fisher, Mark Hamill, Peter Mayhew, Anthony Daniels, Kenny Baker and George Lucas, framed, 27in (68cm) wide.
£1,000-1,500 *CSK*

According to the vendor who worked on the film, only three posters were signed by the cast, and each of these posters had a different image. This poster was won at a raffle held during the 'End of Picture' party.

A pair of painted rubber pointed ear tops, worn by Leonard Nimoy to look like Mr Spock's Vulcan ears in the TV series Star Trek, mounted on board, ears 2.5in (6cm) high.
£900-1,200 *CSK*

Astaire and Kelly, signed by Fred Astaire and Gene Kelly, full length in dancing pose, 8in (20cm) wide.
£50-70 *VS*

Noel Coward's full length dressing gown of black and gold silk, monogram N.C. on breast pocket; together with a letter stating that it was given to the actor Ronnie Ward after a charity matinée performance at Drury Lane, when Ward shared a dressing room with his friend Noel Coward.
£1,500-2,000 *CSK*

A prototype robotic head of painted gold rubber for the character C-3PO from Star Wars, 1977, 20th Century Fox, 9in (22.5cm) wide.
£300-500 *CSK*

A grotesque creature head, of polyurethane foam with isocylate coating finished in acrylic airbrush, with resin teeth and detailed 2-layered jaw, used in the 1986 20th Century Fox film Aliens. **£900-1,200** *CSK*

A guardsman's bearskin cap, with metal plume-ring on left side, c1939, 15in (38cm) high, and a photograph of the Cowardly Lion, the Tin Man and the Scarecrow dressed in Winkie guard uniform in the Witch's castle, 10in (25cm) wide.
£3,000-4,000 *CSK*

A novelty souvenir clock for the film Indiana Jones & The Last Crusade, made out of a film box, the lid forming the face, signed by Steven Spielberg, George Lucas, Alison Doody, Denholm Elliott, Tom Stoppard, Harrison Ford and 11 other members of the cast and crew, 11.5in (29cm) square.
£600-700 *CSK*

A set of 10 limited edition Bert Stern colour portrait photographs of Marilyn Monroe, taken in 1962, 6 weeks before her death, printed in 1978, each signed by the photographer on the margin and numbered 231/250, 19in (48cm) square; a corresponding printed index, and a printed title page, produced by Shorewood Atelier For Woodbine Books Inc. New York, N.Y., inscribed with the number of the set 231/250.
£2,500-3,000 *CSK*

Miscellaneous

An exhibition poster, Warhol, The Tate Gallery, 17 February - 28 March 1971, reproduction in colours, signed Andy Warhol, 30in (76cm) wide. **£500-800** *CSK*

A pair of leather boxing gloves each signed by Henry Cooper in white ink, and a photograph of Henry Cooper and Oliver Reed wearing similar gloves in the boxing sequence of the 1975 20th Century Fox film, Royal Flash, signed and inscribed Best Wishes Henry Cooper, 8in (20cm) wide.   **£200-400** *CSK*

TYPEWRITERS

Oscar Picht produced a number of specialist machines for the blind including typewriters and shorthand from 1899.

These instruments were first manufactured by Wilhelm Ruppert of Berlin and after by Schreib-und-Nähmaschinenfabrik Wernicke, Edelmann & Co.

A Swiss Velograph typewriter, the circular index machine printing upper and lower case, hinged above platen and paper roller, on mahogany base board, c1890, 14in (36cm) wide. **£5,000-7,000** *S*

A German Picht type-wheel model Braille typewriter, with bell, roller inker and Braille letter index for producing visible characters, in original case with base.   **£2,700-3,300** *S*

A Salter Standard typewriter. **£350-450** *CSK*

A Bar-Lock No. 7 typewriter with ornamental copper shield and 16in (41cm) platen. **£400-500** *CSK*

A Moya No. 2 typewriter by The Moya Typewriter Co., Leicester, England with type-sleeve, 3-row keyboard, one cap missing, and a japanned iron cover, baseboard missing.   **£600-800** *CSK*

ARMS AND ARMOUR
Armour

An Italian composite etched full foot armour, including later close helmet, on a stand, c1600.
£6,500-7,500 *S(NY)*

A German composite full armour, partly early 16thC, the helmet mid-16thC, on a stand with mail shirt,.
£5,500-6,500 *S(NY)*

An Italian fluted close helmet, adapted for the Giuoco del Ponte, the one piece skull embossed with a spray of 11 flutes and punched with the letters GP, early 16thC with later additions, 11in (28cm) high. **£4,000-4,500** *S(NY)*

An Italian fluted gorget 'Alla Tedesca', with a composed pair of South German fluted 'Maximillian' full arm defences, damaged, c1520.
£2,000-2,500 *S(NY)*

A pair of Italian cuisses, c1520.
£2,500-3,000 *S(NY)*

A cabasset, formed in one piece, with 'pear stalk' finial to crown, brass rosettes around base, cleaned and restored, c1600.
£200-250 *WAL*

A Cromwellian lobster tail steel helmet, the skull with 6 flutes, 4 piece articulated neck lames with large steel rivets, pierced ear flaps, and an adjustable nasal bar, initialled M.
£800-900 *HSS*

A visored bascinet in late 14thC style, 10.5in (26.5cm) high.
£2,000-2,500 *S(NY)*

A cuirass, probably German, with steel breastplate and backplate, both with brass studs around the perimeter, and a leather waist strap with brass buckle, c1870.
£500-600 *CSK*

Two identical heavy steel breastplates, each with 10 brass studs around the perimeter, and 2 prominent brass fastening studs on the front, one plate stamped 585 at one armhole.
£350-500 *CSK*

A composite crinet for a horse armour, made of 14 plates moving on sliding rivets, restored, 16thC, 31in (78.5cm).
£600-700 *S(NY)*

A Civil War steel helmet, with peeked hinged visor applied with large brass rivets, a single ridge to the skull extending down to a single socket plume holder.
£850-950 *HSS*

A cabasset, formed in one piece, with 'pear stalk' finial to crown, brass rosettes around base, cleaned and restored, c1600.
£200-250 *WAL*

An Indo Persian steel helmet Khula Khud, the one piece skull embossed with masks, foliage and gilding, together with a matching shield, 18in (46cm) diam., and a fore-arm guard.
£550-750 *WIL*

A pair of German or Italian mail sleeves, made of very small riveted steel rings, shaped for the arm, and the cuffs bordered with riveted brass rings of the same size, damaged, 24in (61cm).
£800-900 *S(NY)*

A cabasset, formed in one piece, with 'pear stalk' finial to crown, brass rosettes around base, the brim with a trace of crowned armourer's mark, cleaned and restored, c1600.
£200-250 *WAL*

Crossbows

Daggers

A Lowland Scottish Quillon dagger, with tapering double edged blade, late 16thC, 16.5in (42cm).
£800-1,200 *S*

The reverse side of the blade bears a label inscribed 'Dagger from Battle of Pinkie fought September 1547 recovered from bank of River Esk August 2 1924'.

A Flemish sporting crossbow, with robust steel bow and original string, the string hook inscribed 'I. Gernay', early 18thC, 41.5in (105.5cm) without windlass.
£950-1,000 *S(NY)*

A German sporting crossbow, with detached steel bow, with original string and stirrup, late 17thC, together with 6 crossbow bolts, damaged, 26.5in (67.5cm).
£2,500-3,000 *S(NY)*

A kidney or ballock dagger, possibly English, damaged, c1500, 9in (23cm).
£3,000-3,500 *S*

A Nazi army officer's dagger, by Emil Voos, blade retaining all original polish, plated mounts, orange grip, in a plated sheath.
£150-200 *WAL*

A Nazi Luftwaffe officer's dagger, 2nd pattern, the blade retaining all original polish, grey metal mounts, wire bound yellow grip, bullion dress knot, in its grey metal sheath.
£200-250 *WAL*

A Nazi SS dagger, by Robert Klaas, with inscription on blade, some wear.
£350-400 *WAL*

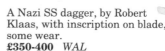

An unmarked Bowie and sheath, blade worn, 5.5in (14cm).
£70-100 *ASB*

A Victorian Gothic dagger, with double edged straight blade etched with foliate scrolls, solid copper gilt hilt, decorated with entwined serpents at base, diced pattern to grip, oval pommel with scrolled decoration, in brown leather covered metal sheath with 3 copper gilt foliate scrolled gothic mounts, blade 7in (18cm).
£250-350 *WAL*

A Nazi Red Cross man's dagger, original polish on the blade, plated mounts, in its black painted metal sheath with plated mounts and original leather frog, some wear.
£250-300 *WAL*

A Sheffield Bowie, for the American market, stag horn grip, nickel silver guard and clipped pointed blade, leather sheath, marked 'George Butler, Trinity Works', 19thC, blade 6in (15cm).
£70-100 *ASB*

A presentation commemorative SAS dagger, a copy of the First Model Fairbairn Sykes fighting knife, the blade blued with gilt inscription and quotation, the hilt and guard gilt, in a presentaiton case with brass plate listing the regimental battle honours, actions and relevant dates, London 1991.
£900-1,200 *S*

This presentation dagger is part of a Limited Edition of 50, specially produced by the Wilkinson Sword Company to commemorate the 50th Anniversary of the SAS, the remainder only being made available to serving or ex-members of the Regiment. This dagger, numbered 1 of 50, is being offered for auction by the organisers of the Golden Jubilee, and all proceeds will be donated to the SAS Regimental Charities.

Swords

A selection of Scottish basket hilted swords.
£350-400 each *ASB*

A Spanish military sword rapier with Bilboa hilt, c1780, 33in (84cm).
£200-270 *ASB*

A British Royal Naval flag officer's sword, the mameluke hilt with ivory grips and gilt brass guard, in its nickel plated scabbard, c1850, blade 31in (79cm).
£700-750 *ASB*

An Indo Persian Shamshir, the mameluke hilt with wooden grips and brass guard engraved with flowers and foliage, the curved single edged blade with 2 fullers, in its tooled leather decorated scabbard with brass mounts, late 18thC, blade 31in (79cm).
£450-500 *ASB*

A silver mounted Peninsular War, presentation sword by Rundell, Bridge and Rundell, London, with inscription, 1811, the double edged blade 32in (81cm).
£3,200-3,600 *CSK*

A Nazi naval officer's dirk, with plain double fluted blade, brass mounts, wire bound white grip, in its brass sheath.
£200-250 *WAL*

A Scottish military backsword, etched in large script 'Sans Peur Et Sans Reproche', iron three-quarter basket guard pierced with traditional patterns, wire bound fishskin covered grip, domed pommel, age wear, part of guard removed, late 18thC.
£370-400 *WAL*

A Shamshir mounted in 2 colours of gold and encrusted with diamonds, presented by Abd-ul-Medshid, Sultan of Turkey, to Prince Alexander Couza, Hospodar of Moldavia and Wallachia, with slender blade of watered steel, the hilt encased in gold, enriched with encrusted patterns of rose diamonds and chased with foliage, in leather-covered wooden scabbard with gold mounts decorated en suite, and complete with its original gold bullion knot, blade repaired, some diamonds lacking, blade 33in (84cm), in its original fitted case.
£12,000-16,000 *S*

A silver gilt Mameluke sword hilt, the quillons cast and chiselled as lions' heads, the eyes of semi-precious stones, gilding worn, 19thC, 8in (20cm) long.
£700-800 *S*

A Peninsula War period officer's sword, the single channelled curved blade engraved with flowers, leaves, martial trophies and other motifs, with crowned G.R. monogram and coat-of-arms, inscribed Major Walter Ross, and Mackintosh & Birnie, London, the gilt brass hilt with inscription, damage to hilt, 37in (94cm).
£2,000-2,500 *MCA*

A Spanish sword believed to have belonged to Fernando Fernandez de Velasco y Sonanes, a claimant to the throne of Charles VII.
£2,500-3,000 *CSK*

An experimental military combination percussion underhammer pistol and cavalry sword, c1860, blade 35.5in (90.5cm).
£1,600-2,000 *S*

A Japanese wakizashi, the bronzed metal handle inlaid with prunus blossom and bamboo in gilt metal, blade signed, 30in (76cm).
£700-800 *HSS*

A Continental swept hilt rapier, with ovoid pommel, S quillons and 2 tier guard rings, the broad double edged blade with armourer's mark to ricasso 'DS' and a crowned wheatsheaf, grip binding missing, c1600, blade 38in (96.5cm).
£1,000-1,300 *ASB*

A German bearing sword with cruciform hilt, the blade etched with scrolling foliage, liturgical scenes and inscribed, dated 1680, blade 33in (83.5cm).
£1,200-1,700 *S*

A gold mounted and jewelled sword, presented by Prince Michael Obrenovitch of Serbia to Prince Alexander Couza of Moldavia and Wallachia, by Mayerhofer and Klinkosch, Vienna, the hilt and scabbard entirely encased in gold and finely cast and chased in high relief, in its original fitted case, the outside covered in red velvet bound in gilt brass and set with a silver escutcheon case with the Arms of Serbia, and the inside lined in velvet and silk and signed by the maker in gilt letters, the blade with small patches of rust, c1861, blade 31in (79cm).
£55,000-70,000 *S*

A North Italian or Venetian Sciavona, with brass kite shaped pommel, leather covered grip and complex multi-bar basket of typical form, the straight double edged blade with maker's mark to the ricasso, 17thC, blade 33.5in (85cm).
£750-800 *ASB*

A medieval sword, in excavated condition, early 15thC, 37in (94.5cm).
£1,700-2,000 *S*

A British heavy cavalry trooper's sabre, with complex steel basket, heavy pommel, wire bound sharkskin grip and long curved blade, c1785, blade 41in (104cm).
£550-600 *ASB*

A Scottish Dragoon officer's sword, the single edged blade with wide fullers, etched blued and gilt decoration including foliage, the Royal Arms of Scotland with the motto 'Nemo me impune lacessit',some wear and damage, blade 30in (76cm).
£500-600 *S*

Blunderbuss

A George III flintlock blunderbuss, by Archer, the action incorporating a half cock, with early safety mechanism, the slightly flared brass barrel stamped with Victorian and Georgian proof marks, top mounted triangular spring bayonet, full walnut stock with brass furniture, and ramrod, 29in (74cm) overall length.
£1,000-1,200 *HSS*

A flintlock blunderbuss, with brass barrel and mounts, spring loaded bayonet, the action and barrel signed 'Dakyn, Nottingham', the figured walnut stock with engraved butt plate, 18thC, 31in (79cm).
£1,000-1,200 *Bea*

Sporting Guns

A 19 bore German or Austrian half stocked flintlock sporting gun, part round, part octagonal barrel with 'spider' foresight, plain lock with 'banana' style lockplate, swan necked cock and pan without frizzen bridle, plain brass furniture and figured walnut stock with horn forend tip, grip tail guard and flat bottomed butt with characteristic cheekpiece, c1780, barrel 36.5in (94cm).
£950-1,000 *ASB*

A double barrelled percussion sporting gun, by Parker Field, inscribed 'Makers to Her Majesty 233 Holborn', and gold rectangular poinçon of W. Parker Field & Sons, signed, c1850, 32in (81cm).
£620-700 *S*

A cased double barrelled tubelock sporting gun, by Joseph Manton of Hanover Square, London, London Proof, No. 8884, barrelsmith's mark of William Fullerd, maker's stamps, patent case hardened locks engraved and signed Joseph Manton Patent, c1821, some damage, 34in (87cm).
£2,200-3,000 *S*

A cased pair of German percussion sporting pistols with detachable stock, by Jacob Kuchenreuter, Regensburg, Liège Proof, with blued and sighted octagonal barrels rifled with 7 grooves, the top flats inlaid with silver scrolls and signed in full in silver, in their brass bound oak case, lined with green baize and containing all but one of the original accessories, mid-19thC, case 30in (76in) long.
£6,200-6,700 *S*

Pistols

A French flintlock holster pistol, by Piraube Aux Galleries à Paris, stock worn, gilt faded in parts, c1725, 20in (50.5cm).
£3,500-4,500 *S*

A German flintlock Kalthoff-system rifled repeating pistol, by Jan Sander, Hanover, c1680, 24in (60.5cm).
£10,000-12,000 *S*

A set of Spanish or Neapolitan pistols, comprising a holster pistol and 2 pocket pistols, with silver gilt mounts, inscribed, mid-18thC, largest 15in (38.5cm).
£5,000-6,000 *S*

A cased pair of double barrelled percussion pistols by J. & W. Wood, Manchester, in a mahogany case with cleaning rod, barrels 4.25in (10.5cm).
£1,200-1,700 *EP*

A cased pair of French breech loading percussion central-fire duelling pistols, by Pauly, Paris, the lock cases signed Invention Pauly Brevetée à Paris, c1815, 21in (52.5cm).
£12,000-17,000 *S*

A pair of Bohemian flintlock pistols, by Leopold Becher, Karlsbad, metal cleaned bright, c1730, 10.5in (26.5cm).
£3,000-3,500 *S*

A pair of French flintlock rifled turn off pistols, by Lehollandois à Paris aux Galleries (Adrien Reynier II), Paris, signed, lightly worn, c1725, 14in (36cm).
£5,000-7,000 *S*

A pair of German flintlock holster pistols, by M. C. Pistor A Cassel, with two-stage barrels swampod at the muzzles, the breeches with brass-lined maker's stamps, stocks with minor age cracks, c1740, 16in (40.5cm).
£2,500-3,000 *S*

A pair of Flemish flintlock double barrelled boxlock pistols, with faceted pommels and engraved iron trigger guards, c1815, small pieces of inlay missing, 12in (30.5cm). **£1,000-1,200** *S*

A flintlock saw handled officer's rifled pistol with detachable stock, by W. Parker, Gunmaker to His Majesty, Holborn, London, Birmingham Proof, with original detachable shoulder stock, chequered at the rear and fitted with blued steel mounts engraved, c1815, stock 28in (71cm). **£3,000-4,000** *S*

A 19 bore Albanian flintlock holster pistol, with a round steel barrel probably from an earlier pistol, miquelet lock with external mainspring and grooved frizzen, brass engraved stock, c1850, barrel 13.5in (34cm).
£250-300 *ASB*

Revolvers

A Birmingham proved 60 bore 6 shot self cocking bar hammer percussion transitional revolver, the octagonal barrel rifled with 9 deep grooves and marked 'Improved Revolver', c1860, barrel 6in (15cm). **£200-270** *ASB*

A cased Colt London Model 1849 pocket revolver, No. 647, .31 calibre, London proof, inscribed 'Address Col. Colt London', 1854, 6in (15cm). **£1,500-1,700** *S*

A cased Colt London Model 1849 pocket percussion revolver, No. 3958, inscribed 'Address Col. Colt London', London proof, 1854, barrel 5in (12.5cm). **£1,300-1,700** *S*

A 150 bore English 6 shot self cocking bar hammer percussion transitional revolver, the barrel marked 'Improved Revolver', c1855, together with a Dixon patent top revolver flask, an ebony handled turnscrew, pewter oil bottle, cap tin and iron pincer type mould, barrel 3.75in (9cm). **£850-950** *ASB*

A pinfire, 4 barrelled pepperbox revolver, by Le Faucheux à Paris, the frame ornately engraved with foliage, underhammer action with ring trigger, 8in (20cm) overall. **£240-270** *L*

Medals and Orders

A 5 shot .31 SA percussion pocket revolver, No. 795, the barrel stamped Bacon Mfg Co. Norwich Conn, some wear and cleaned bright, 8.5in (21.5cm). **£300-400** *WAL*

A Knight of Hanover's Waterloo pair, Lieutenant Colonel G. Desbrowe, Grenadier Guards, 1815. **£3,000-3,500** *S*

The Most Ancient and Most Noble Order of the Thistle (K.T.), Knight's Collar, unmarked but probably by John Campbell of Lundie, 18thC. **£64,000-68,000** *S*

A Bombardment of Acre pair, Lieutenant General T. G. Higgins, Royal Artillery, 1793. **£4,000-4,500** *S*

Queen Margherita, wife of King Umberto I, presentation brooch, by Musy Padre e Figli of Turin, silver gilt and enamel, in the form of an oval badge set with cushion diamonds around the edge, the centre with superimposed royal initial set with rose diamonds, crown above, the base set with stones, in a leather case, Italian, early 20thC. **£1,500-2,000** *S*

A Peninsular War and Waterloo pair, Lieutenant Colonel Lord Charles Fitzroy, P.C., M.P., Grenadier Guards and D.A.A.G., later Vice Chamberlain of the Household, Military General Service, 1793, Waterloo, 1815. **£3,200-3,500** *S*

The Most Ancient and Most Noble Order of the Thistle (K.T.), St Andrew Jewel, by John James Edington of Portland Street, Soho Square, London, the integral suspension loop fully hallmarked and bearing the unusual sun-in-splendour goldmark as well as the date letter k for 1825-26, with 2 further marks on the reverse of the green ground, c1825, 2.5in (6cm) high. **£22,000-25,000** *S*

A Waterloo medal, awarded to Corporal Thomas Greasly, Royal Artillery Driver, with original steel clip-ring and ribbon, 1815. **£250-300** *HSS*

A Crimean War and Indian Mutiny group to a Highlander officer, including dirk, skean dhu and plaid brooch, Lieutenant Colonel Neil Campbell, Cameron Highlanders, all contained within a large glazed display case. **£3,200-4,000** *S*

Order of the Iron Crown, Grand Cross collar chain, by Rothe of Vienna, in gold and enamel, with 37 alternating oak leaf wreaths, Iron Crowns of Lombardy and arabesques, in a fitted case, Austrian. **£9,200-10,000** *S*

Army small gold medal for Nive, 1813, Lieut. Col. James D. West, 1st Regt. Ft. Gds., in circular glazed case, with swivel suspension and a contemporary riband buckle. **£4,000-4,500** *S*

Badges & Plates

A pair of white metal collar badges of the 2nd Cheshire Engineer Volunteers.
£80-90 *WAL*

A Georgian other ranks oval brass shoulder belt plate of The 60th (R. American) Regt., '60' within crowned oval garter.
£320-370 *WAL*

A Victorian other ranks white metal headdress badge of the Sheffield Engineer Volunteers.
£180-200 *WAL*

137 World War II cloth shoulder titles and divisional signs etc., sewn into the lining of a W.R.N.S. other ranks blue jacket, with composition buttons, jacket with minor wear and moth.
£500-550 *WAL*

An officer's badge of the 4th Gurkhas, 'IV' and bugle in the centre of a Maltese Cross resting on crossed kukris, adapted as a desk ornament, 2.5in (6.5cm) wide. **£200-220** *WAL*

An officer's gilt badge of the 1st City of London Engineers.
£100-120 *WAL*

A helmet plate of the 1st Durham Volunteers, Royal Engineers.
£140-160 *WAL*

An other ranks' white metal badge.
£60-70 *WAL*

A badge of the 1st Middlesex Engineer Vols.
£140-160 *WAL*

A Victorian R.E. officer's silver cloak clasp, Birmingham 1892.
£120-140 *WAL*

A cast silver plated glengarry badge of the Scottish Engineers CTC.
£100-120 *WAL*

Headdress

An Austrian Dragoons officer's helmet.
£1,200-1,700 *CSK*

An Austrian Dragoons officer's helmet, the sides of the gilt comb unpainted and lacking chin scales and lining.
£600-800 *CSK*

A trooper's 1871 pattern helmet of the 3rd (Prince of Wales) Dragoon Guards, with black and red plume.
£400-500 CSK

A trooper's brass 1843 pattern helmet of the 2nd The Queen's Dragoon Guards, with ornate brass comb and mounted helmet plate, restored.
£1,400-2,000 *CSK*

An Imperial German Guard Cuirassier helmet, white metal guard star helmet plate, tombak skull, leather backed brass chin scales, leather lining, winged eagle crest, minor damage and repair.
£2,000-2,400 *WAL*

An Austrian Dragoons officer's helmet, of black finished metal with gilt ornaments including the front plate mounted with Franz-Josef I cypher and the chin scales, the comb embossed on each side with a lion and serpent, c1860.
£900-1,000 *CSK*

An officer's blue cloth helmet of the Royal Army Medical Corps, by Hult & Son, 20 Sackville Street, Piccadilly, with gilt fittings including velvet lined chin chain and K.C. Royal Arms helmet plate, with black metal helmet case.
£250-300 *CSK*

A Prussian Infantry officer's quality pickelhaube, of heavy leather with gilt/brass mounts including spike with crosspiece base, fastened with star-shaped studs, flat chin scales, and a German officer's green leather pouch with pouchbelt, both with gilt metal fittings, c1850.
£620-720 *CSK*

A Victorian officer's gilt helmet of The 6th Dragoon Guards (Carabiniers), with gilt mounts, leather backed chin chain and ear rosettes, silver plated helmet plate, padded silk lining, white hair plume with rosette, some damage and worn.
£850-950 *WAL*

A helmet of the 1st Oxfordshire Light Horse Volunteers, of black cloth with red horsehair mane and tuft to the white metal comb, white metal lower edge to patent leather peak, and crown above the badge.
£1,000-1,200 *CSK*

The helmet is fitted with rose pattern side bosses of white metal with matching chin chain lined with velvet and a small rose hook at back for hooking it up.

An officer's helmet of the 2nd Life Guards, complete with chin chain and plume, the elaborate plate having the white metal field to the enamel cross within the Garter, top finial missing.
£2,500-3,500 *CSK*

This helmet belonged to Lieutenant Colonel the Hon. Malcolm Bowes-Lyon (Uncle of Queen Elizabeth the Queen Mother), who served in the Boer War and in the Great War, and was wounded.

A trooper's/NCO's chapka of the Austrian 1st Ulans, with crimson top trimmed with yellow braid, brass chin scales lacking strap ends, eagle front plate and falling hair plume with brass cockade, c1900.
£300-400 *CSK*

An officer's shako of the Royal Dock Yard Battalion, black felt sides and top, black patent leather peak and head band, silver lace top band, gilt laurel and oak wreath plate, leather and silk lining, worn, c1850.
£600-700 *WAL*

An officer's green shako of The Scottish Rifles, black lace and plaited cord trim, patent leather peak, blackened bugle badge, corded boss bearing blackened mullet, black over green feather plume in socket, patent leather chinstrap. **£300-350** *WAL*

An officer's busby of the Royal Gloucestershire Hussars, by Hawkes, 14 Piccadilly, with scarlet bag and crimson and gold cord lines around busby, gilt covered chin chain lined with red velvet and fastening to fine gilt lion's mask bosses and white over red plume with gilt socket and ring and black metal plume case, c1880.
£500-600 *CSK*

A George VI officer's side cap of the Royal Horse Guards, gilt piping, scarlet top, embroidered badge, gilt buttons.
£90-120 *WAL*

An officer's drab cloth side cap of the 12th Frontier Force Regiment, silver piping, scarlet top and front flap, plated badge and buttons, name inside 'Capt. J. Henderson', minor moth damage.
£200-250 *WAL*

An officer's pattern Second Empire chapka of the French 7th Lancers, with blue cloth top, large numbered front plate, chin chain and a crimson hair plume.
£500-600 *CSK*

An officer's blue smoking cap of the 1st Bombay Lancers, scarlet top with gilt braid trim, embroidered '1' on crossed lances badge, plain silk buttons, some wear and moth.
£200-250 *WAL*

A German steel helmet of the Great War, a trench knife, knucklebow and shaped grip of cast alloy with leather sheath, and a water bottle, probably of a British officer, c1900.
£200-250 *CSK*

An officer's peaked cap of the Scots Guards, embroidered peak, red, white and blue silk headband, gilt and silver plated badge with green enamelled centre.
£90-120 *WAL*

An officer's black shako of the South Regiment of West York Yeomanry, with silver lace band and black silk cockade, with white metal ball button, front and back peaks of plain black leather, and a drooping black horsehair plume, with a brass ring, minor refurbishments, some damage, c1825, plume 19in (48cm) long.
£1,000-1,500 *CSK*

This regiment later became the Yorkshire Dragoons.

A cocked hat of an officer of the Royal Dragoons, with large elaborate star loop and regimental mounted gilt button, large tassels and white silk lining, trade label of Catter & Co., 56 Pall Mall, London, in its black metal case, with brass plate engraved Walter B. Barttelot, Esqr., Royal Dragoons, c1841, case 17in (43cm) high.
£500-600 *CSK*

A post-1902 officer's silver plated helmet of The Life Guards, silver plated spike, gilt and silver plated helmet plate, with good red and blue enamelled centre, leather backed chin chain and ear rosettes, leather and silk lining, white hair plume with plain white metal rosette, some minor damage and repairs.
£1,500-2,000 *WAL*

An officer's chapka of Austrian Ulans, with crimson cloth top, ornate chin scales, eagle front plate, and falling hair plume with cockade, c1880.
£450-500 *CSK*

An officer's pattern blue pillbox cap of the East Lothian Yeomanry Cavalry, with gold lace band, an ornate figure in gold to the top and a lining of quilted crimson silk, and a scarlet jacket of the same with very dark blue collar and pointed cuffs, trimmed with gold lace, and matching piping to the back seams, 11 small gilt buttons down the front and winged shoulder cords of twisted gold chain gimp, c1880.
£250-300 *CSK*

Uniforms

An Irish Volunteer colour and tassel, of red silk with a bullion fringe and embroidered with roses, thistles, foliage and a crown incorporating beads and fur, above a harp and with red and gold tassel, some wear, c1798, 22in (56cm) wide.
£4,000-4,500 *S*

Three Victorian practice Standards of the Household Cavalry, of crimson silk damask painted with the same designs as the actual Standards and edged on 3 sides with yellow worsted fringe, 2 being of the Union Flowers pattern and the other of the Royal Arms pattern, some damage, each 33in (84cm) wide, excluding fringe.
£850-950 *CSK*

A post-1902 Lieutenant's full dress blue jacket of The Royal Horse Artillery, scarlet collar, gilt cord and lace trim, including 17 loops with ball buttons to chest, shoulder cords, embroidered collar grenades, name inside 'N. M. McLeod, 27.7.12'; and 2 pairs of matching breeches with broad scarlet stripe.
£370-400 *WAL*

The uniform of an officer of the Royal Horse Guards, including a dress helmet with skull of German silver, a polished steel cuirass, a pair of Wellington boots and wooden stretchers, blue tunic, blue trousers with gold lace at the seams, 2 pairs white leather pantaloons, shabracque, Sam Browne belt and straps, 2 mess waistcoats, various accessories, all contained in a patent zinc lined damp-proof trunk, 1882; and a uniform of a member of the Royal Company of Archers, including bonnet, cap, tunic, frock coat, trousers and 2 belts and blue serge uniform worn in the Egypt 1882 campaign.
£6,500-7,500 *S*

An officer's blue full dress jacket of the Royal Maylor Cavalry, with scarlet facings, silver Russia braid trimming, white metal curb chain wings, and plated buttons with 'RMC' and Prince of Wales' plumes, coronet and motto, 'R. Bateman' on the lining, c1830.
£1,200-1,700 *CSK*

A pre-1922 officer's full dress drab tunic of the 124th Baluchistan Infantry, scarlet facings, gilt lace and braid trim, shoulder cords. **£60-70** *WAL*

A heavy dark green velour table cover, edged all round with wide regimental gold lace and bearing the richly embroidered ornaments from one side of an officer's shabraque of the 14th Light Dragoons, consisting of regimental number XIV and two VR cyphers, each with Royal crest superimposed, 68in (172.5cm) long.
£320-360 *CSK*

An officer's bearskin of the Irish Guards, St. Patrick's blue feather plume, velvet backed graduated link gilt chin chain, leather lining.
£450-500 *WAL*

An officer's dark blue full dress coatee of the King's Cheshire Yeomanry, with scarlet facings and white metal buttons, with 'KCY' within a crowned Garter Star with motto, the collar and cuffs trimmed with silver lace and the back seams with Russia decoration, c1825.
£300-550 *CSK*

A Lieutenant's full dress scarlet tunic of The Queen's Royal Regiment (West Surrey), with blue facings, gilt lace and braid trim, shoulder cords, gilt collar badges, Paschal lamb on torso, gilt buttons, and a pair of overalls with narrow scarlet stripe, some damage, c1925.
£150-200 *WAL*

The shabraque of an officer of the Long Melford Troop of the Suffolk Yeomanry Cavalry, in dark blue cloth with scarlet cloth borders, with large VR cypher in white and crimson silk embroidery beneath crown in coloured silk embroidery, the points lined with black coach-hide.
£700-1,000 *CSK*

A North American Indian beaded waistcoat, the front of black velvet with elaborate floral decoration worked in polychrome beads, plain calico lining and red tie fastenings to front, 19thC.
£600-700 *ASB*

A post World War I officer's scarlet cloth shabraque of the Royal Horse Guards, embroidered crown, 10 battle honour scrolls 'Dettingen' to 'Paardeburg', and Garter star in each quarter, additional scroll 'France and Flanders 1914-18' along the back edge, gilt lace border with blue central stripe.
£550-650 *WAL*

A complete other rank's full dress Elcho grey uniform of the London Scottish, comprising: glengarry cap, doublet, plaid, leather sporran, leather waistbelt with white metal waist belt clasp.
£350-400 *WAL*

A sabretache of the Royal North Devon Yeomanry Cavalry, with its foul weather cover and in its tin case.
£570-620 *WAL*

A Victorian embroidered crimson damask drum banner of the Household Cavalry, bearing the Royal Arms, with silk backing, 48in (122cm) long. **£370-400** *WAL*

A Lancashire Hussars officer's full dress blue jacket and pélisse embellished with gold cord, and crimson nctherwear with gold lace stripes, both jackets with crimson silk lining, together with their crimson and gold barrel-sash and a set of gold caplines with large acorn terminals.
£1,000-1,500 *CSK*

JEWELLERY

A sapphire and cultured pearl flowerhead brooch.
£40-60 *CSK*

A Victorian yellow gold hollow articulated link bracelet with X-mounts, with gold locket, in fitted red leather case.
£1,800-2,200 *GAK*

A 15ct gold and seed pearl swallow brooch.
£350-400 *HSS*

A ruby and diamond brooch, set with rubies with a principal diamond at the foremost flowerhead, the back spray set with small circular cut diamonds, one diamond lacking.
£1,200-1,700 *S(S)*

A star brooch, set with rose diamonds, cut diamonds and chip diamonds.
£1,800-1,900 *RBB*

A 9 ct gold brooch, with cabochon polished amethyst bodies.
£250-275 *HSS*

A gold, opal and rose diamond set locket, glazed within.
£450-475 *S(S)*

A solitaire diamond set platinum ring, 2.75ct. with an inclusion and fissures.
£1,500-1,700 *MJB*

A gentleman's claw set diamond ring, 3ct.
£2,300-2,500 *GAK*

A late Victorian fox's mask stock pin, the mask set with 2 ruby chips for the eyes, on a 9ct gold bar.
£120-180 *HSS*

TUNBRIDGE WARE

A Tunbridge Ware pencil box, by
Thomas Barton, c1870, 8.5in
(21.5cm) long.
£160-190 *AMH*

A Tunbridge Ware writing box,
with inkwell, the mosaic possibly
of Edward, Prince of Wales,
wearing a kilt, holding a parrot in
one hand and a dog in the other,
the design possibly taken from a
Berlin woolwork pattern, c1850,
10in (25cm) long.
£800-850 *AMH*

A Tunbridge Ware stationery box,
by T. Barton, with a label on the
base, c1870, 4in (10cm) high.
£400-500 *AMH*

A Tunbridge Ware caddy, with
single compartment, 4.5in (12cm)
square.
£230-300 *AMH*

Two Tunbridge Ware boxes, 4in
(10cm) long.
£60-70 each *AMH*

A Tunbrige Ware glove box, by
Thomas Barton, labelled, c1875,
9.5in (24cm) long.
£250-300 *AMH*

A Tunbridge Ware snuff box,
c1860, 3in (8cm) diam.
£80-95 *AMH*

A Tunbridge Ware stationery box,
by Edmund Nye, labelled, 6.5in
(16.5cm) wide.
£350-425 *AMH*

Two Tunbridge Ware stamp
boxes:
l. by Thomas Barton, with stamp
stuck on, 1.5in (4cm) high.
£80-100
r. the Queen's head in tesserae,
1.5in (4cm) high.
£150-200 *AMH*

A Tunbridge Ware box, depicting
a lion, 3.5in (9cm) long.
£180-200 *AMH*

A Tunbridge Ware basket, c1860,
4.5in (11.5cm) wide.
£180-225 *AMH*

A Tunbridge Ware tea caddy with
an unusual border, c1850, 8.5in
(21.5cm) long.
£400-475 *AMH*

Two Tunbridge Ware boxes, c1850, larger 4.5in
(11.5cm) long.   **£180-225 each** *AMH*

A Tunbridge Ware watch stand, c1865, 3.5in (9cm) square.
£100-145 *AMH*

A pair of Tunbridge Ware book ends, c1840.
£350-400 *AMH*

Two Tunbridge Ware waxes, smallest 0.5in (1cm) high.
£40-50 *AMH*

A Tunbridge Ware counter box, 2.5in (6cm) high, **£100-145,** and a Tunbridge Ware nutmeg grater, 1.5in (4cm) high.
£80-95 *AMH*

Two Tunbridge Ware teapot pin cushions, c1870, 1.5in (4cm) high.   **£180-225 each** *AMH*

A Tunbridge Ware oak book rack, with cube mosaic ends, 12.5in (32cm) long.
£180-225 *AMH*

A Tunbridge Ware book mark, 1in (2.5cm) diam.   **£30-40** *AMH*

A late Georgian marquetry cribbage board, with Masonic emblem, 12in (31cm) long.
£180-225 *AMH*

Tunbridge Ware match strikers, the centre inscribed 'Go To Bed', c1835, 2in (6.5cm) high.
£50-100 each *AMH*

A Tunbridge Ware ruler, c1840, 15in (38cm) long.
£80-90 *AMH*

A Tunbridge Ware letter opener, c1860, 9.5in (24cm) long.
£40-55 *AMH*

A group of Tunbridge Ware sewing items, comprising: pin cushions, tape measure, and pin wheel.   **£50-150 each** *AMH*

759

AUCTIONEERS

IBBETT MOSELY
25 High Street, SEVENOAKS 456731

A Regular Programme of Sales

of Antique, Victorian and Edwardian Furniture,
Works of Art, Silver, Glass, Watches, China,
Musical Instruments, Jewellery, etc. etc.

Held in our Saleroom at
Sevenoaks.

Also valuations carried out for Probate,
Insurance and Family Division.

Complete house clearances undertaken
with personal supervision.

Storage facilities available for
short periods pending sale.

Chattel Auctions and Valuations

ANDREW PICKFORD

CHARTERED SURVEYORS
FURNITURE AND FINE ART AUCTIONEERS AND VALUERS

Monthly Auction Sales of Antiques
Inventories and Valuations for Probate, Insurance, Family Division and Sale.

Wide selection of over 800 lots of 18th and 19th century furniture, porcelain, glass,
silver and silver plate, brass and copper, jewellery and trinkets, pictures, books,
linen and lace, collectors' items, bric-a-brac, oriental and other carpets.
Viewing on Wednesday (12 noon-7 p.m.) and morning of sale day
on Thursday (9 a.m.)
Catalogues £1.50 by post or £18 by annual subscription
Entries accepted up to 14 days before Sale.

42 ST ANDREW STREET, HERTFORD SG14 1JA
TELEPHONE (0992) 583508 SALEROOM (0992) 501421

Southgate Auction Rooms

London's Largest
Suburban Auction

Sales every Monday 6.30pm

Details 081-886 7888

55 High Street, Southgate
London N14 6LD

Rosebery's

AUCTIONEERS & VALUERS

Antique and Reproduction
Furniture · Silver & Silver Plate
Ceramics & Glass
Carpets & Rugs · Pictures
Musical Instruments
Works of Art · Jewellery

Auctions Held Every Fortnight

★ Free Valuations ★
★ House Clearances ★

Tel: 081-778 4024
Fax: 081-659 9023

The Old Railway Booking Hall
Crystal Palace Station Road
London SE19 2AZ

LLOYDS PARK
AUCTIONS

Monthly quality antique sales
every fourth Friday

Antiques sales every Friday
at 6.30 p.m.

Lots taken in all week.
Viewing all day Friday.
House Clearances
Valuations for probate etc.

Lloyds Park Auctions
89 Grange Road
Walthamstow
London E17
Tel: 081-520 9878

D. M. NESBIT & Company

CHARTERED SURVEYORS
AUCTIONEERS & VALUERS

Monthly sales to include
furniture, porcelain, pottery,
glassware, silver, jewellery, paintings and collectors' items.
Valuations for insurance probate and family division.

Fine Art and Auction Department, Southsea Salerooms,
7 Clarendon Rd., Southsea, Hants. PO5 2ED
Tel: (0705) 864321   Fax: (0705) 295522

AUCTIONEERS

763

AUCTIONEERS

Wingett's

Fine Art Auctioneers

Auctioneers covering the North West

Valuations for Probate and Insurance

Monthly Antique Auctions

Weekly General Sales

**Head Office and Auction Galleries
29 HOLT STREET, WREXHAM, CLWYD
LL13 8DH TEL: (0978) 353553**

Nigel Ward & Morris

CHARTERED SURVEYORS
AUCTIONEERS AND VALUERS

Regular monthly auctions
of Antiques, Objects d'Art
& Collectables
Household Furniture & Effects

On the premises marquee sales

**STUART HOUSE
18 GLOUCESTER ROAD
ROSS-ON-WYE
HEREFORDSHIRE HR9 5BU
(0989) 768320**

**THE BORDER PROPERTY CENTRE
PONTRILAS
HEREFORD HR2 0EH
(0981) 240140**

ROGERS JONES CO.

**FURNITURE & FINE ART AUCTIONEERS
Probate & Insurance Valuers**

Antique Furniture
Collectables and
Paintings every
last Tuesday in the month

General household
sales on
following two Tuesdays

**The Saleroom, 33 Abergele Road,
Colwyn Bay, Clwyd LL29 7RU
Telephone (0492) 532176 24 hrs.
Fax (0492) 533308.**

SPENCER'S

SALEROOM
20 The Square, RETFORD, Nottinghamshire DN22 6BX
(0777) 708633 Fax (0777) 709299
OFFICES
65 Regent Street, CAMBRIDGE CB2 1AB
(0223) 327592
1 Princes Square, HARROGATE, North Yorkshire HG1 1ND
(0423) 500566
42 Silver Street, LINCOLN LN2 1TA
(0522) 536666
21 St Annes Road West, LYTHAM ST ANNES, Lancashire FY8 1SB
(0253) 780202
5 Regent Street, NOTTINGHAM NG1 5BW
(0602) 508833
1 St James' Row, SHEFFIELD S1 1WZ
(0742) 728728

6-8 Specialist Sales held each month
Catalogues available individually or by subscription

Wright-Manley

Beeston Sales Centre, Near Tarporley,
Cheshire CW6 9NJ

Regular Furniture and Fine Art Sales

Fortnightly Collective Sales of
Antique and Modern Furniture

Information: Gerald Tilston
Tel: (0829) 260318

764

Auctioneers
in the Midlands

MEALY'S

Ireland's Leading Fine Art & Rare Book Auctioneers

**Castlecomer
Co. Kilkenny**

**Tel: 056-41229/41413
Fax No: 056-41627**

MORGAN EUANS & CO LTD.

GAERWEN, ANGLESEY
NORTH WALES

Monthly sales of antique furniture, collectables, paintings and 'Welsh' fine art (Saleroom 1). Fortnightly sales of household and general goods (Saleroom 2).

**Head Office: 30 Church Street, Llangefni
Anglesey. (0248) 723303**

Saleroom: (0248) 421582. Fax: (0248) 750146

Established 1846
Monthly Specialist Sales
FURNITURE
WORKS of ART
PORCELAIN & POTTERY
SILVER
PEWTER
CLOCKS
MUSICAL BOXES
BRONZES
BOOKS and PICTURES
BYGONES
ORIENTAL CARPETS

R U S S E L L ,   B A L D W I N   &   B R I G H T

VALUATIONS for all purposes carried out by our qualified staff.
SALES by AUCTION of the contents of Town and Country Houses conducted throughout the West Midlands and Wales.

Enquiries to: The Fine Art Saleroom, Ryelands Rd., Leominster, Herefordshire HR6 8NZ. (0568) 611166
Fax (0568) 611802. Also at Portland Room, Malvern. Tel (0684) 893933

Robert I.
Heyes
& ASSOCIATES

Fine Art Auctioneers and Valuers

**WE OFFER A COMPLETE SERVICE
THROUGHOUT THE NORTH WEST**

Valuations for Probate and Insurance
Regular Specialist Auctions
Complete Contents Cleared

Hatton Buildings
Lightfoot Street
Chester
Tel (0244) 328941
Fax (0244) 310898

766

AYLSHAM
SALEROOMS

*Large pair of bronze garden statuary lions, 44".
Sold at Aylsham Salerooms for £2,500.*

SALES OF
★ ANTIQUES (3-WEEKLY)
★ PICTURES (BI-MONTHLY)
★ BOOKS AND COLLECTORS SALES (BI-MONTHLY)
WEEKLY HOUSEHOLD FURNITURE ETC

**AYLSHAM (0263)
733195**
8 MARKET PLACE, AYLSHAM,
NORFOLK NR11 6EH

G. A. KEY
VALUATIONS FOR SALE
INSURANCE & PROBATE
PURPOSES

Arthur Johnson & sons

The Largest Furniture Auction Complex in the Midlands
6 SPECIALIST SALEROOMS
Around 2,000 lots every Saturday

(0602) 869128 Meadow Lane Nottingham

William H. Brown
FINE ART
— Fine Art Auctioneers and Valuers —

SALES
- *Regular auction sales of antique and fine art at our main salerooms*
- *Regular auction sales of general furniture and effects at all salerooms*
- *Contents sales on vendors' premises*
- *Total House clearance for executors*

VALUATIONS
Valuations and Inventories for Insurance, Probate, Capital Transfer, Capital Gains Tax and Family Division

ADVICE
Free Advisory Service at the Salerooms

SALEROOMS
William H. Brown
(Ken Green)
10 Regent Street
Barnsley
South Yorkshire
S70 2EJ
(0226) 299221

William H. Brown
(Francis Beal)
Paskells Rooms
14 East Hill
Colchester
Essex CO1 2QX
(0206) 868070

*William H. Brown
(Suki Burnett)
Stanilands Auction Rooms
28 Netherhall Road
Doncaster
South Yorkshire
DN1 2PW
(0302) 367766

*William H. Brown
(Robert R. Woods)
Morphets
4-6 Albert Street
Harrogate
North Yorkshire
HG1 1JL
(0423) 530030

William H. Brown
(Ray Young)
The Warner Auction Rooms
16-18 Halford Street
Leicester LE1 1JB
(0533) 519777

*William H. Brown
(James Fletcher)
Olivers Rooms
Burkitts Lane
Sudbury
Suffolk CO10 6HB
(0787) 880305

Brown & Merry
(Stephen J. Hearn)
Brook Street
Tring, Hertfordshire
HP23 5EF
(044282) 6446

REGIONAL OFFICES
1 Market Place
Beverley
North Humberside
HU17 8BB
(0482) 870832

19 Market Square
Northampton
NN1 2DX
(0604) 231866

37-39 Church Street
Sheffield S1 2GL
(0742) 769062

48 Goodramgate
York YO1 2LF
(0904) 621138

*Denotes Members of The Society of Fine Art Auctioneers

AUCTIONEERS

WILLIAM HARDIE LIMITED

Fine Art Consultants and Valuers

Specialist sales of ceramics and decorative arts

141 West Regent Street
Glasgow G2 2SG

Tel: 041-221 6780
Fax: 041-248 6237

Andrew Hartley Fine Arts

Victoria Hall Salerooms
Little Lane, Ilkley, West Yorkshire LS29 8EA
(Tel 0943 816363)

Independent
Furniture and Fine Arts Auctioneers for three
generations. Now fully extended and computerised
premises with two salerooms and carefully graded
general and specialist sales every week.

Anderson & Garland

The Fine Art Sale Rooms
Marlborough House, Marlborough Crescent
Newcastle upon Tyne NE1 4EE
Telephone: (091 232) 6278

 Boulton & Cooper Ltd

Fine Art Auctioneers
Estate Agents
Auctioneers

St Michael's House, Market Place
Malton, North Yorkshire
Tel: (0653) 696151

Tennants

AUCTIONEERS

A complete, nationwide service with free advice
on values and reserves for either a single item, a
complete home clearance or a country house sale.

Tennants, 27 Market Place, Leyburn,
North Yorkshire, DL8 5AS. Tel: 0969 23780

Write for copies of our free full colour News Bulletin.

CUMBRIA AUCTION ROOMS
Fine Art, Antiques and Furniture
Auctioneers and Valuers
Regular Catalogue Sales of Antiques
and Works of Art
Weekly Sales of General Furniture
and Effects
12 LOWTHER STREET, CARLISLE, CUMBRIA CA3 8DA
Telephone: Carlisle (0228) 25259

Charles Edwards Group
(Auctioneers & Valuers)

Monthly and Quarterly Sales
of Whole or Part Estates
Unredeemed Pledges and
Specialist Auctions
Valuations for :- Probate -
Insurance - Private Treaty

4-8 Lynwood Road, Blackburn, Lancashire, Tel. 0254 691748

Lithgow Sons & Partners
(Established 1868)
North East Auctioneers

Antique House
Station Road, Stokesley
Middlesbrough
Cleveland TS9 7AB
Tel: 0642 710158
Fax: 0642 712641

768

DIRECTORY OF SPECIALISTS

This directory is in no way complete. If you wish to be included in next year's directory or if you have a change of address or telephone number, please could you inform us by April 1993. Entries will be repeated in subsequent editions unless we are requested otherwise. Finally we would advise readers to make contact by telephone before a visit, therefore avoiding a wasted journey, which nowadays is both time consuming and expensive.

Any entry followed by (R) denotes a specialist who undertakes restoration work

ANTIQUITIES

London
Astarte Gallery,
Britannia Hotel, Grosvenor
Square, W1
Tel: 071 409 1875

Charles Ede,
37 Brook Street, W1
Tel: 071 493 4944

Faustus Fine Art,
Upper Gallery, 90 Jermyn
Street, SW1
Tel: 071 930 1864

Hadji Baba,
36 Davies Street, W1
Tel: 071 499 9363/9384

Khalili Gallery,
15c Clifford Street, Bond
Street, W1
Tel: 071 734 0202

Jonathan Mankowitz,
Grays in the Mews,
Davies Street, W1

C J Martin,
85 The Vale, Southgate N14
Tel: 081 882 1509

Nigel Mills,
51 Crescent Road, South
Woodford, E18
Tel: 081 504 2569

Pars Antique,
H 16/17 Grays in the Mews,
Davies Street, W1
Tel: 081 399 8801

Simmons & Simmons,
K 37/38 Grays in the Mews,
Davies Street, W1
Tel: 071 629 9321

Thomas Howard Sneyd,
35 Furscroft, George Street,
W1
Tel: 071 723 1976

Surena,
Grays Mews Antique
Market, Davies Mews W1
Tel: 071 493 6762

Annie Trotter and Ian
Parsons,
30 Davies Mews, W1
Tel: 071 629 2813

Nicholas Wright,
42A Christchurch Avenue,
NW6
Tel: 081 459 7123

Dorset
Ancient Forum,
PO Box 356, Christchurch
Tel: 0202 478592

Hants
Phil Goodwin,
3 Apollo Drive, Crookhorn,
Portsmouth
Tel: 0705 266866

Michael Harrison,
Truelocke Antiques, 109
High Street, Odiham
Tel: 0256 702387

Herts
David Miller, 51 Carlisle
Avenue, St Albans
Tel: 0727 52412

Kent
C J Denton,
PO Box 25, Orpington
Tel: 0689 873690

Lancs
H & M J Burke,
Old Packet House Building,
South Worsley

Middx
M & H Kashden,
19 The Lawns, Pinner
Tel: 081 421 3568

Somerset
Fox & Co.,
30 Princes Street, Yeovil
Tel: 0935 72323

Sussex
Agora, 18 Regent Arcade,
East Street, Brighton
Tel: 0273 26663

Yorks
Wilton House Gallery,
95 Market Street,
Pocklington
Tel: 0759 4858

ARCHITECTURAL ANTIQUES

London
Antique Fireplace
Warehouse, 194-196
Battersea Park Road, SW11
Tel: 071 627 1410

Nigel Bartlett,
67 St. Thomas Street, SE1
Tel: 071 378 7895

H Crowther Ltd.,
Garden Leadwork (R)
5 Chiswick High Road W4
Tel: 081 994 2326

Davis & Davis,
Architectural Antiques,
Arch 266, Urlwin Street,
Camberwell SE5 ONF
Tel: 071 703 6525

Fortress, 23 Canonbury
Lane, Islington, N1
Tel: 071 359 5875

Lamont Antiques,
151 Tower Bridge Road, SE1

Lassco, Mark Street, EC2
Tel: 071 739 0448

Miles D'Agar Antiques,
533 Kings Road, SW10
Tel: 071 352 6143

H W Poulter & Son,
279 Fulham Road, SW10
Tel: 071 352 7268

Westland Pilkington
Antiques, The Clergy House,
Mark Street, EC2
Tel: 071 739 8094

Avon
Robert Mills, Unit 3, Satelite
Business Park, Blackswarth
Road, Redfield, Bristol
Tel: 0272 556542

Walcot Reclamation,
108 Walcot Street, Bath
Tel: 0225 444404

Berks
The Fire Place (Hungerford)
Ltd., Old Fire Station,
Charnham Street,
Hungerford
Tel: 0488 683420

Cheshire
Antique Fireplaces, The
Manor House, Tarvin Village
Tel: 0829 40936

Nostalgia, 61 Shaw Heath,
Stockport
Tel: 061 477 7706

Cumbria
The Holme Firth Company,
Holme Mill, Holme, Nr
Carnforth
Tel: 0524 781423

Derbyshire
Havenplan's Architectural
Emporium, The Old Station,
Station Road, Killamarsh, Nr
Sheffield
Tel: 0742 489972

Devon
Architectural Antiques,
Westley, Alswear Old Road,
South Molton
Tel: 076 95 3342

Ashburton Marbles,
Englands Antiques
Fireplaces, Grate Hall, North
Street, Ashburton
Tel: 0364 53189

Bellevue House Interiors,
Fort House, 36 East Street,
South Molton
Tel: 07695 3761

Cantabrian Antiques,
16 Park Street, Lynton
Tel: 0598 53282

Dorset
Talisman Antiques,
The Old Brewery, Wyke,
Gillingham
Tel: 0747 824423

Glos
Architectural Heritage,
Taddington Manor,
Taddington, Nr Cutsdean,
Cheltenham
Tel: 0386 73414

Hayes & Newby, The Pit, 70
Hare Lane, Gloucester
Tel: 0452 301145

Gt Manchester
Antique Fireplaces,
1090 Stockport Road,
Levenshulme
Tel: 061 431 8075

Hereford & Worcs
Bailey's Architectural
Antiques, The Engine Shed,
Ashburton Industrial Estate,
Ross-on-Wye
Tel: 0989 63015

Lancs
W J Cowell & Sons,
Church Hill House, D'urton
Lane, Broughton, Preston
Tel: 0772 862034

Leics
Britains Heritage,
Shaftesbury Hall, 3 Holy
Bones, Leicester
Tel: 0533 519592

Middx
Crowther of Syon Lodge,
London Road, Isleworth
Tel: 081 560 7978/7985

Norfolk
Christopher Bailey (Chimney
Pieces), The Raveningham
Centre, Raveningham,
Lodden, Beccles
Tel: 050 88 439

Oxon
Oxford Architectural
Antiques, The Old Depot,
Nelson Street, Jericho,
Oxford
Tel: 0865 53310

Shropshire
Architectural Antiques,
140 Corve Street, Ludlow
Tel: 0584 876207

Somerset
Wells Reclamation Company, The Old Cider Farm, Wells Road, Coxley, Nr Wells
Tel: 0749 677087 or evenings and weekends 0749 677484

Staffordshire
Old Flames,
133-139 Church Street, Stoke-on-Trent
Tel: 0782 744985

Surrey
Drummond's of Bramley, Birtley Farm, Horsham Road, Bramley, Guildford
Tel: 0483 898766

Glover and Stacey Ltd., Grange Farm, Grange Road, Tongham, Nr Farnham
Tel: 02518 2993

Sussex
Brighton Architectural Salvage,
33 Gloucester Road, Brighton
Tel: 0273 681656

Tyne & Wear
Shiners,
123 Jesmond Road, Jesmond, Newcastle-upon-Tyne
Tel: 091 281 6474

Wilts
David J Bridgwater,
112 High Street, Marshfield, Nr Chippenham
Tel: 0225 891623

Relic Antiques,
Brillscote Farm, Lea, Nr Malmesbury
Tel: 0666 822332

Yorks
Robert Aagaard Ltd., Frogmire House, Stockwell Road, Knaresborough
Tel: 0423 864805

Cupid Architectural,
West Royd Cottage, West Royd Avenue, King Cross, Halifax
Tel: 0422 3763585

The Main Pine Co.,
Grangewood, Green Hamerton, York
Tel: 0423 330451

Manor House Fireplaces, Bankgate Mills, Bankgate, Slaithwaite, Huddersfield
Tel: 0484 846055

Andy Thornton Architectural Antiques Ltd., Ainleys Industrial Estate, Elland
Tel: 0422 3775595

Wales
An Englishman's Home, Old Stores, Sudbrook, Newport
Tel: 0291 423414

M & A Main Architectural Antiques (R), The Old Smithy, Cerrig-y-Drudion, Corwen
Tel: 049 082 491

The Pumping Station, Penarth Road, Cardiff
Tel: 0222 221085

Victorian Fireplaces (Simon Priestley),
Saturdays only: Ground Floor, Cardiff Antique Centre, 69-71 St Mary Street, Cardiff
Tel: 0222 30970
Any other time: Tel: 0222 26049

ARMS & MILITARIA

London
Armada Antiques,
Gray's Antique Market, 58 Davies Street, W1
Tel: 071 499 1087

The Armoury of St James's, 17 Piccadilly Arcade, SW1
Tel: 071 493 5082

Colin C Bowdell,
Gray's Antique Market, 58 Davies Street, W1
Tel: 071 408 0176

Michael C German,
38b Kensington Church Street, W8
Tel: 071 937 2771

Tradition,
5a Shepherd Street, W1
Tel: 071 493 7452

Avon
Chris Grimes Militaria,
13 Lower Park Row, Bristol
Tel: 0272 298205

Co. Durham
Matched Pairs Ltd.,
20 High Street, Spennymoor
Tel: 0388 819500 or 0740 20667 evenings

Glos
HQ 84, 82-84 Southgate Street, Gloucester
Tel: 0452 27716

Hants
Romsey Medal Centre,
5 Bell Street, Romsey
Tel: 0794 512069

Lancs
Rod Akeroyd & Son Antiques, 101-103 New Hall Lane, Preston
Tel: 0772 794947

Garth Vincent
The Old Manor House, Allington, Nr Grantham
Tel: 0400 81358

Norfolk
Anglian Arms,
Market House, Harleston
Tel: 0379 852184 or 0986 875115

Northumberland
David A Oliver,
Pennystane, Church Lane, Thropton, Nr Morpeth
Tel: 0669 20618

Surrey
Casque & Gauntlet Antiques, 55/59 Badshot Lea Road, Badshot Lea, Farnham
Tel: 0252 20745

Alan S Cook, 132 Rydens Road, Walton-on-Thames
Tel: 0932 228328 home

West Street Antiques,.
63 West Street, Dorking
Tel: 0306 883487

Sussex
Military Antiques (by appointment only),
42 Janes Lane, Burgess Hill
Tel: 0444 233516 & 43088

Michael Miller,
The Lamb, 8 Cuckfield Road, Hurstpierpoint
Tel: 0273 834567

Wallis & Wallis,
West Street Galleries, Lewes
Tel: 0273 480208

Worthing Gunshop,
80 Broadwater Street West, Worthing
Tel: 0903 37378

Warwickshire
Arbour Antiques Ltd.,
Poet's Arbour, Sheep Street, Stratford-upon-Avon
Tel: 0789 293453

Yorks
The Antique & Bargain Store,
6 Sunny Bar, Doncaster
Tel: 0302 344857

The Antique Shop,
226 Harrogate Road, Leeds
Tel: 0532 681785

Andrew Spencer Bottomley (by appointment only),
The Coach House, Thongsbridge, Holmfirth
Tel: 0484 685234

Doncaster Sales & Exchange, 20 Copley Road, Doncaster
Tel: 0302 344857

Wales
Hermitage Antiques,
10 West Street, Fishguard
Tel: 0348 873037

ART DECO & ART NOUVEAU

London
Bizarre,
24 Church Street, NW8
Tel: 071 724 1305

Henry Boxer Galleries,
58-60 Kensington Church Street, W8
Tel: 071 376 0425/081 948 1633

Butler & Wilson,
189 Fulham Road, SW3
Tel: 071 352 3045

Chilton, Stand A11/12, Chenil Galleries, 181-183 King's Road, SW3
Tel: 071 352 2163

Church Street Antiques,
8 Church Street, NW8
Tel: 071 723 7415

T. Coakley, Stand D13, Chenil Galleries, 181-183 King's Road SW3
Tel: 071 351 2914

Cobra & Bellamy,
149 Sloane Street, SW1
Tel: 071 730 2823

Editions Graphiques Gallery, 3 Clifford Street, W1
Tel: 071 734 3944

The Facade,
196 Westbourne Grove, W11
Tel: 071 727 2159

Galerie 1900, 267 Camden High Street, NW1
Tel: 071 485 1001

Gallery '25, 4 Halkin Arcade, Motcomb Street, SW1
Tel: 071 235 5178

Patrick & Susan Gould,
L17 Grays Mews, Davies Mews, W!

Jazzy Art Deco, 67 Camden Road, Camden Town, NW1
Tel: 071 267 3342

John Jesse, 160 Kensington Church Street, W8
Tel: 071 229 0312

Lewis M Kaplan Associates Ltd., 50 Fulham Road SW3
Tel: 071 589 3108

Helen Lane, 212 Camden High Street, NW1
Tel: 071 267 6588

The Lamp Gallery,
355 New Kings Road, SW6
Tel: 071 736 6188

John & Diana Lyons Gallery, 47-49 Mill Lane, West Hampstead NW6
Tel: 071 794 3537

Sylvia Powell Decorative Arts, 28 The Mall, Camden Passage, N1
Tel: 071 354 2977

Pruskin Gallery,
73 Kensington Church Street, W8
Tel: 071 937 1994

Ziggy, Portwine Galleries, 175 Portobello Road W11

Cheshire
Nantwich Art Deco & Decorative Arts,
87 Welsh Row, Nantwich
Tel: 0270 624876

Gt Manchester
A S Antiques,
26 Broad Street, Salford
Tel: 061 737 5938

Herts
Ziggy, 2 Morley Cottages, Chells Manor, Stevenage
Tel: 0438 727084

Humberside
Carlton Gallery,
Main Street, Swanland, Hull
Tel: 0482 443954

Kent
Rowena Blackford, Penny Lampard's Antique Centre, 31 High Street, Headcorn
Tel: 0622 890682/861360

Lancs
Decoroy,
105 New Hall Lane, Preston
Tel: 0772 705371

Leics
Birches Antique Shop,
18 Francis Street,
Stoneygate, Leicester
Tel: 0533 703235

Merseyside
Osiris Antiques (Paul &
Carol Wood),
104 Shakespeare Street,
Southport
Tel: 0704 60418 (Eve)
0704 500991 (Day)

Norfolk
Yesteryear Antiques,
24D Magdalen Street,
Norwich
Tel: 0603 622908

Shropshire
Antiques on the Square,
2 Sandford Court, Church
Stretton
Tel: 0694 724111

Expressions, 17 Princess
Street, Shrewsbury
Tel: 0743 51731

Somerset
Decoration, Rosamund
Morgan, Taunton Antique
Centre, Silver Street,
Taunton, every Monday
Tel: 0460 40958 evenings

Suffolk
Victoria & Alan Waine,
Country Collectables, The
Old Surgery, Hall Street,
Long Melford
Tel: 0787 310140

Surrey
Peter & Debbie Gooday, 20
Richmond Hill, Richmond
Tel: 081 940 8652

Sussex
Armstrong-Davis Gallery,
The Square, Arundel
Tel: 0903 882752

Warwickshire
Art Deco Ceramics,
The Ocsbury, 10 Mill Street,
Warwick
Tel: 0926 498068

Rich Designs,
Unit 3-7A,
Waterloo Industrial Estate,
Bidford-on-Avon
Tel: 0789 772111

West Midlands
Smithsonia,
15/16 Piccadilly Arcade, New
Street, Birmingham
Tel: 021 643 8405

Yorks
Dragon Antiques,
10 Dragon Road, Harrogate
Tel: 0423 562037

Mr Muir Hewitt,
Halifax Antiques Centre,
Queens Road, Gibbet Street,
Halifax
Tel: 0422 366657

Scotland
The Rendezvous Gallery,
100 Forest Avenue, Aberdeen
Tel: 0224 323247

Wales
Paul Gibbs Antiques,
25 Castle Street, Conway
Tel: 0492 593429

ART DECO, 60s & 70s

Warwickshire
FAB,
130 Queens Road, Nuneaton
Tel: 0203 382399

ARTS & CRAFTS

London
Paul Reeves, 32B Kensington
Church Street, W8
Tel: 071 937 1594

Simon Tracy Gallery,
18 Church Street NW8
Tel: 071 724 5890

BOOKS

Middx
John Ives, 5 Normanhurst
Drive, Twickenham
Tel: 081 892 6265

BOXES & TREEN

London
Simon Castle, 38B
Kensington Church Street,
W8
Tel: 071 937 2268

Halcyon Days,
14 Brook Street, W1
Tel: 071 629 8811

Alistair Sampson Antiques,
156 Brompton Road, SW3
Tel: 071 589 5272

Avon
Gloria Gibson, 2 Beaufort
West, London Road, Bath
Tel: 0225 446646

Berks
Mostly Boxes,
92-52b High Street, Eton
Tel: 0753 858470

Charles Toller, Hall House,
20 High Street, Datchet
Tel: 0753 42903

Bucks
A & E Foster (appt only),
Little Heysham, Forge Road,
Naphill
Tel: 024 024 2024

Hants
Gerald Austin Antiques,
2A Andover Road,
Winchester
Tel: 0962 869824 Ext.2

Millers of Chelsea,
Netherbrook House, 86
Christchurch Road,
Ringwood
Tel: 0425 472062

Oxon
Key Antiques, 11 Horse Fair,
Chipping Norton
Tel: 0608 643777

Shropshire
Parmenter Antiques,
5 Central Court, High Street,
Bridgnorth
Tel: 0746 765599

Sussex
Michael Wakelin & Helen
Linfield, 10 New Street,
Petworth
Tel: 0798 42417

CAMERAS

London
Jessop Classic
Photographica, 67 Great
Russell Street, WC1
Tel: 071 831 3640

Cliff Latford Photography,
Stand G006 Alfie's Antiques
Market, 18/25 Church Street,
NW8
Tel: 071 724 5650

Vintage Cameras Ltd.,
254/256 Kirkdale, Sydenham
Tel: 081 778 5416 & 5841

Essex
Cliff Latford,
91A East Hill, Colchester
Tel: 0206 564474

Herts
P Coombs,
87 Gills Hill Lane, Radlett
Tel: 0923 856949

CARPETS

London
David Black Oriental
Carpets, 96 Portland Road,
Holland Park, W11
Tel: 071 727 2566

Mayfair Carpet Gallery,
9 Old Bond Street, W1
Tel: 071 493 0126/7

Vigo Carpet Gallery,
6a Vigo Street, W1
Tel: 071 439 6971

Vigo Sternberg Galleries,
37 South Audley Street, W1
Tel: 071 629 8307

Dorset
J L Arditti (Old Oriental
Rugs), 88 Bargates,
Christchurch
Tel: 0202 485414

Essex
Robert Bailey (by appt only),
PO Box 1110, Ongar
Tel: 0277 362662

Glos
Alan Du Monceau,
Millswood, Chalford
Tel: 0453 886970

Herts
Oriental Rug Gallery,
42 Verulam Road,
St Albans
Tel: 0727 41046

Kent
Persian Rugs, R & G King,
Vines Farm, Mathews Lane,
W. Peckham, Maidstone
Tel: 0732 850228

Somerset
Sheelagh Lewis (by appt),
The Garden House,
Selworthy
Tel: 0643 862344

M & A Lewis, Oriental
Carpets & Rugs, 8 North
Street, Wellington
Tel: 082 347 667430

Sussex
Lindfield Galleries,
59 High Street, Lindfield
Tel: 04447 3817

Yorks
Danby Antiques,
61 Heworth Road, York
Tel: 0904 415280

London House Oriental Rugs
& Carpets, London House,
High Street, Boston Spa by
Wetherby
Tel: 0937 845123

Omar (Harrogate) Ltd.,
8 Crescent Road, Harrogate
Tel: 0423 503675

Gordon Reece Gallery,
Finkle Street,
Knaresborough
Tel: 0423 866219/866502

Scotland
Whytock & Reid, Sunbury
House, Belford Mews,
Edinburgh
Tel: 031 226 4911

CLOCKS WATCHES & BAROMETERS

London
Asprey PLC, 165-169 New
Bond Street, W1
Tel: 071 493 6767

Bobinet Ltd., 102 Mount
Street, W1
Tel: 071 408 0333/4

Aubrey Brocklehurst,
124 Cromwell Road, SW7
Tel: 071 373 0319

Camerer Cuss & Co.,
17 Ryder Street, St James's
SW1
Tel: 071 930 1941

Capital Clocks,
190 Wandsworth Road, SW8
Tel: 071 720 6372

Partic Capon,
350 Upper Street, N1
Tel: 071 354 0487

Chelsea Clocks,
479 Fulham Road, SW6
Tel: 071 731 5704
Also at:
69 Portobello Road,
Tel: 071 727 5417

City Clocks (R),
31 Amwell Street, EC1
Tel: 071 278 1154

The Clock Clinic Ltd.,
85 Lower Richmond Road,
SW15
Tel: 081 788 1407

Philip & Bernard Dombey,
174 Kensington Church
Street, W8
Tel: 071 229 7100

Gerald Mathias (R),
R5/6 Antiquarius, 136 King's
Road, SW3
Tel: 071 351 0484

North London Clock Shop
Ltd. (R),
72 Highbury Park, N5
Tel: 071 226 1609

Pieces of Time,
1-7 Davies Mews, W1
Tel: 071 629 2422

Roderick Antique Clocks,
23 Vicarage Gate, W8
Tel: 071 937 8517

R E Rose, FBHI, 731 Sidcup
Road, Eltham, SE9
Tel: 081 859 4754

Strike One (Islington) Ltd.,
51 Camden Passage
Tel: 071 226 9709

Temple Brooks,
12 Mill Lane, NW6
Tel: 081 452 9696

Philip Whyte,
32 Bury Street, SW1
Tel: 071 321 0353

Avon
David Gibson,
2 Beaufort West, London
Road, Bath
Tel: 0225 446646

John & Carol,
Hawley CMBH1, The
Orchard, Clevedon Lane,
Clapton Wick, Clevedon
Tel: 0275 852052

Berks
Richard Barder Antiques,
Crossways House, Nr
Newbury
Tel: 0635 200295

The Clock Workshop,
17 Prospect Street,
Caversham, Reading
Tel: 0734 470741

Medalcrest Ltd.,
Charnham House,
Charnham Street,
Hungerford
Tel: 0488 84157

Times Past Antiques Ltd.,
59 High Street, Eton
Tel: 0753 857018

Bucks
The Guild Room,
The Lee, Great Missenden
Tel: 024 020 463

Cheshire
Peter Bosson Antiques,
10B Swan Street, Wilmslow
Tel: 0625 525250 & 527857

Coppelia Antiques,
Holford Lodge, Plumley Moor
Road, Plumley
Tel: 056 572 2197

Cranford Clocks,
12 Princess Street,
Knutsford
Tel: 0565 633331

Derek Rayment Antiques
(R), Orchard House, Barton
Road, Barton, Nr Farndon
Tel: 0829 270429

Cumbria
Don Burns, CMHBI, The
Square, Ireby, Carlisle
Tel: 096 57 477

Derbyshire
Derbyshire Clocks, 104 High
Street West, Glossop
Tel: 0457 862677

Devon
Merton Antiques, Merton,
Okehampton
Tel: 08053 443

Musgrave Bickford Antiques,
15 East Street, Crediton
Tel: 03632 5042

Dorset
Good Hope Antiques,
2 Hogshill Street,
Beaminster
Tel: 0308 862119

Tom Tribe & Son, Bridge
Street, Sturminster Newton
Tel: 0258 72311

Essex
It's About Time (R),
863 London Road,
Westcliff-on-Sea
Tel: 0702 72574 & 205204

Littlebury Antiques,
58/60 Fairycroft Road,
Saffron Walden
Tel: 0799 27961

Mark Marchant,
3 Market Square, Coggeshal
Tel: 0376 561188

Trinity Clocks,
29 East Hill, Colchester
Tel: 0206 868623

Glos
J & M Bristow Antiques,
28 Long Street, Tetbury
Tel: 0666 502222

Gerard Campbell, Maple
House, Market Place,
Lechlade
Tel: 0367 52267

Colin Elliott, 4 Great
Norwood Street, Cheltenham
Tel: 0242 528590

Montpellier Clocks Ltd., 13
Rotunda Terrace,
Montpellier St, Cheltenham
Tel: 0242 224414

Saxton House Gallery, High
Street, Chipping Camden
Tel: 0386 840278

Southbar Antiques, Digbeth
Street, Stow-on-the-Wold
Tel: 0451 30236

Hants
Charles Antiques,
101 The Hundred, Romsey
Tel: 0794 512885

Evans & Evans,
40 West Street, Alresford
Tel: 096 273 732170

Gerald E Marsh,
32A The Square, Winchester
Tel: 0962 844443

A W Porter & Sons, High
Street. Hartley Wintney
Tel: 025284 2676

Hereford & Worcs
Barometer Shop,
New Street, Leominster
Tel: 0568 3652
also at:
3 Lower Park Row, Bristol
Tel: 0272 272565

G & V Taylor Antiques,
Winforton Court, Winforton
Tel: 05446 226

Herts
Country Clocks (R),
3 Pendley Bridge Cottages,
Tring Station, Tring
Tel: 044 282 5090

Isle of Wight
R Taylor, Alum Bay
Tel: 0983 754193

Kent
Apollo Gallery, 19 Market
Square, Westerham
Tel: 0959 62200

Atropos Antiques,
21 St Johns Hill, Sevenoaks
Tel: 0732 454179

John Chawner Antiques,
44 Chatham Hill, Chatham
Tel: 0634 811147 & 0843
43309

Hadlow Antiques,
No. 1 The Pantiles,
Tunbridge Wells
Tel: 0892 29858

The Old Clock Shop,
63 High Street, West Malling
Tel: 0732 843246

Derek Roberts Antiques,
24/25 Shipbourne Road,
Tonbridge
Tel: 0732 358986

Rochester Fine Arts,
88 High Street, Rochester
Tel: 0634 814129

Malcolm G Styles (R),
Tunbridge Wells
Tel: 0892 30699

Anthony Woodburn, Orchard
House, Leigh, Nr Tonbridge
Tel: 0732 832258

Lancs
Davies Antiques,
32 King Street, Whalley
Tel: 0254 823764

Kenneth Weigh, Signwriting
& Numbering,
9 Links Road, Blackpool
Tel: 0253 52097

Leics
Bonington Clocks,
12 Market Place, Kegworth
Tel: 05097 672900

Clock Replacements (R),
239 Welford Road, Leicester
Tel: 0533 706190

G K Hadfield (R),
Blackbrook Hill House,
Tickow Lane, Shepshed
Tel: 0509 503014

C Lowe & Sons Ltd (R),
37-40 Churchgate,
Loughborough
Tel: 0509 217876

Lincs
Pinfold Antiques,
3 Pinfold Lane, Ruskington
Tel: 0526 832057

Merseyside
T Brown Horological
Restorers (R),
12 London Road, Liverpool 3
Tel: 051 709 4048

Norfolk
Delawood Antiques & Clock
Restoration (R), 10 Westgate,
Hunstanton
Tel: 048 53 2903

Norfolk Polyphon & Clock
Centre, Wood Farm,
Bawdeswell, Nr East
Dereham
Tel: 036 288 230

Oxon
Laurie Leigh Antiques,
36 High Street, Oxford
Tel: 0865 244197

Rosemary & Time,
42 Park Street, Thame
Tel: 084421 6923

Telling Time,
57 North Street, Thame
Tel: 084 421 3007

Witney Antiques,
96-98 Corn Street, Witney
Tel: 0993 703902

Somerset
Michael & Judith Avis (R),
The Barton, Simonsbath,
Minehead
Tel: 064383 428

Shelagh Berryman,
15 The Market Place, Wells
Tel: 0749 76203

Bernard G House,
Mitre Antiques, 13 Market
Place, Wells
Tel: 0749 72607

Edward A Nowell,
12 Market Place, Wells
Tel: 0749 72415

Matthew Willis,
88 Bove Town, Glastonbury
Tel: 0458 32103

Staffordshire
James A Jordan, 7 The Corn
Exchange, Lichfield
Tel: 0543 416221

Suffolk
AN Antiques, Home Farm,
South Green, Eye
Tel: 0379 870367

Antique Clocks By Simon
Charles, The Limes, 72
Melford Road, Sudbury
Tel: 0787 75931

R L Fryatt, Grad BHI (R),
10 Amberley Court, Oulton
Broad, Lowestoft
Tel: 0502 560869

Surrey
BS Antiques, 39 Bridge
Road, East Molesey
Tel: 081 941 1812

Bryan Clisby,
86B Tilford Road, Farnham
Tel: 0252 716436

The Clock Shop,
64 Church Street, Weybridge
Tel: 0932 840407 & 855503

Roger A Davis,
Antiquarian Horologist,
19 Dorking Road, Great
Bookham
Tel: 0372 57655 & 53167

Douglas Dawes (by appt),
Antique Clocks, Linfield
Tel: 0342 834965

Hampton Court Antiques,
75 Bridge Road,
East Molesey
Tel: 081 941 6398

E Hollander Ltd.,
The Dutch House,
Horsham Road, South
Holmwood, Dorking
Tel: 0306 888921

Horological Workshops,
204 Worplesdon Road,
Guildford
Tel: 0483 576496

R Saunders Antiques,
71 Queens Road, Weybridge
Tel: 0932 842601

Geoffrey Stevens,
26-28 Church Road,
Guildford
Tel: 0483 504075

Surrey Clock Centre,
3 Lower Street, Haslemere
Tel: 0428 4547

Sussex
Adrian Alan Ltd.,
4 Frederick Place, Brighton
Tel: 0273 25277

W F Bruce Antiques,
Gardner Street,
Herstmonceux
Tel: 0323 833718

Sam Orr Antique Clocks,
36 High Street,
Hurstpierpoint
Tel: 0273 832081

David & Sarah Pullen,
Bexhill-on-Sea
Tel: 0424 222035

R W Wren, MBHI (R),
4 The Ridge, Hastings
Tel: 0424 445248

Tyne & Wear
T P Rooney, Grad BHI (R),
191 Sunderland Road,
Harton Village,
South Shields
Tel: 091 456 2950

Warwickshire
The Grandfather Clock Shop,
2 Bondgate House, Granville
Court, West Street, Shipston
on Stour
Tel: 0608 62144

J & S Clocks (R)
Warwick Antique Centre,
22 High Street, Warwick
Tel: 0926 495704

Mason Antique Clocks,
Glympton House, 3 New
Road, Water Orton
Tel: 021 747 5751

West Midlands
M Allen (R),
76A Walsall Road, Four
Oaks, Sutton Coldfield
Tel: 021 308 6117

Ashleigh House Antiques,
5 Westbourne Road,
Birmingham
Tel: 021 454 6283

Osborne's (R),
91 Chester Road, New
Oscott, Sutton Coldfield
Tel: 021 355 6667

Wiltshire
Avon Antiques,
26-27 Market Street,
Bradford-on-Avon
Tel: 022 16 2052

P A Oxley, The Old Rectory,
Cherhill, Nr Calne
Tel: 0249 816227

The Salisbury Clock Shop,
107 Exeter Street, Salisbury
Tel: 0722 337076

Allan Smith Clocks,
Amity Cottage, 162
Beechcroft Road, Upper
Stratton, Swindon
Tel: 0793 822977

Yorks
Arcadia Antiques,
The Ginnel Antique Centre,
Harrogate
Tel: 0704 64441

Clocks & Gramophones,
11 Walmgate, York
Tel: 0904 611924

The Clock Shop, Hilltop
House, Bellerby, Nr Leyburn
Tel: 0969 22596

Haworth Antiques (R),
Harrogate Road, Huby, Nr
Leeds
Tel: 0423 734293
also at:
26 Cold Bath Road,
Harrogate
Tel: 0423 521401

Brian Loomes, Calf Haugh
Farm, Pateley Bridge
Tel: 0423 711163

Keith Stones Grandfather
Clocks, 5 Ellers Drive,
Bessacarr, Doncaster
Tel: 0302 535258

Scotland
Browns Clocks Ltd.,
203 Bath Street, Glasgow
Tel: 041 248 6760

DOLLS, TOYS & GAMES

London
Antique Dolls,
Stand L14, Grays Mews, W1
Tel: 071 499 6600

Dr Colin Baddiel,
Stand C12, Grays Mews,
1-7 Davies Mews, W1
Tel: 071 629 2813

Heather & Clifford Bond,
Victoriana Dolls,101
Portobello Road, (Sign of the
Teapot), W11.
Tel: 081 471 9382

Jilliana Ranicar-Breese,
Martin Breese International,
8 Portwine Arcade, 175
Portobello Road (Sats only).
Tel: 071 727 9378

Steve Clark (Chelsea Lion),
Chenil Gallery, 181-183
Kings Road, Chelsea SW3
Tel: 071 352 8653

Stuart Cropper, Grays Mews,
1-7 Davies Mews, W1
Tel: 071 499 6600

The Dolls House Toys Ltd.,
29 The Market, Covent
Garden WC2
Tel: 071 379 7243

Dolly Land, 864 Green
Lanes, Winchmore Hill, N21
Tel: 081 360 1053

Donay Antiques,
35 Camden Passage, N1
Tel: 071 359 1880

Engine n'Tender, 19 Spring
Lane, Woodside, SE25
Tel: 081 654 0386

Pete McAskie,
Stand D10-12 Basement,
Grays Mews Antiques, 1-7
Davies Mews, W1
Tel: 071 629 2813

The Singing Tree,
69 New Kings Road, SW6
Tel: 071 736 4527

Yonna,
C17 Grays Mews, W1
Tel: 071 629 3644

Avon
Bristol Doll's Hospital,
50-52 Alpha Road,
Southville, Bristol
Tel: 0272 664368

The China Doll,
31 Walcot Street, Bath
Tel: 0225 465849

Chester
Dollectable, 53 Lower Bridge
Street, Chester
Tel: 0244 344888

Cornwall
Mrs Margaret Chesterton,
33 Pentewan Road,
St Austell
Tel: 0726 72926

The Millcraft Rocking Horse
Company,
Lower Trannack Mill,
Coverack Bridges, Helston
Tel: 0326 573316

Dorset
Hobby Horse Antiques,
29 West Allington, Bridport
Tel: 0308 22801

Essex
Blackwells of Hawkwell,
Dept C, 733 London Road,
Westcliffe-on-Sea
Tel: 0702 72248

Glos
Lilian Middleton's Antique
Dolls' Shop & Dolls' Hospital,
Days Stable, Sheep Street,
Stow-on-the-Wold
Tel: 0451 30381

Park House Antiques, Park
Street, Stow-on-the-Wold
Tel: 0451 30159

Hampshire
Past & Present Crafts,
19 Ditton Close, Stubbington
Tel: 0329 661377

Hereford & Worcs
Antiques Centre, Blackwell
Street, Kidderminster
Tel: 0562 829000

Kent
Hadlow Antiques, 1 The
Pantiles, Tunbridge Wells
Tel: 0892 29858

The Magpie's Nest,
14 Palace Street, Canterbury
Tel: 0227 764883

Pantiles Spa Antiques,
4,5,6 Union House, The
Pantiles, Tunbridge Wells
Tel: 0892 541377

Oxon
Teddy Bears of Witney,
99 High Street, Witney
Tel: 0993 702616

Surrey
Dorking Dolls House, 23
West Street, Dorking
Tel: 0306 885785

Elizabeth Gant, 52 High
Street, Thames Ditton
Tel: 081 398 0962

Sussex
Dolls Hospital Hastings,
17 George Street, Hastings
Tel: 0424 444117

Doll & Teddy Bear Restorer
(R), Wendy Foster, Minto,
Codmore Hill, Pulborough
Tel: 0798 872707

Rathbone Law,
7-9 The Arcade, Worthing
Tel: 0903 200274

Tyne & Wear
B H Bates (Amusement
Machine Spacialist),
Fairview, Maerway Lane,
Maer, Newcastle
Tel: 0782 680667

West Midlands
Robert Taylor,
Windyridge, Worcester Lane,
Four Oaks, Sutton Coldfield
Tel: 021 308 4209

Woodsetton Antiques,
65 Sedgley Road,
Woodsetton, Dudley
Tel: 0384 277918

Yorks
The Antique & Bargain
Store, 6 Sunny Bar,
Doncaster
Tel: 0302 344857

Doncaster Sales & Exchange,
20 Copley Road, Doncaster
Tel: 0302 344857

John & Simon Haley,
89 Northgate, Halifax
Tel: 0422 822148

Second Childhood,
20 Byram Arcade, Westgate,
Huddersfield
Tel: 0484 530117/603854

Scotland
Stockbridge Antiques & Fine
Art, 8 Deanhaugh Street,
Edinburgh
Tel: 031 332 1366

Wales
Museum of Childhood Toys &
Gift Shop, 1 Castle Street,
Beaumaris, Anglesey,
Gwynedd
Tel: 0248 712498

EPHEMERA

London
Jilliana Ranicar-Breese,
Martin Breese Ltd.,
Martin Breese International,
8 Portwine Arcade, 175
Portobello Road (Sats only)
Tel: 071 727 9378

Dodo (Posters),
286 Westbourne Grove, W11
(Sat 7-4 or by appointment)
Tel: 071 229 3132

Donay,
35 Camden Passage, N1
Tel: 071 359 1880

M & R Glendale,
Antiquarian Booksellers, 9A
New Cavendish Street, W1
Tel: 071 487 5348

Jubilee, 1 Pierrepont Row,
Camden Passage, N1
Tel: 071 607 5462

The Old Ephemera &
Newspaper Shop,
37 Kinnerton Street, SW1
Tel: 071 235 7788

Pleasures of Past Times,
11 Cecil Court, Charing
Cross Road, WC2
Tel: 071 836 1142

Danny Posner, The Vintage
Magazine Company,
39/41 Brewer Street, W1
Tel: 071 439 8525

Avon
Michael & Jo Saffell,
3 Walcot Buildings, London
Road, Bath
Tel: 0225 315857

Bucks
Omniphil Ltd.,
Germains Lodge, Fullers
Hill, Chesham
Tel: 0494 771851
also at:
Stand 114, Grays Antique
Market, 58 Davies Street,
W1
Tel: 081 629 3223

Essex
GKR Bonds Ltd.,
PO Box 1, Kelvedon
Tel: 0376 571138

Hants
Cobwebs, 78 Northam Road,
Southampton
Tel: 0703 227458

Kent
Mike Sturge,
39 Union Street, Maidstone
Tel: 0622 754702

Notts
Neales of Nottingham,
192 Mansfield Road,
Nottingham
Tel: 0602 624141

T Vennett-Smith,
11 Nottingham Road,
Gotham
Tel: 0602 830541

Surrey
Richmond Antiquary,
28 Hill Rise, Richmond
Tel: 081 948 0583

FISHING TACKLE

London
Jess Miller,
PO Box 1461, London W6
Tel: 081 748 9314

Dorset
Yesterday Tackle & Books,
42 Clingan Road,
Southbourne
Tel: 0202 476586

Kent
Alan Clout, 36 Nunnery
Fields, Canterbury
Tel: 0227 455162

Lancs
Brian Bowcock, 15 Round
Hey, Mossley, Tameside
Tel: 0457 832967

Sussex
N Marchant-Lane,
The Old Bakery, Golden
Square, Petworth
Tel: 0798 42872

Scotland
Jamie Maxtone Graham,
Lyne Haugh, Lyne Station,
Peebles
Tel: 07214 304

FURNITURE

London
Antiquum (R)
147 Highgate Road, NW5
Tel: 071 485 9501

Asprey PLC 165-169 New
Bond Street, W1
Tel: 071 493 6767

John Bly, 27 Bury Street,
St. James's, SW1
Tel: 071 930 1292

F.E.A. Briggs Ltd.,
73 Ledbury Road, W1
Tel: 071 727 0909

Butchoff Antiques,
233 Westbourne Grove, W1
Tel: 071 221 8174

Rupert Cavendish Antiques,
610 Kings Road, SW6
Tel: 071 731 7041

Eldridge, 99-101 Farringdon
Road, EC1
Tel: 071 837 0379/0370

Hampstead Antique
Emporium, 12 Heath Street,
Hampstead, NW3
Tel: 071 794 3297

John Keil Ltd.,
154 Brompton Road, SW3
Tel: 071 589 6454

C.H. Major (Antiques) Ltd.,
154 Kensington Church
Street, W8
Tel: 071 229 1162

Mallett & Son (Antiques)
Ltd., 40 New Bond Street,
W1
Tel: 071 499 7411

Michael Marriott Ltd.,
588 Fulham Road, SW6
Tel: 071 736 3110

The Old Cinema,
160 Chiswick High Road, W4
Tel: 081 995 4166

Oola Boola Antiques,
166 Tower Bridge Road, SE1
Tel: 071 403 0794

Phelps Ltd.,
133-135 St. Margaret's Road,
Twickenham
Tel: 081 892 1778 & 7129

Reindeer Antiques,
81 Kensington Church
Street, W8
Tel: 071 937 3754

Alistair Sampson Antiques,
156 Brompton Road, SW3
Tel: 071 589 5272

Arthur Seager Ltd.,
25a Holland Street,
Kensington W8
Tel: 071 937 3262

M. & D. Seligmann,
37 Kensington Church
Street, W8
Tel: 071 937 0400

Stair & Co.,
120 Mount Street, W1
Tel: 071 499 1784/5

Murray Thomson Ltd.,
152 Kensington Church
Street, W8
Tel: 071 727 1727

William Tillman,
30 St. James's Street, W1
Tel: 071 839 2500

O.F. Wilson Ltd.,
Queen's Elm Parade, Old
Church Street, SW3
Tel: 071 352 9554

Robert Young Antiques,
68 Battersea Bridge Road,
SW11
Tel: 071 228 7847

Zal Davar Antiques,
Unit 4, Hurlingham Business
Park, Sulivan Road, SW6
Tel: 071 736 2559/1405

Avon
Cottage Antiques,
The Old Post Office,
Langford Place, Nr. Bristol
Tel: 0934 862597

Berks
Mary Bellis Antiques,
Charnham Close,
Hungerford
Tel: 0488 682620

Biggs of Maidenhead,
Hare Hatch Grange, Twyford
Tel: 0734 403281

Medalcrest Ltd.,
Charnham House,
Charnham Street,
Hungerford
Tel: 0488 684157

The Old Malthouse,
Hungerford
Tel: 0488 682209

Charles Toller, Hall House,
20 High Street, Datchet
Tel: 0753 42903

Bucks
A. & E. Foster (by appt),
Little Heysham, Forge Road,
Naphill
Tel: 024 024 2024

Jeanne Temple Antiques,
Stockwell House,
1 Stockwell Lane, Wavendon,
Milton Keynes
Tel: 0908 583597

Lloyd Loom (R),
Western Turville
Tel: 0296 61 5121

Cambs
Clover Antiques,
5-6 Soham Road, Fordham
Tel: 0638 720250

Simon & Penny Rumble
Antiques,
The Old School, Chittering
Tel: 0223 861831

Cheshire
Coppelia Antiques,
Holford Lodge, Plumley Moor
Road, Plumley
Tel: 056 581 2197

Townwell House Antiques,
52 Welsh Row, Nantwich
Tel: 0270 625953

Cornwall
Pydar Antiques & Gallery,
People's Palace, Off Pydar
Street, Truro
Tel: 0872 510485
Home: 0637 872034

Cumbria
Anthemion,
Broughton Hall, Cartmel,
Grange-over-Sands
Tel: 05395 36295

Haughey Antiques, Market
Street, Kirkby Stephen
Tel: 0930 71302

Fenwick Pattison,
Bowmanstead, Coniston
Tel: 0534 41235

Shire Antiques,
The Post House, High
Newton, Newton in Cartmel,
Nr. Grange-over-Sands
Tel: 0448 31431

Townhead Antiques,
Newby Bridge
Tel: 0448 31321

Derbyshire
Antiques Warehouse,
25 Lightwood Road, Buxton
Tel: 0298 72967/0298 871932

Maurice Goldstone & Son,
Avenel Court, Bakewell
Tel: 0629 812487

Spurrier-Smith Antiques,
28,39 & 41 Church Street,
Ashbourne
Tel: 0335 43669
Home: 0629 822502

Devon
Robert Byles,
7 Castle Street, Bamton
Tel: 0398 31515

McBain of Exeter, Exeter
Airport, Clyst Honiton,
Exeter
Tel: 0392 66261

Dorset
Dodge & Son, 28-33 Cheap
Street, Sherborne
Tel: 0935 815151

Johnsons of Sherborne Ltd.,
South Street, Sherborne
Tel: 0935 812585

Talisman Antiques,
The Old Brewery, Wyke,
Gillingham
Tel: 0747 824423

Durham
Bygone Antiques, Victorian
& Edwardian Furniture,
3/5 McMullen Road,
Darlington
Tel: 0325 461399/380884

Eden House Antiques, 10
Staindrop Road, West
Auckland
Tel: 0388 833013

Essex
F. G. Bruschweiler Ltd.,
41-67 Lower Lambricks,
Rayleigh
Tel: 0268 773761

Stone Wall Antiques,
Trade Warehouse,
Down Hall Road,
Matching Green, Nr. Harlow
Tel: 0279 731440

Glos
Baggot Church Street Ltd.,
Church Street, Stow-on-the-
Wold
Tel: 0451 30370

Paul Cater, High Street,
Moreton-in-Marsh
Tel: 0608 51888

Country Life Antiques,
Grey House, The Square,
Stow-on-the-Wold
Tel: 0451 31564

Gloucester House Antiques,
Market Place, Fairford
Tel: 0285 712790

Huntingdon Antiques Ltd.,
The Old Forge, Church
Street,
Stow-on-the-Wold
Tel: 0451 30842

Painswick Antiques &
Interiors,
Beacon House, Painswick
Tel: 0452 812578

Antony Preston Antiques
Ltd., The Square, Stow-on-
the-Wold
Tel: 0451 31586

Stone House Antiques,
St. Mary's Street, Painswick
Tel: 0452 813540

Studio Antiques Ltd.,
Bourton-on-the-Water
Tel: 0451 20352

Denzil Verey Antiques,
(Specialists in Country Pine),
Barnsley House, Barnsley,
Nr. Cirencester
Tel: 0285 740402

Hants
C. W. Buckingham, Twin
Firs, Southampton Road,
Cadnam
Tel: 0703 812122

Cedar Antiques, High Street,
Hartley Wintney
Tel: 025 126 3252

Mark Collier Antiques,
24 The High Street,
Fordingbridge
Tel: 0425 52555

R.C. Dodson,
85 Fawcett Road, Southsea
Tel: 0705 829481

Lita Kaye of Lyndhurst,
13 High Street, Lyndhurst
Tel: 042 128 2337

Millers of Chelsea Antiques
Ltd., Netherbrook House, 86
Christchurch Road,Ringwood
Tel: 0425 472062

Truelock Antiques,
109 High Street, Odiham
Tel: 0256 702387

Hereford & Worcs
Gavina Ewart,
60-62 High Street, Broadway
Tel: 0386 853371

Great Brampton House
Antiques Ltd., Madley
Tel: 0981 250244

Jean Hodge Antiques,
Peachley Manor, Lower
Broadheath, Worcester
Tel: 0905 640255

Jenning of Leominster,
30 Bridge Street, Leominster
Tel: 0568 2946

Lower House Fine Antiques
(R) Far Moor Lane, Winyates
Green, Redditch
Tel: 0527 25117

Herts
C Bellinger Antiques,
91 Wood Street, Barnet
Tel: 081 449 3467

John Bly,
50 High Street, Tring
Tel: 044 282 3030

Collins Antiques,
Corner House,
Wheathampstead
Tel: 058283 3111

Phillips of Hitchin (Antiques)
Ltd.,
The Manor House, Hitchin
Tel: 0462 432067

Humberside
Geoffrey Mole,
400 Wincolmlee, Hull
Tel: 0482 27858

Isle of Wight
Chris Watts,
60 High Street, Cowes
Tel: 0983 298963

Kent
Atropos Antiques,
21 St. Johns Hill, Sevenoaks
Tel: 0732 454179

Castle Antiques,
1 London Road, Westerham
Tel: 0959 62492

Chislehurst Antiques,
7 Royal Parade, Chislehurst
Tel 081 467 1530

Conquest House Antiques,
Conquest House, 17 Palace
Street, Canterbury
Tel: 0227 464587

Furnace Mill, Lamberhurst
Tel: 0892 890285

Garden House Antiques,
118 High Street, Tenterden
Tel: 05806 3664

La Trobe & Bigwood
Antiques, Motts Farm,
Forge Road, Eridge Green,
Tunbridge Wells
Tel: 0892 863840

John McMaster,
5 Sayers Square, Sayers
Lane, Tenterden
Tel: 05806 2941

The Old Bakery Antiques
(Mr & Mrs D. Bryan),
St. Davids Bridge, Cranbrook
Tel: 0580 713103

Pantiles Spa Antiques,
4,5,6 Union House, The
Pantiles, Tunbridge Wells
Tel: 0892 541377

Steppes Hill Farm Antiques,
Stockbury, Sittingbourne
Tel: 0795 842205

Sutton Valence Antiques,
Sutton Valence, Maidstone
Tel: 0622 843333/843499

Swan Antiques,
Stone Street, Cranbrook
Tel: 0580 712720

Lancs
The Manchester Antiques
Co., 915 Stockport Road
Levershulme, Manchester
Tel: 061 224 7923

Preston Antique Centre,The
Mill, New Hall Lane, Preston
Tel: 0772 794498

West Lancs Exports,
Victoria Mill,
Victoria Street,Burscough
Tel: 0704 894634

Leics
Leicester Antiques Complex,
9 St Nicholas Place,
Leicester
Tel: 0533 533343

Lowe of Loughborough,
37-40 Church Gate,
Loughborough
Tel: 0509 217876

Lincs
Kirkby Antiques Ltd.,
Kirkby-on-Bain, Woodhall
Spa
Tel: 0526 52119/53461

Harwood Tate,
Church Mill, Caistor Road,
Market Rasen
Tel: 0673 843579

Laurence Shaw Antiques,
Spilsby Road, Horncastle
Tel: 06582 7638

Middlesex
Binstead Antqies,
21 Middle Lane, Teddington
Tel: 081 943 0626

J. W. Crisp Antiques,
166 High Street, Teddington
Tel: 081 977 4309

Phelps Ltd.,
133-135 St. Margaret's Road,
Twickenham
Tel: 081 892 1778

Norfolk
Joan Adams Antiques,
Rossendale, The Street,
Rickinghall, Diss
Tel: 0379 898485

Arthur Brett & Sons Ltd.,
40-44 St. Giles Street,
Norwich
Tel: 0603 628171

M. D. Cannell Antiques,
Castell Farm, Beccles Road,
Raveningham
050846 441

Peter Howkins Antiques,
39, 40 & 135 King Street,
Great Yarmouth
Tel: 0493 851180

Roderic Haugh Antiques,
Fairhurst Gallery, Bedford
Street, Norwich
Tel: 0603 614214

Pearse Lukies,
Bayfield House, White Hart
Street, Aylsham
Tel: 0263 734137

The Old Curiosity Shop,
South Walsham Norfolk
Tel: 0605 49204

Rossendale Antiques (Ian
Shaw),
Rossendale, The Street,
Rickinghall, Diss
Tel: 0379 898485

Northants
Paul Hopwell Antiques,
30 High Street, West Haddon
Tel: 0788 510636

Oxon
David John Ceramics,
11 Acre End Street,
Eynsham
Tel: 0865 880786

Rupert Hitchcox Antiques
Warehouse, The Garth,
Warps Grove, Chalgrove, Nr.
Oxford
Tel: 0865 890241

Elizabethan House Antiques,
28 & 55 High Street,
Dorchester-on-Thames
Tel: 0865 340079

Key Antiques, 11 Horse Fair,
Chipping Norton
Tel: 0608 643777

Peter Norden Antiques,
High Street, Burford
Tel: 099 382 2121

Manfred Schotten Antiques,
The Crypt, High Street,
Burford
Tel: 099 382 2302

Telling Time,
57 North Street, Thame
Tel: 084 421 3007

Zene Walker,
The Bull House, High Street,
Burford
Tel: 099 382 3284

Witney Antiques,
96-98 Corn Street, Witney
Tel: 0993 703902

Shropshire

Castle Gate Antiques,
15 Castle Gate, Shrewsbury
Tel: 0743 61011 (eves)

R. G. Cave & Sons Ltd.,
17 Broad Street, Ludlow
Tel: 0584 3568

Dodington Antiques,
15 Dodington, Whitchurch
Tel: 0948 3399

Doveridge House of
Neachley,
Long Lane, Nr. Shifnal
Tel: 090 722 3131/2

F. C. Manser & Son Ltd.,
53/54 Wyle Cop, Shrewsbury
Tel: 0743 51120

Parmenter Antiques,
5 Central Court, High Street,
Bridgnorth
Tel: 0746 765599

Paul Smith, The Old Chapel,
Old Street, Ludlow
Tel: 0584 2666

M. & R. Taylor (Antiques)
53 Broad Street, Ludlow
Tel: 0584 4169

Somerset

Peter Murray Antique
Exports,
Station Road, Burton
Tel: 0749 813728

Edward A. Nowell,
12 Market Place, Wells
Tel: 0749 72415

Staffs

Richard Midwinter Antiques,
13 Brunswick Street,
Newcastle under Lyme
Tel: 0782 712483

Suffolk

David Gibbins Antiques,
21 Market Hill, Woodbridge
Tel: 039 43 3531

Hubbard Antiques,
16 St. Margaret's Green,
Ipswich
Tel: 0473 226033

Michael Moore Antiques,
The Barns, Clare Hall,
Cavendish Road, Clare
Tel: 0787 277510

Peppers Period Pieces (R),
23 Churchgate Street, Bury
St. Edmunds
Tel: 0284 768786

Randolph, 97 & 99 High
Street, Hadleigh
Tel: 0473 823789

Oswald Simpson,
Hall Street, Long Melford
Tel: 0787 77523

Surrey

Albany Antiques,
8-10 London Road, Hindhead
Tel: 0428 605528

Churchill Antiques Gallery
Ltd.,
65 Quarry Street, Guildford
Tel: 0483 506662

Richard Deryn Antiques,
7 Paved Court, The Green,
Richmond-upon-Thames
Tel: 081 948 5005

Dorking Desk Shop,
41 West Street, Dorking
Tel: 0306 883327/880535

Hampshires of Dorking,
51 West Street, Dorking
Tel: 0306 887076

J. Hartley Antiques,
186 High Street, Ripley
Tel: 0483 224318

Heath-Bullock,
8 Meadow, Godalming
Tel: 048 68 22562

Ripley Antiques,
67 High Street, Ripley
Tel: 0483 224981

Anthony Welling Antiques,
Broadway Barn, High Street,
Ripley
Tel: 0483 225384

Wych House Antiques,
Wych Hill, Woking
Tel: 0483 764636

Sussex

A27 Antiques Warehouses,
Chaucer Industrial Estate,
Dittons Road, Polegate
Tel: 032 12 7167/5301

Bursig of Arundel,
The Old Candle Factory,
Tarrant Street, Arundel
Tel: 0903 883456

Richard Davidson,
Lombard Street, Petworth
Tel: 0798 42508

Dycheling Antiques,34 High
Street, Ditchling, Hassocks
Tel: 0273 842929

The Grange Antiques, High
Street, Robertsbridge
Tel: 0580 880577

Humphry Antiques,
North Street, Petworth
Tel: 0798 43053

Lakeside Antiques,
The Old Cement Works,
South Heighton, Newhaven
Tel: 0273 513326

John G. Morris Ltd.,
Market Square, Petworth
Tel: 0798 42305

The Old Mint House, High
Street, Pevensey, Eastbourne
Tel: 0323 762337

David and Sarah Pullen
29/31 Sea Road, Bexhill
Tel: 0424 222035

Peter Semus Crafting
Antiques The Warehouse
Gladstone Lane, Portslade
Tel: 0273 420154

Village Antiques,
2 & 4 Cooden Sea Road,
Little Common, Bexhill
Tel: 042 43 5214

Tyne & Wear

Harold J. Carr Antiques,
Field House, Rickleton,
Washington
Tel: 091 388 6442

Warwickshire

Apollo Antiques,
The Saltisford, Birmingham
Road, Warwick
Tel: 0926 494746

Coleshill Antiques,
High Street, Coleshill
Tel: 0675 462931

Ferneyhough Antiques,
11 Chapel Street, Stratford-
upon-Avon
Tel: 0789 293928

Don Spencer Antiques,
Unit 2, 20 Cherry Street,
Warwick
Tel: 0926 499857

West Midlands

John Hubbard Antiques,
224-226 Court Oak Road,
Harborne, Birmingham
Tel 021 426 1694

Rock House Antiques &
Collectors Centre,
Rock House, The Rock,
Tettenhall, Wolverhampton
Tel: 0902 754995

Wilts

Avon Antiques,
26-27 Market Street,
Bradford-upon-Avon
Tel: 022 16 2052

Robert Bradley,
71 Brown Street, Salisbury
Tel: 0722 333677

Combe Cottage Antiques,
Castle Combe,
Nr. Chippenham
Tel: 0249 782250

Ian G. Hastie, BADA,
46 St. Ann Street, Salisbury
Tel: 0722 22957

Robert Kime Antiques,
Dene House, Lockeridge
Tel: 067 286 250

Melkssham Antiques,
8A King Street, Melksham
Tel: 0225 707291

Monkton Galleries, Hindon
Tel: 074 789 235

K. & A. Welch, 1a Church
Street, Warminster
Tel: 0985 214687/213433
(evenings)

Worcs

Gavina Ewart,
60-62 High Street, Broadway
Tel: 0386 853371

Yorks

Robert Aagaard Ltd.,
Frogmire House, Stockwell
Road, Knaresborough
Tel: 0423 864805
(Specialises in fireplaces)

Barmouth Court Antiques,
Abbeydale House, Barmouth
Road, Sheffield
Tel: 0742 582160/582672

Derbyshire Antiques Ltd.,
27 Montpellier Parade,
Harrogate
Tel: 0423 503115/564242

Bernard Dickinson,
Estate Yard, West Street
Tel: 0756 748257/749285

W. F. Greenwood & Sons
Ltd., 2 & 3 Crown Place,
Harrogate
Tel: 0423 504467

Old Rectory Antiques,
The Old Rectory, West
Heslerton, Malton
Tel: 094 45 364

Robert Morrison & Son,
Trentholme House,
131 The Mount, York
Tel: 0904 655394

R.M.S. Precious,
King William House, High
Street, Settle
Tel: 072 92 3946

Scotland

John Bell of Aberdeen Ltd.,
Balbrogie, By Blackburn,
Kinellar, Aberdeenshire
Tel: 0224 790209

Paul Couts Ltd.,
Linkfield House, 8-10 High
Street, Musselburgh
Tel: 031 665 7759

Letham Antiques,
20 Dundas Street, Edinburgh
Tel: 031 556 6565

Roy Sim Antiques,
21 Allan Street, Blairgowrie,
Perthshire
Tel: 0250 3860/3700

Unicorn Antiques,
65 Dundas Street, Edinburgh
Tel: 031 556 7176

PINE FURNITURE

London

Abbots Antiques,
109 Kirkdale, SE26
Tel: 081 699 1363/5729

Adams Antiques,
47 Chalk Farm Road, NW1
Tel: 071 267 9241

At the Sign of Chest of
Drawers, 281 Upper Street,
Islington N1
Tel: 071 359 5909

The Barewood Company,
58 Mill Lane, W. Hampstead,
NW6
Tel: 071 435 7244

Islington Artefacts,
12-14 Essex Road, Islington,
N1
Tel: 071 226 6867

Scallywag,
187-191 Clapham Road,
Stockwell, SW9
Tel: 071 274 0300

This & That (Furniture)
50-51 Chalk Farm Road,
NW1
Tel: 071 267 5433

Avon

Abbas Combe Pine,
4 Upper Maudlin Street,
Bristol
Tel: 0272 299023

Pennard House Antiques,
3/4 Piccadilly, London Road,
Bath
Tel: 0225 313791

Bucks

For Pine, 340 Berkhampstead Road, Chesham
Tel: 0494 776119

The Pine Merchants, 52 High Street, Gt. Missenden
Tel: 024 06 2002

Cornwall

Pydar Pine, People's Palace, off Pydar Street, Truro
Tel: 0872 510485
Home: 0637 872034

Devon

The Ark Antiques, 76 Fore Street, Topsham
Tel: 0392 876251

Chancery Antiques, 8-10 Barrington Street, Tiverton
Tel: 0884 252416/253190

Country Cottage Furniture, The Old Smithy, Back Street, Modbury
Tel: 0548 830888

Fine Pine, Woodland Road, Harbertonford
Tel: 080 423 465

Glos

Bed of Roses Antiques, 12 Prestbury Road, Cheltenham
Tel: 0242 231918

Country Homes, 61 Long Street, Tetbury
Tel: 0666 502342

Gloucester House Antiques, Market Place, Fairford
Tel: 0285 712790

Denzil Verey Antiques, Barnsley House, Barnsley, Nr. Cirencester
Tel: 0285 740402

Hants

C. W. Buckingham, Twin Firs, Southampton Road, Cadnam
Tel: 0703 812122

Craftsman Furniture Ltd., Castle Trading Estate, Portchester, Portsmouth
Tel: 0705 219911

Grayshott Pine, Crossways Road, Grayshott, Hindhead
Tel: 0428 607478

Millers of Chelsea Antiques Ltd., Netherbrook House, 86 Christchurch Road, Ringwood
Tel: 0425 472062

The Pine Cellars, 39 Jewry Street, Winchester
Tel: 0962 867014

The Pine Co., 104 Christchurch Road, Ringwood
Tel: 0425 473932

Hereford & Worcs

Jennings of Leominster, 30 Bridge Street, Leominster
Tel: 0568 2946

La Barre Ltd., The Place, 116 South Street, Leominster
Tel: 0568 4315

Marshall Bennett Restorations, Eagle Lane, High Street, Cleobury, Mortimer, Nr. Kidderminster
Tel: 0299 270553

S. W. Antiques, Abbey Showrooms, Newlands, Pershore
Tel: 0386 555580

Herts

Out of Town, 21 Ware Road, Hertford
Tel: 0992 582848

Humberside

Bell Antiques, 68 Harold Street, Grimsby
Tel: 0472 695110

The Hull Pine Co., 2/6 Bean Street, Anlaby Road, Hull
Tel: 0482 227169

Paul Wilson Pine Furniture, Perth Street West, Hull
Tel: 0482 447923/448607

Kent

Country Pine Antique Co., The Barn, Upper Bush Farm, Upper Bush, Nr. Rochester
Tel: 0634 717982

Empire Antiques, The Old Council Yard, Gazen Salts, Strand Street, Sandwich
Tel: 0304 614474

Penny Lampard, 31 High Street, Headcorn
Tel: 0622 890682

The Old Bakery Antiques, St. Davids Bridge, Cranbrook
Tel: 0580 713103

Old English Pine, 100 Sandgate High Street, Folkestone
Tel: 0303 48560

The Plough Pine Shop, High Street, Eastry, Dover
Tel:0304 617418

Traditional Furniture, 248 Seabrook Road, Seabrook, Hythe
Tel: 0303 239931

Up Country, The Corn Stores, 68 St. John's Road, Tunbridge Wells
Tel: 0892 523341

Lancs

Cottage Furniture, Queen Street, Farnworth, Bolton
Tel: 0204 700853

Enloc Antiques, Birchenlee Mill, Lenches Road, Colne
Tel: 0282 861417

Utopia Pine, Holme Mills, Carnforth
Tel: 0524 781739

Leics

Richard Kimbell Antiques, Riverside, Market Harborough
Tel: 08584 33444

Riverside Trading, Riverside Industrial Estate, Market Harborough
Tel: 0858 46110/464825

Lincs

Allens Antiques, Moor Farm, Stapleford
Tel: 052 285 392

Stow Away (UK) Ltd., 2 Langton Hill, Horncastle
Tel: 065 82 7445

Norfolk

Rossendale Antiques (Ian Shaw), Rossendale, The Street, Rickinghall, Diss
Tel: 0379 898485

Northants

Acorn Antiques, The Old Mill, Moat Lane,Towcester
Tel: 0327 52788

The Country Pine Shop, Northampton Road, West Haddon
Tel: 0788 510430

Oxon

Julie Strachey, Southfield Farm, Weston-on-the-Green
Tel: 0869 50833/2

Somerset

Chalon, Hambridge Mill, Hambridge, Nr Langport
Tel: 0458 252374

Crewkerne Antiques Centre, 42 East Street, Crewkerne
Tel: 0460 76755

Peter Murray Antique Exports, Station Road, Bruton
Tel: 0749 813728

Pennard House Antiques, East Pennard, Shepton Mallet
Tel: 074986 266

Staffs

Anvil Antiques Ltd., Cross Mills, Cross Street, Leek
Tel: 0538 371657

Aspleys Antiques, Compton Mill, Compton, Leek
Tel: 0538 373396

Directmoor Ltd., The Coppice Farm, Nr Moorcourt, Oakamoor
Tel: 0538 702419

Gemini Trading, Limes Mill, Abbotts Road, Leek
Tel: 0538 387834

Johnsons, Park Works, Park Road, Leek
Tel: 0538 386745

Stone Wares, The Stripped Pine Shop, 24 Radford Street, Stone
Tel: 0785 815000

Suffolk

Michael Moore Antiques, The Barns, Clare Hall, Cavendish Road, Clare
Tel: 0787 277510

Surrey

Richard Deryn Antiques, 7 Paved Court, The Green, Richmond
Tel: 081 948 5005

Grayshott Pine, Crossways Road, Grayshott, Hindhead
Tel: 0428 607478

Manor Antiques, 2 The New Shops, Old Woking
Tel: 0483 724666

Odiham Antiques, High Street, Compton, Guildford
Tel: 0483 810215

F. & L. Warren, The Sawmills, Firgrove Hill, Farnham
Tel: 0252 726713

Wych House Antiques, Wych Hill, Woking
Tel: 0483 764636

Sussex

Drummer Pine, Hailsham Road, Herstmonceux
Tel: 0323 833542/833661

Hillside Antiques, Units 12-13, Lindfield Enterprise Park, Lewes Road, Lindfield
Tel: 04447 3042

Bob Hoare Antiques, Unit Q, Phoenix Place, North Street, Lewes
Tel: 0273 480557

Ann Lingard, Ropewalk Antiques, Ropewalk, Rye
Tel: 0797 223486

Polegate Antique Centre, Station Road, Polegate
Tel: 0323 485277

Graham Price Antiques Ltd., A27 Antiques Complex, Unit 4, Chaucer Industrial Estate, Dittons Road, Polegate
Tel: 0323 487167/487681

Touchwood (Mervyn & Sue), The Square, Herstmonceux
Tel: 0323 832020

Michael Wakelin & Helen Lindfield, 10 New Street, Petworth
Tel: 0798 42417

Wilts

Ray Coggins Antiques, The Old Brewery, Newtown, Bradford-on-Avon
Tel: 02216 3431

Yorks

Early Days, 7 Kings Court, Pateley Bridge, Harrogate
Tel: 0423 711661

Michael Green, Library House, Regent Parade, Harrogate
Tel: 0423 560452

Manor Barn Pine, Burnside Mill, Main Street, Addingham, Ilkley
Tel: 0943 830176

Pine Finds, The Old Corn Mill, Bishop Monkton, Harrogate
Tel: 0765 677159

Smith & Smith Designs,
58A Middle Street North,
Driffield
Tel: 0377 46321

Ireland
Bygones of Ireland,
Westport Antiques Centre,
Lodge Road, Westport,
County Mayo
Tel: 010 353 098 26132

Delvin Farm Galleries,
Gormonston, Co. Meath
Tel: 010 3531 841 2285

Albert Forsythe, Mill House,
66 Carsontown Road,
Saintfield, Co. Down
Tel: 0238 510398

Honans Antiques,
Crowe Street, Gort,
County Galway
Tel: 010 353 9131 407

Luckpenny Antiques,
Kilmurray House, Shinrone,
Birr, Co. Offaly
Tel: 010 353 505 47134

Somerville Antiques,
Moysdale, Killanley,
Ballina, Co. Mayo
Tel: 010 353 96 36275

Old Court Pine, The Square,
Collon, Co. Louth
Tel: 010 353 41 26270

Scotland
A & P Steadman, Unit 1,
Hatston Industrial Estate,
Kirkwall, Orkney
Tel: 0856 5040

Wales
Chapel House Antiques,
(& 32 Pentood Industrial
Estate), Pendre, Cardigan,
Dyfed
Tel: 0239 614868/613268

Heritage Restorations,
Maes y Glydfa, Llanfair,
Caereinion, Welshpool,
Powys
Tel: 0938 810384

Maclean, Dudley & Marie
Thorpe, Tiradda,
Llansadwrn, Dyfed
Tel: 0550 777509

Pine Furniture, Station
Stores, Station Yard,
Goodwick, Fishguard
Tel: 0348 872634

GLASS
London
Asprey PLC,
165-169 New Bond Street,
W1
Tel: 071 493 6767

Phyllis Bedford Antiques,
3 The Galleries, Camden
Passage, N1
Tel: 071 354 1332 or Home:
081 882 3189

Christine Bridge,
78 Castelnau, SW13
Tel: 081 741 5501

W. G. T. Burne (Antique
Glass) Ltd.,
11 Elystan Street, SW3
Tel: 071 589 6074

Delomosne & Son Ltd.,
4 Camden Hill Road, W8
Tel: 071 937 1804

East Gates Antiques,
Stand G006,
Alfies Antique Market,
13-25 Church Street, NW8
Tel: 071 724 5650

Eila Grahame,
97C Kensington Church
Street, W8
Tel: 071 727 4132

Lloyds of Westminster,
5A Motcomb Street, SW1
Tel: 071 235 1010

S. W. Parry (Old Glass),
Stand A4-A5 Westbourne
Antique Arcade,
113 Portobello Road, W11
Tel: 081 740 0248

Pryce & Brise Antiques,
79 Moore Park Road,
Fulham, SW6
Tel: 071 736 1864

Gerald Sattin Ltd.,
25 Burlington Arcade,
Piccadilly, W1
Tel: 071 493 6557

Mark J. West,
Cobb Antiques Ltd.,
39B High Street,
Wimbledon Village, SW19
Tel: 081 946 2811

R. Wilkinson & Son, (R)
5 Catford Hill, SE6 4NU
Tel: 081 314 1080

Avon
Somervale Antiques,
6 Radstock Road,
Midsomer Norton, Bath
Tel. 0761 412686

Dorset
A. & D. Antiques,
21 East Street,
Blandford Forum
Tel: 0258 455643

Quarter Jack Antiques,
The Quarter Jack,
Bridge Street,
Sturminster Newton
Tel: 0258 72558

Hants
Stockbridge Antiques,
High Street, Stockbridge
Tel: 0264 810829

Todd & Austin Antiques &
Fine Art, 2 Andover Road,
Winchester
Tel: 0962 869824

Kent
Castle Antiques,
1 London Road, Westerham
Tel: 0959 62492

Somerset
Abbey Antiques,
52-54 High Street,
Glastonbury
Tel: 0458 31694

Surrey
Shirley Warren,
333B Limpsfield Road,
Sanderstead
Tel: 081 651 5180

Sussex
Rusthall Antiques,
Chateaubriand Antique
Centre, High Street,
Burwash
Tel: 0435 882535

Warwickshire
Sharon Ball,
Unit 1, Stratford-on-Avon
Antique Centre, Ely Street,
Stratford-on-Avon
Tel: 0789 204180

Scotland
William MacAdam,
86 Pilrig Street,
Edinburgh
Tel: 031 553 1364

GRAMOPHONES, PHONOGRAPHS & RADIOS

Avon
The Vintage Wireless Co.
Tudor House, Cossham
Street, Mangotsfield, Bristol
Tel: 0272 565472

Devon
Brian Taylor Antiques,
24 Molesworth Road, Stoke,
Plymouth
Tel: 0752 569061

Yorks
Clocks & Gramophones,
11 Walmgate, York
Tel: 0904 611924

ICONS
London
Maria Andipa, Icon Gallery,
162 Walton Street, SW3
Tel: 071 589 2371

Mark Gallery, 9 Porchester
Place, Marble Arch, W2
Tel: 071 262 4906

INSURANCE & LOSS ADJUSTERS

London
Cameron Richard & Smith
Insurance Services,
Boundary House, 7-17 Jewry
Street, EC3
Tel: 071 488 4554

Cunningham Hart,
59 Compton Road, NW2
Tel: 071 354 3504

JEWELLERY
London
Hirsh Fine Jewels, Diamond
House, Hatton Garden, EC1
Tel: 071 405 6080

Glos
South Bar Antiques
(Cameos), Digbeth Street,
Stow-on-the-Wold
Tel: 0451 30236

Hereford & Worcs
B B M Jewellery,
8 & 9 Lion Street,
Kidderminster
Tel: 0562 744118

Old Curiosity Antiques,
11 Tower Buildings,
Blackwell Street,
Kidderminster
Tel: 0562 742859

Herts
Forget Me Not Antiques,
23 George Street,
St. Albans
Tel: 0923 26472

Kent
Castle Antiques,
1 London Road, Westerham
Tel: 0959 62492

Norfolk
Peter & Valerie Howkins,
39, 40 & 135 King Street,
Great Yarmouth
Tel: 0493 844639

Somerset
Edward A Nowell,
12 Market Place, Wells
Tel: 0749 72415

Sussex
Rusthall Antiques,
Chateaubriand Antique
Centre, High Street,
Burwash
Tel: 0435 882535/0892 20668
(evenings)

Scotland
Bow-Well Antiques,
Monkton House, Old
Craighall, Musselburgh
Tel: 031 665 5733

KITCHENALIA
Lancashire
Kitchenalia, 36 Inglewhite
Road, Longridge, Nr. Preston
Tel: 077 478 5411

Shropshire
Tiffany Antiques,
Unit 3, Shrewsbury Antique
Centre, 15 Princess House,
The Square, Shrewsbury
Tel: (Home) 0270-257425
also at:
Unit 15, Shrewsbury Antique
Market, Frankwell Quay,
Warehouse, Shrewsbury
Tel: 0270 257425

Surrey
Grayshott Pine, Crossways
Road, Grayshott, Hindhead,
Surrey
Tel: 0428 607478

Wales
Chapel House Antiques, 32
Pentwood Industrial Estate,
Pendre, Cardigan, Dyfed
Tel: 0239 614868/613268

LIGHTING

London

Judy Jones 194 Westbourne Grove, W11
Tel: 071 229 6866

The Lamp Gallery,
355 New Kings Road, SW6
Tel: 071 736 6188

Hereford & Worcester

Fritz Fryer,
12 Brookend Street, Ross-on-Wye, Hereford
Tel: 0989 67416

Hertfordshire

J. Marsden, Magic Lanterns and Vestalia Antique Lighting Ltd., 23 George Street, St. Albans
Tel: 0727 65680/53032

LOCKS & KEYS

Notts

The Keyhole, Dragonwyck (R), Far Back Lane, Farnsfield
Tel: 0623 882590

MARINE ANTIQUES

Devon

Temeraire, 63 Brownston Street, Modbury
Tel: 0548 830317

Essex

Littlebury Antiques,
58/60 Fairycroft Road, Saffron Walden
Tel: 0799 27961

METALWARE

London

Christopher Bangs (by appointment only)
Tel: 071 223 5676

Jack Casimir Ltd.,
The Brass Shop, 23 Pembridge Road, Wll
Tel: 071 727 8643

Arthur Davidson Ltd.,
78-79 Jermyn Street, SWl
Tel: 071 930 6687

Alistair Sampson Antiques,
156 Brompton Road, SW3
Tel: 071 589 5272

Avon

Cottage Antiques,
The Old Post Office, Langford Place, Langford, Nr. Bristol
Tel: 0934 862597

Beds

Christopher Sykes Antiques, The Old Parsonage Woburn, Milton Keynes
Tel: 052 525 259/467

Bucks

Albert Bartram,
177 Hivings Hill, Chesham
Tel: 0494 783271

Cumbria

Stable Antiques,
Wheelwright Cottage, 15-16 Back Lane, Sedbergh
Tel: 05396 20251

Glos

Country Life Antiques,
Grey House, The Square, Stow-on-the-Wold
Tel: 0451 31564

Oxon

Robin Bellamy Ltd.,
97 Corn Street, Witney
Tel: 0993 704793

Elizabethan House Antiques,
28 & 55 High Street, Dorchester-on-Thames
Tel: 0865 340079

Key Antiques, 11 Horse Fair, Chipping Norton
Tel: 0608 643777

Suffolk

Brookes Forge Flempton (R), Flempton, Bury St. Edmunds
Tel: 02848 728473
0449 781376 home

Sussex

Michael Wakelin & Helen Linfield, 10 New Street, Petworth
Tel: 0798 42417

Wilts

Avon Antiques,
26-27 Market Street, Bradford-on Avon
Tel: 022 16 2052

Combe Cottage Antiques,
Castle Combe, Chippenham
Tel: 0249 782250

Rupert Gentle Antiques,
The Manor House, Milton Lilbourne, Nr. Pewsey
Tel: 0672 63344

Yorks

Windsor House Antiques
(Leeds) Ltd.,
18-20 Benson Street, Leeds
Tel: 0532 444666

MUSICAL INSTRUMENTS

London

Mayflower Antiques,
117 Portobello Road, W11
Tel: 071 727 0381
(Sats only 7am-3pm)

Avon

Piano Export, Bridge Road, Kingswood, Bristol
Tel: 0272 568300

Essex

Mayflower Antiques,
2 Una Road, Parkeston, Harwich
Tel: 0255 504079

Glos

Vanbrugh House Antiques,
Park Street, Stow-on-the-Wold
Tel: 0451 30797

Oxon

Laurie Leigh Antiques,
36 High Street, Oxford
Tel: 0865 244197

Somerset

Shelagh Berryman, Musical Boxes, 15 The Market Place, Wells
Tel: 0749 76203

Sussex

Sound Instruments, Worth Farm, Little Horsted, Nr. Uckfield
Tel: 0825 750567

ORIENTAL

London

Kotobuki, F10 Alfies Antique Market, Church Street,NW8
Tel: 071 402 0723

Sussex

Linda Loveland Restorations, 18-20 Prospect Place, Hastings
Tel: 0424 441608

PORCELAIN

London

Armin B Allen, 3 Bury Street, St. James's , SW1
Tel: 071 930 4732/0729

Albert Amor Ltd.,
37 Bury Street, St. James's, SW1
Tel: 071 930 2444

Antique Porcelain Co. Ltd.,
149 New Bond Street, W1
Tel: 071 629 1254

Susan Becker,
18 Lower Richmond Road, SW15
Tel: 081 788 9082

David Brower Antiques,
113 Kensington Church Street, W8
Tel: 071 221 4155

Cale Antiques, 24 Cale Street, Chelsea Green, SW3
Tel: 071 589 6146

Belinda Coote Antiques,
29 Holland Street, W8
Tel: 071 937 3924

Craven Antiques, 17 Garson House, Gloucester Terrace, W2
Tel: 071 262 4176

Marilyn Delion, 288 Westbourne Grove, Stand 7, Portobello Market, W11
(Sat only by appointment)
Tel: 071 937 3377

Delomosne & Son Ltd.,
4 Campden Hill Road, W8
Tel: 071 937 1804

H & W Deutsch Antiques,
111 Kensington Church Street, W8
Tel: 071 727 5984

Graham & Oxley (Antiques) Ltd. 101 Kensington Church Street, W8
Tel: 071 229 1850

Grosvenor Antiques Ltd.,
27 Holland Street, W8
Tel: 071 937 8649

Harcourt Antiques,
5 Harcourt Street, W1
Tel: 071 723 5919

Hoff Antiques Ltd.,
66A Kensington Church Street, W8
Tel: 071 229 5516

Klaber & Klaber, 2A Bedford Gardens, Kensington Church Street, W8
Tel: 071 727 4573

Marion Langham,
41A Lower Belgrave Street, SW1
Tel: 071 730 1002

Mayfair Gallery,
46 South Audley Street, W1
Tel: 071 499 5315

Mercury Antiques,
1 Ladbroke Road, W11
Tel: 071 727 5106

St. Jude's Antiques,
107 Kensington Church Street, W8
Tel: 071 727 8737

Gerald Sattin Ltd., 14 King Street, St. James's, SW1
Tel: 071 493 6557

Jean Sewell (Antiques) Ltd.,
3 Campden Street, Kensington Church Street, W8
Tel: 071 727 3122

Simon Spero,
109 Kensington Church Street, W8
Tel: 071 727 7413

Constance Stobo,
31 Holland Street, W8
Tel: 071 937 6282

Nicholas Vandekar Ltd.,
138 Brompton Road, SW3
Tel: 071 589 8481/3398

Venner's Antiques,
7 New Cavendish Street, Wl
Tel: 071 935 0184

Avon

Andrew Dando, 4 Wood Street, Queen Square, Bath
Tel: 0225 422702

Brian & Angela Downes, 9 Broad Street, Bath
Tel: 0225 465352

Berks

The Old School Antiques, Dorney, Windsor
Tel: 0628 603247

Cornwall

Mrs. Margaret Chesterton, 33 Pentewan Road, St. Austell
Tel: 0726 72926

Devon

Paul & Dorothy Stockman, Newton Abbot Antiques, 55 East Street, Newton Abbot
Tel: 0803 215188

David J. Thorn, 2 High Street, Budleigh Salterton
Tel: 039 54 2448

Glos

Gloucester House Antiques, Market Place, Fairford
Tel: 0285 712790

L. Greenwold, Digbeth, Digbeth Street, Stow-on-the-Wold
Tel: 0451 30398

Pamela Rowan, High Street, Blockley, Nr. Moreton-in-Marsh
Tel: 0386 700280

Studio Antiques Ltd., Bourton-on-the-Water
Tel: 0451 20352

Hants

Gerald Austin Antiques, 2A Andover Road, Winchester
Tel: 0962 869824 Ext 2

Goss & Crested China Ltd., 62 Murray Road, Horndean
Tel: 0705 597440

Rogers of Alresford, 16 West Street, Alresford
Tel: 0962 732862

Hereford & Worcs

Antiques Centre, 11 Tower Buildings, Blackwell Street, Kidderminster
Tel: 0562 829000

Gavina Ewart, 60-62 High Street, Broadway
Tel: 0386 853371

M. Lees & Sons, Tower House, Severn Street, Worcester
Tel: 0905 26620

Kent

Beaubush Antiques, 95 Sandgate High Street, Folkestone
Tel: 0303 49099

Castle Antiques, No.l. London Road, Westerham
Tel: 0959 62492

The History in Porcelain Collector, High Street, Shoreham Village, Nr. Sevenoaks
Tel: 09592 3416

Kent Cottages Antiques, 39 High Street, Rolvenden
Tel: 0580 241719

Steppes Hill Farm Antiques, Stockbury, Sittingbourne
Tel: 0795 842205

Wakefield Ceramic Fairs (Fred Hynds), 1 Fountain Road, Strood, Rochester
Tel: 0634 723461

W.W. Warner (Antiques) Ltd., The Green, Brasted
Tel: 0959 63698

Lancs

Burnley Antiques & Fine Arts Ltd., 336A Colne Road, Burnley
Tel: 0282 20143/65172

Leics

Charnwood Antiques, Coalville, Leicester
Tel: 0530 38530

Norfolk

T.C.S. Brooke, The Grange, Wroxham
Tel: 0603 782644

Margaret Corson, Irstead Manor, Neatishead
Tel: 0692 630274

Peter Jackson Antiques, 3 Market Place, Brackley
Tel: 0280 703259/ 0993 882415

Notts

Breck Antiques, 726 Mansfield Road, Woodthorpe
Tel: 0602 605263

Oxon

Castle Antiques, Lamb Arcade, Wallingford, Oxon
Tel: 0491 35166

David John Ceramics, 11 Acre End Street, Eynsham, Oxford
Tel: 0865 880786

Shropshire

Castle Gate Antiques, 15 Castle Gate, Shrewsbury
Tel: 0743 61011 evenings

F.C. Manser & Son Ltd., 53-54 Wyle Cop, Shrewsbury
Tel: 0743 51120

Teme Valley Antiques, 1 The Bull Ring, Ludlow
Tel: 0584 874686

Tudor House Antiques, 33 High Street, Ironbridge
Tel: 0952 433237

Peter Wain, 7 Nantwich Road, Woore
Tel: 0630 817118

Suffolk

Crafers Antiques, The Hill, Wickham Market, Woodbridge
Tel: 0728 747347

Surrey

Elias Clark Antiques Ltd., 1 The Cobbles, Bletchingley
Tel: 0883 843714

Whittington Galleries, 22 Woodend, Sutton
Tel: 081 644 9327

Sussex

Barclay Antiques, 7 Village Mews, Little Common, Bexhill-on-Sea
Tel: 0797 222734 home

Geoffrey Godden, Chinaman, 17-19 Crescent Road, Worthing
Tel: 0903 35958

William Hockley Antiques, East Street, Petworth
Tel: 0798 43172

Leonard Russell, 21 King's Avenue, Newhaven
Tel: 0273 515153

Warwickshire

Coleshill Antiques, High Street, Coleshill
Tel: 0675 462931

Wilts

The China Hen, 9 Woolley Street, Bradford-on-Avon
Tel: 022 16 3369

Mark Collier Antiques,High Street, Downton
Tel: 0725 21068

Melksham Antiques, 8A King Street, Melksham
Tel: 0225 707291

Yorks

Angela Charlesworth, 99 Dodworth Road, Barnsley
Tel: 0226 282097/203688

David Love, 10 Royal Parade, Harrogate
Tel: 0423 565797

Nanbooks, Roundabout, Duke Street, Settle
Tel: 072 92 3324

Wales

Station Stores, Station Yard, Goodwick, Fishguard
Tel: 0348 872634

POTTERY

London

Nicolaus Boston, Chenil Galleries, 181-183 Kings Road, SW3
Tel: 071 352 8790

Britannia, Stand 101, Gray's Market, 58 Davies Street, W1
Tel: 071 629 6772

Cale Antiques, 24 Cale Street, SW3
Tel: 071 589 6146

Gerald Clark Antiques, 1 High Street, Mill Hill Village, NW7
Tel: 081 906 0342/

Belinda Coote Antiques, 29 Holland Street, W8
Tel: 071 937 3924

Marilyn Delion, 228 Westbourne Grove, Stand 7, Portobello Market, W11 (Sat by appointment only)
Tel: 071 937 3377

Richard Dennis, 144 Kensington Church Street, W8
Tel: 071 727 2061

Graham & Oxley (Antiques) Ltd., 101 Kensington Church Street, W8
Tel: 071 229 1850

Jonathan Horne, 66C Kensington Church Street, W8
Tel: 071 221 5658

Valerie Howard, 131e Kensington Church Street, W8
Tel: 071 792 9702

J. & J. May, 40 Kensington Church Street, W8
Tel: 071 937 3575

Mercury Antiques, 1 Ladbroke Road, W11
Tel: 071 727 5106

Sue Norman, L4 Antiquarius, 135 Kings Road, SW3
Tel: 071 352 7217

Jacqueline Oosthuizen, Shop 12, Georgian Village, N1 (Wed & Sat) Tel: 071 226 5893
23 Cale Street, Chelsea
Tel: 071 352 6071/376 3852

Rogers de Rin, 76 Royal Hospital Road, SW3
Tel: 071 352 9007

781

Alistair Sampson Antiques,
156 Brompton Road, SW3
Tel: 071 589 5272

Constance Stobo,
31 Holland Street, W8
Tel: 071 937 6282

Oliver Sutton Antiques,
34C Kensington Church
Street, W8
Tel: 071 937 0633

Nicholas Vandekar Ltd.,
138 Brompton Road, SW3
Tel: 071 589 8481/3398

Avon
Andrew Dando, 4 Wood
Street, Queen Square, Bath
Tel: 0225 5422702

Robert Pugh,
Tel: 0225 314713

Cornwall
Mrs Margaret Chesterton,
33 Pentewan Road, St.
Austell
Tel: 0826 72926

Cumbria
Kendal Studio Pottery,
2-3 Wildman Street, Kendal
Tel: 0539 723291

Devon
Paul & Dorothy Stockman,
Newton Abbot Antiques, 55
East Street, Newton Abbot
Tel: 0803 215188

David J. Thorn, 2 High
Street, Budleigh Salterton
Tel: 039 54 2448

Hants
Goss & Crested China Ltd.,
62 Murray Road, Horndean
Tel: 0705 597440

Millers of Chelsea,
Netherbrook House,
Christchurch Road,
Ringwood
Tel: 0425 472062

Rogers of Alresford,
16 West Street, Alresford
Tel: 0962 732862

Humberside
The Crested China
Company, The Station
House, Driffield
Tel: 0377 47042

Kent
Beaubush House Antiques,
95 High Street, Sandgate,
Folkestone
Tel: 0303 49099

W. W. Warner (Antiques)
Ltd., The Green, Brasted,
Tel: 0959 63698

Lancs
Roy W. Bunn Antiques,
34/36 Church Street,
Barnoldswick, Colne
Tel: 0282 813703

Burnley Antiques & Fine
Arts Ltd., (appts only)
336A Colne Road, Burnley
Tel: 0282 65172

Norfolk
Margaret Corson, Irstead
Manor, Neatishead
Tel: 0692 630274

Northants
Heyford Antiques, 9 Church
Street, Nether Heyford
Tel: 0327 40749

Shropshire
Peter Wain, 7 Nantwich
Road, Woore
Tel: 0630 817118

Suffolk
Crafers Antiques,
The Hill, Wickham Market,
Woodbridge
Tel: 0728 747347

Surrey
Elias Clark Antiques Ltd., 1
The Cobbles, Bletchingley
Tel: 0883 843714

Whittington Galleries,
22 Woodend, Sutton
Tel: 081 644 9327

Sussex
Ron Beech,
1 Brambledean Road,
Portslade
Tel: 0273 423355

Ray & Diane Ginns,
PO Box 129,
East Grinstead
Tel: 0342 326041

Leonard Russell,
21 King's Avenue, Newhaven
Tel: 0273 515153

Tyne & Wear
Ian Sharp Antiques,
23 Front Street,
Tynemouth
Tel: 091 296 0656

Warwickshire
Beehive Antiques,
125 Warwick Road,
Kenilworth
Tel: 0926 55253

Lions Den, 31 Henley Street
Stratford-upon-Avon
Tel: 0789 415802

Wilts
Bratton Antiques,
Market Place, Westbury
Tel: 0373 823021

Yorks
The Antique & Bargain
Store, 6 Sunny Bar,
Doncaster
Tel: 0302 344857

Doncaster Sales & Exchange,
20 Copley Road, Doncaster
Tel: 0302 344857

Nanbooks, Roundabout,
Duke Street, Settle
Tel: 072 92 3324

Scotland
Bow-Well Antiques,
Monkton House, Old
Craighall, Musselburgh
Tel: 031 665 5733

Wales
Chapel House Antiques, 32
Pentwood Industrial Estate,
Pendre, Cardigan, Dyfed
Tel: 0239 614868/613268

Howards Antiques,
10 Alexandra Road,
Aberystwyth, Dyfed
Tel: 0970 624973

Islwyn Watkins,1 High
Street, Knighton, Powys
Tel: 0547 520145/528940

Isle of Man
Rushton Ceramics,
Tynwald Mills, St. Johns
Tel: 0624 801618

RESTORATION

London
K. Restorations,
2A Ferdinand Street, Chalk
Farm, NW1
Tel: 071 482 4021

Plowden & Smith,
190 St. Ann's Hill, SW18
Tel: 081 874 4005

Cumbria
Domino Restorations,
129 Craig Walk, Windermere
Tel: 05394 45751

Devon
Alastair Paul & Co. Ltd.,
Challenge House,
12 Walkham Business Park,
Burrington Way, Plymouth
Tel: 0752 770049

Durham
Eden House Antiques,
10 Staindrop Road, West
Auckland
Tel: 0388 833013

Essex
Clive Beardall, 104B High
Street,Maldon
Tel: 0621 857890

Millside Antique Restoration,
China & Porcelain Restorers,
Parndon Mill Lane, Harlow
Tel: 0279 428148

Glos
S. Rouse & Co.,
99 Gloucester Road,
Cheltenham
Tel: 0242 234361

Humberside
Adrian J. Black,
Alkira, Main Road,
Barnoldby-le-Beck, Grimsby
Tel: 0472 824823

Kent
Antique Restoration &
Polishing
Tel: 0797 270250

Cleaning & Maintenance
Tel: 0227 762822/
071 266 1851

K. J. Garrett (Clocks)
48 Henley Fields
St. Michaels, Tenterden
Tel: 05806 4485

Lincs
Lincolnshire Conservation
Studio,
Metals, frame and ceramic
restoration,
Museum of Lincolnshire Life,
Burton Road, Lincoln
Tel: 0522 533207

Merseyside
Ceramic Restoration Studios,
3 John Street, Biddulph,
Stoke on Trent
Tel: 0782 517849

Sussex
Richard Davidson, Lombard
Street, Petworth
Tel: 0798 42508/43354

Surrey
Robin J. Johnson,
Unit 2, Church Street,
Dorking
Tel: 0306 884244

Wiltshire
Cooks of Marlborough,
High Trees House
Savernake Forest
Marlborough
Tel: 0672 513017/515745

Scotland
Traditional Antique
Restoration, The Stable,
Altyre Estate, Forres Moray
Tel: 0309 72572

SCENT BOTTLES

Kent
Kent Cottage Antiques,
39 High Street, Rolvenden
Tel: 0580 241719

SCIENTIFIC
INSTRUMENTS

London
Jilliana Ranicar-Breese,
Martin Breese International,
8 Portwine Arcade, 175
Portobello Road (Sat only)
Tel: 071 727 9378
(Optical Toys/Illusion)

Arthur Davidson Ltd.,
78-79 Jermyn Street, SW1
Tel: 071 930 6687

Mariner Antiques Ltd.,
55 Curzon Street, W1
Tel: 071 499 0171

Mayflower Antiques,
117 Portobello Road, W11
Tel: 071 727 0381
(Sats only 7am-3pm)

Arthur Middleton Ltd., 12
New Row, Covent Garden
WC2
Tel: 071 836 7042/7062

Trevor Philip & Sons Ltd.,
75A Jermyn Street,
St. James's, SW1
Tel: 071 930 2954/5

David Weston Ltd.,
44 Duke Street,
St. James's, SW1
Tel: 071 839 1051-2-3

Harriet Wynter Ltd.,
(by appointment only)50
Redcliffe Road, SW10
Tel: 071 352 6494

Beds
Christopher Sykes Antiques,
The Old Parsonage, Woburn,
Milton Keynes
Tel: 0525 290259/290467

Essex
Mayflower Antiques,
2 Una Road, Parkeston,
Harwich
Tel: 0255 504079

Glos
Country Life Antiques,
Grey House, The Square,
Stow-on-the-Wold
Tel: 0451 31564

Kent
Hadlow Antiques,
No.1 The Pantiles,
Tunbridge Wells
Tel: 0892 29858

Norfolk
Margaret Corson,
Irstead Manor, Neatishead
Tel: 0692 630274

Humbleyard Fine Art,
3 Fish Hill, Holt,
Tel: 0263 713362

Turret House (Dr. D. H.
Morgan) 27 Middleton
Street, Wymondham
Tel: 0953 603462

Yorks
Arcadia Antiques,
The Ginnel Antique Centre,
Harrogate
Tel: 0704 64441

Scotland
Bow-Well Antiques,
Monkton House, Old
Craighall, Musselburgh
Tel: 031 665 5733

SECURITY

London
Aid-Call, Art Security
Systems,
363 Fulham Road, West
Brompton, SW10
Tel: 071 352 2822

Simba Security Systems
Ltd., Security House,
Occupation Road, SE17
Tel: 071 703 0485

Hampshire
Securikey, PO Box 18
Aldershot
Tel: 0252 311888/9

Oxon
Elsec Security &
Conservation Products,
Littlemore Scientific Eng.
Co., Railway Lane,
Littlemore, Oxford
Tel: 0865 747437

SILVER

London
Asprey PLC, 165-169 New
Bond Street, W1
Tel: 071 493 6767

N. Bloom & Son (Antiques)
Ltd., 40-41 Conduit Street,
W1
Tel: 071 629 5060

Bond Street Galleries,
111-112 New Bond Street,
W1
Tel: 071 493 6180

J.H Bourdon-Smith,
24 Mason's Yard, Duke
Street, St. James's, SW1
Tel: 071 839 4714

H. & W. Deutsch Antiques,
111 Kensington Church
Street, W8
Tel: 071 727 5984

Howard Jones,
43 Kensington Church
Street, W8
Tel: 071 937 4359

S. J. Phillips Ltd.,
139 New Bond Street, W1
Tel: 071 629 6261/2

Gerald Sattin Ltd.,
25 Burlington Arcade,
Piccadilly, W1
Tel: 071 493 6557

S. J. Shrubsole Ltd.,
43 Museum Street, WC1
Tel: 071 405 2712

Cheshire
Watergate Antiques,
56 Watergate Street, Chester
Tel: 0244 44516

Cornwall
Sylvaturo Antiques, Sylvia &
Arthur Zanelli
Tel: 0637 860725

Hereford & Worcs
Lower House Fine Antiques
(R), Far Moor Lane,
Winyates Green, Redditch
Tel: 0527 25117

Kent
Castle Antiques,
1 London Road, Westerham
Tel: 0959 62492

Ralph Antiques,
40A Sandwich Industrial
Estate, Sandwich
Tel: 0304 611949/612882

Steppes Hill Farm Antiques,
Stockbury, Sittingbourne
Tel: 0795 842205

Middlesex
London International Silver
Co. Ltd., Hampton
Tel: 081 979 6523

Oxon
Thames Gallery,
Thameside, Henley-on-
Thames
Tel: 0491 572449

Shropshire
F. C. Manser & Son Ltd.,
53-54 Wyle Cop, Shrewsbury
Tel: 0743 51120

Somerset
Edward A. Nowell,
12 Market Place, Wells
Tel: 0749 72415

Warwickshire
Coleshill Antiques,
High Street, Coleshill
Tel: 0675 462931

Yorks
Georgian House,
88 Main Street, Bingley
Tel: 0274 568883

SPORTS & GAMES

London
Sarah Baddiel, The Golf
Gallery, B12 Grays in the
Mews, Davies Mews, W1
Tel: 071 408 1239

Oxon
The Crypt Antiques,
109 High Street, Burford
Tel: 099382 2302

Somerset
The Billiards Co.,
6 The Courtyard, Bancks
Street, Minehead
Tel: 0643 706165

Surrey
Academy Antiques (Billiard
Tables) No.5 Camphill
Industrial Estate, West
Byfleet
Tel: 0932 352067

TELEPHONES

Kent
Candlestick & Bakelite,
PO Box 308 Orpington
Tel: 081 467 3743

TEXTILES

London
Act One Hire Ltd.,
2a Scampston Mews,
Cambridge Gardens , W10
Tel: 081 960 1456/1494

Matthew Adams,
A1 Rogers Antique Galleries,
65 Portobello Road, W11
Tel: 081 579 5560

Gallery of Antique Costume
& Textiles, 2 Church Street,
Marylebone, NW8
Tel: 071 723 9981

Linda Wrigglesworth,
Grays in the Mews, 1-7
Davies Mews, Wl
Tel: 071 408 0177

Kent
The Lace Basket,
1A East Cross, Tenterden
Tel: 05806 3923

Norfolk
Mrs Woolston,Design House,
29 St. Georges Street,
Norwich
Tel: 0603 623181

Sussex
Celia Charlotte's Antiques,
7 Malling Street, Lewes
Tel: 0273 473303

Wales
Forge Antiques, Synod Inn,
Llandysul, Dyfed
Tel: 0545 580707/580604

WINE ANTIQUES

London
Brian Beat, 38 Burlington
Gardens, W1
Tel: 071 437 4975

Richard Kihl, 164 Regent's
Park Road, NW1
Tel: 071 586 3838

Avon
Robin Butler,
20 Clifton Road, Bristol
Tel: 0272 733017

Beds
Christopher Sykes Antiques,
The Old Parsonage, Woburn,
Milton Keynes
Tel: 0525 290259 290467

Cumbria
Bacchus Antiques.
Longlands at Cartmel
Tel: 05395 36475

WRITING MATERIALS

London
Jasmin Cameron (R),
Stand J6 Antiquarius, 131-141 Kings Road, SW3
Tel: 071 351 4154

ANTIQUE CENTRES AND MARKETS

London
Alfies Antiques Market,13-25 Church Street, NW8
Tel: 071 723 6066

Antiquarius Antique Market, 135/141 King's Road, SW3
Tel: 071 351 5353

Atlantic Antique Centres, 15 Flood Street, SW3
Tel: 071 351 5353

Bermondsey Antique Market & Warehouse, SE1
Tel: 071 407 2040

Bond Street Antique Centre, 124 New Bond Street, W1
Tel: 071 351 5353

Camden Passage Antique Centre, 357 Upper Street, Islington N1
Tel: 071 359 0190

Chenil Galleries, 181-183 King's Road, SW3
Tel: 071 351 5353

Georgian Village, Camden Passage, N1
Tel: 071 226 1571

Grays, 1-7 Davies Mews, 58 Davies Street, W1
Tel: 071 629 7034

Hampstead Antique Emporium, 12 Heath Street, NW3
Tel: 071 794 3297

Antique Centre, 58-60 Kensington Church Street, W8

London Silver Vaults, 53-65 Chancery Lane, WC2.
Tel: 071 242 3844

The Mall Antiques Arcade, 359 Upper Street, N1
Tel: 071 351 5353

The Old Cinema, 160 Chiswick High Road, W4
Tel: 081 995 4166

Avon
Bath Antique Market, Guinea Lane, Paragon, Bath
Tel: 0225 422510

Clifton Antiques Market, 26/28 The Mall,Clifton
Tel: 0272 741627

Great Western Antique Centre, Bartlett Street, Bath
Tel: 0225 424243

Beds
Woburn Abbey Antiques Centre,Wobur
Tel: 05252 290350

Berks
Loddon Lily Antiques Centre, 1 High Street, Twyford
Tel: 0734 342161

Old Barn Antiques, At Country Gardens, Dedworth Road, Oakley Green, Windsor
Tel: 0753 833099

Bucks
Great Missenden Antique Arcade, 76 High Street, Gt. Missenden
Tel: 02406 2819 & 2330

Cambs
Collectors' Market, Dales Brewery, Gwydir Street, Cambridge

Cheshire
Davenham Antique Centre, 461 London Road, Davenham, Northwich
Tel: 0606 44350

Cumbria
Cockermouth Antiques Market, Main Street, Cockermouth
Tel: 0900 824346

J. W. Thornton Antiques Supermarket, North Terrace, Bowness-on-Windermere
Tel: 0229 869745 & 0966 22930/25183

Devon
Barbican Antiques Market, 82-84 Vauxhall Street, Barbican, Plymouth
Tel: 0752 266927

New Street Antique Centre, 27 New Street, The Barbican, Plymouth
Tel: 0752 661165

Sidmouth Antiques Market, 132 High Street (next to Fords), Sidmouth
Tel: 03955 77981

Dorset
Antique Market, Town Hall/Corn Exchange, Dorchester
Tel: 0963 62478

Antique Market, Digby Hall, Sherborne
Tel: 0258 840224

Antiques Trade Warehouse, 28 Lome Park Road, Bournemouth
Tel: 0202 292944

Barnes House Antiques Centre, West Row, Wimborne Minster
Tel: 0202 886275

Wimborne Antique Centre, 21 Newborough Road, Wimborne
Tel: 0202 841251

Essex
Antique Centre, Doubleday Corner, Coggeshall
Tel: 0376 562646

Baddow Antiques & Craft Centre, The Bringy, Church Street, Great Baddow
Tel: 0245 76159

Maldon Antiques & Collectors' Market, United Reformed Church Hall, Market Hill, Maldon
Tel: 07872 22826

Trinity Antiques Centre 7 Trinity Street, Colchester
Tel: 0206 577775

Glos
Antique Centre, London House, High Street, Moreton-in-Marsh
Tel: 0608 51084

Cheltenham Antique Market, 54 Suffolk Road, Cheltenham
Tel: 0242 529812

Cirencester Antique Market, Market Place (Antique Forum Ltd.), Cirencester
Tel: 071 240 0428

Gloucester Antique Centre, 1 Severn Road, Gloucester
Tel: 0452 29716

Tewkesbury Antique Centre, 78 Church Street, Tewkesbury
Tel: 0684 294091

Hants
Winchester Antique & Craft Market, King's Walk, Winchester
Tel: 0962 862277

Hereford & Worcester
Antiques Centre (Old Curiosity), 11 Towers Buildings, Blackwell Street, Kidderminster
Tel: 0562 829000

Leominster Antiques Market, 14 Broad Street, Leominster
Tel: 0568 2189

Herts
By George! Antiques Centre, 23 George Street, St Albans
Tel: 0727 53032

The Herts & Essex Antiques Centre, The Maltings, Station Road, Sawbridgeworth
Tel: 0279 722044

St Albans Antique Market, Town Hall, Chequer Street, St Albans
Tel: 0727 50427

Kent
The Antiques Centre, 120 London Road, Sevenoaks
Tel: 0732 452104

Canterbury Weekly Antique Market, Sidney Cooper Centre, Canterbury (no telephone number)

Castle Antiques Centre, 1 London Road, (next to Post Office), Westerham
Tel: 0959 62492

Hythe Antique Centre, The Old Post Office, 5 High Street, Hythe
Tel: 0303 269643

Noah's Ark Antique Centre, King Street, Sandwich
Tel: 0304 611144

Rochester Antiques & Flea Market, Rochester Market, Corporation Street, Rochester
Tel: 071 262 5003

Sandgate Antiques Centre, 61-63 High Street, Sandgate Folkestone
Tel: 0303 48987

Lancs
The A & D Centre, 56 Garstang Road, Preston
Tel: 0772 882078

Castle Antiques, Moore Lane, Clitheroe
Tel: 0254 35820

Levenshulme Antique Village, Old Town Hall, 965 Stockport Road, Levenshulme
Tel: 061 224 2410

North Western Antique Centre, New Preston Mill (Horrockses Yard), New Hall Lane, Preston
Tel: 0772 794498

Preston Antique Centre, The Mill, New Hall Lane, Preston
Tel: 0772 794498

Leics
Oxford Street Antique Centre Ltd., 16-26 Oxford Street, Leicester
Tel: 0533 553006

Lincs
The Hemswell Antiques Centres,
Caenby Corner Estate, Hemswell Cliff, Gainsborough
Tel: 0427 668389

Lincolnshire Antiques Centre, Bridge Street, Horncastle
Tel: 06582 7794

Norfolk
Antique & Collectors Centre, St Michael at Plea, Bank Plain,
Norwich
Tel: 0603 619129

Coltishall Antiques Centre, High Street, Coltishall
Tel: 0603 738306

Fakenham Antique Centre, Old Congrega-tional Chapel, 14 Norwich Road, Fakenham
Tel: 0328 862941 or home: 0263 860543

Norwich Antique & Collectors Centre, Quayside, Fye Bridge, Norwich
Tel: 0603 612582

The Old Granary Antique & Collectors Centre, King Staithe Lane, Off Queen's Street, King's Lynn
Tel: 0553 5509

Northants
Finedon Antiques Centre, 3 Church Street, Finedon
Tel: 0933 681260

The Village Antique Market, 62 High Street, Weedon
Tel: 0327 42015

Northumberland
Colmans of Hexham (Saleroom & Antique Fair), 15 St Mary's Chare, Hexham
Tel: 0434 603812/605522

Notts
Nottingham Antique Centre, British Rail Goods Yard, London Road, Nottingham
Tel: 0602 54504/55548

Top Hat Antiques Centre, 66-72 Derby Road, Nottingham
Tel: 0602 419143

Oxon
The Antique Centre, Laurel House, Bull Ring, Market Place, Deddington
Tel: 0869 38968

Shropshire
Ironbridge Antique Centre, Dale End, Ironbridge
Tel: 095 245 3784

Shrewsbury Antique Market, Frankwell Quay Warehouse, (Vintagevale Ltd), Shrewsbury
Tel: 0743 50916

Stretton Antiques Market, Sandford Avenue, Church Stretton
Tel: 06945 402 or 0694

Somerset
Crewkerne Antiques Centre, 42 East Street, Crewkerne
Tel: 0460 76755

Taunton Antiques Centre, 27/29 Silver Street, Taunton
Tel: 0823 289327

Staffs
The Antique Centre, 7A The Digbeth Arcade, Walsall
Tel: 0922 725163/5

Barclay House, Howard Place, Shelton, Stoke-on-Trent
Tel: 0782 657674/274747

Rugeley Antique Centre, 161 Main Road, Rugeley
Tel: 08895 77166

Suffolk
Old Town Hall Antique Centre, High Street, Needham Market
Tel: 0449 720773

Waveney Antique Centre, The Old School, Peddars Lane, Beccles
Tel: 0502 716147

Surrey
Antique Centre, 22 Haydon Place, Martyr Road, Guildford
Tel: 0483 67817

Dukes Yard Antique Market, 1A Duke Street, Richmond
Tel: 081 332 1051

Farnham Antique Centre, 27 South Street, Farnham
Tel: 0252 724475

Maltings Market, Bridge Square, Farnham
Tel: 0252 726234

The Old Smithy Antique Centre, 7 High Street, Merstham
Tel: 0737 642306

Victoria & Edward Antiques, 61 West Street, Dorking
Tel: 0306 889645

Sussex -East
Antique Market, Leaf Hall, Seaside, Eastbourne
Tel: 0323 27530

Bexhill Antiques Centre, Old Town, Bexhill
Tel: 0424 210182

Chateaubriand Antique Centre, High Street, Burwash
Tel: 0435 882535

The Collectors Market, The Enterprise Centre, Station Parade, Eastbourne
Tel: 0323 32690

Heathfield Antiques Centre, The Market, Heathfield
Tel: 042 482 387

Antiques Centre, 20 Cliffe High Street, Lewes
Tel: 0273 476148

Flea Market,28 South Way, Newhaven
Tel: 0273 517207

St Leonards Antique Dealers, Norman Road, St Leonards-on-Sea
Tel: 0424 444592

Seaford's Barn Collectors Market, The Barn, Church Lane, Seaford
Tel: 0323 890010

Sussex - West
Mamie's Antiques Market, 5 River Road, Arundel
Tel: 0903 882012

Midhurst Antiques Market, Knockhundred Row, Midhurst
Tel: 073081 4231

Mostyns Antiques Centre, 64 Brighton Road, Lancing
Tel: 0903 752961

Petworth Antiques Market, East Street, Petworth
Tel: 0798 42073

Robert Warner & Son Ltd., South Farm Road, Worthing
Tel: 0903 32710

Treasure House Antiques Market, Crown Yard, Arundel
Tel: 0903 883101

Warwickshire
Antiques Centre, High Street, Bidford-on-Avon
Tel: 0789 773680

Rugby Antiques Centre, 22 Railway Terrace, Rugby

Vintage Antique Market, 36 Market Place, Warwick
Tel: 0926 491527

Warwick Antique Centre, 16-18 High Street, Warwick
Tel: 0962 492482

West Midlands
The City of Birmingham Antique Market, St Martins Market, Edgbaston Street, Birmingham
Tel: 021 624 3214

Wiltshire
Salisbury Antique & Collectors Market, 37 Catherine Street, Salisbury
Tel: 0722 26033

Yorks - North
The Emporium, 4 Skeldergate, York
Tel: 0904 634124

Grove Collectors Centre, Grove Road, Harrogate
Tel: 0423 561680

Harrogate Antique Centre, The Ginnel, Corn Exchange, Harrogate
Tel: 0423 508857

West Park Antiques Pavilion, 20 West Park, Harrogate
Tel: 0423 561758

York Antique Centre, 2 Lendal, York
Tel: 0904 641445

Yorks - South
Treasure House Antiques & Antique Centre, 4-10 Swan Street, Bawtry
Tel: 0302 710621

Yorks - West
Halifax Antique Centre, Queen's Road/Gibbet St., Halifax
Tel: 0422 366657

N. Ireland
London Street Antique Market, 4 London Street, Londonderry
Tel: 0504 371551

Scotland
Bath Street Antique Centre, 203 Bath Street, Glasgow
Tel: 041 248 4229

The Victorian Village, 53 & 57 West Regent Street, Glasgow
Tel: 041 332 0808

Wales
Cardiff Antique Centre, 69-71 St Mary Street, Cardiff
Tel: 0222 230970

DIRECTORY OF AUCTIONEERS

This directory is by no means complete. Any auctioneer who holds frequent sales should contact us for inclusion in the next Edition. Entries must be received by April 1993. There is, of course, no charge for this listing. Entries will be repeated in subsequent editions unless we are requested otherwise.

London

Academy Auctioneers &
Valuers,
Northcote House,
Northcote Avenue, Ealing,
W5
Tel: 081 579 7466

Bonhams, Montpelier
Galleries,
Montpelier Street,
Knightsbridge, SW7
Tel: 071 584 9161

Bonhams, Lots Road,
Chelsea, SW10
Tel: 071 351 7111

Christie Manson & Woods
Ltd.,
8 King Street,
St James's, SW1
Tel: 071 839 9060

Christie's Robson Lowe,
47 Duke Street,
St James's, SW1
Tel: 071 839 4034/5

Christie's South Kensington
Ltd.,
85 Old Brompton Road, SW7
Tel: 071 581 7611

City Forum Auctioneers,
108 Belsize Avenue, NW3
Tel: 071 433 1305

Dowell Lloyd & Co.,
118 Putney Bridge Road,
SW15
Tel: 081 788 7777

Forrest & Co.,
79-85 Cobbold Road,
Leytonstone, E11
Tel: 081 534 2931

Stanley Gibbons Auctions
Ltd.,
399 Strand, WC2
Tel: 071 836 8444

Glendining's,
101 New Bond Street, W1
Tel: 071 493 2445

Hamptons Fine Art
Auctioneers and Valuers,
6 Arlington Street, SW1
Tel: 071 493 8222

Harmers of London Stamp
Auctioneers Ltd., 91 New
Bond Street, W1
Tel: 071 629 0218

Hornsey Auctions Ltd.,
91 New Bond Street, W1
Tel: 071 629 0218

Hornsey Auctions Ltd.,
54/56 High Street, Hornsey,
N8
Tel: 081 340 5334

Jackson-Stops & Staff,
14 Curzon Street, W1
Tel: 071 499 6291

Lewisham Auction Rooms,
165 Lee High Road, SE13
Tel: 081 852 3145

Lloyds Park Auctions,
89 Grange Road,
Walthamstow, E17
Tel: 081 520 9878

Lots Road Chelsea Auction
Galleries,
71 Lots Road, Worlds End,
Chelsea, SW10
Tel: 071 351 7771

MacGregor Nash & Co.,
Lodge House, 9-17 Lodge
Lane, North Finchley,
N12 8JH
Tel: 081 445 9000

Thomas Moore,
217-219 Greenwich High
Road, SE10
Tel: 081 858 7848

Onslow's,
Metrostore,
Townmead Road, SW6
Tel: 071 793 0240

Palmers,
New Octagon House,
17-31 Gibbons Road,
E15
Tel: 081 555 0517

Phillips,
Blenstock House,
7 Blenheim Street,
New Bond Street, W1
Tel: 071 629 6602 and
10 Salem Road, W2
Tel: 071 229 9090

Rippon Boswell & Co.,
The Arcade, South
Kensington Station, SW7
Tel: 071 589 4242

Rosebery's Fine Art Ltd.,
Old Railway Booking Hall,
Crystal Palace Station Road,
SE19 Tel: 081 778 4024

Seven Dials Auction Rooms,
Rear of 59 High Street, E17
Tel: 081 520 5436

Sotheby's,
34-35 New Bond Street, W1
Tel: 071 493 8080

Southgate Auction Rooms,
55 High Street, Southgate
N14
081 886 78880

Avon

Alder King, Black Horse
Agencies,
The Old Malthouse,
Comfortable Place,
Upper Bristol Road, Bath
Tel: 0225 447933

Aldridges, Bath,
The Auction Galleries,
130-132 Walcot Street, Bath
Tel: 0225 462830 & 462839

Allen & Harris,
Bristol Auction Rooms,
St Johns Place, Apsley Road,
Clifton, Bristol
Tel: 0272 737201

Clevedon Salerooms,
Herbert Road, Clevedon
Tel: 0275 876699

Phillips Auction Rooms of
Bath, 1 Old King Street,
Bath Tel: 0225 310609

Phillips Fine Art
Auctioneers,
71 Oakfield Road, Clifton,
Bristol
Tel: 0272 734052

Taviner's Ltd.,
Prewett Street, Redcliffe,
Bristol
Tel: 0272 265996

Woodspring Auction Rooms,
Churchill Road,
Weston-super-Mare
Tel: 0934 628419

Bedfordshire

Wilson Peacock,
The Auction Centre, 26
Newnham Street, Bedford
Tel: 0234 266366

Berkshire

Dreweatt Neate,
Donnington Priory,
Donnington, Newbury
Tel: 0635 31234

R. Elliott,
Chancellors, 32 High Street,
Ascot
Tel: 0344 872588

Holloway's,
12 High Street, Streatley,
Reading
Tel: 0491 872318

Martin & Pole,
12 Milton Street,
Wokingham
Tel: 0734 790460

Thimbleby & Shorland,
31 Great Knollys Street,
Reading
Tel: 0734 508611

Duncan Vincent Fine Art &
Chattel Auctioneers,
105 London Street, Reading
Tel: 0734 594748

Buckinghamshire

Amersham Auction Rooms,
Station Road, Amersham
Tel: 0494 729292

Hamptons,
10 Burkes Parade,
Beaconsfield
Tel: 0494 672969

Geo Wigley & Sons,
Winslow Sale Room,
Market Square, Winslow
Tel: 029 671 2717

Cambridgeshire

Cheffins Grain & Comins,
2 Clifton Road, Cambridge
Tel: 0223 358721/213343

Phillips Auctioneers,
Station Road, St. Ives
Tel: 0480 68144

Grounds & Co.,
2 Nene Quay, Wisbech
Tel: 0945 585041

Hammond & Co.,
Cambridge Place, off Hills
Road, Cambridge
Tel: 0223 356067

Maxey & Son,
1-3 South Brink, Wisbech
Tel: 0945 584609

Cheshire

Andrew Hilditch & Son,
Hanover House, 1A The
Square, Sandbach
Tel: 0270 762048/767246

Robert I Heyes,
Hatton Buildings, Lightfoot
Street, Hoole, Chester
Tel: 0244 328941

Highams Auctions, Waterloo
House, Waterloo Road,
Stalybridge
Tel: 061 303 2924/061 303
1091 also at:
Southgate House, Southgate
Street, Rhodes Bank,
Oldham Tel: 061 626 1021

Frank R Marshall & Co.,
Marshall House, Church
Hill, Knutsford
Tel: 0565 653284

Phillips North West,
New House, 150 Christleton
Road, Chester
Tel: 0244 313936

Phillips Fine Art
Auctioneers,
Trinity House, 114
Northenden Road, Sale,
Manchester
Tel: 061 962 9237

Henry Spencer Inc. Peter
Wilson,
Victoria Gallery, Market
Street, Nantwich
Tel: 0270 623878

Wright Manley,
Beeston Sales Centre,
63 High Street, Tarporley
Tel: 0829 260318

Cleveland

Lithgow Sons & Partners,
The Auction Houses, Station
Road, Stokesley,
Middlesbrough
Tel: 0642 710158 & 710326

Cornwall

Eric Distin Chartered
Surveyors,
54 Fore Street
Saltash

Lambrays, incorporating
R J Hamm ASVA
Polmorla Walk, The Platt,
Wadebridge
Tel: 020 881 3593

W H Lane & Son,
St Mary's Auction Rooms,
65 Morrab Road, Penzance
Tel: 0736 61447

David Lay,
Penzance Auction House,
Alverton, Penzance
Tel: 0736 61414

Phillips Cornwall,
Cornubia Hall, Par
Tel: 072 681 4047

786

Pooley and Rogers,
Regent Auction Rooms,
Abbey Street, Penzance
Tel: 0736 68814

Jeffery's,
5 Fore Street, Lostwithiel
Tel: 0208 872245

Cumbria

Cumbria Auction Rooms, 12
Lowther Street, Carlisle
Tel: 0228 25259

Mitchells,
Fairfield House,
Cockermouth
Tel: 0900 822016

Alfred Mossops & Co.,
Loughrigg Villa, Kelsick
Road, Ambleside
Tel: 05394 33015

James Thompson,
64 Main Street, Kirkby
Lonsdale
Tel: 05242 71555

Thomson, Roddick & Laurie,
24 Lowther Street, Carlisle
Tel: 0228 28939 & 39636

Derbyshire

Noel Wheatcroft & Son,
The Matlock Auction Gallery,
39 Dale Road, Matlock
Tel: 0629 584591

Devon

Bearnes,
Avenue Road, Torquay
Tel: 0803 296277

Bonhams West Country,
Devon Fine Art Auction
House,
Dowell Street, Honiton
Tel: 0404 41872

Michael J Bowman,
6 Haccombe House, Nr
Netherton, Newton Abbot
Tel: 0626 872890

Eric Distin,
Chartered Survyors,
54 Fore Street, Saltash
Tel: 0752 843768/842355

Peter J Eley,
Western House, 98-100 High
Street, Sidmouth
Tel: 0395 513006

Robin A Fenner & Co.,
Fine Art & Antique
Auctioneers,
The Stannary Gallery, Drake
Road, Tavistock
Tel: 0822 617799/617800

Kingsbridge Auction Sales,
85 Fore Street, Kingsbridge
Tel: 0548 856829

McBain's of Exeter,
Exeter Airport,
Clyst Honiton
Tel: 0392 66261

Michael Newman,
Kinterbury House,
St Andrew's Cross, Plymouth
Tel: 0752 669298

Phillips,
Alphin Brook Road,
Alphington, Exeter
Tel: 0392 439025 and
Armada Street, North Hill,
Plymouth Tel: 0752 673504

Potbury's,
High Street, Sidmouth
Tel: 0395 515555

Rendells,
Stone Park, Ashburton
Tel: 0364 5301

G S Shobrook & Co.,
20 Western Approach,
Plymouth
Tel: 0752 663341

John Smale & Co.,
11 High Street, Barnstaple
Tel: 0271 42000/42916

South Street Auctions,
Newport,
Barnstaple
Tel: 0271 788581/850337

Martin Spencer-Thomas,
Church Street Auction
Rooms, Exmouth
Tel: 0395 267403

Taylors,
Honiton Galleries, 205 High
Street, Honiton
Tel: 0404 42404

Ward & Chowen,
1 Church Lane, Tavistock
Tel: 0822 612458

Whitton & Laing,
32 Okehampton Street,
Exeter
Tel: 0392 52621

Dorset

Cottees, Bullock & Lees,
The Market, East Street,
Wareham
Tel: 0929 554915/552826

Hy Duke & Son,
Fine Art Salerooms,
Weymouth Ave, Dorchester
Tel: 0305 265080
also at:
The Weymouth Saleroom,
St Nicholas Street,
Weymouth
Tel: 0305 783488

Garnet Langton Auctions,
Burlington Arcade,
Bournemouth
Tel: 0202 552352

House & Son,
Lansdowne House,
Christchurch Road,
Bournemouth
Tel: 0202 556232

Southern Counties
Auctioneers,
Shaftesbury Livestock
Market,
Christy's Lane, Shaftesbury
Tel: 0747 51735

William Morey & Sons,
The Saleroom, St Michaels
Lane, Bridport
Tel: 0308 22078

Riddetts of Bournemouth, 26
Richmond Hill, Bournemouth
Square, Bournemouth
Tel: 0202 555686

County Durham

Denis Edkins,
Auckland Auction Room,
58 Kingsway,
Bishop Auckland
Tel: 0388 603095

Thomas Watson & Son,
Northumberland Street,
Darlington
Tel: 0325 462559/463485

Wingate Auction Co.,
Station Lane, Station Town,
Wingate Tel: 0429 837245

Essex

Abridge Auction Rooms,
Market Place, Abridge
Tel: 099281 2107/3113

Black Horse Agencies,
Ambrose, 149 High Road,
Loughton Tel: 081 502 3951

William H Brown,
The Auction Rooms,
11-14 East Hill
Colchester Tel: 0206 868070

Cooper Hirst,
The Granary Saleroom,
Victoria Road,
Chelmsford
Tel: 0245 260535

Saffron Walden Saleroom,
1 Market Street,
Saffron Walden
Tel: 0799 513281

Grays Auction Rooms,
Ye Old Bake House, Alfred
Street, Grays
Tel: 0375 381181

Hamptons Fine Art/J.M.
Welch & Son,
The Old Town Hall,
Great Dunmow
Tel: 0371 873014

John Stacey & Sons,
Leigh Auctions Rooms,
86-90 Pall Mall,
Leigh-on-Sea
Tel: 0702 77051

Gloucestershire

Bruton, Knowles & Co.,
111 Eastgate Street,
Gloucester
Tel: 0452 521267

Fraser Glennie & Partners,
The Old Rectory,
Siddington,
Nr Cirencester
Tel: 0285 659677

Hobbs & Chambers,
Market Place,
Cirencester
Tel: 0285 654736 also at:
15 Royal Crescent,
Cheltenham
Tel: 0242 513722

Ken Lawson t/as
Specialised Postcard
Auctions,
25 Gloucester Street,
Cirencester
Tel: 0285 659057

Mallams,
26 Grosvenor Street,
Cheltenham
Tel: 0242 235712

Moore, Allen & Innocent,
33 Castle Street, Cirencester
Tel: 0285 65183

Wotton Auction Rooms,
Tabernacle Road,
Wotton-under-Edge
Tel: 0453 844733

Hampshire

Andover Saleroom,
41A London Street, Andover
Tel: 0264 364820

Fox & Sons,
5 & 7 Salisbury Street,
Fordingbridge
Tel: 0425 652121

GA Fine Art & Chattels, The
Romsey Auction Rooms, 86
The Hundred,
Romsey
Tel. 0794 513331

Hants & Berks Auctions,
82, 84 Sarum Hill,
Basingstoke
Tel: 0256 840707
also at:
Heckfield Village Hall,
Heckfield

Jacobs & Hunt,
Lavant Street, Petersfield
Tel: 0730 62744/5

May & Son,
18 Bridge Street, Andover
Tel: 0264 323417

D M Nesbit & Co.,
7 Clarendon Road, Southsea
Tel: 0705 864321

New Forest Auction Rooms,
Emsworth Road, Lymington
Tel: 0590 677225

Phillips Fine Art
Auctioneers,
54 Southampton Road,
Ringwood
Tel: 04254 473333 also at:
The Red House, Hyde Street,
Winchester
Tel: 0962 862515

Hereford & Worcs

Broadway Auctions,
41-43 High Street,
Broadway Tel: 0386 852456

Carless & Co.,
58 Lowesmoor, Worcester
Tel: 0905 612449

Andrew Grant,
St Mark's House,
St Mark's Close, Worcester
Tel: 0905 357547

Griffiths & Co.,
57 Foregate Street,
WorcesterTel: 0905 26464

Hamptons,
69 Church Street, Malvern
Tel: 0684 892314

Philip Laney & Jolly,
12a Worcester Road, Gt
Malvern
Tel: 0684 892322

Phipps & Pritchard,
Bank Buildings,
Kidderminster
Tel: 0562 822244/6 & 822187

Russell, Baldwin & Bright,
Fine Art Saleroom, Ryelands
Road, Leominster
Tel: 0568 611166

Village Auctions,
Sychampton Community
Centre
Ombersley
Tel: 0905 421007

Nigel Ward & Morris,
Stuart House, 18 Gloucester
Road, Ross-on-Wye
Tel: 0989 768320

Richard Williams,
2 High Street, Pershore
Tel: 0386 554031

Hertfordshire

Bayles,
Childs Farm, Cottered,
Buntingford
Tel: 076 381 256

Brown & Merry,
41 High Street, Tring
Tel: 044 282 6446

Andrew Pickford,
The Hertford Saleroom
106 The Fore Street,
Hertford
Tel: 0992 582249

Pamela & Barry Auctions,
The Village Hall, High
Street, Sandridge,
St Albans
Tel: 0727 861180

Sworders,
Northgate End Salerooms,
Bishops Stortford
Tel: 0279 651388

Humberside North

Gilbert Baitson, FSVA, The
Edwardian Auction
Galleries, Wiltshire Road,
Hull Tel: 0482 500500

H Evans & Sons,
1 Parliament Street, Hull
Tel: 0482 23033

Humberside South

Dickinson, Davy &
Markham,
10 Wrawby Street, Brigg
Tel: 0652 653666

Isle of Man

Chrystals Auctions,
Majestic Hotel, Onchan
Tel: 0624 673986

Isle of Wight

Watson Bull & Porter,
Isle of Wight Auction Rooms,
79 Regent Street, Shanklin
Tel: 0983 863 441

Phillips Fine Art
Auctioneers,
Cross Street Salerooms,
Newport
Tel: 0983 822031

Ways Auction House,
Garfield Road, Ryde
Tel: 0983 62255

Kent

Albert Andrews Auctions &
Sales,
Maiden Lane, Crayford
Tel: 0322 528868
Bracketts,
27-29 High Street,
Tunbridge Wells
Tel: 0892 533733

Lambert & Foster,
102 High Street, Tenterden
Tel: 05806 2083/3233

Canterbury Auction
Galleries,
40 Station Road West,
Canterbury
Tel: 0227 763337

Mervyn Carey,
Twysden Cottage,
Benenden, Cranbrook
Tel: 0580 240283

Stewart Gore,
100-102 Northdown Road,
Margate
Tel: 0843 221528/9

Edwin Hall,
Valley Antiques,
Lyminge, Folkestone
Tel: 0303 862134

Hobbs Parker,
Romney House, Ashford
Market, Elwick Road,
Ashford
Tel: 0233 622222

Ibbett Mosely,
125 High Street, Sevenoaks
Tel: 0732 452246

Kent Sales,
'Giffords', Holmesdale Road,
South Darenth
Tel: 0322 864919

Lawrence Butler & Co, (inc.
F W Butler & Co.),
Fine Art Salerooms, Butler
House, 86 High Street,
Hythe Tel: 0303 266022/3

B J Norris,
"The Quest", West Street,
Harrietsham,
Nr Maidstone
Tel: 0622 859515

Phillips,
11 Bayle Parade, Folkestone
Tel: 0303 45555

Phillips Fine Art
Auctioneers,
49 London Road, Sevenoaks
Tel: 0732 740310

Halifax Property Services,
Fine Art Department,
53 High Street, Tenterden
Tel: 05806 3200
also at:
15 Cattle Market, Sandwich
Tel: 0304 614369

Michael Shortall,
Auction Centres,
Highgate, Hawkhurst
Tel: 0580 753463

Walter & Randall,
7-13 New Road, Chatham
Tel: 0634 841233

Peter S Williams, FSVA,
Orchard End, Sutton
Valence, Maidstone
Tel: 0622 842350

Lancashire

Artingstall & Hind,
29 Cobden Street, Pendleton,
Salford
Tel: 061 736 5682

Capes Dunn & Co.,
The Auction Galleries,
38 Charles Street,
Manchester
Tel: 061 273 6060/1911

Charles Edwards & Co.,
4/8 Lynwood Road,
Blackburn
Tel: 0254 691748

Entwistle Green,
The Galleries, Kingsway,
Ansdell, Lytham St Annes
Tel: 0253 735442

Robt. Fairhurst & Son,
39 Mawdsley Street, Bolton
Tel: 0204 28452/28453

Highams Auctions,
Southgate House, Southgate
Street, Rhodes Bank,
Oldham
Tel: 061 626 1021 also at:
Onward Buildings,
207 Deansgate, Manchester
Tel: 061 834 0068

McKennas, formerly
Hothersall, Forrest,
McKenna & Sons,
Bank Salerooms, Harris
Court, Clitheroe
Tel: 0200 25446/22695

Mills & Radcliffe,
101 Union Street, Oldham
Tel: 061 624 1072

David Palamountain,
1-3 Osborne Grove,
Morecambe
Tel: 0524 423941

J R Parkinson Son & Hamer
Auctions,
The Auction Rooms,
Rochdale Road, Bury
Tel: 061 761 1612/7372

Phillips,
Trinity House, 114
Northenden Road, Sale,
Manchester
Tel: 061 962 9237

Smythe, Son & Walker,
174 Victoria road West,
Cleveleys
Tel: 0253 852184 & 854084

Warren & Wignall Ltd.,
The Mill, Earnshaw Bridge,
Leyland Lane, Leyland
Tel: 0772 453252/451430

Leicestershire

Churchgate Auctions,
The Churchgate Saleroom,
66 Churchgate, Leicester
Tel: 0533 621416

Gildings,
64 Roman Way,
Market Harborough
Tel: 0858 410 414

Noton Salerooms,
76 South Street, Oakham
Tel: 0572 722681

David Stanley Auctions,
Stordon Grange, Osgathorpe,
Loughborough
Tel: 0530 222320

William H Brown,
The Warner Auction Rooms,
16/18 Halford Street,
Leicester Tel: 0533 519777

Lincolnshire

Marilyn Swain Auctions,
Fine Art Dept, Westgate
Hall, Westgate, Grantham
Tel: 0476 68861

Dowse,
89 Mary Street, Scunthorpe
Tel: 0724 842569/842039

Henry Spencer & Sons,
42 Silver Street, Lincoln
Tel: 0522 536666

Thomas Mawer & Son,
63 Monks Road, Lincoln
Tel: 0522 524984

Bourne Auction Rooms,
Spalding Road, Bourne
Tel: 0778 422686

John H Walter,
1 Mint Lane, Lincoln
Tel: 0522 525454

Merseyside

Hartley & Co.,
12 & 14 Moss Street,
Liverpool
Tel: 051 263 6472/1865

Kingsley & Co.,
3-5 The Quadrant, Hoylake,
Wirral Tel: 051 632 5821

Outhwaite & Litherland,
Kingsway Galleries,
Fontenoy Street, Liverpool
Tel: 051 236 6561/

Eldon E Worrall & Co.,
13-15 Seel Street, Liverpool
Tel: 051 709 2950

Norfolk

Ewings,
Market Place, Reepham,
Norwich Tel: 0603 870473

Thos Wm Gaze & Son ,
10 Market Hill, Diss
Tel: 0379 651931

Glennie's,
Marchants Court, St Georges
Street, Norwich
Tel: 0603 633558

Nigel F Hedge,
28B Market Place, North
Walsham Tel: 0692 402881

Hilhams,
Baker Street, Gorleston,
Great Yarmouth
Tel: 0493 662152 & 600700

James Norwich Auctions
Ltd.,
33 Timberhill, Norwich
Tel: 0603 624817/625369

G A Key,
8 Market Place, Aylsham
Tel: 0263 733195

Northamptonshire

Corby & Co.,
30-32 Brook Street, Raunds
Tel: 0933 623722

Heathcote Ball & Co.,
Albion Auction Rooms, Old
Albion Brewery, Commercial
Street, Northampton
Tel: 0604 37263

Lowery's,
24 Bridge Street,
Northampton
Tel: 0604 21561

Merry's Auctioneers,
The Old Corn Exchange,
Cattle Market, 14 Bridge
Street, Northampton
Tel: 0604 32266

Moreton Pinkney,
28 High Street, Daventry
Tel: 0327 703917

Southam & Sons,
Corn Exchange, Thrapston,
Kettering
Tel: 08012 4486

H Wilford Ltd.,
Midland Road,
Wellingborough

Northumberland

Louis Johnson Auctioneers,
Morpeth Tel: 0670 513025

Nottinghamshire

Arthur Johnson & Sons Ltd.,
The Nottingham Auction
Rooms, The Cattle Market,
Meadow Lane, Nottingham
Tel: 0602 869128

Neales of Nottingham,
192 Mansfield Road,
Nottingham
Tel: 0602 624141

John Pye & Sons,
Corn Exchange, Cattle
Market, London Road,
Nottingham
Tel: 0602 866261

C B Sheppard & Son,
The Auction Galleries,
Chatsworth Street, Sutton-
in-Ashfield
Tel: 0773 872419

Henry Spencer & Sons Ltd.,
20 The Square, Retford
Tel: 0777 708633

T Vennett-Smith,
11 Nottingham Road,
Gotham Tel: 0602 830541

Oxfordshire

Green & Co.,
33 Market Place, Wantage
Tel: 02357 3561/2

Holloways,
49 Parsons Street, Banbury
Tel: 0295 253197/8

Mallams,
24 St Michael's Street,
Oxford Tel: 0865 241358

Messengers,
27 Sheep Street, Bicester
Tel: 08692 52901

Phillips Inc Brooks,
39 Park End Street, Oxford
Tel: 0865 723524

Simmons & Sons,
32 Bell Street,
Henley-on-Thames
Tel: 0491 571111

Shropshire

Cooper & Green,
3 Barker Street, Shrewsbury
Tel: 0743 232244

Ludlow Antique Auctions
Ltd., 29 Corve Street,
Ludlow Tel: 0584 875157

McCartneys,
25 Corve Street, Ludlow
Tel: 0584 872636

Perry & Phillips,
Newmarket Salerooms,
Newmarket Buildings,
Listley Street, Bridgnorth
Tel: 07462 762248

Somerset

Dores, The Auction Mart,
Vicarage Street, Frome
Tel: 0373 62257

John Fleming,
4 & 8 Fore Street, Dulverton
Tel: 0398 23597

Greenslades,
13 Hamet Street, Taunton
Tel: 0823 277121also at:
Priory Saleroom, Winchester
Street, Taunton

Gribble Booth & Taylor,
13 The Parade, Minehead
Tel: 0643 702281

Black Horse Agencies,
Alder King, 25 Market Place,
Wells
Tel: 0749 73002

The London Cigarette Card
Co Ltd.,
Sutton Road, Somerton
Tel: 0458 73452

Frome Auction Rooms,
Frome Market, Standerwick,
Nr Frome
Tel: 0373 831010

Nuttall Richards & Co.,
The Square, Axbridge
Tel: 0934 732969

Wellington Salerooms,
Mantle Street, Wellington
Tel: 0823 664815

Staffordshire

Bagshaws,
17 High Street, Uttoxeter
Tel: 0889 562811

Hall & Lloyd,
South Street Auction Rooms,
Stafford
Tel: 0785 58176

Louis Taylor,
Britannia House, 10 Town
Road, Hanley, Stoke-on-
Trent
Tel: 0782 260222

Wintertons,
Lichfield Auction Centre,
Woodend Lane, Fradley,
Lichfield
Tel: 0543 263256

Suffolk

Abbotts (East Anglia) Ltd.,
The Hill, Wickham Market,
Woodbridge
Tel: 0728 746321

Boardman Fine Art,
Station Road Corner,
Haverhill Tel: 0440 730414

Diamond, Mills & Co.,
117 Hamilton Road,
Felixstowe Tel: 0394 282281

William H Brown,
Ashford House,
Saxmundham
Tel: 0728 603232

Lacy Scott,
Fine Art Department, The
Auction Centre, 10 Risbygate
Street, Bury St Edmunds
Tel: 0284 763531

Neal Sons & Fletcher,
26 Church Street,
Woodbridge
Tel: 0394 382263

Olivers, William H Brown,
Olivers Rooms, Burkitts
Lane, Sudbury
Tel: 0787 880305

Phillips,
Dover House, Wilsey Street,
Ipswich
Tel: 0473 255137

Surrey

Chancellors,
74 London Road,
Kingston upon Thames,
Tel: 081 541 4139

Clark Gammon,
The Guildford Auction
Rooms, Bedford Road,
Guildford Tel: 0483 66458

Crows Auction Gallery, Rear
of Dorking Halls, Reigate
Road, Dorking
Tel: 0306 740382

Croydon Auction Rooms
(Rosan & Co)
144-150 London Road,
Croydon
Tel: 081 688 1123/4/5

Ewbank Fine Art,
Welbeck House, High Street,
Guildford
Tel: 0483 232134

Fernhursts,
1 Crossways Corner,
Haslemere Road, Fernhurst,
Haslemere Tel: 0428 653727

Hamptons, Fine Art
Auctioneers & Valuers, 93
High Street, Godalming
Tel: 04834 23567

Lawrences,
Norfolk House, 80 High
Street, Bletchingley
Tel: 0883 743323

Parkins,
18 Malden Road, Cheam,
Surrey
Tel: 081 644 6633 & 612

Phillips Fine Art
Auctioneers, Millmead,
Guildford
Tel: 0483 504030

Wentworth Auction
Galleries, 21 Station
Approach, Virginia Water
Tel: 0344 843711

P F Windibank,
Dorking Halls, 18-20 Reigate
Road, Dorking
Tel: 0306 884556

Sussex - East

Ascent Auction Galleries,
11-12 East Ascent, St
Leonards-on-Sea
Tel: 0424 420275

Burstow & Hewett,
Abbey Auction Galleries and
Granary Salerooms, Battle
Tel: 04246 2374/2302

Clifford Dann Auction
Galleries,
20-21 High Street, Lewes
Tel: 0273 480111

Fryers Auction Galleries,
Terminus Road, Bexhill-on-
Sea
Tel: 0424 212994

Gorringes Auction Galleries,
15 North Street, Lewes
Tel: 0273 472503

Graves, Son & Pilcher, Fine
Arts, 71 Church Road, Hove
Tel: 0273 735266

Edgar Horn's Fine Art
Auctioneers,
46-50 South Street,
Eastbourne
Tel: 0323 410419

Hove Auction Galleries,
1 Weston Road, Hove
Tel: 0273 736207

Raymond P Inman,
Auction Galleries, 35 & 40
Temple Street, Brighton
Tel: 0273 774777

Lewes Auction Rooms,
(Julian Dawson),
56 High Street, Lewes
Tel: 0273 478221

Rye Auction Galleries,
Rock Channel, Rye
Tel: 0797 222124

Wallis & Wallis,
West Street Auction
Galleries, Lewes
Tel: 0273 480208

Watsons,
Heathfield Furniture
Salerooms, The Market,
Burwash Road, Heathfield
Tel: 0435 862132

Sussex - West

Peter Cheney,
Western Road Auction
Rooms, Western Road,
Littlehampton
Tel: 0903 722264 & 713418

Denham's,
Horsham Auction Galleries,
Warnham, Horsham
Tel: 0403 53837/55699

R H Ellis & Sons,
44-46 High Street, Worthing
Tel: 0903 38999

Midhurst Auction Rooms,
Bepton Road, Midhurst
Tel: 073081 2456

Phillips Fine Art
Auctioneers,
Baffins Hall, Baffins Lane,
Chichester
Tel: 0243 787548

Sotheby's in Sussex,
Summers Place,
Billingshurst
Tel: 0403 783933

Stride & Son,
Southdown House, St John's
Street, Chichester
Tel: 0243 780207

Sussex Auction Galleries,
59 Perrymount Road,
Haywards Heath
Tel: 0444 414935

Worthing Auction Galleries,
31 Chatsworth Road,
Worthing
Tel: 0903 205565

Tyne & Wear

Anderson & Garland,
The Fine Art Sale Rooms,
Marlborough House,
Marlborough Crescent,
Newcastle-upon-Tyne
Tel: 091 232 6278

Boldon Auction Galleries,
24a Front Street,
East Boldon
Tel: 091 537 2630

Thomas N Miller,
18-22 Gallowgate,
Newcastle-upon-Tyne
Tel: 091 232 5617

Sneddons,
Sunderland Auction Rooms,
30 Villiers Street,
Sunderland
Tel: 091 514 5931

Warwickshire

Bigwood Auctioneers Ltd.,
The Old School, Tiddington,
Stratford-upon-Avon
Tel: 0789 269415

John Briggs & Calder,
133 Long Street, Atherstone
Tel: 0827 718911

Locke & England,
18 Guy Street, Leamington
Spa Tel: 0926 427988

West Midlands

Biddle & Webb,
Icknield Square, Ladywood
Middleway, Birmingham
Tel: 021 455 8042
Cariss Residential,
20-22 High Street, Kings
Heath, Birmingham
Tel: 021 444 0088

Ronald E Clare,
Clare's Auction Rooms, 70
Park Street, Birmingham
Tel: 021 643 0226

Frank H Fellows & Sons,
Augusta House, 19 Augusta
Street, Hockley, Birmingham
Tel: 021 212 2131

Giles Haywood,
The Auction House, St Johns
Road, Stourbridge
Tel: 0384 370891

James & Lister Lea,
42 Bull Street, Birmingham
Tel: 021 200 1100

Phillips,
The Old House, Station
Road, Knowle, Solihull
Tel: 0564 776151

K Stuart Swash, FSVA,
Stamford House, 2 Waterloo
Road, Wolverhampton
Tel: 0902 710626

Walker Barnett & Hill,
3 Waterloo Road,
Wolverhampton
Tel: 0902 773531

Walton & Hipkiss,
111 Worcester Road, Hagley
Tel: 0562 885555

Weller & Dufty Ltd.,
141 Bromsgrove Street,
Birmingham
Tel: 021 692 1414

Wiltshire

Allen & Harris,
Saleroom & Auctioneers
Dept.,
The Planks (off The Square),
Old Town, Swindon
Tel: 0793 615915

Hamptons,
20 High Street, Marlborough
Tel: 0672 513471

Woolley & Wallis,
The Castle Auction Mart,
Castle Street, Salisbury
Tel: 0722 411422

Yorkshire - East

Dee & Atkinson,
The Exchange, Driffield
Tel: 0377 43151

Yorkshire - North

Boulton & Cooper (Fine
Arts),
St Michael's House, Market
Place, Malton
Tel: 0653 696151

H C Chapman & Son,
The Auction Mart, North
Street, Scarborough
Tel: 0723 372424

M W Darwin & Sons,
The Dales Furniture Hall,
Bedale
Tel: 0677 422846

GA Fine Art & Chattels,
Royal Auction Rooms, Queen
Street, Scarborough
Tel: 0723 353581

Hutchinson Scott,
The Grange, Marton-Le-
Moor, Ripon
Tel: 0423 324264

Christopher Matthews,
23 Mount Street, Harrogate
Tel: 0423 871756

Morphets of Harrogate,
4-6 Albert Street, Harrogate
Tel: 0423 530030

Wells Cundall,
15 Market Place, Malton
Tel: 0653 695581

Stephenson & Son,
Livestock Centre, Murton,
York
Tel: 0904 489731

Fine Arts,
27 Flowergate, Whitby
Tel: 0947 603433

Geoffrey Summersgill,
ASVA,
8 Front Street, Acomb, York
Tel: 0904 791131

Tennants,
Market Place, Leyburn
Tel: 0969 23780

D Wombell & Son, Bell Hall,
Escrick, York
Tel: 090 487 531

Yorkshire - South

Eadon Lockwood & Riddle,
Western Saleroom, Crookes,
Sheffield
Tel: 0742 686294

William H Brown,
10 Regent Street, Barnsley
Tel: 0226 733456

William H Brown,
Stanilands Auction Room, 28
Nether Hall Road, Doncaster
Tel: 0302 367766

Roland Orchard,
Fine Art & Chattels Valuers
& Auctioneers, 55 Copley
Road, Doncaster (call
Monday)
Tel: 0302 340499

Henry Spencer & Sons Ltd.,
1 St James Row, Sheffield
Tel: 0742 728728

Wilkinson & Beighton,
Woodhouse Green, Thurcroft,
Nr Rotherham
Tel: 0709 700005

Yorkshire - West

Audsley's Auctions (C R
Kemp BSc),
11 Morris Lane, Kirkstall,
Leeds 5
Tel: 0532 758787

de Rome,
12 New John Street,
Westgate, Bradford
Tel: 0274 734116

Eddisons,
Auction Rooms, 4-6 High
Street, Huddersfield
Tel: 0484 533151

Andrew Hartley,
Victoria Hall Salerooms,
Little Lane, Ilkley
Tel: 0943 816363

Malcolms No. 1 Auctioneers
& Valuers,
7 Finkle Hill, Sherburn-in-
Elmet, Nr Leeds
Tel: 0977 684971/685334
(24 hours)

Whitby Auction Rooms, West
End Saleroom, The Paddock,
Whitby
Tel: 0947 603433

New Bond Street Auctions,
76 Harry Street, Batley Car,
Dewsbury
Tel: 0924 469381

Phillips,
17a East Parade, Leeds
Tel: 0532 448011

John H Raby & Son,
The Sale Rooms,
21 St Mary's Road,
Manningham, Bradford
Tel: 0274 491121

Windle & Co.,
The Four Ashes, 535 Great
Horton Road, Bradford
Tel: 0274 572998

Channel Islands

Langlois Auctioneers &
Valuers,
Westway Chambers, 39 Don
Street, St Helier, Jersey
Tel: 0534 22441

La Gallais Auctions Ltd.,
36 Hillgrove Street,
St Helier, Jersey
Tel: 0534 66689

Martel, Maides & Le Pelley,
50 High Street, St Peter
Port, Guernsey
Tel: 0481 713463

Ireland

James Adam & Sons,
26 St Stephens Green,
Dublin 2
Tel: 010 3531 760261

Mealys,
Chatsworth Street, Castle
Comer Co. Kilkenny
Tel: 010 353 564 1229

Northern Ireland

Dunmurry Auctions Ltd.,
Barbour Gardens,
Dunmurry, Belfast
Tel: 0232 602815/6

Morgans Auctions Ltd.,
Duncrue Crescent, Duncrue
Road, Belfast
Tel: 0232 771552

Temple Auctions Limited,
133 Carryduff Road, Temple,
Lisburn, Co. Antrim
Tel: 0846 638777

Scotland

John Anderson,
33 Cross Street,
Fraserburgh, Aberdeenshire
Tel: 0346 28878

Christie's Scotland,
164-166 Bath Street,
Glasgow
Tel: 041 332 8134

B L Fenton & Sons,
Forebank Auction Halls, 84
Victoria Road, Dundee
Tel: 0382 26227

Frasers (Auctioneers),
28-30 Church Street,
Inverness
Tel: 0463 232395

William Hardie Ltd.,
141 West Regent Street,
Glasgow
Tel: 041 221 6780/248 6237

J & J Howe,
24 Commercial Street, Alyth,
Perthshire
Tel: 08283 2594

Loves Auction Rooms,
The Auction Galleries, 52-54
Canal Street, Perth
Tel: 0738 33337

Robert McTear & Co
(Auctioneers) Ltd.,
Royal Exchange Salerooms, 6
North Court, St. Vincent
Place, Glasgow
Tel: 041 221 4456

John Milne,
9 North Silver Street,
Aberdeen
Tel: 0224 639336

Robert Paterson & Son ,
8 Orchard Street, Paisley,
Renfrewshire
Tel: 041 889 2435

Phillips in Scotland,
207 Bath Street, Glasgow
Tel: 041 221 8377 also at:
65 George Street, Edinburgh
Tel: 031 225 2266

L S Smellie & Sons Ltd.,
Within the Furniture
Market,Lower
Auchingramont Road,
Hamilton
Tel: 0698 282007

West Perthshire Auctions,
Dundas Street, Cowie,
Perthshire

Wales

Dodds Property World,
Victoria Auction Galleries, 9
Chester Street, Mold, Clwyd
Tel: 0352 752552

Graham H Evans, FRICS,
FRVA,
Auction Sales Centre, The
Market Place, Kilgetty,
Dyfed
Tel: 0834 812793 & 811151

Spencer's John Francis,
Curiosity Salerooms, 19 King
Street, Carmarthen
Tel: 0267 233456

Roger Jones & Co., 33
Abergele Road, Colwyn Bay,
Clwyd
Tel: 0492 532176

King Thomas,
Lloyd Jones & Company, 36
High Street, Lampeter,
Dyfed
Tel: 0570 422550

Morgan Evans & Co. Ltd.,
30 Church Street, Llangefni,
Anglesey, Gwynedd
Tel: 0248 723303/77582
Morris Marshall & Poole,
10 Broad Street, Newtown,
Powys
Tel: 0686 625900

Phillips in Wales Fine Art
Auctioneers,
9-10 Westgate Street, Cardiff
Tel: 0222 396453

Rennies,
1 Agincourt Street,
Monmouth
Tel: 0600 712916

Wingett's,
22 Holt Street, Wrexham,
Clwyd
Tel: 0978 353553

INDEX

LAKESIDES FURNITURE FEATURES STRONG, CLASSIC DESIGNS
WHETHER FOR THE AMERICAN OR EUROPEAN MARKET.
USING ONLY OLD OR WELL SEASONED MATERIALS, THE HIGHEST
QUALITY IS ASSURED

OUR SKILLED CRAFTSMAN MAKE EACH PIECE INDIVIDUALLY TO
EXACT STANDARDS THEREFORE WE CAN TAILOR TO SPECIFIC NEEDS.
WE CAN ALSO MANUFACTURE CUSTOMISED DESIGNS IN A
VARIETY OF MATERIALS.